# COMMUNIST CHINA

*A System-Functional Reader*

*Edited with an Introduction by*

## Yung Wei

*Memphis State University*

Charles E. Merrill Publishing Company
*A Bell & Howell Company*
Columbus, Ohio

# MERRILL POLITICAL SCIENCE SERIES

Under the Editorship of

John C. Wahlke

Department of Political Science

SUNY at Stony Brook

ISBN: 0-675-09167-5

Library of Congress Catalog Card Number: 79-174781

1   2   3   4   5   6   7   8   —   76   75   74   73   72

Printed in the United States of America

# PREFACE

Ever since the emergence of a communist regime on the Chinese mainland, interest has been growing among scholars, businessmen, government officials, and the general public in the study of this huge, populous, and seemingly mysterious nation. The Korean War, the conflicts in Indo-China and other parts of Southeast Asia, and the development of nuclear capabilities by the Chinese Communists have sharpened interest in knowledge of that nation.

More recently, President Nixon's announcement of a visit to China by May 1972, has generated much speculation as to possible developments from the forthcoming meeting between Nixon and Chou En-lai as well as its implication to the relations among other countries of the world. As a result, public discussion and debates on issues related to China are now frequently held among various social, political, and religious groups. Courses and seminars on China have entered the curricula not only of leading universities and colleges, but also of smaller undergraduate institutions. Even some high schools in the United States are now offering courses on China to their students.

This phenomenal growth of interest in, and the demand for courses on, China has made increasingly evident the shortage of adequate textbooks covering the various aspects of political systems in the Chinese setting. Yet the current status of China studies is such that while essays of high quality are scattered in various professional journals, few scholars feel that they have sufficient reliable and consistent data to write an original book covering the Chinese Communist political system in its totality. In this situation a book of readings is called for. The present anthology is prepared in response to the need to fill this gap on China studies.

Three important features should be noted in this book. First of all, it is organized with the system-functional framework. By adopting this kind of theoretical framework as the basis for selecting and organizing the materials, the book places the Chinese Communist political system in its rightful place in social and political sciences; that is, as a political system sharing the common structures and functions of other political systems, not merely as problems in American foreign policy, nor as a unique system with idiosyncratic features which defy comparative analysis. Consequently, the selections were grouped into the general categories of the system-functional analysis such as political culture, political socialization, political communications, political integration, elite recruitment, and the allocation processes.

A second feature of this book is its interdisciplinary approach. Since a system-functional framework has been adopted as the organizational format, the text is able to incorporate not only materials on the operation of formal governmental structures, but also discussion and analysis on the roles played by other informal social-political structures such as the family, the kinship system, and the school in their relations with the political system. As a result, the book has a strong interdisciplinary flavor, including the contributions not only of political scientists, but also of historians, sociologists, psychologists, and economists, on various aspects of the Chinese polity.

The last important feature of this book is that it is one of the first books on the post-Cultural Revolution China. Close to half of the selections were published in or after 1966. In one way or another, these materials deal with the consequences of this unprecedented event on the social and political structures of the Chinese society on the mainland. The inclusion of these up-to-date materials will definitely place the readers in a better position to understand the more recent developments in that part of the world.

It must be pointed out that although this book of readings has been edited with an analytical framework, most of the selections in it are not beyond the grip of intelligent laymen. In other words, it is the belief of this editor that advanced training in social science and China studies is not indispensable for the understanding of most selections in this book.

A number of people have assisted in the production of this book. First of all, I would like to take this opportunity to express my gratitude to the authors and publishers for permission to use their materials. I am indebted to Professors John C. Wahlke of the State University of New York, Lucian W. Pye of M.I.T., Chalmers Johnson of the University of California, Berkeley, and Michel Oksenberg of Columbia University, for reviewing the organizational format and the selections of the book. Their encouragement has been an important factor for me in undertaking the present task. Professors Parris Chang of Pennsylvania State University and Derek Waller of Vanderbilt University have helped me collect some of the materials as well as making suggestions on the book, for which I am deeply grateful. I also want to extend my thankfulness to Professors John Beifus and Jacob Silver, both my colleagues at Memphis State University, for their editorial assistance to the book; and to Mrs. Laura Ingram, the capable secretary of the Political Science Department at Memphis State University, for her invaluable service in typing the draft. Finally, I want to thank my wife, Ning, who has tolerated my frequent absences from home and my negligence in performing my part of the household chores. It was through her constant self-denial and persistent emotional support that this book was completed.

# CONTENTS

vii

# SECTION TWO: SOCIAL STRUCTURE AND POLITICAL SOCIALIZATION 111

# SECTION THREE: ELITES, GROUPS, POLITICAL PARTICIPATION, AND COMMUNICATION 174

# SECTION FOUR: POLITICAL INTEGRATION, POLITICAL STRUCTURE, AND THE ALLOCATION PROCESSES 295

# THE CHINESE COMMUNIST POLITICAL SYSTEM: AN INTRODUCTION

Few events that have occurred after the Second World War have had more impact on world politics than the emergence of a totalitarian, communist political system on the Chinese mainland in 1949. In less than twenty years since its formal establishment as an independent political entity, Communist China has made itself an important actor in international relations through a series of actions affecting various nations of the world. Among these actions are a war with the United States in Korea, the development of nuclear capabilities, the split with the Soviet Union, and the export of revolutionary ideas of a "people's war" as well as open support for subversive, rebellious activities in various parts of the world. As a result of these activities, few political leaders of any nation would plan, implement, and evaluate their foreign policy without taking into account the possible reaction of the communist political system on the Chinese mainland.

## The Importance of China Studies in Social and Political Science

While political leaders throughout the world are concerned with the behavior of the Chinese Communist political system because of a practical preoccupation with its influence on world politics, social and political scientists are interested in studying this new political system for more basic and theoretical reasons. One of the major reasons for their interest in Communist China lies in the fact that it occupies the Chinese main-

1

land, which is the seat of a society having a continuous social and political structure for more than three thousand years.[1] Thus, to study Communist China in this context represents an effort to keep tracking social and political developments in one of the oldest living civilizations of the world.

A second reason for studying Communist China is to be found in the enormous dimension of this political system in terms of the size of its territory and of the population under its domination. Indeed, it rules one-fourth of the people on earth and is the biggest country in Asia, with a central location in the eastern part of that continent.

The third reason for an interest in Communist China among social and political scientists is that it is the largest communist nation in the world, not excepting the Soviet Union. The success or failure of this communist regime[2] will have a decisive impact on the communist movements in various parts of the world. More recently, the Sino-Soviet split with all its consequent effects on communist parties and governments throughout the world has further intensified concern for the role played by Communist China in the unity or division of the communist camp.

The final reason that has motivated social and political scientists to study Communist China is that the communist regime on the Chinese mainland stands not only for a totalitarian political system of tremendous dimension but also for a distinct model of political development which differs both from the Western democratic model and the Soviet communist model. An understanding of this regime would shed much light on the nature of totalitarian rule and the process of political development of the emerging nations in Asia, Africa, and Latin America.

## The Chinese Communist Political System: A Brief Review of History

Concomitant with an intense interest in the Chinese Communist political system among social and political scientists in the United States, there are various problems associated with the study of this communist regime. Before discussing the problems involved in China studies, however, a brief review of the history of this new political system in the Chinese setting is necessary.

We may roughly divide the history of Communist China into five periods. The first period lasted from 1949 to 1952. This was a period in which the Chinese Communists consolidated their control over the population through a series of measures such as the land reform, thought re-

---

[1]Counting from the Chou Dynasty (1122–256 B.C.) which is generally accepted by historians as the first Chinese dynasty with a reliable historical record.

[2]Both "Communist China" and "communist regime" are used as synonyms of "the Chinese Communist political system" here.

form, class struggle, and the "three-anti" and "five-anti" movements.[3] By adopting these measures, the Chinese Communists succeeded in suppressing or eliminating the so-called "counterrevolutionary" elements in the Chinese society, by which they meant those who either had associated with the Nationalist Government or were uncooperative with the new regime. Millions of people were imprisoned or executed in the process, which served the function of clearing out the residual resistance among the populace against the new political and social order.

In October 1950, Communist China entered into the Korean War by sending a "voluntary army" into North Korea to fight with the North Koreans against the South Koreans and the UN forces made up primarily of armed forces from the United States. At about the same time, Chinese Communist troops made expeditions into Tibet and subdued it to Chinese political control. The occupation of Tibet paved the way for future conflicts with India on border issues. The war in Korea was settled with an armistice in July 1953, which the Chinese Communists boasted was a success of halting "American Imperialism" in Eastern Asia.

The second period of communist rule in China, which covered the time from 1953 to 1957, was probably the most successful period for the communist regime. With the implementation of the First Five-Year Plan, the communist regime made notable achievements in the development of heavy industry, the expansion of irrigation systems, and the building of new roads and bridges connecting important urban centers and the rural areas. An intensive effort was also made in expanding the educational system, which substantially raised the literacy rate of the people on the Chinese mainland, especially those in the countryside.

The progress made by the Chinese Communists during this period was manifested in the increasing volume of exports from Communist China to other nations. It was also recognized and witnessed by foreign visitors who went to the Chinese mainland at that time. So much was Chairman Mao satisfied with the material progress achieved toward the end of this period that he proclaimed in February 1957 the principle of peaceful resolution of conflicts among the people,[4] and invited criticism of party and government from the populace in general and the intellectuals in particular. The extent of disenchantment and the severity of the criticisms that followed the invitation far exceeded Mao's and the party's expectation. A quick reverse of policy was made in July 1957, and the counter-attacks against the "bourgeois rightists" began. The result was a large scale prosecution of those who had voiced criticisms against the commu-

---

[3]See Theodore H. E. Chen and Wen-Hui C. Chen, "The 'Three-Anti' and 'Five-Anti' Movements in Communist China," *Pacific Affairs* 26 (March 1953); also see *Current Background* (Hong Kong: U.S. Consulate General, March 26, 1952), No. 168.

[4]See Mao Tse-tung, *On the Correct Handling of Contradictions Among the People* (Peking: Foreign Language Press, 1960).

nist regime during the so-called "One Hundred Flowers Bloom" period and a return to tight physical and mental control of the population by the regime.

Despite the turmoils in the political arena, in mid-1957 economic conditions of Communist China showed continuous improvement. By August 1958, Mao and his colleagues had decided to collectivize further the economic activities in China with the launching of the Second Five-Year Plan. The essence of the Second Five-Year Plan was embedded in a single phrase — "The Great Leap Forward." This movement was marked by the backyard steel drive as a method to boost industrial output, and the amalgamation of collective farms into "people's communes" as an innovative structure to promote agricultural products.[5]

The ability of the regime to mobilize the people of China in huge collectives for farming and construction work during this period was impressive indeed. But the results of the "Great Leap Forward" movement were not what the Chinese Communists had anticipated. By the end of 1959, economic dislocations and natural calamities had turned the "Great Leap Forward" into what some China specialists called the "Great Leap Backward." In addition to economic setbacks at home, Communist China was also faced with problems in its relations with other political systems. One of the major developments in the international front for the Chinese Communists was its split with the Soviet Union.

While students of Chinese politics still have different interpretations on the causes of the split, it is generally agreed that the criticisms of the commune system by the Soviet leaders and the lack of full support from the Soviet Union for the Chinese Communists' adventure in the Taiwan Strait in 1958 were the primary factors leading to the deterioration of relations between these two communist nations. Significant differences between leaders of Communist China and the Soviet Union on ideological issues also had some effect on the split. The results of the split were the withdrawal of Soviet technicians from mainland China and the near complete cessation of Soviet aid to Communist China.

Following the setbacks in the "Great Leap Forward" movement, leaders in Communist China gradually came to the realization that some relaxation of the commune system was necessary. One form of modifying the communes was to permit the peasants to operate a small private lot and to sell the products for a profit. This and other measures of relaxation gradually brought about a recuperation from the near collapse of the economy.

---

[5]The purposes of rural communes was specified by the Central Committee of the Chinese Communist Party, "Resolution on the Establishment of People's Communes in the Rural Areas," in *The Chinese Communist Regime: Documents and Commentary*, ed. Theodore H.E. Chen (New York: Praeger, 1967), pp. 223-27.

From 1962 to 1965, the Chinese Communists increasingly emphasized the importance of self-reliance as a means of solving the problems confronting the regime. Intensive propaganda campaigns were launched throughout the Chinese mainland to indoctrinate the people into believing in the importance of not relying upon any foreign government or on alien advisers and teachings, but to rely solely upon the Chinese people themselves. On the international front, a short but intensive military conflict broke out between the troops of Communist China and India, which resulted in defeat for the Indians. But other than holding some limited border areas taken from India (which both the Communist Chinese and the Nationalists claimed to be Chinese territories), Communist China did not enlarge the war and a *de facto* peace settlement was soon established.

One of the most important developments in Communist China during this period was probably the explosion of the first nuclear device at Lop Nor in Sinkiang in October 1964. Soon afterward, in May of the next year, a second nuclear explosion was set off in the same area. Within a few months after the second explosion of a nuclear device by Communist China, Lin Piao released the famous article on "Long Live the Victory of the People's War," in which he specified the tactics of revolutionary struggles against "reactionary" governments of the world and expressed confidence in the eventual downfall of the bourgeois imperialists, led by the United States.

During the 1962-65 period of recuperation and reassessment of party policies, serious disagreements seemed to have developed among top party leaders. The disagreements bore primarily on the problem of whether the party should put greater stress on ideological purity or on the need of practical, professional knowledge in the educational system, the recruitment of party and government officials, and the selection of directors of economic and agricultural activities. This controversy on what is now called the "redness versus expertness" issue gradually developed into a power struggle between those who argued for more pragmatic policies and those who emphasized the importance of ideological commitments. The latter had the blessing of Mao Tse-tung.

By June 1966, conflicts between the two groups came to the open with the sudden organization of millions of high school and university students into "red guards" and the so-called "Great Proletarian Cultural Revolution" was thus begun. Many party leaders were verbally assailed, publicly humiliated, and brutally tortured; a number of them committed suicide. Government and party headquarters were seized by red guards; objects reminiscent of China's traditional past were destroyed; violent conflicts between the supporters of the red guards and their opponents, and among the different factions of red guards, spread throughout the country. In some areas, serious military confrontations occurred. In southern China, bodies of those who were killed in the conflicts were thrown into rivers; some of these were carried as far as Hong Kong and Macao. For a time, the whole Chinese Communist political system appeared to be on the verge of anarchy and provincial military rule was a reality in many parts of China.

The full effect of the "cultural revolution" is still being analyzed by the specialists in the field. The immediate consequences of the upheaval include the removal of Liu Shao-chi as the head of the government; the purge of Teng Hsiao-p'ing, P'eng Chen, Lu Ting-yi, Chou Yang, and many other important party officials; the enactment of a new party constitution, which formally established Lin Piao as the vice-chairman of the Chinese Communist Party, thus making him heir-apparent to Mao;[6] and the emergence of large numbers of military leaders into the core-elite position in the power structure of the Chinese Communist political system.

It will take some time before we can arrive at an accurate evaluation of the more hidden and profound damages inflicted by the "cultural revolution" on the Chinese Communist regime on mainland China. But we can be quite sure that this event, unprecedented in the history of Chinese polity, or anywhere in the world, is going to have long-lasting effects both on the communist regime and on the social and political life of the Chinese people as a whole.

## Problems Associated with the Study of the Chinese Communist Political System

Having briefly reviewed the history of the Chinese Communist political system in the past twenty years, we may now turn to some of the problems involved in the study of this political system. Generally, four basic problems may be distinguished in the study of Communist China by scholars in the West.

First, there is the problem of orientation. The field of China studies has been dominated by sinologists for years. A basic assumption of sinologists is that unless one knows China in its totality — its history, language, customs, and the cultural traits of the Chinese people — one

---

[6]It should be noted, however, that Chou En-lai, the Premier of mainland China, can very likely be a rival to Lin Piao in succeeding Mao. The frequent appearance of Chou at diplomatic functions, including the receiving of U.S. ping-pong players in Peking in April 1971, has generated much speculation among Western observers of Chou En-lai's future leadership role in Communist China. Chou's recent meeting with Henry Kissinger and his invitation to President Nixon to visit mainland China have further reinforced this sort of speculation. See *Newsweek*, April 26, 1971, pp. 19–20; and *Life*, July 30, 1971, pp. 18–26.

is not qualified to study that country. Following this logic, the study of China is to be limited to a few scholars who have made China studies their life career. This kind of assertion has discouraged quite a number of young social scientists from making China their field of specialization.

The second problem relates to the difficulty of the Chinese language. It is a language based on ideographic symbols, namely, the "characters." One has to memorize several thousand characters before he is able to read original Chinese materials. Even after one manages to remember the meanings of a sizable number of characters, the habit of Chinese writers of using complex phrases, idioms, and allusions poses further problems. As a result, not only beginning students but also quite a few established scholars who have made China their field of concentration rely on materials translated into English as their basic source of information.

The third kind of problem related to Chinese studies is to be found in the lack of theoretical constructs in most of the studies that have been conducted in this field. Lacking a theoretical framework as a guide, many research workers on Communist China have ended up with pure descriptive analysis of rough data or broad generalizations supported only by speculative observations. This lack of concern with theory has prevented a systematic growth of empirical and comparable knowledge on the Chinese Communist political system, and has retarded a mutual fertilization of research results of China studies and those of other social and behavioral sciences.

Finally, there is the problem of obtaining hard data on Communist China. Before 1959, the government of the People's Republic of China occasionally allowed reporters and writers from Western nations to visit the mainland on predetermined routes and with "tourist guides." A number of impressionistic, but nevertheless on-the-spot, reports resulted from these trips. After 1959, with the deterioration of the domestic situation and the increasing hostilities toward the Western nations, the Soviet Union, and other "revisionist" communist countries, it became increasingly difficult for individuals from the West to gain access to Communist China.[7] Consequently, students of Communist China must rely on the official documents and broadcasts released by the Communist government, newspapers published in the Chinese mainland, interviews with refugees in Hong Kong and Taiwan, and the confidential reports occasionally brought out by intelligence agents and defected communist

---

[7]However, with the invitation of the U.S. ping-pong team to visit mainland China in April 1971, Peking seemed to have relaxed its long-imposed restrictions on travels to the Chinese mainland by Westerners in general and the Americans in particular. See reports in *Newsweek*, April 26, 1971, pp. 14–20.

personnel. For a serious scholar interested in first-hand data, this situation is indeed less than desirable.

With all the above-mentioned problems and difficulties in China studies, some solutions, nevertheless, have been found. There is, first of all, a general understanding among social and political scientists that one does not have to know the several thousand years of history of China or to understand the classical Chinese language before he is qualified to examine contemporary problems in the Chinese setting. It is feasible for a person with the preliminary ability to read vernacular Chinese and with a knowledge of post-eighteenth-century China to do quality work on modern China.

As for the problem of language, an increasing number of universities and colleges have started offering courses on Chinese, with the emphasis on enabling the students to read materials written in modern Chinese within a reasonable period of time. Also, language training centers have been established in Taiwan and Hong Kong with native instructors to teach Western students to learn the language. As a result, a growing number of younger scholars in the United States have obtained not only a proficiency in reading contemporary Chinese but also an ability to speak it as well.

With regard to the problem of lack of theoretical development in China studies, a small minority of students of China studies have taken account of this shortcoming and are attacking the problem with vigor and perseverance.[8] Their contributions have already begun to have great effect on the direction of research in the field.

The greater problem in studying Communist China is the lack of data. For any empirical science to grow, the availability of reliable data is essential. Variation in the availability and reliability of data frequently has led to variation in the interpretation of events in the real world. But this problem of lacking sufficient first-hand data is not a unique problem, limited only to China studies. It is rather a common problem in the study of any closed political system, be it modern or traditional, communist or fascist. With the progress of modern research techniques such as content analysis and multivariate analysis, secondary data can also yield important information on the political system under examination. In this respect, the progress we have made on the studies of the Soviet Union can serve as an example. Hence we may conclude that although

---

[8]Examples can be found in the selections in the present reader and those in A. Doak Barnett, ed., *Chinese Communist Politics in Action* (Seattle: University of Washington Press, 1969); for a discussion on the methodology of China studies, see Chalmers Johnson, "The Role of Social Science in China Scholarship," *World Politics* 17 (January 1965): 256–71; and Michel Oksenberg, "Sources and Methodological Problems in the Study of Contemporary China," in Barnett, *op. cit.*, pp. 577–606.

the study of the Chinese Communist political system may pose more problems in research than other political systems, these problems are neither unique nor insoluble. And the recent achievements in China studies have emphatically demonstrated this point.

It should be acknowledged at this point that by the systematic application of various theoretical models and by painstaking analysis of available data, students of Communist China have produced a great deal of objective knowledge on the nature and behavior of the communistic political system in mainland China. Among these new areas of information are the relations between the family, the community, and the state; the shifting of loyalty from the family to the state; the process of political socialization in Communist China; the use of mass media by the Communists to control the behavior of the Chinese people; the social background, skill, and mobility of the Chinese Communist elites; and so on.[9] It is this kind of material that has made the present book possible.

## Organization of the Selections on Communist China

Following a system-functional framework we have grouped sections on Communist China into five sections. Section one serves as an overall introduction to the history, the environment, and the political myth of the Chinese Communist political system. It contains essays on the geography, the people, the culture, and the history of Communist China since its establishment in 1949. It also includes analyses of the authority crisis, the theory of a people's war, and the cult of Mao in Communist China.

Section two concerns itself mainly with the relationship between the social structure and the political system in Communist China, and the process of political socialization under the communist regime. Selections in this section cover discussion of the impact of communist revolution on the Chinese family and village life, the theory and practice of communist education, the sociopsychological process of thought reform, the socialization of the mind by the Chinese Communists through the monopoly of the mass media, and the level of political participation on mainland China.

Section three is devoted to analysis of the political elites and various important political groups in Communist China. Materials in this section probe into the social backgrounds, the skills, and the mobility of the top-ranking political leaders as well as the local political elites in an urban center. The nature of the cultural revolution and its impact on

---

[9]Since nearly all of these materials are included in the present book we shall not cite them here.

the leadership of the political system, the roles of the Communist party, the trade unions, the peasant associations, and the armed forces in the political struggles and decision-making process within the system, are also examined in turn.

Section four deals with the problems of political integration and the process of allocation of values among members of the political system. It includes discussion of the efforts made by the Communists led by Mao Tse-tung to integrate different sections of the Chinese society and the minority groups into a unified polity to strive for communist goals. It also contains materials focusing on the principles and process of allocating material benefits and of providing legal justice and protection to various groups of people on mainland China.

Finally, in section five, we have selected several essays concerning the external relations of Communist China, its capability, and its reactions and adjustments to a changing world. The topics covered by materials in this section include the basic factors affecting the foreign policy of Communist China; Mao Tse-tung's revolutionary strategy and the international behavior of the Communist Chinese; the process and effect of Sino-Soviet conflict; and the conventional as well as the nuclear capability of Communist China as related to its ideological goals, military strategy, and foreign relations.

## Studying Communist China: The Need of Comparative Analysis and Application of Theories and Methods of the Behavioral Sciences

After one has read some parts of the materials in this book, he must ask himself several questions: How can we relate research on the Chinese political system to the various areas of interest in political science? In what manner can knowledge produced by China studies benefit the field of political science, or vice versa? The answers lie in the adoption of a comparative perspective and in the application of the theories and methods of the behavioral sciences, particularly those which have been successfully applied to the study of political behavior.[10]

---

[10]There are voluminous discussions on the importance of comparative study and the application of behavioral-science theories and methods among political scientists nowadays. To get a general notion, consult Gabriel A. Almond, "A Functional Approach to Comparative Politics," in *The Politics of the Developing Areas*, ed. Gabriel A. Almond and James S. Coleman (Princeton: Princeton University Press, 1960), pp. 3–66; Almond, "A Developmental Approach to Political System," *World Politics* 17 (January 1965): 183–214; David Easton, *A Framework for Political Analysis* (Englewood Cliffs, N. J.: Prentice-Hall, 1965), pp. 1–22; Karl W. Deutsch, *The Nerves of Government, Models of Political Communication and Control* (New York: The Free Press, 1966), pp. 3–21.

In terms of comparative analysis, we may compare the Chinese Communist political system with other political systems along several mutually complementary spectrums over time and space. For instance, we may place Communist China on the familiar traditional-transitional-modern spectrum and see how it differs from other political systems in terms of the relationship between the social and economic conditions of a society and its political style and development. Comparison along this line will help us gain much insight into the appeal of the Chinese version of communism for countries in Asia, Africa, and Latin America.

We may also, of course, compare Communist China with other nations of the world along the line of a competitive–semicompetitive–authoritarian model.[11] Using this classification of political systems, we may compare the Chinese Communist political system with other political systems in terms of the degree of "openness" and "competitiveness" in the process of performing interest articulation, interest aggregation, elite recruitment, rule making, and other functions. There must be a word of warning here, however; we must be careful not to let our ideological preference lead us to jump to quick, subjective conclusions as to the nature of the political system on the Chinese mainland, and thus lose sight of the real purpose of the comparison.

A third type of comparison can be made between Communist China and other communist nations against an orthodox-revisionist spectrum. By doing this, we may see how the differences on the commitment to the original Marxist-Leninist dogma have affected the behavior of the communist nations. We may also see how the historical, geographical, and cultural elements of a society can lead to different interpretations and application of the communist political myth to fit local conditions.

Finally, we may, and should, compare the Chinese Communist political system with the Nationalist political system on Taiwan. There have been comparisons between the two systems by people who are either highly sympathetic or antagonistic toward one of the regimes. Understandably, the results are not the kind of information we need for empirical political analysis. What we need is detached and dispassionate comparison based upon empirical data and with some kind of theoretical framework. Given the common cultural and historical roots[12] of the two systems, one could well serve as a control group for another. In so doing, we may examine the effect of different political systems on the

---

[11]James S. Coleman, "Conclusion: The Political Systems of the Developing Areas," in Almond and Coleman, *The Politics of the Developing Areas, op. cit.,* pp. 532–76.

[12]This is an assumption and is subject to challenge. Through careful empirical research, one may find there are already significant differences in the memory, norms, and values between members of the two political systems.

life of a huge number of Chinese people who, until twenty years ago, lived within one single polity.

In addition to these comparative approaches, which have already been widely used in political science research, especially in the field of comparative politics, we should also make an effort to apply some, if not all, of the theories of social and behavioral sciences to the study of the Chinese Communist political systems. There is no reason why we cannot apply system theory, structural-functional theory, decision-making theory, and communication theory to China studies. We do not deny the fact that there may not be enough reliable data concerning the Chinese political systems and that there is the danger of superficially testing a theory against very meager and shaky data. But by applying some kinds of systematic theories, it will at least make us aware of the need for more consistent and reliable data as well as the ways to collect them.

Besides empirical theories, sophisticated research methodology is another important factor that has heightened the development of political science. In this connection, we see no reason why research methods such as content analysis, statistical analysis and inference, sample survey (in Taiwan and Hong Kong at the present time), information retrieval, and computer analysis cannot be applied to collect and analyze data on China. Some younger political scientists have recently applied some of the methods and obtained significant results.[13] What we need is to have more political scientists follow the same path.

Other than the application of empirical theories and methods, there should also be more cooperation and division of labor among China specialists. China is a vast nation. To study it in its totality is a tremendous job for any single scholar. Therefore, we may want to try to concentrate our research on smaller geographical units such as regions, provinces, cities, and villages; or on more limited analytical areas such as political culture, political socialization, political communication, elite recruitment, and so forth. There should be more teamwork between China specialists whose mother tongue is English and those whose native language is Chinese. Many mistakes in translation and interpretation can thus be avoided.

To attack the problem of the lack of empirical data, a data archive fashioned after the Inter-University Consortium for Political Research or other data banks might be established. This will greatly increase the pace of dissemination of available information on China and enhance the opportunities for comparative analysis.

In the development of any science, a new field always poses more problems than solutions, more questions than answers, and more com-

---

[13]See Barnett, *op. cit.*

plexities than regularities. But these are precisely the ingredients that make a field interesting to serious scholars, for it constitutes a challenge to the intellectual capacity of those who have chosen to pursue it. With the increasing application of theories and methods of behavioral science, and with the increasing number of well-trained political scientists who have an interest in China studies, we have reasons to believe that the myths surrounding the Chinese political systems will gradually disappear, just as the myths which have held for many years about the political behavior of American people have been unfolded.

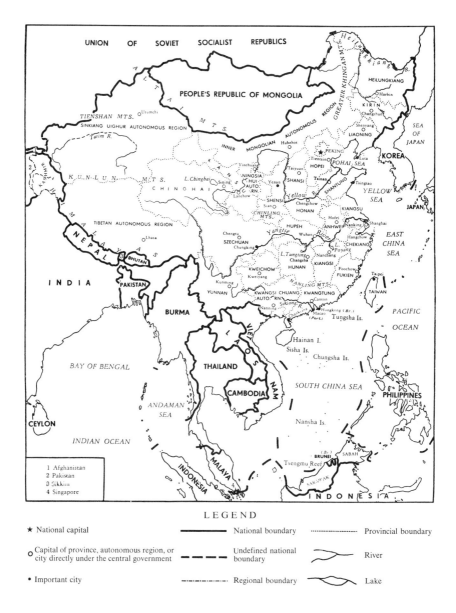

## LEGEND

★ National capital

o Capital of province, autonomous region, or city directly under the central government

• Important city

National boundary

Undefined national boundary

Regional boundary

Provincial boundary

River

Lake

From Jen Yu-ti, *A Concise Geography of China* (Peking: Foreign Language Press, 1964). [The Government of the Republic of China (Nationalist China) has thus far refused to recognize the government of the People's Republic of Mongolia and considers the territories under its control a part of China. — Ed.]

## MAP 1
## Mainland China: A Simple Map

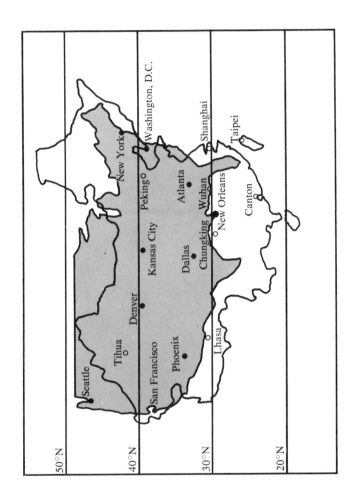

Prepared by Yung Wei.

MAP 2
Communist China and the United States: A Comparison
of Sizes and Geographical Locations

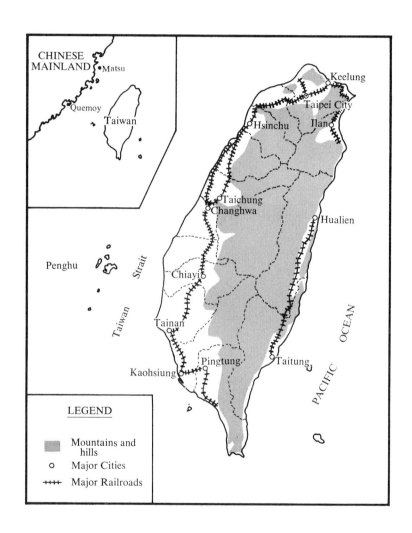

CHINESE MAINLAND

Matsu

Quemoy

Taiwan

Penghu

Strait

Taiwan

LEGEND

Mountains and hills

○ Major Cities

┼┼┼┼ Major Railroads

Keelung

Taipei City

Hsinchu    Ilan

Taichung
Changhwa

Hualien

Chiayi

Tainan

Pingtung    Taitung

Kaohsiung

PACIFIC OCEAN

Prepared by Yung Wei.

## MAP 3
## Taiwan, Republic of China

# HISTORY,
# GEOGRAPHY,
# AND POLITICAL MYTH

No political system is free from the influence of the historical past, geographical foundation, and cultural heritage of the society within which it operates. History constitutes the common "memory" of the members of the political system. Geography provides the physical and demographic basis of a political system, which affects the capacity and goals of that system. Cultural heritage gives the members of a system shared beliefs, values, and norms, which shape their behavior in the interactions among themselves and toward the outside world. All of these factors affect the inputs of a political system. Variations in the history, geography, and culture of different societies often lead to variation in the types of demand and support received by the political systems.

As we have pointed out in the introduction, the political system which the Chinese Communists inherited from the Nationalists has a long, continuous, and generally glorious history parallelled by few political systems of the world. As a result, the Chinese people are extremely conscious of their historical past and are immensely proud of the achievements of their ancestors. Thus to save China from the humiliations suffered at the hands of the Western nations after the nineteenth century, to restore its previous dominating position in East Asia, and to reassert its role as a major nation in international relations have been the primary concerns of all Chinese political leaders of modern time.

One does not have to read all the writings of Mao Tse-tung to detect his concern with the invasion and exploitation of China by Western nations and Westernized Japan. For him, to resist foreign repression and to regain the glory and status which China had enjoyed in the past is a primary goal of the communist revolution in China. The realization of this goal is important not only in the emancipation of the "suppressed classes" in the Chinese society, but also of those of the world.

For the past twenty years, the Chinese Communists have devoted themselves to the goal of making China a strong communist nation. In this respect, they have met with serious limitations in the geographical and demographical environments. China is a large nation in terms of the size of its territory and population; but it is not a rich nation in terms of natural resources, agricultural products, and industrial development.

China has sufficient reserves and production of coal, copper, and iron, but is short of oil, chromium, cobalt, and nickel. Nearly half of the territories of China consist of deserts, high-rising mountains and plateaus, and other wastelands. Only about ten percent of the total area of China is cultivated. With the agricultural products of this small portion of cultivated land, one-fourth of the world's population must be supported. It is not surprising, therefore, that the Chinese people have one of the lowest standards of living among the nations of the world.

The large number of poor, hunger-stricken peasants of China provided the Chinese Communists with great potential for political agitation and support. However, it also proved to be a serious liability to the modernization efforts of the communist leaders after they had gained control of the Chinese mainland.

Of the 750 million people of China,* approximately 6 percent are a non-Chinese (Han) minority. Though not very important in terms of overall population, the minority ethnic groups occupy nearly half of the territories of mainland China in the northern, northwestern, and southwestern regions. The territories settled by minority groups are important to the Chinese Communist political system both as an outlet for the overcrowded population in the eastern and southern parts of China and as the frontiers of national defense. In recent years, because of Communist China's conflicts with the Soviet Union and India, its policies toward minority-occupied areas such as Inner Mongolia, Sinkiang, and Tibet have become increasingly important in the decision-making process of the Chinese Communists.

To hold such a vast nation together, the rulers of traditional China have relied upon a political myth of benevolent monarchy. For thousands of years the emperors of China depended upon the service of a small group of Confucianist scholars to rule the huge mass of the illiterate peasants. Under the so-called "Mandate of Heaven" theory, the emperor had the power to rule because he was the "Son of Heaven," who

*No census has been taken on the Chinese mainland since 1953. Recent estimates of the current population of Communist China vary anywhere from 700 million to 800 million.

had been delegated such a power by Heaven (God). In actuality, however, whether the emperor still had the mandate or not was determined by his ability, or willingness, to follow the advice of the learned Confucianist scholars and maintain peace and prosperity within the empire. When an emperor failed in this, it was interpreted by the people as the loss of the "Mandate of Heaven" by the emperor and revolution to overthrow a decadent dynasty was justified.

When the Chinese Nationalists overthrew the Manchu dynasty in 1911, they rejected the "Mandate of Heaven" myth of the traditional dynasties and replaced it with nationalism and democracy. But they still tried to preserve Confucianism as the cultural basis of the Chinese society. Their efforts in this respect have not been successful, owing to the rapid social disorganization resulting from the intrusion of foreign economic and cultural forces, the conflicts between warlords, a protracted war with Japan, and the continuous harassment and challenge from the Communists.

The Chinese Communists, on the other hand, reject both the traditional political structure and its cultural-ideological foundation — Confucianism. For the Chinese Communists, Confucianism is an ideology representing and protecting the interests of the "exploiting classes" of traditional China—among them the landlords, the bureaucrats, and merchants. To replace Confucianism and nationalism, the Chinese Communists introduced what they believed to be orthodox Marxism-Leninism.

A closer examination of what the Chinese Communists regard as true Marxism-Leninism leads most scholars of Chinese communism to conclude that what the Chinese Communists claim to be the "true and pure" communism has already been adapted and revised by the leaders of the Chinese Communist party, notably Mao Tse-tung, to suit the local conditions of China and to fit the revolutionary experience of the Chinese Communist movement. The most important revision or contribution of Mao Tse-tung to Marxism-Leninism is found in his emphasis on the role of the peasantry in the communist revolution. Based upon his experience in the communist movement in China, Mao concluded that winning the support of the peasantry and the occupancy of the rural areas is the only sure way for a communist revolution to succeed.

Mao's theory has recently been expanded by Lin Piao (or actually by himself, but published in the name of Lin Piao) to make it applicable to the revolutionary situation of the world. Taking North America and Europe as the urban areas of the world and the vast underdeveloped regions of Asia, Africa, and Latin America as their rural surroundings, Lin calls for unification of all the "exploited" peoples of the "rural areas" of the world to defeat the imperialist, exploitative classes in the capitalist strongholds of the "urban areas."

Whether the rejection of the Confucianist past has functioned to fulfill the goals of the Chinese Communists is subject to debate among students of Chinese communism. Yet judging by the severity of the attack against traditional Chinese cultural symbols and institutions during the Great Proletarian Cultural Revolution, we have reason to believe that there must be a residual attachment of the Chinese people on the mainland toward the sociocultural order of the "older society."

Certain China experts are even of the opinion that while attacking the traditional culture of China, the communist leaders have adopted, consciously or unconsciously, traditional methods to maximize their control of the populace of the Chinese mainland. The excessive, unrestrained deification of Mao Tse-tung in recent years seems to lend support to their thesis. Hence, it may be concluded that it is very difficult for a political system to rid itself of the influence of its cultural heritage, even with a prototype totalitarian, communist regime such as Communist China.

# I
# The Chinese Communist Political System: Its Heritage And History

## 1. China's Heritage and the Communist System

*Ping-ti Ho*

It is fairly safe for students of Chinese history to say that the current revolution that has been going on in mainland China since 1949 will overshadow in nature and scope the one which from the late third century B.C. onward swept away the remnants of feudalism and ushered China into two thousand years of imperial rule. For many students of world history, the present Chinese revolution deserves to be ranked with the French and Russian revolutions as one of the most momentous events in recent centuries. In spite of various domestic difficulties and international setbacks within a short span of seventeen years, the Chinese Communists have profoundly altered the form and substance of the Chinese society, including the destruction of the pre-1949 power elite — an aspect which is regarded by two leading experts of Communist China to be the mark of a true revolution.[1] It is with a full awareness of the profundity of the many-sided changes, therefore, that I undertake the task of analyzing certain salient aspects of China's heritage in the hope that they may help to sharpen our perception of the present. While in this paper China's heritage is approached fairly comprehensively from the geographic-ethnic, demographic, political, social-educational, and economic points of view, I purposely eschew the legacy of the traditional tributary system and its likely influence on present-day China's international policy and behavior. This is partly because the focus of this first

---

[1]Franz Schurmann, *Ideology and Organization in Communist China* (Berkeley: University of California Press, 1966), p. 2; Chalmers Johnson, *Revolution and the Social System* (Stanford, Calif.: Stanford University Press, 1964), p. 8.

Reprinted from Ping-ti Ho and Tang Tsou, eds., *China in Crisis* (Chicago: University of Chicago Press, 1968), 1:1–9, by permission of the author and the publisher.

Conference is on historical background and Communist China's internal policies and partly because, of all aspects of Chinese history, China's international relations are the most studied and best understood in the West.

# I

However much China experts may differ in their appraisals of the strengths and weaknesses of mainland China as a major power, they are unanimous in recognizing the basic fact that much of its impact on the outside world is due to its sheer physical size and the location of its frontiers. It seems pertinent therefore to begin a survey of China's heritage with a brief review of the growth of modern China as a geographic and ethnic entity.

Even after the legal secession of Outer Mongolia, the People's Republic of China still embraces an area of 3,657,765 square miles, which makes it the second largest country in the world. The consolidated land mass of China, which stretches longitudinally from the Pamir and the "roof of the world" to the Pacific Ocean and latitudinally from the cool northern Eurasian steppe to the tropics of southern Asia, gives it a commanding position in the continent of Asia. To use some erstwhile interesting geopolitical expressions, China and the Soviet Union share the "heartland" of the Eurasian land mass but China alone possesses the important warm-water east Eurasian "rimland." China's deep concern with and potent influence on Korea and Vietnam — two areas which may be regarded as its traditional and strategically vital "rimlands" — make it the chief target of the United States' long-range world policy. While the revolutionary development in military technology during and after World War II has considerably invalidated certain fundamental assumptions of geopolitics, the very fact that China, notwithstanding its relative military and industrial weakness, has almost replaced the Soviet Union as the most urgent concern of the United States must be partially accounted for by its physical size and strategic geographic location.

One striking fact which is not too clearly known to students of world affairs is that throughout much of its long history China was actually a far smaller country than it is today. Historically, the area under abiding effective Chinese jurisdiction lies south of the Great Wall, which in modern times is called China Proper. China Proper, with an area of about 1,532,800 square miles, amounts to only one-half of that of the United States. It is true that at the peak of the Han (B.C. 206-220 A.D.) and T'ang (618-907) empires the Chinese reached as far west as present Russian Turkestan and that the Mongol empire is the largest in the annals of man. But the westward expansions of Han and T'ang were ephemeral at best and the Mongol empire was too loosely organized to leave any permanent imprint. It was during the last dynasty of Ch'ing (1644-1912) that China was geographically transformed from China Proper to what from the historian's point of view may be called "Greater China."[2]

The first important contribution that the Manchus made to the growth of China as a geographic and ethnic entity was the addition of Inner Mongolia and Manchuria to China Proper. Thanks to their geographic propinquity to the Mongols and especially to their farsightedness, the early Manchu rulers had worked out, even before the conquest of China in 1644, a long-range policy toward the Mongols of Inner Mongolia, which was continued and amplified down to the very end of the dynasty in 1912. The policy consisted of perennial intermarriage between the Manchu imperial clan and Mongol princedoms, periodic conferring of noble ranks on the various strata of the Mongol ruling class, the endorsement of Lamaism as the official religion for the Mongols, and the setting up of administrative machinery from *aimaks* ("principalities"), *chigolgans* ("leagues"), down to *hoshigo* ("banners"), a system which not only suited Mongol customs but also allowed the Manchus to play a policy of divide and rule. In addition, a significant number of Mongols were incorporated into the Eight Banner system and into central and provincial administration. Although early Ch'ing statutes prohibited the Chinese from entering the domains reserved for Mongol nomads, the imperial government from the late seventeenth century onward connived at Chinese immigration to Inner Mongolia, especially at times of famine. Chinese immigration at first received also the tacit blessing of Mongol nobles who found their new role as *rentiers* profitable. Wherever sizable Chinese agricultural colonies were established, the imperial government set up regular local administrations, that is, counties and prefectures. By late Ch'ing times Chinese migrations to the northern steppe had reached much larger scales, and Inner Mongolia had become increasingly Sinicized. Similar Chinese migrations to Manchuria, where the Manchus originated, have made Manchuria thoroughly Chinese, despite the onslaughts of Czarist Russia and Japan.

The need in the late seventeenth and early eighteenth centuries to defend Khalkha or Outer Mongolia from the warlike Zunghars of northern Chinese Turkestan led the Manchus to a long series of wars which resulted in the establishment of Chinese suzerainty over Outer Mongolia and Tibet and the conquest of Kokonor and Chinese Turkestan. All these vast outlying areas, together with Inner Mongolia, were supervised from

---

[2]Much of this section is taken from my article, "The Significance of the Ch'ing Period in Chinese History," *Journal of Asian Studies*, 26, no. 2 (1967).

Peking by *Li-fan yüan,* or Court of Colonial Affairs.[3] The effectiveness of Manchu control of these far-flung areas varied in inverse proportion to the magnitude of such difficulties as distance, terrain, transportation of men and supplies, and financial resources. An indication that the complex Ch'ing system of control was by and large viable may be seen from the following facts: Chinese Turkestan and Kokonor were made into new provinces of Sinkiang and Chinghai, respectively, in 1884 and 1928; the imperial resident and garrisons of Lhasa were not withdrawn until after the fall of the dynasty in 1912; and Outer Mongolia did not legally secede from China until after the end of World War II.

From 1840 onward the Manchu empire was greatly weakened by successive international wars and domestic rebellions. Various imperialist powers began to launch their onslaughts on the peripheries of the Manchu empire. Step by step, Russia, Britain, France, and Japan reduced the question of the legal statuses of China's outlying territories and dependent states to an almost purely academic one. For every party had learned from *Realpolitik* that the true status of any of these disputed areas depended on China's ability to exert effective control. It is this rude historical lesson that prompted the People's Republic of China to seize the first opportunities to rush its army into Sinkiang and Tibet. Because of the secession of Outer Mongolia, the area of the People's Republic of China is approximately 606,000 square miles smaller than that of the late Manchu empire, which in turn had shrunken considerably from its fullest extent attained before 1800.

Any review of the evolution of China as a geographic and ethnic entity would be misleading without pointing out that the extension of China's internal frontiers, if less spectacular than empire building, is historically equally important. Although the history of the extension of China's internal frontiers is practically as old as Chinese history itself, it was from the 1720's onward that a more energetic policy of Sinicization was directed against various non-Chinese ethnic groups who constituted a majority in a number of mountainous enclaves in the southwestern provinces of Yunnan, Kweichow, Szechwan, and Kwangsi, and in the central Yangtze provinces of Hunan and Hupei. The core of this policy was to replace the native tribal system with Chinese local administration. To a more limited extent, it was applied also to parts of Kansu, Kokonor, Chinese Turkestan, and eastern Tibet, the latter becoming Sikang province during the Nationalist period. Even the last few years of Manchu dynasty witnessed a recrudescence of this policy in Sikang, in response

---

[3]The predecessor of *Li-fan yüan* was the *Meng-ku ya-men* (Office for Mongolian Affairs), which came into being in 1634 at the latest. See *Ch'ing T'ai-tsung shih-lu,* chap. 18, p. 32b. In 1638 the name of this office was changed to *Li-fan yüan.*

to Britain's growing influence in Tibet. In its broader aspects, this Ch'ing policy of Sinicization of non-Chinese ethnic groups considered the feasibility of carrying out limited economic and social reforms and included such measures as the setting-up of county and prefectural schools and of local quotas for degree-holders as a means of gradual cultural assimilation. Needless to say, the late Ch'ing, the early Republican, and the Nationalist governments were so beset by domestic difficulties and international crises that they fell far short of the long-range goals set by statesmen of the 1720's.

There is every indication that the historical movement of consolidating China's internal frontiers, which up to the end of the imperial age was confined to China Proper, Inner Mongolia, and Manchuria, has since the founding of the People's Republic of China in 1949 been extended to the vast outlying regions of Sinkiang, Chinghai, Sikang, and Tibet. Superficially, the policy of the present Peking regime toward the fifty or so national minorities seems to be a reversal of the traditional policy of suppression and forced Sinicization, for it has conferred on them constitutional rights of self-rule and regional administrative and cultural autonomy. These constitutional rights, together with some genuine efforts on the part of Peking to help them in agriculture, stock-raising, industry, education, public health, and social reform, have led some Western observers to believe that there has been a complete reorientation of policy.[4]

Yet it may be argued that the basic reason the Peking government has adopted a more enlightened approach to the problem of national minorities is its exuberant confidence in its ability to exert potent control over all minority areas, and in the strength of Chinese culture gradually to assimilate all the non-Han ethnic groups, which—after all—constitute only 6 per cent of the total national population.[5] Whereas the Manchu empire was severely handicapped by difficulties of distance, terrain, and communication, the People's Republic of China has at its disposal more varied and effective instruments of control. We need mention only such factors as, for example, the presence of significant numbers of the People's Liberation Army (PLA) in all outlying areas of national minorities including Tibet; the impending completion of the Peking-Lanchow-Sinkiang Railway, which already has reached Urumchi, capital of Sinkiang; the completion of three trunk roads which link Sinkiang, Chinghai,

---

[4]Josef Kolmas, "The Minority Nationalities," *Bulletin of the Atomic Scientists,* "China Today," June, 1966, pp. 71–75.

[5]The 1953 census gave the total minority population as 35,320,360. Numerically the more important groups are the Chuang (6,611,455), Uighur (3,640,125), Hui (Moslems, 3,559,350), Yi (3,254,269), Tibetan (2,775,622), Miao (2,511,339), Manchu (2,418,931), Mongolian (1,462,956).

Sikang, and Tibet with the rest of China; the establishment of colleges and universities in Sinkiang and Inner Mongolia and of nationality institutes in Peking, Lanchow, Hsining (capital of Chinghai), Wuhan, Chengtu, Nanning and Kunming, which have attracted thousands of non-Han students; the migration of significant numbers of Chinese technological personnel to the northwest where they serve as additional catalysts to inter-ethnic acculturation; and the increasing use of various mass media and of party cadres and native activists to transform the national minorities socially, ideologically, and organizationally. Peking can afford to grant the various non-Han ethnic groups regional administrative and cultural autonomy because of its unprecedented position of strength vis-à-vis them.

In spite of the constitutional rights granted to the national minorities, we find a remarkable continuity between traditional and present policies. Historically, the extension of internal frontiers often contained an element of coercion and was not infrequently accompanied by bloodshed. Even Peking's seemingly enlightened policy toward the national minorities has on occasions required the use of military force. The pacification of the unrest of the Uighurs and Kazaks in Sinkiang in recent years and the suppression of the armed revolt of the Tibetans in 1959 are outstanding examples. The cynic could say that Peking respects the constitutional rights of national minorities only to the extent that they do not resist its imposition of far-reaching social reform. It should be pointed out, however, that, for all its high-handed measures and its technical violation of some non-Han groups' constitutional rights, Peking is not unconcerned with the welfare of the downtrodden within various national minorities. For example, the 1959 revolt was engineered by the old Tibetan ecclesiastical and temporal interests because Peking was determined to emancipate Tibetan commoners from the *ula* (feudal *corvée*) and other economic and social abuses. In fact, even in the late imperial age some farsighted provincial and local officials in the southwest realized that the fundamental solution for the problem of national minorities was for Chinese authorities to eliminate, by force if necessary, the inherent injustice in the non-Han tribal system, although the high price for implementing such a policy made the imperial government reluctant to sanction anything more drastic than palliatives. Put in a proper historical perspective, therefore, the present Peking government's policy toward national minorities is an amplification rather than a reversal of the traditional.

In view of Peking's vastly improved means of control, it is not unlikely that the historical movement of consolidating China's internal frontiers will be reasonably successfully extended, for the first time in Chinese history, from China Proper to "Greater China."

## II

Another important inheritance which China has received from the past is its large population. Prior to the Ch'ing, the peak officially registered population was 60,000,000, although there is strong reason to believe that during certain earlier periods, such as the latter halves of Sung (960-1279)and Ming (1368-1644), the population may well have exceeded 100,000,000. In spite of the wars and turmoil of the twelfth and mid-fourteenth centuries which exacted heavy tolls of human lives, the general demographic trend during the past millennium was toward growth, mainly because of two long-range revolutions in land utilization and food production. The first was brought about by an ever-increasing number of varieties of early-ripening and relatively drought-resistant rice, consequent upon the introduction of the Champa rice from central coastal Indochina at the beginning of the eleventh century. Throughout subsequent centuries the early-ripening rice was responsible for the conquest of hilly regions where the topsoil was sufficiently heavy and rainfall or spring water was adequate and made feasible the double-cropping system for which China's rice area is famous.[6] The second revolution in land utilization began with the introduction in the sixteenth century of such American food crops as maize, the sweet potato and the peanut, which, along with a much later arrival, the Irish potato, enabled the Chinese—hitherto mainly a plain and valley folk—systematically to tackle dry hills, mountains, and sandy loams.[7] As a result of centuries of gradual dissemination of these new crops, large areas of new land were opened up and China's food supply became much more abundant than during pre-Sung times.

Yet, like other pre-industrial populations, China's population could not grow at a sustained high rate over a long period unless institutional and economic factors other than agricultural production were also favorable. As has been discussed in detail in my *Studies on the Population of China, 1368–1953*,[8] such a combination of unusually favorable economic and institutional factors did exist in the century from the dawn of domes-

---

[6]Ping-ti Ho, "Early-Ripening Rice in Chinese History," *Economic History Review*, new series, 9, no. 2 (1956).

[7]Ping-ti Ho, "The Introduction of American Food Plants into China," *The American Anthropologist*, 57, no. 2, pt. 1 (1955); and "American Food Plants in China," *Plant Science Bulletin* (The Botanical Society of America), 2, no. 1 (1956).

[8]Cambridge, Mass.: Harvard University Press, 1959.

tic peace and prosperity in 1683 to the late eighteenth century. Consequently, China's population shot up to 300,000,000 by 1800 and even
an increasingly unfavorable population-land ratio could not prevent the
population from reaching 430,000,000 by 1850. It was precisely at this
juncture where a vastly increasing population was straining at resources
and a large part of it living near the margin of subsistence, that the
Taiping, Nien, and Moslem rebellions broke out in succession.

The decimation of the population of central and lower Yangtze provinces, the Huai River area and the northwest brought about by the rebellions of the third quarter of the nineteenth century at best conferred upon
the nation a brief breathing spell and failed to redress the old population-
land ratio. The absence of major technological revolution has made it
impossible for China to broaden the scope of her land economy to any
appreciable extent. But although the economy failed to make a breakthrough, the ideal of benevolent despotism of the late seventeenth and
early eighteenth centuries was dead once and forever. After the downfall
of the Manchu dynasty, an era of warlordism was ushered in at a time
when the nation had so little economic reserve that natural calamities
exacted disproportionately heavy tolls of human lives. Even during
twenty-two years of Nationalist rule, the nation hardly enjoyed a year
without war, civil or international. Small wonder, then, that the 1953
census yielded a total of 583 millions, which gives a total gain of a mere
35.5 per cent in 103 years and an average annual rate of growth of only
0.3 per cent.

After the Communist takeover in 1949, however, population growth
is reported to have been rapid. The return of peace and order, the beginnings of large-scale industrialization, and especially the nationwide
health campaign apparently have stimulated population growth. During
the past six centuries the Chinese population has responded quickly to
favorable economic and political conditions but has failed to show the
same alacrity in adjusting itself to hard times. The result has been an
almost progressive deterioration in the national standards of living since
the late eighteenth century. Whether history will repeat itself or whether
the new China can achieve a rate of economic growth greater than her
current rate of population growth remains to be seen. But the existence
of so large a population, currently estimated to be in the neighborhood
of 700,000,000 (more than 40 per cent under seventeen years of age), is
a major factor to be reckoned with in world politics. . . .

## 2. The Chinese Communist Regime: A Brief Review

*Theodore H. E. Chen*

### Early Beginnings

The Chinese Communists came to power in 1949. Official policy during the period immediately following the establishment of the new regime was marked by caution and moderation. The Communists did not want to alarm the people, who had been more interested in peace and the cessation of civil strife than in ideology or party politics. To allay public fears, they declared that there would be no abrupt changes. Business people were encouraged to carry on and assured of due profit. Teachers were told that their work would not be interrupted. Even the missionaries were given the impression that they would be able to continue their educational and evangelical work without drastic curtailment.

Official declarations during this initial period promised to protect private property and private enterprise. Religious freedom was guaranteed. The peasants were given land and the satisfaction of private ownership of the land they tilled. Little was said about socialism and Communism; these were distant goals to be attained only after a long transitional period in which the major concern was to build up a strong, independent, and prosperous nation.

This period of moderation did not last long. Its termination was hastened when, in 1950, the new regime decided to play a major role in the Korean War. In the name of a national emergency, the Communists adopted repressive measures to stamp out latent as well as overt opposi-

Reprinted from Theodore H. E. Chen, ed., *The Chinese Communist Regime: Documents and Commentary* (New York: Praeger, 1967), pp. 3–10 by permission of the author, Praeger Publishers, Inc., and Pall Mall Press Ltd.

tion and to tighten their control over the population. A campaign for the "suppression of counterrevolutionaries" was launched in the latter part of 1950, and the ensuing months saw a crescendo of mass trials, mass executions, and wholesale persecution of all who were believed or suspected to be hostile to the new regime. At the same time, a fierce "class war" was waged against landlords in the countryside and the bourgeoisie in the cities, resulting in further persecution and more deaths. Millions of people met sudden and violent death; many more were condemned to long-term hard labor in camps. These campaigns against the "enemies of the people" left no doubt among the people that the Communists would brook no interference with what they were setting out to do.

Reporting to the Fourth Session of the First National People's Progress on June 26, 1957, Prime Minister Chou En-lai noted with satisfaction the success of the new regime in consolidating its power and using it to lead the country toward socialism. Five major campaigns, he said, had paved the way for the consolidation of state power: (1) the agrarian reform to destroy feudalism and the landlord class; (2) the Resist America and Aid Korea movement to combat American imperialism and root out its evil influences on Chinese life; (3) the suppression of counterrevolutionaries to liquidate opposition; (4) the "three anti" and "five anti" campaigns[1] against the bourgeoisie; and (5) ideological remolding to change the outlook, thought patterns, and basic loyalties of the Chinese people, especially the intellectuals. These campaigns were the instruments by which control was tightened during the period from 1950 through 1952.

By the end of 1952, the Communists felt confident enough to terminate officially the initial period of moderate policies and to launch openly their plans for socialism as a prelude to Communism. The Korean War was entering a quiescent phase, with negotiations in process toward some kind of formal armistice. The rural and urban population had been brought under control, and the intellectuals had undergone intensive "thought reform." The First Five-Year Plan was launched on January 1, 1953.

## Five-Year Plans

Then followed five years of intensive reconstruction marked by positive achievements and substantial material progress. A good start was made in industrialization. New buildings and wide streets gave Peking and other

---

[1]See the introduction to Chapter V in Theodore H. E. Chen, ed., *The Chinese Communist Regime, Documents and Commentary* (New York: Praeger, 1967), pp. 183–95.

big cities a look of modernization. New roads, new irrigation works, and new schools were being constructed. Production rose; manufactured goods were exported to other lands as proof to China's neighbors of the success of the Five-Year Plan. Visitors from abroad were impressed by the cleanliness and orderliness of the streets, as well as the immense energy of the people engaged in constructive enterprises. They saw a new China rising, united and moving ahead under the leadership of a stable and efficient government.

The Communists were at the height of their pride and confidence at the beginning of 1958. The Second Five-Year Plan, which was to be even more spectacular than the first, was announced with much fanfare. The nation would not only move at an increased pace; it would take a "Great Leap Forward." China was to overtake Britain industrially in fifteen years. The farms and factories would produce "more, faster, better, and more economically."

The year of the Great Leap Forward was also the year of the dramatic steel drive and the communes. Most of these grandiose plans, however, remained on paper. A combination of circumstances led to economic dislocations and reverses which nullified many of the gains made under the First Five-Year Plan. Industrialization virtually came to a halt. Agricultural production lagged. Shortage of food and consumer goods caused a decline in public morale. Refugees sought haven in Hong Kong or abroad.

The economic crisis, which became more acute after 1959, continued until 1962. Realizing the necessity of major changes in policy, the Communists adopted emergency measures that finally checked the deterioration of the economy. It took time, however, to put new life into the economy and to offset the losses sustained during the period of dislocations. Before further progress was possible, it was first necessary to try to return to the level of development attained in 1957-58. The Second Five-Year Plan, scheduled to last until 1962, had faded away without even an obituary. Three years of "adjustment" intervened before a mild Third Five-Year Plan was announced, to begin in 1966.

## Cultural Revolution

The ideological aspect of its program also posed serious problems for the regime. It has been noted that ideological remolding was one of the "five campaigns" that the regime relied upon for the consolidation of its power. Actually, thought reform was involved in all the five campaigns: The class struggle against the landlords and the bourgeoisie, the attack on

American influence on Chinese life, and the assault on "bourgeois ideology" and bourgeois behavior all constituted important phases of the Communist "ideological struggle."[2] It should also be observed that ideological remolding cannot be accomplished in one stroke; it is a continuous campaign with intermittent periods of relative intensity and severity. Among these periods in China have been the thought reform of 1951-52, with intellectuals making confessions of their failings; the anti-rightist campaign that followed the "contending of the Hundred Schools and blooming of the Hundred Flowers"[3] in 1957; the subsequent demand that intellectuals sign pledges of "heart surrender," vowing to surrender their whole heart, without reservation or condition, to the Communist Party; and the controversy over "Redness versus expertness," in which the official line maintained that it was not enough to train persons with expert knowledge and skills but, even more important, they should be imbued with the correct political ideology in order to become thoroughly "Red." New problems have continued to arise to disturb and distress the ideological molders, and the pressure for thought reform has had to persist unabated.

The Sino-Soviet dispute produced serious problems not only in the economic and political realms, but also in the ideological struggle. Anti-revisionism injected a new stimulant into the campaign for ideological orthodoxy and led to a witch hunt for any indications of thought or attitude that might be at variance with the Party line. A campaign against nonconforming historians, philosophers, and writers seemed to merge in 1966 with a struggle for power within the Communist Party. Important figures in the Party hierarchy and well-known intellectuals who had enjoyed official approbation were put on the black list of "revisionists" and "anti-Party conspirators." Scholars were accused of teaching and spreading anti-Marxist ideas by minimizing the importance of the class struggle or stressing the material aspects of happiness, such as food and comfort. Writers were attacked for voicing indirect criticism of the regime through political satire and ridicule of historical rulers who had ignored the welfare of the people. Even some Party leaders were branded "revisionists" because they did not fully support the program of large-scale collectivization. To combat the rising wave of bourgeois ideas, a "great cultural revolution" of vast proportions was launched. The full effects of this revolution remain to be seen; they are likely to go far beyond the political

---

[2]See Theodore H. E. Chen, *Thought Reform of the Chinese Intellectuals* (Hong Kong: University of Hong Kong Press; New York: Oxford University Press, 1960), Part 1.

[3]This refers to a brief period in 1957 when the intellectuals were encouraged to speak their minds. The result was a flood of severe criticism of the Communists.

field and leave deep scars in the fabric of social and cultural life on the Chinese mainland.

## Forces at Work

In 1966, Communist China did not have the poise and confidence it had exhibited in 1958. In terms of political unity and national stability, the regime seemed to have retrogressed. The popular enthusiasm and the vitality of a dynamic society that so impressed the world in the 1950's seemed to have been overshadowed by internal strife and tensions. What had happened?

The positive achievements of the 1950's stemmed from a combination of circumstances. At the time of the Communist assumption of power, China had emerged from an eight-year war with Japan, only to find itself torn by intensified civil strife. Political instability and economic chaos had discouraged constructive work, and there had been little incentive for long-range planning. History, however, provides ample evidence of the capacity of the Chinese people for hard work and creative activities. Some of the greatest achievements of China have taken place during periods of relative peace and stability — in the long dynasties of Chou, Han, T'ang, Sung, Ming, and the early years of Ch'ing. But the disheartening experiences of a weakened and hard-pressed nation in the nineteenth and the twentieth centuries discouraged and frustrated the people, who were unable to give expression to their latent abilities and creative energies.

In the 1930's, under a government that could at least claim nominal unity after years of division and warlordism, and in a wave of national patriotism stimulated in part by the threat of external aggression, there had been a release of energy resulting in a few years of constructive progress. During the few years prior to the outbreak of war in 1937, China made substantial progress in education, public health, fiscal reform, road-building, rural development, and various phases of material reconstruction. Foreign observers who visited China or served as advisers in various capacities at this time had high praise for the accomplishments of the regime. Optimists averred that a new era was dawning.

The prospect of progress and prosperity came to an abrupt end with the outbreak of war in 1937. What happened to wartime China and the declining morale of the people in the postwar years is a story that does not need to be told here. Suffice it to say that after eight years of a devastating war with Japan, followed by a prolonged civil war, the people of China wanted peace more than anything else. They wanted a stabilization of conditions which would enable them to work and plan in order to get things accomplished. They welcomed the cessation of civil strife that came with Communist victory, and they were eager and relieved to settle down to a peaceful and industrious life.

This brief review of past events suggests that a large part of the credit for the achievements of the 1950's belongs to the hard-working people of China, apart from the government. The material progress and economic prosperity that the island of Taiwan has seen since 1950 also lends support to the contention that, given a reasonable degree of peace and stability, the people of China are capable of outstanding accomplishments, regardless of the form of government under which they live.

At the same time, due recognition must be made of the ability of the Communists to arouse the enthusiasm of the people and to stimulate their pride in positive achievements. Communist propaganda made a strong appeal to national pride; the slogan "The Chinese people have now stood up" helped to raise national morale from the abyss of dejection and depression. Inspired by the vision of a strong and prosperous nation, the people responded enthusiastically to the call for hard work and sacrificial devotion.

Credit must also be given to the Communists for their ability to mobilize the people and marshal their energies and capabilities in the fulfillment of projected plans. The Communists did bring something new to the Chinese scene. Their experience in discipline and organization enabled them to introduce efficiency and orderliness in public enterprises. They forged an intricate system of government and Party administration that exercised authority in all parts of the country. They established a network of mass organizations reaching into all phases of social, economic, and political life. They extended the "iron discipline" of their Party to the nation at large and brought all sectors of the population under their control. By means of rectification campaigns and such devices as criticism and self-criticism in small groups, and by an unrelenting effort to prevent and weed out any "deviations" in thought and action, they were able to reduce corruption and assure the enforcement of orders and decrees.

Effective control was facilitated by a unified leadership that showed few signs of factionalism. The top leaders were singularly devoted to what they believed to be the right cause. By a combination of astute propaganda, effective organization, strict discipline, and a unified and dedicated leadership, the Communists were able to direct the energies and capabilities of the Chinese people into constructive projects. They cleverly combined an appeal to idealism and national pride with veiled forms of coercion, and the fact that punitive action by a powerful Party-state could be quick and relentless made it easier to obtain the "voluntary" submission of the masses. Ruthless suppression of any latent as well as overt opposition also served to convince the population that it would be wiser to submit than to resist.

It took tremendous feats of organization to assemble hundreds of thousands of people to work on the construction of dams, to stage the huge rallies celebrating such events as the founding of the new regime on October 1, or to arrange for simultaneous demonstrations all over the country on a designated day to oppose American imperialism. It was no simple matter to develop mass organizations embracing major sectors of the population — for example, the Sino-Soviet Friendship Association, trade unions, youth groups, the women's federation, and organizations of teachers, scientists, writers, artists — with each local group subordinate to the next higher one in a hierarchy culminating at the national head-quarters. It was no easy task to get millions of people to go out on the streets to kill flies, mosquitoes, or sparrows on a given day, or to take part in a fertilizer-collecting drive. These things the Communists were able to achieve on a nation-wide scale.

## Setback

A different picture, however, presented itself in the 1960's. The popular enthusiasm that characterized the earlier mass campaigns and made pos-sible the production records of the First Five-Year Plan seemed to have declined. The image of a united and dedicated leadership was blurred by what appeared to be a deep-seated factional struggle among the upper echelons of the Party. Unrest among intellectuals was still prevalent after successive campaigns of ideological remolding. Even young people — products of Communist indoctrination — were found wanting in ideolog-ical firmness, sometimes hostile to the established order. Somehow or other, the slogans and the propaganda appeals that had stirred the masses in the first decade no longer seemed effective. The shake-up within the Party leadership, the renewed attack upon intellectuals, and a demand for drastic changes in education testified to the fact that the regime was in the midst of a crisis that went deeper than economic difficulties.

The waning of popular enthusiasm probably began with the economic shortages of 1959 and afterward, and with the institution of the com-munes,[4] demanding radical changes in the Chinese way of life. The de-cline of production in the communes was in no small measure due to a

---

[4]See Chapter V of Chen, *The Chinese Communist Regime*, for further discussion of the communes.

lack of motivation. People who had in the first decade responded to the call to work hard for a strong and prosperous country now wondered if they had labored only to lose what they considered precious—their land, their family life, and their traditions. They had accepted the need to sacrifice present comforts for a better tomorrow, but now they began to wonder if tomorrow would ever come. True, the Communists quickly revised their initially ambitious plans for communization; they did not push collectivization beyond the public mess halls, service centers, and nurseries for the care of infants. Moreover, they gave a part of the collectivized land to the peasants to be cultivated as private plots. The very fact that the private plots proved to be the healthiest part of the rural economy showed that the peasants had no enthusiasm for the communes and the collectivization program of the Communists.

From another point of view, the Sino-Soviet dispute must have exacerbated the internal psychological problems confronting the Communists. During the first few years of the regime, the Sino-Soviet Friendship Association was the biggest mass organization in the country. Headed by no less a person than Liu Shao-ch'i, it flooded the country with intensive propaganda praising "the Soviet Union, our teacher" and honoring Joseph Stalin, "the savior of mankind." During the "Hundred Flowers" period of "free criticism," no one was allowed to criticize the Soviet Union. Soviet advisers were exalted as "Big Brothers" who had come to assist China in the most selfless spirit. The Soviet model was held up as a guide in industry, in education, and in all reforms. Russian replaced English as the most important foreign language.

Then the Party line was completely reversed when the Sino-Soviet dispute became acute. No longer selfless "Big Brothers," the Russian "revisionists" were now attacked and reviled as severely as the imperialist Americans. The erstwhile Russian model was now shunned, and the Russian language was no longer stressed. The intellectuals and the nationalist-minded patriots who in early years had been skeptical of the wholesale introduction of Russian influence may have been secretly amused by the belated realization that Soviet dominance was no better than any other form of foreign influence, but the masses must have been greatly confused by the switch of Party line. The reversal of what had been repeatedly affirmed in nation-wide propaganda must have created in many minds a serious doubt as to the veracity of the "truths" imparted in Communist propaganda. Once such doubts begin to grow in the public mind, the whole structure of Communist propaganda, a major pillar of the regime, may start to weaken.

In the upheaval of the mid-1960's, therefore, the Communists were not grappling with economic or political problems as such, but with the state of mind that had created them. While the popular enthusiasm of the first decade was the product of popular attitudes that the Communists were able to exploit and direct to fulfill their plans, the decline of morale in the 1960's was the result of a state of mind that tended to question or even resist the official plans and policies. In the opinion of this writer, it is a recognition of the need to change the public mood that lies behind the new emphasis on a "cultural revolution." . . .

# II

# The Environment of the
# Chinese Communist System


## 3. The Physical and Demographic Setting

*Chang-tu Hu, et al.*


### Geography and Population

An area of four million square miles and a population of well over six hundred fifty million people make China one of the largest and most populous countries in the world today. It compares favorably with the other Pacific nations in natural resources and geographical location. Though possessing an extensive coast line with many good harbors on the eastern seaboard, China developed as a land power rather than as a sea power, the fertile plains of North China being the historic center of Chinese expansion and influence.

Besides a certain resemblance in size and contour, China and the United States, lying largely in the same latitudes (25° N. to 45° N.), share a comparable, continental-type climate and vegetation. There is, however, a marked difference in topography. Whereas the United States, bounded by two oceans, tends toward an equal development of east and west, China expands from the loess highland and the central plains eastward and southward to the sea. In the northwest, China has a vast hinterland of deserts and plateaus screened off from Soviet Central Asia by high mountain ranges. The borders between southwestern China and India and Burma are as yet undelimited.

A majority of Chinese cities are found in the central, eastern, and southeastern areas favored by a temperate climate and gentle terrain. The west, though known to abound in natural resources, has remained

Reprinted from Chang-tu Hu, et al., *China: Its People, Its Society, Its Culture* (New Haven: HRAF Press, 1960), pp. 40, 42–50, 54–58, 64–69, 85–88, by permission of the author and the publisher.

only partially explored because of its adverse terrain and climate. Improved transportation and communications will doubtless change this development pattern. Exploration, irrigation, and reclamation projects in the northwest and southwest have been incorporated in the Communist government's five-year plans and the industrialization of Manchuria is fast transforming it into an area comparable to the northern New Jersey-New York complex.

**Physical Setting.** Extending over 2,500 miles from its Pacific coast to the Pamir plateau in Central Asia, China exhibits great variety in topographical relief. Surrounding the plateau of Tibet in the southwest are mountains the loftiest of which rise over 25,000 feet while some depressions in the Turfan basin in Sinkiang are 141 feet below sea level. The Mongolian plateau, the world's widest, stretches for a distance of over 2,000 miles. The desolate high plateaus in Tibet and Tsinghai (Kokonor), enclosed by mountain ranges, contrast with such rich lowlands as the Red Basin of Szechwan and the lake basins along the middle and lower Yangtze valley. Great fertile plains, particularly in the coastal delta area of the great rivers, are located amidst large masses of hills and uplands.

*Mountains, Rivers, and Harbors.* From the Pamirs, a central mountain knot of all the mountains of Asia, four major limbs of the Central Asia ramparts extend toward China. The Altai, T'ien Shan, Kunlun, and Himalayan mountain systems each consist of several parallel chains and form the chief watersheds of all the principal rivers in China. Their passes afford natural land routes between China and its neighbors in Mongolia and Central Asia.

The Altai and Himalayan systems form the natural boundaries of China in the northwest and southwest; the T'ien Shan divides Sinkiang; the Kunlun system branches all over the country, forming the backbone or skeleton of its topography. Running eastward from the Pamirs, the Kunlun system divides the Tarim basin of Sinkiang from the high plateaus of Tibet, then branches off into three separate chains: (1) the Altin Tagh-Nan Shan ranges in the north, which divide the inland drainage of the Mongolian plateau from the Yellow River; (2) the Tsinling-Ta-pieh ranges in the center, which form the major watershed between the Yellow River and the Yangtze; and (3) the Thanglha Ri range in the south, which meets the eastern end of the Himalayan system in Sikang and northwestern Yunnan.

In addition to these four major systems are two mountain groups in the northeast and southeast, the so-called Sinic mountains, which seem to have no direct relation to any of the major systems in the west. In between the mountains of the northern group are valley plains, such as the Chiao valley plain between T'ai Shan and Lao Shan in the peninsula of Shantung; and the Sungari-Liao plain surrounded by Hsing-an Ling (Khingan), Ch'ang-pai Shan, and the Jehol hills in Manchuria. The southern ranges, the Nan Ling, form a major geographical divide between the lower Yangtze and the various short independent streams which flow separately into the southwestern China Sea.

Since the general topography of China orientates toward the east, all the great rivers flow eastward to the Pacific. In the northeast, the Amur (Hei-lung Chiang) drains a great part of the Manchurian basin as it winds along its 2,500-mile course. Though navigation is limited to small steamers and native craft, these can go as far as the confluence of its two upper reaches and even beyond during the flood season. Other Manchurian rivers include the Liao Ho, the chief river in southern Manchuria, as well as the Tumen and the Yalu, which form the boundary between China and Korea. Carrying very little ordinary shipping, the importance of the Yalu lies primarily in hydroelectric power development and in its timber traffic.

The main river of North China, and the second largest in the country, is the Yellow River (Huang Ho), which acquires its characteristic yellowish muddy color from the tributary rivers of the loess plateau of Kansu. From Kansu it winds 2,980 miles through the northern provinces eastward to Shantung where it empties into the Gulf of Chihli (Po Hai). The Yellow River valley includes an area of 600,000 square miles. Abundant silt and an almost unvarying water level limits its transportation capacity, creating as well a control problem. To keep the flow channeled, the Chinese have been continuously building up its embankments with the result that the present river bed is 16 feet or more above the general level of the surrounding plain, held to its course by man-made levees. Along its lower course, the Yellow River floods regularly, particularly in late summer and early autumn, and no important towns have grown up along its banks.

Central China is drained mainly by the Yangtze and its numerous tributaries. The Yangtze (Ch'ang Chiang) is by far the largest river in China. From sources only 50 miles (as the crow flies) from those of the Yellow River, it travels 3,237 miles, draining over 700,000 square miles. From the confluence of its two headwaters in the upland of southern Tsinghai, it flows southward to western Szechwan as the Chin-sha Chiang; then, beyond the great bend in northwestern Yunnan it turns sharply to the east and traverses the whole length of Central China to the East China Sea.

The Yangtze can be divided into three parts: a torrential upper course that includes many rapids and falls; a middle course of 960 miles, on parts of which (such as the Yangtze gorges) navigation is limited to junks and river steamers of no more than 200 tons; and a lower course of 1,062 miles navigable by both coastal and ocean-going vessels. On its way to the sea, the Yangtze is divided by the Ch'ung-ming Island into two channels. The southern channel, known as Wu-sung, has a deeper entrance closer to Shanghai, from which ocean-going vessels can sail up to Hankow, 630 miles inland.

In Central China, the Huai Ho and the Fu-ch'un Chiang are next to the Yangtze in importance. The Fu-ch'un Chiang is one of the main rivers along the Chekiang coast. The Huai, the largest river between the Yangtze and the Yellow, is unique in that it is the only long river without a natural outlet, and consequently it frequently floods.

Important rivers that drain the southeastern coastal regions are the Min Chiang and the Chu Chiang (Pearl River). The Min is navigable over most of its course although upstream navigation is rather difficult in the flood season. The Pearl, the chief river in Kwangtung and Kwangsi, is the fourth largest river in China and its valley covers a drainage area of 150,000 square miles. The Pearl is a general name for a network of three waterways, which meet south of Canton to form a big estuary consisting of many channels separated by a number of islets. The main eastern channel, Hu Men (Boca Tigris), enters the sea near Hong Kong, while the main western channel flows close to Macao.

Farther southwest are two independent rivers, the Mekong (Lan-ts'ang Chiang) and the Red River (Yüan Chiang), of which only the upper courses are in Chinese territory. Both flow southward through a large part of Indochina before entering the sea, but are unnavigable in China.

Pacific drainage accounts for 50 percent of China's total drainage area; inland drainage, 39 percent; and the Indian Ocean and the Arctic, the remaining 6 and 5 percents respectively. Today, with Outer Mongolia and Tannu Tuva independent, none of the Arctic drainage except a small portion of the upper Irtysh (one of the upper reaches of the Ob River) via the Zaisan Nor is in China Proper. Fairly long stretches of the upper reaches of the principal rivers of the Indian Ocean drainage are in China, but these rivers enter the sea through other nations' territories. The Salween (Nu Chiang), the Irrawaddy, and the Tsangpo (Ya-lu-ts'ang-pu) all have their sources in the mountainous regions of Tibet and western Szechwan. The Tsangpo flows eastward from its Himalayan home to drain southern Tibet, then bends abruptly south to India, where under the name of Brahmaputra it merges with the Ganges to empty into the Bay of Bengal. The upper courses of both the Salween and Irrawaddy drain a large portion of western Yunnan before they reach the sea by way of Burma.

Inland drainage covers a number of upland basins in the vast dry interior of North and Northwest China. Due to meager rainfall and difficult terrain, the inland rivers are as a whole rather small and lack outlets to the sea. They generally flow into lakes or die in the desert, most of them entirely inside China. The Tarim, the longest inland river in the country, consists of numerous streams coming down from the mountains in southern Sinkiang.

While the inland rivers are valuable for irrigation in the dry interior of northern and northwestern China, their water supply from the snow-clad mountains is rather limited. On the other hand, the upper courses of the Red River, Mekong, Salween, and Irrawaddy provide potential sources for the development of waterpower in the plateaus of Southwest China. There are too many torrents and rapids, especially in the summer monsoon season, to make navigation possible. No transportation is available along their courses except on some parts of the upper Red River, the upper Irrawaddy, and the east-west stretch of the Tsangpo, where small native craft are sometimes seen. At 12,000 feet the Tsangpo or upper Brahmaputra is the highest navigable river in the world.

The coast line of China extends from the mouth of the Yalu River in the northeast to the mouth of the Pei-lun River in the south. It forms a great arc with the peninsulas of Liaotung and Shantung in the north and that of Luichow in the south protruding respectively into the Yellow Sea and the South China Sea. The coast is separated from the Pacific Ocean by a chain of islands and archipelagos, such as Liu-ch'iu, Taiwan, Pescadores (P'eng-hu), Hainan, and the Pratas (Tung-sha), Paracel (Hsi-sha), and Spratly (Nan-sha) groups, which not only gives China a continuous series of partially enclosed coastal seas like the Gulf of Chihli, the Yellow Sea, the East China Sea, and the South China Sea, but also forms the two great gulfs of Liaotung in the north and Tonkin in the south.

The general configuration of the coast line comes to a length of 2,500 miles. If the minor inlets are included, the distance amounts to nearly 7,000 miles. Of this total, some 3,000 miles are sandy and the rest, rocky. The sandy coast is characterized by wide, relatively flat beaches on a shore line of long straight stretches coupled with sweeping curves. The adjoining country is often low and flat with marshes or lakes. Shoals and generally shallow water are usual along these sandy coastal areas although good natural harbors, as at Shanghai, can be found at the mouths of the larger rivers. In contrast, the rocky parts of the coast of China are often highly indented. Fairly deep seas broken by numerous islands and islets are characteristic of these coastal areas. Such conditions create many good natural harbors but the characteristics of the hinterlands, hilly to mountainous, limit the exploitation of these coastal features. Thus no port of importance has been developed except at or near the mouth of a large river, as at Canton. The big port planned for South China is to be situated at Huang-pu (Whampoa) on the estuary of the Pearl River.

Other ports of importance are An-tung at the mouth of the Yalu River, Port Arthur (Lü-shun), and Dairen (Ta-lien) on the Liaotung Peninsula. Port Arthur is the leading naval base and Dairen the chief commercial port of Manchuria. There are also three developed ports along the Shantung coast; Chefoo (Yen-t'ai) on the north; Wei-hai-wei, not far from the tip of the peninsula; and Tsingtao, lying on its southernmost part at the entrance to the bay. Farther south, numerous good harbors can be found all along the coast. Some of the moderately developed ports are Yin-hsien (Ningpo), Foochow, Amoy, Swatow, and Chan-chiang.

*Climate.* Although most of China lies inside the temperate belt, it has an extreme continental climate with a summer temperature (especially in Central and South China) higher than that of the tropics and a winter cold which in the far north is more severe than in the frigid zone. In winter the temperature decreases rapidly from south to north, ranging from an average of 60° F. south of the Nan Ling range to about 40° F. along the middle and lower Yangtze valley, to just below freezing or about 30° F. in the North China plain and southern Manchuria, and to well below freezing at about 0° F. and −17° F. in central and northern Manchuria respectively. In summer the temperature is more nearly uniform over the whole country, with a July mean of 80° F., but northern China has much cooler nights and a shorter hot period than southern China.

Rainfall is essentially seasonal, most of it occurring in the summer. The amount of precipitation decreases from south to north, with an annual average of 60-80 inches in the Pearl River valley and the hilly land along the southeastern coast, 40-60 inches in the Yangtze valley, about 25 inches over the North China plain, and less than 10 inches in the interior. To the northeast, in the Manchurian basin, the rainfall varies from about 30 inches in southeastern areas to less than 10 inches in the Barga district and the eastern Gobi.

Most of the late summer rain along the southeastern coast is due to typhoon influence. Typhoons bring some cooling, a temporary relief from the prolonged summer heat, but also cause damage to crops and to a considerable degree determine the type planted. The crops grown along the southeastern coast of China are therefore predominantly low standing—peanuts and sweet potatoes are common—in preference to higher standing crops that would be more easily damaged by typhoons.

*Soils.* The soils of China can be classified into three main groups: non-acid or sweet soil in the north, acid soil in the south, and neutral soil in the central area. The leaching effect of the non-acid soil is weakened by flat topography, low annual rainfall, and limited irrigation whereas the acid soil of the south is subjected to leaching by hilly terrain and abundant rainfall. For climatic reasons more crops are raised in the southern regions where the soil is poor than in the northern areas where the soil is rich. The nonacid soil region represents the wheat area, and the acid soil region, the rice area.

The transitional belt of neutral, slightly acid soil includes western Hupeh, southern Shantung, the Yangtze delta, and northern Szechwan. The deltaic plains, both north and south, such as the lower Yangtze valley plain and the Pearl River delta, are all only slightly leached, contain a fair percentage of calcium and other soluble minerals, and are quite fertile.

Broadly speaking, the productivity of the land in China corresponds to the distribution of the population. The populous areas are the valley plains of the winter wheat and millet area (the loess plateau of Northwest China), the winter wheat and kaoliang area (the North China plain and Shantung highland), the Szechwan rice-growing area (Red Basin), the rice and wheat area (the lower Yangtze valley plain), and the double-cropping rice area of the Pearl River delta. The Yangtze delta and the Red Basin of Szechwan, which have slightly leached and weak acid soils, are the most densely populated areas.

**Political Divisions.** Politically, China is divided for administrative purposes into a number of provinces and autonomous regions (see the map, Political Divisions, 1959). The eighteen provinces of China Proper south of the Great Wall were the core of Chinese political influence, which later extended to the border regions of Manchuria, Mongolia, Sinkiang, and Tibet. Together they constitute what is generally known as Greater China.

At present there are seventeen provinces in China Proper. In the north are the four provinces of Hopeh, Honan, Shansi, and Shantung. In the northwest are the two border provinces of Shensi and Kansu. In Central China are the four provinces of Anhwei, Kiangsi, Hupeh, and Hunan; to the east, the two provinces of Kiangsu and Chekiang. In the southwest interior are the three provinces of Szechwan, Yunnan, and

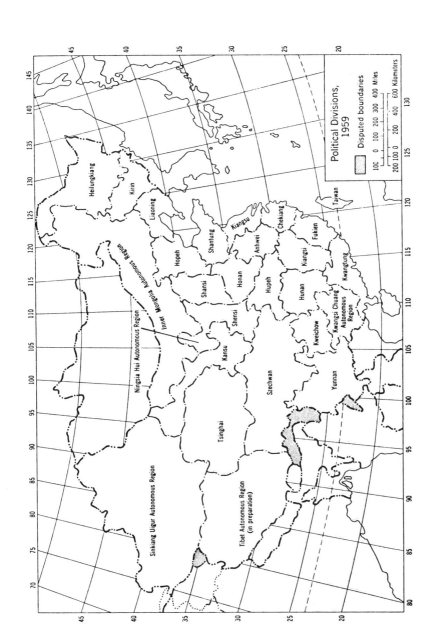

Political Divisions, 1959

Disputed boundaries

Kweichow. In South China are the two coastal provinces of Fukien and Kwangtung; Kwangsi, formerly a province, has been made into an autonomous region of the Chuang people.

Some of the outlying regions of Greater China have become provinces, while others have more recently been made into autonomous regions. In Manchuria are the three provinces of Liaoning, Kirin, and Heilungkiang. At the western end of Kansu is Sinkiang, also known as Chinese Turkestan; formerly a province, it is now an autonomous region of the predominant Uigur population. Southwest of Kansu is the province of Tsinghai, formerly a part of Inner Tibet with a large Tibetan population. Sikang, formerly a province carved out from Szechwan and Tibet, has lost its provincial status and been incorporated into Szechwan. Preparations are being made to incorporate Tibet as an autonomous region. The Autonomous Region of Inner Mongolia consists of Chahar and Suiyuan, parts of Jehol and Kansu, and the western part of Manchuria. Ningsia is now an autonomous region of the Hui people. Outer Mongolia, formerly a Chinese dependency, has become the Mongolian People's Republic. On the other hand, Taiwan (the official Chinese name for Formosa) has been included as a Chinese province.

Today there are twenty-two provinces (including Taiwan), five autonomous regions (including Tibet), and a number of smaller autonomous areas established along ethnic lines. There are also two special municipalities administered directly by the central government; Peking, the capital city, and Shanghai. All other municipalities, including the former special municipality of Tientsin, are under provincial control. There are an estimated 100 provincial municipalities, 2,000 counties, and some 80 autonomous administrative units in the country. . . .

**Population.** Well over 650 million people live in China today if the estimates made on the basis of the 1953 census—a population of approximately 583 million and a 2 percent annual increase—are correct. These millions form an immense reservoir of manpower vitally important to the rapid industrialization of China but also generate pressures and problems for the Communist regime as well as the other nations of the world.

The Communists began their preparations for a nationwide census, the first since 1909, shortly after assuming power in 1949. In June 1953, as part of the registration for the general elections at the primary level, each voter was directed to fill out a census questionnaire, giving his name, domicile, sex, age, and nationality. The total population figure of 601,938,035 published in November 1954 by the State Statistical Bureau included, however, more than 7.5 million Chinese on Taiwan and approximately 12 million Chinese abroad, reducing to about 583 million the population actually living in mainland China at the time of the census. Those who were directly surveyed and registered amounted to 574 million.

Study of population statistics for China over the past three hundred years reveals a steady growth from 70 million in 1650 to 583 million in 1953 — a more than eightfold increase. (If a population of 150 million in 1650, given in another source, were used, the increase would still be almost fourfold in three hundred years.) The present 2 percent annual rate of increase, if maintained, will result in a population by 2000 of at least 1.5 billion, or more than half the present world population.

The phenomenal growth of the Chinese population is largely due to a high birth date. In the past this was countered by a similarly high death rate resulting from a low standard of living and poor sanitation as well as frequent calamities such as famines, floods, and wars. But during the twenty-two years of the Nationalist rule (1927-49) the birth rate was estimated to be thirty-five per thousand and the death rate twenty-five per thousand, representing a yearly net gain of ten persons per thousand. This rate of increase is already quite high when compared with that in such countries as Sweden, Switzerland, Belgium, and England. In one of its studies the Communist government has set the present average birth rate at thirty-seven and the death rate at seventeen for a natural increase of twenty per thousand. The lower death rate has been attributed to the government's successful public health work, the improvement in living conditions, and the decrease in the infant death rate.

It has been commonly presumed that India, Japan, and China, generally speaking, have more males than females, and past Chinese population estimates often indicated an unusual preponderance of males over females. As recently as 1927 the Chinese government, in a population report of twelve provinces, showed the sex ratio to be 124 : 100. Previous investigations revealed an even greater excess of males. This may be due in part to the traditionally low position of women in society, which used to lead to the abandonment of baby girls, but may also reflect the tendency not to report females, especially young ones, in past years. The nearly equal sex ratio of recent years is therefore one indication of the new social status enjoyed by women. The 1953 census, covering a directly registered population of 574 million, reports 297,553,518 males and 276,652,422 females, a sex ratio of 107: 100, much lower than any previous ratio. It agrees, however, with the normal distribution of sexes among many other peoples and there seems to be little doubt of its validity.

Of the 574 million Chinese, 338,400,00 persons belonged to the age group of eighteen and over, constituting 59 percent of the total registered population. Of this group 1,850,000 persons were eighty to ninety-nine years old; 3,384 had reached the age of one hundred or more, the oldest recorded age being one hundred fifty-five (sex not given). On the other hand, 235,200,000 persons belonged to the age group of seventeen and under, constituting 41 percent of the total registered population. Of this group 89,500,000 were children up to four years of age, 63,100,000 were between five and nine, and 82,600,000 were from nine to seventeen. With forty-one persons out of every one hundred in the seventeen-and-under group, the source of China's manpower in the next few decades will be very large indeed.

The life expectancy of the Chinese has never been very high. Judging from the results of recent sample studies, the life expectancy of the present-day Chinese at birth is 31.9 for males and 34.2 for females; at the age of 20 the figures are 35.6 and 39.3 respectively; at 40 they are 23.5 and 25.6; at 60 they are 11.5 and 12.1. Compared with other Asian nations, life expectancy in China is slightly higher than in India, but less than in Japan.

A comparison of the age compositions of the populations in China and in the United States reveals a general similarity in age distribution for the group between five and fifty-four, and life expectancy figures within this group seem to be much the same in both countries. There are important differences, however, in the four or under and fifty-five or over categories. A higher Chinese birth rate, even though offset to a certain extent by a higher infant mortality rate, results in a much higher proportion of infants four years old or younger in the Chinese population. The United States population, on the other hand, reflects a longer life expectancy at fifty-five and over in a higher percentage of people in this age group. . . .

## Ethnic Minorities

The Chinese Communists use the term "minority nationalities" to designate ethnic minorities within the People's Republic of China. A minority nationality is defined as a community of common origin, bound together by a common language, a continuous area of residence, and a sense of group identity in economic and social matters as well as in standards of behavior and other distinctive traits. Physiological elements are considered secondary although marked physical differences exist between the various nationalities in China.

In the past the Han-Chinese attitude toward the non-Han ethnic groups was that of the bearers of a high civilization toward primitive tribal peoples. Steeped in age-old prejudice, the Han-Chinese had formed misconceptions based largely upon incorrect and improbable tales rather than on their own observations and personal contact.

In recent years, however, a significant change has taken place in the Chinese attitude toward the minority peoples. During the Nationalist administration a minimal effort was made to allay the traditional Han-Chinese prejudice toward these groups, to discourage categorization of them as "barbarians" and "aborigines," as well as to assimilate them into the national norm.

While also trying to minimize group divergences, the Chinese Communists have recognized that at the present stage the millions of minority peoples can achieve social and cultural progress only in their own accustomed patterns and habits of living. Present efforts are therefore concentrated on bringing the leaders of the ethnic groups into closer association with the government and on training the minority youths in Chinese schools and universities to undertake the task of social and economic transformation among their own people. In economic, cultural, political, educational, and public health activities, the Communist government endeavors to diminish the differences among the groups without trying actually to absorb them into Han-Chinese culture. The goal of Communist nationalities policy is to remove the factors that had for centuries caused them to defy the central government and, through better communications and direct contact, to bring them under effective control. The government has, however, shown by its recent suppression of the Tibetans that it will not tolerate more than a mild degree of resistance among these groups.

**Classification and Distribution.** There are probably few areas in the world where so many ethnic groups have lived together for so many centuries as in China. These groups, distributed over a wide area both in the hinterlands and the border regions, have undergone a complicated historical process of migration, assimilation, and transformation. Moreover, designations for these people have changed from time to time, making it difficult sometimes to trace the origin of particular groups or to keep track of their movements from one region to another.

The minority nationalities, constituting about 6 percent of China's 650 million population, are concentrated mainly in seven border regions: (1) Manchuria; (2) Inner Mongolia; (2) Sinkiang, Tsinghai, and Kansu; (4) Tibet; (5) Szechwan, Yunnan, and Kweichow; (6) Kwangtung and Kwangsi; and (7) Taiwan (see the map, Minority Nationality Areas). Ten of the non-Han ethnic groups have a population from one million to over six million. Among them, the Koreans in Manchuria are immigrants from Korea; the Manchus, who were of Tungus origin, have become completely Sinicized; and the Hui, descendants of Turkic-Uigur soldiers and merchants who moved to China more than a thousand years ago, have lost much of their racial identity through intermarriage with the Han-Chinese. Aside from these, the more important and distinctive non-Han ethnic groups in China are the Mongols, the Uigurs, the Tibetans, the Miao-Yao, the Chuang, the Yi, and the Puyi.

The Mongols constitute the major ethnic groups on the Mongolian steppes and are divisible into three groups: the Eastern Mongols, the largest group in Inner Mongolia, related to the Khalka of Outer Mongolia; the Western Mongols, or Oirat; and the Northern Mongols, or Buryat. Small numbers of Mongols are found in Sinkiang, Manchuria, and Kansu. Other ethnic groups in Inner Mongolia include the Daur, Orochon, Yakat, Solon, and Tungusic immigrants from Manchuria. All are relatively unimportant numerically.

The Uigurs (New Uigurs, or Eastern Turks) live mainly in the southern part of Sinkiang and generally call themselves after the names of their adopted cities. Other groups in Northwest China include the Hui, Kazak, Kirghiz, Monguor, Tadjik, Tatar, and Uzbek.

The Tibetans are distributed principally in Tibet and in the Chamdo region of Szechwan; some are found in Tsinghai and Kansu, where their neighbors include the Monguor, Salar, and Turki.

The Miao and Yao, though not closely related, are often classified together. They constitute one of the most important groups in South and Southwest China. The Miao are distributed widely over the mountainous areas of Kweichow and Yunnan in the west to Hunan, Kwangtung, and Kwangsi in the central south. The Kwangtung group, located on Hainan Island, is descended from Miao soldiers brought there centuries ago by the Chinese government to quell the rebellious Li. The Miao are subdivided into such groups as the Red, Black, Blue, White and Flowery Miao. The Yao inhabit the mountainous regions of Kwangtung and Kwangsi.

The Chuang, numbering over six and one half million, constitute the largest of the ethnic minorities in China. This Thai-speaking group is located principally on the plains and in the valleys of western Kwangsi.

The Yi (Lolo) are located principally in the Liang Shan area on the borders of Szechwan and Yunnan.

The Puyi (Chungchia) are distributed in low marshy areas around Kuei-yang and in southwestern Kweichow province.

Many of these minority nationalities are indigenous groups that settled in their homes in ancient times; others moved to their present locality only in recent centuries. Although their migratory routes were different, they seem to have followed a general southward movement from the deserts and plateaus of the north to the Yellow River plains, or from

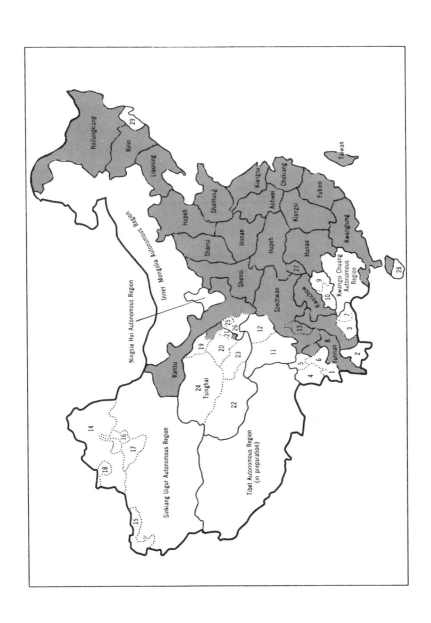

central south and southwest regions toward the tropics. While northern groups like the Mongols, Manchus, and Tungus have repeatedly pressed southward and have just as often been pushed back to their original abode by the Han-Chinese, southern groups such as the Thai and Miao penetrated beyond the Chinese national boundary into Burma, Indochina, and Thailand. . . .

## NATIONALITY AUTONOMOUS DISTRICTS (CHOÙ)*

*Yunan*

1. Te-hung (Thai and Chingpo)
2. Hsi-shuang-pa-na (Thai)
3. Hung-ho (Hani and Yi)
4. Nu-chiang (Lisu)
5. Ti-ch'ing (Tibetan)
6. Ta-li (Pai)
7. Wen-shan (Chuang and Miao)
8. Ch'u-hsiung (Yi)

*Kweichow*

9. Southeastern Kweichow (Miao and Tung)
10. Southern Kweichow (Puyi and Miao)

*Szechwan*

11. Kan-tzu (Tibetan)
12. A-pa (Tibetan)
13. Liang-shan (Yi)

*Sinkiang Uigur Autonomous Region*

14. I-li (Kazak)
15. K'e-tzu-le-su (Khalka)
16. Ch'ang-chi (Hui)
17. Pa-yin-kuo-leng (Mongol)
18. Po-erh-ta-la (Mongol)

*Tsinghai*

19. Hai-pei (Tibetan)
20. Hai-nan (Tibetan)
21. Huang-nan (Tibetan)
22. Yü-shu (Tibetan)
23. Kuo-lo (Tibetan)
24. Hai-hsi (Mongol, Tibetan and Kazak)

*Peking Review*, Vol. II, No. 21, May 26, 1959, p. 9.

*Kansu*

25. Lin-hsia (Hui)
26. Southern Kansu (Tibetan)

*Hunan*

27. Western Hunan (Tuchia and Miao)

*Kwangtung*

28. Hainan (Li and Miao)

*Kirin*

29. Yen-pien (Korean)

**Relations with Han-Chinese.** Relations of the ethnic minorities with the dominant Han-Chinese have not been without strain and tension. The history of the frequent conflicts and wars between the Chinese and various tribal groups on the country's borders discloses in fact certain recurrent patterns. The ethnic groups of the south and southwest, such as the Miao, Yao, Chuang, and Yi, mostly agriculturists, would rebel whenever the local Chinese government became weak or oppressive, only to be reconquered by superior Chinese forces after a few years of resistance. The numerous campaigns undertaken by the government to quell these uprisings resulted in further penetration of Chinese influence into the remote mountainous regions and valleys, once the strongholds of these groups. To govern them more efficiently, the Chinese government adopted a policy of ruling the natives through native chieftains; this *t'u-ssu* (native official) system, first introduced as early as the third century A.D., was eminently successful in later centuries. The Han-Chinese were also successful in building up and training an army of one tribal group to be used in fighting against another whenever expedient.

Sometimes native officials were assigned Han-Chinese assistants to protect the interests of the Han-Chinese population in the area, but these officials also came under the supervision of the provincial authority, to whom they had to pay taxes and for whom they had to provide soldiers in case of war. The *t'u-ssu* system, most fully developed and organized during the Ming dynasty (1368-1644), was not abolished until the twentieth century, when the territories of these minority groups were put under direct government administration. Among some groups like the Tibetans and Yi, the power of the tribal chieftains never was broken and their continued rule was the cause of local disturbances in the republican period (1912-49). The Thai chieftains in southwestern Yunnan at the Burma border also continued to function up to recent times, serving as buffers in border conflicts.

The pattern of conflict in the north and northeast, somewhat different from the south's, was also on a larger scale. The mainly nomadic and more warlike groups along China's vast northern frontier at times grew strong enough to seize large parts of Chinese territory and twice succeeded in conquering the whole country and establishing their own rule. In the thirteenth and fourteenth centuries, the Mongols established a vast Asian empire with its seat of government in modern Peking. The Manchus were the masters of China for almost three hundred years until their power was broken in 1911. After World War II the Mongols in Outer Mongolia, backed by the Soviet Union, obtained official Chinese recognition of their independence and brought the nominal Chinese suzerainty there to an end.

As a corollary to these contacts over the centuries a great number of individuals from the minority groups, attracted to the more advanced Chinese civilization, were assimilated to the Chinese people. Chinese colonization of the frontiers also resulted in a preponderance of Han-Chinese in some minority regions, especially in Manchuria, where they constitute 95 percent of its population; the Manchus, on the other hand, have almost completely lost their group identity. This is a typical example of the gradual spread and penetration of Chinese cultural and political influences into the border regions and the absorption of the minority people through intermarriage and acculturation. Other minority groups in Manchuria, like the Mongols and Tungus, have also been absorbed by the Han-Chinese, and only the Koreans there present problems different from the others. For one thing, the Koreans in Manchuria are more steeped in western civilization and more productive than the Chinese. Furthermore, unlike the more modernized Russians who even in their own settlements at Harbin are outnumbered by the Chinese, and unlike the Japanese who have never considered Manchuria their permanent home, the Koreans settle mostly in areas where they outnumber the Chinese and where they persist in preserving their cultural traditions without even learning the Chinese language. The establishment by the Communist government of the Yen-pien Korean Autonomous District in Manchuria is evidence of the ethnic integrity of the Koreans and a matter of some international significance.

In Inner Mongolia also, the Han-Chinese outnumber the Mongols and other ethnic groups. It has been estimated that there is a total Chinese population of five million, most of them in southeastern Mongolia, compared to about one million Mongols. The Mongols vary in culture and degree of Sinification. The sedentary groups, as mentioned before, have adopted much of the Chinese way of life. The most Sinified groups are found in the southeastern area and among the Tumet of the former Suiyuan province, which the Chinese have colonized. On the whole, neither the Mongols nor the smaller Tungusic groups, most of them nomads, seem to have had much conflict with either the agricultural and urban-oriented Han-Chinese communities or the Chinese administration in these regions. The establishment by the Communist regime of the Inner Mongolia Autonomous Region aims to reduce what tension might have existed in the past.

Relationships between the Han-Chinese and the minority nationalities in the west and northwest, however, have been tense. There has been a definite racial antagonism between the Han-Chinese and the other ethnic groups in these areas. An old and deep animosity exists between the Turkic people and the Chinese due partly to the greater efficiency and industriousness of the Chinese, who have managed to displace the Turkic people in much of their agricultural work. The Kazak, a proud and freedom-loving people, dislike any political supervision and are known to have avoided tax collectors by crossing the national borders to Soviet Russia. Successive Hui uprisings were put down at the cost of much bloodshed. The Salar, who have a reputation for being fanatical Moslems, participated in all the Hui uprisings of recent centuries.

The question of Tibetan independence presented a serious problem to the Chinese. Tibet had won a quasi-independent status from the weakened Chinese government at the beginning of the twentieth century and did not surrender this status until after its penetration in 1950 by the Communist forces. An agreement was reached between the Peking government and the Lhasa authority for the autonomy of Tibet and the organization of a preparatory committee for the Autonomous Region of Tibet with the Dalai Lama as chairman; nevertheless, friction and antagonism developed between Chinese and Tibetans. The lack of co-operation from local authorities forced the Communists to postpone the proposed land reform. By 1958 uprisings of the Khamba tribes broke out with the tacit support of the Lhasa officials; these led to the rebellion in Lhasa itself, the subsequent flight of the Dalai Lama to India in March 1959, and his public denunciation of the Chinese occupation. After having suppressed the rebellion, the Communists abolished the local government and handed its functions and powers to the preparatory committee, elevating the Panchen Lama to acting chairmanship. In July 1959 a resolution by the preparatory committee called for the abolition of serfdom and the reduction of land rents. Thus Tibet which has been most resistant to Chinese influences is being compelled to overhaul its centuries-old social and political structure. . . .

# III

# The Political Myth and Goals

## 4. The Chinese Society and Communist Revolution

*Mao Tse-tung*

### Chinese Society

**1. The Chinese Nation.** China is one of the largest countries in the world, her territory being about the size of the whole of Europe. In this vast country of ours there are large areas of fertile land which provide us with food and clothing; mountain ranges across its length and breadth with extensive forests and rich mineral deposits; many rivers and lakes which provide us with water transport and irrigation; and a long coastline which facilitates communication with nations beyond the seas. From ancient times our forefathers have laboured, lived and multiplied on this vast territory. . . .

The Chinese nation is known throughout the world not only for its industriousness and stamina, but also for its ardent love of freedom and its rich revolutionary traditions. The history of the Han people, for instance, demonstrates that the Chinese never submit to tyrannical rule but invariably use revolutionary means to overthrow or change it. In the thousands of years of Han history, there have been hundreds of peasant uprisings, great and small, against the dark rule of the landlords and the nobility. And most dynastic changes came about as a result of such peasant uprisings. All the nationalities of China have resisted foreign oppression and have invariably resorted to rebellion to shake it off. They favour a union on the basis of equality but are against the oppression of one nationality by another. During the thousands of years of recorded history, the Chinese nation has given birth to many national heroes and revolutionary leaders. Thus the Chinese nation has a glorious revolutionary tradition and a splendid historical heritage.

Reprinted from Mao Tse-tung, *Selected Works of Mao Tse-tung* (Peking: Foreign Language Press, 1965), 2:305, 306–10, 312–21, 323–27, 329–31.

**2. The Old Feudal Society.** Although China is a great nation and although she is a vast country with an immense population, a long history, a rich revolutionary tradition and a splendid historical heritage, her economic, political and cultural development was sluggish for a long time after the transition from slave to feudal society. This feudal society, beginning with the Chou and Chin Dynasties, lasted about 3,000 years. . . .

The principal contradiction in feudal society was between the peasantry and the landlord class.

The peasants and the handicraft workers were the basic classes which created the wealth and culture of this society.

The ruthless economic exploitation and political oppression of the Chinese peasants forced them into numerous uprisings against landlord rule. There were hundreds of uprisings, great and small, all of them peasant revolts or peasant revolutionary wars . . . The scale of peasant uprisings and peasant wars in Chinese history has no parallel anywhere else. The class struggles of the peasants, the peasant uprisings and peasant wars constituted the real motive force of historical development in Chinese feudal society. For each of the major peasant uprisings and wars dealt a blow to the feudal regime of the time, and hence more or less furthered the growth of the social productive forces. However, since neither new productive forces, nor new relations of production, nor new class forces, nor any advanced political party existed in those days, the peasant uprisings and wars did not have correct leadership such as the proletariat and the Communist Party provide today; every peasant revolution failed, and the peasantry was invariably used by the landlords and the nobility, either during or after the revolution, as a lever for bringing about dynastic change. Therefore, although some social progress was made after each great peasant revolutionary struggle, the feudal economic relations and political system remained basically unchanged.

It is only in the last hundred years that a change of a different order has taken place.

**3. Present-Day Colonial, Semi-Colonial and Semi-Feudal Society.** As China's feudal society had developed a commodity economy, and so carried within itself the seeds of capitalism, China would of herself have developed slowly into a capitalist society even without the impact of foreign capitalism. Penetration by foreign capitalism accelerated this process. Foreign capitalism played an important part in the disintegration of China's social economy; on the one hand, it undermined the foundations of her self-sufficient natural economy and wrecked the handicraft industries both in the cities and in the peasants' homes, and on the other, it hastened the growth of a commodity economy in town and country.

Apart from its disintegrating effects on the foundations of China's feudal economy, this state of affairs gave rise to certain objective conditions and possibilities for the development of capitalist production in China. For the destruction of the natural economy created a commodity market for capitalism, while the bankruptcy of large numbers of peasants and handicraftsmen provided it with a labour market.

In fact, some merchants, landlords and bureaucrats began investing in modern industry as far back as sixty years ago, in the latter part of the 19th century, under the stimulus of foreign capitalism and because of certain cracks in the feudal economic structure. About forty years ago, at the turn of the century, China's national capitalism took its first steps forward. Then about twenty years ago, during the first imperialist world war, China's national industry expanded, chiefly in textiles and flour milling, because the imperialist countries in Europe and America were preoccupied with the war and temporarily relaxed their oppression of China.

The history of the emergence and development of national capitalism is at the same time the history of the emergence and development of the Chinese bourgeoisie and proletariat. Just as a section of the merchants, landlords and bureaucrats were precursors of the Chinese bourgeoisie, so a section of the peasants and handicraft workers were the precursors of the Chinese proletariat. As distinct social classes, the Chinese bourgeoisie and proletariat are new-born and never existed before in Chinese history. They have evolved into new social classes from the womb of feudal society. They are twins born of China's old (feudal) society, at once linked to each other and antagonistic to each other. However, the Chinese proletariat emerged and grew simultaneously not only with the Chinese national bourgeoisie but also with the enterprises directly operated by the imperialists in China. Hence, a very large section of the Chinese proletariat is older and more experienced than the Chinese bourgeoisie, and is therefore a greater and more broadly based social force.

However, the emergence and development of capitalism is only one aspect of the change that has taken place since the imperialist penetration of China. There is another concomitant and obstructive aspect, namely, the collusion of imperialism with the Chinese feudal forces to arrest the development of Chinese capitalism.

It is certainly not the purpose of the imperialist powers invading China to transform feudal China into capitalist China. On the contrary, their purpose is to transform China into their own semi-colony or colony.

To this end the imperialist powers have used and continue to use military, political, economic and cultural means of oppression, so that China has gradually become a semi-colony and colony. . . .

It is thus clear that in their aggression against China the imperialist powers have on the one hand hastened the disintegration of feudal society and the growth of elements of capitalism, thereby transforming a feudal into a semi-feudal society, and on the other imposed their ruthless rule on China, reducing an independent country to a semi-colonial and colonial country.

Taking both these aspects together, we can see that China's colonial, semi-colonial and semi-feudal society possesses the following characteristics:

(1) The foundations of the self-sufficient natural economy of feudal times have been destroyed, but the exploitation of the peasantry by the landlord class, which is the basis of the system of feudal exploitation, not only remains intact but, linked as it is with exploitation by comprador and usurer capital, clearly dominates China's social and economic life.

(2) National caiptalism has developed to a certain extent and has played a considerable part in China's political and cultural life, but it has not become the principal pattern in China's social economy; it is flabby and is mostly associated with foreign imperialism and domestic feudalism in varying degrees.

(3) The autocratic rule of the emperors and nobility has been overthrown, and in its place there have arisen first the warlord-bureaucrat rule of the landlord class and then the joint dictatorship of the landlord class and the big bourgeoisie. In the occupied areas there is the rule of Japanese imperialism and its puppets.

(4) Imperialism controls not only China's vital financial and economic arteries but also her political and military power. In the occupied areas everything is in the hands of Japanese imperialism.

(5) China's economic, political and cultural development is very uneven, because she has been under the complete or partial domination of many imperialist powers, because she has actually been in a state of disunity for a long time, and because her territory is immense.

(6) Under the twofold oppression of imperialism and feudalism, and especially as a result of the large-scale invasion of Japanese imperialism, the Chinese people, and particularly the peasants, have become more and more impoverished and have even been pauperized in large numbers, living in hunger and cold and without any political rights. The poverty and lack of freedom among the Chinese people are on a scale seldom found elsewhere.

Such are the characteristics of China's colonial, semi-colonial and semi-feudal society.

This situation has in the main been determined by the Japanese and other imperialist forces; it is the result of the collusion of foreign imperialism and domestic feudalism.

The contradiction between imperialism and the Chinese nation and the contradiction between feudalism and the great masses of the people are the basic contradictions in modern Chinese society. Of course, there are others, such as the contradiction between the bourgeoisie and the proletariat and the contradictions within the reactionary ruling classes themselves. But the contradiction beween imperialism and the Chinese nation is the principal one. These contradictions and their intensification must inevitably result in the incessant growth of revolutionary movements. The great revolutions in modern and contemporary China have emerged and grown on the basis of these basic contradictions.

## The Chinese Revolution

**1. The Revolutionary Movements in the Last Hundred Years.** The history of China's transformation into a semi-colony and colony by imperialism in collusion with Chinese feudalism is at the same time a history of struggle by the Chinese people against imperialism and its lackeys. The Opium War, the Movement of the Taiping Heavenly Kingdom, the Sino-French War, the Sino-Japanese War, the Reform Movement of 1898, the Yi Ho Tuan Movement, the Revolution of 1911, the May 4th Movement, the May 30th Movement, the Northern Expedition, the Agrarian Revolutionary War and the present War of Resistance Against Japan — all testify to the Chinese people's indomitable spirit in fighting imperialism and its lackeys.

Thanks to the Chinese people's unrelenting and heroic struggle during the last hundred years, imperialism has not been able to subjugate China, nor will it ever be able to do so. . . .

**2. The Targets of the Chinese Revolution.** Since the nature of present-day Chinese society is colonial, semi-colonial and semi-feudal, what are the chief targets or enemies at this stage of the Chinese revolution?

They are imperialism and feudalism, the bourgeoisie of the imperialist countries and the landlord class of our country. For it is these two that are the chief oppressors, the chief obstacles to the progress of Chinese society at the present stage. The two collude with each other in oppressing the Chinese people, and imperialism is the foremost and most ferocious enemy of the Chinese people, because national oppression by imperialism is the more onerous. . . .

In the face of such enemies, the principal means or form of the Chinese revolution must be armed struggles, not peaceful struggle. For our enemies have made peaceful activity impossible for the Chinese people and have deprived them of all political freedom and democratic rights. Stalin says, "In China the armed revolution is fighting the armed counter-revolution. That is one of the specific features and one of the advantages of the Chinese revolution." This formulation is perfectly correct. Therefore, it is wrong to belittle armed struggle, revolutionary war, guerrilla war and army work.

In the face of such enemies, there arises the question of revolutionary base areas. Since China's key cities have long been occupied by the powerful imperialists and their reactionary Chinese allies, it is imperative for the revolutionary ranks to turn the backward villages into advanced, consolidated base areas, into great military, political, economic and cultural bastions of the revolution from which to fight their vicious enemies who are using the cities for attacks on the rural districts, and in this way gradually to achieve the complete victory of the revolution through protracted fighting; it is imperative for them to do so if they do not wish to compromise with imperialism and its lackeys but are determined to fight on, and if they intend to build up and temper their forces, and avoid decisive battles with a powerful enemy while their own strength is inadequate. Such being the case, victory in the Chinese revolution can be won first in the rural areas, and this is possible because China's economic development is uneven (her economy not being a unified capitalist economy), because her territory is extensive (which gives the revolutionary forces room to manoeuvre), because the counter-revolutionary camp is disunited and full of contradictions, and because the struggle of the peasants who are the main force in the revolution is led by the Communist Party, the party of the proletariat; but on the other hand, these very circumstances make the revolution uneven and render the task of winning complete victory protracted and arduous. Clearly then the protracted revolutionary struggle in the revolutionary base areas consists mainly in peasant guerrilla warfare led by the Chinese Communist Party. Therefore, it is wrong to ignore the necessity of using rural districts as revolutionary base areas, to neglect painstaking work among the peasants, and to neglect guerrilla warfare.

However, stressing armed struggle does not mean abandoning other forms of struggle; on the contrary, armed struggle cannot succeed unless co-ordinated with other forms of struggle. And stressing the work in the rural base areas does not mean abandoning our work in the cities and in the other vast rural areas which are still under the enemy's rule; on the contrary, without the work in the cities and in these other rural areas, our own rural base areas would be isolated and the revolution would suffer defeat. Moreover, the final objective of the revolution is the capture of the cities, the enemy's main bases, and this objective cannot be achieved without adequate work in the cities. . . .

**3. The Tasks of the Chinese Revolution.** Imperialism and the feudal landlord class being the chief enemies of the Chinese revolution at this stage, what are the present tasks of the revolution?

Unquestionably, the main tasks are to strike at these two enemies, to carry out a national revolution to overthrow foreign imperialist oppression and a democratic revolution to overthrow feudal landlord oppression, the primary and foremost task being the national revolution to overthrow imperialism.

These two great tasks are interrelated. Unless imperialist rule is overthrown, the rule of the feudal landlord class cannot be terminated, because imperialism is its main support. Conversely, unless help is given to the peasants in their struggle to overthrow the feudal landlord class, it will be impossible to build powerful revolutionary contingents to overthrow imperialist rule, because the feudal landlord class is the main social base of imperialist rule in China and the peasantry is the main force in the Chinese revolution. . . .

**4. The Motive Forces of the Chinese Revolution.** Given the nature of Chinese society and the present targets and tasks of the Chinese revolution as analysed and defined above, what are the motive forces of the Chinese revolution?

Since Chinese society is colonial, semi-colonial and semi-feudal, since the targets of the revolution are mainly foreign imperialist rule and domestic feudalism, and since its tasks are to overthrow these two oppressors, which of the various classes and strata in Chinese society constitute the forces capable of fighting them? This is the question of the motive forces of the Chinese revolution at the present stage. A clear understanding of this question is indispensable to a correct solution of the problem of the basic tactics of the Chinese revolution.

What classes are there in present-day Chinese society? There are the landlord class and the bourgeoisie, the landlord class and the upper stratum of the bourgeoisie constituting the ruling classes in Chinese society. And there are the proletariat, the peasantry, and the different sections of the petty bourgeoisie other than the peasantry, all of which are still the subject classes in vast areas of China.

The attitude and the stand of these classes toward the Chinese revolution are entirely determined by their economic status in society. Thus the motive forces as well as the targets and tasks of the revolution are determined by the nature of China's socio-economic system.

Let us now analyse the different classes in Chinese society.

*1. The Landlord Class.* The landlord class forms the main social base for imperialist rule in China; it is a class which uses the feudal system to exploit and oppress the peasants, obstructs China's political, economic and cultural development and plays no progressive role whatsoever.

Therefore, the landlords, as a class, are a target and not a motive force of the revolution. . . .

*2. The Bourgeoisie.* There is a distinction between the comprador big bourgeoisie and the national bourgeoisie.

The comprador big bourgeoisie is a class which directly serves the capitalists of the imperialist countries and is nurtured by them; countless ties link it closely with the feudal forces in the countryside. Therefore, it is a target of the Chinese revolution and never in the history of the revolution has it been a motive force. . . .

The national bourgeoisie is a class with a dual character.

On the one hand, it is oppressed by imperialism and fettered by feudalism and consequently is in contradiction with both of them. In this respect it constitutes one of the revolutionary forces. In the course of the Chinese revolution it has displayed a certain enthusiasm for fighting imperialism and the governments of bureaucrats and warlords.

But on the other hand, it lacks the courage to oppose imperialism and feudalism thoroughly because it is economically and politically flabby and still has economic ties with imperialism and feudalism. This emerges very clearly when the people's revolutionary forces grow powerful. . . .

*3. The Different Sections of the Petty Bourgeoisie Other than the Peasantry.* The petty bourgeoisie, other than the peasantry, consists of the vast numbers of intellectuals, small tradesmen, handicraftsmen and professional people.

Their status somewhat resembles that of the middle peasants, they all suffer under the oppression of imperialism, feudalism and the big bourgeoisie, and they are being driven ever nearer to bankruptcy or destitution.

Hence these sections of the petty bourgeoisie constitute one of the motive forces of the revolution and are a reliable ally of the proletariat. Only under the leadership of the proletariat can they achieve their liberation. . . .

*4. The Peasantry.* The peasantry constitutes approximately 80 per cent of China's total population and is the main force in her national economy today.

A sharp process of polarization is taking place among the peasantry.

First, the rich peasants. They form about 5 per cent of the rural population (or about 10 per cent together with the landlords) and constitute the rural bourgeoisie. Most of the rich peasants in China are semi-feudal in character, since they let a part of their land, practise usury and ruthlessly exploit the farm labourers. But they generally engage in labour themselves and in this sense are part of the peasantry. The rich-peasant form of production will remain useful for a definite period. Generally speaking, they might make some contribution to the anti-imperialist struggle of the peasant masses and stay neutral in the agrarian revolutionary struggle against the landlords. Therefore we should not regard the rich peasants as belonging to the same class as the landlords and should not prematurely adopt a policy of liquidating the rich peasantry.

Second, the middle peasants. They form about 20 per cent of China's rural population. They are economically self-supporting (they may have something to lay aside when the crops are good, and occasionally hire some labour or lend small sums of money at interest); and generally they do not exploit others but are exploited by imperialism, the landlord class and the bourgeoisie. They have no political rights. Some of them do not have enough land, and only a section (the well-to-do middle peasants) have some surplus land. Not only can the middle peasants join the anti-imperialist revolution and the Agrarian Revolution, but they can also accept socialism. Therefore the whole middle peasantry can be a reliable ally of the proletariat and is an important motive force of the revolution. The positive or negative attitude of the middle peasants is one of the factors determining victory or defeat in the revolution, and this is especially true after the agrarian revolution when they become the majority of the rural population.

Third, the poor peasants. The poor peasants in China, together with the farm labourers, form about 70 per cent of the rural population. They are the broad peasant masses with no land or insufficient land, the semi-proletariat of the countryside, the biggest motive force of the Chinese revolution, the natural and most reliable ally of the proletariat and the main contingent of China's revolutionary forces. Only under the leadership of the proletariat can the poor and middle peasants achieve their liberation, and only by forming a firm alliance with the poor and middle peasants can the proletariat lead the revolution to victory. Otherwise neither is possible. The term "peasantry" refers mainly to the poor and middle peasants.

5. *The Proletariat.* Among the Chinese proletariat, the modern industrial workers number from 2,500,000 to 3,000,000, the workers in small-scale industry and in handicrafts and the shop assistants in the cities total about 12,000,000, and in addition there are great numbers of rural proletarians (the farm labourers) and other propertyless people in the cities and the countryside.

In addition to the basic qualities it shares with the proletariat everywhere — its association with the most advanced form of economy, its strong sense of organization and discipline and its lack of private means of production — the Chinese proletariat has many other outstanding qualities.

What are they?

First, the Chinese proletariat is more resolute and thoroughgoing in revolutionary struggle than any other class because it is subjected to a threefold oppression (imperialist, bourgeois and feudal) which is marked by a severity and cruelty seldom found in other countries. Since there is no economic basis for social reformism in colonial and semi-colonial China as there is in Europe, the whole proletariat, with the exception of a few scabs, is most revolutionary.

Secondly, from the moment it appeared on the revolutionary scene, the Chinese proletariat came under the leadership of its own revolutionary party — the Communist Party of China — and became the most politically conscious class in Chinese society.

Thirdly, because the Chinese proletariat by origin is largely made up of bankrupted peasants, it has natural ties with the peasant masses, which facilitates its forming a close alliance with them.

Therefore, in spite of certain unavoidable weaknesses, for instance, its smallness (as compared with the peasantry), its youth (as compared with the proletariat in the capitalist countries) and its low educational level (as compared with the bourgeoisie), the Chinese proletariat is nonetheless the basic motive force of the Chinese revolution. . . .

6. *The Vagrants.* China's status as a colony and semi-colony has given rise to a multitude of rural and urban unemployed. Denied proper means of making a living, many of them are forced to resort to illegitimate ones, hence the robbers, gangsters, beggars and prostitutes and the numerous people who live on superstitious practices. This social stratum is unstable; while some are apt to be bought over by the reactionary forces, others may join the revolution. These people lack constructive qualities and are given to destruction rather than construction; after joining the revolution, they become a source of roving-rebel and anarchist ideology in the revolutionary ranks. Therefore, we should know how to remould them and guard against their destructiveness. . . .

**5. The Character of the Chinese Revolution.** Since Chinese society is colonial, semi-colonial and semi-feudal, since the principal enemies of the Chinese revolution are imperialism and feudalism, since the tasks of the revolution are to overthrow these two enemies by means of a national and democratic revolution in which the bourgeoisie sometimes takes part, and since the edge of the revolution is directed against imperialism and feudalism and not against capitalism and capitalist private property in general even if the big bourgeoisie betrays the revolution and becomes its enemy — since all this is true, the character of the Chinese revolution at the present stage is not proletarian-socialist but bourgeois-democratic.

However, in present-day China the bourgeois-democratic revolution is no longer of the old general type, which is now obsolete, but one of a new special type. We call this type the new-democratic revolution and it is developing in all other colonial and semi-colonial countries as well as in China. The new-democratic revolution is part of the world proletarian-socialist revolution, for it resolutely opposes imperialism, *i.e.*, international capitalism. Politically, it strives for the joint dictatorship of the revolutionary classes over the imperialists, traitors and reactionaries, and opposes the transformation of Chinese society into a society under bourgeois dictatorship. Economically, it aims at the nationization of all the big enterprises and capital of the imperialists, traitors and reactionaries, and the distribution among the peasants of the land held by the landlords, while preserving private capitalist enterprise in general and not eliminating the rich-peasant economy. Thus, the new type of democratic revolution clears the way for capitalism on the one hand and creates the prerequisites for socialism on the other. The present stage of the Chinese revolution is a stage of transition between the abolition of the colonial, semi-colonial and semi-feudal society and the establishment of a socialist society, *i.e.*, it is a process of new-democratic revolution. This process, begun only after the First World War and the Russian October Revolution, started in China with the May 4th Movement of 1919. A new-democratic revolution is an anti-imperialist and anti-feudal revolution of the broad masses of the people under the leadership of the proletariat. Chinese society can advance to socialism only through such a revolution; there is no other way.

The new-democratic revolution is vastly different from the democratic revolutions of Europe and America in that it results not in a dictatorship of the bourgeoisie but in a dictatorship of the united front of all the revolutionary classes under the leadership of the proletariat. . . .

The new-democratic revolution also differs from a socialist revolution in that it overthrows the rule of the imperialists, traitors and reactionaries in China but does not destroy any section of capitalism which is capable of contributing to the anti-imperialist, anti-feudal struggle.

. . . The Chinese revolution at the present stage must strive to create a democratic republic in which the workers, the peasants and the other sections of the petty bourgeoisie all occupy a definite position and play a definite role. In other words, it must be a democratic republic based on a revolutionary alliance of the workers, peasants, urban petty bourgeoisie and all others who are against imperialism and feudalism. Only under the leadership of the proletariat can such a republic be completely realized.

**6. The Perspectives of the Chinese Revolution.** Now that the basic issues—the nature of Chinese society and the targets, tasks, motive forces and character of the Chinese revolution at the present stage—have been clarified, it is easy to see its perspectives, that is, to understand the relation between the bourgeois-democratic and the proletarian-socialist revolution, or between the present and future stages of the Chinese revolution.

There can be no doubt that the ultimate perspective of the Chinese revolution is not capitalism but socialism and communism, since China's bourgeois-democratic revolution at the present stage is not of the old general type but is a democratic revolution of a new special type—a new-democratic revolution—and since it is taking place in the new international environment of the Nineteen Thirties and Forties characterized by the rise of socialism and the decline of capitalism, in the period of the Second World War and the era of revolution. . . .

# 5. Mao Tse-tung's Theory of People's War

*Lin Piao*

The Chinese revolution is a continuation of the Great October Revolution. The road of the October Revolution is the common road for all people's revolution. The Chinese revolution and the October Revolution have in common the following basic characteristics: (1) Both were led by the working class with a Marxist-Leninist party as its nucleus. (2) Both were based on the worker-peasant alliance. (3) In both cases state power was seized through violent revolution and the dictatorship of the proletariat was established. (4) In both cases the socialist system was built after victory in the revolution. (5) Both were component parts of the proletarian world revolution.

Naturally, the Chinese revolution had its own peculiar characteristics. The October Revolution took place in imperialist Russia, but the Chinese revolution broke out in a semi-colonial and semi-feudal country. The former was a proletarian socialist revolution, while the latter developed into a socialist revolution after the complete victory of the new-democratic revolution. The October Revolution began with armed uprisings in the cities and then spread to the countryside, while the Chinese revolution won nation-wide victory through the encirclement of the cities from the rural areas and the final capture of the cities.

Comrade Mao Tse-tung's great merit lies in the fact that he has succeeded in integrating the universal truth of Marxism-Leninism with the concrete practice of the Chinese revolution and has enriched and developed Marxism-Leninism by his masterly generalization and summation of the experience gained during the Chinese people's protracted revolutionary struggle.

Reprinted from Lin Piao, "Long Live the Victory of People's War," *Peking Review*, September 3, 1965, pp. 22–27.

Comrade Mao Tse-tung's theory of people's war has been proved by the long practice of the Chinese revolution to be in accord with the objective laws of such wars and to be invincible. It has not only been valid for China, it is a great contribution to the revolutionary struggles of the oppressed nations and peoples throughout the world.

The people's war led by the Chinese Communist Party, comprising the War of Resistance and the Revolutionary Civil Wars, lasted for twenty-two years. It constitutes the most drawn-out and most complex people's war led by the proletariat in modern history, and it has been the richest in experience.

In the last analysis, the Marxist-Leninist theory of proletarian revolution is the theory of the seizure of state power by revolutionary violence, the theory of countering war against the people by people's war. As Marx so aptly put it, "Force is the midwife of every old society pregnant with a new one."

It was on the basis of the lessons derived from the people's wars in China that Comrade Mao Tse-tung, using the simplest and the most vivid language, advanced the famous thesis that "political power grows out of the barrel of a gun."

He clearly pointed out:

> The seizure of power by armed force, the settlement of the issue by war, is the central task and the highest form of revolution. This Marxist-Leninist principle of revolution holds good universally, for China and for all other countries.

War is the product of imperialism and the system of exploitation of man by man. Lenin said that "war is always and everywhere begun by the exploiters themselves, by the ruling and oppressing classes." So long as imperialism and the system of exploitation of man by man exist, the imperialists and reactionaries will invariably rely on armed force to maintain their reactionary rule and impose war on the oppressed nations and peoples. This is an objective law independent of man's will.

In the world today, all the imperialists headed by the United States and their lackeys, without exception, are strengthening their state machinery, and especially their armed forces. U.S. imperialism, in particular, is carrying out armed aggression and suppression everywhere.

What should the oppressed nations and the oppressed people do in the face of wars of aggression and armed suppression by the imperialists and their lackeys? Should they submit and remain slaves in perpetuity? Or should they rise in resistance and fight for their liberation?

Comrade Mao Tse-tung answered this question in vivid terms. He said that after long investigation and study the Chinese people discovered that all the imperialists and their lackeys "have swords in their hands and are out to kill. The people have come to understand this and so act after the same fashion." This is called doing unto them what they do unto us.

In the last analysis, whether one dares to wage a tit-for-tat struggle against armed aggression and suppression by the imperialists and their lackeys, whether one dares to fight a people's war against them, is tantamount to whether one dares to embark on revolution. This is the most effective touchstone for distinguishing genuine from fake revolutionaries and Marxist-Leninists.

In view of the fact that some people were afflicted with the fear of the imperialists and reactionaries, Comrade Mao-Tse-tung put forward his famous thesis that "the imperialists and all reactionaries are paper tigers." He said,

> All reactionaries are paper tigers. In appearance, the reactionaries are terrifying, but in reality they are not so powerful. From a long-term point of view, it is not the reactionaries but the people who are really powerful.

The history of people's war in China and other countries provides conclusive evidence that the growth of the people's revolutionary forces from weak and small beginnings into strong and large forces is a universal law of development of class struggle, a universal law of development of people's war. A people's war inevitably meets with many difficulties, with ups and downs and setbacks in the course of its development, but no force can alter its general trend towards inevitable triumph.

Comrade Mao Tse-tung points out that we must despise the enemy strategically and take full account of him tactically.

To despise the enemy strategically is an elementary requirement for a revolutionary. Without the courage to despise the enemy and without daring to win, it will be simply impossible to make revolution and wage a people's war, let alone to achieve victory.

It is also very important for revolutionaries to take full account of the enemy tactically. It is likewise impossible to win victory in a people's war without taking full account of the enemy tactically, and without examining the concrete conditions, without being prudent and giving great attention to the study of the art of struggle, and without adopting appropriate forms of struggle in the concrete practice of the revolution in each country and with regard to each concrete problem of struggle.

Dialectical and historical materialism teaches us that what is important primarily is not that which at the given moment seems to be durable and yet is already beginning to die away, but that which is arising and developing, even though at the given moment it may not appear to be durable, for only that which is arising and developing is invincible.

Why can the apparently weak new-born forces always triumph over the decadent forces which appear so powerful? The reason is that truth is on their side and that the masses are on their side, while the reactionary classes are always divorced from the masses and set themselves against the masses.

This has been borne out by the victory of the Chinese revolution, by the history of all revolutions, the whole history of class struggle and the entire history of mankind.

The imperialists are extremely afraid of Comrade Mao Tse-tung's thesis that "imperialism and all reactionaries are paper tigers," and the revisionists are extremely hostile to it. They all oppose and attack this thesis and the philistines follow suit by ridiculing it. But all this cannot in the least diminish its importance. The light of truth cannot be dimmed by anybody.

Comrade Mao Tse-tung's theory of people's war solves not only the problem of daring to fight a people's war, but also that of how to wage it.

Comrade Mao Tse-tung is a great statesman and military scientist, proficient at directing war in accordance with its laws. By the line and policies, the strategy and tactics he formulated for the people's war, he led the Chinese people in steering the ship of the people's war past all hidden reefs to the shores of victory in most complicated and difficult conditions.

It must be emphasized that Comrade Mao Tse-tung's theory of the establishment of rural revolutionary base areas and the encirclement of the cities from the countryside is of outstanding and universal practical importance for the present revolutionary struggles of all the oppressed nations and peoples, and particularly for the revolutionary struggles of the oppressed nations and peoples in Asia, Africa and Latin America against imperialism and its lackeys.

Many countries and peoples in Asia, Africa and Latin America are now being subjected to aggression and enslavement on a serious scale by the imperialists headed by the United States and their lackeys. The basic political and economic conditions in many of these countries have many similarities to those that prevailed in old China. As in China, the peasant question is extremely important in these regions. The peasants constitute the main force of the national-democratic revolution against the imperialists and their lackeys. In committing aggression against these countries, the imperialists usually begin by seizing the big cities and the main lines of communication, but they are unable to bring the vast countryside completely under their control. The countryside, and the countryside alone, can provide the broad areas in which the revolutionaries can manoeuvre freely. The countryside, and the countryside alone, can provide the revolutionary bases from which the revolutionaries can go forward to final victory. Precisely for this reason, Comrade Mao Tse-tung's theory of establishing revolutionary base areas in the rural districts and encircling the cities from the countryside is attracting more and more attention among the people in these regions.

Taking the entire globe, if North America and Western Europe can be called "the cities of the world," then Asia, Africa and Latin America constitute "the rural areas of the world." Since World War II, the proletarian revolutionary movement has for various reasons been temporarily held back in the North American and West European capitalist countries, while the people's revolutionary movement in Asia, Africa and Latin America has been growing vigorously. In a sense, the contemporary world revolution also presents a picture of the encirclement of cities by the rural areas. In the final analysis, the whole cause of world revolution hinges on the revolutionary struggles of the Asian, African and Latin American peoples who make up the overwhelming majority of the world's population. The socialist countries should regard it as their internationalist duty to support the people's revolutionary struggles in Asia, Africa and Latin America.

The October Revolution opened up a new era in the revolution of the oppressed nations. The victory of the October Revolution built a bridge between the socialist revolution of the proletariat of the West and the national-democratic revolution of the colonial and semi-colonial countries of the East. The Chinese revolution has successfully solved the problem of how to link up the national-democratic with the socialist revolution in the colonial and semi-colonial countries.

Comrade Mao Tse-tung has pointed out that, in the epoch since the October Revolution, anti-imperialist revolution in any colonial or semi-colonial country is no longer part of the old bourgeois, or capitalist world revolution, but is part of the new world revolution, the proletarian-socialist world revolution.

Comrade Mao Tse-tung has formulated a complete theory of the new-democratic revolution. He indicated that this revolution, which is different from all others, can only be, nay must be, a revolution against imperialism, feudalism and bureaucrat-capitalism waged by the broad masses of the people under the leadership of the proletariat.

This means that the revolution can only be, nay must be, led by the proletariat and the genuinely revolutionary party armed with Marxism-Leninism, and by no other class or party.

This means that the revolution embraces in its ranks not only the workers, peasants and the urban petty bourgeoisie, but also the national bourgeoisie and other patriotic and anti-imperialist democrats.

This means, finally, that the revolution is directed against imperialism, feudalism and bureaucrat-capitalism.

The new-democratic revolution leads to socialism, and not to capitalism.

Comrade Mao Tse-tung's theory of the new-democratic revolution is the Marxist-Leninist theory of revolution by stages as well as the Marxist-Leninist theory of uninterrupted revolution.

Comrade Mao Tse-tung made a correct distinction between the two revolutionary stages, *i.e.*, the national-democratic and the socialist revolutions; at the same time he correctly and closely linked the two. The national-democratic revolution is the necessary preparation for the socialist revolution, and the socialist revolution is the inevitable sequel to the national-democratic revolution. There is no Great Wall between the two revolutionary stages. But the socialist revolution is only possible after the completion of the national-democratic revolution. The more thorough the national-democratic revolution, the better the conditions for the socialist revolution.

The experience of the Chinese revolution shows that the tasks of the national-democratic revolution can be fulfilled only through long and tortuous struggles. In this stage of revolution, imperialism and its lackeys are the principal enemy. In the struggle against imperialism and its lackeys, it is necessary to rally all anti-imperialist patriotic forces, including the national bourgeoisie and all patriotic personages. All those patriotic personages from among the bourgeoisie and other exploiting classes who join the anti-imperialist struggle play a progressive historical role; they are not tolerated by imperialism but welcomed by the proletariat.

It is very harmful to confuse the two stages, that is, the national-democratic and the socialist revolutions. Comrade Mao Tse-tung criticized the wrong idea of "accomplishing both at one stroke," and pointed out that this utopian idea could only weaken the struggle against imperialism and its lackeys, the most urgent task at that time. The Kuomintang reactionaries and the Trotskyites they hired during the War of Resistance deliberately confused these two stages of the Chinese revolution, proclaiming the "theory of a single revolution" and preaching so-called "socialism" without any Communist Party. With this preposterous theory they attempted to swallow up the Communist Party, wipe out any revolution and prevent the advance of the national-democratic revolution, and they used it as a pretext for their non-resistance and capitulation to imperialism. This reactionary theory was buried long ago by the history of the Chinese revolution.

The Khrushchev revisionists are now actively preaching that socialism can be built without the proletariat and without a genuinely revolutionary party armed with the advanced proletarian ideology, and they have cast the fundamental tenets of Marxism-Leninism to the four winds. The revisionists' purpose is solely to divert the oppressed nations from their struggle against imperialism and sabotage their national-democratic revolution, all in the service of imperialism.

The Chinese revolution provides a successful lesson for making a thoroughgoing national-democratic revolution under the leadership of the proletariat; it likewise provides a successful lesson for the timely transition from the national-democratic revolution to the socialist revolution under the leadership of the proletariat.

Mao Tse-tung's thought has been the guide to the victory of the Chinese revolution. It has integrated the universal truth of Marxism-Leninism with the concrete practice of the Chinese revolution and creatively developed Marxism-Leninism, thus adding new weapons to the arsenal of Marxism-Leninism.

Ours is the epoch in which world capitalism and imperialism are heading for their doom and socialism and communism are marching to victory. Comrade Mao Tse-tung's theory of people's war is not only a product of the Chinese revolution, but has also the characteristics of our epoch. The new experience gained in the people's revolutionary struggles in various countries since World War II has provided continuous evidence that Mao Tse-tung's thought is a common asset of the revolutionary people of the whole world. This is the great international significance of the thought of Mao Tse-tung.

## Defeat of U.S. Imperialism and Its
## Lackeys by People's War

Since World War II, U.S. imperialism has stepped into the shoes of German, Japanese and Italian fascism and has been trying to build a great American empire by dominating and enslaving the whole world. It is actively fostering Japanese and West German militarism as its chief accomplices in unleashing a world war. Like a vicious wolf, it is bullying and enslaving various peoples, plundering their wealth, encroaching upon their countries' sovereignty and interfering in their internal affairs. It is the most rabid aggressor in human history and the most ferocious common enemy of the people of the world. Every people or country in the world that wants revolution, independence and peace cannot but direct the spearhead of its struggle against U.S. imperialism.

Just as the Japanese imperialists' policy of subjugating China made it possible for the Chinese people to form the broadest possible united front against them, so the U.S. imperialists' policy of seeking world domination makes it possible for the people throughout the world to unite all the forces that can be united and form the broadest possible united front for a converging attack on U.S. imperialism.

At present, the main battlefield of the fierce struggle between the people of the world on the one side and U.S. imperialism and its lackeys on the other is the vast area of Asia, Africa and Latin America. In the world as a whole, this is the area where the people suffer worst from imperialist oppression and where imperialist rule is most vulnerable. Since World War II, revolutionary storms have been rising in this area, and today they have become the most important force directly pounding U.S. imperialism. The contradiction between the revolutionary peoples of Asia, Africa and Latin America and the imperialists headed by the United States is the principal contradiction in the contemporary world. The development of this contradiction is promoting the struggle of the people of the whole world against U.S. imperialism and its lackeys.

Since World War II, people's war has increasingly demonstrated its power in Asia, Africa and Latin America. The peoples of China, Korea, Viet Nam, Laos, Cuba, Indonesia, Algeria and other countries have waged people's wars against the imperialists and their lackeys and won great victories. The classes leading these people's wars may vary, and so may the breadth and depth of mass mobilization and the extent of victory, but the victories in these people's wars have very much weakened and pinned down the forces of imperialism, upset the U.S. imperialist plan to launch a world war, and become mighty factors defending world peace.

Today, the conditions are more favourable than ever before for the waging of people's wars by the revolutionary peoples of Asia, Africa and Latin America against U.S. imperialism and its lackeys.

Since World War II and the succeeding years of revolutionary upsurge, there has been a great rise in the level of political consciousness and the degree of organization of the people in all countries, and the resources available to them for mutual support and aid have greatly increased. The whole capitalist-imperialist system has become drastically weaker and is in the process of increasing convulsion and disintegration. After World War I, the imperialists lacked the power to destroy the newborn socialist Soviet state, but they were still able to suppress the people's revolutionary movements in some countries in the parts of the world under their own rule and so maintain a short period of comparative stability. Since World War II, however, not only have they been unable to stop a number of countries from taking the socialist road, but they are no longer capable of holding back the surging tide of the people's revolutionary movements in the areas under their own rule.

U.S. imperialism is stronger, but also more vulnerable, than any imperialism of the past. It sets itself against the people of the whole world, including the people of the United States. Its human, military, material and financial resources are far from sufficient for the realization of its ambition of dominating the whole world. U.S. imperialism has further weakened itself by occupying so many places in the world, over-reaching itself, stretching its fingers out wide and dispersing its strength, with its rear so far away and its supply lines so long. As Comrade Mao Tse-tung has said, "Wherever it commits aggression, it puts a new noose around its neck. It is besieged ring upon ring by the people of the whole world."

When committing aggression in a foreign country, U.S. imperialism can only employ part of its forces, which are sent to fight an unjust war far from their native land and therefore have a low morale, and so U.S. imperialism is beset with great difficulties. The people subjected to its aggression are having a trial of strength with U.S. imperialism neither in Washington nor New York, neither in Honolulu nor Florida, but are fighting for independence and freedom on their own soil. Once they are mobilized on a broad scale, they will have inexhaustible strength. Thus superiority will belong not to the United States but to the people subjected to its aggression. The latter, though apparently weak and small, are really more powerful than U.S. imperialism.

The struggles waged by the different peoples against U.S. imperialism reinforce each other and merge into a torrential world-wide tide of opposition to U.S. imperialism. The more successful the development of people's war in a given region, the larger the number of U.S. imperialist forces that can be pinned down and depleted there. When the U.S. aggressors are hard pressed in one place, they have no alternative but to loosen their grip on others. Therefore, the conditions become more favourable for the people elsewhere to wage struggles against U.S. imperialism and its lackeys.

Everything is divisible. And so is this colossus of U.S. imperialism. It can be split up and defeated. The peoples of Asia, Africa, Latin America and other regions can destroy it piece by piece, some striking at its head and others at its feet. That is why the greatest fear of U.S. imperialism is that people's wars will be launched in different parts of the world, and particularly in Asia, Africa and Latin America, and why it regards people's war as a mortal danger.

U.S. imperialism relies solely on its nuclear weapons to intimidate people. But these weapons cannot save U.S. imperialism from its doom. Nuclear weapons cannot be used lightly. U.S. imperialism has been condemned by the people of the whole world for its towering crime of dropping two atom bombs on Japan. If it uses nuclear weapons again, it will become isolated in the extreme. Moreover, the U.S. monopoly of nuclear weapons has long been broken; U.S. imperialism has these weapons, but others have them too. If it threatens other countries with nuclear weapons, U.S. imperialism will expose its own country to the same threat. For this reason, it will meet with strong opposition not only from the people elsewhere but also inevitably from the people in its own country. Even if U.S. imperialism brazenly uses nuclear weapons, it cannot conquer the people, who are indomitable.

However highly developed modern weapons and technical equipment may be and however complicated the methods of modern warfare, in the final analysis the outcome of a war will be decided by the sustained fighting of the ground forces, by the fighting at close quarters on battlefields, by the political consciousness of the men, by their courage and spirit of sacrifice. Here the weak points of U.S. imperialism will be completely laid bare, while the superiority of the revolutionary people will be brought into full play. The reactionary troops of U.S. imperialism cannot possibly be endowed with the courage and the spirit of sacrifice possessed by the revolutionary people. The spiritual atom bomb which the revolutionary people possess is a far more powerful and useful weapon than the physical atom bomb.

Viet Nam is the most convincing current example of a victim of aggression defeating U.S. imperialism by a people's war. The United States has made south Viet Nam a testing ground for the suppression of people's war. It has carried on this experiment for many years, and everybody can now see that the U.S. aggressors are unable to find a way of coping with people's war. On the other hand, the Vietnamese people have brought the power of people's war into full play in their struggle against the U.S. aggressors. The U.S. aggressors are in danger of being swamped in the people's war in Viet Nam. They are deeply worried that their defeat in Viet Nam will lead to a chain reaction. They are expanding the war in an attempt to save themselves from defeat. But the more they expand the war, the greater will be the chain reaction. The more they escalate the war, the heavier will be their fall and the more disastrous their defeat. The people in other parts of the world will see still more clearly that U.S. imperialism can be defeated, and that what the Vietnamese people can do, they can do too.

History has proved and will go on proving that people's war is the most effective weapon against U.S. imperialism and its lackeys. All revolutionary people will learn to wage people's war against U.S. imperialism and its lackeys. They will take up arms, learn to fight battles and become skilled in waging people's war, though they have not done so before. U.S. imperialism like a mad bull dashing from place to place, will finally be burned to ashes in the blazing fires of the people's wars it has provoked by its own actions. . . .

# 6. The Political Dynamics of the Cult of Mao Tse-tung

*James T. Myers*

In the period since the beginning of the Great Proletarian Cultural Revolution (GPCR) a substantial amount of attention has been drawn to the personality and leadership cult of Mao Tse-tung. While this is very likely in large measure a function of the volume and quality of the served to spotlight an important feature of the Chinese political system. rhetorical excesses produced by the great upheaval, it has nevertheless It is the purpose of this article to present the cult not merely as the object of an old man's vanity[1] (though this is certainly an element), nor as an object of ridicule (for which it is an easy target), but as a significant operative feature of the Chinese Communist political system, which must properly be analyzed within the context of the dynamic action of Chinese leadership politics.

In the analysis of the manipulation of the Mao cult presented here, an attempt is made to identify specific "constructs" and stages in the development of the cult. The term "construct" is selected to reflect the element of conscious manipulation so basic to the development of the cult. These constructs are (1) the cult of Mao as a Marxist-Leninist prophet leader, which corresponds to the earliest stages of the cult's

---

[1]This is essentially the view presented in more sophisticated form by Robert Jay Lifton in his *Revolutionary Immortality: Mao Tse-tung and the Chinese Cultural Revolution* (New York: Vintage Books, 1968), pp. 91–95. He writes, "Mao apparently requires the immortalizing corpus for his 'romantic' sense of self and history, his image of the heroic confrontation with the powers of heaven and earth" (p. 92). This view is challenged in Richard Pfeffer's review of Lifton's volume, *The China Quarterly*, No. 38 (April-June 1969): 166–70. Pfeffer writes, "The cult of personality should not be taken as a sophisticated manifestation of Mao's vanity. Quite the contrary seems to be true: the cult of personality consistently has been used instrumentally to achieve ends more significant than the enhancement of Mao's self-image" (p. 168).

Prepared by the author for this anthology; a longer paper on the same subject was delivered by the author at the First Sino-American Conference on Mainland China, Taipei, Taiwan, Republic of China, December 14–19, 1970.

development; (2) the cult of Mao as the "great savior" of the Chinese people, corresponding to the second stage of development beginning in 1949-1950; (3) the cult as a weapon in the intra-elite struggle beginning with 1956; (4) the quasi-magical ritualistic cult of Mao which appears with the opening stages of the GPCR in 1966.

While there is a correspondence between the initial appearance of a construct and the stage of development at which it appears, this should not be interpreted as signifying the exclusive use of one construct at any given time. All constructs are brought into play in the later stages of the cult's development.

## Mao As Party Leader—1942-1949[2]

The earliest use of the conscious manipulation of Mao's image is associated with the effort to establish his credentials and position as undisputed leader of the Communist Party of China (CPC) beginning in the early 1940's.

In studying the phenomenon of a leadership cult in a modern Communist setting one studies a particular variation of this phenomenon. While striking institutional similarities may exist between contemporary manifestations of culted leadership and historical manifestations as, for example, the glorification of Pharoah or of Chinese Emperor, there are equally important differences which must be taken account of. It is in a communist system, founded upon the scientific validity of a world order revealed by Marx and Engels[3] and developed by Lenin and his successors, that the claim to ideological omnicompetence has become a decisive factor in the political struggle over party formulation.

There need be, of course, no direct relationship between the "correctness" or predictive accuracy of the leader involved and his successes in the political arena. Predictive accuracy may enhance the political fortunes of a Communist leader but more often ideological "correctness" flows from a firm position of political superiority. The successful leader, that is, is able to proclaim, with authority, his superior understanding of

---

[2]The date 1949 is selected here to reflect the appearance of a new construct of the cult at that time. As the discussion below seeks to show, the effort to enlarge Mao's image as Party leader continues to the present. Throughout, the growth of the cult proceeds as symbol is added to symbol. In the analysis presented here, the appearance of a new construct of the cult merely signifies the addition of new symbols or new dimensions to the total fabric of the cult. It is this point which the periodization is intended to reflect.

[3]Engels said of his friend, "Just as Darwin discovered the law of development of organic nature, so Marx discovered the law of development of human history." Frederick Engels at the graveside of Karl Marx, Marx & Engels, *Selected Works*, 2 Vols. (Moscow: Foreign Languages Publishing House, 1958), 2:153–54.

contemporary problems as well as future developments as a result of the superior power position he enjoys relative to his rivals or potential rivals within the ruling elite.[4]

While ideological "correctness" may be a function of the political strength of the leader, rather than the reverse, nevertheless the rhetoric of political power struggles in a communist system is always framed in terms of the ideological correctness or superior scientific understanding of the combatants. Because of the scientific world view provided by Marxism-Leninism the opponent is not simply characterized as a bad or unsavory character. He must usually also be "wrong" or "incorrect." In a system based upon the validity of the Marxian analysis there cannot be two or more "correct" ways to reach the Communist millenium. Absolute doctrine demands one and only one authoritative interpretation.

This interpretation, then, is provided by the leader, the great man who becomes the wellspring of all social and political wisdom so far as the movement he leads is concerned. For Mao this assertion of doctrinal supremacy came with the formal inauguration of the Cheng Feng movement in the early months of 1942. The movement represented an attempt by the CPC leadership to bring greater discipline into the rapidly growing numbers of the Party rank and file and to assert the doctrinal supremacy of the Party center represented by Mao Tse-tung and his "thought."[5]

During the early 1940's as Mao continued to solidify his control over the CPC, more claims were advanced for his leadership. A greater prominence was given to his theoretical contributions. The new Constitution adopted by the CPC Seventh National Congress in 1945 declared:

> The Communist Party of China guides its work *entirely* by the teachings which unite the theories of Marxism-Leninism with the actual practice of the Chinese revolution—the thought of Mao Tse-tung—and fights any dogmatist or empiricist deviations.[6]

Moreover, as Professor William F. Dorrill points out, it was during this period, "after Mao had gained an absolutely unassailable position of control over the Party apparatus (that) the entire Kiangsi historical

---

[4]Cf. William F. Dorrill's observation in connection with the revision of the historical record of the Kiangsi period ". . . in the CPC it has always been an important matter for leaders in power to be able to identify themselves with the successes of the Party and, above all, to be able to absolve themselves of any responsibility for failures that are encountered." "Transfer of Legitimacy in the Chinese Communist Party: Origins of the Maoist Myth," *The China Quarterly*, No. 36 (October-December 1968), 47.

[5]See e.g., "Reform in Learning, the Party, and Literature," in Boyd Compton, *Mao's China: Party Reform Documents, 1942–1944* (Seattle: University of Washington Press, 1952), pp. 9ff.

[6]*Current Background* (hereafter *CB*), (United States Consulate General, Hong Kong), No. 8 (September 14, 1950). (Emphasis added.)

record was radically revised."[7] In 1945 the Central Committee issued an official interpretation of the Party's history with special emphasis on the period 1931-1934, in which, Professor Dorrill observes, "the successes and failures of the CPC were invariably linked to the presence or absence of Mao Tse-tung's leadership.[8]

In the years prior to 1949, therefore, as Mao sought to bolster his claim as leader of the CPC, his "correctness" in using and interpreting Marxist-Leninist doctrine was cited as a principal source from which his legitimacy was derived. The earliest manipulation of the Mao image occurred almost entirely within the framework of Party leadership. The more familiar aspects of hero worship usually associated with the cult developed only later. Observing Mao at Yenan, Edgar Snow asserted:

> . . . while everybody knew and respected him, there was—as yet at least —no ritual of hero worship built up around him. I never met a Chinese Red who drooled 'our great leader' phrases, I did not hear Mao's name used as a synonym for the Chinese people . . . (Yet) the role of his personality in the movement was clearly immense.[9]

The relationship between Mao and his Party in the late 1930's and 1940's appears to have been a symbiotic one with Mao lending his personal charisma to the Party while at the same time claiming his special relationship to the institution and its ideological foundation as the basis of his legitimacy as leader. The effort during the 1940's was directed toward transferring the popularity and personal charisma of Chairman Mao *to* the Party, while at the same time attempting to cement his position *within* the Party. Despite differences of outlook, goals, and temperament with Liu Shao-ch'i and others concerning Party bureaucratic structures and means to achieve revolutionary goals, Mao clearly grasped the vital importance of a Leninist-style revolutionary party in these early years.[10] The fact that Mao later turned against the commissars

---

[7]*Op. cit.*, p. 54.

[8]*Ibid.*, p. 45.

[9]Edgar Snow, *Red Star Over China* (New York: Grove Press, 1961), p. 74.

[10]Professor John W. Lewis suggests that Mao did not "grasp the pivotal importance of the political commissar and in the end has turned on the commissars while restoring revolutionary chaos in an effort to preserve his own charismatic role." "Leader, Commissar, and Bureaucrat: The Chinese Political System in the Last Days of Revolution," in Ping-ti Ho and Tang Tsou, eds., *China in Crisis* (Chicago: The University of Chicago Press, 1968), 1:451. Also cf. Leonard Shapiro and John W. Lewis, "The Roles of the Monolithic Party Under the Totalitarian Leader," *The China Quarterly*, No. 40 (October-December 1969), 50. Cf. Mao Tsetung, "Reform in Learning, the Party, and Literature," *loc. cit.*, p. 9. Also, cf. the assertion by Conrad Brandt, Benjamin Schwartz, and John K. Fairbank: "The proper understanding of the Leninist concept of party lies at the very heart of the whole *cheng-feng* movement." *A Documentary History of Chinese Communism* (Cambridge, Massachusetts: Harvard University Press, 1952), p. 354.

after 1956 appears more a function of the direction and quality of the growth of the Party machine in power during the early 1950's, the emergence of certain latent differences with Liu Shao-ch'i and the Party bureaucrats, and the general impulse toward the diminution or routinization of charisma in post-revolutionary regimes.

The symbiotic relationship between leader and Party was even more apparent after 1949 as the new government made strenuous efforts to publicize and enlarge the apparently considerable appeal of Mao Tse-tung as the great national unifier — the savior of the Chinese people.

## Authority Crisis and Miranda—1949-1956

The propaganda efforts undertaken during the first years of the new regime to establish Mao as the unifying hero-figure of his nation were of great importance for the leaders of the CPC. The leaders of the Chinese political system, like those of other types of systems, have sought to endow their actions with legitimacy, to promote within the system a belief that the "structure, procedures, acts, decisions, policies, officials, or leaders of government possess the quality of 'rightness,' propriety, or moral goodness, and should be accepted because of this quality—irrespective of the specific content of the particular act in question."[11]

One of the most important elements of a support system is the authorizing political myth, the "pattern of basic political symbols" which is current in a society.[12] In a revolutionary system where new social institutions and structures are to replace the old, the attempt is made, through the manipulation of political symbols, to create belief in and support for the newly-created authorization myth of the new revolutionary state. Within the authorizing myth, those symbols of sentiment and identification which Lasswell and Kaplan term "miranda" serve the function of arousing "admiration and enthusiasm" and "setting forth and strengthening faiths and loyalties . . . thereby providing a basis for solidarity."[13] It is in this latter context that the manipulation of the symbols of the Mao cult is particularly relevant. In assuming his new role as leader of all the Chinese people, Mao's great natural popularity was combined with an intensive campaign of revolutionary propaganda to enlarge and reinforce his image as the savior of the long-suffering Chinese people, as the embodiment of the values and principles upon which the new state

---

[11]Robert A. Dahl, *Modern Political Analysis* (Englewood Cliffs, N. J.: Prentice-Hall, 1965), p. 19.

[12]Harold D. Lasswell and Abraham Kaplan, *Power and Society: A Framework for Political Analysis* (New Haven, Conn.: Yale University Press, 1952), p. 116.

[13]*Ibid.*, p. 119.

was founded, and as sage of the new order.[14] As old social and political institutions and structures were uprooted, the glorification of Mao Tsetung was aimed at establishing Mao as the symbol of national unity, a figure around whom the toiling masses of China could rally and with whom they could identify their future hopes and dreams.[15] The style or the spirit of the early glorification effort was a manifestation of the apparently genuine personal appeal of Chairman Mao in the early years and of the need of the Chinese people for a unifying heroic figure to lead them in the construction of a "more satisfying culture."[16]

In this effort the Chinese gave wide publicity both to Chairman Mao's greatness and brilliance and to his commonalty as well. Pictures of Mao came to adorn every home, every school, every public office and factory. He presided over huge mass rallies on important national ceremonial occasions and saw millions of Chinese shout the greater glory of his name. Mao made tours to the countryside as well, mingling with the common people, his presence calling forth a wide variety of poetic imagery. He became at once the Marxist-Sage Emperor and a sort of Chinese Everyman. One of the best known songs of the Communist movement, which had, by 1949, been elevated almost to a par with the National Anthem proclaimed:

> The East is Red
> The Sun Rises
> On the Horizon of China
> Appears the Great Hero Mao-Tse-tung . . .
> He is the Great Savior of the People

Mao was painted as a great, wise, and kind father—(or better, perhaps, uncle) figure who had brought his flock to the threshold of abundance and would lead them on to greater and more glorious victories in the future. He was lauded in speeches, articles, and editorials as a brilliant theorist and military strategist and was the recognized authority on everything from art to nightsoil collecting. In addition, the

---

[14]There was an attempt, in Prof. Pfeffer's words, "to legitimize roles and institutions through association with a beloved and respected leader." Richard M. Pfeffer, "The Pursuit of Purity: Mao's Cultural Revolution," *Problems of Communism*, November-December 1969, p. 19.

[15]Michel Oksenberg makes essentially the same point, linking the expansion of the Mao cult in the 1960's to the expansion and improvement of communications and transportation facilities and the resultant disintegration of social institutions which are taking root," he writes, "resort to the unifying symbol of the ruler . . . may be an appropriate response." Michel Oksenberg, "Comments" on a paper by John W. Lewis, Ping-ti Ho and Tang Tsou, eds., *op. cit.*, 1:500.

[16]Anthony F. C. Wallace, "Revitalization Movements," *American Anthropologist* 58 (April 1956): 265. Wallace's seminal study offers important insights into the development of the Mao cult.

effort to elevate Mao's standing within as a Marxist-Leninist Party leader continued, especially with the great campaign to publicize Mao's "philosophical" works, *On Practice* (1950) and *On Contradiction* (1952) which were said to have been produced originally in July and August, 1937.[17] Likewise, a new systematic effort to affirm the historical correctness of the Maoist leadership was contained in Hu Chiao-mu's long pamphlet "Thirty Years of the Chinese Communist Party,"[18] which also received wide publicity.

Of equal importance was the development of the CPC during the early 1950's as the central legitimizing institution in China. As Party and government functions and roles became regularized, there was a clear tendency in the direction of transferring the personal charisma of Mao Tse-tung to the Party — of establishing the institution rather than its Chairman personally as the source of legitimacy for other institutions, structures, and programs.

Though the symbiotic relationship between Mao and the Party which he led continued to exist for the most part during the early years of the new regime, with the shift from a guerrilla army-based party to a ruling party in power—a party which inevitably developed its own independent bureaucratic personality — the relationship between leader and institution began to change. Indeed, the seeds of one of the several problems which later precipitated the GPCR appear to have been contained in this developing relationship between Mao (and the "Maoists" associated with him) and the CPC bureaucrats in the years prior to the Eighth CPC Congress in 1956.

## Intra-elite Conflict—1956-1966

Beginning about 1956 yet another new dimension was added to the cult as it was brought into play as a weapon by Mao and his allies (and in

---

[17]A substantial controversy among students of Chinese affairs has arisen as to the validity of the 1937 date assigned by the Chinese to these two essays. The differing views are best represented by Stuart R. Schram, *The Political Thought of Mao Tse-tung* (New York: Praeger, 1963), pp. 43–44, and Arthur A. Cohen, *The Communism of Mao Tse-tung* (Chicago: University of Chicago Press, 1964), p. 24. Also, cf. the articles by Stuart Schram and Arthur Cohen, "Maoism: A Symposium," *Problems of Communism*, September-October 1966. Both Schram and Cohen seem to agree that Mao failed to make the grade as a first-rate Marxist dialectician. Perhaps the most interesting discussion of Mao's failings as a Marxist philosopher is offered by Karl A. Wittfogel, "Some Remarks on Mao's Handling of Concepts and Problems of Dialectics," *Studies in Soviet Thought* 3 (December 1963), which deals with Mao's incomplete 1940 philosophical essay, "On Dialectical Materialism."

[18]Peking: Foreign Languages Publishing House, 1951. The essay was also published in five installments in *People's China* beginning with volume 4, number 2, July 16, 1951.

some cases by those who hoped to profit by association with Mao) in a growing power struggle related primarily, though not exclusively, to domestic, political, social, and economic policies.

As suggested above, the early 1950's had witnessed a considerable growth in the civilian Party bureaucracy. These years had also seen the Maoist charisma transferred, to a substantial degree, to the CPC. Related to this development was the progressive inability of the Maoists and their opponents to reconcile their differences; an inability founded, as Michel Oksenberg asserts, upon "the irreconcilable controversy between Scientific Marxism-voluntarism."[19] It was in the struggle against the non-Maoist Party bureaucrats in this period, during which the bureaucrats became increasingly intrenched, that the cult became a major weapon to be used by the Chairman against his opponents; a weapon used first to help gain support for the Great Leap Forward (GLF), and following the failure of the experiment, used in the attempt to regain for Mao personally and for the Maoist vision a place of pre-eminence in domestic policy formation.

During the middle 1950's Chairman Mao continued to be pictured as a rather kindly father-figure whose mere presence was sufficient to stir the hearts of the masses. A typical report in the Chinese press stated that:

> Chairman Mao . . . had a stout build, a swarthy face with a reddish glow, greying hair; he wore a half-new grey-colored uniform and black shoes. He had in his hand an ordinary folding fan. What could be more appealing to human emotions?[20]

The initial phases of the great leap, however, brought an intensive nationwide campaign to build the Mao image to even more heroic proportions. During the summer and fall of 1958 Mao made extensive tours of China's rural areas in connection with the big push for the communization of agriculture. The widest possible press coverage was given to these tours in which Mao was pictured as generating great enthusiasm

---

[19] Michel Oksenberg, "Comments," *loc. cit.*, p. 490.

[20] Shanghai, *Lao Tung Pao*, August 3, 1957. This is an important part of the personal image of Mao which persisted until it was largely drowned out by the more grandiose claims of the cultural revolution. Mao was pictured as a simple, hardy peasant who led a Spartan existence. One of the men who guarded Mao's living quarters in Peking wrote, "The door screen for protection against the sun was made of reeds and the appointments within were very simple. Except for a bookcase full of books, a cot, a desk, and several chairs, there was nothing. Chairman Mao's clothes are simplicity itself. His silver-grey gown he has worn for several years, his shoes have lost their color; even his swimsuit has been patched." *Chung Kuo Ch'ing Nien* (China Youth), February 1, 1959.

among the masses and inspiring them by his radiant presence to put forth unprecedented effort. A visit by Chairman Mao was even said to serve as a rejuvenating tonic for old folks. One report declared that:

After Chairman Mao visited Tassukou, several old men in the happiness home left the institution to return to labor.[21]

In addition, Mao's "thought" began to receive its first serious and extensive treatment in the burgeoning glorification campaign. The Chinese press was filled with reference to the benefits to be derived from correctly internalizing Mao's thought. Reports poured in of the formation throughout the country of study groups to discuss Mao's writings.[22] Mao's thought was said to generate a tremendous spirit of self-sacrifice among the people, and its historical necessity was cited.[23] Likewise, Mao's military thought was the subject of numerous articles and speeches.[24] Mao's physical vigor also became highly praised. He was reported to have swum the mighty Yangtze "guerrilla style" on seven separate occasions in September, 1958, at the age of 65![25] In addition, a number of articles had begun to appear in 1957 written by persons who had been with Mao on the Long March. Each extolled his bravery, unselfishness, stamina, foresight, and feeling for the masses.[26] The praise for Mao seemed boundless. At the height of the great leap on National Day 1958 the *People's Daily* declared:

Today in the era of Mao Tse-tung, heaven is here on earth . . . Chairman Mao is a great prophet . . . Each prophecy of Chairman Mao has become a reality. It was so in the past; it is so today.[27]

This was, in fact, the first full-scale attempt to apotheosize the person and thought of Mao Tse-tung. That it occurred at this exact time is, of course, no accident. It came at a time when Mao had only recently been faced with the unpleasant consequences of the 100 flowers episode and when he was enmeshed in a bitter struggle with high-ranking members of the CPC over his plan to attempt a leap into the future through an im-

---

[21]K'ang Yao, "Eulogy to the People's Communes in Hsushui," *CB*, No. 520, September 30, 1958.

[22]See e.g., *Jen Min Jih Pao* (Peking), May 14, 1958.

[23]See e.g., the article by Ch'en Po-ta, *Hung Ch'i*, July 16, 1958.

[24]See e.g., Chu Teh's speech delivered on the 31st anniversary of the founding of the PLA, *NCNA* (Peking), July 31, 1958. Also cf., *Chieh Fang Chün Pao*, May 23, 1958.

[25]Cf. Richard L. Walker, "Chairman Mao and the Cult of Personality," *Encounter*, June 1960.

[26]See e.g., "Days with Chairman Mao," *People's China*, No. 13, 1957.

[27]*Jen Min Jih Pao*, Peking, October 1, 1958.

mense effort of the human will. The criticism of the 100 flowers period which saw the omniscience of the Great Helmsman questioned and the Party subjected to abuse might have been sufficient to call forth such a campaign. That the serious miscalculation which brought forth this criticism was followed closely by the challenge of those who opposed the radicalization of domestic policies made it imperative that an attempt be made to bolster Mao's image and reputation. The campaign seems to have had a two-fold objective; first, to create a generally favorable disposition toward the great leap programs among the ordinary Chinese whom these programs would most directly affect; and second, to reinforce and expand if possible the still enormous prestige enjoyed by Mao Tse-tung in the top echelons of the Party.

In the latter connection an attempt was made, first, to show that Chairman Mao enjoyed great popularity among the common people of China, and that he generated great waves of enthusiasm wherever he went. Secondly, there was an attempt to play to the nostalgic sentiments of the Long March veterans with the series of articles recalling Mao's leading role in that heroic struggle, and a reminder, should one be needed, of the long-time ties which bound the old comrades together. Third, and very important, was the effort expended toward demonstrating the historical "correctness" of Mao's thought. Stripped of their flowery rhetoric the statements glorifying the thought of Mao Tse-tung said to the Party leaders that Mao had been right in the past, that the revolution had succeeded as a result of his brilliant leadership, and that he was therefore likely to be right again and his critics wrong. The Party veterans were certainly aware of the importance of Mao's leading role in directing the affairs of the Party in the decades from the mid-1930's, and statements asserting his historical correctness seem calculated to reinforce that awareness. The push to glorify Mao's military thought was perhaps even more important given the fact that he stood opposed by his Minister of Defense and Army Chief of Staff. Finally, the extensive coverage given to Mao's alleged marathon swims in the Yangtze (a spectacle to be repeated at the height of the Cultural Revolution) must have been intended to assure the Party leaders that Mao was still hale and hearty, and capable of vigorous physical as well as mental activity.

The plans for the great leap went through, of course, over what must have been substantial although not decisive opposition. While neither the campaign to glorify Mao and his thought nor the natural position of great esteem he occupied made the great leap a success, they almost certainly saved him from a more ignominious fate than the one he in fact suffered when his grand experiment was seen to be a failure.

For Mao the cumulative effect of the three Central Committee meetings of 1958-1959 represented a serious political setback even though he was himself not subjected to public criticism or held up to ridicule. Clearly his great prestige and image as the founder of the new Chinese state saved him from public abuse at the hands of his enemies. It would appear that, next to the decline of Mao's credibility and influence in top Party circles, the most important political development of the conferences was the emergence of Lin Piao as a figure of growing political importance. Lin may already have become by late 1959, the dominant figure in the Mao faction next to Chairman Mao himself. Indeed, next to Chairman Mao, spiritually if not always physically close to the Great Helmsman, is precisely where Lin Piao was to be found henceforth.

As a result of the decision to cast his lot with Mao Tse-tung at top level Party meetings in 1958 and 1959, Lin Piao developed a considerable proprietary interest in the Chairman's hero cult.

Almost immediately following the Lushan meeting Lin Piao emerged as one of the chief patrons and the PLA as a principal vehicle for the spread of the new and expanded cult of Chairman Mao; a cult which assumed new dimensions and additional importance in the maneuvering for political power in China during the ensuing period. The cult was to be a major weapon against the increasingly entrenched Party bureaucracy which regarded the reimposition of Maoist voluntarist programs with keen disfavor. Because Lin Piao had decided to stake his political fortunes on a close association with Chairman Mao, he too had a substantial interest in preserving and increasing the Mao reputation. "Chairman Mao" as a symbol, contrasted with Mao the actual political ally, became of increasing importance to Lin and the other protectors of the cult as they attempted to insure that the Thought of Mao Tse-tung (TMTT) and the mentality it was intended to induce among the toiling masses of China (a condition which I shall refer to as "Maoness") would outlive the Chairman himself and would continue to be under their control and manipulation.

In general outlines the post-Lushan glorification of Chairman Mao saw (1) an attempt to repair the damaged prestige of the Chairman resulting from his association with the Great Leap Forward; (2) the effort by Lin Piao to reassert Party supremacy in the PLA and to infuse its ranks with TMTT thereby bringing about the condition of Maoness; (3) the subsequent campaign to make the Maoness and Mao-style of the PLA the model for the entire country; (4) and most important perhaps, the attempt by the Maoist faction to establish in the cult a power base which would be independent of the Party as a legitimizing institution.

The celebrations marking the tenth anniversary of the founding of the Chinese People's Republic provided a convenient occasion for the opening of this new campaign to glorify Chairman Mao. In a major statement Lin Piao asserted the importance of Chairman Mao's "personal" leadership in building China's military strength.[28] In an access of glorification Liu Lan-t'ao cited Mao as the "most outstanding contemporary revolutionist, statesman and theoretician of Marxism-Leninism."[29] A "folk song" published in *Hung Ch'i* proclaimed:

> Chairman Mao is infinitely kind
> Ten thousand songs are not enough to praise him.
> With trees as pens, the sky as paper
> And an ocean of ink,
> Much would still be left unwritten.[30]

Mao's physical vigor was praised by Li Chi-shen who compared him to the "millennial pine tree" always "green and growing ever more vigorously through the ages."[31]

Similar sentiments were expressed throughout the year which followed with another great outpouring of praise coming at the 1960 National Day celebrations. The publication of volume 4 of Mao Tse-tung's *Selected Works* which coincided with the National Day celebration also brought a new nationwide campaign to glorify Mao's "thought" and to persuade the masses to study this newest volume of his writings.

At the same time, Lin Piao was pressing his campaign to deal with the disaffection in the PLA and to glorify the thought of Mao Tse-tung within its ranks. A resolution adopted in October, 1960, by an enlarged meeting of the Party Military Affairs Commission, chaired by Lin Piao, and dispatched as a secret document to regimental level, maintained that "Mao Tse-tung's thought, whether in the past, at present, or in the future, serves always as the guide in building up our army."[32] It was at this meeting that Lin Piao presented the "four relations"[33] (later to become known as the "four firsts") which were hailed as a "creative application of Mao Tse-tung's thought." Lin was thus already becoming cited

---

[28]Lin Piao, "Take Giant Strides, Holding Aloft the Red Flag of the Party's General Line and the Military Thinking of Mao Tse-tung," *Hung Ch'i* 19 (October 1, 1959). Cf. *Peking Review* 40 (October 6, 1959).

[29]Liu Lan-t'ao, "The Chinese Communist Party Is the Supreme Commander of the Chinese People in Building Socialism," *Jen Min Jih Pao* (Peking), September 28, 1959.

[30]*Hung Ch'i*, November 1959.

[31]*Jen Min Jih Pao* (Peking), September 27, 1959.

[32]*Kung Tso T'ung Hsün* (Work Bulletin of the PLA), translated in *The Politics of the Chinese Red Army*, J. Chester Cheng, ed. (Stanford, California: Hoover Institution Publications, 1966), Bulletin No. 3, October 20, 1960.

[33]The relationship of (1) men to weapons, (2) various kinds of work to political work, (3) general administrative work to ideological work, (4) book ideology to living ideology.

(within the ranks of the PLA at any rate) as the person who correctly and "creatively" applied Mao's teachings, in very much the same fashion as Mao himself was said to have creatively applied the teachings of Lenin and Stalin. The resolution advocated as "principal measures" to be carried out by those concerned, an "intensive, repeated, and widespread" campaign of "propaganda about the great significance of Mao Tse-tung's thought"; the transmission of the "instructions of Comrade Mao Tse-tung"; an effort to pursue the "serious study of Mao Tse-tung's works" and the use of the "sharp weapon of Mao Tse-tung's thought to display the brilliance of our revolution," and other similar activities. These extracts are but a brief example of the type of exhortation which was repeated endlessly within the ranks of the PLA in the years which followed and which eventually became standard fare for the civilian population as well.

This effort and the subsequent campaigns to emulate Lei Feng and Wang Chieh[34] were part of the larger attempt to make the PLA and its personnel models of Maoness for the entire country. The *Jen Min Jih Pao* gave formal proclamation to the campaign in February, 1964, with an editorial titled, "The Whole Country Must Learn from the PLA."[35] The Maoness of the PLA particularly as revealed in the "four firsts" policy and the "three-eight" style of work[36] subsequently became the model for the entire country.[37]

---

[34]See e.g., "Notification on the Propaganda and Study of Comrade Lei Feng's Exemplary Deeds in the Whole Army," issued by the General Political Department of the PLA, February 9, 1963. *Union Research Service* 31:864. Also, cf., *The Diary of Wang Chieh* (Peking: Foreign Language Press, 1967). For the "Learn from Lei Feng" movement among youth see e.g. "Actively Conduct Class Education Among Urban Youths," *Chung Kuo Ch'ing Nien Pao* (Peking), September 13, 1963; "Strengthen Class Education for Rural Youths," *ibid.*, July 27, 1963; Editorial, *ibid.*, November 8, 1965. For the campaign to "Emulate Wang Chieh" see e.g. "To Be a Financial and Trade Worker of the Wang Chieh Type" (Peking), *Ta Kung Pao*, November 13, 1965; " 'Emulate Wang Chieh' Becomes a Common Purpose of Teachers and Students" (Peking), *Kuang Ming Jih Pao*, November 9, 1965; cf. *Union Research Service* 41 (November 26, 1965). Also cf. *Chieh Fang Chün Pao*, Editorial, November 8, 1965.
[35]*Jen Min Jih Pao* (Peking), February 1, 1964.
[36]This style of work was said to have been condensed by Mao Tse-tung into three phrases and eight characters. The phrases are (1) keep a firm, correct political orientation, (2) work hard and live plainly, (3) be flexible in strategy and tactics. The eight Chinese characters form four English words: (1) unity, (2) vigor, (3) seriousness, (4) liveliness. Cf. "propagate the 'Three-Eight' Working Style Throughout the Entire Country," *Jen Min Jih Pao*, Editorial (Peking), February 23, 1964.
[37]See e.g., "Commercial Departments Should Learn from the PLA," *Jen Min Jih Pao*, Editorial, February 20, 1964. For the youth of the country urged to "go all out in learning from the PLA," see e.g., Peking, Domestic Service in Mandarin, February 21, 1964. For the establishment of PLA-style political departments in various government organizations see e.g., *Ta Kung Pao* (Peking), April 4, 1964 in *Union Research Service* 35 (May 29, 1964).

In fact, the Mao-Lin group had come already to count on the PLA as the most reliable, if, indeed, not the *only* reliable instrument at its command; and this, perhaps, not without good reason. The glorification of Chairman Mao and TMTT in the years leading up to the cultural revolution was probably carried out as a sort of partnership enterprise. Mao's belief that the regular Party apparatus had become unreliable and shot-through with incompetents (correct from his point of view) dictated his reliance on his powerful ally Lin Piao and on the PLA which, it was hoped, Lin could make responsive to his will. Lin Piao needed Chairman Mao and the Mao cult as well. As suggested above, he particularly needed "Chairman Mao" the symbol and the concomitant Maoness and TMTT which he had expended such effort to glorify. For Lin Piao the strategy of forming a close, even intimate, association with Mao Tse-tung was eminently sensible. Prior to the outbreak of the Cultural Revolution Lin had never ranked higher than seventh in the Party hierarchy. He could have little hope of substantially advancing his position by siding with the moderates or anti-Maoists in the Party. He could scarcely have expected to displace Liu Shao-ch'i, Teng Hsiao-p'ing or Chou En-lai by throwing his forces in with their own. By casting his lot with Chairman Mao, however, by becoming, in fact, the principal pillar of Maoist support, he could hope to gain the inside track for the top position in China once Mao was gone. Lin therefore linked his political fortunes to his association with Chairman Mao as closest comrade-in-arms, and to the underpinning of TMTT which he would "creatively" develop. Indeed, Lin Piao gradually became the object of a growing hero cult of his own, based primarily upon his "close" relationship with Chairman Mao. The full dimensions of this development, which accelerated significantly during the GPCR, have yet to be seen.

The strategy of the Mao-Lin group and the purpose of the alliance was two-fold. First, in view of the suspected unreliability of the regular Party apparatus they hoped to create a more reliable revolutionary mass base for their future activities by infusing the young of the country and the ranks of the PLA with the "cog" mentality and unswerving loyalty to Chairman Mao of the martyred heroes Lei Feng and Wang Chieh. Second, they were attempting to make the highly sloganized TMTT under their manipulation[38] an independent source of legitimacy to undercut, thereby, the support and influence enjoyed by Liu Shao-Ch'i and his allies in the Party bureaucracy.

The attempts of Mao and his supporters to establish a source of authority outside the Party, however, represented only a part of the political

---

[38]It should be recalled that the little red book *Quotations from Chairman Mao*, was originally produced under the direction of Lin Piao for use in the PLA.

struggle during the years preceding the Cultural Revolution. The manipulation of the cult was combined with a continued pressure by the Maoists within the Party and in other political structures as well, for the reimposition of Maoist programs. Unfortunately, from the Maoist point of view none of these attempts was very successful. The thrust of the "Socialist Education Campaign" which grew out of the Tenth Plenum of the Party Central Committee in September, 1962, had resulted in a policy which was "left in form but right in essence," according to the Maoists' later evaluation.[39] Nor had the campaign to win the membership of the Communist Youth League over to the side of the Mao forces met with much success.[40] Likewise, the trade unions elected to remain somewhat neutral or non-Maoist[41] as the crisis in the top Party leadership mounted during the late summer and fall of 1965. In addition, the growth of the Chairman's hero cult may itself have become a source of friction. Certainly many intellectuals had found Mao's style and the excessive glorification of his person and thought repugnant. One has only to consider the attacks by Wu Han and Teng T'o.[42] The literary critics were not simply calling for a thaw or a liberalization. They were engaging in vicious personal attacks on the Great Helmsman himself.

It seems clear that, in almost every important respect, the manipulation of the cult during the years following the GLF failed to achieve the Maoist purpose. The Party bureaucrats remained entrenched and in those instances where Maoist slogans or rhetoric had been adopted it appears to have been an exercise in "waving the Red Flag to oppose the Red Flag." Nevertheless, the buildup of the cult had not been entirely without positive value. The considerable preparation made toward establishing TMTT as a source of authority independent of the Party became of even greater importance to the Maoists once the decision was made in 1966

---

[39]See Mao's wall poster "Bombard the Headquarters" (August 5, 1966), *Peking Review* 33 (August 11, 1967). Also cf., "Completely Smash the Bourgeois Headquarters," *ibid.*

[40]Cf. the "Resolution of the Third Plenary Session of the Ninth CYL," adopted on April 20, 1966 (Peking), *Chung Kuo Ch'ing Nien Pao*, May 4, 1966.

[41]See e.g., "Combining Labor and Rest," *Jen Min Jih Pao*, Editorial, June 21, 1965. Also cf. "One Must Maintain the Combination of Labor with Rest" (Peking), *Ta Kung Pao*, Editorial, November 10, 1965. For a full analysis of the significance of the trade union movement during this period see *China News Analysis* (Hong Kong) 627 (September 2, 1966).

[42]Cf. Yao Wen-yüan, "On the New Historical Play *Dismissal of Hai Jui*" (Shanghai), *Wen Hui Pao*, November 10, 1965; and Wu Han, "Self-Criticism on *Dismissal of Hai Jui*" (Peking), *Jen Min Jih Pao*, December 30, 1965. Also cf. Yao Wen-yüan, "On 'Three Family Village'," Shanghai, *Wen Hui Pao*, May 10, 1966. Two of the most famous essays by Teng T'o appeared in the official fortnightly publication of the CPC Peking Committee—"Great Empty Talk," *Ch'ien Hsien* 21 (1961), and "Special Treatment for Forgetfulness," *Ch'ien Hsien* 14 (1962).

that violent overthrow of the Party would be necessary. Under these circumstances the central legitimizing role was thrust, albeit only temporarily, upon Mao and his Thought, as the Party was destroyed to await re-creation according to Mao's design. Moreover, while the campaigns were not necessarily successful in their larger socio-political implications, they did provide a substantial foundation for the further advance and growing glorification of Lin Piao throughout the course of the GPCR.[43]

## Magic and Ritual—1966-1969

With the beginning of the Great Proletarian Cultural Revolution in 1966 yet another construct of the cult, the quasi-magical and ritualistic cult, became fully articulated. This development is interesting for two reasons. First, it accompanied the attempt by the Maoist faction to bypass, indeed to eliminate, the regular Party apparatus, to take their appeal directly to the people. Second, alongside the allegedly scientific pretensions of the previous constructs of the cult there appeared a new order of claims for Mao and his thought which took as their point of origin Chinese mythology or tales of the supernatural. While it was claimed that the principal object of the cult, Mao's thought, remained essentially "scientific" or "Marxist" in its underpinnings, the manipulators of the cult felt it necessary or expedient to underplay the twentieth century aspects of the cult and to stress its new magical elements in an attempt to promote widespread acceptance by the broad mass of the Chinese people.

Beginning about mid-January 1966, following a news hiatus of nearly two months duration (coinciding with the first weeks of Mao's nearly six-months absence from public view), the *Chieh Fang Chün Pao* and the Canton *Yang Ch'eng Wan Pao* began to feature a new campaign to "bring politics to the fore." The campaign, which received its impetus from the Political Work Conference of the PLA held in Peking from December 30, 1965 to January 18, 1966, displayed a number of elements already familiar from the earlier development of the cult. The leading address of the conference was delivered by Hsiao Hua, both Mao Tse-tung and Lin Piao being absent. Hsiao Hua announced that the "central item on the agenda" of the conference was to "examine and sum up the political work in the past two years and to study how to implement Comrade Lin Piao's 5-point principle of keeping politics in the fore. . ." "Putting politics first," Hsiao declared, means "putting Mao Tse-tung's thinking first. We must take Mao Tse-tung's thinking as our criterion in all

---

[43]Cf. James T. Myers, "The Rise of Lin Piao," *Journal of Southeast Asia and the Far East* 2 (1969).

aspects of our Army's work and in all our words and deeds."[44] The call
to keep politics in the fore was subsequently taken up in a series of *Chieh
Fang Chün Pao* Editorials over the next few months.[45] At about the same
time there appeared in the Canton *Yang Ch'eng Wan Pao* an Editorial
which marked a renewed effort to glorify the role and the importance of
TMTT. The Editorial divided the development of Marxism into three
stages. The third and final period which began following the close of
World War II saw Mao Tse-tung become the principal exponent of
Marxism-Leninism. The Editorial asserted:

> In the new, great and revolutionary epoch, it is the thought of Mao Tse-
> tung which has comprehensively and systematically developed Marxism-
> Leninism—the peak of contemporary Marxism-Leninism.[46]

A later Editorial asserted that "the thought of Mao Tse-tung is the bril-
liant peak of contemporary Marxism-Leninism."[47] In the months which
followed the initial declaration of TMTT as the "peak," the *Yang Ch'eng
Wan Pao* became a major spokesman for the Maoist counterattack, the
Peking press being still under the control of P'eng Chen and the CPC
Peking Municipal Committee.[48]

Other familiar elements of the cult were also brought into play amid
intensified political maneuvering, as Mao returned to Peking in the wake
of the armed occupation of the capital city by units of the PLA loyal to
Lin Piao. In view of the fact that Mao was reported to have made only
one appearance in public between his disappearance from Peking in November and his famous swim on July 16, 1966, the publicity surrounding
this event must once again, as in 1958, have been intended to reassure
wavering Party leaders that Mao was in sound health. According to the
report, Chairman Mao "stayed in the water a full sixty five minutes, cov-

---

[44]Hsiao Hua, "Hold High the Great Red Banner of the Thought of Mao Tse-
tung, and Resolutely Implement the 5-Point Principle of Bringing Politics to the
Fore," *NCNA* (Peking), January 24, 1966.

[45]See e.g., "Forever Bringing Politics to the Fore," February 4, 1966; "In Tackling
Living Ideas, We Must Tackle Fundamentals," February 7, 1966; "The Most Im-
portant and Fundamental War Preparations," February 14, 1966; "Politics Com-
mand Military Affairs, Politics Command Everything," February 18, 1966; "Regard
Chairman Mao's Books as the Highest Directive for All Work Throughout the
PLA," May 2, 1966.

[46]"The Peak of Development of Marxism" (Canton), *Yang Ch'eng Wan Pao*,
Editorial, February 2, 1966. Translated in *SCMP* 3641 (February 18, 1966).

[47]"More on the Peak of Development of Marxism" (Canton), *Yang Ch'eng Wan
Pao*, Editorial, April 5, 1966. Translated in *SCMP* 3678 (April 15, 1966).

[48]See e.g., the following *Yang Ch'eng Wan Pao* articles: "On Bringing Politics to
the Fore," Editorial, February 5, 1966; "The Busier the Work, the Greater the
Necessity to Bring Politics to the Fore," February 18, 1966; Chao Tzu-yang, "Ev-
eryone Can Study Chairman Mao's Works and Anyone Having Revolutionary
Aspirations Can Study Them Well," March 2, 1966; "An Unprecedented Way of
Tackling Living Ideas," Editorial, March 26, 1966.

ering a total distance of almost fifteen kilometers." When news of this event spread through Wuhan, the report continues, "Everybody was saying: 'Our respected and beloved leader Chairman Mao is in such wonderful health.' "[49] The following day the *Jen Min Jih Pao* declared:

> The fact that Chairman Mao is in such wonderful health and brimming with such energy is a matter of the greatest happiness for the entire Chinese people.[50]

And the *Chieh Fang Chün Pao* declared, "Chairman Mao's good health is the happiness of all the people of China and the people throughout the world."[51] All of this would at least tend to reinforce a strong suspicion that the swim was intended to counter rumors of a real or suspected illness during Mao's long absence from public view.

Of equal importance was the effort beginning in August to demonstrate the love of the masses for Chairman Mao. The immense rallies held in Peking following the appearance of the Red Guards saw eleven million or so "revolutionary fighters" from all parts of China, many shedding "tears of joy," come to proclaim the greater glory of Chairman Mao.[52] To this point then, during the opening stages of the GPCR, the manipulation of the symbols of the cult revolved around several already familiar elements: (1) the assertion of the political reliability of the PLA and its loyalty to Mao, (2) a reaffirmation of the "correctness" of TMTT, (3) the confirmation of the soundness of Mao's health, and (4) a demonstration of the love of the masses for Chairman Mao.

As indicated above, however, this effort was accompanied by the introduction of several entirely new elements in the manipulation of the cult. It was claimed, for example, that Mao's thought was *"Fa Pao,"* a magical or supernatural weapon.[53] The enemies of the Great Helmsman were no longer characterized as simply enemies of the state or of the people. They became "devils," "demons," "monsters," "apparitions and spectres," and other supernatural creatures.[54] This type of rhetoric, which has diminished since its high-point in 1966, may have reflected a note of desperation by Mao's close entourage as the GPCR met unexpectedly stiff resistance. Though the supernatural element has been played down in

---

[49]*NCNA*, English (Wuhan, July 25, 1966).

[50]"Follow Chairman Mao and Advance in the Teeth of the Great Storms and Waves," *Jen Min Jih Pao*, Editorial (Peking), July 26, 1966.

[51]*Chieh Fan Chün Pao*, Editorial, July 26, 1966.

[52]For a description of these rallies see *Peking Review* 35, 37, 39, and 41 (1966).

[53]*Kuang Ming Jih Pao* (Peking), August 5, 1966. Cf. H. C. Chuang, *The Great Proletarian Cultural Revolution: A Terminological Study*, Studies in Chinese Communist Terminology, No. 12, Center for Chinese Studies, Institute of International Studies (Berkeley: University of California, 1967), pp. 36–37.

[54]H. C. Chuang, *op. cit.*, pp. 22–24.

the last few years, the claims for the miraculous or magical effects of the proper application of Mao's thought have continued to mount. It has not yet been asserted that Mao can raise the dead or cure infirmities by the laying-on of hands, but short of this there are few miracles left to claim. Indeed, the internalization of Mao's thought has recently been said to be an aid in the curing of cancer victims[55] and deaf-mute children.[56] This appears to be a part of a general effort to persuade people to tighten their belts and through a dedication to the Maoist principles of commitment, sacrifice, service, etc. (as best exemplified by the numerous heroes of the PLA), to achieve better results with the resources at hand in what will undoubtedly continue to be difficult times for China.

The GPCR also brought a subtle shift in the manipulation of the cult, associated with the growing ritualization in the cult's celebration. By mid-1968 there appears to have developed in some cases a definite ritual for paying respect to Chairman Mao. One such ritual described follows much the form of a Christian church service with (1) a processional, (2) reading of verse, (3) sermon, and (4) recessional or benediction. A report of a Heilungkiang rally affirming loyalty to Chairman Mao was described as follows:

> After opening ceremonies to the strains of (1) "The East Is Red" and (2) a recital of quotations from Mao Tse-tung, (3) a directive to hold high the great red banner of Mao Tse-tung's thought, vigorously grasp class struggle, and do a good job on the production of summer-ripening crops . . . was read . . . the rally ended with the song (4) "Sailing the Seas Depends on the Helmsman."[57]

At the same time the trend has been increasingly to emphasize Mao's thought or other symbolic aspects of his existence as contrasted with his physical presence. Though Mao has been present at great ceremonial occasions, as for example, at the immense Red Guard Rallies in 1966, he has largely (entirely in the case of the 1966 rallies) remained mute while Lin Piao delivered the major address. Thus in a sense even though present on these occasions, his presence has been largely symbolic. Indeed, as the ceremonial position of Lin Piao has risen the public role of Mao himself, the physical corpus, has become increasingly irrelevant. This is not to say that Mao no longer wields important political power. The exact role played by Mao in domestic political events is still very much a matter

[55]See e.g., "A Communist Full of Revolutionary Vigour," *Peking Review* 17 (April 25, 1969) for the story of cancer victim Ma Yi; and "My Life Belongs to the People, I Will Fight to the Last Day of My Life," *Peking Review* 52 (December 27, 1968) for the story of cancer victim Yu Chun.

[56]John Gittings, "Sing Along with Chairman Mao," *Far Eastern Economic Review* (Hong Kong) 21 (May 18–24, 1969).

[57]Heilungkiang Provincial Service in Mandarin, May 23, 1968.

of debate. Nevertheless, Mao's public role has become increasingly symbolic and less substantive. As the celebration of the Mao cult has become more ritualistic, it has at the same time become largely de-personalized, and Mao himself has become more and more important as a spiritual presence. Thus, for example, it is possible for the editors of the *Peking Review* to produce a major article on party building composed entirely of Mao's past utterances.[58] Mao himself is no longer in any way vital to such a process of production. Whole essays may be produced from fragments of his body of work in very much the same way that a Christian cleric might produce a sermon from the recorded words of Jesus.

There is, moreover, a growing trend toward idolatry in the celebration of the Mao cult. It is no longer necessarily Mao himself who receives the accolades of his loyal subjects. More and more the proper acts of devotion are performed before a portrait of the Great Helmsman. We read, for example, that the entire company of one PLA engineering corps unit "took a solemn oath before Chairman Mao's portrait."[59] According to the same report a group of paraders later converged on the *Chung Nan Hai* "carrying pledges written on red paper" which they read "in front of the big portrait of Chairman Mao,"[60] while still another group of workers "solemnly pledged before the portrait of Chairman Mao."[61] One cancer victim, Miss Ma Yi, was, according to a report, delivering a speech "propagating Chairman Mao's revolutionary line" to a meeting of some six thousand persons when she became dizzy and unable to stand. When she raised her head, however, "she saw the lofty image of Chairman Mao in a portrait over the platform and was immediately filled with warmth. Her energy restored, she walked back to the platform and continued her speech."[62] Yet another loyal subject, one Ho Chen-wu, a representative of the "Tenth Company of the Engineering Corps in the Snow-Bound Highlands Boundlessly Loyal to Chairman Mao" (apparently the official, full name of the company as it appears within quotation marks in the original), appears to have had a visionary experience: "Looking at the lights over *Chung Nan Hai* which he had thought about day and night, he seemed to see Chairman Mao standing before him." Whereupon he delivered the following highly interesting pledge to Chairman Mao:

> Chairman Mao, Chairman Mao! I am resolved to take the deputy supreme commander Lin as the glorious example all my life in creatively studying your works.[63]

---

[58]"Chairman Mao on Party Building," *Peking Review* 15 (April 11, 1969).
[59]*Peking Review* 15 (April 11, 1969): 8.
[60]*Ibid.*, p. 10.
[61]*Ibid.*
[62]*Peking Review* 17 (April 25, 1969): 27.
[63]*Peking Review* 15 (April 11, 1969): 11.

If these few examples are indeed indicative of an important shift in the development of the cult, as they clearly seem to be, there can be little doubt that they represent a move to prepare the way for a smooth transfer of power once Mao passes from the scene. The principal beneficiary of this shift in the celebration of the cult appears to be Lin Piao. It is Lin who appears as the spokesman and interpreter for the thought of Chairman Mao. Beginning with the mass rallies of 1966 it has been Lin Piao who has delivered the major political addresses, as he did at the Ninth Party Congress — though, of course, his ideas are always presented as creative applications of the thought of Chairman Mao. Withal, Lin's own modest but substantial personality cult has continued to grow.

From a somewhat modest beginning, a hero cult af sizeable proportions glorifying Lin Piao gradually blossomed forth. It has been asserted, for example, that, "Comrade Lin Piao has given the most correct, scientific and highest Marxist-Leninist evaluation of the all-illuminating thought of Mao Tse-tung."[64] And further that, "Comrade Lin Pao has made the most comprehensive, correct and scientific appraisal of Chairman Mao and Mao Tse-tung's thought."[65] The parallels between this assessment of Lin Piao's "correct" evaluation of TMTT and the glorification in the middle and late 1950's of Mao's correct "summing-up" and application of the doctrines of Lenin and Stalin are indeed striking. The Chinese Navy also added to the burgeoning cult of Lin Piao. A decision adopted by the PLA Navy on Lin Piao's now famous inscription, "Sailing the seas depends on the helmsman; making revolution depends on Mao Tse-tung's thought," declared that this inscription "is a great truth that holds true for the entire world." The Navy decision further declared that:

> Vice Chairman Lin Piao is the one who holds highest the great red banner of Mao Tse-Tung's thought, comprehends Mao Tse-Tung's thought, and applies it best. Vice Chairman Lin Piao is our best model in the entire Party in the study, application, propaganda, and defense of Mao Tse-tung's thought. He is always a brilliant example for us to learn from.[66]

More recently Lin has been referred to, in terms hitherto reserved for Mao Tse-tung alone, as "Our respected and beloved Vice Chairman Lin

---

[64]Yang Ch'eng-wu, "Thoroughly Establish the Absolute Authority of the Great Supreme Commander Chairman Mao and His Great Thought," *Peking Review* 46 (November 10, 1967): 18.

[65]*Ibid.*, p. 24.

[66]"PLA Navy Adopts Decision on Vice Chairman Lin's Inscription," *NCNA* (Peking), December 18, 1967.

Piao,"[67] and, proclaims the new CPC Constitution, "Comrade Lin Piao is Comrade Mao Tse-tung's close comrade-in-arms and successor."[68]

Thus it appears that in this latest development of the cult the groundwork has been set for Lin to remain on earth as the interpreter and guide while Mao himself is elevated to a spiritual pantheon with Marx and Lenin, remaining to be worshipped on earth through symbols and icons. He will as well, it is hoped, be worshipped through devotion to his thought which will remain, under the manipulation of Lin Piao and Mao's other successors, as the continuing foundation of legitimacy for the post-Mao Chinese leadership. Only time will allow us to judge the success or failure of this effort or even, for that matter, if the effort will continue. One fact, however, stands out quite clearly. The ceremonial ascendancy of Lin Piao during the Cultural Revolution has placed him in an excellent position to assume leadership after Mao's passing. He has clearly eclipsed all of his rivals (except, of course, Mao Tse-tung himself), at least in terms of the output of the Party Propaganda Department, and his growing personality cult shows no signs that it may diminish.

## Conclusion

One of the ironies of the recent upheaval in China is that the PLA—the principal pillar of Maoist support—should in the end have prevented the realization of Mao's ambition. The GPCR might not have succeeded for a variety of other reasons but the fact remains that it was the PLA which put the brakes on Mao's attempt to purify the Party through violent revolution. This fact combined with the continued existence of a flourishing cult which glorifies Mao and his thought cannot fail to have produced a situation with serious built-in tensions. One sees a curious arrangement in which all rhetoric emanating from Peking is Maoist rhetoric, while at the same time the task of administering the country is, for the most part, in the hands of precisely the sort of persons Mao sought to eliminate through the GPCR. Perhaps the most outstanding example of this strange situation is the case of Huang Yungsheng whose reward for being consistently attacked by Red Guards in Canton as an anti-Maoist, was his elevation to the position of Chief of the PLA General Staff. This apparent dichotomy between rhetoric and

---

[67]*NCNA* (Peking), International Service in English, April 20, 1969.

[68]The Constitution of the Communist Party of China (adopted by the Ninth National Congress of the CPC on April 14, 1969), *Peking Review* 18 (April 30, 1969): 36.

reality gives rise to important questions as to what will serve to guide the leaders of the Chinese nation through the years ahead; to aid them in seeking and implementing solutions to the monumental problems confronting any Chinese leaders. In view of the apparent incapacity of TMTT to provide a useful and realistic guide for the future development of China, at least in the view of China's "pragmatists," it is important to question what possible alternatives are available to serve as the programmatic guides and authorizing myths of the post-Maoist political order. The answer poses a dilemma which may be difficult to solve. We have been told that Mao Tse-tung has developed the theories of Marx, Engels, Lenin, and Stalin to a new and higher stage beginning with his ascendency to the position of "greatest contemporary" Marxist-Leninist theoretician in the late 1950's. The Chairman's publicists claimed that the center of gravity of Marxist-Leninist development had shifted to the East, and that Marxism-Leninism had been elevated to its "highest stage" and "brilliant peak" in TMTT. If, as it appears, many of those holding real power in China consider TMTT inadequate to the task of solving China's vast problems any solution will have to be based on a non-Maoist commentary on the sacred texts. Since the highest stage in the development of Marxist-Leninist thought has reached in TMTT, however, any attempt to return to any earlier stage, or even worse, to borrow from the Soviet experience, would be open to the still potent charge of revisionism. This dilemma, created by the growth of the cult may require some very nimble ideological manipulation to overcome.

The manipulation of the cult over the years, therefore, while it may at certain times have aided the Maoists in gaining a temporary advantage or averting a disaster (e.g., 1958, 1965), appears to have failed in achieving the principle objectives of Mao and his supporters. Following the initial disillusionment of 1958-1959 with the Maoist programs, there has been, in the top circles of the Party, neither widespread acceptance of the claims of the cult nor substantial implementation of the programs of Mao and his supporters. The moderates and rightists in opposition paid lip service to the heroic deeds and doctrines of the Great Helmsman and made no attempt to interfere with the buildup of his image. But they were not swayed in their policy decisions by the growing claims of Mao's omniscience which they voiced along with the Maoists. The anti-Maoists were later accused of "waving the Red Flag to oppose the Red Flag" and this they did. They sang the praises of Mao Tse-tung while attempting to overcome the nearly disastrous effects of his domestic programs.

The open use of armed force and the increasing reliance of the Maoists on the Army as their principal pillar of support, indicate at least a tacit admission of the failure of the buildup of the cult to achieve the desired results. For the principal objective of the propaganda claims, from Mao's point of view, was precisely to create a situation where the resort to force would be unnecessary. In the final analysis, Lin Piao alone appears to have advanced his lot substantially the manipulation of the cult, having worked his way to the top of the leadership pyramid and prepared the way to succeed Mao.

# 7. Political Myth and Personality:
## The Authority Crisis

*Lucian W. Pye*

China is not only Communist it is a developing country. Strangely this second dimension of China has been more appreciated in the popular press and in official policies than in scholarly research. Academically there has been little inclination to apply to the analysis of Communist China the concepts and theories that have given such vitality to the study of political and economic development in the rest of the Afro-Asian world. Among scholars the division has been sharp between those working on Communist China and those working on political and economic development. Each group has gone its separate way, and there has been remarkably little intellectual exchange. The China specialists have seemingly taken on some of the pride of their country of study and have been anxious to stress its world-shaking importance, often, possibly quite unintentionally, giving the impression that the rest of the underdeveloped countries are insignificant in comparison. This has helped to spread the impression that China's problems and those of the other transitional societies have little in common. The students of development, on the other hand, have steadfastly ignored Communist China and have generally displayed a strong distaste for any serious analysis of communism. For these people Communist China smacks too much of the Cold War, a reality they accept at times when justifying the importance of development but which they prefer to live without. Although the search for theories of political, social, and economic development has sought to avoid excessive partisanship, the implicit bias of most scholars in the

Reprinted from Lucian W. Pye, *The Spirit of Chinese Politics, A Psychocultural Study of the Authority Crisis in Political Development* (Cambridge, Mass.: M.I.T. Press, 1968), pp. 1–11, by permission of The M.I.T. Press, Cambridge, Massachusetts and the author.

field has been toward democratic development; hence there has been a feeling that the blatantly Communist example of China can properly be ignored.

Possibly an even more significant element in this curious scholarly omission is the fact that China was a transitional society long before the world fully appreciated the inherent difficulties of modernization. If we were now to review the twentieth-century experiences of the Chinese in the light of what we currently know about the difficulties of achieving advancement in the Afro-Asian world we should have to revise many, if not most, of the conventional judgments and evaluations of Chinese performance. Throughout the 1920's and 1930's the Chinese received low marks and a bad press from scholars, diplomats, and journalists because everyone measured their efforts to modernize against the standards of the European world and not against those that are currently being applied to transitional societies in the former colonial areas. During these early decades of the century when China was seeking to break out of the traditional institutional molds there was little general understanding of the extraordinary complexity of economic and political development. At that time China stood largely alone in the rest of the world as an independently developing society; the rest of the still traditional and pre-nation-state societies were held together and given administrative order largely through colonial rule. Thus, in the decades when China was passing through the first phases of modernization, the world was not nearly as tolerant as it is now of the violence, confusion, and ineffectualness characteristic of developing societies.

During this period China was compared only with Japan, a country we now realize had unique potentialities for development. Certainly no other developing country in today's world has the likelihood of matching the Japanese record in modernization. The common Confucian-Buddhist tradition and the historic Japanese borrowing of Chinese culture, however, tended only to confuse the issue by suggesting that the Japanese experience should be relevant for judging Chinese potentialities.

The feeble afterglow of the 1911 Revolution, the period of the pathetic Phantom Republic in Peking, Sun Yat-sen's impotent efforts at economic planning, the sordid interplay of warlords, the students' explosive but ineffectual nationalism, the venal corruption of bureaucrats and office holders, the Nationalist government's shallow propagandist pretensions of progress—all seemed to suggest that something was wrong with the Chinese, that they lacked the ability to build a polity and to run a country. Since the forces of frustration and conflict inherent in the developmental process were being contained throughout the rest of Asia, Africa, and the Middle East by the intervention of European power, no one could envisage standards appropriate for measuring Chinese performance.

Now that the world has seen innumerable "phantom republics" in the ex-colonial world, the period of the early twenties in Peking seems less preposterous. The common phenomenon of military rule in postindependence societies makes the emergence of the Chinese military and the rule by warlords less disgraceful and more sociologically understandable.[1] Indeed, considering the intellectual vitality and the exciting traffic in ideas of the warlord period, military rule in China was seemingly less handicapping to development than it has been in most contemporary cases.

If we use the measures of progress currently applied in the Afro-Asian world, we see that significant advances in Chinese development occurred in the 1930's and 1940's. During this period, increasing numbers of Chinese were trained in modern skills, and elite cadres were developed in a variety of fields and were eager and able to perform the functions necessary in a modern secular society. The war against Japan, which has generally been thought to show up Chinese weaknesses, was in fact a remarkable performance for a transitional society. It is questionable today whether any developing country could, with almost no outside assistance, mobilize so large a proportion of its human and material resources for so long a period of time. The Americans who knew wartime China were largely disappointed and frustrated because they expected too much of their ally. Today we are wiser and expect less of a transitional society.

The reason for attempting to analyze contemporary China in the light of our knowledge about political development in other countries is less to achieve justice in historical evaluations and more to discover what may be unique and what may be universal in China's experiences with modernization. Although we cannot as yet say how successful the Chinese will be in time, we can certainly begin to isolate the ordinary and the peculiar in their pattern of development. It is at this point that a comparative perspective is critical.

The Chinese themselves would insist that because of the historic greatness of their civilization their experiences with modernization must be significantly different from those of other traditional societies with less impressive histories. In their minds China represents the agonies of a great civilization in turmoil and not just a traditional culture adapting to modern ways.

---

[1] For a general discussion of the military and the problems of political development see John Johnson, ed., *The Role of the Military in the Underdeveloped Areas* (Princeton, N.J.: Princeton University Press, 1961).

The key problem that has plagued a hundred years of efforts to respond to the challenge of a dynamic outside world has been the inability of the Chinese to reconcile the manifest accomplishments of their traditional civilization with the requirement that their society would have to be radically made over. According to the straightforward logic that greatness should sire greatness the Chinese felt they had the right to expect that their philosophically sophisticated traditional civilization, with its partially urbanized way of life, should give them unquestionable advantages in accommodating to the demands of the modern world. Yet these manifest advantages may also have been subtle and intractable liabilities for truly effective development. In clinging to both the legitimacy and the virtues of a past civilization the Chinese have necessarily inhibited their commitments to change and to modernization.

It is rarely appropriate to take seriously the historical pretensions of a people, but there are grounds for recognizing that the Chinese experience in modernization has differed in certain critical respects from the typical pattern of transitional societies. It is equally proper to discount the earlier Chinese protestations that they were unique in their suffering from the Western impact and the current Communist claim of having a unique "Chinese model" for all developing societies. Yet there are deeper analytical reasons for believing that the Chinese experience has been significantly different.

It will be the theme of this book that the critical difference between the Chinese and most of the other developing countries begins with the fact that the Chinese have been generally spared the crises of identity common to most other transitional systems. The basic problem in development for the Chinese has been that of achieving within their social and political life new forms of authority which can both satisfy their need to reassert a historic self-confidence and also provide the basis for reordering their society in modern terms.

We shall have to reserve for later discussion the complex implications for national development of the Chinese sense of historical greatness; at this point we need only note that in the modern era the Chinese have had little doubt about their identities as Chinese, and the more they have been exposed to the outside world the more self-consciously Chinese they have become. Indeed, their psychological sense of cultural and social identity has in many respects blurred the extent of regional, class, and linguistic divisions in Chinese society. Thus, the Chinese have not been psychologically confused over who they are, instead they have been distressed and frustrated over the fact that they have been weaker and poorer on the world scene than they have felt it right and proper for them to be. Modernization has created for them a long-persisting sense of dissatisfaction with their leaders and deep cravings for the decisive power of truly effective authority. It has given them a crisis of authority.

An authority crisis arises when the cultural and psychological bases for the legitimacy of political power are radically undermined by the developmental process. This can occur, in the first instance, when the traditional political forms of authority prove to be manifestly incapable of coping with the problems and demands of modernization. Legitimacy always needs competence; nothing so shatters the mystique of authority as helplessness. But beyond the question of the legitimacy of political institutions, the authority crisis gains depth and pervasiveness as the other structures of society lose their capacities to command easy compliance. Without the reinforcing powers of the social, religious, and cultural institutions that give form and order to the entire social structure a vacuum of authority appears.

In the last analysis, however, the acuteness of the authority crisis stems from disruptions in the prime socializing institution of the society, the family. The critical problem, ironically, is that the family does not necessarily lose any of its potency in socializing the offspring even when it is disrupted and weakened as a social and economic unit. The young will still be taught abiding sentiments and concepts about authority no matter what the fate of the family as an adult institution. Indeed, paradoxically, the very weakening of the family as a social institution tends frequently to increase the sense of dependency of the young. In short, in spite of all the disruptions of a society under the pressure of modernization the most intimate processes of learning can continue to operate, producing people who may still expect much from authority.

The authority crisis thus involves far more than just the problem of establishing new sentiments and beliefs in legitimacy. Attitudes and sentiments about authority are shaped by both the earliest socialization experiences and the later cognitive political socialization process, and widespread frustration can occur when there is a serious breakdown in the continuity and reinforcing elements of these two socialization processes. The earlier process may produce people who cannot easily adjust to a political system with weakened forms of authority, because they have internalized various forms of dependency on an ordered social system. The failure of public authority can then release anxieties and produce frustration and aggression. Manifestations of such aggressive behavior may in turn produce not only increased anxieties but the release of sentiments that can only complicate the re-establishment of new forms of authority.

An authority crisis thus has several dimensions. At the most manifest level it calls for the creation of the myth of legitimacy for new governmental institutions. It becomes serious, however, only when this collective political process is complicated by an earlier socialization process in which sentiments about authority constitute a peculiarly important element of the individual's basic personality. Specifically, this is likely to occur when the ego-ideals that helped to shape the superego involve an inordinate awe of parental authority, as happens when a culture places unqualified stress upon filial piety. Thereafter the individual is likely to have a permanent ambivalence: On the one hand he feels a deep need for such an idealized authority, while on the other he can never find in reality an authority that can satisfy his ideals. The individual is left expecting more of authority than reality permits; he may also have problems about governing his own behavior, for in the process of molding his personality many of the mechanisms for controlling his emotions are inevitably tied to his ideals of authority and order.

In China the process of modernization was seen from the very beginning as a Western challenge to Chinese authority. At first the threat was to the authority of the Manchu dynasty, but quickly it became apparent that the requirement of performing in a world dominated by foreign concepts and practices would bring into question the authority of the Confucian traditions and of the whole Chinese imperial system.

Inevitably the system collapsed, and after 1911 the Chinese were thrown into a state of prolonged disarray as they desperately sought to find for themselves forms of authority that could meet the demands of modernization without violating too greatly their cultural concepts of the proprieties of government. From 1911 to 1916 the Chinese wavered between a return to some form of monarchy and an irrevocable commitment to republicanism. With the death of Yuan Shih-k'ai the option of monarchy disappeared, but the profound weaknesses of the republican governments that followed meant that authority increasingly gravitated to the provinces and to regional leaders.

The rebuilding of Chinese society now came to founder on the issue of provincial versus central authority. The subtle but profound processes of social and economic change tended to aggravate issues about the relative jurisdiction of different authorities. The introduction of the telegraph and the railroad, for example, raised this question directly, since central and provisional authorities were soon competing for the control and management of the revenues raised in different localities. The requirements of modern financing for such national systems conflicted with the age-old accommodation that imperial authorities had had with local authorities, and provincial governors naturally expected to have the first say about the disposition of any revenues collected in their territories.

Lacking authority, the Chinese system in the 1920's failed to mobilize the necessary resources for modernization and national development. Any essential effort by a provisional authority to press ahead with social development became a challenge to the concept of a national authority; and any attempt by a presumed national authority to encourage modernization tended to disrupt the legitimacy of the more localized authorities, who were in fact closer to the great masses of the people. During the years from 1916 to 1927 when the warlords dominated the political scene the crisis of authority became increasingly acute; more and more Chinese were frustrated by the lack of a coherent and decisive system of authority that could unambiguously resolve all the jurisdictional issues between central and local authorities, between public and private authorities, and between the authority of the family and clan and the authority of the school and government.

As long as the Chinese were plagued with this crisis of authority it was impossible for their governments to advance national political development, because they could not meet the essential requirements of penetrating more thoroughly into the society and mobilizing human and material resources more extensively than had been possible in the traditional system. Out of the frustrations the stage was set for widespread receptivity to one-party rule, first by the Kuomintang and then by the Communists. Yet the problem of authority was not to be solved quite so easily. Imposed national authority could only be a façade as long as the Chinese had deeper problems about the moral basis of legitimacy and authority. The attempts by Nationalist and Communist leaders to press the pace of national development tended in the decades of the 1930's and 1940's to provoke moral issues and hence raise questions about the intentions and moral proprieties of those with power. By its very nature a crisis of authority means that power is limited by the suspicion that it lacks a proper moral basis, and hence lacks legitimacy. The more the Nationalists tried to achieve substantive advances the more they seemed to raise suspicions about their ultimate intentions.

Throughout this whole period the central articulated theme of Chinese politics was revolution and nationalism. The emotional content of the Chinese sense of revolution was singular in that it dwelt upon the need for a strong and more complete authority. Instead of picturing revolution as an assault by the weak upon the strong so as to do away with a dominating and repressive authority, the Chinese have tended to conceive of revolution as the collective assertion by a people of their need for more, not less, authority.

What is distinctive about the Chinese sense of nationalism is that it has come in great waves, with massive outbursts of great emotions, which quickly subside as the people sink back into their normal state of accepting their Chineseness as the most obvious thing in the world. The ease with which national activities are quickly drained of any significant emotion suggests not a problem of national identity but rather one of handling affect in relations beyond the confines of the family and clan. For the Chinese there has been an element of artificiality in expressing strong emotions about such distant and abstract relationships as the bonds of the national community.

By relying so much upon the family to instill civic attitudes about authority, the Chinese political culture has had to pay a high price, for the individual has always been taught not to make emotional commitments outside of the institution of the family. Thus the great problem that the Chinese have had in modern times with the control of affect in nonkin relationships has been linked directly to the question of authority.

Today in the Great Proletarian Cultural Revolution and in the movements of the Red Guards we see the same themes bedeviling the Chinese. Revolution still means that those in authority have failed to live up to expected standards, and the demand of the revolutionaries is for a more complete disciplining of life. Similarly, we still see the problem of vacillation between overcharged emotionalism and routinized performance as the Chinese continue to work at developing new patterns for the commitment of their emotions in non-kinship relationships.

Before we turn to the more psychological aspects of the Chinese authority crisis we need to review some of the historical and social factors that set the stage for their problems with modernization. We shall first want to isolate some characteristics of the classical Chinese political system that have persisted into modern times and that have impeded modernization. The peculiar relationship between the political realm and the society in traditional China produced a system in which government continued to be remarkably insensitive to the consequences of change in the rest of the society. Thus the authority crisis in China was further intensified by the way in which men who had little exposure to the modern world could continue to be the nation's leaders. From this analysis of the character of the Chinese political elite we shall go on to a more detailed examination of the reasons why the Chinese have not been troubled by problems of national identity. We shall then return to a discussion of the psychological basis of the Chinese political culture.

# SOCIAL STRUCTURE
# AND
# POLITICAL SOCIALIZATION

One way to understand the nature of a political system is to examine the relationship between that political system and other social systems in a society. Knowledge of the delineation and maintenance of the boundaries between the political system and the social systems, the differentiation of social and political roles, and the degree of structural specialization between the social and political systems, has helped social and political scientists to classify various societies into primitive, traditional, transitional, and modern systems.

The Chinese society has been described by social scientists as a typical example of traditional systems. It has been variously called the society of "oriental despotism," the society of "the literati," and the "gentry's" society by Karl Wittfogel, Max Weber, and Fei Hsiao-t'ung. Several special features existed in the traditional Chinese society. First, there was a vast bureaucratic structure under a monolithic and hierarchical imperial government. Second, individuals who had passed the civil service examination constituted the backbone of the bureaucracy. Familiarity with, and belief in, the Confucianist ideology was essential to pass this examination. Since in traditional China only the land-owning class had the means and leisure to prepare for the examination, which was theoretically open to all, most of the successful candidates came from that class.

Third, the power of the imperial government ordinarily did not penetrate into the local social structures. Instead, control of the local community was exercised through the "gentry," i.e., the landed scholar-officials, in various localities. The gentry served as an intermediary between the political authority of the imperial government and the common people. Theirs was a dual function. On the one hand, they helped carry out the orders of the imperial government; on the other hand, they served as the spokesmen of the people in the local community, protecting them from being overly exploited by the representatives of the central government.

The last and the most important feature of the society of traditional China is the predominance of the family as one of the most important social structures. From the cradle to the grave, an individual in traditional China was protected as well as possessed by his family and the extended kinship group—the clan. The family and the clan had a collective responsibility to see that all of their members had adequate means of support and security. The birth, education, marriage, illness, and death of an individual were all events demanding involvement and concern not only from the members of his immediate family but also from those of the extended kinship group.

Obedience to the head of the family was considered the supreme virtue in such a society. Obedience to parents was extended to the authority of the teacher, the community leader, the various government officials, and eventually, the emperor. Consequently, filial piety was considered a prerequisite to the loyalty required toward the state. Hence, failure in observing the norms of filial piety not only would invite social punishment but would also damage a person's relationship with the state; the latter was particularly important for an individual who was associated with government affairs or who had an ambition to participate in them.

With the 1911 Republican Revolution, the imperial Manchu government collapsed but the traditional social structure persisted. Generally speaking, the Nationalists made little effort to change the structure of authority within the local communities of rural China. In many instances, they co-opted and utilized the local leaders, usually of scholar-landlord background, to establish control in the countryside. Partially because of this, the Nationalists were unable to fully carry out the land reform programs envisioned by Dr. Sun Yat-sen in his theory of "People's Livelihood" until they moved to Taiwan in 1944.[1]

Unlike the Nationalists, the Chinese Communists from the very beginning were determined to bring a fundamental change to the social

---

[1]After retreating to Taiwan, the Chinese Nationalists have successfully implemented a peaceful and step-by-step land reform on the Island which climaxed with "The Land to the Tillers" program. For a detailed account of the process of land reform on Taiwan and its socioeconomic impacts, see Martin M. C. Yang, *Socio-Economic Results of Land Reform in Taiwan* (Honolulu: East-West Center Press, 1970).

structure of China. One of the primary targets of the Communist Revolution has been the elimination from the Chinese society of the "exploiting classes," by which they mean primarily the capitalists in the cities and the landlords in the countryside. During the first several years of communist occupation of the Chinese mainland, large scale mass trials of factory owners in the cities and of landlords in the villages were conducted with great ferocity. Hundreds of thousands of individuals who were accused of being the exploiters of the people lost their lives in the process.

Aside from the landlords, another primary target of the communist attack on the social institutions has been the family system of China. As a radical, antitraditional and antibourgeoisie political movement, it was only natural for the Chinese Communists to take drastic measures to minimize the influence of the role of the family in the "new society." Rebellion against parental authority, especially among youth with parents of "questionable" social and political background, is openly encouraged by political authority on mainland China.

The first step taken by the Chinese Communists to change the family system of China was the promulgation of the new marriage law of 1950. This law gave the women of China, especially those in the countryside, more rights and privileges in their marriage relationships. Although the new law led to an increased number of divorces on mainland China, it provided the Chinese women, who had been the victims of many unhappy marriages in traditional China, more freedom and independence. During the period of the Great Leap Forward, the Chinese Communists took another important step in releasing women from their homes by establishing public mess halls, nurseries for the children, and nursing homes for the elders. The practice was not very successful and gradually subsided along with the relaxation of the commune system.

With the upsurgence of the Great Cultural Revolution, a renewed attack against parental authority, concern for one's family, and respect for the figures of traditional authority was staged on mainland China. Accusation of one's parents and criticism and prosecution of teachers by teenagers in elementary and high schools were openly encouraged by the political authority. The effects of these activities on the social fabric of the Chinese society on the mainland are yet to be measured. There is evidence, however, that they have dealt a crucial blow to the hierarchy of social and even of political order in the Chinese society under the communist rule.

All the above mentioned measures taken by the Chinese Communists —the new marriage law, the commune system, and the attacks against authority figures in the Chinese society during the Cultural Revolution—

are aimed at achieving one goal: to convert the Chinese people on the mainland from a people whose loyalty usually has been directed to the family and kinship group to a people with an intense loyalty toward the State. To achieve this goal, the Chinese Communists do not rely solely on coercive measures. A more important and more subtle method has been used; that is, to inject new values and beliefs into the thinking of the Chinese people through political socialization.

When the Chinese Communists took over mainland China in 1949, they were faced with a two-fold mission of political socialization. First, they had to overhaul the educational system left by the Nationalists so that the children of the post-1949 period would learn a new set of values and norms compatible with the communist ideology. This they have done with great vigor and resolution. A second mission in connection with the socialization efforts of the Chinese Communists was to reeducate the adult population, who had lived under the Nationalist rule for decades, so that they would become, if not ardent supporters, at least passive subjects of the new regime.

To fulfill this second mission, centers of "socialist education" were established in many parts of China. Western-trained intellectuals, co-opted former Kuomintang officials and officers, college students, and even some foreigners were sent to these centers for reeducation. Stories told by individuals who had been in these reeducation centers focused wide attention among observers in the Western world on the so-called "brain-washing" techniques of the Chinese Communists.

Essentially, what constituted the techniques of "brain-washing" included coercion, exhortation, therapy, and realization. By depriving an individual involved in the process of his basic physical needs and comfort, by isolating him from the outside world, by exposing him to a specially arranged environment, and by creating intense mental stress, the Chinese Communists were able to produce confession, self-criticism, and open repentance. Although the immediate effects of the thought reform seemed to be quite impressive, the process has been proved to have only short-term effects on an individual. Once the milieu of the thought reform was removed, gradual rehabilitation of most of its victims has been achieved.

In regard to the socialization efforts of the Chinese communists, one of the most frequently asked questions has been this: After twenty years of rule on the Chinese mainland, have the Chinese Communists succeeded in creating a new political culture in the Chinese society? To answer this question, one must be able to obtain first hand data by interviewing a selected sample of people on the Chinese mainland, which of course is presently impossible.

Judging by the renewed attack against traditional values and institutions during the Cultural Revolution, we have reason to believe that there must be some residual influence of traditional values and norms on the behavior of the people on the Chinese mainland, at least enough to have worried Mao and his followers. Of special interest in this connection was the attack staged by the Cultural Revolution groups against Liu Shao-chi, the purged chairman of the People's Republic of China, for relying too much on the concept and methods of Confucianism in his writings. This ironic fact fully demonstrates the difficulty involved in the replacement of traditional social-political ideology with a completely new set of political beliefs and norms in a short period, no matter how much effort has been put into it by the new political regime.

# IV

# Social Structure and
# the Political System

## 8. The Chinese Family and Communist Revolution

*C. K. Yang*

### The Chinese Family in Traditional Society

Communist consideration of the remaking of the family as one of the basic measures in the transformation of traditional Chinese society shows that the Communist leadership has a full realization of the vital role of the family and the broader kinship system in the traditional social structure. Economically, the family has been the most important unit of organization in production, for not only has agriculture been almost exclusively a family undertaking but also in industry and commerce the family has been the most numerous organizational unit in investment and operation. There is hardly one major aspect of traditional social life that is not touched by the ties and influence of the family. It is somewhat difficult for an upper- or middle-class urban Chinese in his twenties today to visualize how dominant a part the family once played in public and private life during the earlier part of his father's generation.

In the early years of the twentieth century many of society's economic, educational, religious, recreational, and even political functions were intimately tied to the family institution. From cradle to grave the individual was under the uninterrupted influence of the family regarding his physical and moral upbringing, the formation of his sentiments and attitudes, his educational training, his public career, his social associations, his emotional and material security. In the Chinese community, particularly in the rural areas, there have been only a few social organizations or associations outside the family to serve the individual's social

Reprinted from C. K. Yang, *The Chinese Family in the Communist Revolution* (Cambridge, Mass.: M.I.T. Press 1959), pp. 5–7, 11–20, by permission of The M.I.T. Press, Cambridge, Massachusetts, and the author.

needs. Consequently, throughout his life the individual constantly struggled with problems concerned with the relations of parents and children, husband and wife, elder and younger brothers, the "in-laws," uncles, cousins, nephews, grandparents and grandchildren, and other members of the complex kinship circle.

Beyond the kinship circle the individual might have to deal with government officials, with his teacher or craft master, his colleagues, his employer or employees, and his neighbors and friends. But many of these social relations came through direct or indirect kinship contacts, and they were often patterned after the family system in structure and in values. Hence government officials were often referred to as "parent-officials" (*fu mu kuan*) and the people as "children people" (*tzu min*). The relationship between master and apprentice, or between teacher and student, operated on a simulated father-and-son basis. A solemn ceremony of a sacred character was used to introduce a new student to his teacher and an apprentice to his master, in order to establish the pseudo-kinship bond. And the devotion and reverence expected of a student or apprentice by the teacher or master was of the same type expected from a son by his father. Stores, handicraft shops, and farms employed mainly relatives, and the kinship bond was pervasive in the system of basic economic relations. Friends and neighbors addressed each other in fraternal or other kinship terms. Conversations between friends were punctuated with appellations like "elder brother" and "younger brother" and "uncle," even though the parties were not related as such.

Various forms of fraternal and sororal organizations stood out prominently among the few organized associations which existed beyond the kinship ties. The membership of most traditional social associations, from fraternities, sororities, and literary societies of the gentry to the business and craft guilds of the urban centers, was structured according to age and generation factors. The secret societies regarded their founders as "ancestors" and treated them with ancestor-worship rites. Their organization was patterned closely after the kinship structure, and authority was exercised through a hierarchy of generational status and age levels. The initiation of a new member was frequently done by drinking a few drops of each other's blood so as to establish the "blood tie" and to impart a measure of realism to the simulated kinship bond. Secret societies have played an important part in the life of certain segments of the traditional society, particularly among traveling entertainers, patent-medicine venders, and urban transportation workers, who had to operate outside the home territory where the kinship system was based, and among the poor peasants whose kinship ties were insufficient to meet their social and economic needs.

Under a social situation so thoroughly permeated with actual or simulated kinship ties it is to be expected that many of the kinship values should have general validity for society as a whole, and that the family should perform the function of being the training ground for general citizenship for society and for the state. An example is the so-called Five Cardinal Relations (*wu lun*, meaning the five basic norms of social order), which constituted the foundations of traditional social values. Mencius states that in "the relations of humanity—between father and son there should be solidarity and affection; between sovereign and minister, righteousness; between husband and wife, attention to their separate functions; between old and young, a proper order; and between friends, fidelity."[1] It is to be noted that heading the Five Cardinal Relations of humanity is the relation between father and son, and that of the five relations three belong to the kinship realm. The two non-kinship relations, those between ruler and officials and between friends, also rely partly for their actual operation on the moral strength of loyalty and status concepts required of the three kinship relations. In this sense, the mores of non-kinship relations may be regarded as an extension of the mores of kinship relations.

These Five Cardinal Relations, centering upon kinship ties, formed the core of social and moral training for the individual almost from the beginning of his consciousness of social existence until he became so conditioned to it that his standard of satisfaction and deprivation was based upon it, and the complex and extensive web of kinship ties created a feeling of a closed universe from which there seemed to be no escape, except perhaps death. The large number of suicides resulting from the strain of family relations among women is a reflection of this situation. Here, for the unfortunate few, social pressure from the family institution appeared weightier than life itself, and the pain of death was considered lighter than the torture of living in a society which provided little outlet and security for a deviant from the traditional ideal of the family institution.

Such was the place of the traditional Chinese family and the broader kinship system in the general picture of social life about half a century ago. At present this situation still exists widely in rural communities and to a lesser extent among certain sections of the urban population. This is particularly so in mountainous sections of the country where confinement of the population in valleys discourages migration and accentuates the earthbound character and the kinship orientation of the peasant communities. . . .

---

[1] *The Works of Mencius*, tr. James Legge (Shanghai, 1949), Book III, Part 1, ch. 4.

## The "Family Revolution"

In the past the traditional family could function rather smoothly in spite of the many innate dissatisfactions of the women or the young with its authoritarian character, chiefly because of the dominance of the kinship factor in the old social pattern. In such a pattern the family and the larger kinship group formed a relatively warm atmosphere in which the individual found not merely economic security but also the satisfaction of most of his social needs. Beyond this warm atmosphere lay what the traditional individual considered the cold and harsh world wherein his treatment and fate became unpredictable. Consequently, the women and the young accepted their traditional status as dictated by the way social life was traditionally organized.

But this pattern of social organization became increasingly incompatible with the new needs that arose with China's gradual integration into the modern industrial and nationalistic world. The past three-quarters of a century of floundering efforts at transferring the family and kinship relations to modern economic and political undertakings produced endless contradictions between the particularistic and the universalistic patterns of social life.[2] From such contradictions developed the accelerating trend of change in the traditional family and its old role in the organization of social life, a change that proceeded by popular demand from the educated young for a "family revolution" from the second decade of the present century. There was little success in overcoming the incongruity between the kinship tie as an organizational requirement in the traditional order and the need for objective qualifications for individuals as components of modern economic and political structures. Moreover, the particularistic nature of the kinship-oriented pattern of social organization divided the population into numerous small, self-confined, and loosely interrelated kinship units, while the mass organization of modern industrial society and the national state demanded intimate integration between the social and economic organs based on universal standards for the individuals.

This incompatibility seems to have been in the awareness of China's modern leading reformers whose ideological movements aimed at guiding China into a modern industrial state. K'ang Yu-wei, who led China's first organized modern reform in 1898, pointed out that the "abolition" of the traditional family was a condition for proper performance of modern public duties.[3] But his reform movement proved abortive. Save

---

[2]See Talcott Parsons, *The Social System* (Illinois: Glencoe, 1951), pp. 85–87.
[3]K'ang Yu-wei, *Ta t'ung shu* (The Great Commonwealth), (Shanghai, 1923), Part I.

for his unwitting pioneering influence in weakening the Confucian orthodoxy by inspiring a change of attitude, he and his reform movement had little direct effect on the traditional kinship system. Sun Yat-sen, the leading revolutionist to rise on the heels of K'ang's failure, sensed the same incompatibility when he urged the expansion of "familism and clannism" into nationalism. Although he advanced no specific steps for such transformation, the Republican revolution of 1911 which he fathered did have serious effects on the subsequent change of the traditional family institution.

Some students underestimate this revolution as merely a change of political formality from monarchy to a nominal republic, devoid of any serious social significance. Actually, it started the trend toward destroying the theoretical applicability of Confucian kinship ethics to the operation of the state, thus undermining the traditional dominance of the family in social and political life. Furthermore, the collapse of the monarchy brought the abolition of the old imperial laws which compelled conformity to the traditional family institution based on Confucian orthodoxy. Subsequent laws on kinship relations promulgated by various governments under the Republic increasingly veered away from the traditional pattern. This had at least the negative significance of undermining the strength of the traditional family institution by reducing that part of its compulsory character which was founded upon formal political control. Also gone with the monarchy was the encouragement given by the government to such acts of devotion to the ideals of the traditional family as erecting memorial arches for unusually chaste widows or temples for outstanding filial sons. The effective symbolistic value of such old objects erected before the Republic steadily wore thin with the passing years. Finally, the revolution of 1911 attracted into its ranks many women whose demand for a new feminine role in a different family institution was no less strong than their demand for a new political order. These women, though few in number, planted the seed for the many subsequent popular movements that were to seriously affect the continued operation of the traditional family institution.

These influences continued to brew in the political chaos of the young Republic while the problem of social and cultural reform claimed increasing public attention. A great ideological upheaval, the New Culture Movement or Renaissance, which started in 1917, broke out in full force in the May 4th Movement of 1919. In this movement of multiple significance the term "family revolution" was introduced into the consciousness of the public. It was used by leaders and protagonists of the movement as a slogan, and by the conservative old generation as a reprimand to rebellious youngsters who struggled to deviate from the traditional family institution. It became current parlance in the rising cry of the times for a change in the way of life as the political revolution gradually unfolded into its social and cultural phases.

There was no organized platform for this popular movement called the "family revolution," but its main objectives were clearly suggested in its slogans, catch-words, and the increasing volume of its literature. It demanded a new role for women in the family as well as in society in general terms of sex equality; it advocated freedom of social association between opposite sexes; it demanded marriage by free choice and love, not by parental arrangement; it called for greater freedom for the young; it vaguely urged a new family institution similar to the Western pattern.

Ill-defined and poorly coordinated as some of these objectives were, they did form a sufficiently coherent group of new ideas that served to focus the public's attention upon the problem of remaking the traditional family and of gathering sympathetic forces for group action. The roots of Western inspiration were unmistakable in this movement. From the May 4th Movement to the late 1920's, Ibsen's plays on women's status and the family gained wide circulation in Chinese, became successful stage productions in large cities, and brought forth spirited discussions. But the main preoccupation of the movement then was still with the traditional family institution. Books, pamphlets, and articles on the family problem appeared in growing numbers, firing broadsides at the ancient institution as being destructive of human rights, decadent in moral character, and as discouraging the spirit of independence and progress. The institution that had withstood some two millennia of dynastic changes and foreign invasions and all their political and economic devastations now came to be viewed as symbolizing all of China's sins and weaknesses. The new demands and the proffered solutions, however untried and incoherent in some respects, were pictured as the road to happiness and strength. Nationalistic sentiments which began to surge forth with increasing force in the decade following World War I in China as well as elsewhere helped to impress these arguments on the minds of the public.

Aside from the rising nationalistic sentiments, many other forces stimulated by the May 4th Movement added strength to the family revolution. One was a concentrated attack on the absolutism of the Confucian orthodoxy and the social institutions modeled after it. Keynotes of the attack were: "skepticism toward all ancient teachings," "down with *Confucius and Company*" (the latter term meaning the traditional schoolroom and its Confucian classical teachings) and the "man-devouring doctrine of ritualism." This branch of the New Culture Movement called for a complete re-evaluation of traditional learning and institutions and for a new cultural orientation in the light of modern science and democracy.

As the "new current of thought" won widening acceptance in a decade of raging polemics following World War I, Confucian orthodoxy together with its kinship values and the family institution molded after it were no longer a matter of "sacred" character enjoying deep reverence and unquestioned conformity from the people and supported by compulsory political power. They became subjects for secular discussions and popular attacks from the educated young—so much so, in fact, that it was fashionable for modern Chinese intellectuals to criticize Confucianism. The result was a serious loss of prestige and strength by the Confucian orthodoxy. As the family institution was deeply enmeshed in the matrix of Confucian ideology and its institutions, it could not help but be weakened by this development.

The call for skepticism toward the old cultural heritage and a new orientation for the future found the most attentive listeners among modern educated young men and women, who felt the most strain from the rigid sex and age stratifications in the traditional family and society. The rise of the youth movement and the women's movement, as phases of the May 4th Movement, lent important support to the family revolution and in fact became inseparable parts of it. In a sense, the family revolution developed as a rebellion of the educated young of both sexes against the traditional social order.

Such a rebellion, breaking out within the family circle, was naturally viewed with alarm and even terror by the older generation, who found the process increasingly difficult to stop. Under the driving and infectious demand for freedom and equality, and in the growing destruction of unquestioned conformity to traditional institutions in general, many traditional families, mainly among the urban upper and upper-middle classes, were forced to undergo certain fundamental changes by the mid-1920's; and the family problem was pushed into the fore of the nation's attention along with other vital political, social, and economic issues of the day.

By this time another great upheaval was rapidly sweeping across China, bringing the stress of a political storm to bear increasingly upon the old social institutions. This was the so-called Second Revolution, which began with the early years of the second decade of the present century and culminated in Chiang Kai-shek's Northern Expedition of 1926 and in the establishment of the Nationalist government in Nanking a year later. The decade from 1927 to the full-scale Japanese invasion of China in 1937 saw the development of the Chinese Communist Party as a military and political power in the "red areas" that studded many parts of the country.

In this turbulent decade social and political forces served to accelerate the pace of the family revolution—although the term was by this time losing its impact of novelty and was less frequently heard. A vital feature of the period was the youthfulness and the Western educational background of the men who came into power, whether in the Nationalist or in the Communist camp. When Chiang Kai-shek led his expeditionary forces northward from Canton in 1926, he was but a young man of forty, and Mao Tse-tung, present head of the Chinese Communist Party, was only thirty-three. Young and modern educated men came to fill an increasing proportion of government offices at all levels.

Although the Republican revolution of 1911 had abolished the imperial laws which supported the traditional family institutions, old officials who manned the government in the early Republican years still exercised their political power largely in the Confucian mode in which they had been raised and trained, and the Republican laws, when enforced at all, were more frequently than not given a Confucian interpretation. But by the late 1920's the gap was fast widening between the Confucian mentality and the attitudes of the young politicial leadership, and consequently not only the *de jure* but also the *de facto* political control of the traditional family institution dwindled rapidly, particularly in the cities. So overwhelming was the ideological swing away from the Confucian orthodoxy and the social institutions molded by it that repeated restorationist efforts in the 1930's, such as local government orders to reinstate Confucian classics into the school curriculum and the Confucian tenet of the New Life Movement of the Nationalist regime, were unable to turn the tide. Although the scene of ideological struggle was enacted mainly in the cities, the new influence spread to an ever-increasing proportion of the population, especially among those who could afford a modern education.

Against this ideological background, the family revolution persisted on its course set by the previous period. Literature on the subject continued to pour forth from the growing number of mechanical presses. Increasing social contacts between the young of opposite sexes, growing numbers of marriages resulting from romantic love, and "small families" on the Western model were among the visible results wrought by this process of change. These were living examples of a cause that had come to be embraced by an entire generation of the modern educated young. The youth movement and the women's movement continued to expand and to exert influence upon the development of the family situation. Anti-Communist measures frequently caused setbacks to these movements by hitting many of their organizations as Communist fronts, but this did not affect the spreading struggle among the young against the traditional family and their persistent clamor for its reform.

The Law of Kinship Relations promulgated by the Nationalist government in 1930 incorporated many of the ideological objectives of the family revolution, although many of the basic principles of the traditional family institution were retained.[4] Aside from the question of logical coherence and the lack of effective general enforcement, this compromise law stood as a crystallization of the persistent trend of change in the traditional family, a change which had been brewing for a quarter of a century.

It was true that this trend mainly affected the modern intelligentsia, the majority of whom stemmed from the upper and upper-middle classes in the cities. The importance of this group could not be measured entirely by its small numerical size because of its strategic function in giving direction to the social change and its dominant position in such mechanisms of social control as the government. But the influence of the family revolution in this period was definitely spreading, though slowly, to the urban middle class and a small portion of the city workers. The younger generation of the well-to-do landowners in the countryside also became increasingly affected by the new ideological trends as they went to the cities for a modern education, but, as they soon became identified with the urban intelligentsia and no longer remained members of rural communities, the countryside was not much affected by modern ideological movements.

It is obvious that the gradual change of the traditional family was not the result of ideological agitation alone without the operation of other supporting social and economic factors. The confinement of the family revolution and its related ideological movements mainly to the cities was due precisely to the presence of collaborating social and economic forces in the urban areas and the weakness or absence of such forces in the rural communities.

There was, for example, the concentration of modern educational facilities and the modern press in the cities, which operated as disseminating agents for new ideas about the family and other social institutions which were being challenged by the "new currents of thought." The rapid development of women's education and coeducation since the New Culture Movement was a particularly important influence. Similarly significant was the growth of urban occupational opportunities for women, which provided the economic ground for women's claims for a higher status in the family and in society. The city, with its greater social and economic mobility, offered more fertile ground than the rural community for the dissemination of modern democratic ideas incompatible with the authoritarian characteristics of the traditional family. The growing specialization of social and economic functions, including the commercialization of recreation, undermined the traditional self-sufficiency of

---

[4]*The Civil Code of the Republic of China*, tr. Hsia Tsin-lin (Shanghai, 1931), pp. 249–291.

the family by reducing many of its functions and thus lessening the individual's dependence upon it. Above all, the accelerating development of modern industry and the emergence of an urban economy geared to its needs after World War I worked to destroy the particularism of the old kinship-oriented social pattern, and compelled some kind of change in the mode of family life.

Growing population mobility, with frequent prolonged physical separation of some members from the family, affected the continued operation of the traditional family organization, which required constant, close contact among the members. Increased population mobility stemmed from a number of social situations, notably the steady deterioration of the handicraft and agricultural economy, the expansion of urbanization, and the high frequency of famines and wars. In the eight years of war against the Japanese invasion (1937-1945), there was no new ideological wave on the reform of the family, but the pouring of millions of modern-minded coastal refugees into the hitherto isolated Southwest undoubtedly aided the disintegration of many traditional families and the formation of new ones on the model promoted by the family revolution. When the curtain of enemy occupation was lifted by the Japanese surrender of 1945, the cities revealed a scene of family life marked by physical separation of members and deviation from the traditional standards, departing further from the Confucian pattern than in any preceding period.

## The Communist Revolution and the Chinese Family

In 1949, four years after the Japanese surrender, when the Chinese Communists took over the reins of national political power, China entered upon a period in which drastic political revolution was but one phase of a comprehensive movement aimed at recasting the entire traditional social order by coordinated plans and compulsory measures. The reform of the Chinese family, along with the remaking of other major social institutions, became a part of an over-all drastic social change.

This crisis for the family institution contained no new substance. As already shown, this institution had been changing under constant stress and strain for the preceding three decades; and the Communist crisis, so far as the family was concerned, represented but a more drastic development of the same process, which was now being urged on under a different leadership and in a different manner.

Neither was the effort at altering the family institution anything new with the Communists. Long before the establishment of the Communist regime in 1949, members of the Communist movement had been playing a vital part, along with other reformers and intellectuals, in developing the family revolution and its supporting ideological movements. Ch'en Tu-hsiu, one of the founders of the Chinese Communist Party, ranked with Hu Shih in the New Culture Movement and in the relentless assault against the ideological and institutional citadel of Confucian orthodoxy. Particularly vital was Ch'en's place in initiating and developing the youth movement and the women's movement. Communists in general had been strategic in the agitating and organizing efforts of these movements. The Chinese Communist Party was co-author with the Kuomintang of the Second Revolution, which had serious effects on the development of the family revolution. (Present Communist interpretation of modern Chinese history claims Communist Party leadership in the May 4th Movement and the Second Revolution.) The actual development of the family situation in the "red areas" that came into existence after 1928 has remained largely unrecorded, but scattered information has indicated uncompromising Communist endeavor in changing both the traditional family institution and the kinship-oriented pattern of social organization in those areas.

Many sources of popular information in China for the past thirty years have pictured the Communists as iconoclasts toward the family as a social institution. Ch'en Tu-hsiu was charged by his political enemies with advocating the practice of "communal property and communal wives;" and the charge of practicing "communal wives" was directed against the "red areas" in the early 1930's.[5] There was a disquieting rumor of "forced assignment of wives" by the Communists in 1948 and 1949, a rumor so persistent and widespread that it caused a marriage boom in localities in the paths of the advancing Communist columns in their southward conquest because parents were hurriedly marrying off their daughters in an effort to save them from becoming "assigned wives."

It is probably true that relatively light restrictions were placed upon marriage and divorce in the "red areas" before 1949. This can be seen in such available documents of the period as the Marriage Regulations of the Chinese Soviet Republic and the Temporary Marriage Regulations, both promulgated in 1931 by the Chinese Soviet Republic, and the Marriage Regulations of the Border Area of Shansi, Chahar, and Hopei provinces. But there seems to be no substantiation to the charge of either the practice of "communal wives" or the discarding of the family as a social institution.

---

[5]See, for example, "Absolute Proof of the Communists' Practice in Communal Wives," in *Kuang-ming chih-lu* (The Road of Light) vol. I, no. 7–8 (Nanking, June 1931), 1–7.

Facts as observed in Communist China after 1949 indicate no evidence for any of these allegations. The promulgation of the new Marriage Law on May 1, 1950, and the nationwide efforts at its enforcement by the Communist government through the network of organizations under its command seem clear indications of a Communist policy toward the family which insisted upon drastic reform of the traditional family but fully retained the family as a basic social institution. Even under the people's commune, the family remains the basic social unit, though vastly reduced in its functions. An unmistakable sign of Communist policy was seen in the complex responsibilities involved in divorce by the new Marriage Law, responsibilities that weigh particularly heavy on the husband. Hence the drastic reform of the traditional family demanded by the Communists should not be taken as an iconoclastic view of the family as a social institution.

The reason for the Communist policy of reshaping the traditional family seems plain. The Communist regime is bent on building an industrial society on the socialistic pattern, and it is fully aware of the incompatibility between such a society and the kinship-oriented structure. Also important for the political purpose of the regime is the incompatibility between the individual's traditional loyalty to the family and the new requirements of his loyalty to the state and to the Communist Party.

Up to the Communist accession to power, the family revolution had proceeded largely as a part of a process of spontaneous social change in modern China. The inauguration of the Communist regime, particularly after the promulgation of the new Marriage Law, brought a different development. Change of the traditional family is no longer left to a spontaneous process but is subjected to the compulsory power of law and the pressure of a powerful, well-organized mass movement; and it is coordinated with other aspects of the Communist social, economic, and political revolution.

# 9. Traditional Social Structure and Communist Goals

*John Wilson Lewis*

The Communist task of restructuring social obligations was a particularly delicate one in China because of the reverent attitude of Chinese toward their kin and other relationships within the traditional society.[1] From the individual's point of view, his bonds of kinship, friendship, common origin, and common experience (particularly *t'ung-hsüeh* or school-mates) established a more or less permanent pattern of obligations. Obliged to immediate family members, kinsmen, and schoolmates, among others, the individual Chinese found himself in a relatively fixed place in the social order, for which the Confucian system provided moral jus-tification, personal assurance of correctness, and a sense of continuity. Although the Chinese pattern of social relationships was not strikingly

---

[1] A selected list of works consulted in the preparation of this section includes Fei Hsiao-t'ung, *China's Gentry: Essays in Rural-Urban Relations* (Rev. and ed.; Chicago: University of Chicago Press, 1953); Francis L. K. Hsü, *Under the An-cestor's Shadow: Chinese Culture and Personality* (New York: Columbia University Press, 1948); W. La Barre, "Some Observations on Character Structure in the Orient: II, The Chinese, Parts One and Two," *Psychiatry*, IX (1946), 215–237, 375–396; Olga Lang, *Chinese Family and Society* (New Haven: Yale University Press, 1946); Lin Tsung-yi, "A Study of the Incidence of Mental Disorder in Chi-nese and other Cultures," *Psychiatry*, XVI (1953), 313–336; David S. Nivison, "Communist Ethics and Chinese Tradition," *Journal of Asian Studies*, XVI, no. 1 (November, 1956), 51–74; Arthur H. Smith, *China in Convulsion* (New York: F. H. Revell Co., 1901); Arthur H. Smith, *Chinese Characteristics* (Enlarged and rev. ed.; New York: F. H. Revell Co., 1894); Arthur H. Smith, *Village Life in China* (New York: F. H. Revell Co., 1899); C. K. Yang, *The Chinese Family in the Communist Revolution* (Cambridge, Mass.: Technology Press, 1959); and C. K. Yang, *A Chinese Village in Early Communist Transition* (Cambridge, Mass.: Technology Press, 1959).

Reprinted from John Wilson Lewis, *Leadership in Communist China* (Ithaca, N. Y.: Cornell University Press, 1963), pp. 247–64, by permission of the pub-lisher and author.

different from that in other patrilineal, agricultural societies, long continuous development and Confucian values made most Chinese believe that
their society organized on patrilineal lines was not only unique but was
morally the best. Reinforced by habitual obligations and Confucian
values, the Chinese belief in the moral superiority of their society manifested itself in their attitude of reverence toward particularistic social relationships.

Based on the structure of social ties, an elaborate code of behavior
was developed and perpetuated in China. Deference to elders, material
support of the aged, reverence for ancestors, dispensing of influence
among friends (*jen-ch'ing*), and loyalty to social groups were emphasized
for succeeding generations of Chinese youth and were rigidly defined and
enforced. Families, lineage, villages, and voluntary associations were the
permanent elements of the institutional network which gave specific content, and controlled the individual's response, to his social obligations.
The emphasis was on social relations which were elaborately structured
and discrete; and the Chinese social obligations applicable to those relations were well known and enduring.

As was natural in a society which emphasized well-defined social relationships, the relationships of a Chinese with kinsmen, friends, classmates,
colleagues, acquaintances, and the local elites—to name only some of the
possibilities—were formalized and identified by a recognized system of
nomenclature. The Chinese viewed this formal system in terms of the intimacy of social ties on a "scale" measuring the "social distance" from the
individual. At the intimate or *li-mao* (good manners) end of the scale,[2]
relationships were clear, unequivocal, direct, and based on the exercise of
personal influence. At the less intimate or *k'o-ch'i* (politeness) end of the
scale (new acquaintances, distant relatives, officials), relationships were
apt to be relatively more equivocal and indirect. Throughout the scale of
relationships, there were variations and exceptions to the general pattern
of obligations actually forthcoming, and naturally all relationships were
expected to manifest a balance of good manners and politeness. When
the relative intimacy of the scale decreased to such an extent that the
distinguishing act of personal recognition disappeared, the clear-cut obligations were reduced to a jumbled list of platitudes without moral sanction and social acceptance. Non-Chinese have described this lack of
obligation to strangers in China as "the cheapness of human life in
China" and "the lack of a Chinese social consciousness." More accu-
rately, the obligations of acquaintance were so demanding that Chinese

---

[2]This scale of intimacy contained the values of *hsiao* (filial piety), *i* (righteousness), *jen* (benevolence), *chung* (loyalty), and *ai* (love) which complemented
the prescribed Confucian relationships.

were reluctant to commence casual relationships with strangers or to establish even *ad hoc* contacts outside the close pattern.

Political relationships thus generally fell outside the range of social relationships — even *k'o-ch'i* relationships — for which there existed social obligations in practice. The "social distance" between leaders and led simply exceeded the distance in which social obligations were operative. The mutual exclusiveness of socially unrelated Chinese in general critically influenced contacts in the traditional polity. Within the bureaucracy, minimal political obligations were either frustrated by "social distance" or corrupted by bringing together in a single part of the apparatus, by accident or design, members obliged by the particularistic bonds of kinsmen, friends, fellow schoolmates, or fellow townsmen. On the one hand, the limited range of obligations prevented the bureaucracy from penetrating the intimate social groups; on the other hand, social obligations distorted the operation of "related" members within the bureaucracy. Moreover, despite a generalized acceptance of the imperial hierarchy and the classical political platitudes, which theoretically stipulated mutual obligations between the elite and general population, the hierarchy and the platitudes were insufficient to bridge the lack of obligations between society and polity. In general, the Chinese peasants felt that their own organizations should fulfill all but the most formal "national" functions in a well-ordered society.

The social structure presented the bureaucracy with opportunities as well as limits and distorting pressures. For example, Chinese officials attempted to manipulate the social structure through the family and lineage. When manipulation was not feasible, however, the officials outside the lineage enforced edicts or collected taxes with the aid of police and armies. An example of partially effective adaptation of the social structure for police control was the *pao chia* system.[3] This system of collective responsibility made each head of a household (*hu*) responsible for the acts of the household members. In one of the most common variations of this system, similar responsibility was given to the head of ten households (*p'ai*), one hundred households (ten *p'ai* or one *chia*), and one thousand households (ten *chia* or one *pao*). Political obligations such as derive from concepts of "citizenship" or "rule of law" were for practical purposes nonexistent. Traditional political relationships, however much masked by other language, were more or less identical with applications of force when conducted on an intergroup basis and were relatively limited in scope. Those political relationships which relied on

---

[3]See the excellent study by Kung-chuan Hsiao, *Rural China: Imperial Control in the Nineteenth Century* (Seattle: University of Washington Press, 1960), esp. chaps. ii-iii.

measures of force were strongly differentiated from, and in direct conflict with, social relationships.

The smaller Chinese political parties — including in some respects Kuomintang factions — that existed from 1911 to 1949 were political associations governed by the *li-mao* rules of intimate personal obligations and factional exclusiveness. Within these parties, the membership usually clustered around a former professor, a core of alumni of a particular academy or university, or a respected journalist. The inner ties of association were derived more from particularistic relationships than from common ideological programs or formal organizations. This personal quality, which can be traced to the traditional social relationships, partly explains the failure of the other political parties to offer the Chinese people an effective alternative to Communist domination during the civil war period.

The Marxist-Leninists were the first to provide China with a consistent ideology of national political power based on a thoroughgoing, reciprocal relationship between leaders and led. This relationship, which is particularly important at the production team level in the countryside, has created a special tone and character for the Chinese Communist Party, differentiating its working methods from those of the other Chinese political parties. The key to the Communist leadership and organization in China is the party's dedication of its primary effort to creating a new structure within the leadership (including the working cadres) and between the cadres and masses. Put differently, Chinese Communist cadres formulated operational principles which would permit them to penetrate the intimate or face-to-face social groups within the general society but which would enable them to resist succumbing to the obligational pulls from within those groups. Equally important, the party cadres endeavored to restructure the social obligations by selectively pressing certain useful habits drawn from the *li-mao* pattern. The party's mass line may be considered the prototype of the new and ideal social relationships which blind polity and society and yet allow political cadres to manipulate the society for political purposes.

To achieve the merger of polity and society, party leaders selectively utilized advantageous traditions in political thought as well as in social practice. For example, leading cadres exploited the tradition in Chinese theory that politics had been part of an undifferentiated whole, despite the fact that intergroup politics contradicted the idealized human relationships prescribed by Confucian ethics. Chinese thought exhibited a predilection for the unity of knowledge, and dominant philosophical and value theories usually linked human action to social obligation (although this linkage was not made as frequently in Taoism and Buddhism as in

Confucianism). Chinese theory did not distinguish social from political obligation, and the society was thus denied conceptual limits on political power. The society was, of course, the presumed source of political values, and the preoccupation with inviolable classics constituted a limitation on political action. By focusing on the conceptual continuum of all obligations and by denying the validity of the classics, party leaders hope to legitimatize their unlimited authority in the minds of the Chinese people. The Chinese political tradition, however, did not provide for a full equivalence between political and social obligations. This the Chinese Communists seek to achieve.

The Communist-directed transformation of China has entailed three principal changes from the viewpoint of the individual.[4] First, the social horizons of a Chinese in the new social system, having the "collectivity of the whole people" as its objective, are expanded far beyond the *li-mao k'o-ch'i* pattern to coincide with the Communist-controlled state. Second, creation of a nationwide collectivity has required the fostering of new obligations based on the prescribed mass relationships. Third, the traditional obligations and loyalties of a direct personal character are being reformed in order to create the new synthesis of leaders and the masses. The new common loyalties and obligations, which when created would make force unnecessary, fundamentally derive from one's identity as a member of the "people" and as a Chinese — not from kinship, friendship, or other particularistic relationships. In creating the new universalism, the Communists have attempted to redirect and expand the social habit of face-to-face obligations and to eliminate the habit of avoiding political leaders. Honoring mutual obligations between Communists and the broad masses is guaranteed by force, however, until obligations prescribed by ideology become habitual and force is supplanted by inner, personal compulsion. Also underlying the three major changes worked by the Communists has been the replacement of the "natural" and habitual social systems by a structure of more self-consciously created relationships which are logically derived from the Marxist-Leninist dialectic. The Communist leadership has identified the key actions necessary to inculcate and activate the new relationships and has developed organizational techniques to carry those actions into operation.

The party leaders have used the political techniques of peaceful and nonpeaceful suasion to bridge the transition from old to new patterns during a period in which new obligations have not yet become habitual. In particular, party cadres establish small groups for study and produc-

---

[4]This paragraph is based on Fan Jo-yü, "Why We Abolished the Feudal Patriarchal System" (in Chinese), *Hung-ch'i* [Red Flag], no. 5, March 1, 1960, pp. 19–27.

tion in which new types of intimate relationships are cultivated to replace the former *li-mao* ties. The small size of these groups permits the development of reciprocal obligations in general agreement with traditional schemes. Under party supervision, these obligations are nurtured and then closely examined and criticized in order to bring them into conformity with the requirements of the Communist collectivity and party leadership. Family members are dispersed when assigned to small groups, and this prevents family dominance within a single group from distorting the Communist aims of these groups, although evidence presented in the previous chapter would suggest the possibility of single-family dominance within some leadership cells. The party guides the participation and performance of small-group members and painstakingly motivates each member to change his attitudes and to develop new obligations.

During the transitional period, a flexible system of political control is adapted to foster the establishment of the desired obligational patterns. According to Mao Tse-tung, since the establishment of socialism (in 1955-1956) the major contradictions in China are those which are nonantagonistic.[5] To resolve these nonantagonistic contradictions, Mao advocated education (discussion, criticism, and persuasion) and administrative orders as effective and complementary techniques.[6] In accordance with dialectical materialism, administrative orders and laws are considered a part of the superstructure and must serve the economic base and the development of socialist construction.[7] All laws are initiated by the party which then "organizes discussions on the bills and has them amended repeatedly before submitting them to the National People's Congress for discussion and approval."[8] Legal organs must reject the "reactionary bourgeois" principles of "assumption of innocence" and the "judge's freedom of conviction"[9] and must adopt instead, as "weapons" for resolving contradictions and promoting socialism under party leadership, the mass line method of leadership. For the "people," the resolution of nonantagonistic contradictions follows the lead of the party and takes place during popular participation in "great leap" production, debates, rallies, and study and during such symbolic exercises as the annual "love the people month" sponsored by the public security forces.[10] Under this system the cadres of the police and other public security organs

---

[5]Mao Tse-tung, *On the Correct Handling of Contradictions Among the People* (Peking: Foreign Language Press, 1957), pp. 7–32.

[6]*Ibid.*, p. 16.

[7]*Jen-min jih-pao* [People's Daily], February 18 and March 6, 1958.

[8]*Ibid.*, December 24, 1957.

[9]*Ibid.*

[10]See, for example, Hsinhua News Agency release, March 26, 1960, in *Survey of China Mainland Press* (SCMC), no. 2229 (1960), pp. 2–3.

work among the people, who in turn are expected "on their own initiative" to disclose criminal acts and expose "counterrevolutionaries." Outside the "people," reform through labor, executions of "spies" and "counterrevolutionaries," and the unique Communist system of "suspended death sentences" continue the dictatorship for the flexible category of "the enemy."[11]

Since the Communist victory in 1949, the most conspicuous assaults on the family-based social structure have been the replacement of the family-owned land system with agricultural collectives and communes and a rigid control of social communication. Before these revolutionary changes could be achieved, however, a decade of basic training of party cadres in intensive, collective relationships in party and mass organizations had been completed. The objectives were to substitute a new "comradeship" for traditional relationships and common ideology for familial values and to instill or preserve characteristics of li-mao intimacy among Chinese in general and between cadres and the worker-peasant classes. Inculcated to live their own lives according to the new obligational precepts of Marxism-Leninism, thousands of Communist cadres set out in 1949 to bring to China what they had learned in study groups and work teams during the previous decade at Yenan (and the guerrilla areas) and in the People's Liberation Army.

These cadres accelerated and directed the social revolution in the Chinese family which was well under way before the Communists came to power. Party cadres exploited the disintegration of the family system by skillfully manipulating the emotions of youth alienated from their parents and of parents denied security and respect. Communist leaders held out the party comradeship and organizations as legitimate social alternatives to the once-pervasive family loyalties and organized structure. Simultaneously, party cadres sought to establish new codes of social morality. They demanded, for example, a rigid conduct with respect to women and eliminated prostitution, polygamy, the buying and selling of female children, infanticide, and arranged marriages. The party leaders endeavored to change the limited focus of the family so as to make the family "a source of progress," with "political life in first position."[12] The family system, the Communists hold, is the product of the social mode of production, and the new family pattern must keep

---

[11]Mao, *On the Correct Handling*, pp. 27–32; Lo Jui-ch'ing, "The Struggle between Revolution and Counter-Revolution in the Past Ten Years," *Ten Glorious Years* (Peking: Foreign Languages Press, 1960), pp. 357–359.

[12]Li Chung-ying, *Ko-ming-che ko-jen sheng-huo yü cheng-chih ti kuan-hsi* [The Relationship of a Revolutionary Individual's Life and Politics] (Peking: T'ung-su tu-wu ch'u-pan she, 1956), pp. 24–27.

pace with the Marxist-Leninist revolution.[13] In a series of articles for the guidance of youth, a Communist writer advocated the abolition of the family as a financial unit; separate eating, working, and study habits for family members; and the relegation of sex life to a minor position.[14] Given these changes, the writer concluded, the family would no longer be the basic unit which organizes society. Since women and men will become equal so far as labor is concerned,[15] the working masses will have "little time for their family activities, because they are mostly engaged in participating in the collective activities during their spare time."[16]

## Major Communist Goals for Chinese Society

Mao's immediate objectives stated in *On People's Democratic Dictatorship* (1949) for strengthening the state power were basically attained with the liquidation of the landlords and other "class enemies" between 1949 and 1953. Toward the end of 1952, the party Central Committee inaugurated the second phase of its social goals with the "general line for the period of transition to socialism." The major objectives for this transitional period were the "simultaneous development of socialist revolution and socialist construction" and the step-by-step socialist transformation of agriculture, handicraft industry, and capitalist industry. This second phase of social policy, which is still partly in effect, began in full force with the First Five-Year Plan (1953-1957), during which time rural collectivization, socialization of industry and commerce, the "hundred flowers" reform of intellectuals, and the purging of "rightist" elements in the first stages of the 1957 rectification campaign brought progress toward the socialist goal. With these major changes achieved by 1957, Mao Tse-tung in *On the Correct Handling of Contradictions among the People* restated the basic tasks set in 1949: "Our basic task is

---

[13]See *Hsin chien-she* [New Construction], no. 4, April 7, 1960, in *SCMM*, no. 214 (1960), pp. 1–10, and *Hsin chien-she*, no. 5, May 5, 1960, in *SCMM*, no. 219 (1960), pp. 1–7.

[14]*Chung-kuo ch'ing-nien* [China Youth], no. 4, 1960, in *ECMM*, no. 210 (1960), pp. 38–39; *Shan-hsi jih-pao* [Shansi Daily], March 8, 1958, in *SCMP*, no. 1789 (1958), pp. 23–26.

[15]See "Speech by Comrade Teng Ying-chao," *Eighth National Congress of the Communist Party of China* (Peking: Foreign Languages Press, 1956), II, 225–235. A comprehensive collection on official policy toward women is *Fu-nü yün-tung wen-hsien* [Documents of the Women's Movement] (Hong Kong: Hsin min-chu ch'u-pan she, 1949).

[16]*Chung-kuo ch'ing-nien*, p. 39. The translation has been slightly altered to conform to the original.

no longer to set free the productive forces but to protect and expand them in the context of the new relations of production."[17] The line for this new task was capsulized in the 1958 "general line for socialist construction"—"to build socialism by exerting our utmost efforts, and pressing ahead consistently to achieve greater, faster, better and more economical results."

The post-1957 "basic task" of the Chinese people under the leadership of the Chinese Communist Party was broken into five parts during discussions on the Second Five-Year Plan (1958-1962). These five "fundamental tasks" of the Plan were

> (1) to continue industrial construction with heavy industry as its core and promote technical reconstruction of the national economy . . . ; (2) to carry through socialist transformation, and consolidate and expand the system of collective ownership and the system of ownership by the whole people; (3) to further increase the production of industry, agriculture and handicrafts and correspondingly develop transport and commerce . . . ; (4) to make vigorous efforts to train personnel . . . ; and (5) to reinforce the national defences and raise the level of the people's material and cultural life.[18]

These five tasks centered in socialist industrialization, which was scheduled for completion "within a period of three Five-Year Plans."[19] "In three five-year plans or perhaps a little longer," Mao Tse-tung said in 1957, "China's annual steel output can be raised to 20,000,000 tons or more."[20] Although Mao stated that "heavy industry is the core of China's economic construction,"[21] the Chinese Communist Party Central Committee late in 1959 proposed the "supplementary" policy that "agriculture is the foundation of the national economy," a policy which acknowledged the devastating significance of two years of agricultural setbacks.[22]

The Chinese Communists have lauded the rapid transition in China to an industrial society. "We did in ten years more than our ancestors had done in hundreds and even thousands of years," a Communist leader (T'ao Chu) wrote in 1959.[23] In all cases, the fundamental causes of this

---

[17]P. 30.

[18]See, for example, Chou En-lai, "Report on the Proposals for the Second Five-Year Plan," *Eighth National Congress*, I, 280–281.

[19]*Ibid.*, p. 281.

[20]Mao, *On the Correct Handling*, p. 68.

[21]*Ibid.*, p. 67.

[22]For a typical discussion of this policy, see Liao Lu-yen, *The Whole Party and the Whole People Go In for Agriculture in a Big Way* [September 1, 1960] (Peking: Foreign Languages Press, 1960), pp. 1–7.

[23]*Nan-fang jih-pao* [Southern Daily], September 30, 1959, in *SCMP*, no. 2130 (1959), pp. 23–27; *Wen-hui pao* [Cultural Exchange] (Hong Kong), October 2, 1959, in *SCMP*, no. 2118 (1959), p. 19. The quotation is found in the latter citation.

swift transformation are given as "the correct leadership of the great Chinese Communist Party and the great leader Comrade Mao Tse-tung, the guidance of the general line applicable in our country during the period of transition, and the guidance of the general line for socialist construction."[24] In an all-encompassing way, the party has done on a grand scale what Wang Kuo-fan did in the "paupers' cooperative" on a small scale, but the party also leads the total socialist transformation of China by its leadership guidance of the whole as well as of the parts.

Since the extraordinary crisis in agricultural production began in 1959-1960, the cadres of the party have been even more insistent on the leadership of the Communist Party as the "fundamental guarantee for the victory of all our undertakings."[25] Despite the increase in disciplinary and control measures during that crisis, the party leadership techniques have remained remarkably consistent and, as in the past, have even been strengthened in the crisis rather than yielding to desperation and irrationality. The party leadership has not always been successful and at times has miscalculated, but it has shown a critical attitude toward its own mistakes. "All our cadres," Vice-Premier Li Fu-ch'un said in 1960, "must improve their way of doing things in the spirit of scorning difficulties strategically and taking full account of them tactically."[26] On the same theme of difficulties, Li added that the party cadres must be "ambitious and bold in the cause of socialist construction."[27] He stated that the party cadres must be "diligent" and "down-to-earth" in addition to having a clear-cut direction toward "far-sighted goals."

The avowed objectives of industrialization[28] and commune regimentation under party leadership have been to achieve "the socialist system and the concerted efforts of a united people."[29] Given these conditions

---

[24]*Wen-hui pao*, p. 23.

[25]Li Fu-ch'un, *Raise High the Red Flag of the General Line and Continue to March Forward* [August 16, 1960] (Peking: Foreign Languages Press, 1960), pp. 35 ff. See also Liu Shao-ch'i, "The Political Report," *Eighth National Congress*, I, 95–111.

[26]Li Fu-ch'un, *op. cit.*, p. 37; this is a paraphrase of a statement made by Mao Tse-tung in 1946 and popularized by an editorial in *Hung-ch'i*, no. 19, October 1, 1960, pp. 13–17.

[27]Li Fu-ch'un, *op. cit.*, p. 37.

[28]The few statistics released by the Central People's Government on economic production before 1961 indicated some important increases despite major setbacks in agriculture. (*Peking Review*, no. 8, 1961, pp. 5–8). For example, steel production reportedly rose from 13,350,000 tons in 1959 to 18,450,000 tons in 1960. Compared with 1957, the gross value of industrial output in 1960 increased nearly threefold, the average annual rate being "more than 40 per cent." No comparable figures were released in 1962. (See *Peking Review*, no. 1, 1962, pp. 9–10.) By October, 1962, no plans had been announced concerning the end of the Second Five-Year Plan (1958–1962) or the inauguration of a Third Five-Year Plan.

[29]Mao, *On the Correct Handling*, p. 65.

of socialism and unity, a "dialectical reversal" of China's international and domestic position has been predicted by Mao Tse-tung. He said in 1957: "China's situation as a poor country denied her rights in international affairs will also be changed—a poor country will be changed into a rich country, a country denied her rights into a country enjoying her rights—a transformation of things into their opposites."[30] To effect this reversal, the Communists have maintained the priority for the establishment of the socialist system of relationships which they regard as fundamental to economic construction. Party leaders have continued the rectification movements into 1962[31] and have relentlessly advocated "radical changes in human relations" through the utilization of the rectification techniques of criticism and self-criticism.[32] Taking the broad view, Liu Shao-ch'i in 1958 stated that "the tasks of the Party at present are, on the basis of the rectification campaign, to continue to handle contradictions among the people, systematically improve the work of the state, strengthen the work of Party organizations at all levels, and work unswervingly for the implementation of the general line."[33] Liu particularly emphasized the crucial importance of rectification in a statement which still remained in full force in 1962: "The present task is to effect a thorough and systematic readjustment in the relationships between people, rooting out the capitalist and feudal survivals of bygone days and building completely new socialist relations."[34] Presumably the changes in social relationships, which would be along the lines suggested in the previous section, would set the stage for the "dialectical reversal." That reversal would usher in the period of "transition to communism."

The Communist society is the final goal of the Chinese Communists. Yet, from current Communist revelations on utopia, it is difficult to differentiate the Communist society from what exists currently or what will supposedly exist in the socialist society after the "dialectical reversal." For example, forums conducted on the topic of the transition to communism in China merely reiterate either the Central Committee resolution of August 29, 1958 ("commune resolution"), that "people's communes are the best form for the attainment of socialism and gradual transition to communism" or Liu Shao-ch'i's statement that under communism there will be "no exploiters, oppressors, landlords, capitalists, imperialists, fascists, oppressed, exploited, or darkness, ignorance, and

---

[30]*Ibid.*, pp. 64–65.
[31]See *Peking Review*, no. 4, 1961, p. 6; *ibid.*, no. 8, 1961, p. 8; and *Jen-min jih-pao*, April 3, 1962.
[32]Liu Shao-ch'i, "Report on the Work of the Central Committee," *Second Session of the Eighth National Congress of the Communist Party of China* (Peking: Foreign Languages Press, 1958), p. 26.
[33]*Ibid.*, p. 52.
[34]*Ibid.*, p. 53.

backwardness."[35] However, communes exist in the China of the pre-Communist era, a China which allegedly vanquished most of the various villains on Liu's list before the establishment of the communes. Adding to the confusion, the forums on communism attempt to adhere to the vague criteria for moving to communism set forth in the August, 1958, resolution and repeated in the subsequent Central Committee resolution of December 10, 1958. These criteria or prerequisites for the Communist society were summarized as follows:

> Some years after that [transition to socialism] the social product will become very abundant; the communist consciousness and morality of the entire people will be elevated to a much higher degree; universal education will be achieved . . . ; the differences between worker and peasant, between town and country, between mental and manual labour . . . and the remnants of unequal bourgeois rights . . . will gradually vanish; and the function of the state will be limited to protecting the country from external aggression; and it will play no role internally.[36]

The well-worn Marxist pronouncements that the Communist society will witness the abolition of classes, political parties, and the state (except for the "administration of things" by rotating officials) were subtly modified in 1956, when *People's Daily* stated that in a Communist society "there will still be contradictions among people . . . [and] there will still be a struggle between people, though its nature and form will be different from those in class societies."[37] Moreover, the Communist society will not be a society of ease, although it will presumably be a society of plenty. "Persons who think a Communist society will breed lazy bones always regard laziness as a common nature of mankind having nothing to do with social conditions."[38] Attributing laziness and the desire for ease to the system of private property, the Chinese Communists hold that "conscious and selfless labor as an aspect of the Communist spirit" will grow in the struggle toward communism.[39]

---

[35]See, for example, *Hsin chien-she*, no. 4, April 7, 1959, in *Extracts from China Mainland Magazines (ECMM)*, no. 171 (1959), pp. 26–27, and Liu Shao-ch'i, "On the Cultivation of the Communist Party Member" (in Chinese), *Hung-ch'i*, no. 15–16, August 1, 1962, p. 15.

[36]"Resolution on Some Questions concerning the People's Communes," *Sixth Plenary Session of the Eighth Central Committee of the Communist Party of China* (Peking: Foreign Languages Press, 1958), pp. 25–26.

[37]"On the Historical Experience of the Dictatorship of the Proletariat" [April 5, 1956], *The Historical Experience of the Dictatorship of the Proletariat* (Peking: Foreign Languages Press, 1959), p. 11.

[38]*Wen-hui pao*, October 23, 1958, in *SCMP*, no. 1900 (1958), pp. 2–5.

[39]*Ibid.*, p. 5.

Not only will people struggle and work hard under communism, but they will also have leaders despite the scheduled disappearance of the party organization. The importance of leadership, *Red Flag* wrote in 1959, "is a universal law of social life within the easy comprehension of all."[40] The form of leadership applicable to the future Communist society was clarified somewhat in 1957 by Lu Ting-yi.[41] The future society, Lu declared, would be organized according to the principle of democratic centralism. Democratic centralism is currently the organizational principle of the Chinese Communist Party, the Chinese state, mass organizations, industries and enterprises, the army, and the communes. All organizations under the *direct* leadership of the Communist Party are organized according to democratic centralism. . . . Given the clues provided by Lu Ting-yi, it is probable that the Chinese Communists understand totalitarianism as the integration and systematization of Chinese society—and later all human society—within the framework of democratic centralism. This is their mechanism for comprehending the totality and adjusting current leadership techniques to promote it. In a Communist society, Lu Ting-yi said, "the question of democracy will still exist; however, it will not be democracy within the framework of 'democracy and dictatorship' but democracy within the framework of 'democracy and centralism.' "[42] . . .

---

[40]*Hung-ch'i*, no. 24, December 16, 1959, p. 14. The Chinese Communists, however, accept Lenin's dictum that a rotation of public offices will occur in the period of communism. As stated in a recent organizational manual: "In the period of communism, the concept of cadre will be taught with new meaning; that is, everybody can be a cadre."

[41]Lu Ting-yi, "Wo-men t'ung tzu-ch'an-chieh-chi yu-p'ai ti ken-pen fen-ch'i" [The Basic Difference between the Bougeois Rightists and Us], speech given on July 11, 1957, at the fourth session of the First National People's Congress, in *She-hui-chu-i chiao-yü k'o-ch'eng ti yüeh-tu wen-chien hui-pien* [Collected Readings and Documents for the Curriculum in Socialist Education] (Peking. Jen-min ch'u-pan she, 1959), pp. 94–95.

[42]*Ibid.*

# V

# Political Socialization

## 10. Communist Education: Theory and Practice

*C. T. Hu*

Paradoxically, the contemporary phase of China's development under Communism is at once an extreme form of Westernisation and a partial reversion to traditional patterns. The totalitarian character of the present régime is not only reminiscent of the ancient autocratic order but is attributable to that tradition for its acceptance and acquiescence. On the ideological front, the state of confusion of thought, compounded by almost a century's cultural dislocation, has been brought to an abrupt end, with the promulgation of Marxism-Leninism as the state ideology which, though antithetic to Confucian orthodoxy in every essential way, is equally pervasive. Inasmuch as the ideological reconditioning of the Chinese nation is first and foremost an educational task, education has become the exclusive concern of the Communist state. Moreover, within the Marxian ideological framework, the pursuit of concrete national goals requires the education of the Chinese people. Hence there are two major aspects in the study of Chinese education under Communism: Fundamental principles and actual implementation; in short, theory and practice.

There is, strictly speaking, very little in the Chinese Communist educational literature that can be regarded as educational theory as such. What has been labelled by the Chinese Communists as educational theory is no more than the extension and application of certain aspects of dialectical materialism, as expounded by Marx, Lenin, Stalin and Mao, to the direction of educational affairs. Since the Communist doctrine stresses the unity of theory and practice, as well as the importance of "concrete objective conditions," any educational policy or measure can

Reprinted from C. T. Hu, "Communist Education: Theory and Practice," *The China Quarterly* 10 (April-June 1962): 84–97, by permission of the author and the journal.

be introduced and promoted or criticised and abandoned in the name of either theory or practice.


## The Ideological Basis: The First Triad


Of particular significance and relevance to education are three basic concepts of dialectical materialism, as interpreted by the Chinese Communists. The first is the classification of human thought, insofar as the laws of the development of the world are concerned, into the metaphysical and the dialectical, which represent two mutually opposed world outlooks. Mao Tse-tung wrote in his *On Contradiction*:

> For a very long period of history both in China and in Europe, metaphysics formed part of the idealist world outlook and occupied a dominant position in human thought. In the early days of the bourgeoisie in Europe, materialism was also metaphysical. The Marxist materialist-dialectical world outlook emerged because in many European countries social economy had entered the stage of highly developed capitalism, the productive forces, the class struggle and the sciences had all developed to a level unprecedented in history, and the industrial proletariat had become the greatest motive force in historical development. Then among the bourgeoisie, besides an openly avowed, extremely bare-faced reactionary idealism, there also emerged vulgar evolutionism to oppose materialist dialectics.[1]

In this one short passage one comes across a number of the familiar phrases of Communist jargon: class struggle, bourgeoisie, proletariat, productive forces, capitalism, reactionary idealism and materialist dialectics. No useful purpose can be served by raising philosophical questions about any one of these terms, nor is it relevant to ask if the majority of the Communist followers understand the meaning and implications of these terms. It is, however, exceedingly important to bear in mind that, by categorising all human thought according to such a scheme, there now exists a simple formula by which all thinking and action can be judged. The metaphysical world outlook is equated with idealism, is adhered to by the bourgeoisie, is reactionary, and therefore is opposed to both human progress and scientific truth. On the opposite side is the dialectical world outlook which is founded on the objective scientific truth, represents the irresistible forward running current of history, is supported by the proletariat, and promises the Communist millennium. Thus the line between right and wrong, friend and enemy, progress and

---

[1]Mao Tse-tung, "On Contradiction," in *Selected Works of Mao Tse-tung* (London: Lawrence and Wishart, 1954), Vol. 2, p. 14.

reaction is irrevocably drawn, with the party leadership enjoying the exclusive prerogative of interpretation. Ideological rigidity forbids deviation in thought yet allows sufficient tactical latitude for the party itself. The state of confusion of thought in modern China has been brought to an end; education now proceeds in an atmosphere of controlled uniformity.

The second concept concerns practice, with even greater and more direct implications for education. To quote Mao Tse-tung once more:

> Knowledge starts with practice, reaches the theoretical plane via practice, and then has to return to practice. The active function of knowledge not only manifests itself in the active leap from perceptual knowledge to rational knowledge, but also—and this is the more important—in the leap from rational knowledge to revolutionary practice. The knowledge which enables us to grasp the laws of the world must be redirected to the practice of changing the world, that is, it must again be applied in the practice of production, in the practice of the revolutionary class struggle and revolutionary national struggle, as well as in the practice of scientific experimentation. This is the process of testing and developing theory, the continuation of the whole process of knowledge.[2]

The nature of knowledge is thus defined. Since search for knowledge is the prime objective of education, any form of education that fails to attain knowledge through practice according to the prescribed formula of production, class struggle, and national struggle is worse than no education at all. If, by classifying human thoughts into two fundamental opposing world views in favour of the dialectical, the Communists seek to create a monolithic pattern of ideological conformity, this emphasis upon practice tends to determine both the nature of knowledge and the meaning of education. Ideologically, the Chinese educational tradition can thus be negated on the ground that it was divorced from practice, hence its failure to lift China out of primitive agrarianism, to eliminate class exploitation, to achieve national power, and to reap the benefits of modern science. The feverish action-oriented form of education in China today can be understood only in terms of this fundamental consideration.

The third part of the triad is the class character of education and culture in general. Culture and education are regarded as concrete expressions of the politics and economics of a given society, and the politics and economics are determined by the class character. With respect to China, there are two aspects in Mao Tse-tung's analysis of the problem of culture. The first concerns his interpretation of China's culture before the Communist revolution, which he described in the following terms:

---

[2]Mao Tse-tung, "On Practice," *ibid.*, Vol. 2, pp. 292, 297.

There is in China an imperialist culture which is a reflection of the control or partial control of imperialism over China politically and economically. This part of culture is advocated not only by the cultural
organisations run directly by the imperialists in China but also by a
number of shameless Chinese. All culture that contains a slave ideology
belongs to this category. There is also in China a semi-feudal culture
which is a reflection of semi-feudal politics and economy and has as its
representatives all those who, while opposing the new culture and new
ideologies, advocate the worship of Confucius, the study of the Confucian canon, the old ethical code and the old ideologies. Imperialist culture and semi-feudal culture are affectionate brothers, who have formed
a reactionary cultural alliance to oppose China's new culture. This reactionary culture serves the imperialists and the feudal class, and must
be swept away.[3]

The "reactionary culture" must be condemned and swept away because it served only the interests of the exploiting classes which were
allied with imperialism and semi-feudalism. This forms the negative
aspect of Mao's interpretation. In a positive sense, Mao advocated the
new-democratic culture which can only be led by the "proletarian cultural
ideology, by the ideology of communism, and cannot be led by the
cultural ideology of any other class."[4] It is, in a word, the culture of the
broad masses under the leadership of the proletariat.

## The Fundamental Principles: The Second Triad

Although there have been tactical retreats on the educational front since
the Communist takeover, the three fundamental concepts concerning the
dialectical world outlook, the search for true knowledge through practice,
and the development of a proletarian culture have remained the very
foundation upon which education rests. In this respect, there seems to
be a remarkable degree of ideological consistency in the Communist
régime, because the educational principles laid down in the Common
Programme, which served as the basic guiding rules of the land until the
adoption of a constitution in 1954, specifically called for the creation of
a culture and education of the New Democracy, "that is, nationalistic,
scientific, and popular."[5] These make up the second triad of nationalism,

---

[3]Mao Tse-tung, "On New Democracy," *ibid.*, Vol. 3, p. 141.
[4]*Ibid.*, p. 145.
[5]Article 41 of the Common Programme, adopted by the Chinese People's Political Consultative Conference which functioned as the highest law-making organ
immediately after the Communist seizure of power in 1949. Chapter V of the Programme deals with culture and education; it is translated in *New China: Three
Views* by Otto B. van der Sprenkel, Michael Lindsay, Robert Guillain (London:
Turnstile Press, 1950), pp. 199–216.

scientism and popularism which, unlike the first, which provides the ideological basis, sets up the educational objectives for the régime to strive for. The achievement of these objectives requires action; now that the Communists are in power, they lose no time in remoulding Chinese education according to the ideological dictates.

There can be little doubt that nationalism has been one of the most pervasive and dynamic forces in modern China which the Communists have manipulated to their fullest advantage. To achieve the nationalistic goal through education, two major strategies have been employed. On the positive side, the Chinese people are taught to cherish their great cultural tradition, reminded of the lasting achievements of their fore-fathers, the vastness and richness of their land and the tremendous potentials for the betterment of mankind.[6] Negatively, the humiliation of the Chinese nation during the past century, the sufferings of the Chinese people, and the degradation of China to the status of a semi-colony are ascribed to the unrelenting aggressions on all fronts by the arrogant and vicious imperialists. If the "victory" of the Chinese people in free-ing themselves has broken the political bondage of semi-colonialism, the vestiges of imperialist culture and education still present the most serious obstacle to the achievement of the culture of New Democracy.

It is for the "nationalistic" purpose that all Western-sponsored insti-tutions of education were the first ones to be subjected to the fury of educational reorganisation, and in less than three years, from early 1950 to the fall of 1952, all schools with foreign affiliations were "reorganised" out of existence.[7] Labelled as agencies of imperialist cultural aggression, the foreign-supported schools were declared to be hotbeds for the spread of individualism, liberalism, and bourgeois decadence, all implacable enemies of the culture of New Democracy. Similarly, the Western-trained intellectuals, their repentance and profession of faith in the new order notwithstanding, were subjected to the severest dosages of thought reform.[8]

The "scientific" part of the triad involves two directly related objec-tives. The first has to do with the acceptance of the Communist definition of knowledge, discussed above, which can be scientific only when it is dialectical and derived through practice. Within such an ideological

---

[6]See, for example, a collection of essays entitled *Lun Ai-kuo chu-i ti Chiao-yu* (*Essays on Education for Patriotism*), by Hsu T'e-li and others (Peking: The Masses' Bookstore, 1951).

[7]For further information on the fate of foreign-supported schools of higher edu-cation, see C. T. Hu, "Higher Education in Mainland China," in *Comparative Edu-cation Review*, Vol. 4, No. 3, February 1961, p. 163.

[8]For a thorough and up-to-date analysis of the thought reform of intellectuals, see Theodore H. E. Chen, *Thought Reform of the Chinese Intellectuals* (Hong Kong University Press, 1960).

framework, scientific education means specifically the development of modern science and technology to expedite the process of industrialisation and national development. Concrete educational efforts in this direction have been both numerous and concentrated and fall under three general categories. On the highest level is the Chinese Academy of Sciences, which has steadily expanded over the past twelve years. The number of its research institutes increased from thirty-one in 1952 to 170 in 1958, with a corresponding increase in trained personnel which for the year 1958 was close to 30,000 strong.[9] The Academy is responsible for the training of scientists in all major fields of specialisation who form the nucleus of an expanding army of scientific manpower. Below the Academy are the institutions of higher and secondary education, the majority of which are devoted to the training of engineers, technicians of all types, medical personnel, and other specialists. On the lowest level are the "broad masses of the people," who are taught not only to read and write but also the rudiments of modern science and technology, consisting, at the present stage, of primarily labour-saving devices. Underlying the whole educational process of scientism is the principle of "walking on two legs," which demands the combination of theory and practice, new and old, Western and Chinese.

The idea of popularism has grown out of the concept of class struggle, and it is in this important respect that it differs from the phenomenon of popularisation of education in non-Communist countries. Concerning the class structure of Chinese society, Mao Tse-tung wrote as early as 1926 an essay entitled "Analysis of the Classes in Chinese Society," in which he classified the Chinese population into five major classes, representing three basically different positions with respect to the Chinese revolution: Those for it, those against it, and those wavering between the two.[10] Since the culture and educational system of China before the Communist revolution were those favoured by the oppressing and anti-revolutionary classes, the culture and education of New Democracy must serve the needs of the masses under the leadership of the proletariat. Needless to say, the Communists are fully aware of the educational needs of the nation at a time of all-out national construction which cannot be accomplished without a literate and technically competent populace. Therefore, from both the ideological viewpoint of class struggle and the practical viewpoint of the nation's educational needs, popularism in

---

[9]Leo A. Orleans, *Professional Manpower and Education in Communist China* (Washington: National Science Foundation, 1960), p. 111.

[10]Mao-Tse-tung, "Analysis of the Classes in Chinese Society," in *Selected Works of Mao Tse-tung*, op. cit., Vol. 1, pp. 13–20.

education must be held up as one of the major goals. The slogan "intellectualise the proletariat; proletarianise the intellectuals!" reveals in a nutshell the true meaning of the movement towards popularism.

Different means have been employed to popularise education. Of first importance has been the steady expansion of education on all levels. Enrolment in full-time institutions is reported to have increased by leaps and bounds, with a corresponding increase in the number of schools. In 1958, the government claimed that 85 per cent. of all school age children were in attendance.[11] With the advent of the "Great Leap Forward" in 1958, the informal part of education has received encouragement and attention, resulting in the creation, sometimes almost overnight, of literally thousands of spare-time schools and Red-and-Expert colleges. These schools are undoubtedly far below standard and in some cases exist no more than in name, but nevertheless they are indicative of the extent to which the goal of popularism has been sought. The class character of the students has also shifted in favour of the proletariat, which by Chinese definition includes both agricultural and industrial workers. According to official reports, the percentage of students of working class origin has increased from 19.1 per cent. in 1951 to 48 per cent. in 1958 for higher education, and that of students in secondary schools from 51.3 per cent. to 75.2 per cent.[12] This is known as "opening the doors of schools for peasants and workers"; in other words, the "intellectualisation of the proletariat." At the same time, the "proletarianisation of the intellectuals" has proceeded according to party dictates, largely through thought reform, intensive indoctrination, and participation in productive labour. By and large, the quality of education in the present phase of development seems to indicate a downward trend, that is, as a result of the heavy demands made upon the students, the Communists have been more successful in bringing the intellectuals down than in raising the proletariat up.

Under Communism, a new generation of "educated Chinese" is slowly emerging. If the earlier phase of modern Chinese education which began about a century ago had created a group of intellectuals with little in common with their traditional predecessors in orientation, outlook and temperament, the present generation has gone even further in renouncing the educational heritage of the recent past. This is the real meaning of popularism.

---

[11] A breakdown of the enrolment for 1958 gave 86,400,000 for elementary schools; 10,000,000 for all types of secondary schools; and 660,000 for higher institutions. See *Wei-ta ti shih-nien* (*Ten Great Years*) (Peking: People's Publishing House, 1959), p. 170.

[12] *Ibid.*, p. 178.

Foundations of Educational Policy: The Third Triad

By 1958, the Communist Party and the Communist state under its control were sufficiently convinced of the "correctness" of the Party line and satisfied with the progress along the road to Socialism up to that point that an all-out and nation-wide movement known as the "Great Leap Forward" was launched. As education formed an integral and important part of this national assertion, fundamental policy decisions concerning education were proclaimed jointly by the Chinese Communist Party and the State Council on September 19, 1958, in which it was stated that "the policy of educational work of the Party is to make education serve proletarian politics, and to combine education and production labour. In order to carry out this policy, educational work must be led by the Party."[13] Thus there appeared yet another triad, namely, politics, production, and Party control.

To the Communists, the term politics is all-inclusive in its implications. By proletarian politics is meant, therefore, the whole intricate process of establishing a new national polity based upon the leadership of the proletariat, of which the Communist Party is the vanguard. Being aware that the Communist millennium must be created by a people completely immersed in Communist ideology, the Party leadership indeed see no other alternative than to assign to politics the highest priority in all educational tasks. It is significant to note, in this connection, that the Party organisation in China has no educational department as such, and that all major decisions concerning education are made by the Party hierarchy on the recommendations of the Department of Propaganda. In view of the role of the Communist Party in the functioning of the Chinese state, it is clear that the Ministry of Education is no more than an administrative organ through which Party decisions are carried out. The obvious implication is that education, in so far as the Party is concerned, is primarily a propaganda function, with indoctrination of the population as its ultimate aim.

Ideological indoctrination is the essence of the political part of the triad and takes precedence over all other aspects of education. Consequently all persons, and especially educational workers and students, are graded, selected and treated according to their "political consciousness." Academic excellence is, to be sure, desirable and encouraged, but it must be accompanied by political reliability as a result of proper indoctrination. The term "Red and Expert" is, in this sense, particularly pertinent and revealing, for being Red has been, at least until recently, more important than being Expert, and the objective of education is to train

---

[13]Reported in the *People's Daily* (*Jen-min Jih-pao*), September 20, 1958.

a new generation of ideologically trustworthy and technically competent Chinese.

References have been made to the ideological framework when discussing the first triad. Our concern here is with the means by which the political objectives of education are achieved. A variety of methods are in use, ranging from the simple technique of repeating slogans to the highly complex process of thought reform. Broadly speaking, however, these methods fall under two categories, the formal or doctrinal part and the informal or action part, which, according to the Communist scheme, complement each other and unify theory and practice.

On the formal and doctrinal side there are the political subjects of instruction which consist of Dialectical Materialism, Foundations of Marxism and Leninism, History of the Chinese Revolution, Political Economy, and the like. The titles and the manner of presentation of the courses may vary from level to level and from institution to institution, but they are "musts" in all cases, be it the People's University or a rural spare-time school. Moreover, instruction is given, in most cases, by Party cadres operating in educational institutions. Passive acceptance of the doctrines never suffice, and such devices as "Study Groups," "criticism and self-criticism," and "thought struggle sessions" are resorted to from time to time not only to prevent deviation but also to insure complete and absolute belief in the new faith. The informal and action part of indoctrination takes many forms, mostly in organised political activities of one sort or another. Teachers and students have in the past twelve years engaged in several large-scale campaigns, beginning with the first land reform movement in 1950, followed by the Resist-America Aid-Korea movement in 1951, the Three-Anti- and Five-Anti movements of 1952, the Blooming and Contending of 1957, the Great Leap Forward of 1958, and more recently the movement to increase agricultural production. These are political activities of considerable duration and scope, to which must be added a large number of short-term action programmes, such as mass demonstrations against the French and British during the Suez crisis and against Eisenhower's visit to the Far East in 1960.

At the present stage, there is every indication that political indoctrination is receiving the utmost emphasis in all educational activities. The régime seems perfectly aware of the effect of such emphasis upon the quality of education, but as long as the principle of making education serve the needs of proletarian politics is adhered to, political indoctrination will continue to receive the highest priority and constitute the major form of education.

In an article entitled "The Great Revolution and Development in our Country's Educational Task," the Chinese Minister of Education made the following statement concerning the position of politics in education:

The great revolution in education further solved the problem of the relationship between education on the one hand and politics on the other. The capitalist class hypocritically chanted "education for education's sake" and "leave the students out of politics." But we insist that education must be in the service of proletarian politics and that all undertakings must be combined with political thought, because only in this way can we train the type of personnel who are both red and expert. For this reason, we hold up as the soul of all school work the political education of Marxism-Leninism and the political task of the Party. Moreover, we have put into effect the guiding principle of "let politics be the commander-in-chief" in all fields of cultural and scientific education.[14]

With respect to the policy of combining education with production, there are two readily discernible reasons by which the policy is justified. One is related to the fundamental ideological consideration of the nature of knowledge and the importance of practice in the acquisition of knowledge. To engage in productive activities is to combine practice with theory, and thus to acquire true knowledge. Also, productive labour is believed to be the surest way to eliminate the class character of education. Through productive labour the socially aloof and ideologically unwholesome intellectuals are made mindful of the dignity and honour of physical work and are proletarianised in the process. The other reason lies in the actual and acute need of the nation for total mobilisation of human resources for national development. An expanding army of students, particularly on the secondary and higher education level, is an extremely important asset, in that they have considerably more to offer to national construction than the unskilled workers, numerous though they are. Therefore, for both ideological and economic reasons, the school system itself has been adjusted and developed in such a way as to facilitate the combination of education with productive labour.

Within this context, there are now three major types of schools in China, namely, the spare-time schools, half-work half-study schools, and full-time schools. The spare-time schools are designed for the purpose of elevating the cultural level and technical competence of the masses and are, as the name itself indicates, organisationally flexible. Drawing students from the rural communes, industrial plants, and urban residential districts, these schools range from open-air literacy classes to technical training on farms and in factories. Since all participants, including instructional staff, have their regular tasks to perform, these

---

[14]*Chien-kuo Shih-nien (Ten Years of National Construction)* (Hong Kong: Chiwen Publishing Co., 1959).

schools represent one form of mass education in which production comes before education. Because the state has encouraged local authorities to assume major responsibility for the organisation and operation of spare-time schools, and because of the diversity in objectives, resources, background of students and other factors, there exist no set pattern or criteria by which the spare-time schools can be properly described or classified. There are, however, common problems besetting these schools both in the mental and physical realms. Over-emphasis upon political indoctrination in spare-time school instruction, often given in addition to regular political meetings of one form or another, has given rise to mental dissipation or resentment, while the compulsory nature of such schools has contributed to physical exhaustion, the working hours being long and arduous.

In the half-work half-study schools students are required to participate in active production in a large variety of fields on a half-day, half-week, or sometimes half-month basis. Both in organisation and in curriculum these schools display a higher degree of articulation and co-ordination. In many cases they are middle schools under the supervision of government agencies which make arrangements with industrial or technical institutions for the provision of technical training and guidance for students, while the regular working force in return receive school instruction when the students are at work. Here education and production receive equal attention.

Forming the backbone of the nation's school system are the full-time schools which are subject to the overall control and supervision of the state in matters relating to organisation, administration, finance, curriculum, admission, graduation, and assignment of work. To combine education with production, different means are employed on different levels of schooling. For children below the secondary level, stress is laid upon the cultivation of the correct attitude towards work. Whenever feasible, children are encouraged to perform manual labour in school, not so much for production as to prepare them for participation in "socialist construction." On the secondary and higher education level, production becomes an integral part of education, and production in this case covers a wide range of activities. University students majoring in Chinese language and literature compile dictionaries; geology students explore parts of the country for minerals; and students in economics or banking work in state operated enterprises. Engineering institutes not only train their students in laboratory plants; they fulfil production quotas assigned by the state. The following report illustrates the extent to which education has been combined with productive labour:

Labour has become a formal part of our school curriculum. Schools everywhere have established factories and farms. According to statistics submitted by 323 institutions of higher education, there are now 738 factories and 233 farms, the latter having a total cultivated area of 140,000 *mou* of land. During 1958 and 1959, 386,000 students put in altogether 36,460,000 working days of work, with a total output valued at 1,380,000,000 *yuan*. All that we have belongs to the Party.[15]

It is idle to speculate on the effect of politics and productive labour upon education, although it is generally known that there is deep-seated dissatisfaction with the present state of educational affairs. Inasmuch as there is dissatisfaction and public scepticism, the third cardinal policy calling for party control of education is indeed a necessity, for without it other educational goals would be impossible to reach. The reaffirmation of this policy by no less a personage than Mao Tse-tung himself in 1958 was, therefore, not merely a reiteration of a familiar tune or theme, but an authoritative statement of the official party position concerning education, a position that tolerates no interference in educational matters from other quarters.

The timing of reaffirming party leadership in education was significant. It coincided with the "Great Leap Forward" and signalled the end of the earlier policy of tolerating to a certain degree the so-called old intelligentsia and their limited role in formulating educational policies. With the reaffirmation of this policy, all criticisms directed against various aspects of Chinese education were silenced and positive measures were taken to insure complete and unquestioning implementation of Party directives in the realm of education. These measures included intensified Party work among the students, the strengthening of the power and authority of Party representatives in schools, and the control of academic and administrative affairs by the state through the Party apparatus. In August 1959, one newspaper reported that among the 60,000 or more graduates from institutions of higher education in 1959, the number of Party and Communist Youth League members had reached a record high, with the Peking Normal University claiming as high a proportion as 85 per cent.[16] In virtually all schools, the Party secretary, with the Party machinery functioning at the lowest level and covering all ranges, now wielded absolute power over all essential aspects of school life, ranging from curriculum designing and examination procedures to student selection.

---

[15]A report by the Chairman of the All-China Students Union, *Hong Kong Times*, February 11, 1960.
[16]*Kuang-ming Daily*, August 24, 1959.

A delegation to the All China Conference of Advanced Socialist Workers in Education, Culture, Health, Physical Education, and Press, held in Peking in the summer of 1960, made the following remarks concerning Party leadership:

> The educational and cultural task of our country is a task of socialism. It is an instrument for the consolidation of proletariat dictatorship, and it is at the same time an instrument for the Communist education of our people. The fundamental principle is that education and cultural work must serve proletarian politics and socialist economic construction. In order to accomplish this, education must be led by our Party. Within the realm of education and culture, the struggle between the bourgeoisie and the proletariat, and the struggle between capitalism and socialism have manifested themselves in many forms. Over a long time, the focus of contention has always been centred on the fundamental problem of Party leadership. Prior to 1957, despite the fact that we had made great gains in educational and cultural work, we were not able to consolidate, in time, the leadership of the proletariat. As a result, the bourgeois rightists, taking advantage of this condition, began to challenge the party on all fronts, shouting such slogans as "the Party is incapable of leading educational work," "education for education's sake," and "separate labour from mental work." . . . The thorough crushing of the vicious attacks by the bourgeois rightists has firmly established the indisputable correctness of our Party's educational and cultural policy, has paved the way for even greater progress, and has made possible the Great Leap Forward on all fronts.[17]

## Conclusions

The revolt against tradition and the deepening of sweeping changes in modern Chinese education form one important part of the transformation of the most populous nation on earth. The traditional system and pattern of education, like all other facets of Chinese national life, proved totally inadequate in the face of an unprecedented challenge from the West. With the abandonment of traditional education came the weakening and later the disintegration of the ideological, moral and political fabric of old China. However valiant the efforts of the educational reformers during the transitional period, the general conditions which prevailed in China since its confrontation with the West prevented the gradual and healthy growth of a new educational system to serve the needs of a nation in transformation. Foreign aggression, civil strife and economic distress

---

[17]*People's Daily*, June 2, 1960.

combined to render educational development difficult, while confusion on the intellectual front produced cynicism and despair. The Communist revolution is thus the culmination of China's century-long search for a new place in a new world.

In studying Chinese educational development under Communism, the totalitarian character of the new régime must assume first importance. It is precisely because of its totalitarianism that there now exists a government with absolute power, dominated by a disciplined, militant and dynamic political party. Through the government machinery and the Party apparatus, the Communists now control all aspects of national activity, including the re-education of the entire populace. By insisting upon party leadership in education, the régime is now able to pursue its educational goals with remarkable singleness of purpose and a degree of effectiveness and forcefulness that have no precedence in Chinese history. Totalitarianism, moreover, has brought about ideological uniformity and, at least in the present phase, succeeded in suppressing all real and potential challengers to Party doctrine. Through thought control and reform, the Chinese people are being moulded according to the image of the new Socialist Man, made to see the world and its history from the dialectical view, taught to love, hate and work in compliance with Party dictates.

Aggressive nationalism has replaced traditional humanism, and the major objective of education is now the maximisation of national power by means of industrialisation, for which scientism provides the key. Education has become, because of this overriding consideration, an integral part of the gigantic plan for national construction, to be coordinated with other phases of development. Thus the types of schools, the number of students, the method of selection, the content of education, as well as the assignment of graduates to jobs are all determined by the state according to a plan which is only a part of yet another larger plan. The political, social, economic and intellectual meaning of education has been rigidly defined by the state which permits no deviation or divergence of view. Education must serve the needs of proletarian politics.

If by totalitarian means the state has achieved complete control over the material and human resources of the nation, and in the field of education has claimed impressive achievements, the very magnitude of the task can cause a mistake or miscalculation to have disastrous consequences. The commune movement resulted in an economic crisis of alarming proportions, and the subsequent mobilisation of manpower for agricultural work dealt a severe blow to education on all levels, if for no other reason than the necessity of reducing the hours of instruction. There is, however, every indication that the régime remains as determined as ever in pursuing its educational goals, and given the organisational advantage of the Party and the dedication of its members, there is little reason to doubt that education will continue to develop according to the Party-formulated plans. The way in which education develops will determine the way in which the whole society develops, and in recognition of this relationship between education and society, it is imperative that we study China's educational developments with the care and attention they deserve.

## 11. Why Communists Must Undertake Self-Cultivation

*Liu Shao-ch'i*

Why must Communists undertake to cultivate themselves?

In order to live, man must wage a struggle against nature and make use of nature to produce material values. At all times and under all conditions, his production of material things is social in character. It follows that when men engage in production at any stage of social development, they have to enter into certain relations of production with one another. In their ceaseless struggle against nature, men ceaselessly change nature and simultaneously change themselves and their mutual relations. Men themselves, their social relations, their forms of social organization, and their consciousness change and progress continuously in the long struggle which as social beings they wage against nature. In ancient times, man's mode of life, social organization, and consciousness were all different from what they are today, and in the future they will again be different.

Mankind and human society are in process of historical development. When human society reached a certain historical stage, classes and class struggle emerged. Every member of a class society exists as a member of a given class and lives in given conditions of class struggle. Man's social being determines his consciousness. In class society the ideology of the members of each class reflects a different class position and different class interests. The class struggle constantly goes on among these classes with their different positions, interests, and ideologies. Thus it is not only in the struggle against nature but in the struggle of social classes that men change nature, change society and at the same time change themselves.

Reprinted from Liu Shao-ch'i, *How To Be A Good Communist* (Peking: Foreign Language Press, 1964), pp. 1–9, 45–47.

Marx and Engels said:

> Both for the production on a mass scale of this communist conscious-
> ness, and for the success of the cause itself, the alteration of men on a
> mass scale is necessary, an alteration which can only take place in a
> practical movement, a *revolution*; this revolution is necessary, therefore,
> not only because the ruling class cannot be overthrown in any other way,
> but also because the class *overthrowing* it can only in a revolution suc-
> ceed in ridding itself of all the muck of ages and become fitted to found
> society anew.

That is to say, the proletariat must consciously go through long periods
of social revolutionary struggles and, in such struggles, change society
and change itself.

We should therefore see ourselves as in need of change and capable
of being changed. We should not look upon ourselves as immutable, perfect and sacrosanct, as persons who need not and cannot be changed.
When we pose the task of remolding ourselves in social struggle, we are
not demeaning ourselves; the objective laws of social development demand it. Unless we do so, we cannot make progress, nor fulfill the task of
changing society.

We Communists are the most advanced revolutionaries in modern history; today the changing of society and the world rests upon us and we
are the driving force in this change. It is by unremitting struggle against
counter-revolutionaries and reformists that we Communists change society and the world, and at the same time change ourselves.

When we say that Communists must remold themselves by waging
struggles in every sphere against the counter-revolutionaries and reformists, we mean that it is through such struggles that they must seek to
make progress, and must enhance their revolutionary quality and ability.
An immature revolutionary has to go through a long process of revolutionary tempering and self-cultivation, a long process of remolding, before he can become a mature and seasoned revolutionary who can grasp
and skillfully apply the laws of revolution. For in the first place a comparatively immature revolutionary, born and bred in the old society, car-
ries with him remnants of the various ideologies of that society (including
its prejudices, habits, and traditions), and in the second he has not been
through a long period of revolutionary activity. Therefore he does not
yet have a really thorough understanding of the enemy, of ourselves, or
of the laws of social development and revolutionary struggle. In order
to change this state of affairs, besides learning from past revolutionary
experience (the practice of our predecessors), he must himself participate in contemporary revolutionary practice, and in this revolutionary

practice and the struggle against all kinds of counter-revolutionaries and reformists, he must bring his conscious activity into full play and work hard at study and self-cultivation. Only so can he gradually acquire deeper experience and knowledge of the laws of social development and revolutionary struggle, acquire a really thorough understanding of the enemy and ourselves, discover and correct his wrong ideas, habits and prejudices, and thus raise the level of his political consciousness, cultivate his revolutionary qualities and improve his revolutionary methods.

Hence, in order to remold himself and raise his own level, a revolutionary must take part in revolutionary practice from which he must on no account isolate himself. He cannot do so, moreover, without subjective effort, without self-cultivation and study, in the course of practice. Otherwise, it will still be impossible for him to make progress.

For example, several Communists take part in a revolutionary mass struggle together and engage in revolutionary practice under roughly the same circumstances and conditions. It is possible that the effect of the struggle on these Party members will not be at all uniform. Some will make very rapid progress and some who used to lag behind will even forge ahead of others. Other Party members will advance very slowly. Still others will waiver in the struggle, and instead of being pushed forward by revolutionary practice will fall behind. Why?

Or take another example. Many members of our Party were on the Long March; it was a severe process of tempering for them, and the overwhelming majority made very great progress indeed. But the Long March had the opposite effect on certain individuals in the Party. After having been on the Long March they began to shrink before such arduous struggles, and some of them even planned to back out or run away and later, succumbing to outside allurements, actually deserted the revolutionary ranks. Many Party members took part in the Long March together, and yet its impact and results varied very greatly. Again, why?

Basically speaking, these phenomena are reflections in our revolutionary ranks of the class struggle in society. Our Party members differ in quality because they differ in social background and have come under different social influences. They differ in their attitude, stand, and comprehension in relation to revolutionary practice, and consequently they develop in different directions in the course of revolutionary practice. This can clearly be seen in your Institute as well. You all receive the same education and training here, and yet because you differ in quality and experience, in degree of effort and self-cultivation, you may obtain different or even contrary results. Hence, subjective effort and self-cultivation in the course of revolutionary struggle are absolutely essential, indeed indispensable, for a revolutionary in remolding himself and raising his own level.

Whether he joined the Revolution long ago or recently, every Communist who wants to become a good, politically mature revolutionary must undergo a long period of tempering in revolutionary struggle, must steel himself in mass revolutionary struggles and all kinds of difficulties and hardships, must sum up the experience gained through practice, make great efforts in self-cultivation, raise his ideological level, heighten his ability and never lose his sense of what is new. For only thus can he turn himself into a politically staunch revolutionary of high quality.

Confucius said, "At fifteen, my mind was bent on learning. At thirty, I could think for myself. At forty, I was no longer perplexed. At fifty, I knew the decree of Heaven. At sixty, my ear was attuned to the truth. At seventy, I can follow my heart's desire, without transgressing what is right." Here the feudal philosopher was referring to his own process of self-cultivation; he did not consider himself to have been born a "sage."

Mencius, another feudal philosopher, said that no one had fulfilled "a great mission" and played a role in history without first undergoing a hard process of tempering, a process which "exercises his mind with suffering and toughens his sinews and bones with toil, exposes his body to hunger, subjects him to extreme poverty, thwarts his undertakings, and thereby stimulates his mind, tempers his character, and adds to his capacities." Still more so must Communists give attention to tempering and cultivating themselves in revolutionary struggles, since they have the historically unprecedented "great mission" of changing the world.

Our Communist self-cultivation is the kind essential to proletarian revolutionaries. It must not be divorced from revolutionary practice or from the actual revolutionary movements of the laboring masses, and especially of the proletarian masses. Comrade Mao Tse-tung has said:

> Discover the truth through practice; and again through practice verify and develop the truth. Start from perceptual knowledge and actively develop it into rational knowledge; then start from rational knowledge and actively guide revolutionary practice to change both the subjective and the objective world. Practice, knowledge, again practice, and again knowledge. This form repeats itself in endless cycles, and with each cycle the content of practice and knowledge rises to a higher level. Such is the whole of the dialectical materialist theory of knowledge, and such is the dialectical materialist theory of the unity of knowing and doing.

Our Party members should temper themselves and intensify their self-cultivation not only in the hardships, difficulties and reverses of revolutionary practice, but also in the course of smooth, successful, and victorious revolutionary practice. Some members of our Party cannot withstand the plaudits of success and victory; they let victories turn their heads, become brazen, arrogant, and bureaucratic and may even vacillate, degenerate, and become corrupted, completely losing their original revolutionary quality. Individual instances of this kind are not uncommon among our Party members. The existence of such a phenomenon in the Party calls for our comrades' sharp attention.

In past ages, before proletarian revolutionaries appeared on the scene, practically all revolutionaries became corrupted and degenerated with the achievement of victory. They lost their original revolutionary spirit and became obstacles to the further development of the revolution. In the past hundred years of China's history, or to speak of more recent times, in the past fifty years, we have seen that many bourgeois and petty-bourgeois revolutionaries became corrupted and degenerated after gaining some success and climbing to power. This was determined by the class basis of revolutionaries in the past and by the nature of earlier revolutions. Before the Great October Socialist Revolution in Russia, all revolutions throughout history invariably ended in the supersession of the rule of one exploiting class by that of another. Thus, once they themselves became the ruling class, these revolutionaries lost their revolutionary quality and turned around to oppress the exploited masses; this was an inexorable law.

But such can never be the case with the proletarian revolution and with the Communist Party. The proletarian revolution is a revolution to abolish all exploitation, oppression, and classes. The Communist Party represents the proletariat which is itself exploited but does not exploit others, and it can therefore carry the Revolution through to the end, finally abolish all exploitation and sweep away all the corruption and rottenness in human society. The proletariat is able to build a strictly organized and disciplined party and set up a centralized and at the same time democratic state apparatus; and through the Party and this state apparatus, it is able to lead the masses of the people in waging unrelenting struggle against all corruption and rottenness and in ceaselessly weeding out of the Party and the state organs all those elements that have become corrupt and degenerate (whatever high office they may hold), thereby preserving the purity of the Party and the state apparatus. This outstanding feature of the proletarian revolution and of the proletarian revolutionary party did not and could not exist in earlier revolutions and revolutionary parties. Members of our Party must be clear on this point, and—particularly when the Revolution is successful and victorious and when they themselves enjoy the ever greater confidence and support of the masses—they must sharpen their vigilance, intensify their self-cultivation in proletarian ideology and always preserve their pure proletarian revolutionary character so that they will not fall into the rut of earlier revolutionaries who degenerated in the hour of success.

Tempering and self-cultivation in revolutionary practice and tempering and self-cultivation in proletarian ideology are important for every Communist, especially after the seizure of political power. The Communist Party did not drop from heaven but was born out of Chinese society. Every member of the Communist Party has come from this society, is living in it today, and is constantly exposed to all its evils. It is not surprising then that Communists, whether they are of proletarian or non-proletarian origin and whether they are old or new members of the Party, should carry with them to a greater or lesser extent the thinking and habits of the old society. In order to preserve our purity as vanguard fighters of the proletariat and to enhance our revolutionary quality and working ability, it is essential for every Communist to work hard to temper and cultivate himself in every respect. . . .

### A Party Member's Personal Interests Must Be Unconditionally Subordinated to the Interests of the Party

Personal interests must be subordinated to the Party's interests, the interests of the local Party organization to those of the entire Party, the interests of the part to those of the whole, and temporary to long-term interests. This is a Marxist-Leninist principle which must be followed by every Communist.

A Communist must be clear about the correct relationship between personal and Party interests.

The Communist Party is the political party of the proletariat and has no interests of its own other than those of the emancipation of the proletariat. The final emancipation of the proletariat will also inevitably be the final emancipation of all mankind. Unless the proletariat emancipates all working people and all nations—unless it emancipates mankind as a whole—it cannot fully emancipate itself. The cause of the emancipation of the proletariat is identical with and inseparable from the cause of the emancipation of all working people, all oppressed nations, and all mankind. Therefore, the interests of the Communist Party are the emancipation of the proletariat and of all mankind, are communism and social progress. When a Party member's personal interests are subordinated to those of the Party, they are subordinated to the interests of the emancipation of the class and the nation, and those of communism and social progress.

Comrade Mao Tse-tung has said:

At no time and in no circumstances should a Communist place his personal interests first; he should subordinate them to the interests of the nation and of the masses of the people. Hence, selfishness, slacking, corruption, striving for the limelight, etc., are most contemptible, while selflessness, working with all one's energy, wholehearted devotion to public duty, and quiet hard work are the qualities that command respect.

The test of a Party member's loyalty to the Party, the Revolution, and the cause of Communism is whether or not he can subordinate his personal interests absolutely and unconditionally to the interests of the Party, whatever the circumstances.

At all times and on all questions, a Party member should give first consideration to the interests of the Party as a whole, and put them in the forefront and place personal matters and interests second. The supremacy of the Party's interests is the highest principle that must govern the thinking and actions of the members of our Party. In accordance with this principle, every Party member must completely identify his personal interests with those of the Party both in his thinking and in his actions. He must be able to yield to the interests of the Party without any hesitation or reluctance and sacrifice his personal interests whenever the two are at variance. Unhesitating readiness to sacrifice personal interests, and even one's life, for the Party and the proletariat and for the emancipation of the nation and of all mankind—this is one expression of what we usually describe as "Party spirit," "Party sense" or "sense of organization." It is the highest expression of Communist morality, of the principled nature of the party of the proletariat, and of the purest proletarian class consciousness.

Members of our Party should not have personal aims which are independent of the Party's interests. Their personal aims must harmonize with the Party's interests. If the aim they set themselves is to study Marxist-Leninist theory, to develop their ability in work, to establish revolutionary organizations, and to lead the masses in successful revolutionary struggles—if their aim is to do more for the Party—then this personal aim harmonizes with the interests of the Party. The Party needs many such members and cadres. Apart from this aim, Party members should have no independent personal motives such as attaining position or fame, or playing the individual hero, otherwise they will depart from the interests of the Party and may even become careerists within the Party. . . .

## 12. Thought Reform: The Cultural Perspectives

*Robert Jay Lifton*

Where did the Chinese Communists learn their reform skills? How did they get to be such master psychologists?

These are questions I have frequently been asked, and as often as not the questioner has in mind a theory of his own: the Chinese have studied Freud or individual psychology, or Kurt Lewin on group dynamics, or Pavlov on conditioned reflexes. The first two of these theories (Freud and Lewin) are products of a cultural and professional ethnocentrism among Western psychiatrists and social scientists; actually, neither Freud nor Lewin has had much influence in China or Russia. The Pavlovian theory is more generally held. It is based on a chain of associations that goes something like this: Pavlov—Russian scientist— supported by Soviet regime—Soviets use his theory of conditioned reflex for propaganda purposes—they taught his techniques to the Chinese — result, thought reform. But there is no convincing evidence that thought reform developed this way. It is true that academic psychology in Communist China does follow the Soviet lead in emphasizing Pavlovian theory, but academic psychologists apparently have had nothing to do with thought reform. And even in the Soviet Union, according to an American authority, there has been nothing to indicate that psychiatrists or psychologists have shaped confession or indoctrination techniques, or even that Pavlovian theory has been an important model for

Reprinted from Robert Jay Lifton, *Thought Reform and the Psychology of Totalism, A Study of "Brain-Washing" in China* (New York: W. W. Norton, 1961), pp. 388–98, by permission of the author and publisher. Copyright © 1961 by Robert Jay Lifton.

propaganda approaches.[1] In all three of these theories there is the twentieth-century tendency to single out the scientific specialist both as the fountain of all knowledge and the perpetrator of all evil. Moreover, all of them neglect the two great historical forces which shaped thought reform: Chinese culture and Russian Communism.

The Russian Communist contribution to thought reform is immediately apparent in much of the content and many of the forms of the process: the allegedly scientific Marxist-Leninist doctrine; the stress upon criticism, self-criticism, and confession as features of "ideological struggle"; the organizational techniques of "democratic centralism"; the combination of utopian imagery and iron discipline; the demands for purity of belief and absolute obedience; and the practice of informing upon others in the service of the Party. Certainly, many of the pressures used to extract confessions in penal thought reform closely resemble techniques used by the Russians during the great Soviet purge trials of the late 1930's: the irresistible demand for an admission of criminal guilt, however distorted or false, and the prolonged interrogations, physical pressures, and incriminating suggestions used to obtain it.[2] Eastern European Communist nations have employed similar confession methods, for instance, in the widely publicized cases of Cardinal Mindszenty, William Oatis, and Robert Vogeler.

Russian Communist influences are also responsible for thought reform's immense stress upon sin and evil, and for its continual manipulation of feelings of guilt within all who take part in the program. Such a focus upon sin and guilt has never been prominent in traditional Chinese culture. These Soviet Russian contributions are in turn derived from the many cultural influences which fed modern Communism: the Judeo-Christian religious tradition, the utopian secular ideologies of the eighteenth century, mystical elements of German romanticism, and the authoritarian excesses of traditional Russian and Byzantine culture, including the heritage of the Russian Orthodox church.

But after acknowledging these Russian and Western debts, we must still ask why it was the Chinese who developed thought reform. Other Communist countries have, to be sure, used elaborate propaganda tech-

---

[1]Raymond A. Bauer, "Brainwashing: Psychology or Demonology?", *Journal of Social Issues* (1957) 13:41–47. See also, by the same author, *The New Man in Soviet Psychology*, Cambridge, Harvard University Press, 1952.

[2]These trials are discussed in Nathan Leites and Elsa Bernaut, *Ritual of Liquidation*, Glencoe, Ill., The Free Press, 1954. They were fictionalized, with great psychological accuracy, by Arthur Koestler in the novel, *Darkness at Noon*, New York, Macmillan, 1941. Both of these books deal with the special ethos of the "old Bolshevik." F. Beck and W. Godin, *Russian Purge and the Extraction of Confession*, New York, Viking Press, 1951, conveys vividly the experiences within a Soviet prison of outsiders caught up in the great purge.

niques and various psychological pressures, but never with thought reform's meticulous organization, its depth of psychological probing, or its national scale. Nowhere else has there been such a mass output of energy directed toward changing people. In Russia confessions have generally been associated with the purge — the "ritual of liquidation"; in China, confession has been the vehicle for individual re-education. What is the source of this special *reform* emphasis?

Communist leaders reveal the source in some of their thought reform writings. Liu Shao-chi, for instance, in "How to be a Good Communist" enjoins Party neophytes to pursue diligently their "self-cultivation." And he quotes as an example the experience and the words of none other than Confucius himself:

> At fifteen, I had my mind bent on learning. At thirty, I stood firm. At forty, I had no doubts. At fifty, I knew the decree of Heaven. At sixty, my ear was an obedient organ for the reception of truth. At seventy, I could follow my heart's desire, without transgressing what was right.

Liu also makes reference to the Confucian disciple who said: "I reflect on myself three times a day," and to the Book of Odes which suggests that one cultivate oneself "as a lapidary cuts and files, carves and polishes." He refers to the Confucian principles expressed in the following quotation from *The Great Learning:*

> The ancients who wished to illustrate illustrious virtue throughout the kingdom first ordered well their own states. Wishing to order well their own states, they first regulated their families. Wishing to regulate their families, they first cultivated their persons. Wishing to cultivate their persons, they first rectified their hearts. Wishing to rectify their hearts, they first sought to be sincere in their thoughts. Wishing to be sincere in their thoughts, they first extended to the utmost, their knowledge. . . . from the Son of Heaven down to the mass of the people, all must consider the cultivation of the person the root of everything besides.[3]

These principles echo in the thought reform program, although Liu does of course emphasize the Communists' needs to stress materialism rather than classical "idealism," and to achieve their self-cultivation not through passive meditation but rather by means of active participation in the Communist movement.

Yet the concept of self-cultivation is distinctly Confucian, as is Liu's injunction to Communist cadres that each "watch himself when alone."

---

[3]*The Great Learning*, in *The Four Books*, translated by James Legge, London, Perkins, 310–313. All subsequent references to Confucian writings are to this translation.

Liu and other Communist theorists may refer to these traditional principles in order to introduce the alien words of Marx, Lenin, and Stalin in a familiar idiom: but this Confucian idiom does have deep emotional meaning even for anti-Confucian reformers, and it is this lingering Confucian spirit which has caused the Chinese Communists to make an ideological fetish of moralistic personal re-education.

Similarly, the Confucian principle of "rectification of names" (which according to the Sage was the first and most important task for a new ruler) has important bearing upon thought reform's approach to the reshaping of identity. In both cases, "rectification" means changing not the "name" or category of man, but rather changing the man himself until he fits that category — the Confucian or Communist ideology, of course, being the arbiter of proper standards. This principle is expressed in Confucius' demand, "let the ruler be ruler, the minister be minister; let the father be father and the son, son," and in the Communist demand that the intellectual be the "progressive" or "proletarian" intellectual or the "good Communist." For Confucianism shares with Communism the assumption that men can and should remake themselves, first as part of a process of changing their environment, and then as a means of adapting themselves to their environment. Both systems always involve a subtle interplay between role and identity: one first learns the more or less formal requirements for thought and behavior, and only much later becomes in his essence the thing aspired to. This is called achieving complete "sincerity."

And in Confucianism, just as in thought reform, the ideal of sincerity is made almost sacred:

> Sincerity is the way of heaven. The attainment of sincerity is the way of men. He who possesses sincerity is he who, without an effort, hits what is right, and apprehends without the exercise of thought; — he is the sage who naturally embodies the *right* way. He who attains to sincerity is he who chooses what is good and firmly holds it fast.[4]

This Confucian (and later neo-Confucian) notion of sincerity depends very much upon the principle of harmony: harmony within, permitting one to act correctly in an automatic fashion, and harmony without, enabling one to find his proper behavior in relationship to other men. To be sincere, in traditional China, meant to possess an inner urge toward fulfilling one's obligations, including both the desire and the means for conforming to the filial ideology. Only the sincere man could give full

---

[4]*The Doctrine of the Mean*, Legge, 394.

expression to his nature, possess genuine self-knowledge, exact a beneficial influence upon others, and achieve a complete union (both organic and mystical) with Heaven and Earth. Thought reform is a way to achieve such sincerity in relationship to Communist doctrine. As in Confucianism, it is finding the correct path; as in neo-Confucianism it is combining knowledge and action. And the man who is truly sincere, like his Confucian and neo-Confucian counterparts, is said to possess superhuman powers.[5]

These traditional Chinese themes could be expressed in thought reform only because they were also consistent with Marxist-Leninist principles. And this double fit has enabled the Chinese Communists to pursue them so energetically. Marxist-Leninist writings, for instance, are replete with references to personal reform; a similar Chinese cultural tradition has enabled Chinese Communists to be good Marxists. Communist practice in any country requires role-playing and identity change; but the Chinese bring to this a more concrete and explicit — not to say diligent — emphasis. In the matter of sincerity, Leninists too stress uniting theory and practice; but it is thought reform's combination of Marxist-Leninist (including Christian and Russian) with Confucian influences that has produced the bizarre extremes described in this book: for when the Eastern notion of The Way was combined with the Western ideal of credal purity, sincerity came to mean nothing short of absolute submission.

It is impossible to document all the ways in which traditional Chinese and Russian Communist styles come together in thought reform, but a few of the more important convergences are worth listing. We have already noted the great sweep of both Confucianism and Communism; both cover all aspects of human existence in their stress upon loyalty and orthodoxy. In addition, both have a tradition of benevolent leadership by a small élite, within a strongly authoritarian framework. They also share an emphasis upon the responsibility of the individual person to the larger human group, upon his impotence when he stands alone, and upon the dangers of deviant individual initiative. In both there is the conviction that human nature is essentially good, although the extent to which both seek to control human behavior makes one wonder whether their advocates really believe this. The Russian Communist reliance upon emotionally charged slogans has an analogue in the traditional Chinese style of thinking in wholes rather than in parts, of using proverbs and metaphor

---

[5]See David S. Nivison, "Communist Ethics and Chinese Tradition," *The Journal of Asian Studies* (1956) 16:51–74; and the same author's "The Problem of 'Knowledge' and 'Action' in Chinese Thought since Wang Yang-ming," *Studies in Chinese Thought*, 112–145.

to envelop a subject emotionally as well as intellectually.[6] There is some similarity (along with a good deal of difference) between the Soviet Communist dualism of the dialectic and the traditional Chinese dualism of *Yin* and *Yang*.[7] The traditional blood brotherhood of Chinese rebel bands and secret societies resembles Communism's sense of cloak-and-dagger intimacy and moral mission. The Soviet Communist stress upon personal confession (the main source of this ethic for thought reform) had some relationship to the traditional Chinese practice of requiring local officials to accept blame for such things as natural catastrophes and to "confess" that their own unworthiness may have been responsible. And in the prison setting, Russian Communist pressures to confess (themselves apparently derived from practices of the Tsarist *Okhrána*) come together with a traditional Chinese custom of requiring a prisoner to confess his crime before being judged, while granting the judge considerable latitude in the methods he could employ to extract this confession.[8]

How did this blending of cultural styles occur? The extensive thought reform program which the Communists had ready at the moment of the takeover was obviously the product of years of preparation. I was fortunate in being able to discuss this question in some detail with Mr. Chang Kuo-t'ao, one of the leading figures of the early Chinese Communist movement until his defection in 1938. According to Mr. Chang, the Communists began to employ systematic, if crude, reform techniques as early as the late 1920's. Communist leaders commanding small and relatively isolated military units began to devote much attention to the problem of winning over captured enemy soldiers and groups among the general population. Their task was complicated by the difference among their prospective converts: peasants, opium-smoking bandits, disgruntled conscripts in the Kuomintang armies, old-time Kuomintang supporters, uninvolved bystanders, and idealistic intellectuals. They first utilized international Communist principles, learned from Soviet contacts, dealing with "agitation and propaganda." But very soon they began to modify these and develop their own programs derived from their special Chinese environment.

---

[6]Lily Abegg, *The Mind of East Asia*, Thames and Hudson, London, 1952, Chapters 2 and 3.

[7]In terms of logic, both follow the "law of opposition," rather than the traditional Western pattern of the "law of identity"; but their difference lies in the Chinese emphasis upon "adjustment" in relationship to this opposition, in contrast to the Marxist emphasis upon "struggle." See Chang Tung-sun, "A Chinese Philosopher's Theory of Knowledge," *The Yenching Journal of Social Studies* (Peking, 1939), 1:155–189.

[8]Robert Van Gulik, *The Chinese Bell Murders*, New York, Harper Bros., 1958, 258.

They approached uneducated peasants on a simple colloquial level. Ordinary enemy soldiers were first treated with unexpected "leniency"; then they were encouraged to vent all of their grievances against such past authorities as landlords and officers (to "vomit bitter water"); next they were taught to recognize the social evils of the Kuomintang regime as the source of their suffering ("dig the bitter roots"). The soldier was then offered an opportunity to remain with the Communists — to join the "one heart movement" to combat Chiang Kai-shek and create a new China; or he was given the option of returning to his home village as a person ostensibly sympathetic to the Communist cause. As in later programs, participants quickly became themselves active reformers: peasant soldier captives showing signs of "progress" were encouraged to circulate among new arrivals with similar class backgrounds, and help in the latter's "vomiting" and "root digging" by recounting their own happy reform experiences.

With captured officers the Communists employed more sophisticated and individualized approaches. After separating the officer from his men, they would assign to him some of their most articulate and persuasive spokesmen, and then subject him to prolonged analytic discussions of his personal relationship to the Chinese Civil War. Struggle procedures were used upon the most recalcitrant, and those known to be responsible for the death of large numbers of Communists were often executed; but there was an attempt to win converts whenever possible.

Chang emphasized that, with both officers and men, the Communists were consciously aware of the importance of setting an impressive personal example in their own dedication, discipline, and personal morality. After their first more or less experimental military efforts, the Communists proceeded in twenty years of trial-and-error improvement to make their program increasingly efficient. They extended the reform efforts to Japanese prisoners captured during the thirties and later to American prisoners captured during the Korean war. But their main efforts were concentrated upon their own countrymen during the phases of the long Chinese Civil War, so that by the time of the takeover, they had learned how to apply them quickly and effectively to entire armies of prisoners.

The reform program specifically for intellectuals, as opposed to that for military captives, was developed by Communist groups operating in the outlying border areas during the Yenan period (1935-45). In order to absorb the large numbers of intellectuals, sympathetic but inexperienced (at least in the ways of revolution), who made their way to these Communist areas, a number of special training centers were set up. Those in the Yenan area of northwest China — the Anti-Japanese University,

North Shensi Academy, and Marx Lenin Institute (later renamed Lu Hsun Academy) — gave rise to the thought reform programs for intellectuals we have been studying.

Here, as elsewhere, the Communists started with a prescribed Russian Communist model: the Yenan institutions were set up as replicas of Sun Yat-sen University in Moscow, an early training center for Chinese Communist intellectuals. This model was then adapted to their own revolutionary style. The Communists improvised as they went along, hardly following a precise scientific "methodology." Indeed, Mr. Chang felt that an important factor in the introspective *hsüeh hsi*, or group study process, was the isolation of many of these early institutions, and the lack of qualified teachers and textbooks, so that much of the subject matter studied had to come from the participants. This comment, while far from a full explanation, does make clear how important the external circumstances were under which the Chinese Communist revolutionary movement synthesized Chinese and Russian Communist themes. Nor were Chinese improvisations always approved by Russian advisors. Chang mentioned that on several occasions Chinese Communist leaders were criticized for being "too much influenced by Confucian ethics." Yet this moral and psychological emphasis seemed to come naturally to them; according to Chang, they were "good psychiatrists." And although the Nationalists made similar efforts to "reform" Communists and Communist sympathizers in special "repentance camps," their efforts were (according to Chang and many other observers) much more clumsy and much less effective.

Perhaps the crucial step in the development of the Communist reform program for intellectuals was the *Cheng Feng* (literally, reform of work style or "spirit") conducted within the Communist Party, mostly in Yenan, from 1942 to 1944. (Mr. Chang was no longer with the Communists then; my information here is based on written studies and on the impressions of my subjects.) During this campaign, the basic techniques, as well as the widely-circulated *Reform Documents* from which I have been quoting, were evolved.

At the time of the *Cheng Feng*, the Party faced the problem of the threat of unorthodoxy among its heterogeneous recruits, and especially among its intellectuals; it was also confronted with the task of Sinifying a Marxist movement whose ideology had heretofore been entirely foreign, and it had to invigorate intraparty morale.[9] It is of the greatest significance that the Chinese Communists solved these problems through personal confession and re-education, that these forms of introspection

---

[9]Boyd Compton (trans.), *Mao's China: Party Reform Documents 1942–44*, Seattle, University of Washington Press, 1952, xv-lii; C. Brandt, B. Schwartz, and J. Fairbank, *A Documentary History of Chinese Communism*, Cambridge, Mass., Harvard University Press 1951, 372–375.

were used to produce within each Party member the desired blend of Leninism and Chineseness, along with a sense of personal revitalization. From this movement the Chinese Communists' own ideology (mostly in the form of "the thought of Mao Tse-tung") emerged; the importance of this ideology lay not in any brilliant originality, but more in its organizational and psychological usefulness, and in the renewed sense of group identity to which both the campaign and its ideology contributed. After the *Cheng Feng*, the die was cast; just a year later, "the documents of the movement had become Party dogma, and the reform process had become a continuing organizational mechanism."[10] Even such a brief outline of the history of thought reform confirms what I have already suggested—that the reformers evolved their psychological skills by combining elements from their cultural heritage and their own revolutionary needs with principles of Russian Communist theory and practice.

One other important factor in the Chinese heritage also played a part in the evolution of reform techniques: human-centered psychological skills. No other civilization has paid so much attention to the conduct of human relationships. An American anthropologist has claimed that "Chinese culture has developed inter-personal relationships to the level of an exquisite and superb art."[11] It is not that Chinese are incapable of obtuseness and insensitivity; but a particular kind of psychological mindedness has long been cultivated in Chinese life. The Chinese family, with its characteristically complicated inner maneuvering, has been an excellent psychological training ground: in order to be "proper," Chinese children have had to learn to be aware of the emotional currents in their milieu. And this personal emphasis has extended from the family into the rest of Chinese life: whether performing official duties or seeking personal objectives, Chinese have always put great stress on exerting influence upon the people involved—and there is only a fine line between influence and manipulation. These human-centered skills have been carefully nurtured over centuries, and emphasized at the expense of technical achievements (even the gods play psychological games).[12] In this sense, thought reform is the modern totalitarian expression of a national genius.

But the spirit in which these human-centered skills are used in thought reform is certainly alien to the traditional Chinese cultural style. In the past, the stress was upon individual and social harmony; the ideal was

[10]Compton, *op. cit.*, xlvi.

[11]Weston LaBarre, "Some Observations on Character Structure in the Orient: II. The Chinese," *Psychiatry* (1946) 9:215–237.

[12]Once during a discussion with one of my Chinese interpreters, I mentioned the interest of American psychiatrists in the subject of interpersonal relations. His immediate reply was "What else *is* there?" In this interest in what goes on between people, there is something Sullivanian in every Chinese. See also John H. Weakland, "The Organization of Action in Chinese Culture," *Psychiatry* (1950) 13:361–370.

that of quiet wisdom and unbroken calm. The *chuntze,* or superior Confucian man, was expected to be contemplative and reserved in his bearing: "the master was mild yet dignified; majestic and yet not fierce; respectful and yet easy."[13] Above all, he was to be in full control of his emotions: "if a man be under the influence of passion, he will be incorrect in his conduct."[14] For the withdrawn Taoist sage, restraint was equally essential: "So long as I love calm, the people will be right themselves."[15] Such a cultural stress upon moderation, balance, and harmony—which we may call a *cult of restraint*—insures a certain degree of preservation of self.

Thought reform has the opposite ethos, a *cult of enthusiasm* (*enthusiasm* in the religious meaning of rapturous and excessive emotional experience),[16] with a demand for total self-surrender. It is true that thought reform implies a promise of a return to restraint, and of an attainment of relaxed perfection some time in the mystical Communist future, just as Confucius claimed that these ideals had existed during an equally mystical past or "golden age"—but enthusiasm and restraint, once established, are not always so easily controlled.

The spirit of enthusiasm seems to have entered China from the outside, carried in on the ideological wings of Western nationalism, international Communism, and displaced Judeo-Christian demands for ecstatic repentance and histrionic remorse. Yet the intellectual descendants of the staid literati have shown themselves to be quite capable of orgiastic display—in fact, more capable of it than their counterparts in Western Communist countries who have a much greater tradition for this type of emotional excess. Apparently any culture, or any person within a culture, is potentially capable of either restraint or enthusiasm, depending upon individual and collective historical experience. Those cultures in which restraint has been long maintained (again we may use the analogy of the individual) are likely to experience an explosive emotional breakthrough once the restraint begins to loosen; and the new enthusiasm becomes the means of putting to rout what remains of the older pattern.

Just as thought reform draws upon psychological skills of both traditional China and Western Communism, it also brings out the inquisitional tendencies of both worlds. From each of the two great cultural

---

[13]*Confucian Analects,* Legge, 94.

[14]*The Great Learning,* Legge, 326.

[15]*The Texts of Taoism,* translated by James Legge, London, 1891, Part I, 70.

[16]Ronald Knox, *Enthusiasm,* London, Oxford University Press, 1950. See also William Sargent, *Battle for the Mind,* New York, Doubleday, 1957, for a different approach to relating thought reform to ecstatic religious practice.

streams, it stresses what is most illiberal. Inquisitorial dogmatism, skill-ful human-centered manipulation, and ecstatic enthusiasm combine within it to produce an awesome quality. Consequently, relatively mod-erate Russian and Eastern European Communists look warily at China's totalism (and Stalinism); and people like Bishop Barker (something of an enthusiast himself) envy the energies and the psychological clever-ness of a respected rival. For in breaking out of its traditional cult of restraint, while retaining its old penchant for the reordering of human emotions, China has created a cult of enthusiasm of such proportions that it must startle even the most immoderate Christian or Communist visionary.

# ELITES, GROUPS, POLITICAL PARTICIPATION, AND COMMUNICATION

The study of political elites has been one of the important foci of political analysis in recent years. By examining the social background, the paths of recruitment, and the skills of the political elites of various nations, valuable information has been obtained on the nature, scope, and directions of change of many political systems. According to system-functional theorists in political science, political recruitment is an important function through which members of particular subcultures of the society are inducted into important specialized roles in the political system.

Among the variables which have an effect on the pattern of elite recruitment in a political system, the most important is probably political ideology. In almost every political system, the criteria and the institutional arrangement of elite recruitment are affected by the prevailing ideology of that system. In Imperial China, the myth of the "rule of the virtuous" was sustained by a strict examination in which knowledge of the Confucianist moral code was the base for selection. In Western democratic systems, the myth of "rule of, by, and for the people" is reinforced by a recruiting system based mainly upon free, competitive election of government officials. In communist systems, the Marxist idea that "the working class should rule" constitutes a major criterion in the selection of party cadres and members of the state bureaucracy.

Few political systems, however, have been able to apply fully the criteria set down by the political ideology in the actual process of recruitment. In this regard, the communist political systems, including Communist China, are no exceptions. Despite the vehement attack against the traditional ruling classes of China—the landlords, scholar-officials, and merchants—a large percentage of early communist leaders in China were sons of members of these groups. Most of the Chinese Communist party elite were highly educated and had studied in foreign countries such as France, Russia, and Japan.

In many aspects, the social background of the Chinese Communists has been very similar to that of the Kuomintang party elite. Members of both parties' elites come from the upper socioeconomic bracket of the social strata of the Chinese society, representing more of the traditional ruling elements of China than the illiterate mass of poor peasants and laborers. Thus it may be concluded that so far as social background of the Chinese communist elite is concerned, there has been a serious discrepancy between ideology and reality.

Although the actual background of the Chinese communist leaders does not correspond to the ideology of proletarian rule, there has been a noticeable increase of individuals of lower socioeconomic origin in the Chinese Communist party elite since 1949. This is especially true at the local and provincial level. Apparently the communist leaders have made a genuine effort to meet the criteria set down by the communist ideology. In doing so, however, the Chinese Communists have been facing a serious dilemma, i.e., the problem of "redness versus expertise."

To put it in very simple terms, the problem of "redness versus expertise" refers to a dilemma faced by the Chinese Communists in recruiting individuals to fill important political roles; that is, whether they should emphasize the length of association with the Chinese communist movement, belief in Marxism-Maoism, and loyalty toward the Chinese communist party of the prospective candidates; or whether they should stress education, specialization, and personal ability in the recruiting processes. In short, it is a matter of which should come first: political reliability or individual capacity? The dilemma lies in the fact that individuals with intense loyalty toward the party do not always possess the skills needed to perform a task, while on the other hand, those having specialized skills may not have a strong attachment to communist ideology.

When the Chinese Communists were still a group of guerrilla fighters with a very simple organizational structure, the problem of "redness versus expertise" was not a serious one. Devotion to the cause of communist revolution was unquestionably the most important criterion for recruitment into the party elite. But after the Chinese Communists had established a permanent governmental structure on the Chinese mainland, differentiation of and specialization in various types of jobs relating to the governing process became inevitable. As time went on, the Chinese

Communists found themselves more and more in need of the services of the experts with special skills, such as the natural scientists, the engineers, medical doctors, and administrators to carry out their ambitious goals in the social, economic, and technological development of China.

To Mao Tse-tung, recruitment of individuals with specialized skills, yet with limited experience with the communist movement and little devotion to the fulfillment of communist ideology, constituted a serious threat to the maintenance of ideological purity of the system, which threatened a "restoration of the capitalist rule" in China. Nevertheless, for other Chinese communist leaders with a more pragmatic outlook toward nation-building, such as Liu Shao-chi and his followers, it was necessary and beneficial for the system to recruit and to rely upon the specialists so long as they were under effective supervision of the communist party.

Conflicts between these two schools of thought came into the open during the Great Leap Forward period. It broke out again more recently during the Great Proletarian Cultural Revolution. One of the major crimes of the "revisionist traitors" led by Liu, according to supporters of Mao, was the encouragement or tolerance of the bureaucratization of party structure which has allegedly led to the deterioration of, and deviation from, the "mass line" of Marxism-Leninism. It was therefore necessary for the masses to rebel and to destroy the bureaucratized and degenerated party organizations.

In their struggles against each other, both the followers of Mao and those of Liu appealed to various social and political groups for support. The students were the first group to be involved. Although the students constituted the forefront of the cultural revolution, they were not the only group whose support was sought by the dueling factions. In one way or another, peasants, workers, bureaucrats, party officials, and the military were all involved in the struggle. Violent conflicts occurred between the students and party officials and bureaucrats as well as between the students and workers. Blood was also shed when different factions within these groups struggled for control over the organizations of their respective groups. Throughout the Cultural Revolution, the peasants and the people's Liberation Army generally remained out of the conflict. The peasants resisted the disturbance created by the activities of the students in the countryside. For fear of affecting agricultural production, this kind of resistance from the peasants was tolerated by the authorities in Peking.

As for the Army, their role in the Cultural Revolution was to maintain an adequate level of control of the conflicts between various groups. Yet, by the sheer fact that they had a near monopoly on the means of violence, they were able to exploit the situation to greatly expand their influence in the political arena, taking advantage of the decline of the party-bureaucratic elite. As a result, Lin Pao, a spokesman of the military elite, became the Vice-Chairman of the Party and heir-apparent of Mao Tse-tung. A great number of other military leaders were also able to gain membership in the Central Committee of the Chinese Communist Party in the Ninth Party Congress.[1]

Throughout the turmoils in Communist China, one thing has become apparent—Mao Tse-tung has never given up the "mass line" as the single most important strategy for controlling the country and expanding his personal authority among the Chinese people. Time and again, he broke the regular routines of the functioning of the communist system and tried to achieve what he believed to be the goals of communism in China. The "Hsia-fang (go to the lower ranks) movement," "The Great Leap Forward," and the "Great Cultural Revolution" are but some of the more notable examples. Through these movements, Mao was able to generate a level of political participation rarely exceeded by other political systems, past or present. Mao also was able to establish a communication apparatus which was so penetrating and omnipotent that it rivaled those developed by Nazi Germany in the 1930s. The result was a political system which closely approaches the stereotype of a "mass society."[2]

But mass society is not without its problems. With the continuous state of "crisis politics," and with the destruction of all intermediate groups between the elite and mass, there is the danger of having the mobilized members of the political system refuse to retreat from the extremist movements originally initiated by the leaders of a totalitarian system themselves. The result could either be a release of overcharged enthusiasm in suicidal wars against other political systems, or a turnabout of the direction of attack of the masses against the system itself.

---

[1]For a list of new members in CCP Politbueo, see appendix one.

[2]Cf. William Kornhauser, *The Politics of Mass Society* (New York: The Free Press, 1959).

# VI
# The Political Elites


## 13. The Social Characteristics of Chinese
## Party Elites

### Robert C. North and Ithiel de Sola Pool

For the greater part of three decades the Kuomintang and the Communist Party have fought each other with all the bitterness of a class war. On the surface the rival interests involved in this conflict seem clear, for here are all the superficial characteristics of a struggle between masses on the one hand and classes on the other. The policies of the Kuomintang and the way of life of its leaders have again and again lent credence to the picture that its enemies propagate, namely, that the Kuomintang is simply a landlord clique. Moreover, the utilization by the Communists of peasant discontent, together with their insistent profession of a Marxian ideology, has created the strong impression that their movement is a movement of the masses. But an examination of membership data raises the question: how far does the character of Kuomintang and Communist leaderships support or contradict these preconceptions?

It is certainly true that Communist Party leaders differ from Kuomintang leaders in social and economic background. Indeed, the leaders of the right, center, and left within the Kuomintang also differ in these respects. But before considering these differences, we ought to take into account a number of rather striking similarities. For despite all the detailed differences, we find ourselves forced to concede that a major portion of the elite of both movements came from quite similar high social strata, and responded to similar Western and native influences during their years of growth and education.

Reprinted from Robert C. North and Ithiel de Sola Pool, "Kuomintang and Chinese Communist Elites," in Harold D. Lasswell and Daniel Lerner, eds., *World Revolutionary Elites: Studies in Coercive Ideological Movements* (Cambridge, Mass.: M.I.T. Press, 1965), pp. 376–87, by permission of The M.I.T. Press, Cambridge, Massachusetts.

## Common Characteristics

In both parties, the leaders have been drawn most frequently from a relatively thin upper layer of the Chinese population. In both parties these men were often the sons of landlords, merchants, scholars, or officials, and they usually came from parts of China where Western influence had first penetrated and where the penetration itself was most vigorous. All of them had higher educations, and most of them had studied abroad. The leaders of both parties, despite a relatively high status in private life, showed a reluctance or perhaps an inability to establish private careers. The majority were alienated intellectuals, men and women whose Western educations isolated them from the main currents of Chinese society. In the chaos of modern China, these persons became full-time professional politicians specializing, for the most part, in military violence or in party administration. Whichever party they belonged to, Communist or Kuomintang, they differed from the Imperial elite, which we described at the beginning of this study (cf. pp. 319-328) in that they were drawn from a much wider circle. It is true that the sons of scholar-officials continued to enter politics—and very successfully—but more noteworthy, perhaps, is the fact that recent revolutions in China have brought forward the sons of the *nouveau-riche* compradors, other business classes of coastal cities, the sons of landlords, and recently, even, the sons of wealthy peasants. On the other hand, despite plebeian protestations of the Communists, the relatively smaller mass of proletarians have continued to enjoy only limited access to the elite.

The basic similarity in social origins of the largest portion of both Kuomintang and Communist leaders is emphasized by figures on their fathers' occupations and social status (cf. Table 1). The 1945 Central Committee of the Chinese Communist Party contained eight sons of landlords, two sons of merchants, and one son of an official. Against these eleven men of high social status, there were also eleven sons of peasants, of whom six were wealthy peasants. There were also two sons of workers. And the composition of the Politburos from the beginning until 1945 was similar. For these ten leading bodies (including, as in all our Politburo tabulations, the First Congress in 1921 and the "ruling clique" of August 1927) contained, in all, five sons of landlords, two sons of merchants, four sons of officials, and one son of a scholar. Against these twelve men of upper-class origin, there were ten sons of peasants, of whom six were wealthy peasants. There were also two sons of workers. Thus we find about half of the Communist elite drawn from upper-class and middle-class families, and another quarter from the prosperous section of the peasantry.

**TABLE 1**
**Father's General Occupation**

| | Kuomintang CEC's 1924, 1926, 1929 | | Communist Politburo | | Communist CEC 1945 | |
|---|---|---|---|---|---|---|
| | No. | % | No. | % | No. | % |
| Wealthy landlord or scholar-landlord | 10 | 21.3 | 3 | 12.5 | 7 | 23.3 |
| Scholar-official | 3 | 6.4 | 4 | 16.7 | 3 | 10.0 |
| Scholar | 3 | 6.4 | 1 | 4.2 | | |
| Merchant-scholar or wealthy merchant | 7 | 14.9 | | | 1 | 3.3 |
| Upper class, indeterminate | — | — | — | — | 1 | 3.3 |
| | | 48.9 | | 33.3 | | 40.0 |
| Other landlords | 4 | 8.5 | 2 | 8.3 | 1 | 3.3 |
| Other merchants | 15 | 31.9 | 2 | 8.3 | 1 | 3.3 |
| Professional revolutionary | 2 | 4.3 | — | | | |
| Wealthy peasant | — | | 6 | 25.0 | 6 | 20.0 |
| Middle class, indeterminate | — | | — | | 3 | 10.0 |
| | | 44.7 | | 41.7 | | 36.7 |
| Other peasants | 3 | 6.4 | 4 | 16.7 | 5 | 16.7 |
| Workers | — | | 2 | 8.3 | 2 | 6.7 |
| | | 6.4 | | 25.0 | | 23.3 |
| Total known | 47 | | 24 | | 30 | |
| Don't know | 23 | | 18 | | 14 | |
| Total | 70 | 100.0 | 42 | 100.0 | 44 | 100.0 |

In the Kuomintang elite all but three of the fifty-one members of the first three Central Executive Committees whose occupations we know were upper or upper-middle class. Aside from these three (all sons of medium or poor peasants), there were fourteen sons of landlords, three sons of officials, and three sons of scholars whose occupations we cannot further identify. In addition there were twenty-two sons of merchants who, although middle-class, enjoyed less prestige than would merchants in the West.

In this and some later tabulations we include only the first three committees because the informants who provided the data had enjoyed close contacts with earlier, rather than later, members of the Kuomintang.

It is not easy to secure material concerning the social and economic status of Chinese leaders. They have been traditionally reticent about revealing information on the source or level of an individual's income. Moreover, many leaders, especially among the Communists, lived underground for many years at a stretch, assumed revolutionary names, and covered their movements with utmost caution. Nevertheless, a few broad conclusions can be drawn from the reports of Western businessmen, missionaries, and travelers who succeeded in establishing close personal relationships with influential Chinese. Such informants have materially aided this study by reporting on Chinese leaders they have known, providing information on source of income and occupation of father, and offering subjective ratings of financial status. The resultant data on Politburo members have been relatively full, owing to the fact that members of this body are few in number.

On the basis of these data it is clear that both elites have drawn heavily from limited circles of the population. There may be support for the impression that the social origins of Kuomintang leaders were higher than those of the Communist elite, but three cautions must be observed. Note first that many of the middle-class Kuomintang leaders were merchants' sons, of limited social status. Second, note the large number of "don't knows." For about one third of the members of the first three Kuomintang CEC's and for over 40 per cent of the CCP Politburo members we do not know the fathers' occupations, and there is no ground for assuming that these men had the same backgrounds as did those whose status we know. Usually, leaders whose origins are unreported in biographical sources are those of lower-class origins; prominent parents are likely to be known. This generalization certainly applies to Kuomintang leaders, for their ideology is such that they normally prefer to publicize reputable origins. With Communists, however, the pattern is quite the opposite, both in China and elsewhere. They prefer to hide upper-class backgrounds and to feature or even fabricate proletarian origins.

Thus, among the Communist "don't knows" there is probably a higher proportion of upper-class parents than among Kuomintang "don't knows." This is one reason for suspecting that the relatively small difference in the social status of fathers of Kuomintang and Communist leaders is not significant.

A third factor also tends to emphasize the fallacy in assuming that Kuomintang leaders came from higher social backgrounds than Communist leaders. Since our data ran out after 1929, we used Kuomintang CEC's only through that date. If we limit our examination to Politburos appointed up to and through that same year, we find that only three of the Politburo members were sons of peasants and that only one member was the son of a proletarian, while eight were sons of upper-class or middle-class parents. Clearly, then, *in both the Communist Party and the Kuomintang* the plebeians entered later. This is not to deny the possibility, of course, that there may have been a genuine difference between parties in the number of plebeians. The point to be noted, however, is that both parties drew heavily on the upper ranks of the population for recruiting their leadership (cf. Table 2).

TABLE 2
Status of Fathers of Politburocrats
(Showing Entry of Plebeians after 1927)

| Politburo | Upper and Middle | Lower |
|---|---|---|
| 1921 | 4 | —— |
| April 1, 1927 | 4 | 1 |
| July 13, 1927 | 4 | —— |
| August 1927 | 3 | 2 |
| 1928 | 3 | 2 |
| January 1931 | 4 | 1 |
| June 1931 | 4 | —— |
| 1934 | 7 | 3 |
| 1937 | 5 | 2 |
| 1945 | 9 | 3 |

It is not at all surprising that the Kuomintang included in its leadership a number of persons born to wealth and prominence, but it is worthy of note that among Communist leaders, too, we find, for example, three fathers who were wealthy landlords, one who was both a wealthy landlord and an official, and in addition to these, three men who listed their fathers respectively as statesmen, Mandarin, and provincial governor.

So, too, members of the two elites are similar in the educations they have received. Aside from two members of the Politburo and one other member of the 1945 Central Committee of the Communist Party, all the elite members on whom we have information enjoyed a higher education (cf. Table 3). Some went to universities in China or abroad, some had classical Chinese educations, some attended military schools; but, with the rarest exceptions, they were trained men. Despite the revolutionary character of recent Chinese history, political involvement did not truncate their education as it did in the cases of so many Soviet and Nazi leaders. Despite the poverty of China and the very small proportion of families able to afford higher educations for their sons, leaders simply did not arise by making their own way through channels outside normal educational patterns.

**TABLE 3**
**Education of Elite Members**

|                          | Kuomintang CEC | Politburo |
| ------------------------ | -------------- | --------- |
| No higher education      | 2              | 2         |
| Chinese education only   | 123            | 2         |
| Foreign education        | 136            | 25        |
| Total known              | 261            | 29        |
| Don't know               | 26             | 13        |
| Total                    | 287            | 42        |

Once touched by an education, the hitherto fatalistic peasant boy who has looked forward to a life no different from that of his ancestors gradually achieves a consciousness of progress and an awareness of the good things that technology can provide. And whatever his local background, the man trained as an engineer is impressed by the fact that in his own country the number of factories, and hence of jobs, is limited, with foreign "imperialists" filling most of the top positions of a technical nature. Soon he concludes that, born in the West, he would have a job and command a factory, but that, short of a thoroughgoing revolution, he can look forward to no better prospect than unemployment in his own backward country. So, too, the man trained as a banker or chemist feels a similar lack of opportunities in his field. So it is for these and innumerable other reasons, some of them exceedingly subtle and complex, that students tended to provide the leadership for both Communist and "bourgeois nationalist" movements.

The impact of Western thought upon such people has provided fuel for anti-Western movements. This impact on both Kuomintang and Communist elites is indicated by figures showing the geographical distribution of institutions that have provided elite members with their educations. (cf. Table 4) In the case of each elite the majority have been educated abroad. Out of 261 Kuomintang CEC members whose educational careers we know, 138 were educated abroad, and out of 29 Politburo Members whose educational careers we know, 25 were educated abroad. Rus-

**TABLE 4**
**Universities Attended***

| | Kuomintang CEC | | Politburo | | Communist CEC | |
|---|---|---|---|---|---|---|
| | No. | % | No. | % | No. | % |
| Chinese university | 86 | 33.0 ⎤ | 13 | 44.8 | 23 | 54.8 |
| Chinese military school | 88 | 33.7 ⎬ China | | | | |
| Chinese classical education | 15 | 5.7 ⎦ | | | | |
| Japanese university | 42 | 16.1 ⎤ Japan | | | | |
| Japanese military school | 26 | 10.0 ⎦ | 5 | 17.2 | 5 | 11.9 |
| United States | 40 | 15.3 | 2 | 6.9 | 1 | 2.4 |
| France | 13 | 5.0 | 6 | 20.7 | 12 | 28.6 |
| Germany | 13 | 5.0 | 2 | 6.9 | 3 | 7.1 |
| Great Britain | 15 | 5.7 | | | | |
| Belgium | 2 | .8 | | | 1 | 2.4 |
| Soviet Union | 14 | 5.4 | 20 | 69.0 | 25 | 59.5 |
| Other | 3 | 1.1 | | | | |
| None | 2 | .8 | 2 | 6.9 | 3 | 7.1 |
| Total known | 261 | 100.0 | 29 | 100.0 | 42 | 100.0 |
| Don't know | 26 | | 13 | | 2 | |
| Total | 287 | | 42 | | 44 | |

*This table is nonadditive, since the same individual may go to several universities.

sian training accounts for the higher proportion of foreign training among Communist leaders, but if we leave Russian education aside, we still find that 38 per cent of the leaders of the Communist Party had been trained in advanced capitalist countries.

As awareness of the role of students might lead us to expect, the leaders of both the Kuomintang and the Communist Party were young. Not only did these revolutionists join the movements in their student years, but they rose to positions of leadership fast. Both elites tended to age over the years, but until 1945 no Kuomintang CEC had an average age of over forty-five, and no Politburo had an average age over forty (cf. Table 5 for full figures). From 1921 through 1931 in fact the average of each Politburo ranged between twenty-seven and thirty-three, while that of each Kuomintang CEC was either forty-two or forty-three. After that the average ages of both groups started to rise till in 1945 it was forty-nine for the Politburo and fifty-one for Kuomintang CEC. Even these figures are a little low as compared to those for other elites reported in the Hoover Institute Studies, but they are in the usual range. It is only in times of revolutionary change, however, that one finds an elite whose average age is in the thirties or early forties. In a stable society political leadership is likely to be a function of achieved status. "Notables" (to use Max Weber's term) from other fields of life are recruited to give prestige and standing to the political machines. A political elite of notables is necessarily of reasonable advanced age—usually averaging in

**TABLE 5**
**Average Ages of Party Elites**

| Party Elites | Average Age of Members |
|---|---|
| *Kuomintang CEC* | |
| 1924 | 43.3 |
| 1926 | 44.6 |
| 1929 | 43.8 |
| 1931 | 42.6 |
| 1935 | 48.9 |
| 1945 | 54.9 |
| *Communist Politburo* | |
| 1921 | 29.4 |
| April 1927 | 33.4 |
| July 1927 | 27.3 |
| August 1927 | 29.0 |
| 1928 | 30.0 |
| January 1931 | 29.0 |
| June 1931 | 28.4 |
| 1934 | 35.2 |
| 1937 | 39.3 |
| 1945 | 48.9 |
| *Communist Party CC* | |
| 1945 | 46.8 |

the fifties. An exception is the elite in an aristocratic society where a person may be a notable from birth. In such a society, however, he is likely to remain in politics till a fairly advanced age; so the average, although lower than in a democratic society where all must work their way up, is still apt to be well up in the forties. Modern China has certainly not been an aristocratic society in that sense. Neither the Kuomintang nor Communist elites have been born to their positions. They have achieved them by effort, but in the revolutionary conditions that existed they could achieve them rapidly by going directly into politics without establishing an outside reputation first.

As a matter of fact, we find that few of the leaders of either Kuomintang or Communist Party had extrapolitical careers. The overwhelming majority were professional politicians who devoted most of their adult life to party struggles. This we expect to be true of a Communist Politburo. A Politburo member must conform to the Leninist ideal of a professional revolutionary. Following the Politburo pattern in this respect, the 1945 Central Committee of the Communist Party consisted also of professional revolutionists. (cf. Table 6) Forty-five per cent made their careers in party organization; another 39 per cent made careers of the army. Thus 84 per cent were professionally engaged in revolutionary struggle. Most of the remainder of the CC were presented as coming directly from the work benches. Any large Communist body is required to have some such proletarians as showpieces. How many of them in reality were primarily laborers and how many were primarily Communist functionaries is impossible to say, but even if all five were primarily laborers they were still but a sprinkling. In addition to these persons there were one educator and one journalist, and no persons with any other major career. Thus the Central Committee, like the Politburo, was clearly a body of professional party activists.

TABLE 6
Careers of 1945 Communist Central Committee Members

|  | Number | Percentage |
| --- | --- | --- |
| Party organization and administration | 20 | 45.5 |
| Military | 17 | 38.6 |
| Labor | 5 | 11.4 |
| Education | 1 | 2.3 |
| Journalism | 1 | 2.3 |
| Total | 44 | 100.0 |

What is surprising is that the situation was almost identical in the Kuomintang, as shown in Table 7. Fifty-one per cent of all Kuomintang CEC members made their careers in party organization. Thirty-six per cent had military careers. Thus 86 per cent were, above all, professional politicians. Of the residue we do not know the occupation of 3 per cent; 6 per cent were in education, and 3 per cent in journalism. This leaves a total of 2 per cent, or six individuals, whose primary career was in any part of the entire remaining range of businesses and professions.

TABLE 7
Careers of Kuomintang Executive Committeemen (in Percentages)

|  | 1924 | 1926 | 1929 | 1931 | 1935 | All CEC 1945 Members |
|---|---|---|---|---|---|---|
| Organization and administration | 58.3 | 55.6 | 55.6 | 63.9 | 45.4 | 50.2 | 50.5 |
| Military | 25.0 | 25.0 | 41.7 | 33.3 | 42.9 | 37.2 | 35.9 |
| Education | 4.2 | 5.6 | — | — | 5.0 | 6.3 | 5.6 |
| Journalism | 4.2 | 2.8 | 2.8 | 2.8 | 2.5 | 3.1 | 2.8 |
| Other | 4.2 | 2.8 | — | — | 1.7 | 1.8 | 2.1 |
| Don't know | 4.2 | 8.3 | — | — | 2.5 | 1.4 | 3.1 |
| Total | 100.0 | 100.0 | 100.0 | 100.0 | 100.0 | 100.0 | 100.0 |
| (Number) | (24) | (36) | (36) | (36) | (119) | (223) | (287) |

This does not imply that only these six individuals made money by business or professional activities. With the widespread corruption in the Kuomintang it goes without saying that a career in politics or the army was likely to be associated with extensive private business activity; but we may still distinguish between businessmen, few in number, who got into politics on the side, and the many politicians who seized upon the number of business opportunities that were made available by the very nature of a given political office. The picture may be clarified by looking at the main sources of income of the members of the first three CEC's. (Such data are not available for the other bodies in our sample.) The members of the CEC whose main income was from their party or government or army salary were outnumbered by more than two to one by those whose main source of income was nonpolitical (see Table 8). Yet, as we have seen, their main career activity was political. Most of their time was spent on politics, but most of their income came from private enterprise. This apparent contradiction is explained when we realize that very few (six out of forty-three) had a major source of private *earned* income. Most of those with large private incomes lived on rent or interest. Their business dealings were not such as to conflict with the active pursuit of politics as a career.

Thus we see that the leaders of both the Kuomintang and the Communist Party were young, Western-educated, and Western-oriented professional politicians. (The term "Western" includes the U.S.S.R.) They were without roots in the normal enterprises of civilian life. Alienated and relatively hopeless of their futures in traditional careers, many

**TABLE 8**
**Sources of Income of Kuomintang CEC Members, 1924-1929**

| | | |
|---|---|---|
| Salaries | | |
| Government | 2 | |
| Party | 8 | |
| Military | 4 | |
| Total political | | 14 |
| Land rents | 12 | |
| Interest on | | |
| investments | 11 | |
| Business | | |
| Large | — | |
| Medium | 2 | |
| Small | 1 | |
| Professional fees | 2 | |
| Wages | 1 | |
| Total private | | 29 |
| Don't know | | 27 |
| Total | | 70 |

found in revolutionary party politics new and appealing opportunities. Turning to the muddied waters of politics, they made their careers in the three main channels of political activity: organization, violence, and symbol manipulation.

In China the symbol specialists were relatively few as compared to their role in some other states. In the Hoover Institute Elite Studies we have found that the balance between these three kinds of political specialist is a highly significant index to the nature of the society. Among the stable cabinets in the West, for example, we found the role of army officers in Germany far greater than in Britain, France, or the United States, although even in Germany they were only about one third as frequent as in either party in China. In the Politburo we found that in the course of time the specialists on organization and domestic violence supplanted the specialists on persuasion. In the Nazi elite we found that the specialists on organization dominated the specialists on persuasion. In the French Third Republic, however, the reverse was true: there the specialist on persuasion had the leading role.

In China, revolutionary chaos gave the specialist on violence (i.e., the military careerist) a larger role than anywhere else so far studied, and the role of the symbol specialists (lawyers, journalists, teachers) was considerably reduced. In both the Communist Party and the Kuomintang, persons with organizational and administrative careers consituted about half of the elite. Next most numerous were persons with military careers, who made up about one third and increased in number with the passage of time. The residue is small, but it is interesting to note that among all the remaining professions education and journalism were the only ones sufficiently frequent to be of note. The non-persuasive professions—e.g., engineering—were completely out. Lawyers, the dominant symbol specialists in stable Western elites, were here completely absent. But then lawyers have never played the same role in China as in the West. The few ideologizers included in the elite were those who could make a mass appeal.

The dominance of men of violence is an index of the intensity of revolutionary struggles. The young elite in China, seeing no stable future for themselves in the backward economy of their homeland, were expressing a self-confirming expectation. In their hopelessness of stable careers they turned to violent politics, which, in fact, ultimately destroyed the chances for stable evolution. The career opportunities outside of politics gradually narrowed, and the standard of living gradually declined. This, plus the shattering of the old society, plus the slow spread of Western stimuli, and thus political activity, to ever wider circles of the population, gradually lowered the social status of the political elite.

# 14. The Urban Bureaucratic Elite in Communist China

## Ying-mao Kau

Let me begin the examination of the bureaucratic elite of Wuhan* by pointing out some of its more obvious characteristics. The upper part of Figure 1 shows three major sociological attributes of the 157 senior bureaucrats in the samples used for this study.[1] First, males were predominant; second, the elite members were recruited primarily from men with extensive backgrounds; and, third, the overwhelming majority of the members of the elite sampled were "outsiders," in the sense that they were not born and brought up in Wuhan.[2]

It is not surprising to find only a small proportion of women leaders in any Chinese group. In Wuhan 10 out of 156 senior bureaucrats tabulated (6 per cent) were women. However, the data will become more meaningful if put in historical and comparative perspective. In premodern China, even during the Ch'ing and Nationalist periods, virtually no women ever occupied any top bureaucratic offices (even at the local levels).[3] Under Communist rule it is now common to find women mak-

---

*Formed by the three cities of Hankow, Han-Yang, and Wu-ch'ang in Hupeh Province. Wuhan is the largest industrial city in central China. [Ed.]

[1]The total number tabulated for each category includes only those on whom information on that specific category is available, so the figure is ordinarily smaller than the total sample of 157.

[2]Many other major socioeconomic characteristics of the elite, such as age, geographical mobility, associational membership, and so on, which are obviously important for any elite analysis, are not discussed here, mainly because the data available are so fragmentary that no meaningful statistical analysis can be made.

[3]See. for example, various studies of traditional China's bureaucratic mobility, in Johanna M. Menzel (ed.), *The Chinese Civil Service: Career Open to Talent?* (Boston: Heath, 1963).

Reprinted from Ying-mao Kau, "The Urban Bureaucratic Elite in Communist China: A Case Study of Wuhan, 1949-65," in A. Doak Barnett, ed., *Chinese Communist Politics in Action* (Seattle: University of Washington Press, 1969), pp. 226–38, 252–65, by permission of the author and publisher.

ing up about 10 per cent of the cadres.[4] This suggests that women in China are now playing a more active and significant role in politics than

## FIGURE 1
### Socio-Political Characteristics of the Elite

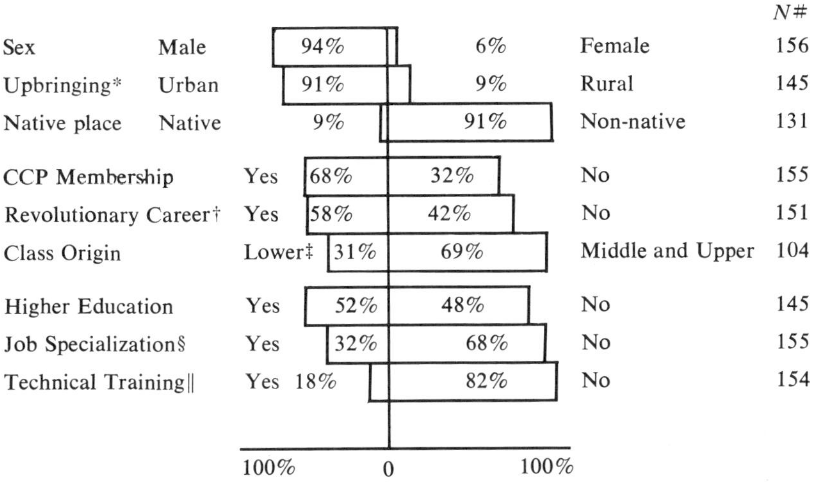

N#

| | | | | | |
|---|---|---|---|---|---|
| Sex | Male | 94% | 6% | Female | 156 |
| Upbringing* | Urban | 91% | 9% | Rural | 145 |
| Native place | Native | 9% | 91% | Non-native | 131 |
| CCP Membership | Yes | 68% | 32% | No | 155 |
| Revolutionary Career† | Yes | 58% | 42% | No | 151 |
| Class Origin | Lower‡ | 31% | 69% | Middle and Upper | 104 |
| Higher Education | Yes | 52% | 48% | No | 145 |
| Job Specialization§ | Yes | 32% | 68% | No | 155 |
| Technical Training‖ | Yes | 18% | 82% | No | 154 |

100%        0        100%

*Upbringing refers to the urban or rural setting in which leaders spent their youth.
†Those who joined the Communist movement before 1945 are considered to have had a revolutionary career.
‡Lower class origin includes both worker and peasant family origins.
§Eight years or more of consistent service in one functional area of political or administrative activity is considered to represent job specialization for the purpose of this study.
‖Technical training refers to technical training at, or equivalent to, the college level.
#Numbers for each category include only those on whom information is available. Thus they are smaller than the total of 157 in the sample.

they were before. Although half of the women cadres in the sample specialized in work related mainly to women's organizations, some did occupy other posts of power and importance. Hsia Chih-yü, for instance, once held the directorship of the powerful Organization Department of the Municipal Party Committee; and Ling Sha for a time headed the Bureau of Culture and Education of the municipal government.[5]

The pattern of elite socialization experiences in terms of an urban-rural dichotomy reveals that an extremely high proportion of the sample (90.8 per cent of 145) had grown up in an urban environment—

---

[4]For example, women constituted roughly 10 per cent of the entire Chinese Communist Party membership in 1956.

[5]In the mid-1950's Hsia was first promoted to the post of assistant to the minister of light industry and later named deputy minister of food industry. Ling became president of Peking Normal College in 1955.

they had received either their secondary or higher education in the cities or had worked in the cities for an extensive period of time during their youth.[6] The data thus imply that some degree of "urbanism" was virtually a prerequisite for an urban bureaucratic career. In view of the fact that Wuhan is one of the most advanced urban centers in China, this finding should not surprise us. What appear to be important are its implications. The data call our attention to the popular hypothesis about the "ruralism" of the Chinese Communist leadership. It is often contended that the Communist leaders were strongly rural oriented because of their protracted rural-based guerrilla activities and thus were not "qualified" to rule the cities. There was, however, little sign of "ruralism" in the top bureaucratic elite of Wuhan.[7]

Urban living provides education, skills, and know-how which have now become the key prerequisites for entering highly professionalized bureaucracies in the cities. A lack of urban socialization experiences in youth would therefore tend to block access to modern education and training, and, as a result, would block access to professional urban careers. The finding that only an extremely small proportion of the members of Wuhan's bureaucratic elite (9 per cent) were drawn from the rural sector would appear to support this hypothesis.

The current Chinese Communist policy of discouraging rural youth from seeking schooling and careers in the cities, effective since the latter 1950's, will undoubtedly have a very far-reaching impact by limiting the opportunities of rural youth for advancement and mobility.[8] Furthermore, as will be shown below, since the urban bureaucracy constitutes a major channel of upward mobility to provincial and national leadership, a rural cadre will clearly have far less chance than his urban counterpart in competing for the upper rungs of the bureaucratic ladder.

Another important finding revealed in Figure 1 is that only 12 out of a total of 131 leading cadres whose native places (*chi kuan*) could be ascertained were natives of Wuhan in the sense that their parents or ancestors had established permanent residence there before their birth. If six "democratic personages" and two intellectuals are subtracted from

---

[6]For comparison with urban-rural mobility in the Ch'ing period, see P'an Kuang-tan and Fei Hsiao-t'ung, "City and Village: The Inequality of Opportunity," in Menzel (ed.), *Chinese Civil Service*, pp. 9–21.

[7]In his study of Tangshan city, John W. Lewis has found that the Communists recruited continuously from the urban area during the thirties and forties. Lewis, "Political Aspects of Mobility."

[8]See, for example, the directive of the State Council of December 18, 1957, banning unauthorized migration to the cities. *Kuang-ming Jih-pao* (Bright Daily), December 19, 1957.

this tiny group of twelve native cadres, there were only four natives in the entire sample who would be ranked as real political and administrative leaders in Wuhan. Among these four, none had advanced beyond the level of bureau head. In contrast, there were many cases where "outsiders" were assigned from other cities or provinces directly to bureaucratic posts in Wuhan, including such formally elective offices as the mayorality or deputy mayoralities.[9] Being a native of Wuhan, it appeared, in no way constituted an asset in placement or advancement in the city.

This finding inevitably raises the question as to why so few ranking native cadres of Wuhan were assigned to work in their own native place. The sociological maxim that urban population, particularly that of a rapidly industrializing and urbanizing city, is generally composed of immigrant "outsiders" may provide a partial explanation. But perhaps a more pertinent reason can be found in the deep-rooted traditions of China's bureaucratic system. Beginning in imperial days, officials were in principle not to be assigned to posts in their own native *hsien* or provinces. Briefly, two reasons may have accounted for this. In the first place, working in his home district, an official could more easily be induced to commit bureaucratically undesirable acts because of extensive kin ties and personal obligations. Secondly, the imperial court was ever suspicious that a mandarin could more easily conspire against the imperial authorities in his own home base, because of these same ties and obligations.[10] Although there is no way to test empirically the extent to which "traditionalism" still exists in China today, such reasoning, in slightly altered forms, appears to influence Communist behavior.[11]

The small number of senior cadres recruited from the native populace, however, was compensated for by a larger number of leaders (29 per cent) drawn from the surrounding province of Hupeh. Approximately one-third of the non-native members of the Wuhan elite were from China's coastal provinces; and another third came from the northern and central regions. Only three were from the border areas and vast regions of the West. These data reveal that the overwhelming majority of those belonging to the elite were recruited from the coastal provinces

---

[9]One of the most striking cases was the transfer of Hsüeh Pu-jo in 1961 from the Honan Provincial Government to the post of deputy mayor of Wuhan, which was formally an elective office.

[10]Cf. Ch'ü T'ung-tsu, *Local Government in China under the Ch'ing* (Cambridge, Mass.: Harvard University Press, 1962), pp. 14–35.

[11]The periodic campaigns against localism, sectarianism, and "independent kingdoms" serve as a clear indication of the leadership's suspicion of local power. See Oksenberg, "Paths to Leadership," pp. 3–4.

and Central China, the most modernized sector of the nation.[12] This pattern of distribution presents a striking parallel with our earlier finding on the "urbanism" of the elite. Both findings tend to validate the conclusion that senior members of the bureaucratic elite in China were recruited predominantly from individuals who were from the urban sector or had urban backgrounds.

The middle section of Figure 1 sets forth the characteristics of the 157 leaders sampled in terms of three variables which may be considered political in nature. The data indicate that, first of all, the elite was strongly dominated by Chinese Communist Party (CCP) members (68 per cent); next, over one-half of the members of the elite (58 per cent) were career revolutionists in the sense that they had made their career in the Communist movement before the beginning of the Third Revolutionary Civil War (1946-49); and, finally, a minority of 30 per cent of the 104 leaders in the sample on whom information on family backgrounds was available were from worker or peasant families.

The characteristics deserve further comment. The dominance of Communist Party members was, of course, to be expected. What appeared to be significant, however, was the predominance of old cadres among the 108 Party members in the sample (see Table 1). Ranked according to the standard periods of Party seniority, over 82 per cent of the members of the elite who were Party members had Party seniority at least equivalent to "liberation cadre" level (1946-49). Only 15 per cent joined the Party during the Third Revolutionary Civil War (1946-49), while only three leaders (roughly 3 per cent of the 108 Party cadres) were men who joined the Party after 1949. In the early 1950's, all Party members who held posts at the level of bureau chief and above were at least "Yenan cadres." These and similar findings lend strong support to the long-standing impression of scholars in the field that Party seniority was indeed a major criterion in assignment and advancement to high-ranking posts in the government.[13]

The proportion of non-Communists within the bureaucratic elite (32 per cent), small as it might appear to be, highlights some important features of Wuhan's political recruitment. In the first place, the data suggest that the monopoly of high ranking posts by the CCP was not so complete as generally believed. At least until 1965, non-Communists

---

[12]John W. Lewis has pointed out the significance of the influence of the level of socioeconomic development on Chinese politics in his article, "The Study of Chinese Political Culture," *World Politics*, XVIII, No. 3 (April, 1966), 503-24.

[13]In his case study of the bureaucracy of a ministry, A. Doak Barnett has also found that Party seniority played a significant role in assignment. See Barnett, "Social Stratification and Aspects of Personnel Management in the Chinese Communist Bureaucracy," *China Quarterly*, No. 28 (October-December, 1966), pp. 23-25.

## TABLE 1
### Party Members Among Members of the Elite Ranked by Party Seniority

| Party Seniority | N | Percentage |
|---|---|---|
| Long March cadres (1921–35) | 30 | 27.8% |
| Yenan cadres (1935–40) | 43 | 39.8% |
| Anti-Japanese cadres (1941–45) | 16 | 14.8% |
| Liberation cadres (1946–49) | 16 | 14.8% |
| Post-Liberation cadres (1949) | 3 | 2.8% |
| Total | 108 | 100.0% |

with talent and ambition could find their way into senior bureaucratic positions in Wuhan. It is clear that talent was needed by the bureaucracy for efficiency just as much as political loyalty was desired by the Party for control. Secondly, the distribution of the forty-nine non-Communist members of the elite by political affiliation reveals that just over two-thirds of them (67.3 per cent) belonged to "democratic parties," while the remaining one-third were non-party affiliated personages (*wu-tang-p'ai jen-shih*). Leaving aside for the moment the political impotence of the "democratic parties" and the uncertain role of mass organizations in Communist China, the fact remains that "democratic" leaders and non-party-affiliated persons were normally selected from various important occupational groups and professional organizations to represent these groups and organizations. This suggests that "interest groups," whether in the form of mass organizations or "democratic parties," were not completely eliminated. They continued to play some roles, though highly circumscribed, in politics under Communist rule.

The mass organizations and "democratic parties" served as channels of political recruitment and were used as means for advancement by those highly trained professionals and formal social and business leaders who for one reason or another remained outside the Communist Party. As such, the mass organizations and "democratic parties" were among the few legitimate channels of mobility still open to non-Party leaders. Take Ch'en Ching-yü, for example. As a member of the national bourgeoisie, he apparently was not eligible for CCP membership. However,

## TABLE 2
### Distribution of Non-Communist Leaders

| Party Affiliation | N | Percentage |
|---|---|---|
| "Democratic party" leaders | 33 | 67.3% |
| Non-party affiliated leaders | 16 | 32.7% |
| Total | 49 | 100.0% |

being chairman of both the local Democratic Construction Association and the Federation of Industry and Commerce of Wuhan, he steadily ascended the ladder of the city's bureaucratic hierarchy and, finally, in 1957 was promoted to become deputy governor of Hupeh Province.

For others, the "democratic parties" and mass organizations served as a stepping stone into the CCP hierarchy. Yü Chin-t'ang and Yüan Wen were typical of these cases. Yü and Yüan originally belonged to the local Democratic Construction Association and the Revolutionary Committee of the Kuomintang, respectively. Their leadership among the intellectuals and apparent devotion to the new government seem to have won them membership in the CCP in the mid-fifties. They were subsequently elected to the Municipal Party Committee, in 1959, and were even put in charge of the Party's United Front Work Department and the city's Civil Affairs Bureau. In the light of cases such as these, it would be a mistake to dismiss entirely the political function of the "democratic parties" and mass organizations in China. (See also the discussion below on the contributions of functional expertise by the non-Party leaders.)

Another finding of considerable importance derived from the same middle section of Figure 1 discloses that slightly over two-thirds (69 per cent) of the 104 members of the elite tabulated for class background were from the middle and upper socioeconomic strata. Even within the group of leaders who were also CCP members, the proportion of those with middle- and upper-class origin still stood at 62 per cent.

In comparison with the situation during the Ch'ing and Kuomintang (KMT) periods, the data show that, under Communist rule, men of lower-class origin appear to have better access to elite status.[14] Yet, the data also demonstrate that the Communist recruitment system in Wuhan did not work as much as one might have expected in favor of cadres with lower-class background. In other words, the leadership of Wuhan was by no means drawn mainly from what Sigmund Neumann called the "marginal men" belonging to "marginal groups" of society.[15] Class origin, important as it may have been (particularly in the recruitment

---

[14]For the Ch'ing period, Robert M. Marsh has found that only 13.7 per cent of the officials listed in *T'ung Kuan Lu* were from the commoner families. See his article, "Formal Organization and Promotion in a Pre-Industrial Society," *American Sociological Review*, XXVI, No. 4 (August, 1961), 550. Robert C. North has shown that only 6 to 19 per cent of the members of the Central Executive Committee of the Kuomintang, during 1924–31, were of poor merchant and peasant origin. See Robert C. North, "Kuomintang and Chinese Communist Elites," in Lasswell and Lerner (ed.), *World Revolutionary Elites*, p. 453. See also Menzel (ed.), *Chinese Civil Service*, pp. 20–45.

[15]Sigmund Neumann, *Permanent Revolution* (2nd. ed.; New York: Praeger, 1965), p. 62.

of new cadres at lower levels in the post-1949 period), clearly did not carry as much weight as other political attributes, such as Party membership and seniority.

Drawing from the data in Figure 1 again, we can analyze (from the data in the lower section) the members of the elite in terms of whether they had higher education, job specialization, and technical training. These three variables were chosen as rough indicators of the elite's non-politically oriented achievement and expertise.

The data show slightly over half of the 145 members of the elite tabulated (52 per cent) had some education beyond the secondary school level. According to present-day Chinese standards, the top elite as a whole might be considered well educated.[16] In contrast to this better than average educational background, the Wuhan elite appears to have had a relatively low degree of job specialization, measured in terms of the length of uninterrupted service in one of the major functional areas of government administration. Only 32 per cent of the 155 bureaucrats tabulated, for example, had stayed in one of the regime's five main functional areas of work (namely, political and legal work, education and culture, industry and communications, finance and trade, and agriculture and forestry) for more than eight years.[17] Limited comparable data available on the senior bureaucrats of other countries would seem to support the impression, stated above,[18] that this suggests a relatively low degree of job specialization.

The last part of Figure 1 further indicates that the Wuhan elite as a whole was also poorly trained professionally and technically: only 18 per cent of the 154 tabulated had technical training at college level. This figure, together with earlier findings, strongly suggests that a large proportion of the Wuhan bureaucratic corps was composed of political "generalists" (as opposed to job-experienced or job-trained "specialists"),

---

[16]For example, of the ninety-seven Central Committee members of the CCP in 1958, seventy-three of them (74 per cent) appear to have received education at the college level, including training in military academies. Chao Kuo-chün, "Leadership in the Chinese Communist Party," *Annals of the American Academy of Political and Social Science*, CCCXXI (January, 1959), 47.

[17]The percentage would presumably have been different if we had had more complete information on the career history of every member of the elite covering the entire eighteen-year period under study.

[18]Studies of the federal bureaucrats of the United States government (GS-15 and above), for instance, show that approximately 70 to 85 per cent of the top bureaucrats have served in only one of the thirty-odd standard (organizational) fields throughout their entire government career, which normally has ranged from twenty to thirty years. It should be further noted that the functional fields as defined in the United States Civil Service are much more refined than the five to eight broad areas used in Communist China. Stanley, *The Higher Civil Service*, pp. 31–34, 137. John J. Corson and R. Shale Paul, *Men Near the Top* (Baltimore: The Johns Hopkins Press, 1966), pp. 116–18, 175–76.

a proportion larger than one would ordinarily expect in a highly modernized bureaucracy.[19]

This combination of a reasonably high level education with a relatively low level of professionalism is probably attributable to two major factors. First, the "higher education" which many of these Communist leaders received appears to have been primarily of the type offered by institutions such as the Anti-Japanese War College under the auspices of the CCP during World War II, or in higher Party schools in the post-1949 period, both of which were fundamentally designed for general political education and revolutionary training. Thus, even though on paper they appeared to be highly educated, they were not really technically trained. Second, the lack of an effective assignment and transfer system after the Communist takeover of the government apparently further reduced the opportunities available to bureaucrats to specialize and accumulate functional expertise (a fact which will be considered further in the discussion on the personnel transfer system, below).

## Distribution of Functional Expertise

The sociology of Wuhan's bureaucratic elite analyzed in the preceding section focuses primarily on the elite as a whole. This analysis tells us little, however, about differences between the Communist and non-Communist leadership elements in terms of their relative levels of technical expertise and job specialization.

Table 3 presents the distribution of Party and non-Party members of the elite by higher education, job specialization, and technical training. Although the data indicate that the highly educated were almost equally divided between the Party and non-Party groups (45 per cent to 55 per cent), the breakdown of leaders with job specialization stood clearly in favor of the non-Party group by approximately two to one (65 per cent to 35 per cent). What seemed most striking of all was the one-sided distribution of technical skills in favor of the non-Party group; in fact, virtually all professional skills (93 per cent) were supplied by this group. This finding strongly reinforces the speculation that the

---

[19]For comparable data available on the United States and Soviet elites, see Lowi, *At the Pleasure of the Mayor*; Stanley, *Higher Civil Service*; Hough, "In Whose Hands the Future?" For the elites of other countries, see, for example, Thom Kerstiens, *The New Elite in Asia and Africa* (New York: Praeger, 1966); Clement H. Moore, *Tunisia Since Independence* (Victoria, Australia: Longmans, 1965); Wendell Bell, *Jamaican Leaders* (Berkeley and Los Angeles: University of California Press, 1964); Robert A. Scalapino and Junnosuke Masume, *Parties and Politics in Contemporary Japan* (Berkeley and Los Angeles: University of California Press, 1962).

TABLE 3
Distribution of Functional Expertise Between Party and
Non-Party Groups

| Political Affiliation | TOTAL | | E+ | | S+ | | T+ | |
|---|---|---|---|---|---|---|---|---|
| | N | Percentage | N | Percentage | N | Percentage | N | Percentage |
| Party members | 106 | 68% | 34 | 45% | 17 | 35% | 2 | 7% |
| Non-Party members | 49 | 32% | 41 | 100% | 32 | 65% | 26 | 93% |
| Total | 155 | 100% | 75 | 100% | 49 | 100% | 28 | 100% |

E+ = Leaders with higher education.
S+ = Leaders with job specialization.
T+ = Leaders with technical training.

Communist members of the elite may have received higher level education without being professionally and technically trained. Table 3 also shows a slightly higher degree of job specialization among Party leaders, a finding which results from the number of cadres who started a specialized bureaucratic trade in the post-1949 period. These findings demonstrate clearly that in spite of the fact that there were twice as many Party cadres as non-Party cadres among the Wuhan elite, the latter as a whole disproportionately contributed the technical skills and expertise which the bureaucracy needed.

TABLE 4
Distribution of Functional Expertise Among Party
and Non-Party Members

| 106 PARTY MEMBERS | | | 49 NON-PARTY MEMBERS | | |
|---|---|---|---|---|---|
| P+ | N | Percentage of P+ | P− | N | Percentage of P− |
| P + E + | 34 | 32.0% | P − E + | 41 | 83.6% |
| P + S + | 17 | 16.0% | P − S + | 32 | 67.0% |
| P + T + | 2 | 1.8% | P − T + | 26 | 53.0% |

P+ = Party members.
P− = Non-Party members.
E+ = Leaders with higher education.
S+ = Leaders with job specialization.
T+ = Leaders with technical training.

Using the same set of data as shown in Table 3, Table 4 presents a different set of percentages to show the distribution of functional expertise between Party and non-Party leaders in each achievement category. The table indicates that non-Party bureaucrats as a group were clearly much better educated, specialized, and trained (84, 67, and 53 per cent for the non-Party elites in each category as opposed to 32, 16, and 2 per cent for the Communists). This finding is complementary with that in Table 3. The non-Party bureaucrats achieved greater technical expertise not only because a larger proportion of them were more professionally and technically trained but also because they served more consistently in one functional area for a longer period of time.

To shift the focus of analysis from the relative strength of technical expertise of the Party and non-Party groups to the question of recruitment criteria, a less obvious characteristic of Wuhan's bureaucratic system may be detected from the data in Table 4; the fact that the overwhelming majority of non-Party members of the elite were better educated, were more specialized, and had greater technical skill implies that they may have been recruited because of these technical qualifications.[20] In contrast, the fact that only a very small minority of the skilled and specialized leaders were Communist cadres would seem to suggest that most of the Party members may have been recruited for reasons other than their technical qualifications and competence. Political qualifications such as seniority, loyalty, and Party membership must have been the key factors that operated in their favor. Moreover, the data in Table 4 also show that as many as seventy-two Communist cadres in the sample (68 per cent) had none of the three technical achievement attributes. This means that the non-job-trained or non-job-experienced Communist cadres constituted a group far exceeding in numbers the total number of all non-Communist leaders in the sample. This pattern of distribution strongly suggests that political attributes as determinants of bureaucratic recruitment seemed to carry much greater weight than technical achievements. To state this finding differently, it seems clear that political criteria in general took priority over achievement criteria in recruitment. This appears to be particularly true in cases where conflict occurred between these two sets of criteria, and the leadership had to choose.

The dominance of political attributes was equally apparent in job assignments. Cross tabulation of the Party seniority of members of the elite and the types of jobs they held, as shown in Table 5, yields a relatively high contingency coefficient of 0.666, with the chi-square significance value and its corresponding probability standing at 63.006 and .001 respectively.[21] These figures suggest a fairly high degree of correlation between the two variables measured. In other words, with technical expertise held constant, the more political seniority a cadre possessed, the more likely he was to receive a post of political impor-

---

[20]This speculation, however, does not necessarily preclude other possible motivations of a political nature. As noted earlier, in the period immediately following the takeover, the Party recruited a considerable number of non-Party intellectuals and personages for united front purposes.

[21]A note on the meaning of Karl Pearson's contingency coefficient may be found below.

tance and power. In fact, the powerful and politically sensitive jobs, such as those in public security, personnel, and education, were virtually monopolized by cadres with high Party seniority, while non-Party officials were normally assigned to offices of lower political sensitivity and power, such as those in forestry, public health, and construction.

If we assume that the order of political sensitivity from high to low would be roughly equivalent to the order of technical complexity from low to high, the data in Table 5 also show that most non-Communist members of the elite held posts on a high technical level, while the Communists filled jobs of low technical orientation. This finding indicates that the non-Party leaders' higher level of technical competence

### TABLE 5
### Political Seniority and Job Assignment

| Political Sensitivity of Jobs | POLITICAL SENIORITY | | | | | | | |
|---|---|---|---|---|---|---|---|---|
| | Long March and Yenan Cadres | | Anti-Japanese and Liberation Cadres | | Non-Party Cadres | | Total | |
| | N | Percentage | N | Percentage | N | Percentage | N | Percentage |
| Highly sensitive | 54 | 75.0% | 21 | 60.0% | 7 | 16.3% | 82 | 54.7% |
| Sensitive | 18 | 25.0% | 12 | 34.3% | 15 | 34.9% | 45 | 30.0% |
| Not sensitive | 0 | 0.0 | 2 | 5.7% | 21 | 48.8% | 23 | 15.3% |
| Total | 72 | 100.0% | 35 | 100.0% | 43 | 100.0% | 150 | 100.0% |

Chi sq. = 63.006   NDF        = 4
CC        = 0.544    CC/max. CC = 0.666

may have played a part in their assignment to technical jobs. However, the fact that many Communist leaders in Wuhan who—on the basis of the available evidence—had no technical expertise or job-oriented skills were also found in jobs with a high technological orientation would seem to suggest that, in these cases, political considerations outweighed technical considerations. . . .[22]

## Changing Patterns of Elite Recruitment and Mobility

The profile of the bureaucratic elite of Wuhan analyzed in the preceding sections is derived primarily from the aggregate data, which covered the entire time span of sixteen years under study. This profile reveals

---

[22]It should be noted that using Party seniority as the indicator of political qualification alone may be questionable in some cases. A. Doak Barnett, for example, has pointed out in his study that Party seniority may suggest degrees of organizational skills and administrative ability. Barnett, "Social Stratification," p. 16.

some highly significant characteristics which, as expected, do not fully conform to the "ideal-type" modern bureaucracy that Max Weber conceptualizes. Although the Wuhan bureaucracy had recruited some men with needed talents and expertise, and showed some signs of professionalism, the structure and process of its recruitment and mobility were still under the strong influence of political priorities. The profile also shows that a relatively high rate of elite turnover and interorganizational transfer prevailed in this bureaucracy, and that the leadership has apparently not succeeded in developing a personnel system which could effectively build up a pool of professional manpower to expedite bureaucratic modernization. This over-all portrait, one should hasten to add, is basically "static" in nature. It does not convey the dynamics of its development or highlight the changes that have taken place and the direction in which this bureaucracy has been evolving.

In this section we shall attempt to examine the Wuhan bureaucracy from a time-series perspective, so that we can assess the major changes and trends of development since the Communist takeover. For this task, the Municipal People's Council may again serve as a convenient focus of analysis. Comparison of the membership composition of the MPC over time in terms of its members' major qualifications and institutional roles will highlight the changing patterns of recruitment and mobility. Moreover, changes in tenure and turnover rate of the MPC membership over time may be used to measure the trend of leadership continuity and professionalization.

Figure 2 presents the distribution of the major qualifications of MPC members elected during the five sessions of the MPC in the period from 1950 to 1961. The qualifications chosen for analysis here, as before, include Party membership, revolutionary career, and worker and peasant class origin — representing political attributes — on the one hand, and higher education, job specialization, and technical training—representing achievement attributes (of a nonpolitical nature) — on the other. Close examination of this graph reveals a very significant pattern of change over the years. The importance of political attributes appears to have declined consistently from 1949 through 1958, with a sharp drop in 1952. Though this trend of decline was slightly reversed in 1961, the gain was not significant. In contrast, the importance of achievement attributes showed a gradual over-all rise over time. This was particularly evident in the areas of job specialization and technical training. The level of education declined somewhat after 1955, yet, it should be noted, its 1961 percentage was not only still higher than that for 1950-52 but also at the top of all attributes. The significance of an increase in educational qualifications becomes more meaningful if considered in conjunction with

FIGURE 2
Political and Achievement Attitudes of Members of
the MPC, 1950–61
(in Percentage of the Total Members in Each Category)

Percentage

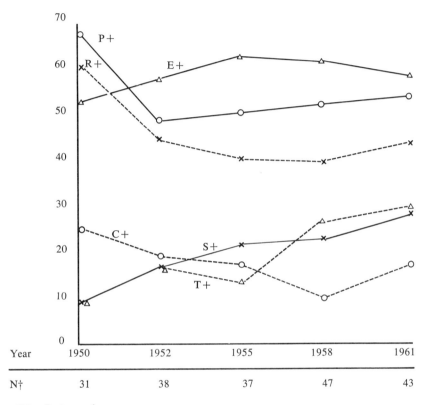

| Year | 1950 | 1952 | 1955 | 1958 | 1961 |
|------|------|------|------|------|------|
| N†   | 31   | 38   | 37   | 47   | 43   |

P+ = Party members.
R+ = Leaders with revolutionary career.
E+ = Leaders with higher education.
C+ = Leaders of worker and peasant class origin.
T+ = Leaders with technical training.
S+ = Leaders with job specialization.
    *Percentages represent the proportion of members in each attribute category to the total membership in each session. Since each member normally exhibits more than one attribute, and they are counted for each one, the combined total of percentages for each selected session exceeds 100 per cent.
    †The total number of MPC members in each session.

the decrease in the number of Party members and those with revolutionary careers. In 1950 there were more MPC members with Party membership (68 per cent) or revolutionary careers (61 per cent) than with higher education (55 per cent). This pattern was sharply reversed in 1952, however. The level of higher education reached its peak in 1955, at 65 per cent, well over the respective percentages of 41 per cent and 43 per cent for Party membership and revolutionary careers.

The contrast between the distribution pattern for 1950 and that for 1961 in each attribute category reveals that the political attributes, without exception, showed signs of decline, while all the achievement attributes emerged stronger. Though the degree of difference was by no means striking, the trend itself was highly significant. In the Weberian sense, this trend testified to some improvement of the professional quality of the bureaucracy during the years studied. More men with technical expertise, professional experience, and better educational background, instead of men with political qualifications only, were being recruited, though very slowly, into the senior bureaucratic positions in Wuhan.

Although the analysis of major qualifications of MPC members reveals some tendencies of the Weberian type, further examination of the composition of the MPC in terms of members' major political and social roles (or institutional identifications) fails to show the same trend. The MPC, as suggested earlier, brought together local leaders who played various formal leadership roles; and membership in the council was a symbol of elite status. The primary institutional roles that each of the MPC members played outside of the council may be divided into five basic categories: (1) Party elite members, (2) leading government administrators, (3) "democratic party" personages, (4) mass organization leaders, and (5) high level technical experts and intellectuals. Figure 3 presents the role composition of the MPC between 1950 and 1961, indicating the number of elite members in each role category in proportion to the total membership of the MPC. The figure demonstrates a striking growth of the Party's representation over the years, which expanded from an initial 19 per cent in 1950 to 33 per cent in 1961. This increase seems to imply that the Party, by virtue of its ever-expanding representation, played an ever-increasing role in the city's bureaucratic and administrative processes. In other words, there was a clear trend toward Party dominance of the bureaucracy. If the presence of military leaders in the MPC could also be interpreted as a sign of political control, then the formal reappearance of two local military leaders in the MPC following 1958, after a lapse of seven years, could also be cited as an indication of this trend.[23] In contrast to the expansion of the Party's representation, it should be noted, the representation of administrators and professional

---

[23]The immediate reasons for the reappearance of military leaders in municipal posts might have been related to the political unrest caused by the Hundred Flowers movement and the Anti-Rightist campaign in 1957–58, and to the ascendence of the People's Liberation Army's political role following Lin Piao's takeover of control of the military in 1959.

## FIGURE 3
### Role Composition of the MPC, 1950–61
### (in Percentage of the Total Members in Each Role Category)*

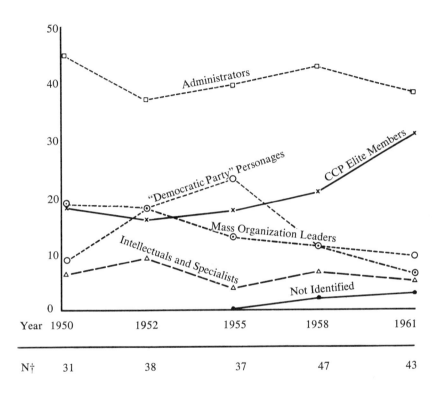

*Each member is classified only once by his most salient official role. Thus, the combined total of percentages for each session stands at 100 per cent.
†The total number of MPC members in each session.

specialists remained at about the same level, with some signs of fluctuation and minor decline.

Another conspicuous trend shown in Figure 3 was the decline of the representation in the bureaucracy of leaders of the "democratic parties" and mass organizations. This decline might be attributable partly to the increasing professionalization of the urban government and partly to the diminishing function of the "united front" organizations for purposes of power legitimization.[24] In conjunction with the trend of Party dominance,

[24]One indication of the trend was the elimination of the representation of model workers after 1955.

as discussed above, it is instructive to note that the decline of the representation of mass organization and "democratic parties" failed to boost that of professional administrators and experts. Instead, it was the Party that filled the positions given up by leaders of the mass organizations and "democratic parties."

The trend of bureaucratic development in Wuhan, in short, showed a somewhat mixed pattern, involving simultaneously the rise of professionalization and increased Party control. More qualified and specialized bureaucrats were recruited into positions of authority and power in the sixties than in the fifties. However, a countertrend of intensification of Party control over government administration appears to have been accelerated also. If a bureaucracy of both "red" and "expert" was what the Communist leadership had consciously planned to achieve, the findings would seem to confirm that the Party had made progress in that general direction.[25]

In contrast to the above findings, which suggest that the bureaucracy of Wuhan achieved only a limited gain in the intake of professional expertise and the expansion of administrative authority, progress in other areas appears to have been rather more impressive. Let us again take the MPC as the point of departure. The membership turnover of the MPC during 1950-61, as presented in Table 6, showed a remarkably steady decline over the years. The high annual turnover rate of 19.3 per cent in 1950-52 was reduced by two-thirds, to 6.6 per cent per year, in the 1958-61 period. The high rate in 1950-52 may have resulted from the *san-fan* purge, yet that purge was by no means the only contributing factor. Take the 1955-58 rate of 13.6 per cent for example. In spite of the heavy toll among the non-Party members of the elite during the *fan-yu* movement (1957-58), the turnover rate was still lower than that of the preceding period (14.7 per cent). Thus, it is reasonable to assume that if it were not for the fact that the trend of decline was already in progress then, the net rate for this period would have been as high as that for the early 1950's.

A survey of the patterns of mobility year by year from 1949 through 1965 also demonstrates a trend toward leadership stabilization in Wuhan. Figure 4 summarizes the annual distribution in percentages of those promoted, those demoted, and those remaining at the same rank (un-

---

[25]The current upheaval of the Cultural Revolution has raised serious doubt as to whether the leadership is still strongly concerned about the building of a bureaucracy balanced with both "red" and "experts." Violent attacks on the Party as well as state bureaucracies by the Maoists and Red Guards suggest that the leadership in charge is determined to put the "reds" in absolute command at the expense of the "experts."

## TABLE 6
### Membership Turnover of the MPC, 1950–61

| Year | Total Number of Leaders | NUMBER OF LEADERS LEFT | | NUMBER OF LEADERS ENTERED | | AVERAGE ANNUAL RATE OF TURNOVER* |
|------|------|------|------|------|------|------|
| | | N | Percentage | N | Percentage | Percentage |
| 1950 | 31 | | | | | |
| | | 10 | 32.3% | 17 | 44.7% | 19.3% |
| 1952 | 38 | | | | | |
| | | 17 | 44.7% | 16 | 43.3% | 14.7% |
| 1955 | 37 | | | | | |
| | | 13 | 35.1% | 22 | 46.7% | 13.6% |
| 1958 | 47 | | | | | |
| | | 11 | 23.4% | 7 | 16.3% | 6.6% |
| 1961 | 43 | | | | | |

*Average annual rate of turnover for the entire period: 13.5 per cent.

changed). It indicates that 1949 was clearly a year of "collective" upward mobility for many Communists and their supporters who started their government careers following the Communist victory. Of those for whom 1949 career information was available, 79 per cent appear to have received their first governmental assignment or to have been promoted in that year. This group of "collectively" promoted leaders, contrary to the popularly held impression, was not necessarily confined to the Communist cadres. In fact, a considerable number of democratic personages were also recruited into the Wuhan government in this period. Motivated by a variety of considerations and desiring to create an attractive image of the new government and the united front, the Communist leadership in the early period of takeover seems to have preferred recruiting fresh "democratic" personages and leading intellectuals into government rather than promoting the officials left over from the Nationalist government.[26]

After the 1949 "mobility boom," the upward mobility rate in 1950 dropped sharply, to 25 per cent of the sample. In the next six years a trend of upward mobility persisted, showing a moderate increase during 1950-55 and a startling leap up to 51 per cent in 1956. After that, a reverse trend emerged. The rate of upward mobility began to fall consistently, though it fluctuated from time to time. This new trend of overall decline implies that after 1956 fewer leaders were constantly on the move in the bureaucratic hierarchy, and that a trend toward manpower stabilization had emerged. This decline in upward mobility was also clearly reflected in the corresponding rise in the proportion of leaders remaining in the same rank. In short, statistical analysis of mobility

---

[26]The best indication of this, of course, was the fact that only a small number of the "retained" personnel attained the ranks of the elite.

**FIGURE 4**
**Pattern of Mobility, 1949–65**
**(in Percentage of Total Members by Year)**

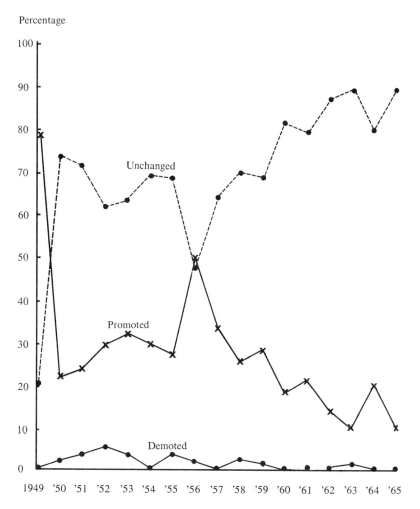

patterns over the years reveals that the Wuhan bureaucracy has tended toward leadership stabilization since 1957.

The actual stabilization of the top administrative and Party leadership in Wuhan provided the most convincing evidence of this trend. In the first eight years of Communist rule, 1949-56, Wuhan had four mayors and ten deputy mayors. This means that the average tenures for mayors and deputy mayors in this period were only twenty-two and twenty-four months, respectively, representing a turnover rate of approximately 50 per cent per year through 1956.[27] In sharp contrast Liu Hui-nung, the fifth mayor of Wuhan under Communist rule, has remained in office ever since November, 1956. (If he has not been purged during the current Cultural Revolution, his tenure is now over ten years.) At the same time, it should be noted that the average tenure of the deputy mayors increased from two years to seven years after 1956.

Moreover, leadership stabilization occurred not only in the municipal government but also in the city's Party leadership, in a similar pattern. In the first eight years, the top leadership of the Party also changed hands four times, registering an average tenure of twenty-one months for the Party secretary (or first secretary) and thirty-two months for the deputy secretaries (including second and third secretaries, or first, second, and third deputy secretaries). These figures represented, respectively, turn-over rates of 57 per cent and 38 per cent per year. Nevertheless, Sung K'an-fu took over as first secretary in 1956, and he appears to have remained in that post through 1966.[28] Furthermore, the average tenure for the other Party secretaries since 1956 has stretched to six years. The parallel between the stabilization pattern affecting government leadership and that affecting Party leadership in Wuhan strongly suggests that the leadership stabilization was a significant trend, rather than a random development.[29]

## Conclusion

In his theory of modern bureaucracy, Max Weber predicted two major trends of bureaucratic development: an increase in structural differentiation and specialization of bureaucracy, and a growing intake of professional talent and expertise.[30] These trends, as aspects of the

[27]Data on the Soviet bureaucracy suggest that in the last two decades directors in the vast majority of important plants have held their posts for five to ten years or even longer. Jerry Hough, "The Soviet Concept of the Relationship between the Lower Party Organs and the State Administration," *Slavic Review*, XXIV, No. 2 (June, 1965), 227.

[28]It is not clear whether Sung has been purged during the Cultural Revolution. At any rate, his name has not been mentioned in the press since mid-1966.

[29]The trend toward leadership stabilization appears also to have been evident in the mass organizations, such as the Communist Youth League and the Federation of Industry and Commerce. Structural and organizational stabilization appears also to have emerged in this period. Structural changes within the bureaucracy were greatly reduced. It should be noted, however, that the long average tenure of seven to ten years that senior bureaucrats were enjoying by the mid-1960's may have created problems of different types, namely, lack of mobility for younger cadres, recruitment stagnation, and generational tensions.

[30]Parsons (ed.), *Max Weber*; Victor Thompson, *Modern Organization* (New York: Knopf, 1961), pp. 10-57.

modernization process, both reflect and facilitate government and administrative efficiency.

In a formal structural sense the bureaucratic system of Wuhan appears to have been fully equipped for many years with the features of the "ideal type." Like many other modern bureaucracies, it has developed highly differentiated, specialized structures. However, conclusions derived from an analysis of this formal structure alone, without careful examination of the personnel and operational aspects of the system, will be superficial and even misleading.

As found in the course of this analysis, the prevailing recruitment and mobility system of the Wuhan bureaucracy did not, as of 1965, appear to have made fully operational its elaborate and differentiated structures in the direction that Weber predicted.[31] The composition of the leadership corps was biased in favor of "political generalists" rather than "professional specialists." The majority of the members of the elite appear to have been recruited and moved up the bureaucratic hierarchy mainly by virtue of their political merits and qualifications, rather than because of professional training and expertise. This phenomenon, however, does not imply that the leadership was totally unaware of the importance of professional expertise to the bureaucratic outputs and administrative efficiency. Periodic debates in China over the contradiction between "red" and "expert," and between "politics in command" and "professionalism in command," indicate clearly that the leadership was quite aware of the stakes involved. Yet, preoccupation with the desire to preserve its monopoly of political power and other political concerns have apparently prevented the leadership from developing a recruitment and mobility system oriented toward maximizing the intake of professional expertise, on the one hand, and using manpower in the most rational way possible to support bureaucratic modernization, on the other. As long as the charismatic Mao and his militant followers retain their rigid outlook, as they do in the current Cultural Revolution, maintaining that "politics is the soul, the supreme commander," and that it is not only worthless but also incorrect to "get one's job done without letting politics take command,"[32] it is not likely that the basic characteristics of the contemporary Chinese bureaucracy will be changed.

---

[31]Readers are reminded again that the preceding analysis represents a case study of a specific urban bureaucracy and its senior elite. Thus many generalizations drawn from this study are not intended to apply uniformly to the bureaucracies in all sectors and at all levels in China. Lower level cadres in the countryside, for example, may exhibit features quite different from what we have found in Wuhan. However, some comments regarding the general impact of Communist policies on the Wuhan bureaucracy may be valid for the Chinese bureaucracy as a whole. Needless to say, a complete and accurate knowledge of the Chinese bureaucratic system will require more comparative and microscopic studies which cut across sectors and levels.

[32]NCNA, Peking, 1729 GMT, May 17, 1966.

The trend of development as highlighted in the time-series analysis of this study, however, has revealed highly significant features of change. In the first place, the bureaucracy of Wuhan has shown over the years some positive, though still quite feeble, signs of professionalization, as measured by its increasing intake of expertise and talent. But a trend toward intensification of political control over the bureaucracy has also emerged since the late fifties.

Political campaigns—whether in the name of *cheng-chih kua-shuai* (put politics in command), or of *cheng-chih t'u-ch'u* (give politics prominence)—were all directed toward enhancing the power of militant revolutionaries vis-à-vis the authority of professional bureaucrats. Nothing illustrated this trend better than the systematic introduction, since 1962, of the political work departments (*cheng-shih kung-tso-pu*) and the appointment of a large number of military personnel in non-military organizations.[33] Modeled on the operation of the People's Liberation Army's (PLA) political department system, this group of new political commissars, with exclusive control of political and personnel matters, began to overshadow, if not totally destroy, the authority of professional administrators.[34] Under these circumstances the division of labor between "political" and "technical" work, naturally, became extremely difficult, if not completely impossible, to maintain. No administrator could possibly insist that his work was purely technical and, as such, should not be subject to political intervention. Moreover, the launching of the Cultural Revolution and the violent assault on the bureaucracy and on "bourgeois" professionalism amounted to a declaration of "war" against the bureaucracy by the militant Maoists. This "war" obviously is going to have a most destructive effect on the moderate gains that the Chinese bureaucracy has achieved the hard way over the past seventeen years.

Second, the study also indicates that 1957 was a landmark year in Wuhan's bureaucratic development. The relatively high rate of cadre mobility and turnover characteristic of the post-liberation period began to slow down after that year; and the top leadership of Wuhan began to stabilize. High personnel mobility and turnover, of course, tends to create a faster rate of political recruitment, more active political participation by the populace, and broader sharing of political power. Thus, political mobility, as John W. Lewis has pointed out, tends to play the important function of generating political support and legitimacy for a

---

[33]An excellent account of the "political work department" system may be found in Chalmers Johnson, "Lin Piao's Army and Its Role in Chinese Society," Part 2, *Current Scene*, IV, No. 14 (July 15, 1966), 1–11.

[34]Detailed information on the power, structure, and operational process of the political department system within the PLA may be found in a collection of Communist documents under the title *Fei-chün Cheng-chih Kung-tso T'iao-li* (Regulations on Political Work of the Bandit Army) (Taipei: Ch'ing-pao-chü, 1965).

new government.[35] However, fostering high political mobility without giving due attention to such bureaucratic problems as personnel staffing, the training of manpower, and the continuity of leadership may easily lead to overstaffing, manpower waste, and leadership instability. These troubles may be compounded if high mobility is accompanied by a system of transfer and assignment not carefully designed to facilitate manpower training and specialization.

During the first eight years of Communist rule, the bureaucracy in Wuhan appears to have developed these symptoms. The rapid political recruitment and upward mobility following the seizure of power seem to have strongly boosted the prestige and legitimacy of the Communist leadership. But by the mid-fifties the problems of overstaffing and manpower waste in the bureaucracies began to create difficulties for the leadership and eventually forced it to resort to drastic measures such as *ching-chien* and *hsia-fang* movements during the second half of the fifties. By the end of the 1950's these drastic measures had succeeded in correcting the previous excesses, and a new trend toward stabilization began to set in. As a result of the leadership's strong push to reduce mobility, and even to promote downward mobility, the government apparently traded one evil for another. Judging from the long tenure (seven to ten years) which many top members of the elite had enjoyed in the mid-1960's, one suspects that the high turnover of the early fifties slowed down because of the need for a short stage of stabilization in the late fifties, which was followed by a swing to the other extreme of excessively long tenure, low mobility, and stagnation in the sixties. This stagnation, in fact, may have been one of the major causes of the widespread criticism of the regime, political resentment, and discontent which steadily grew within various key sectors of population; it may also have been responsible for tensions between the old guards and new cadres and even for the emergence of "localism" which has occurred in the 1960's.[36]

---

[35]Lewis, "Political Aspects of Mobility in China's Urban Development," *American Political Science Review*, LX, No. 4 (December, 1966), 908–10.

[36]Tensions of these sorts were vividly seen in Communist documents such as *Kung-tso T'ung-hsün* (Bulletin of Activities) for the period between January 1 and August 26, 1961; and *Fan-kung Yu-chi-tui T'u-chi Fu-chien Lien-chiang Lu-huo Fei-fang Wen-chien Hui-pien* (Collected Documents Captured During an Anti-Communist Raid on Lien-chiang Hsien, Fukien Province) (Taipei: Ch'ing-pao-chü, 1964). Particularly relevant to our study are the tensions between the old and new cadres, which may have stemmed from three major sources: (1) the old cadres, acting out of their instinct of self-preservation, tried to hold on to their positions, while the new ones aspired to advance; (2) the existence of a wide gap of experience, education, and training between the old guards and the new recruits; and (3) the lack of support and respect for the superior cadres from the subordinates because of the former's failure to show knowledge and expertise commensurate with their positions and superior to that of the latter.

How to maintain a moderate rate of political mobility so that the leadership can attain a high degree of both political legitimacy and bureaucratic efficiency is, of course, a task of supreme importance to China's bureaucratic development. This task will be particularly crucial in the period following the Cultural Revolution.

Third, the analysis of the recruitment and mobility processes in Wuhan clearly reveals that the leadership commanded tremendous power to influence the course of bureaucratic development. The powerful Organization Department of the Party, through its systematic control of personnel offices in all the government bureaucracies and mass organizations, had a virtual monopoly of control over cadre recruitment, mobility, and transfer.[37] It had the power not only to dictate over-all policies and priorities regarding criteria and rate of recruitment, but also to examine, approve, or reject each individual candidate. This power has been evident in the Party's membership recruitment campaigns in the past, for example. The Party has repeatedly demonstrated its ability to designate specific membership qualifications, rates of recruitment, and even sectors of the population to be recruited from over specified periods of time. Moreover, the Party has also shown an indisputable power to rectify and purge cadres selectively, under Party guidance.[38]

The centralized character of recruitment and mobility processes in China and the Party's ability to monopolize control suggest that the leadership was wholly responsible for the course of China's bureaucratic development. The influence of social and economic trends on the course of the development of bureaucracy, important as it may be, is primarily a factor of long-term significance. As this study of the Wuhan bureaucracy indicates, there have been few signs of the emergence of a new generation of "technocrats" able to give a fresh outlook to those operating the system. As of 1965, there was little doubt that the nature of the system was primarily a product of the leadership's deliberate policy choices.

If there is to be a sharp change in the direction of China's bureaucratic development, obviously the initiative will have to come from the leadership. If the leadership were to decide today to moderate its fanatic drive toward *cheng-chih t'u ch'u* (giving prominence to politics) and reestablish the balance of priorities between "red" and "expert," it would

---

[37] An excellent discussion of personnel control by the Party may be found in Barnett, "Social Stratification and Aspects of Personnel Management in the Chinese Communist Bureaucracy," *China Quarterly*, No. 28 (October-December, 1966), pp. 18–20, 29–34.

[38] The ability to control recruitment is best illustrated by the large-scale recruitment of urban industrial workers in 1950–52 and that of intellectuals in 1955–56. The *san-fan* in 1951–52 and the *fan-yu* in 1957–58 are probably the best examples of purges.

be reasonable to expect that such a decision would have an immediate and direct effect on the patterns of cadre recruitment and mobility and, thus, in the long run on the outlook of the entire bureaucratic system. Such a decision (which is extremely unlikely to take place so long as the "Maoists" are in charge) would obviously be the most crucial factor in determining whether the modernization and professionalization of China's bureaucracy is to be achieved in a comparatively short time or to be delayed for another one or two generations. Furthermore, any change in the direction of bureaucratic development in China would certainly in turn exert an impact of strategic importance on China's long-term economic and technological modernization.[39] In this regard, the significance and implications of the current Great Proletarian Cultural Revolution as a power struggle between Mao's charismatic leadership and the bureaucracies' institutionalized authority, and between the "radical revolutionists" and the "pragmatic bureaucrats," cannot be overemphasized.

---

[39]This observation does not necessarily imply that political leadership is always dysfunctional and should be completely eliminated from bureaucracy. Even Max Weber himself admitted that the continued existence of political leadership is not only inevitable but to some degree essential for meaningful development of political order. What appears to be particularly critical today in China's bureaucratic system is the regime's excessive emphasis on political priorities and hostility toward bureaucratic authority and professionalism. A more balanced system which pays equal attention to political leadership and to professional authority is probably what China needs most in its quest for modernization. For a succinct discussion of Weber's view on the need for political leadership in bureaucracy, see Alfred Diamant, "The Bureaucratic Model: Max Weber Rejected, Rediscovered, Reformed," in *Papers in Comparative Public Administration*, ed. by Ferrel Heady and Sybil L. Stokes (Ann Arbor: Institute of Public Administration, University of Michigan, 1962), pp. 67–69.

# VII
# The Political Groups,
# Political Participation, and Communication

## 15. Occupational Groups and the Cultural Revolution

### Michel Oksenberg

This article analyzes the interests and power of seven occupational groups in China: the peasants, industrial workers, industrial managers, intellectuals, students, Party and government bureaucrats, and military personnel. The evidence comes from two sources: (1) the activities of the members of these groups during the Cultural Revolution; and (2) revelations in the wall posters and Red Guard newspapers about their behavior from 1962 to 1966. The article concludes that the configuration of power and influence among these groups will be an important determinant of Chinese politics in the years ahead.

### Analytical Approach

A few years ago, when the totalitarian model of politics in Communist countries was in its heyday, little attention was paid to the ability of various groups in society to influence public policy. The totalitarian model led analysts to concentrate upon the dictator, his whims, the political intrigue among those around him, and the control mechanisms which forced the populace to obey his commands. Barrington Moore and Isaac Deutscher stood out among the analysts of Soviet politics in the early 1950's for their willingness to look beyond Moscow to the power and influence of major groups in society.[1] Now, the totalitarian model

---

[1]Barrington Moore, *Terror and Progress USSR: Some Sources of Change and Stability in the Soviet Dictatorship*, Harvard University Press, 1954, and Isaac Deutscher, *Russia: What Next*, Oxford University Press, 1953.

Reprinted from Michel Oksenberg, "The Political Group, Political Participation and Communication," in *The Cultural Revolution: 1967 in Review*, Michigan Papers in Chinese Studies, No. 2 (Ann Arbor, Michigan: Center for Chinese Studies, 1968), pp. 1–44, by permission of the author and publisher.

has lost its earlier attraction, having proven unable to account for social change. Meanwhile, the approach employed by Moore and Deutscher has begun to win a wider audience, in part because in the early 1950's they suggested the possibilities of significant evolution in the USSR. Recently, Barrington Moore's study of the social origins of democracy and dictatorship again has displayed the analytical power of a study of the interrelationships among key groups in society.[2]

The Cultural Revolution provided a remarkable opportunity to view the structure of Chinese society in the 1960's. Prior to 1965, that view was obscured by the carefully nurtured image of a monolithic society led by a unified, cohesive elite. In 1966-67, the image was destroyed, revealing that the rulers were deeply divided and locked in bitter struggle. As the rulers lost their ability to provide unified, coherent guidelines to the nation, the various segments of society became more able to pursue their own interests. As a result, the Cultural Revolution made it possible to analyze the concerns of the major groups in society and their relative abilities to achieve their interests.

Before the substantive portions of the paper are presented, its analytical framework should be made clear. The analysis has four major conceptual underpinnings. The first concept involves the nature of groups and the ways they are able to articulate their interests. In common parlance, "group" has one of two meanings. One meaning is an "association," a collection of individuals who are formally organized for a purpose. When "interest groups" are discussed in the United States, people have the "association" in mind—a collection of individuals pursuing their common interests in concert. Another definition, more suited to the Chinese case, considers a group to be an aggregate of individuals with similar attributes, roles, or interests. Whether the members of the aggregate become aware of their similarity and form an association depends upon the context. But it is possible for the members of the aggregate, acting separately, to behave in the same way because of the similarity of their positions. In these terms, then, peasants can react to government policy as a group, that is, as an aggregate of individuals making similar decisions.

A second concept embodied in the analysis is that unorganized groups or aggregates can affect the policy formulation process. In democratic countries, aggregates have little trouble forming associations and gaining access to the key centers of decision making. In non-democratic countries, aggregates continue to pursue their interests, but since they are unable to organize, they must adopt different techniques. Manipulation

---

[2]Barrington Moore, *Social Origins of Dictatorship and Democracy*, Beacon Press, 1966.

of information, passive resistance, non-compliance, and cultivation of friends in high places of government are some of the indirect methods which enable groups to influence policy. The important research question, as far as China is concerned, is to determine how and to what extent each aggregate registers its demands.

A third aspect of the analysis is that some groups in society have a greater ability than others to influence policy. A number of factors determine what groups have the greatest power, but key among them are the degree of their organization, the relationship of these groups to the means of production, the values and attiudes of the particular culture, the international situation, and the interrelationship among various groups. The process of industrialization involves the removal, often violently, of some groups from the locus of power, and their replacement by new groups.

Finally, the fourth underpinning of group analysis is the notion that, to a considerable extent, politics involves the attempts by powerless groups to obtain power, while groups with power struggle to retain it. Moreover, the politics of a country to a large extent reflects the conflicts within the groups that have power. In societies where the military has power, for example, national politics comes to involve inter-service rivalries, conflicts between senior and junior officers, and disputes between central headquarters and regional commands. If one can chart the distribution of power among various groups in a society, then one can predict what some of the important public policies and political issues will be.

The application of these concepts to the events in China in 1966-67 must not be misinterpreted as an attempt to explain the Cultural Revolution. Rather, this paper analyzes the Cultural Revolution for what it tells about one aspect of the structure of Chinese society. The seven broad occupational groups into which the Chinese Communists divide their society — peasants, intellectuals, industrial managers, industrial workers, students, Party and Government bureaucrats, and the military — are examined briefly and crudely, with the following questions in mind: What were some of the salient characteristics of these groups? What did the members of these aggregates perceive to be in their interest? Did the aggregates have any common group interests, and if so, what were they? How did they pursue their interests? What power did they have to enforce their demands?

These questions are not easily answered. Without the opportunity to do field research, it is difficult to ascertain what people perceive to be in their interests. The activities of the members of different occupational groups during 1966-67 and statements in the wall posters and Red Guard newspapers about their attitudes and behavior provide some clues. In addition, occupational groups appear to have some similar characteristics, no matter what country is under investigation; the literature on the roles and behavior of members of these groups in the developing countries then provides inferences about some of their likely interests in China. Further, some information is available on the perceived interests of different occupational groups in pre-Communist China. By seeking convergence among the different sources of information, the analyst can roughly identify occupational group interests at the present time. It is harder to estimate the ability of these aggregates to articulate their interests and affect public policy, but surely the relevant data here include actual instances of members of these groups influencing important political decisions or public policy clearly reflecting the interests of the group.

An analysis of the activities of occupational groups during the Cultural Revolution admittedly provides only a limited perspective upon the extraordinary complex events of 1966-67. But no single vantage will suffice in interpreting history of such sweeping proportions. Some of the valuable perspectives employed in other essays on the Cultural Revolution and purposefully eschewed here include analysis in terms of elites,[3] bureaucratic phenomena,[4] problems of industrialization,[5] and the Chinese political culture.[6] By approaching the Cultural Revolution from the perspective of occupational group interests, one of the oldest methods of political analysis, one hopefully will acquire additional insights into the structure of Chinese society and its relationship to the Chinese political system.

## Peasants

**Peasant Interests.** An important desire of most peasants probably is to be free to cultivate, reap, market, and consume their crops; they wish to have less extracted from them, and more goods available for purchase

---

[3]For an analysis stressing this approach, see Philip Bridgham, "Mao's Cultural Revolution," *China Quarterly*, No. 29, January-March 1967, p. 1–35.

[4]Analyses stressing this approach include: Franz Schurmann, "The Attack of the Cultural Revolution on Ideology and Organization," in Tang Tsou and P'ing-ti Ho, ed., *China's Heritage and the Communist Political System*, University of Chicago Press, 1968 forthcoming, and Chalmers Johnson, "China: The Cultural Revolution in Structural Perspective," *Asian Survey*, Vol. VIII, No. 1, January 1968, p. 1–15.

[5]Analyses stressing this approach include: John W. Lewis, "The Leaders and the Commissar: The Chinese Political System in the Last Days of the Revolution," in Tang Tsou and P'ing-ti Ho, ed., *China's Heritage, op. cit.*; and Richard Baum, "Ideology Redivivus," *Problems of Communism*, May-June 1967, p. 1–11.

[6]An analysis stressing this approach is Richard Solomon, "Communication Patterns and the Chinese Revolution," a paper delivered to the annual meeting of the American Political Science Association, September 1967.

at lower prices. Peasants particularly demand political quietude during the planting and harvesting seasons. They also want their government to protect them from disorder and the ravages of nature. In addition, to the extent that their aspirations have risen, China's peasants also want better educational opportunities for their children, more welfare, greater security, and a standard of living comparable to urban dwellers.

**Articulation of Peasant Interests.** Peasants have no associations to voice their demands. Nonetheless, the Cultural Revolution provided ample evidence that the peasants had brokers embodying and representing their interests. Recalling the disaster of the Great Leap, when peasant desires had been disregarded, many among the Peking leadership strove to anticipate peasant reaction to proposed policies. Moreover, upon occasion, outbreaks of violence in the countryside forced the officials to pay attention to peasant grievances.

The brokers came primarily from three sources: the officials in agricultural agencies, regional officials whose power stemmed in part from the performance of agriculture in their areas, and military officers. A number of leading agricultural officials, in particular Teng Tzu-hui, T'an Chen-lin, and Liao Lu-yen, were accused in the *ta-tze-pao* of seeking to expand private plots and free markets, to restrict the power of the communes, and to assign brigade plots to individual households, thereby restoring production responsibility to the family.

Teng, T'an, and Liao, in effect, were voicing the interests of their peasant constituents. The reason for their action seems clear. The performance of the agencies which they led was judged largely by agricultural production. They depended upon the peasants to fulfill the targets for which the agencies were held responsible. It was in their interest, therefore, to argue for measures and to secure targets congruent with peasant interests.

Similarly, regional officials occasionally represented the interests of the peasants in their area. The purge of Li Ching-ch'uan of Szechuan has proven fascinating in this regard. If the charges against him are accurate, Li was keenly aware of the peculiarities of the Szechuan agricultural system, and sought to win exemptions from the uniform, nationwide regulations Peking sought to impose. He took exception, for example, to marketing regulations which Mao had endorsed. He pointed out that (because of the terrain and scattered population) rural markets in Szechuan were different from the rest of the country.[7]

The military also had a vested interest in peasant morale. To the People's Liberation Army fell the unpleasant task of suppressing peasant

---

[7] Radio Kweiyang, June 28, 1967.

unrest. Moreover, soldiers were recruited in the countryside, and troop morale was adversely affected by disenchantment at home.[8] The PLA conducted periodic surveys of troop morale, and monitored letters from home. When the surveys and monitoring revealed disenchantment at home, the military command apparently voiced its concern. As a result of these channels of communication, some military officers became particularly sensitive to the problems of the peasants and upon occasion acted as their representatives. This is precisely what P'eng Teh-huai was doing at Lushan in 1959 when he expressed the discontent of the peasants with the commune system.[9]

In addition to representation by brokers, peasants acted on their own behalf. Such actions included failure to comply with directives — for example, hiding production and concentrating on private plots — and sporadic violence. The *Work Bulletin* described peasant violence in Honan province in 1960, while during the first half of 1967 there were persistent reports of small peasant uprisings and of an illegal influx of peasants into many Chinese cities.[10]

These means of voicing their interests, when combined with surveys measuring rural discontent and the visits by higher level officials to the countryside, added up to a general awareness in Peking of the desires and problems of the peasants.

**Sources of Peasant Strength and Weaknesses.** The power of the peasants to enforce their demands, however, was limited by the fact that they had no organization which could be considered their own. One wall poster indicated that some peasants were acutely aware of this problem:

> Workers have their unions, soldiers have theirs, and Party workers have a body to represent their interests. Why don't we have unions? . . . .
> The peasants have no voice. They have only "formal" democracy. At the Second Conference of our Poor and Lower Middle Peasants Association, no decisions were made by us. All we had was a few days of free board and lodging.[11]

As anthropologists stress, peasants must overcome innumerable difficulties to become an organized, articulate, enduring political force.[12]

---

[8]J. Chester Cheng, ed., *The Politics of the Chinese Red Army*, Hoover Institution, 1966. See pp. 12–19 for example.
[9]See *Peking Review*, No. 35, August 25, 1967, pp. 6–7 and No. 36, September 1, 1967, p. 14; Tokyo *Mainichi*, August 22, 1967.
[10]See *China News Analysis*, No. 645 and 647. For a dramatic account of one such uprising, see Joint Publications Research Service (henceforth JPRS) 44, 052, January 17, 1968, p. 16–23.
[11]*China Topics*, YB 415, February 23, 1967, part III.
[12]See especially Eric Wolf, *Peasants*, Prentice Hall, 1966, p. 91; and Mehmet Bequirj, *Peasantry in Revolution*, Cornell, 1966, p. 14–15.

Concerned with sheer survival and possessing only limited horizons, most peasants enter the political process rarely or not at all. They must depend upon sympathetic brokers to transmit their concerns to those who control the resources they want; barring that, their only recourse is non-compliance or violence.

This is particularly true in China, where the peasants are now bonded to the land. Owning only a small percentage of the land they till, unable to move without a hard-to-obtain permit, forced to deposit savings in state-regulated credit cooperatives which restrict withdrawals, peasants are largely at the mercy of lower level Party and government bureaucrats.

But it is easy to underestimate the power of the peasant aggregate. China's rulers must be at least somewhat responsive to the demands of the peasants because of their numbers (roughly 80% of the population) and their economic importance. Roughly 35% to 45% of China's net domestic product, for example, comes from the agricultural sector, and the bulk of China's exports are agricultural and agriculturally derived products.[13]

The Cultural Revolution demonstrated that political power still was rooted to a considerable degree in control over the peasants and agricultural surpluses. The purges of Li Ching-ch'uan, the powerful Szechuan official, and T'ao Chu, the former Kwangtung official, show how these men were somewhat responsive to peasant demands in order to encourage the peasants to develop the potential of their areas. On the other hand, officials in grain-deficit areas, more dependent upon allocations from central government storehouses, were less able to resist Peking directives. Heilungkiang, Shantung, Shansi, Kweichow, Tsinghai, Peking, and Shanghai—all grain-deficit areas—were among the first to respond to Peking's call in early 1967 to establish Revolutionary Committees. (There undoubtedly were other reasons for their response.) Here are indications of the persistence in China of the intimate relationship between power and agriculture. The peasant has not yet lost his crucial role as a source of bureaucratic power.

**Peasants During the Cultural Revolution.** The course of the Cultural Revolution indicates that by 1967 even the radicals were somewhat sensitive to peasant needs. The two strongest efforts to subdue the Cultural Revolution came precisely at those moments when the peasants proba-

---

[13]For summary discussions of the role of agriculture in the Chinese economy, see especially: Alexander Eckstein, *Communist China's Economic Growth and Foreign Trade*, McGraw-Hill, 1966, p. 47; Marion Larson, "China's Agriculture under Communism," in Joint Economic Committee of the United States Congress, *Economic Profile of Mainland China*, Government Printing Office, 1968, Vol. I, esp. p. 205; and Feng-hua Mah, "Public Investment in Communist China," *Journal of Asian Studies*, Vol. XXI, No. 1, November 1961, p. 46.

bly most desired order. Although earlier efforts had been made, the Red Guards were finally told to cease their marches and return home in early February 1967 on the eve of the spring planting. The PLA received more vigorous orders than usual to assist the peasants in spring planting. These February directives, coming on the heels of widespread signs of peasant unrest, were issued only 45 days after the December 15th directive extending the Cultural Revolution to the countryside.[14] This apparently calmer situation prevailed until early summer, when the turmoil increased. As the fall harvest neared, however, the Peking authorities again recognized the constraints imposed by China's essentially rural character; in late August and early September, they took stringent measures to control the Cultural Revolution.[15]

The peasant desire to be left alone was recognized in other ways. There is remarkably little evidence that the agitational activity which marked the Cultural Revolution in the urban areas spread to the countryside.[16] To judge from the provincial radio broadcasts, the main undertaking of the Cultural Revolution in the countryside was the propagation of Mao's thought, primarily through the organization of Mao-study groups. In spite of all the condemnations, there were very few reports of actual seizure of the private plots or restriction of free markets. The announcements of a good harvest in 1967 further reflected the fact that the Cultural Revolution essentially had by-passed the rural areas. In short, the evidence strongly suggests that the interests of the peasants elicit a response from China's rulers.

## Industrial Managers and Industrial Workers

Since the divergent interests of industrial managers and workers are what strike most Americans, it is wise to recall their common interests in China. Both usually have a vested interest in uninterrupted production, in protecting factory equipment from damage, and in maintaining industrial prosperity and growth. In China, both have a vested interest in the evolving factory management system, in view of the welfare and housing benefits it bestows upon them. Moreover, the deep economic depression following the Great Leap very possibly had underscored to many the

---

[14]*China Topics*, No. 415, February 23, 1967.
[15]Crucial here was Chiang Ch'ing's speech of September 5, 1967. An excellent summary of this period is in Chalmers Johnson, "China: The Cultural Revolution in Structural Perspective," *op. cit.,* p. 10–15.
[16]John R. Wenmohs, "Agriculture in Mainland China — 1967," *Current Scene,* Vol. V, No. 21, December 15, 1967.

commonality of manager and worker interests in resisting attempts by other groups to intrude upon their domain. In spite of common interests, however, industrial manager and worker have rarely joined together to influence the course of Chinese politics.

Against this background, the events from December 1966 to February 1967 assume historical significance. They suggest that China's industrial sector has begun to come of political age. With a few exceptions, the industrial managers and workers, apparently acting in concert, resisted the efforts by parts of the bureaucracy and organized students to intrude upon areas they deemed to be their prerogatives. Within one month of the decision to extend the Cultural Revolution to the factories, the order was quietly but significantly tempered. If China's rulers had been unified in their support of the spread of the Cultural Revolution to the factories, the ability of the industrial managers and workers to temper its course would have been questionable. But the move was initiated only by a radical segment within the Party and government bureaucracy, who required student support. More noteworthy, the considerable opposition within the bureaucracy indicated that since the Great Leap, the industrial managers and workers had acquired strong allies among the top officials.

The exact story of industrial cities in late 1966 and early 1967 has yet to be told, but enough is known to warrant a brief description.[17] In the stormy period following the August 1966 Eleventh Plenum, the Red Guards were repeatedly told that they were not to enter factories without prior approval of the factory employees, nor to interfere with production. One of the strongest warnings came in a November 10, 1966, *People's Daily* editorial, which said,

> Revolutionary students should firmly believe that the worker and peasant masses are capable of making revolution and solving their problems by themselves. No one should do their work for them. Special attention must also be paid to preventing interference with production activities . . . from the outside.[18]

---

[17]As a start, however, see: Evelyn Anderson, "Shanghai Upheaval," *Problems of Communism,* January-February, 1968, p. 12–22; "Sources of Labor Discontent in China: The Worker Peasant System," *Current Scene,* Vol. VI, No. 5, March 15, 1968; Andrew Watson, "Cultural Revolution in Sian," *Far Eastern Economic Review,* April 20, 1967, April 27, 1967, and May 4, 1967; and Neale Hunter, "The Cultural Revolution in Shanghai," *Far Eastern Economic Review,* June 1, 1967, June 22, 1967, and July 6, 1967.

[18]"More on the Question of Grasping the Revolution Firmly and Stimulating Production," *Jen-min Jih-pao* (People's Daily, henceforth, *JMJP*), November 22, 1966, in *Survey of the Chinese Mainland Press* (henceforth *SCMP*), No. 3825, pp. 1–4.

But by December 9, the earlier policy was reversed and a more radical policy was adopted; the Red Guards were encouraged to enter the factories. In early December, in contrast to the November 10th editorial, a Red Guard newspaper could state,

> Chairman Mao has taught us, "The Young intellectuals and young students of China must definitely go among the worker and peasant masses. . ." The cultural revolutionary movement must expand from the young people and students to the workers and peasants.[19]

The formal decision allowing the students to enter the factories, promulgated on December 9, was made public in the important *People's Daily* editorial of December 26th.[20]

Five days later, the annual *People's Daily* New Year editorial indicated that there was considerable opposition to the measure. The editorial stated, "Any argument against carrying out a large-scale cultural revolution in factories and mines and in rural areas is not correct."[21] According to the rules of Pekingology, this sentence indicates that a strong debate was being waged. Moreover, by mid-January it was clear that the industrial managers and workers were undermining the December 9th directive. Rather than allowing the Red Guards to enter the factories, which might have led to damage of equipment, the factory managers encouraged their employees to leave the factories and travel to Peking to voice their grievances. Factory managers paid bonuses to their workers, promoted many of them, and gave them travel fare. Protesting Red Guard activities, it appears, factory workers went on strike, probably living off the bonuses paid them by their factory managers.

The joint activities of managers and workers, assisted by some Party and government bureaucrats, were described in an "Open Letter" which stated:

> In recent days. . . , a handful of freaks and monsters have cheated the misled . . . worker masses, to put forward many wage, welfare, and other economic demands to the leadership and administrative departments. . . These administrative departments and leaders, acceding to these demands and not caring whether it is in accord with state policy or not, sign their names to hand out generously a lot of state funds.[22]

Those who encouraged the workers to put forth their economic demands were accused of setting the "revolutionary workers movement onto the devious road of trade unionism."

---

[19]JPRS 40, 274, p. 34.
[20]For another analysis, see *China News Analysis*, No. 644.
[21]*Peking Review*, No. 1, January 1, 1967, p. 12.
[22]Radio Foochow, January 9, 1967.

The situation in Shanghai became particularly critical. The railroad network was partially paralyzed due to a high rate of employee absenteeism, with serious disruptions from December 27 to January 9. Public utility services in Shanghai were disrupted; shipping in the Shanghai harbor was adversely affected. Similar reports came from throughout the country. By mid-January, Radio Peking and the New China News Agency (NCNA) had reported instances of worker's strikes and sabotage in such major cities as Tientsin, Shenyang, Chengtu, Chungking, Sian, Canton, and Hangchow.

Within a month of the December 9th directive, the radical attack upon the industrial sector had produced near-chaos. The first response of the leaders of the radical Party and government bureaucrats and their Red Guard student supporters was to win allies among the workers and to encourage conflict between managers and workers. Special appeals were made to the temporary factory employees (Factories have two types of employees on their pay roll—permanent employees, who are paid according to the set wage scale, receive fringe benefits, and have a regular rank; and temporary employees, who are employed on special contract, receive lower wages, and can be dismissed easily during a recession). To gain the favor of the temporary employees, the radicals blamed Liu Shao-ch'i for originating the temporary employee system. They implied that one of the purposes of the Cultural Revolution was to abolish the distinction between permanent and temporary labor. At the same time, the radicals atempted to isolate the factory managers from their worker allies. The managers were attacked as anti-Maoists; the workers were excused for being duped. A series of student-worker meetings was arranged to build good will.

The tacit alliance, particularly between managers and permanent employees, held firm and the government had to take stringent measures to restore industrial production. On January 15, Chou En-lai cautioned the Red Guards against hasty action. He implied that the action in Shanghai was too rash, adding that "we must. . . . see to it that business organizations truly carry out business operations."[23] Two days later, the CCP Central Committee and State Council jointly issued regulations to strengthen urban public security work.[24] On January 28th, an article by Mao Tse-tung entitled "On Correcting Mistaken Ideas in the Party," stressing the virtues of discipline and order, was reprinted, while on the next day, the State Council prohibited industrial workers from visiting their rural ancestral homes during the Chinese New Year. The efforts to keep the workers in the city, to keep the chaos in the cities from spreading to the countryside, and to restore urban order were receiving primary attention. To win back the permanent employees, on February 17

---

[23]*SCMP*, No. 3913, p. 2.
[24]For texts, see *China Topics*, No. 418, March 8, 1967.

the Central Committee and the State Council decided to retain the distinction between permanent and temporary workers.

The stringent measures did not produce immediate results. They were intended to restore the confidence of the industrial worker, but they did little to assuage the fears of the factory managers, former capitalists, trade union leaders, and economic planners. The industrial sector apparently did not begin to return to normal until these groups also were mollified. To restore industrial calm, the vehement charges of "economism" levelled against the industrial managers began to be dampened in February. The press concentrated its attack upon "anarchists," meaning the Red Guards who persisted in their attacks on managers. The slogan so prominent in December and early January, "To Rebel is Justified," gave way to expressions of concern for the sanctity of property.

In view of the tacit manager-worker alliance, and the initial attempts both to split this alliance and divide the workers, the CCP Central Commitee letter of March 18 has very special importance. Addressed jointly to the industrial workers and their leaders, the document officially recognized their common interests. Extremely mild in tone, the letter represents an almost total abandonment of the policy outlined in the December 26, 1966 *People's Daily* editorial extending the Cultural Revolution to the factories. The support given to the factory managers in the March 18 directive is worth quoting:

> As masters of the country, all workers *and staff* in factories and mines must, in the course of the Cultural Revolution, heighten their great sense of responsibility and protect State property effectively...
> The Party Central Committee believes that in all factories and mines, the majority of cadres are good or relatively good. (emphasis mine)[25]

The mere issuance of these instructions did not restore industrial peace. The PLA also was instructed to enter factories to maintain discipline.[26] Workers who had joined the radicals were difficult to control, and factional strife among workers was a frequent phenomenon. Reports of worker absenteeism persisted. The effort to put factory production on a firm footing remained an elusive goal for the rest of the year.

Although these developments were important, the main significance of the events in China's cities from December, 1966 to February, 1967 should not be lost. In the heat of the Cultural Revolution, the industrial managers and workers, acting together, were able to alter drastically the intended course of the Cultural Revolution. The working class and their managers have moved closer to the center of power in Chinese politics.

[25]*SCMP*, No. 3904, p. 9.
[26]For more detailed chronology see *China Quarterly*, No. 30, p. 209, 232–233.

## Intellectuals

In the broadest terms, intellectuals have three tasks. First, they pass the values and accumulated knowledge from one generation to another. Second, they increase the sum total of knowledge and create new works of art. Third, intellectuals criticize the society in which they live and point out alternative ways of ordering their society. Intellectuals can be distinguished according to the relative emphasis they place upon these roles. Thus, the teacher primarily transmits the knowledge of his generation to his students. The nuclear physicist is responsible for providing new information. The political satirist criticizes his society.

Depending upon the values of the society and the demands of the most powerful groups in the political arena, the particular roles performed by intellectuals command somewhat different rewards.[27] The Cultural Revolution demonstrated the political values of each of these roles in China.

**Social Critic.** The social critic was totally vulnerable to political control, as the attacks upon Wu Han and the Three Family Village with which he was associated revealed. To recall briefly, the historian Wu Han wrote on the virtues of the Ming minister Hai Jui.[28] Hai Jui had criticized a Ming emperor's alleged neglect of the peasants, and was removed from office as a result. Mao Tse-tung and those around him charged that Wu Han was using the story of Hai Jui as an allegory to attack Mao and defend P'eng Teh-huai, the dismissed Minister of Defense who had also protested against his leader's peasant policy. Mao, in short, was able to remove Wu Han and others after demonstrating that they were playing the role of social critic. This is not surprising for a society in which the distinction between criticism and disloyalty has often been blurred.

**Transmitters of Values and Knowledge.** The Cultural Revolution also showed that the transmitters of values and knowledge serve at the pleasure of the dominant political groups. As Mao's earlier optimism about the fate of the communist revolution gave way to a more pessimistic appraisal, he became more concerned with the educational process. While optimistic, he could afford to be lenient toward the past, for he believed

---

[27]For a general discussion, see Edward Shils, "The Intellectuals in the Political Development of the New States," in John Kautsky, ed., *Political Change in Underdeveloped Countries*, John Wiley, 1962, p. 195–235.

[28]For the editorials attacking Wu Han and the Three Family Village, see *The Great Socialist Cultural Revolution in China*, Peking: Foreign Language Press, 1966–67, 1–3. A collection of the satires attacking Mao which appeared in the Peking Press in the early 1960's was reprinted in Taiwan: *Teng T'o shih-wen hsuan-ch'i*, Taipei: Freedom Press, 1966.

China would not remain its captive. Later, the accumulated knowledge of the past and those who propagated it became threatening.

Several factors help to explain the political weakness of the propagandists, teachers, artists, and other transmiters of culture and knowledge. First, they had no economic allies, for few people's livelihoods depended upon them. Second, they were divided internally. Some younger "transmitters," such as the idealogues who came to the fore in late 1966 — Wang Li, Yao Wen-yuan, Ch'i Pen-yu, and Kuan Feng — apparently were ready to assist in the removal of their superiors. Third, many "transmitters" had strong enemies among their students. Initially, the weight of tradition and knowledge and its concomitant responsibilities rests heavy upon students, and they tend to resent those who place it upon them. Students therefore were ready allies of the political groups who attacked the propagandists and teachers.

**Researchers.** At the very moment the critics were condemned and the teachers were attacked, the press pointedly praised other intellectuals for developing nuclear weaponry, synthesizing insulin, and improving medical techniques.[29] The increasing importance of China's scientific community enables this segment of the intellectuals to exert its claims. A reasonable assumption is that many scientists are willing to recognize the supremacy of any political leader, so long as they are able to pursue their intellectual interests. This seems to be the tacit bargain struck during the Cultural Revolution. In the 1966-67 reports of their work, scientists always paid homage to the inspiration they derived from Chairman Mao. In exchange, Mao appears to have made fewer demands upon the time of scientists during this campaign than he did during the Great Leap Forward. For example, the twelfth point of the Sixteen Point Central Committee Directive on the Cultural Revolution specifically exempted the scientists, stating:

> As regards scientists, technicians, and ordinary members of working staffs, as long as they are patriotic, work energetically, are not against the Party and socialism, and maintain no illicit relations with any foreign country, we should in the present movement continue to apply the policy of "unity, criticism, unity." Special care should be taken of those scientists and scientific and technical personnel who have made contributions.[30]

Among China's intellectuals, the scientists fared best in 1966-67. Unlike peasants, industrial managers, or workers, who were able to defend

---

[29]*Peking Review*, No. 1, January 1, 1967, p. 15.
[30]*Peking Review*, No. 33, August 12, 1966, p. 10.

their interests only after an initial attack against them, the scientists saw their interests taken into account *prior* to the Cultural Revolution. Since their role in China's industrialization effort is valued by other groups in society, they appear to have representation at the center of power.


## Students


The Cultural Revolution suggests that Chinese students in many ways resemble students everywhere, particularly in the underdeveloped world. Four tendencies among Chinese students seem particularly noteworthy: idealism, deep ambivalence toward authority, highly developed consciousness of their student identity, and low capacity to form associations. These four characteristics must be analyzed at greater length.

**Student Idealism.** With respect to their idealism, Seymour Lipset put it well in a general essay on the topic: "Educated young people . . . tend disproportionately (to their numbers) to support idealistic movements which take the ideologies and values of the adult world more seriously than does the adult world itself."[31] Lipset's observation seems applicable to China. During the Cultural Revolution, as during the Hundred Flowers Campaign of 1957, the students did not reject the ideals of the adult world, but rather criticized adults for not practicing their ideals. Moreover, as Lipset would predict, many Chinese students adamantly refused to compromise on matters they deemed of principle. Theirs was a movement in pursuit of the millennium.

Several factors seem to have produced their radicalism, not the least of which was that the students had been the target of intensive ideological campaigns, especially from 1962 on. The majority of the Red Guards it should be remembered, were the first total products of the Chinese Communist educational system.[32] The values transmitted in these schools, glorifying revolution and Mao-Tse-tung, apparently had an impact.

Another reason for student radicalism was their limited stake in the *status quo*. The Red Guards drew a particularly enthusiastic response not from college students but from the younger, middle school students, precisely the segment of youth which had invested the least time and effort in

---

[31]Seymour Lipset, ed., *Student Politics*, Berkeley: Institute of International Studies, 1966, p. 140.

[32]Not all Red Guards were students, it should be noted, nor were all students Red Guards. Though in this section I discuss the student sector of Chinese Society with particular focus upon the more radical students, my remarks may be applicable to Chinese youth in general.

planning a career. Moreover, in the Chinese cultural context, students can more easily afford to be radical than adults because of their more limited familial obligations. Certainly one of the striking and credible revelations during the Cultural Revolution concerns the familial interests of the older cadres in China. As they matured and assumed demanding adult roles, the former student radicals of the 1920's and 1930's, acting as good Chinese, paid increasing attention to the fortunes of their families. They made sure that their descendents received a good education, and even established special schools for the families of cadres. They saw to it that their children married into decent families and obtained good jobs.[33] And in many instances, the revolutionary leaders of China seem to have enjoyed close, warm relations with their children and grandchildren. These concerns apparently sapped their revolutionary zeal, for rapid social change would have made it impossible for them to assure the continuity of their family. This may be one of the major reasons why students have been so important in China's radical movements. Away from home, with neither children nor dependent parents, students were relatively unencumbered by the net of mutual obligations which confine adult Chinese. They were free to be radical.

**Ambivalent Attitudes of Students Toward Older Generation.** Another characteristic of students, their tendency to regard the older generation with deep ambivalence, also helps to explain their idealism and zealotry. On the one hand, the Cultural Revolution indicated that many students seek the emotional support and intellectual guidance of an older authority figure. On the other hand, the Cultural Revolution also showed that many students tend to regard the older generation with distrust. In China, as elsewhere, a generational gap has developed. Some of the causes of the gap can be identified.

Many students apparently resented the fact that the older generation had the jobs and power which they wanted. The Red Guards concentrated their attacks upon those parts of the bureaucracy which had been most reluctant to promote youth. According to some refugee informants, the Party apparatus — particularly the secretariat on each governmental level and the Organization Department — placed the greatest stress upon seniority as a criterion for employment and promotion.[34] At the same time, the PLA and the finance and trade fields appear to have been more willing to reward youth. The PLA, with its "up or out" promotion system, guarantees to its younger members opportunities for upward mobility in

---

[33]See *China Topics,* No. 427, May 23, 1967, Section F; JPRS, 41, 514.
[34]This point is stressed throughout in A. Doak Barnett and Ezra Vogel, *Cadres, Bureaucracy, and Political Power in Communist China,* Columbia University Press, 1967.

the organization. The finance and trade system, expanding with the economy, probably was somewhat more able to offer employment opportunities to students. Not suprisingly, then, while the students were quick to "bombard the headquarters" of the Party apparatus, they were less concerned with bureaucratism in the PLA and the finance and trade system. In sum, their zealous conduct toward the older generation partly reflected a frustration in employment opportunities.

But this was not the only source of generational tensions. The Cultural Revolution also indicated that many Chinese students resented their elders placing unwanted responsibilities on their shoulders. Urban students in particular began to feel these burdens in their high school days, as they first contemplated the problems of career, marriage, filial obligations, and maintenance of traditions. The student violence toward both teachers and parents in July and August, 1966 underscored the hostility with which youth viewed those in charge of disciplining them.[35]

Yet another cause of the generational tensions was the different environments in which the older generation and the students were reared. Many older cadres, Mao included, viewed the younger generation with apprehension, fearful that their education in a peaceful China did not imbue them with a spirit of self-sacrifice and dedication to change.[36] Students also were keenly aware of the gap that separated them from the older revolutionary generation. As early as 1963, an article in the journal *China Youth* put the problem as seen by youth quite well:

> In discussing heroic persons, frequently one hears many youth say such things as, "The era creates heroes," "Only when a drop of water flows down a mountain can it become part of a wave. Our lives are in an era of peaceful construction. We are water on a plain and only can advance slowly and quietly."
>
> The feelings go to such lengths that some youth believe they were born at an unfortunate time. They say, "If I were born thirty years earlier, I certainly would have participated in the Long March; if I were born twenty years earlier, I certainly would have been a hero in the anti-Japanese war. If I were ten years older, I certainly would have compiled a war record in Korea."[37]

This passage points both to the generational gap which youth perceived, and more significantly, to their desire to narrow that gap. In other words, the above quotation reveals the eagerness of some youths to seize

---

[35]For one discussion of antagonistic student-teacher relations, see Radio Canton, Regional #2, April 3, 1967.

[36]See James Townsend's excellent study, *The Revolutionization of Chinese Youth*, Berkeley: Center for Chinese Studies Monograph, 1966.

[37]*China Youth*, No. 7, 1963, p. 11.

an opportunity to "make revolution," and thereby to join the portion of the older generation whose exploits they admire. Under the communists as well as in traditional times, Chinese moral education makes considerable use of models whom students are taught either to follow or shun.[38] Teenagers are conditioned to search for model men to emulate, and they search for models among older men as well as among youth. Thus, the ambivalent attitude of students toward the older generation becomes understandable. While they resented the burdens the elders place upon them, they depended upon the elders to provide them with models of moral action.[39]

Many students in China, the Red Guards' experience suggests, adopted the model of the Chinese revolutionary tradition, with the romanticism and heroism they assocated with it. In this, they follow Mao. Leaders who successfully associated themselves with this tradition and who were sympathetic to problems of youth acquired student support. On the other hand, the students seemed prone to reject the adult's world of bureaucracy, which to them meant examinations and the need to plan careers. They considered as negative examples the men who, they were told, were responsible for bureaucracy — Liu Shao-ch'i, Teng Hsiao-p'ing, P'eng Chen, et al.

The accounts of Chou En-lai's appearances among the students give the impression of a leader who successfully bridged the generational gap and enjoyed a special rapport with the students. (His support among the students in the early days of the Cultural Revolution, in turn, may have added to his power within leadership circles.) One such account told of a Chou En-lai visit to Tsinghau University. Displaying magnificent command of Mandarin, Chou stated:

> In regard to your school, only by coming into your midst will one penetrate the masses. Nevertheless, now that I have come, I am still barely scratching the surface. (Audience: No!) No? I am sincere, let us think it over. If I do not go to your class room, your dormitory, and your dining room, how can I dissolve the unnecessary estrangement, unnecessary opposition, and unnecessary misunderstanding among you? Yet, you may ask me: Why are you so selfish? I am not! It is not being selfish. I feel bad that the problems were not solved satisfactorily by my talk last time. . . . . . I heard that, after my talk here last time, your problems were not satisfactorily solved, and that you posted three large-letter bulletins about me. They were too few. Reading over my speech again, I feel that you did not post enough large-letter bulletins. Many of your suggestions are correct.

---

[38]See Donald Munro, "Maxims and Realities in China's Educational Policy," *Asian Survey*, Vol. 7, No. 4, April, 1967, p. 254–272.

[39]See Richard Solomon, *The Chinese Revolution and the Politics of Dependency*, MS., University of Michigan, 1966.

I wish to discuss my views once more. One must ceaselessly examine oneself. As I already mentioned last time, one must work, learn, and reform all one's life.[40]

The speech was delivered in a rain, but Chou apparently refused offers to hold an umbrella over him, saying, "You gave me a Red Guard arm badge. Similar to you, we also steel ourselves in the great storms." At the end of his talk, Chou led the students in singing of "Sailing the Seas Depends on the Helmsman." His was a masterful performance of a 68-year-old man successfully bridging the generational gap. The response he elicited is testimony to the importance of this aspect of the problem of youth in China today.

**Student Consciousness.** A third aspect of student life made evident in the Cultural Revolution was its intensity. College students and even many high school students lived on large campuses; their dormitories were crowded. In the suburbs of Peking, for example, several large university campuses were in close proximity. In such an environment, as at large American universities, students had little contact with faculty. They formed their own community, and acquired a high consciousness of their identity as students. In fact, some of Marx's observations about the sources of working-class consciousness are applicable to the rise of student consciousness: large numbers of people massed together, in similar positions, having a high rate of interaction. In addition, Chinese students, particularly those attending Peking University and Tsinghua University, were aware of the role of their predecessors in the May Fourth and December Ninth movements. It was therefore, in a sense, natural for the students to respond, as a group, to Mao's initial call for a student movement.

Moreover, student self-awareness probably was intensified during 1966-67. Group consciousness tends to be heightened by the kind of conflict that students experienced in 1966-67. In addition, student consciousness probably developed as their parochial, regional loyalties were weakened through the nationwide marches and "linking up" activities.

**Student Inability to Organize.** A fourth characteristic, an especially fascinating aspect of the Cultural Revolution, was the students' inability to form effective associations, in spite of the constant exhortations to do so. Intense factional disputes marked Red Guard activities almost from their inception. While the issues involved in the disputes are not entirely clear, in part they appear to reflect the factional strife among the elite. Mao and the group around him organized Red Guard groups in the summer of

[40]JPRS 41, 313, June 8, 1967, p. 14–21.

1966 to assist them in their attacks upon perceived enemies in the Party and government bureaucracy. Very soon thereafter, other officials began organizing Red Guard groups loyal to them.

As the conflicts between these Red Guard groups intensified and spread throughout the country, particularly from January to August, 1967, it apparently became possible for other students to form their own, unaffiliated organizations. The students of China, accustomed to a highly structured environment, suddenly found themselves in a near-chaotic situation. Previously, students were told which organizations were good, which were bad; they had little choice in organizational affiliations. Now, they had to choose among virtually indistinguishable organizations, recognizing that the wrong affiliation could ruin their careers. Little wonder, then, that in such an environment, with little previous experience in forming associations, the students failed miserably. They rapidly degenerated into quarreling, disruptive groups. Unaccustomed to the process of compromise and decision, debates over seemingly trivial issues apparently quickly became problems symbolic of the struggle between the two roads of capitalism and socialism. Coercion became the only way to re-establish order among the youth. The PLA dispatched units to schools; several young rowdies were executed in stadiums and the spectacle televised.

Another related phenomenon also appeared at this time. Unable to associate effectively, some youths simply withdrew from any political activity. Withdrawal apparently was widespread enough to deserve comment from one of Shanghai's leading papers, *Wen-hui Pao*. An editorial in the paper stated:

> There has emerged a number of people who do not pay attention to state affairs and who remain outside the revolutionary movement. These people can be called wanderers.
> They are people who entertain the attitude of non-intervention toward the life-and-death struggle between the proletariat and the bourgeoisie. Whenever they are required to reveal their attitude, they usually just issue a vague statement. Instead of fighting. . . . they wander around school campuses, parks, and streets. . . They pay no attention to proletarian politics and become dispassionate onlookers.
> Some are the so-called veteran rebels who, after a long period of time, became tired of the civil wars among the mass organizations to which they belonged. Instead of seeking ways to stop civil wars and fighting the common enemy, they flew the flag of truce in order to avoid trouble.[41]

The editorial confirms a predictable development. The Red Guards were intended in part to build a sense of community among youth. While

---

[41]Radio Shanghai, July 9, 1967.

undoubtedly becoming more conscious of their identity, instead of acquiring a sense of belonging, the youth probably became more aware of their isolation and their inability to form associations. Moreover, unattainable expectations were probably aroused among some youth in the course of the Cultural Revolution. The sense of isolation and the disappointments appear to have led to alienation or anomie rather than to commitment, the *Wen-hui Pao* editorial suggests.

**Students during the Cultural Revolution.** With the four characteristics of Chinese youth as revealed during 1966-67 —their radicalism, ambivalence toward authority, sense of identity, and low capability of association — it is now possible to summarize the ability of the students to affect public policy during the Cultural Revolution. At the outset, the eager students were easily mobilized to attack the bureaucrats in the culture and education system. This occurred by September, 1966. Mao and his associates saw that they had forged a powerful organizational weapon. The brutal Red Guard attacks upon defenseless victims in August and September, 1966, however, soon made clear that the weapon would not be easily controlled. The mass rallies held from August to October in Peking were perhaps envisioned as a method for providing the youth with an emotional catharsis that would reduce their lust for violence.[42] At the same time, the energy of the youth was tapped by Mao and the radicals around him to attack provincial level Party organizations throughout the country.

But for tens of millions of youths demanding participation in revolutionary activity, the dragging out of a couple hundred provincial and municipal level Party secretaries only whetted the appetite. The youth appear to have kept pressing for more and bigger targets. In early December, 1966, as mentioned earlier, the industrial sector was opened, while on December 15, the rural sector was opened. With the resistance encountered in both these sectors, they were removed from the list of targets in late January. The leaders of China cast about for diversionary targets and in February and March, foreign embassies in Peking bore the brunt of Red Guard hostility. But this too had its limits. Several foreign countries were in no mood to tolerate such diplomatic outrages. In March, the target was narrowed to Liu Shao-ch'i, Teng Hsiao-p'ing, T'ao Chu, and the other "top Party persons in authority taking the capitalist road." At the same time, students were encouraged to return to school.

The rebellious force which the leaders had unleashed eight months earlier was not easy to contain, however. In search of new targets, the

---

[42]This theme is suggested in Philip Bridgham, "Mao's Cultural Revolution," *op. cit.*

more radical students next wanted to take on the army. One reason for the increased animosity among many students toward the army was the role it played in quelling factional strife among youth. Following the July defiance of Peking's orders by the Wuhan garrison commander Ch'en Tsai-tao, students apparently increased the pressure to be given the army as a target; some of the ultra-radicals in Mao's entourage supported the student demands. In late August this target was firmly denied to them and new efforts were then made to open schools. By late fall, 1967, the Red Guards were less frequently in the news, and in January, 1968, a call came for a rectification campaign in Red Guard organizations. The main youth organization prior to the advent of the Red Guards, the Communist Youth League (CYL), rarely mentioned during 1967, began to be mentioned again in early 1968. The radical student movement had run its course, and an effort was being made to re-establish control over youth. In sum, youth were on the periphery of the political arena prior to mid-1966, had been allowed to enter the center by the radicals to wreak their havoc and steel themselves in revolution in 1966-67, and were being pushed to the periphery again by the army and the moderates in the Party and government in 1968.

**Student Potential to Affect Future Policy.** Several factors make it unlikely that student interests will be as peripheral to the political process as they were from 1950 to 1965. The memory of the Red Guards will linger on in the minds of bureaucrats, who probably will be somewhat more responsive to the demands of youth as a result. In addition, the youth have learned some lessons about voicing their interests which they are not likely to forget. Moreover, demographic trends probably will force the rulers to be particularly sensitive to the problems of youth. Their rapidly increasing numbers place an undeniable burden upon existing educational facilities and force the rulers to provide them with employment.

Further, the leaders will have to cope with the widespread cynicism, alienation and anomie among students, a result of the broken promises of 1966 that idealistic and perhaps opportunistic students soon would be able to make important contributions to the pursuit of Mao's utopian vision. Only months after they made these promises, the leaders were coercing students to return to the same stations they had occupied prior to the Cultural Revolution. In the next few years, the idealistic appeals that worked in 1966 are unlikely to work again. The leaders probably will find that they can restore student confidence only by fulfilling specific demands for educational and employment opportunities.[43]

---

[43]The argument is derived from G. William Skinner's theory of a compliance cycle in China. See his important, "Compliance and Leadership in Rural Communist China," a paper delivered to the 1965 Annual Meeting of the American Political Science Association.

In addition, the problem of unequal educational opportunities for youth will certainly persist in the coming decades. According to an estimate by the American demographer John Aird, to achieve universal secondary education by 1985, the secondary educational system would have to enroll a minimum of six million additional students per year, a virtually impossible rate of expansion.[44] In view of their deep commitment to building an egalitarian society, the rulers will probably again feel called upon, as they were during the Cultural Revolution, to alleviate the tensions that develop as some youths enjoy upward mobility while others return to the countryside.

As a result of these factors, one aspect of the Cultural Revolution, its emphasis upon the problems of youth, may foreshadow future Chinese politics. In this sense, the Cultural Revolution may have signalled a partial return of youth to the political position they held prior to communist rule.

## Party and Government Bureaucrats

Prior to the Cultural Revolution, the Chinese Communists described the organizational trinity that ran their country as the Party, the government, and the army (*tang, cheng, chun*). But in February, 1967, when Mao and his entourage called for the formation of "Three-Way Alliance" organizations in the provinces and cities, they referred to a new trinity: (1) the Party *and* the government; (2) the army; and (3) the revolutionary mass organizations. Although the Party and the government retained their separate identity, the delineation between them, which had been so carefully preserved in theory prior to 1966, was blurred.

The lumping together of Party and government in the Three Way Alliance merely gave explicit acknowledgment to a development which students of Chinese politics had long recognized. The overlapping membership in the two organizations, the existence of Party organizations within the government, and the close supervision by the Party of government activities made it difficult to distinguish between the two.

Mao's placement of Party and government in the same category in February, 1967 was the logical outcome of the intense Party involvement in governmental affairs which began during the Great Leap. In oversimplified terms, the First Five Year Plan (1953-57) was run by people in the governmental apparatus; the burden of economic development fell upon their shoulders. The Party remained a vanguard organization; mem-

---

[44]John Aird, "Population Growth and Distribution in Mainland China," Joint Economic Committee of U.S. Congress, *An Economic Profile of Mainland China*, Vol. II, p. 341–403.

bers of the Party apparatus exercised broad control over the government but remained aloof from day-to-day details, in order to preserve their organizational and ideological purity. By 1957 however, the officials in governmental apparatus had become enmeshed in the society they were trying to change. Mao was alarmed by the alacrity with which government officials were increasingly bureaucratized from 1953 to 1957. So, in the Great Leap of 1958-60, he committed his vanguard organization, the CCP, directly to the battle to modernize China. But by 1965, many members of the CCP also had lost their reformist zeal. Inextricably intertwined with the entire society, the Party had come to contain within it all the contradictions, particularist loyalties, and tensions of Chinese society at large. In a sense, by 1966, Mao had used up two organizations in the pursuit of his vision.

In essence, the Cultural Revolution was an attempt by Mao and his associates to remove those government and Party cadres whom he perceived to be ineffective and to draw upon a fresh organization — the PLA — in the modernization effort. But such a design obviously did not coincide with the interests of the Party and government cadres, who wished to retain their jobs and protect the power of their organizations. (The reaction of the military officers, many of whom also opposed Mao's plans, is discussed below.) By the beginning of 1968, it appeared that most bureaucrats, with the exception of those at the top echelons on each level, had successfully resisted efforts to dislodge them. As a group, the Party and government bureaucrats retained their positions of power.

**Bureaucratic Power and Vulnerabilities.** What explains the ability of the bureaucrats to withstand the attacks upon their positions? Three obvious factors stand out. The performance of the routine tasks required for society to survive, from preventing epidemics to the merchandising of goods, depended upon the bureaucrats. To attempt to remove them, as nearly happened in Shanghai in early 1967, would result in the total disruption of society. In addition, the network of organizations developed under communist rule helped to unify the country. As Mao discovered in 1967, a concerted effort to destroy these organizations brought China to the precipice of civil war. Finally, in contrast to other aggregates in Chinese society, such as the peasants, the industrial workers and managers, and the intellectuals, the bureaucrats had their own organizations and enjoyed direct access to the policy formulation process. They were thus better equipped to defend their interests.

While these considerations help to explain why the bureaucrats as an aggregate remained in power, they do not explain the power of individual bureaucrats. Many individuals were able to build positions of considerable strength through their skilled use of personal ties, the manipulation of channels of communication, and the wise allocation of the resources at their disposal. Moreover, the opportunity to act in their own interest was increased by the discretion they enjoyed in making decisions, a discretion that arose in part from the vaguely worded directives they received from Peking.

Several factors made the individual Party or government bureaucrat vulnerable to outside control, particularly his dependence upon superiors to provide money and materials and to grant him promotions. Since these have been explored in the existing literature on contemporary Chinese politics, they need not be discussed here.[45] But in addition to the commonly mentioned techniques for maintaining discipline within the bureaucracy, two others deserve comment because of their prominence in the Cultural Revolution. First, the thorough files (*tang-an*) detailing their behavior over extended periods of time made individual bureaucrats vulnerable to innumerable distorted charges, all allegedly based on the record. Second, perhaps to an extent previously underestimated in earlier studies, the leaders of China have based their legitimacy upon the ideas and symbol of Mao Tse-tung. The denial of that symbol to an individual bureaucrat made it impossible for him to justify his role.

A word of caution is in order before we examine the sources of bureaucratic power and vulnerability in greater detail. The examples cited in the discussion below come from the indictments of top-level officials. Not all bureaucrats had the opportunity to engage in such activities. Nonetheless, the themes probably are applicable to the practices of lower-level officials, such as bureau chiefs and commune directors. A striking aspect of the purge documents is that they tend to confirm the picture of bureaucratic politics on the mainland obtained from former lower-level cadres interviewed in Hong Kong.

**Personal Ties**. Development of a network of reliable friends and loyal subordinates was a crucial part of building an invulnerable position. The purge of Li Ching-ch'uan, for example, revealed how this leader in China's Southwest apparently had built an apparatus loyal to him. He was accused of getting "hold of a number of lackeys and scattering them throughout the Southwest."[46] Prime examples cited were the appointment of his long-time colleagues Yen Hung-yen and Chia Chi-yun to the positions of First Secretary of Yunnan and Kweichow, respectively. Li appar-

---

[45]In particular, see Audrey Donnithorne, *China's Economic System*, Allen and Unwin, 1967, esp. last chapter, and Barnett and Vogel, *Cadres, Bureaucracy . . .*, *op. cit.*

[46]Radio Kweiyang, June 4, 1967.

ently also was quick to remove subordinates who displayed disloyalty to him. More interesting, he appeared willing to employ and perhaps protect officials who were under a political cloud in Peking. He was accused of "taking in traitors and renegades and placing them in very important positions in the Southwest."[47] (P'eng Teh-huai was the most noteworthy example, having obtained a position in the CCP Control Commission in the Southwest Bureau.) Finally, Li was careful to retain his contacts in Peking. Circumstantial evidence suggests that Li and the Southwest Bureau maintained a staff office in Peking to provide information on central politics and to lobby for the Southwest's interests.[48] The denunciations of Li also suggest that he maintained warm relations with several former associates, particularly Politburo members Ho Lung and Teng Hsiao-p'ing, after they moved to Peking.

T'ao Chu's proteges were mentioned by name. For example, T'ao was said to have promoted his disciple Wen Min-sheng, the deposed Governor of Honan, seven times in fourteen years, and "Wen showed his gratitude by lauding T'ao Chu to the sky."[49] In fact, one of the clearest indications of the development of cliques came with T'ao Chu's rise to national prominence in the summer of 1966. Following him to Peking were three first secretaries in the Central-South: Wang Jen-chung of Hopeh, Chang P'ing-hua of Hunan, and Yao Wen-t'ao of Canton. When T'ao fell in late December, 1966, all three officials fell with him.

**Control of Communication Channels.** Another source of power, closely related to personal ties, was control over the channels of information. To establish extensive control over the communication network that extended beyond one's organization required the assistance of loyal subordinates and friends outside one's agency. Again, the purge of Li Ching-ch'uan provided some fascinating details of how a high level bureaucrat sought to seal his area and control the data that flowed from it. One charge against Li claimed:

> He never sent proper reports to the Party Central Committee and Chairman Mao, but rather sent in false reports.[50]

As an example of Li's behavior, Radio Chengtu described Li's alleged attempt in 1962 to portray Szechuan as in the grip of a spring drought

---

[47]*Ibid.*
[48]JPRS 42, 349, August 25, 1967, p. 63; *China Topics*, No. 437, August 18, 1967, p. 9.
[49]Radio Chengchow, October 12, 1967.
[50]Radio Kweiyang, June 4, 1967; Radio Chengtu, October 26, 1967.

that would seriously affect agricultural production. The broadcast continued:

> The old Szechuan Daily printed a report entitled "Welcome Rain Falls Throughout the Province." Li Ching-ch'uan, who was at a conference in Peking at this time, then rushed to telephone Szechuan to vigorously criticize this and forbid its publication. After 1962, the press and radio in Szechuan were instructed that they could only say "increase of production," not "bumper harvest" or still less, "great bumper harvest." The rate of production increase for units of county level and above was not to be reported. Thus, Li deliberately sealed off news from Chairman Mao.[51]

Naturally, Mao was one of the key targets in the manipulation of information. One reasonable hypothesis about Chinese politics is that a crucial part of the game centers on attempts to control what Mao reads. This hypothesis is supported by yet another charge against Li:

> In 1966, just when the black gang element Peng Chen was organizing his "February Report Outline," he came specially to Szechuan with a handful of confederates to hold secret talks with Li Ching-chuan. After returning to Peking, Peng telephoned Li to tell him: "Chairman Mao is reading the local (i.e., provincial as opposed to national—M. O.) papers every day." Peng urged Li to have more repudiation articles printed in the Szechuan papers. . .[52]

The list of techniques employed by ingenious officials to control the flow of communications from their organizations is a long one. The ones cited above —falsifying statistics, suppressing weather reports, and editing the news in anticipation of Mao's desires—merely scratch the surface. Escorting visiting officials to model, Potemkin-type areas, tapping telephones, and enforcing strict censorship apparently were other favorite techniques. The low turnover rate among local officials, particularly at the provincial level, often enabled a bureaucrat to develop an extensive web of personal contacts and to establish effective control over the flow of communications out of his unit. Though firm evidence is hard to obtain, the scattered examples gain credibility because of their strong resemblance to the way bureaucrats operated in traditional China.

**Control of Resources.** Another source of a bureaucrat's power was his control over material resources, which he often used to enhance his posi-

---

[51]Radio Chengtu, October 13, 1967.
[52]Radio Chengtu, September 15, 1967.

tion. The charges against T'ao Chu, though perhaps exaggerated, illustrate the practice:

> The foundation of industry in Kwantung, especially light industry, is comparatively good. If we resolutely implement Chairman Mao's instruction to make use of the original industry, then we can do a better job in supporting industry in the interior of China. However the counterrevolutionary T'ao Chu stubbornly resisted and opposed Chairman Mao's instructions. . . T'ao said: "We should build a complete industrial system in Canton."
>
> In order to achieve this "industrial system," T'ao did not actively help, make use of, reform, and develop the original enterprises, especially in small and poorly equipped street industry and handicraft enterprises. He held that this kind of industry was backward and could not be developed further. . . . He blindly chased after "big," "foreign," and "new," trying his best to demand capital and equipment from the Center. . .[53]

Similar charges of increasing the wealth of his area at the expense of the center were made against Liu Chien-hsun, the former First Secretary of Honan, who emerged unscathed in 1968 as head of Honan's provincial revolutionary committee.[54] In violation of instructions from Peking, Liu allegedly encouraged peasants to plant peanuts for sale to the state by promising them that in addition to the cash payments for each *chin* of marketed peanuts, the state would sell them one *chin* and two ounces of reasonably priced grain. Under this incentive system, Liu apparently hoped that the provincial warehouses would be filled with more peanuts, a valuable commodity producing vegetable oil. But his policy also caused a decrease in Honan's grain production, since peanuts were grown on land that otherwise would have been planted in grain. As a result, Honan, a grain-deficient province at the time, increased its dependence upon grain allotments from the center. In the five years Liu worked in Honan (1961-66), the province allegedly received over six billion *chin* of grain shipped by the Central Committee. The saying in Honan supposedly was: "Eat in Kwangtung and burn coal from Shansi." When the Central Committee directed Liu to abolish his program of guaranteed state sale of grain in exchange for marketed peanuts, he proved reluctant to comply.

**Discretion in Policy Formulation.** As these examples indicate — and many similar instances can be cited — the head of a unit often wished to enhance the ability of his unit to bargain effectively with competing units. In many instances, moreover, he was able to succeed because of the wide

---

[53]Radio Canton, December 1, 1967.
[54]JPRS 43, 357, November 16, 1967, p. 29–30.

discretion he enjoyed in formulating policy. The discretion was not as much the result of deliberate decentralization as it was the result of the vaguely worded directives he received.

This aspect of the environment in which Chinese bureaucrats worked needs to be placed in broader perspective. The information obtained during 1966-67 indicates that at least since the Tenth Plenum of 1962, the Central Committee of the CCP was deeply divided over a large number of issues. The disunified elite were unable to provide decisive, bold leadership to the bureaucracy. The divisions among the rulers were smoothed over through the issuance of vague directives. Often these were drafted by erstwhile colleagues of Mao such as Liu Shao-ch'i and P'eng Chen, who based their directives upon Mao's even more vague oral instructions. Examples are several important directives on rural policy issued during the 1960's, which have recently become available. What characterizes all of them is their ambiguity and sterility.[55] Instead of issuing explicit written orders, the top leaders apparently preferred to shape policy through a series of personal *ad hoc* conferences and trips to the provinces. The denunciations of Liu, Teng, and P'eng, for instance, indicated that these officials made frequent appearances in the provinces to inspect conditions, discuss problems, and deliver instructions. However, it seems that such conferences and appearances usually did not produce more precise directives.

This situation yielded both advantages and disadvantages to the bureaucrat. On the one hand, he was able to interpret the instructions in the light most favorable to his unit. Such behavior should not necessarily be viewed cynically, for most bureaucrats probably considered themselves loyal to Chairman Mao and the Party center, and had come to believe sincerely that the interests of their units coincided with the national interest. Yet, while the bureaucrat inevitably tended to bend the vague directives to suit his interests, thereby strengthening his unit, at the same time he was vulnerable to the accusation of deliberately misinterpreting the directives. Moreover, the higher level leaders who drafted the vague directives were open to the charges that they had violated the spirit of Mao's oral statements.

The conduct of the Four Clearances campaign in China's countryside in 1963-65 provided an excellent example.[56] In late 1962, Mao expressed dissatisfaction with the caliber and honesty of rural, basic-level cadres.

---

[55] The Hoover Institution has a complete file of these directives obtained from GRC authorities in Taiwan.

[56] For discussion of "Four Clearances," see Charles Neuhauser, "The Chinese Communist Party in the 1960's," *China Quarterly*, No. 32. Also, Richard Baum and Frederic Teiwes, *Ssu-Ch'ing: The Socialist Education Movement of 1962–1966*, Berkeley: Center for Chinese Studies, 1968.

However, while calling for a "Four Clearance" campaign to improve the situation, he did not address himself to the problem of standards. Instead, he handed the problem to Liu Shao-ch'i. In 1967, Mao claimed that Liu had violated his instructions by setting too high standards. Mao accused Liu of wishing to purge an excessive number of basic-level cadres, making them scapegoats for peasant discontent that should have been directed toward Liu. Despite Mao's claims, Liu's directives appear to have been so vague that no standard was clearly stated. The responses to Liu's directive were not uniform. Some provincial officials did not push the campaign, and during the Cultural Revolution they were accused of ignoring the problems of cadre corruption and the spread of capitalism. Other officials placed heavy emphasis upon Four Clearances, and in 1966-67, they were accused of unjustly condemning local cadres, thereby protecting Liu Shao-ch'i. In sum, the vagueness of the directives meant that when accused of anti-Maoist activity, a bureaucrat was unable to prove that he had not violated them.

**The Dossier.** Another source of a bureaucrat's vulnerability was the thorough dossier of his past activities. Rare was the Chinese bureaucrat who, at some point in his career, had not engaged in some form of conspicuous consumption, had not spoken somewhat disparagingly about the political system, had not barked orders to a subordinate rather than employing mass line techniques, or had not associated with "bad elements." Such activities often were recorded in his dossier, and were there to be used against him if the need arose. Subordinates who disliked their superior but were unable to damage him in any other way could fill their superior's files with charges of misconduct. Also in the dossier were remarks made during periods in which CCP policy was moderate. One such period occurred in 1961-62, when most leaders—again including Mao—stressed the need of restoring the economy through material incentives. But such speeches appeared damning if reproduced out of context in 1966-67, when Mao stressed class struggle and the evils of material incentives.

As the purge swept the bureaucracy, contending factions tried to obtain the dossiers of their rivals in order to gather "black materials" on them. Not surprisingly, during the Cultural Revolution, there were constant reports of illegal seizures of personnel files, and repeated efforts were made to re-establish central control over them. A bureaucrat rightfully feared that his dossier contained enough evidence to condemn him, if it fell into malicious hands. The dossier made the bureaucrat vulnerable to the control of the man who held it.

**Bureaucratic Claim to Legitimacy.** Another source of bureaucratic vulnerability stemmed from the nature of the regime's claim to legitimacy.

Although in the 1950's China's leaders justified their right to rule by nationalistic and economic appeals, through time they have increasingly based the claims of their legitimacy upon the sanctity of the thought of Mao Tse-tung. Thus, the authority of the bureaucrats was justified neither because their commands made the average Chinese more prosperous nor because their actions built a better China, but because their rule was in accordance with the thought of Mao Tse-tung. The power-holders in China had equated the right of rule with being a disciple of Mao Tse-tung. Whoever manipulated the symbol of Mao—and when Mao was vigorous, he manipulated it—controlled the bureaucrat's claim to legitimacy.

Once an individual bureaucrat's loyalty to Mao was questioned and his dossier was made public, his power—based upon his network of friends, his control over information, and the allocation of his limited resources—gradually eroded. Other bureaucrats sought to disassociate themselves from him, for fear that they might be labelled part of his gang. He became a target for and suffered the humiliation of struggle. He was isolated.

**Strategy for Survival.** Working under the intense physical and psychological pressure of the Cultural Revolution and realizing his vulnerability to purge, the individual bureaucrat had political survival as his main objective. The strategies he employed were to cling tenaciously to the source of his legitimacy by claiming that he was a good Maoist, to seal his unit off from outside interference, as much as possible, and to secure the continued support of his loyal subordinates. These tactics were not sufficient to protect all officials, but, given their crucial social role, most Party and government bureaucrats weathered the storm and remained in positions of power as the Cultural Revolution subsided in early 1968.

## Military

To appreciate the power and influence of the military in Chinese society, one must understand the position of the PLA during the Cultural Revolution. While most analysts agree that the PLA played a crucial role in 1966-67, they differ in their evaluations.

**The PLA Rise to Power.** Some analysts stated that the military had taken over. Impressive evidence exists to support this contention. PLA units were dispatched to factories and schools, where the troop commanders assumed important leadership functions. The PLA, already deeply immersed in such tasks as running the railroads and organizing propaganda prior to the Cultural Revolution, increased its responsibilities in these vital areas. When one looked at the top official in each of the provinces, one found that although a few of the new and surviving officials had careers within the CCP, most were former military officers. Some of them, such as Li Yuan in Hunan or Li Ts'ai-han in Kweichow, had risen from obscurity; their names were not listed in the standard biographic guides to China's leaders. In Peking, the national holidays were presided over by military men. Newspaper editorials throughout 1967 stressed the crucial role performed by the PLA in society. In 1967, Mao's closest comrade-in-arms and his likely successor was said to be the Minister of Defense and head of the Military Affairs Committee, Lin Piao. The nationally debated issues reflected the concerns of the military apparatus: the amount of time the army should spend in physical training versus the amount of time spent on the study of Mao's works, the role of the PLA troops stationed in factories and schools, the relations between the military and other sectors of society, the obligations of the regional garrison commanders to obey the center, and even the role of the navy in domestic peace keeping functions. When the leaders of the country are drawn from the military, when the issues debated in the press are of particular relevance to the military, and when the military stationed its troops in non-military units throughout the country, the evidence strongly suggests that a military takeover occurred.

Moreover, there were signs that the rise of the PLA was the result of a conscious rivalry with the CCP. The PLA had intimate organizational links with the Red Guards, who led the attacks upon the CCP apparatus. One of the key Red Guard units, for example, came from the Peking Aviation Institute, a school with close PLA connections. Some Red Guard newspapers also spoke of an organizational rivalry between the Party and the PLA. For instance, the Ministry of Railways and the PLA shared jurisdiction over the railways. The Minister of Railways, Lu Cheng-ts'ao, was accused of wanting to control the armed railroad personnel, who were under PLA command. Lu allegedly maintained:

> The Public Security Ministry controls its own public security forces. Why shouldn't the Railway Ministry control railway forces?[57]

Lu was accused of "wanting to usurp the power and authority of the PLA."

Invective in a similar vein had been directed earlier against Ten T'o, the dismissed editor of *Peking Daily*:

---

[57]JPRS 41, 249, June 2, 1967, p. 46–67.

We must warn Ten T'o and his ilk that the right to "contend" is not allowed in the PLA, and the fighters of the people will wipe out those who dare to stick their nose into the army under the pretext of contention.[58]

These quotes hinting at a possible PLA-CCP rivalry lend weight to an interpretation of the Cultural Revolution that stresses a PLA takeover from the Party.

On the other hand, several factors made it misleading simply to state that the military seized power in China. First, the military apparatus in China lacked clear cut organizational identity and was thoroughly interwoven with the CCP. The commanders of the PLA who acquired power in 1967 probably were also CCP members. The rise to power of PLA commanders can be seen as a shift in the balance of power within the Party, with CCP members serving in the military sector taking power from those in charge of such internal Party work as organization and propaganda.

Second, not all elements in the military enhanced their position in 1966-67. In fact, many leaders of the PLA were purged. The most noteworthy cases included the dismissals of Chief-of-Staff Lo Jui-ch'ing, the head of the Political Department, Hsiao Hua, and Marshal Ho Lung, but the purge extended to garrison commanders, department heads, political commissars, and others.[59] If one is to speak in organizational terms, one cannot speak of a PLA takeover; one must speak of the seizure of power by specific units within the PLA. But here, no discernable pattern emerges, although there are some tantalizing hints. For instance, in recent years three newly appointed regional commanders came from the Shenyang garrison command,[60] Kiangsi province was occupied during the Cultural Revolution by troops dispatched from the Tsinan garrison command,[61] and the Wuhan rebellion was quelled, in part, through the dispatch from Shanghai of a naval force attached to the East China fleet.[62] A hypothesis that merits testing is that several army, navy, and air commands (such as Shenyang and Tsinan), perhaps owing allegiance to Lin Piao, acted together, that forces from these units occupied various areas, and that the newly risen military personnel were drawn primarily from these units. But until firm evidence is uncovered, such hypotheses must be held in abeyance. Thus, the unqualified assertion that the PLA

---

[58]Radio Peking, May 24, 1966.
[59]In *China News Summary*, No. 188–194.
[60]*Ibid.*
[61]Radio Nanchang, September 6, 1967 and October 9, 1967.
[62]Radio Wuhan, October 22, 1967.

had risen to power glosses over the difficult yet crucial problems of a complex process within the PLA which led to the promotion of some and the purge of other military figures.

A third reason that the image of a "military takeover" needs qualification was its incompleteness. Many government and Party officials, even at higher levels, survived. Hunan provides a convenient example. Li Yuan and PLA unit 6900, which had been garrisoned in Hengyang, began to dominate news items from Ch'angsha. But Li appears to be the leader of a group that includes Hua Kuo-feng and Chang Po-sen, both of whom have long records of leadership in Party and government affairs in Hunan. Hua was First Secretary of Hsiang-t'an Special District in Hunan in the early 1950's, served as head of the provincial government's Culture and Education Office and the Party's United Front Department in the late 1950's, and was an active Party secretary and Vice Governor in the early 1960's. Chang's tenure in Hunan also dates back to the early 1950's, when he was head of the Provincial Party Finance and Trade Department. The Hunan pattern was observable elsewhere. Leaders of the PLA won positions of power, but their rise was not accompanied by the total removal of leading government and Party bureaucrats.

A fourth consideration against labelling the enhanced power of the military as a "takeover" was the noticeable reluctance of some military leaders to assume their new roles in domestic affairs. Military commanders in China were concerned with the capacity of their forces to fight against foreign powers. As the PLA became increasingly involved with domestic functions in the 1960's, of necessity it sacrificed some of its capacity to wage war. Lo Jui-ch'ing apparently was one of the officials opposed to the policy. Moreover, since the PLA automatically created enemies when it tried to restore order between conflicting groups and individuals, local commanders were reluctant to become involved. If the PLA intervened on the side of one Red Guard organization, the other side became disenchanted. If the PLA tried to work out compromises, then the organizations accused the PLA of not settling the dispute on the basis of principles. During the early part of 1967, many PLA commanders apparently tried to shield their units from the turmoil, but the spreading chaos could be dampened only through military intervention. To a certain extent, it was less that the PLA eagerly seized power than that it reluctantly filled an organizational vacuum.

**Sources of PLA Power.** Even with these qualifications, it remains true that the PLA significantly increased its power and influence. Part of the explanation for this rests in Mao's confidence in Lin Piao and the PLA, a confidence inspired by the political program carried out in the army from 1959 to 1965. Because the PLA stood apart from civilian society, ideological indoctrination probably could be carried out more effectively in the PLA than in other institutions in society. The effectiveness of the program in the PLA led Mao, who perhaps failed to discern the inherent differences between military and non-military organizations, to display impatience with the comparatively inefficient indoctrination efforts undertaken by the Party propagandists in civilian society, and to replace them with PLA personnel.

Another factor involved in the rise of the military was a personnel policy which enabled it to retain its vigor and extend its influence. Whereas other organizations in Chinese society frequently lacked institutionalized retirement processes, had aged leaders, and suffered from clogged channels of upward mobility, the PLA was able to transfer its older and less competent members to non-military organizations. Not only did the transfer of veterans to positions in government, Party, and industry enable the PLA to solve its own internal problems of mobility and retirement, but it also meant that the PLA saturated the non-military organizations with men whose loyalties may in part have belonged to the military.

A further reason for the rise of the PLA was the increased importance of the foreign and domestic functions it performs. In foreign affairs, the leaders of China believed themselves to be encircled by hostile powers. They give primacy to the acquisition of a nuclear capability. In the tense situation of the mid-1960's in East Asia, with problems of national defense a prime concern, it was perhaps natural that military men came to play a more vital role in national politics.

Domestically, although firm documentation is lacking, it appears that the rulers increasingly had to rely on coercive means to control the population. As their ability to elicit a mass response through idealistic appeals diminished and their initial wide-spread support waned, the leaders administered a more harsh criminal law. With the population growth and the possibly growing gap between urban and rural living standards, the rulers had to exercise increasingly stringent control over population movements. In 1966-67, the situation became acute, and force of arms became a major way of restoring law and order. Those who wielded the instruments of coercion, people associated with the PLA and the public security forces, rose to power as the demand for their skills increased.

Yet another source of military power was its control of rail, air, and major river transport, giving its members and their allies a mobility which people in other organizations lacked. During the rapidly evolving political situation in 1966-67, access to air transport proved especially important. Chou En-lai, for example, was able at several crucial junctures to fly to trouble spots to negotiate or mediate disputes. In other instances, key groups were flown to Peking. One day after the May 6th incident in Chengtu, for instance, several of those involved were already in Peking to discuss the Szechuan situation with Chou, Ch'en Po-ta, K'ang Sheng, and Chiang Ch'ing. Further, to communicate their message to the peasants, perhaps indicating an inability to use a recalcitrant propaganda apparatus, the leadership airdropped leaflets to peasants in Kwangsi and Hupeh province in the spring.[63]

An additional reason for the enhanced power of military personnel may have been their relative self-sufficiency. In contrast to members of other hierarchies, their organization produced a considerable portion of the goods they consumed. Moreover, the PLA had an important role in directing the machine-building industries, the mining and extractive industries, and the agricultural reclamation projects in China's border provinces. When production and delivery schedules fell behind, as happened in early 1967, the army may have been in a better position to sustain itself. (This observation, however, is a logical inference rather than an adequately documented conclusion.)

In sum, the principal reasons for the rise of the PLA were similar to those for the increased importance of the military in many of the economically developing countries.[64] It won the confidence of the national leader. It stood somewhat isolated from society, thereby retaining a vigor and *élan* which the CCP inevitably lost when it became so involved in societal affairs that its parts came to represent particular interests. The post-service affiliations of former military personnel enabled the PLA to extend its influence to other organizations. Its control of resources enabled it to have an independent base of power. Because the PLA and the public security forces were the coercive agents of the ruler, these organizations came to the fore as the maintenance of the state increasingly rested upon cocrcion. Moreover, since the reasons for their rise are likely to persist, military personnel seem destined to be at the center of Chinese politics for the foreseeable future.

## Conclusion

The power and influence of the major occupational groupings in Chinese society, as revealed in the Cultural Revolution, can now be briefly summarized. The peasants influenced policy indirectly; their interests were

---

[63]Radio Wuhan, March 8, 1967; Radio Nanning, February 28, 1967.
[64]See, for example, Lucian Pye, "Armies in the Process of Political Development," in his *Aspects of Political Development*, Little Brown, 1966, p. 172–187.

voiced by sympathetic government and Party bureaucrats and the military leaders. The top policy formulators tried to anticipate peasant reactions primarily because of their economic importance.

In one of the significant aspects of the Cultural Revolution, the industrial managers and the industrial workers displayed their power to act swiftly and to affect policies ruinous to their interests. Members of these occupational groups appear to be acquiring increased power as China industrializes.

Intellectuals, increasingly differentiated in the roles they perform, differed in their ability to alter policy affecting them. Social critics were totally vulnerable to control, and teachers were shown basically to serve at the pleasure of the ruler. Scientific and technical personnel, however, saw their interests taken into account, particularly if they were engaged in research that gained them firm supporters among the military.

The students demonstrated that, when allied with elements of the bureaucracy and the military, they could become a powerful force, but that without allies, they were unable to remain a politically dominant group. Nonetheless, a study of youth suggests that their problems demand urgent attention, and for this reason their demands probably will elicit a continued response from those at the center of power.

Though many government and Party bureaucrats were purged, they displayed their ability to survive as an occupational group at the center of power. Their functions proved vital; moreover, they had learned some of the tactics necessary to defend their interests.

Finally, members of the military apparatus moved to the very center of power during the Cultural Revolution. An analysis of the sources of their power and influence indicates that their importance will persist.

This summary, however, has several limitations which should be made explicit. The occupational groups analyzed are broadly defined; in reality, each category includes many kinds of positions. For example, instead of analyzing Party and government bureaucrats as one group, a more rigorous analysis would examine the interests and power of the bureaucrats in the various functional systems into which the Party and government were divided; finance and trade, agriculture, forestry, and water conservancy, industry and communications, culture and education, law enforcement, and so on. A more rigorous analysis of industrial workers would distinguish among skilled and unskilled workers in large, medium, and small factories. Their attitudes and ability to affect public policy were probably different.

In addition, this article's exclusive focus upon occupational groups neglects other important ways of subdividing the population, such as into geographical, attitudinal, ethnic, or class groups. Indeed, one would gain considerable insight into Chinese politics by asking the question: What does the Cultural Revolution tell us about the relative power and influence of people in different geographic areas in China? Moreover, there is considerable evidence that conflict within the occupational groups was often based upon class and status groups. Among students, apparently, conflict sometimes broke out between children of cadres and children from less favored backgrounds. (The important United Action Red Guards, for instance, reportedly drew its strength from the children of cadres.) The conflict between the permanent and temporary workers was a struggle between two classes. Conflict between bureaucrats often involved disputes between high-ranking and low-ranking cadres. The pro-Maoist leaders apparently tended to draw strong support from the lower classes and status groups, a facet of the Cultural Revolution that does not become clear if one focuses solely upon occupational groups.

Moreover, the Cultural Revolution provides a narrow and unusual time span from which to view the interests and power of occupational groups. They were able to act upon their interests, in part, because of the diminished capacity of the elite to provide effective leadership. (One reason for their reduced capacity, however, was the increased ability of occupational groups to defend their interests. The two phenomena were inter-related.) If the rulers recapture their former strength, or if they resort to different techniques in order to elicit a response (for example, an increased use of material incentives), then the interests and abilities of various groups to affect policy will change.

Finally, another limitation of the exclusive focus upon group interests and power is its neglect of other important subjects, such as the role of ideas. A satisfactory explanation for the persistence of radical thought in China, so crucial for an understanding of the Cultural Revolution, must go beyond an analysis of student radicalism and the interests of occupational groups, for the radicals were found among all of them.[65] Ultimately, for a thorough understanding of Chinese politics one must integrate group analysis with an analysis of the leaders and the culture and ideas that move them.

In spite of these limitations, however, occupational group analysis enables one to approach China from a fresh vantage point. Transitory factors affecting Chinese politics, such as the power of a particular individual, factional rivalries, or a war on China's border, are blotted out in order to highlight more permanent developments. A clearer picture

---

[65]For sensitive studies of some of the sources of radicalism, see Maurice Meisner, *Li Ta-chao and the Origins of Chinese Marxism*, Harvard University Press, 1967, and Olga Lang, *Pa Chin and his Writings,* Harvard University Press, 1967.

emerges of the occupational groups that will exercise the greatest demands upon the top leaders, no matter who those leaders might be.

This study suggests that in the years ahead, China's leaders will confront several occupational groups that will effectively articulate their interests: the military personnel, the government and Party bureaucrats, and increasingly, the industrial managers and workers. Moreover, the leaders will have to pay urgent attention to the problems of students, and respond to the demands of scientists and technicians. They will face considerable constraints in formulating their policies toward the peasants. It is highly likely that Chinese politics is moving into an era marked by intense bargaining between a weakened central leadership, its authority seriously eroded during the Cultural Revolution, and powerful occupational groups. The leaders will not be in an enviable position, as they attempt to reconcile and mediate the conflicting demands made by these groups.

# 16. Minor Parties in Communist China

*George P. Jan*

One of the characteristics of the Communist regime on the mainland of China thirteen years after its establishment is its continued tolerance of the existence of minor parties. This policy of the Communist party of China (hereafter C.P.C.) raises some interesting questions. Why does the C.P.C. continue to tolerate the existence of these minor parties? To what extent can these minor parties exert influence on the policies of Communist China? What are these parties and who are their leaders? What is their legal status in Communist China?

At the beginning of the People's Republic of China in 1949, there were 11 minor parties in the "coalition government."[1] One of them, the Chinese People's National Salvation Association, dissolved itself "honorably" on December 18, 1949, because it considered that its mission had been accomplished.[2] Two other minor parties, the Association of the Comrades of San Min Chu I and the Kuomintang Association for Promoting Democracy, were subsequently merged with the Kuomintang Revolutionary Committee and suspended their separate activities. Therefore, today there are only eight minor parties in Communist China.[3]

The elements of these minor parties are extremely complex. There are overlappings in their party membership. One individual often belongs

---

[1] *Parties Collaborating with the Communists* (Fu Ni Tang Pai) (Taipei, Taiwan: Investigation Bureau, Ministry of Interior, the Republic of China, 1950), p. 1.

[2] *Materials for the Study of the Great Charters of the People* (Jen Min Ta Hsien Chang Hsueh Hsi Tze Liao) (Tien Tsin, China: Lien Ho Tu Shu Chu Pan Sho, 1950), p. 171.

[3] *People's Handbook* (Jen Min Shou Tso) (Peking: Hsin Hua Shu Tien, 1959), pp. 263–264.

Reprinted from George P. Jan, "Minor Parties in Communist China," *Current History*, September 1962, pp. 174–77 and 183, by permission of the author and journal.

to more than one minor party. In general, members of these minor parties can be classified into four major categories. The first category consists of leftist intellectuals. Their cooperation with the Communists is motivated by their patriotic sentiment and idealistic convictions. They were dissatisfied with the Kuomintang one-party rule and the unjust political, social and economic conditions in China. They believed that the Communist party could correct the evils of China. Most of them were not Communists although many of them had illusions about the Communist party. To this very day few of them are Communist party members. In this category, there are many outstanding Chinese scholars in various fields. Many leaders in the minor political parties belong to this category, especially members of the China Democratic League.

The second category consists of the Kuomintang (the Chinese Nationalist Party) members who are opposed to Chiang Kai-shek. Most of them are frustrated former Kuomintang officials and generals. Most of them, at one time or another, occupied high positions in the Kuomintang government. But they lost favor with Chiang Kai-shek or turned against him. This category includes most of the members of the Kuomintang Revolutionary Committee.

The third category consists of persons who are relatively unknown in Chinese politics. They are neither established scholars nor one-time high-ranking Kuomintang officials, but are for the most part opportunists trying to get government jobs through the bargaining power of the minor parties. This category includes many of the rank and file members of all the minor parties.

The fourth category consists of Communists who disguised themselves as non-Communists and penetrated into minor parties before 1949, such as Chou Hsin-min of the China Democratic League.[4] After 1949, the C.P.C. openly encouraged the Communists to join the Democratic League. In the last analysis, although all these minor parties are pro-Communist, not very many of their members are card-bearing Communists.[5] Even the official analysis of the Nationalist government on Taiwan did not classify most of their members as Communists.[6]

The original political platforms of these minor parties were not Communistic in orientation. For instance, the policy of the China Demo-

---

[4]Chu, Chu-yang, *How the Chinese Communist Party Treated the Democratic Parties* (Chung Kung Zen Yang Tui Tai Min Chu Tang Pai) (Kowloon: Yiu Lien Chu Pan Sho, 1952), p. 49.

[5]*The Bright Road for Intellectuals* (Chi Shih Fen Tze Te Kuang Ming Tao Lu) (Canton, China: Kuang Ming Chu Pan Sho, 1952), p. 42. This is an official publication of the Chinese Democratic League.

[6]See *Parties Collaborating with the Communists*. The nature and composition of the minor parties in Communist China were analyzed at some length in this official publication of Nationalist China.

cratic League before 1949 resembled, in many ways, the concept of a multi-party parliamentary system.[7] While all the minor parties have their constitutions and platforms, in reality, they are organized on the basis more of personal following than specific principles. They rely on cooperation between well-known leaders and their respective personal followings. Because they hated the Kuomintang one-party rule, these parties allied themselves with the C.P.C. to oppose the Kuomintang. In 1949, they joined hands with the C.P.C. under a coalition government and thus established the People's Republic of China, generally referred to as Communist China. By now, for all practical purposes, the minor parties no longer have independent principles and policies contrary to those of the C.P.C. The best evidence to prove this point is the "Joint Message of Greetings to Chairman Mao" signed by six minor parties in 1960. In this message, the minor parties pledged to Mao that they would lean to socialism, listen to him and follow the C.P.C.[8]

The membership of these minor parties is unknown to outsiders. The only organizations that know their exact membership are perhaps the parties themselves and the C.P.C. However, it is safe to say that their membership cannot be large. Another interesting aspect about the minor parties is their financial support. There is evidence to indicate that they receive subsidy from the Communist government.[9] This gives the C.P.C. another means of controlling these parties.

The most active year of the minor parties under communism was 1949 when the Chinese People's Political Consultative Conference (hereafter C.P.P.C.C.) held its first session. Under the category of party delegates in the C.P.P.C.C., there were 14 "democratic parties." Two of these were official Communist organizations, the Communist Party of China and the China New Democracy Youth Corps. Eleven of these were pro-Communist parties but not official Communist organizations. The "independents" were pro-Communist leaders claiming to be non-partisan independents.[10]

---

[7]*Political Report of the Plenary Session of the Second Central Committee of the China Democratic League* (Min Chu Tung Meng Erh Chung Chuan Hui Cheng Chi Pao Kao) (Shanghai: Headquarters of the China Democratic League, 1947), p. 2.

[8]*Current Background* (Hong Kong: American Consulate General, 1960), No. 639, p. 67.

[9]*The Nature and Function of the China Democratic League* (Chung Kuo Min Chu Tung Men Te Hsing Chi Yu Jen Wu) (Canton, China: Kuang Ming Chu Pan Sho, 1950), p. 11. This is an official publication of the China Democratic League. Government subsidy is provided in Item 3 of Chapter 8 of the Constitution of the China Democratic League.

[10]*Documents on the Establishment of the People's Republic of China* (Chung Hua Jen Min Kung Ho Kuo Kai Kuo Wen Hsien) (Hong Kong: Hsin Min Chu Chu Pan Sho, 1949), pp. 14–19.

In the C.P.P.C.C. the Communist party refused to have more delegates than the Kuomintang Revolutionary Committee and the Democratic League.[11] Superficially it appeared that the latter two parties had equal representation with the Communist party. However, a close examination of the membership revealed the hypocritical gesture of the Communists. In the C.P.P.C.C. of 1949, 165 delegates were labeled as party delegates, 116 as regional delegates, 71 as military delegates, 235 as delegates from civic organization and 75 as special delegates. There were 662 delegates altogether including alternates.[12] Although the Communist party had equal representation with the Kuomintang Revolutionary Committee and the China Democratic League under the category of party delegates, the regional delegates and the military delegates were all Communists, and so were most of the delegates from civic organizations. The special delegates were mostly former Kuomintang officials who surrendered to the Communists and pro-Communist "independent leaders." The reality was that about two-thirds of the delegates in the C.P.P.C.C. were Communists, placing the C.P.P.C.C. under the effective control of the Communist party.

In the government established in 1949 under the Common Program adopted by the C.P.P.C.C., Mao Tse-tung was elected Chairman of the Central People's Government Council. Of the six Vice Chairmen of the same Council three were non-Communists. Of the 55 members of the same Council about 22 were non-Communists. The Premier of the Government Administrative Council was Chou En-lai. He was assisted by four Vice Premiers of whom two were non-Communists. Of the sixteen members of the Government Administrative Council nine were non-Communists. Of the thirty ministers and commissioners in the central government nine were non-Communists. The minor parties also occupied a number of subministry positions. Shen Chun-ju, a leader of the Democratic League, was even given the position of the President of the Supreme People's Court, roughly the counter-part of the Chief Justice of the United States.[13]

However, the minor parties felt the pressure of the C.P.C. not long after the first session of the C.P.P.C.C. In 1950, the C.P.C. ordered all the minor parties to revise their party programs.[14] They had to pledge support of the policies of the C.P.C. against the interest of their own

---

[11]*Materials for the Study of the Great Charters of the People*, p. 14.

[12]*Documents on the Establishment of the People's Republic of China*, p. 13.

[13]This analysis is based on the writer's examination of the name lists of the high-ranking government officials in the Central Chinese Government. See *Documents of the People's Political Consultative Conference* (Jen Min Cheng Hsieh Wen Chien) (Peking: Hsin Hua Shu Tien, 1950), on various pages.

[14]Chu, Chu-yang, pp. 49–50.

classes. The C.P.C. forbade the minor parties to try to build up a large following. In 1951, the C.P.C. specified the groups from which each minor party might recruit members.[15]

For instance, in December, 1950, the Central Committee of the China Democratic League adopted a resolution concerning the development of the League's organization. In this resolution, the League decided that it should recruit members from bourgeois intellectuals, cultural and educational workers. It decided that it would not develop its organization in the People's Liberation Army including security forces, military organizations, military schools and military enterprises, nor intelligence agencies, revolutionary universities,[16] agencies dealing with diplomatic affairs, nor among minority nationalities. It also decided not to develop its organization in small cities and rural areas, and only to develop its organization in large cities which were political, economic and cultural centers.

These decisions were obviously made under the pressure of the C.P.C. for they seriously limited the area of activities of the Democratic League. This meant that the activities of the League were excluded not only from many government agencies, but also from rural areas, small cities and minority nationalities. This was a change from the League's policy before 1949 when it insisted on sharing political power in the central government as well as in local governments under a coalition government.[17]

The adoption of the constitution in 1954 further reduced the influence of the minor parties in the Communist government. Under the "Constitutional Government" of Communist China, the C.P.P.C.C. was reduced to a consultative institution according to Article 13 of the Common Program. It is no longer the legislature of the national government. The National People's Congress, the new national legislature, is not elected on a party basis. Of the 1226 deputies to the National People's Congress (hereafter N.P.C.) in 1954 the overwhelming majority were Communists. Of the 65 members of the Presidium of the N.P.C. in 1954, the majority were Communist deputies.[18] The N.P.C. also adopted the committee system to handle legislative bills. A close examination shows that in all the committees in 1954, the majority were Communists.

---

[15]Harold C. Hinton, " 'Democratic Parties': End of An Experiment?" *Problems of Communism*, No. 3, Vol. 7, 1958, p. 42.

[16]These are special universities for the training of career revolutionaries for the Communist regime.

[17]*Political Report of the Plenary Session of the Second Central Committee of the China Democratic League*, p. 26.

[18]*Documents of the First Plenary Session of the First National People's Congress of the People's Republic of China* (Chung Hua Jen Min Kung Ho Kuo Ti Yi Chieh Chuan Kuo Jen Min Tai Piao Ta Hui Ti Yi Tse Hui Yi Wen Chien) (Peking: Jen Min Chu Pan Sho, 1954), p. 146.

In the constitutional government of 1954, the minor party leaders were given some ten ministerial positions plus a number of subministry posts. Superficially, it seemed that the minor parties maintained roughly the same strength in the central government as they had done before 1954. Nevertheless, there were some major changes in the constitutional government in comparison with the government established under the Common Program in 1949. For instance, the number of deputy chiefs of state, the vice chairmen of the Central People's Government Council, was reduced from six to one. Therefore, all the five former non-Communist deputy chiefs of state were dropped. Although the position of deputy chief of state is more a position of prestige than influence, the Communists felt the need in 1949 to share this prestige with the minor parties. This made the government look more like a coalition government.

In 1954, the Communists apparently felt that they no longer needed to share this prestige with the minor parties. Tung Pi-wu, an old-time Communist leader, replaced Shen Chun-ju as the President of the Supreme People's Court. All the Vice Premiers were Communists, as compared to two non-Communist Vice Premiers out of a total of four Vice Premiers before 1954. Of the 15 Vice Chairmen of the National Defense Committee only 4 were former Kuomintang Generals; all the rest were Communists. Through further collectivization of the rural areas after 1954, the activity of minor parties at the local level became increasingly difficult.

By 1958, when the people's communes were introduced, the activity of minor parties in the countryside was virtually impossible. By the end of 1958, Communist China organized all the peasants into communes. Later, the Communists established many communes in smaller cities and a limited number of communes in large cities. Nowhere in the commune organization was the role of minor parties mentioned; the C.P.C. is the only party organization in the communes.

After the rectification and anti-rightist campaigns of 1957, the rightists were subdued. In the Second National People's Congress beginning in 1959 the strength of minor parties was further reduced. Of the 62 members of the Standing Committee of the N.P.C. only about a dozen or so were non-Communists. In the central government in 1959, of the 30 ministries and 32 commissions and agencies under the direct supervision of the Premier only about 10 were headed by non-Communists. In the central government today headed by Liu Shao-chi, all important positions above ministry level are headed by Communists with only a few exceptions.

It is true some of the minor party leaders were given positions in the Communist government. But do they have real power and influence?

The position of the minor party leaders who participate in the government can be evaluated from a report submitted to the Standing Committee of the N.P.C. in 1956 by Li Wei-han, Director of the United Front Work Department of the C.P.C. Central Committee. In his report, Li pointed out that some Communist officials did not respect the authority of the non-Communist officials in the government, nor did they cooperate with non-Communist officials.[19]

It is safe to say that members of the minor parties who work in the Communist government do not have real political power concerning decision-making or even day-to-day routine administration. Although some of them are appointed as heads of ministries or commissions, actual power is in the hands of the vice ministers or deputy commissioners. The minor party leaders who head ministries or commissions or lower level government agencies are only figureheads.

The minor parties do not perform the function of opposition nor can they supervise the C.P.C. by criticism. A few minor party leaders who were naive enough to criticize the C.P.C. during the "Hundred Flowers Bloom" period in 1957 were ruthlessly purged. The participation of the minor parties in the Communist government is obviously not in the tradition of the multi-party parliamentary system that is practiced in the West.

The participation of minor parties in the Communist government is a false pretense of shared authority, a masked exercise of Communist one-party totalitarian dictatorship.

What will be the future of the minor parties in Communist China? The Communists have assured them that the united front will be continued beyond the attainment of socialism; as long as the C.P.C. exists, the minor parties will continue to exist.[20] But how sincere is this Communist assurance? The fate of the minor parties depends upon the policy of the C.P.C. The period of massacre is over in Communist China unless serious situations call for it. There is no indication that the Communists want to liquidate these parties by force. On the contrary, the C.P.C. has adopted a long range policy designed to reform these parties step by step. This is the so-called "soft-breeze-and-light-drizzle" policy.[21] This means that the minor parties will be transformed into socialist parties slowly and gently like a soft breeze and light drizzle. The process of transformation will be long, but it will be steady.

---

[19]*Documents of the Third Plenary Session of the First National People's Congress of the People's Republic of China* (Chung Hua Jen Min Kung Ho Kuo Ti Yi Chieh Chuan Kuo Jen Min Tai Piao Ta Hui Ti San Tse Hui Yi Wen Chien) (Peking: Jen Min Chu Pan Sho, 1956), p. 296.

[20]*The People's Daily* (Jenmin Jihpao), September, 1956, p. 1.

[21]*Current Background*, No. 639, 1960, p. 3.

# 17. Political Participation

*James Townsend*

One of the striking features of the Chinese political system is the degree to which a uniform style of participation pervades all popular political activities. To a great extent, this uniformity is a result of the CCP's conscious and persistent efforts to structure Chinese political life in accordance with its doctrine. Nevertheless, the Chinese political landscape has not been totally malleable to Party manipulation, and the Chinese style of participation reveals certain disadvantages and failures, as well as advantages and successes, from the Party's point of view. A description of political life in Communist China must include, therefore, analysis of the main characteristics of the Chinese style of participation and an attempt to evaluate their consequences.

## Characteristics of Participation

Political participation assumes many forms in China but certain characteristics are common to all of them. The common qualities emerge more clearly from analysis of the organizational setting in which participation occurs, the nature of political relationships among those who participate, the way in which political issues are defined, the primary objective of political action, and the manner in which popular action on major issues is coordinated. Analytical distinctions such as these are not so sharp in practice but they serve to illustrate the main characteristics of mass political life.

Reprinted from James Townsend, *Political Participation in Communist China* (Berkeley, Calif.: University of California Press, 1967), pp. 174–86, by permission of the author and The Regents of the University of California.

**The organizational setting — small-group activities.** The most characteristic organizational setting for political participation in China is the small group. There are, of course, many types of political activity in which people participate in large numbers. Parades, rallies, the mass "trials" of counterrevolutionaries and landlords during the early years of the regime, general meetings of members in production teams and residents' committees, basic-level congresses — all of these are more or less regular gatherings of large numbers of citizens which certainly have some political significance for the participants. For the most part, however, these gatherings involve little discussion or response among those present. They have symbolic and ritualistic importance and they are useful for the transmission of information, but they are inadequate organizational devices for the type of popular participation that the CCP wishes to produce. It is the small group, which can elicit response from every member and check this response against daily behavior, that plays the critical role in the Chinese style of participation.

In the most precise sense, the small group is a unit with a fixed membership of not more than fifteen people who meet regularly (daily or weekly) for well-organized purposes and activities.[1] Its most common form is the political study group in which members engage in lengthy discussion of study materials under the guidance of a group leader. The key aspect of the study group is the "criticism and self-criticism" that requires every member to express his views, criticize himself, and submit to the criticism of others in the group. The small study group is a regular feature in Party life, in "thought reform," in most schools (including colleges and universities, cadre training schools, and the "institutes of socialism" for bourgeois and intellectual elements), and in certain occupational situations, such as government offices and enterprise management, where there is a relatively high educational level among small working groups. It is also an irregular feature of political life for the entire population, appearing during the mass movements or in units not mentioned above where there is a high degree of "activism."

Small-group activity in a more general sense is a universal form of political organization even where the conditions of fifteen-member limits and tightly organized study and criticism are not met. At all times and in all places, the Party follows the general principle of dividing members of social units into groups small enough to permit some discussion and personal contact between leaders and members. Thus, there are small

---

[1] For general discussions of the small group, see John Wilson Lewis, *Leadership in Communist China* (Ithaca, 1963), pp. 157–160, and H. F. Schurmann, "Organization and Response in Communist China," *Annals*, Vol. 321 (January, 1959).

groups in the factories, residents' small groups in the cities, work groups within the production teams, voters' small groups during elections, and temporary small groups among those in attendance at all major meetings and congresses. In addition, there are countless meetings of very small numbers of people which, though informal in composition and manner of convening, are still important and deliberate parts of the Party's organizational arrangement of political participation. In all of these groups, whether they conform closely to the ideal study group or not, there is personal response to guided political discussion and a testing of every individual's political standpoint.

The use of the small group as the typical setting for popular political activity has many advantages. First, by assigning to cadres and activists responsibility for the guidance of small units of specified membership, it enables group leaders to verify by personal observation the transmission of Party policy to the citizenry. The Party's historical experience in mobilizing an illiterate and politically apathetic population has taught it the importance of such verification. Second, the small group makes politics more vivid and memorable by placing it in a setting where face-to-face discussion is possible. The CCP constantly reminds cadres that personal participation makes politics meaningful and that "what is learned in debate is unforgettable"; the small group facilitates the realization of these principles. Finally, since the small group normally consists of people who live or work together, it brings formidable social pressure to bear on its members. The Chinese Communists capitalize on pressures for associational conformity, which are particularly strong in the Chinese tradition, to enhance the persuasiveness of their doctrine and reinforce their demands for political unanimity.

**Political relationships — direct contact and moral leadership.** The doctrinal assertion that leaders are legally responsible to the masses and that people's congresses are "supreme organs of power" is an inaccurate definition of political relationships in Communist China. In fact, the Party seriously emphasized the legal aspects of the state structure only during 1954-1956. A much more consistent theme than observance of "socialist legality" has been a deep suspicion of the development of "bureaucratism" and "formalism" as a consequence of the necessary institutionalization of Communist political power. As we have seen, the long-term trend of Chinese Communist politics has been toward an emasculation of the state structure in general and representative bodies in particular, even though this trend has not been entirely due to the desires of Party leaders. The ineffectiveness of the state structure in obvious contradiction of Party theory is not due simply to CCP cynicism.

It reflects an even stronger theoretical conviction that the mass line and "socialist democracy" depend on an organic, intuitive relationship between cadres and masses rather than on institutional and legal controls. Two important aspects of this relationship are an emphasis on direct contacts between cadres and masses and an insistence on the moral quality of CCP leadership.

The importance of direct contacts has been noted many times in this study, particularly in references to small-group activities, but the best example is the operation of "democratic management" in basic-level political units. "Democratic management" (*min-chu kuan-li*) was one of the fundamental principles of the "Model Regulations" for higher APC's and became the object of a Party enforcement campaign in 1957. A Central Committee statement of March 15, 1957, listed three items as the critical elements of democratic management: (1) APC cadres must make periodic financial statements directly to the members; (2) cadres must discuss all cooperative affairs with the members, and especially with experienced peasants; (3) cadres must participate in production to gain experience and set a good example for the masses.[2] Democratic management in the APC's did not wholly ignore the functions of members' congresses, but a "democratization of management" movement that followed the formation of rural communes in the latter part of 1958 demonstrated that representative bodies played only a minor role in commune "democracy." The literature of this movement focused on two matters: first, the direct solicitation of mass discussion and opinion, and second, the "democratization" of cadre work style.[3]

Solicitation of mass opinion depended mainly on an immense variety of meetings between cadres and masses and on the use of *tatzupao* (large hand-written posters posted publicly for all to read). *Tatzupao* were said to be "powerful means of mass participation in managment" because they enabled the masses to express their opinions at any time. Democratization of cadre work style was the "central key to carrying out democratic management." Once a cadre achieved a democratic work style, he would be "one with the masses" and would automatically govern in accordance with their needs. Cadres were to achieve this style by direct association with the masses and by personally experiencing their living and working conditions. The "four-togethers" — eating, living, working, and consulting with the masses — and the "six to's" — making regular visits to the

[2]"Min-chu Pan-she San-hsiang Ts'o-shih" (Three Measures for Democratic Management of Cooperatives), *JMJP*, March 19, 1957.
[3]This discussion draws on many reports of the movement; in particular, see *JMJP*, November 19, 1958; November 29, 1958; and December 4, 1958.

fields, nurseries, "happiness homes" (for the aged), hospital, mess halls, and members' homes — were typical slogans for encouraging cadres to "democratize" management by democratizing themselves.

The systematic way in which the CCP solicits and publicizes letters and visits to officials is further evidence of the directness of political relationships in China. In June, 1951, the central government adopted regulations calling on all local and higher-level governments to establish departments for handling letters from the people and information bureaus or reception rooms for receiving visitors.[4] The regulations stated proper departments or officials for speedy answer or resolution and that "model cases" of special educational value should be publicized after disposition. A conference of the North China Bureau of the CCP Central Committee in November, 1952, followed with more detailed regulations. The North China directives specified the bureaucratic procedure for dealing with letters, reemphasized the importance of prompt and careful handling of people's letters and calls, called for closer Party supervision of the process, and noted that basic-level work would have to be strengthened to avoid a growing tendency for people to run to higher levels for resolution of their questions and problems.[5]

The focus of handling letters and calls has shifted over the years. Initially, it was the solicitation of accusations from the people against possible counterrevolutionaries or "bad elements" who had slipped into the Party and government. After 1955, emphasis shifted to rationalization proposals and to complaints about public facilities, marketing, food distribution, and so forth. Whatever their content, however, letters and calls transmit popular views and problems directly to responsible units, where their handling and publicizing builds the image of a Party and government that are intimately connected with the masses. Of course, the system gives the letter-writer or visitor no control over the person whom he petitions. The 1951 "Decision" even stated that "questions of a fault-finding or probing nature that are presented to the government by counterrevolutionaries assuming the name of the people should not be answered." The significant point is that so much of local government's information about popular conditions and so many solutions of the pub-

---

[4]"Kuan-yü Ch'u-li Jen-min Lai-hsin ho Chieh-chien Jen-min Kung-tso ti Chüeh-ting" (Decision on the Work of Handling People's Letters and Receiving People's Calls), *Chieh-fang Jih-pao* (Liberation Daily), June 9, 1951.

[5]"Chung-kung Chung-yang Hua-pei-chü Kuan-yü Ch'u-li Jen-min Lai-hsin Chieh-chien Jen-min Ch'ün-chung Kung-tso ti Chih-shih" (Directive of the North China Bureau of the CCP Central Committee on the Work of Handling People's Letters and Receiving the Masses' Calls), *T'ien-chin Jih-pao* (Tientsin Daily), December 9, 1952. A separate directive on procedure accompanied this document.

lic's minor problems are due to direct letters or visits from the masses rather than to the representative structure.[6]

In the Chinese political system, then, the citizen characteristically enters into direct contact with cadres who, theoretically, have an intuitive understanding of popular problems as a result of personally experiencing the living conditions of the masses. What is missing from this idealistic conception of political relationships is the element of popular control over leaders, since formal institutions do not fulfill this function. The CCP answers by claiming that it is the *quality* of Communist leadership, rather than institutional controls, that ensures "democracy" and observance of mass demands. Cadres are "naturally" responsible to the people because of their adherence to a doctrine which demands that they be responsible. The doctrine itself is the real source of authority, basing its claims to legitimacy on its superior morality; those who follow this doctrine have a moral claim to political leadership on the grounds that they alone can lead society along the right path.[7] There is, then, a natural political elite in China composed of those people who accept and follow the superior morality of Communist doctrine. They are the people who "ought to be elected" and who will always deserve their positions if they follow the doctrine correctly. As "good Communists," they will naturally govern in the interests of the people. Obviously, however, they are also obedient to Party orders and, in case of conflict, Party orders take precedence over mass demands. It is equally obvious that an "immoral" cadre may lose his understanding of the masses by failure to maintain his direct contacts with them and yet remain safe from popular (though not necessarily Party) retaliation.

**Definition of issues — political education.** The only political issues in China that can become the rallying point for mass participation are those that the Party introduces and defines. The classic proof of this statement

---

[6] In 1962, about 500,000 people in Kiangsu alone wrote letters and paid visits to government officials, and 80 percent of their problems had been resolved by February, 1963; NCNA, Nanking, February 20, 1963, in *SCMP*, No. 2937 (March 13, 1963). After the 1953–1954 elections in one *ch'ü* in Port Arthur–Dairen, 3,068 proposals had been forwarded to cadres by the people themselves as compared to only 486 from people's deputies; *Lü-ta Jen-min Jih-pao* (Port Arthur–Dairen People's Daily), April 1, 1954.

[7] See Lewis, *Leadership in Communist China*, pp. 38–47, for a discussion of the relationship between Communist morality and political leadership. The CCP's claim to moral, as well as historical, justification for its rule is prominent in Liu Shao-ch'i's essay, "How To Be a Good Communist." See Howard L. Boorman, *"How To Be a Good Communist:* The Political Ethics of Liu Shao-ch'i," *Asian Survey*, Vol. 3, No. 8 (August, 1963); a Chinese text of the new edition of this essay is in *Hung Ch'i* (Red Flag), 1962, Nos. 15–16.

was the "hundred flowers" episode in which some individuals tried to initiate debate on unauthorized issues. The result, after brief success, was either absolute rejection of the issues or continued debate only on grounds defined by the Party. Of course, the Party can neither predict nor totally control the issues and opinions that may arise at any given time. What it can do, however, is prohibit widespread discussion of an issue until it has defined its position and then insist that discussion resolve itself in support of this position. As one writer has said: "In fact, we can have incorrect opinions that differ from Party policy, but only if the masses can say what they wish and support Party policy and if opinions that oppose incorrect opinions can also emerge. This is a very natural thing since opinions that are incorrect and differ from [Party] policy cannot represent mass interests and will receive the opposition of correct opinions that do represent mass interests."[8] The Party, then, assumes responsibility not only for defining all political issues but also for overcoming spontaneous differences from its position on these issues. The technique by which the Party informs the masses of political issues and the "correct" positions on them is political education.

Political education in Communist China covers an enormous range of topics, but, so far as possible, there is one common theme in the treatment of all of them. This theme is the attempt to present political education in such a way that it relates to the personal experience of the citizen and thereby gives him some grounds for identifying with the Party position. Even more basically, political education must be simple enough at the start to convince the citizen that it is within his rights and abilities to debate political issues at all. The organization of a "political theory study group" in a Shanghai residents' small group illustrates this problem. The women involved in the group were all about forty years old and most were "semiliterate." Understandably, the first attempts at "theoretical study" produced great frustration and disillusionment. Recognizing the problem, the group leaders switched to study materials that were much closer to the "daily lives and tastes of the housewives." Interest grew rapidly thereafter and the "superstitious viewpoint about studying theory was smashed."[9] Even when "superstitions" about political participation have been overcome, however, the Party continues to translate political issues into terms of personal experience.

Two common pedagogical devices demonstrate this process. One is the use of contrasting "models" to highlight the differences in "correct" and

---

[8]Wang Han-chih, "I-k'ao Ch'ün-chung, Cheng-ch'üeh Kuan-ch'ieh Cheng-ts'e" (Rely on the Masses, Correctly Carry Out Policy), *Shih-shih Shou-ts'e* (Current Events), 1961, No. 17, p. 9.

[9]*Wen-hui Pao* (Literary News) (Shanghai), August 26, 1958.

"incorrect" policies and behavior and to provide, in the correct "model," an example for imitation. The models employed may be two workers or peasants, two cadres, two labor units, or even two sets of ideas or work styles. In all cases, however, the models clarify Party-approved issues and policies by offering concrete examples of the "good" and "bad" that the people may imitate and reject respectively. A second device is to explain political issues by reference to incidents and personalities that already have personal significance for some or all of the audience. For example, the CCP defends its general program by contrasting living conditions in the "new" and "old" societies and by urging people to talk about the injustice and oppression they suffered before 1949; whenever possible, cadres will identify the old order with specific landlords and local officials who have now been overthrown. Old soldiers will extol the CCP and its leaders with reminiscences about their experiences in the anti-Japanese and civil wars. When the Party attacks American imperialism, cadres urge the people to recall unpleasant incidents with Americans during the years before 1949, while PLA veterans recite the American "atrocities" they witnessed in Korea. China's "semicolonial" history will be raised to identify with political struggles throughout the Afro-Asian world. By such references, the Party solicits personal involvement and identification with distant political issues and programs. The good cadre, of course, will not limit himself to explaining policies in terms of local experiences, but will reverse the process as well by generalizing on the "political significance" of every local incident or dispute.

Political education takes many different forms that vary greatly in their intensity and scope of application. The most intense and the most limited in scope is "thought reform."[10] Thought reform relies on a tightly controlled environment and the threat or use of force to challenge the subject's entire past life and political beliefs, convince him of his "guilt" and the necessity for reform, and then rebuild a new ideological character by intensive study under constant criticism and supervision. It is unquestionably the most thorough and effective form of political education that the CCP employs and it suggests the Party's general ideological aims for the entire population. Nevertheless, the Party does not, and cannot, subject all Chinese to an "educational" process of such intensity. Those who have undergone thought reform, or a reasonably close approximation of it, include some Party members, most intellectuals and political prisoners, and those who have attended the "revolutionary universities" and other training schools specifically designed to remold the thought of the students.

---

[10]See Robert J. Lifton, *Thought Reform and the Psychology of Totalism* (New York, 1961), especially the analytical definitions of thought reform and "totalism" in chaps. 5 and 22.

A second form of political education is political study, which is one of the primary techniques of thought reform but is a far less intensive experience. It demands individual participation in a discussion process that exposes the individual to group criticism, compels him to examine his most basic beliefs, and leads him to at least a surface statement of his acceptance of the Communist viewpoint. Unlike thought reform, however, it does not involve total isolation from outside contacts or the threat of physical punishment, and it does not necessarily lead to a written confession or even a conclusive decision on whether or not the individual has "reformed." Every Chinese has probably participated in political study at some time, but only a minority of the population experiences it as a regular form of political education. The technique is, however, sufficiently familiar to both cadres and masses that the Party can organize political study at the mass level whenever it wishes.[11] Probably the major limitation on the overall effectiveness of political study is the great variation in the quality of study. Political study among peasants is not what it is among intellectuals, even though the format may be the same, and the performance of two study groups of similar composition may be quite different, owing to the different abilities of their group leaders. Political study is a powerful technique for political education and participation, but it is extremely vulnerable to variations in the ability and enthusiasm of its participants.

Political propaganda is the least intensive and most universal form of political education in China. It is total in its coverage and virtually continuous, although the intensity will always vary with the political demands of the moment. Many meetings among the masses that are identified as "study" are actually in this category since they involve no outside preparation and very little response by the participants. Political meetings in rural areas, for example, frequently consist of little more than a lecture by a cadre or a current events session (based on a radio broadcast or a newspaper reading to the group). Such meetings are informative and may stimulate some interchange of opinion, but they are not political study in the sense that we have defined it.

Political education in Communist China defines political issues and educates the people in the policies of the ruling party and the nature of the state system, but it also tries to raise their political consciousness and convince them of the necessity for political action. This aspect of political education explains its intensity and pervasiveness. If only under-

---

[11]For examples of how mass study is organized, see Liu Wan-pang, "Lai-an Hsien Shih Tsen-yang Tsu-chih ho Chien-ch'ih Kung-nung Ch'ün-chung Hsüeh Li-lun ti" (How Laian Hsien Organized and Maintained the Worker-Peasant Masses' Study of Theory), *Hung Ch'i*, 1960, No. 3, pp. 30–33; and Yü Ch'ing-ho, *et al.*, "I-ko Shou-huo-yüan Li-lun Hsüeh-hsi Hsiao-tsu" (A Salesclerks' Theoretical Study Group), *Hung Ch'i*, 1960, No. 7, pp. 36–40.

standing and passive obedience were the goal, a lesser effort would suffice. But political education has the task of making the masses see political issues and feel the need for action in the same way that the Party does. The "Socialist and Communist Education Movement" carried out in the rural communes from September, 1958, to the spring of 1959 is a perfect example of this process. Since the communes were already formed when the movement got under way, its purpose was not simply to explain the commune system and ensure mass obedience in joining. The movement's goal was to guarantee the future of the communes by persuading the peasants that the communes were necessary and by destroying the "individualism and particularism" that inhibited voluntary peasant acceptance of the communes. One discussion of the movement pointed out:

> Individualism and particularism are like a stubborn skin disease; today you drive it out, tomorrow it rushes back; you drive it out here, it rushes back there. In saying this are we saying that individualism and particularism can never be driven out? No, we are only saying that we must use the method of long-term, patient persuasion and education with respect to individualism and particularism; we must use the method of communist ideological education. Individualism and particularism will not be truly exterminated until every commune member possesses communist ideology.[12]

The Party knows that the people must obey its orders, but it cannot be sure that they will actively support Party policies until political education has raised their political consciousness and implanted the communist viewpoint in their minds.

**The objective of political action — execution of Party policies.** The primary objective of all the acts through which the Chinese citizen participates in politics is execution of Party policies. In a limited sense, some forms of political participation do not aim directly at this objective. There is, for example, mass participation in patriotic ceremonies, in the management of strictly local affairs on which the Party has no specific position, and in many educational activities that do not focus on particular policies. However, the Party tries to link all of these activities to realization of the CCP's political program. Patriotic ceremonies may stress loyalty to the nation or state, but national loyalty is inseparable from loyalty to the Party and must be demonstrated by support for Party policies. Cadres constantly tell members of residents' committees and production teams that proper management of their units is a contribu-

---

[12]*JMJP*, October 9, 1958.

tion to socialist construction. And political education, as we have just noted, never loses sight of the ultimate objective of action. From the Party's point of view, therefore, the test of mass political participation is whether or not it leads to active support of CCP policies. One who goes through the motions of participation without developing "activism" is guilty of political passivity which, in effect, is opposition. There is no freedom to abstain from political action in China.

By insisting that the people participate "consciously and voluntarily" in the execution of Party policies, the CCP politicizes all areas of life into which its authority penetrates. This is not to say that all areas of life are political. Although there is no theoretical limit to the extension of Party authority, in practice the Party does not attempt to regulate everything. Nevertheless, the range of behavior that the CCP tries to influence or control is extremely great. Consider, for example, the "socialist" or "patriotic" pact. These pacts are agreements among neighbors to observe certain standards of conduct on the grounds that interests of state or socialist construction are involved. In one "socialist neighborhood pact" in Peking, the residents agreed to the following obligations: To strengthen unity and mutual assistance, help neighbors who are busy or sick, criticize others for their shortcomings, and accept criticism in return; to prevent fires, restrain "bad people" from inciting incidents, and observe regulations requiring the reporting of the arrival and departure of visitors; to accept responsibility for cleaning streets, ditches, and toilets and for killing all flies and mosquitoes; to maintain personal health and hygiene by bathing, changing clothes, washing hands before eating, washing all food, and dressing children carefully with an eye to the weather; to be "diligent and frugal" in managing the household, thinking up ways to economize on food, clothing, coal, water, and electricity; to participate in study for the elimination of illiteracy and to read the newspaper regularly; to respect all policies and decrees of the government, respond to every call of the government, participate in all activities and pass on information to those who cannot attend meetings.[13] One might well question the Party's ability, or desire, to hold the signers of such an agreement to their promises. The point, however, is precisely the fact that the signers themselves are to enforce the pact because they have accepted the Party's assertion that all these acts have a wider political significance.

The CCP's insistence on popular support for all of its policies makes the range of political action in China extremely wide. Popular political action includes not only such obvious categories as electoral participa-

---

[13]*JMJP*, August 17, 1958. For other examples of "patriotic pacts" see *Ch'ang-chou Jih-pao* (Changchow Daily), April 19, 1958, and April 29, 1958.

tion, service as a cadre or activist, or participation in the decisions of small units such as production teams and residents' committees, but also involvement in the execution of tasks that the Party has defined as essential for the victory of socialism over its enemies. By far the most important task of this sort is increasing production. From 1949 to the present, the CCP has consistently cited increased production and willingness to work as the primary evidence of popular political activism. Popular assistance in internal security work—the supervision and apprehension of political and social criminals—has been next in importance, although it no longer receives the emphasis that it did up to 1955. Another critical area is mediation of all kinds of disputes. The mediation committees in the communes and urban neighborhoods, usually dominated by women, perform services that are of great assistance to the Party and which, incidentally, tend to reduce the role of the state legal structure at the lowest levels. The Party also stresses mass implementation of various measures in the fields of sanitation, health, pest riddance, and conservation of scarce products and resources. Social reform was a major field for mass action in the early years of the regime, but it has gradually given way to movements for economic and technological progress and for ideological reform.

**Coordinating political action — the mass movement.** On nearly all major national issues, the Chinese political process culminates in a mass movement that coordinates in one general campaign all the organizational and educational efforts that prepare the citizen for political action. Mass movements are the most characteristic expression of the Chinese style of political participation. Like general election campaigns in Western democracies, they are the most significant events in mass political life and the symbol of the basic objectives of political participation. As "the most concentrated and salient form of expression of the mass line" and "the climax of the revolutionary action of the masses,"[14] the mass movement relies on direct action by an enthusiastic and totally mobilized population to bring Party policies to fruition. The essence of the movement is its ability to stimulate mass activism, thus avoiding reliance on specialists and state organs, while retaining Party leadership to prevent spontaneous or undisciplined action.[15]

The CCP adopted the mass movement during its formative years as a revolutionary party when direct popular action had to compensate for

---

[14]Li-Yu-pin, "The Great Victory of the Mass Line in the Institutes of Higher Education," *Chung-kuo Ch'ing-nien* (China Youth), 1959, No. 24, in *SMM*, No. 199 (February 8, 1960).
[15]See "Speech by Comrade Lo Jui-ching," *Eighth National Congress of the Communist Party of China*, II (Speeches), 109–112.

other political and material weakness. Even after 1949, widespread popular activism was essential for the success of the far-reaching social, economic, and political changes initiated by the Party. It was not until 1956, at the Eighth Party Congress, that Chinese Communist leaders began to express some reservations about the mass movements, hinting that they were necessary during the "revolutionary" period but that they were unsuitable for a state that had settled its internal political struggles and was erecting a stable governmental structure.[16] It is significant that the CCP recognized the fundamental difference between mass movements and institutionalized political action, and even more significant, therefore, that it chose mass movements as the driving force of the Great Leap. In 1959, Chou En-lai spoke approvingly of the "series of mass movements" that had "advanced like waves" on the economic, political, and ideological fronts of the socialist revolution, enabling the masses to retain their revolutionary enthusiasm without "cooling down" and continually raising their political consciousness for the further development of the revolution.[17] Liu Shao-ch'i stated that mass movements under centralized Party guidance "can certainly become the most dynamic and constant factor facilitating the economic leap forward;" he acknowledged that they would "upset some production regimes," but only those that were already "outdated" and a hindrance to production.[18]

The Party's unrestrained enthusiasm for mass movements subsided after the economic setbacks of 1959-1961. By 1961, the mass movement as a technique for raising industrial production had disappeared.[19] At the same time, the CCP relaxed the constant mass mobilization and indoctrination that had been the foundation of the Great Leap. However, there is no indication that the Party has ceased to regard the mass movement as one of its most potent political weapons. It has conceded that the mass movement cannot substitute for technical competence in production, but the revival of national campaigns for ideological indoctrination in 1963-1965 shows that the Party still relies on the assistance of co-ordinated mass action in executing its policies. The CCP's reluctance to give up the mass movement is understandable. It has great emotional

---

[16]See the speeches by Liu Shao-ch'i and Tung Pi-wu, cited in chap. iv, notes 64 and 65 of *Political Participation in Communist China*.

[17]Chou En-lai, "A Great Decade," in *Ten Glorious Years* (Peking, 1960), pp. 55–56.

[18]Liu Shao-ch'i, "The Victory of Marxism-Leninism in China," in *ibid.*, pp. 23–24.

[19]Franz Schurmann, "China's 'New Economic Policy'—Transition or Beginning," *China Quarterly*, No. 17 (January–March, 1964), p. 86. In an editorial of October 26, 1959, translated in *CB*, No. 602 (November 5, 1959), *JMJP* had stated that the belief that mass movements could not be used in industrial production was "bourgeois thinking" on the part of "rightists."

appeal for Party veterans who rose to power on a movement that seemed to demonstrate the superiority of human enthusiasm and effort over material resources; the "guerrilla mentality" and a mystical faith in mass action help to explain the extravagant use of mass movements in the Great Leap. However, the Party's reliance on the mass movement rests not only on faith but also on its proven ability to concentrate popular energies behind the Party's current tasks. . . .

# 18. Communication and Politics

*Frederick T. C. Yu*

Persuasive communications play a conspicuous part in the total policy of the Chinese Communist regime. The rulers in Peking do not govern China solely by naked force. They have always depended upon hypnotic indoctrination and stirring propaganda to mobilize the minds and effort of the population, to carry out tasks of the party leadership, and to facilitate control of the nation.

To be sure, persuasive communications are indispensable political tools in all Communist or totalitarian societies. For in a Communist state solidarity and achievement depend upon ideological unanimity,[1] and communications provide the model with which to conform. But the extensive and vigorous manipulation of communications in Communist China is a startling new phenomenon—new both to China and to world Communism. Although the idea of controlling the thinking and action of the populace is not totally strange in China, no precedent can be

---

[1] Friedrich and Brzezinski refer to this as "passion for unanimity" which, they observe, "make the totalitarians insist on the complete agreement of the entire population under their control to the measures the regime is launching." They add that "the totalitarian regimes insist that enthusiastic unanimity characterize the political behavior of the captive population." See Carl J. Friedrich and Zbigniew K. Brzezinski, *Totalitarian Dictatorship and Autocracy*, Cambridge, Mass., Harvard University Press, 1956, p. 132.

Reprinted from Frederick T. C. Yu, "Communications and Politics in Communist China," in Lucian W. Pye, ed., *Communications and Political Development* (Princeton: Princeton University Press, 1963), pp. 259–66, by permission of the author and publisher. Copyright © 1963 by Princeton University Press; Princeton Paperback, 1967, Social Science Research Council. A major part of the research was done while the writer was a postdoctoral fellow at Harvard University and the Massachusetts Institute of Technology recently under a Ford Foundation grant, which he wishes gratefully to acknowledge. All observations and conclusions are, of course, strictly his own and do not in any way reflect those of the administration or personnel of the Ford Foundation.

found in Chinese history for mass ideological conversion of the sort now being attempted by the Communists. Although many of Peking's principles of propaganda and techniques of persuasion are obviously borrowed from or inspired by the Soviet Union, the Bolshevik attempt to remould the thinking of the Russian population (not just party members and government cadres) in the post-1917 era does not warrant comparison with the Chinese Communist performance in intensity, scope, and skill.

To understand the incredibly important role of persuasive communication in Communist China it is important to keep in mind the Communist belief that "thought determines action." The *Jen Min Jih Pao* put it this way: "Work is done by man, and man's action is governed by his thinking. A man without the correct political thinking is a man without a soul. If politics does not take command—i.e., if the proletarian ideology does not take command—there can be no direction. In every work we undertake, we must always insist that politics take command and let political and ideological work come before anything else. Only when we are both thorough and penetrating with our political and ideological work can we guarantee the accomplishment of our task."[2]

In other words, if people can be made to think "correctly," according to the Communist reasoning, they can naturally act "correctly." The Chinese Communists seem to be singleminded about this, and their press is flooded with stories of how various tasks are accomplished under almost impossible conditions mainly because "the correct political and ideological work takes command." It may be the task of killing 1,700,000 catties of flies in one day in Peking;[3] it may be the task of making Chinese intellectuals "turn over their hearts to the Party."[4] How much truth there is in such stories is not the point; what is significant is the Communists' nearly fanatic faith in their "correct political and ideological work."

The Communist "political and ideological work" is more often known as propaganda (*hsien chuan*) or persuasion ( *shuō fu*). In the lexicon of the Chinese Communists this is also called "ideological warfare" or "political warfare," which is supposed to be "vigorously, gallantly, and ceaselessly fought" on every conceivable front. It is, as some Communists put it, "the basic working method of the Party."[5]

---

[2]*Jen Min Jih Pao* (*People's Daily*, Peking), editorial, November 11, 1960.
[3]*Ibid.*, May 26, 1958.
[4]*Ibid.*, April 28, 1958. This refers to the *Chiao Hsin Yun Tung* (Campaign to Give Hearts) which was supposedly initiated by the "democratic parties" in China following the "Hundred Flowers" campaign in 1958 as a pledge of their loyalty to the party.
[5]Yu Kuang-yuan, "To Develop the Ideological Education of Marxism-Leninism from the Discussions on the Story of Wu-Hsun," *Hsueh Hsi* (*Study*, Peking),IV, 6 and 7, June 1, 1951, p. 59.

The Chinese Communists are not content merely with producing obedient, docile subjects. They have a new gospel to preach and a new world to build; they want converts and believers. They require enthusiastic support of the people, not just silent acceptance. They expect all people in China to be enthusiastic in accomplishing every task of the party, not from necessity but from conviction. They must therefore capture and reshape the minds of the entire population.

This is a big order. For this means no less than an all-out ideological assault on one-fifth of the human race. Nevertheless, this is exactly the objective of the whole intricate design of propaganda or "political and ideological work" of the party. This is the task which the Communists have set out to do with their penetrating system of persuasive communications — a task on which they have spent more time, effort, and energy than on any other activity in the country.

## I. Communist Doctrine and Communication Theory

It has been said that "in the Soviet system, there is not a theory of state and a theory of communication; there is only one theory."[6] Essentially the same thing can be said about communications in Communist China.

This does not mean that the Communists do not theorize about communications. It merely suggests that the Marxist-Leninist dogma which shapes the whole course of development of every Communist society necessarily determines the theory and pattern of every policy and activity of the party. In other words, the best place to start an investigation of the theory and policy of communication in a Communist country is the Communist ideology itself.

Three aspects of the Chinese Communist ideology are especially important in the realm of communication: class consciousness, the mass line, and unity of theory and practice.

**Class Consciousness.** The Chinese Communist revolution is a class struggle, and the entire course of Chinese Communist propaganda and agitation stems from one fundamental concept: class consciousness. The central purpose of propaganda, so a favorite Communist cliché goes, is to "awaken, heighten, and sharpen the class consciousness of the masses," from which the real strength or power of the party is supposed to be generated.

Defining politics as "nothing but a centralized form of class struggle," Ai Ssu-chi, one of China's leading theoreticians, makes this point ex-

---

[6]Wilbur Schramm, *Responsibility in Mass Communication*, New York, Harper, 1957, p. 81.

plicitly clear when he writes: "There are only two kinds of political tasks: one is the task of propaganda and education, and the other is the task of organization. Both aim at raising the level of political consciousness of the revolutionary class, uniting with the forces of the revolutionary classes and fighting for the ruling power."[7]

Class consciousness is, for Marx, the basis of political consciousness. But Lenin further develops the idea — and this is perhaps his greatest contribution to the propaganda of Marxism—that class consciousness left to itself becomes entirely bound up in the "economic struggle" and will be confined to a mere "trade-unionist" consciousness. Therefore Lenin hammered on the idea that class consciousness must be awakened, educated, and brought into the battle in a larger sphere than the worker-employer relations alone, and that this task should be assigned only to an elite group or professional revolutionaries, "the conscious vanguard of the proletariat."[8]

This Leninist interpretation of class consciousness prevails in Communist China. Liu Shao-chi, Red China's chief of state, has the following to say: "We should lead the masses forward, but there should be no commandism. We should be intimately connected with the masses, but we should reject tailism.[9] We should start from the level already attained by the masses in developing their consciousness and leading them forward.[10] With us, therefore, everything is dependent on and determined by the people's consciousness and self-activity, without which we can accomplish nothing and all our efforts will be in vain. . . . When the masses are not fully conscious, the duties of Communists . . . in carrying out any kind of work is to develop their consciousness by every effective and suitable means. This is the first step in our work which must be done no matter how difficult it is or how much time it will take."[11]

**The Mass Line.** "The fundamental policy of the party," according to the Communists, "is the policy of the mass line."[12]

Like class consciousness, this "mass line" has acquired a quality of sacredness in China. The Communists talk forever about the "harmoni-

---

[7]Ai Ssu-chi, *Li Shih Wei Wu Lun She-Hui Fa Chan Shih Chiang I* (*Historical Materialism — Lectures on History of Social Development*), Peking, Workmen's Publishing Co., June 1951, first rev. ed., pp. 83–86.

[8]See Jean-Marie Domanach, "Leninist Propaganda," *Public Opinion Quarterly,* Summer 1951. See also Alex Inkeles "Communist Propaganda and Counter Propaganda," *Proceedings of the 28th Institute of the Norman Wait Harris Memorial Foundation* (1952); stenographic transcription of this lecture is on file in the Social Relations Reading Room, Harvard University.

[9]This follows the Soviet attack on the tendency to drag at the tail of the masses, or *khvostizm*, as it was called by Lenin. See Alex Inkeles, *Public Opinion in Soviet Russia,* Cambridge, Mass., Harvard University Press, 1950, p. 2.

[10]Liu Shao-chi, *On the Party,* Peking, Foreign Language Press, 1950, p. 66.

[11]*Ibid.*, pp. 5, 7, 8.

[12]*Jen Min Jih Pao* (*People's Daily*, Peking), December 11, 1958.

ous unity with the masses," "the viewpoint of the masses," "wisdom of the masses," "sanction of the masses," etc. According to them, almost every program or policy of the party is "demanded," "desired," and "initiated" by the masses. For instance, it is almost always the "creative initiative" and "highly elevated political consciousness" of the masses that result in their "volunteering" to go to the Korean front, "demanding" the punishment of rightists in the Hundred-Flower Movement, or "petitioning" for the realization of the commune program.

But how does this mass line operate? And how is it related to class consciousness and communication?

The answer can be found in the Communist formula: "the policy and methods of work of the party must originate from the masses and go back to the masses." A cynical interpretation of this would be that the Communists are trying to make the ideas of the party sound as if they were ideas of the people. It is perhaps more accurate to say that the Communists always attempt to transform the feeling or sentiments of the masses into an idea or notion which seemingly represents what the masses want but actually expresses what the party intends. As early as 1943 Mao preached: "We should go into the midst of the masses, learn from them, sum up their experiences so that these experiences will become well-defined principles and methods, and then explain them to the masses (through agitation work), and call upon the masses to put them into practice in order to solve their problems and lead them to liberation and happiness."[13]

This "mass line" was explained more fully by Mao at another occasion when he wrote: "In all practical work of our party, correct leadership can only be developed on the principle of 'from the masses, to the masses.' This means summing up (i.e., co-ordinating and systematizing after careful study) the views of the masses (i.e., views scattered and unsystematic), then taking the resulting ideas back to the masses, explaining and popularizing them until the masses embrace the ideas as their own, stand up for them and translate them into action by way of testing their correctness. Then it is necessary once more to sum up the view of the masses, and once again take the resulting ideas back to the masses so that the masses give them their wholehearted support. . . . And so on, over and over again, so that each time these ideas emerge with greater correctness and become more vital and meaningful."[14]

---

[13]Mao Tse-tung, *Selected Works*, London, Lawrence and Wishart, Ltd., 1956, Vol. 4, p. 153.

[14]*Ibid.*, p. 113. This quotation is from a resolution on methods of leadership drafted by Mao on behalf of the Central Committee of the Communist Party. The resolution was passed on July 1, 1943 by the party's Politburo. The Chinese text of the resolution is available in the *Cheng Feng Wen Hsien* (*Documents of the Party's Ideological Remoulding Movement*), Hong Kong, Hsin Min Chu Ch'u Pan She, 1949, pp. 139–144.

So much importance is attached by the Chinese Communists to this method of "mass line" that it is formalized as general guide to action in the party constitution: "Whether or not the party leadership is correct depends upon the party's ability to analyze, systematize, summarize, and consolidate the opinions and experiences of the masses, to transform them as the policy of the party and then to return them, through *propaganda, agitation,* and *organization,* to the masses as their own guide to thinking and action."[15]

**Unity of Theory and Practice.** "If you want to know the theory and methods of revolution," declared Mao in his often quoted article entitled *On Practice,* "you must participate in the revolution."[16] His explanation: "All truths are obtained through direct experience."

It must be remembered that Chinese Communism as an ideology consists of a variety of components ranging from basic beliefs, such as "labor creates the world," to utopian promises, such as "the elimination of classes." It also prescribes tasks to be accomplished and goals to be achieved.

While outright opposition to the doctrine is obviously forbidden in a Communist society, mere passive compliance with the ideology is equally unacceptable. To the Chinese Communists, apathy is a cardinal sin. Everyone must take part in *tou cheng* (struggle).

Thus, in terms of persuasion, it is not enough for a peasant in a commune to shout that he loves Communism, that he detests feudalism, and that he adores communes. He has to show by action that he has actually "benefited" from the wisdom of Marxism-Leninism. This means that he has to "accuse," "attack," or "eliminate" the "reactionary elements," participate actively in the tasks assigned by the cadres, "contribute" his labor or production to the government to express his "gratitude" to the Communist party.

The faith must be practiced. Hence the entire process of mass persuasion is forever built around one central task of one kind or another. The tasks vary, but each represents a goal prescribed by the party and creates an opportunity for the people to unite their faith with practice in an approved manner.

One needs only a casual look at the Communist record since 1949 to discover that for twelve years the entire nation has always engaged in one major mass movement along with large-scale campaigns for different sections of the population during a particular time. To name chrono-

---

[15]*Chung Kuo Kung Chan Tang Chang Cheng (Constitution of the Chinese Communist Party),* Peking, Jen Min Chu Pan She, 1956, p. 8.
[16]*Mao Tse-tung Hsien Chi (Selected Works of Mao Tse-tung),* Peking, Jen Min Publishing Co., 1953, Vol. 1, p. 276.

logically only a few: Land Reform, *Hsueh Hsi* (study), Resist-America Aid-Korea, Propaganda Networks, Democratic Reforms in Factories, Mines, and Enterprises, Ideological Remoulding, Three-anti and Five-anti, Suppression of Counter-Revolutionaries, Five-Year Plans, Agricultural Coops, "Hundred Flowers," National Reconstruction Through Austerity and Diligence, Reform through Work, "Big Leap Forward," "General Line of Socialist Development," Production of Steel and Iron, and People's Commune.

This is not to say that every Communist movement serves mainly the ideological function of the party. That would be stretching somewhat the role of mass persuasion in Communist China. It merely suggests that the policy of communication is synchronized with every task of the party and that it is through the tasks that some major objectives of propaganda are achieved. Here is the way the Communists have stated their position:

"It is always important to grasp every opportunity which can push our revolution one step further. Always give full support to complete one central task, mobilize the broad masses and attract them to the general slogan at the time. We must know that revolution is a mass movement, and that actions of the masses must concentrate only on one or at most a few definite and clearly-expressed objectives. . . . After one central task is completed, replace it with another central task. Substitute one general slogan for another new slogan. This is the forward-going law of revolution. It is also the law of gradually elevating mass consciousness and organizational ability."[17]

## II. The Communication System

The Chinese Communists have developed a crude but strangely effiicient communication system which reaches almost every segment of the population and which controls virtually all the avenues to the Chinese mind. A French correspondent who visited Red China in 1956 reported: "The head of a good Chinese citizen today functions like a sort of radio receiving set. Somewhere in Peiping buzzes the great transmitting station which broadcasts the right thought and the words to be repeated. Millions of heads faithfully pick them up, and millions of mouths repeat them like loud-speakers."

This must sound hard to believe since Communist China, despite its ambitious program of modernization, continues to be handicapped by a high illiteracy rate and inadequate communication facilities. But one

[17] *Hsueh Hsi* (*Study*, Peking), February 10, 1952, p. 44.

must not think of mass communication in Communist China in terms of the conventional mass media such as newspapers, magazines, radio, television, and motion pictures. Though important, they do not make up the entire communication system in China. The Communists depend upon a variety of communications channels and devices that are rarely considered tools for "mass communication" as the words are understood in the United States. These include blackboard newspapers, *tatzepao* (handwritten posters), street corner plays, folk dances, songs, poetry, plain face-to-face communication used by millions of oral agitators known as "propagandists" (*hsien chuan yan*) in China, and various means of thought reform.

Some features of this communication system are Communist, some are traditionally Chinese, and some are strictly inventions of the Chinese Marxists. Together they suggest something of a revolution in communication. Motivated by the general goals of Chinese Communism and guided by a new communication elite, this revolution has resulted in new images, new symbols, a new language, a new audience, new communication channels, new communication methods and behavior of the masses. . . .

# 19. Communication Patterns and the Chinese Revolution

*Richard H. Solomon*

The strategy for gaining power which Mao Tse-tung and other Party leaders gradually evolved seems to have placed great emphasis on the exploitation of weak communication links, based on both the emotional and structural gaps between the peasantry and the established élite. The weak lateral linkages which we saw in our respondents' expectations of peer interaction found political manifestation in the factional conflicts and lack of co-operation between local "warlord" forces which were ostensibly allied to the dominant Nationalist régime. The breakdown in effective working relations between these military forces, as they competed for influence with the central Nationalist authorities and sought to establish or maintain positions of local military dominance, created the conditions whereby a weak Communist movement could survive. As Mao wrote in 1928: "The prolonged splits and wars within the White Régime provide a condition for the emergence and persistence of one or more small Red areas under the leadership of the Communist Party amidst the encirclement of the White Régime. . . . If only we realise that splits and wars will never cease within the White Régime in China, we shall have no doubts about the emergence, survival, and daily growth of Red political power."[1]

Weak links among its opponents reduced the threat to the Red Army. Similarly the "vertical" fragmentation between the peasants and the established élites at either local or national levels provided opportunities

---

[1] Mao Tse-tung, "Why Is It That Red Political Power Can Exist in China?" in *Selected Works of Mao Tse-tung* (Peking: Foreign Languages Press, 1961–1965), Vol. I, p. 65.

Reprinted from Richard H. Solomon, "Communication Patterns and the Chinese Revolution," *China Quarterly* 32 (October-December 1967): 101-10, by permission of the author and journal.

both for destroying the effectiveness of the existing political order and for building the Party's own base of mass support. From a communications perspective, Mao's strategy for gaining power might be summarised as an effort to take advantage of the weak links between leader and led, to break down the established channels of political information flow and control, and then within this newly widened gap to insert a Party organisation which would work to establish its own channels of propaganda, intelligence, and political control among a "liberated" peasantry.

The Party early developed a variety of techniques for breaking down the links between established leadership and the led. Propaganda appeals were aimed at overcoming the anxiety which had been the basis of the peasants' passivity, and then transforming it into hatred for those who had brutalised and exploited the peasants. Selective terror and assassination were used to eliminate or drive away the opposition leadership, and military action was carried out to destroy the forces which supported the established order. This process of widening the gap between established authority and the people was recently described by a peasant from Shensi. He recalled the arrival of the Communist armies at the end of their "Long March":

> To begin with, people were afraid and said that Communists were murderers, but when they came here they were ordinary people and they always said: "Divide up the land and fight against landowners and despots." *They talked a lot and held lots of meetings* and at the meetings we used to stand up and shout, "Yes, Yes!" but we did not really believe in them or that they had any real power.
>
> But in April 1935 the Red Army defeated an armed counterrevolutionary landowners' corps ten *li* from here. They killed the leader of the southern district ... and took lots of booty ... they also killed other counter-revolutionaries. Then the people saw that the Red Army did have power, and so *we stopped driving into the town with our taxes and goods.* Instead, we organised ourselves into guerrilla bands. . . .
>
> *We no longer went to the town and we no longer sold grain to the town and we paid no taxes, and those who were KMT no longer dared live out in the country, but began to run away. The town was isolated....* When tax collectors came, we took them prisoner, and, if any were decent we let them go; the others we killed. *So the town became quite isolated.*[2]

A number of recent studies have indicated that the Communists had rather mixed success in destroying the control linkages between their opponents and the peasantry. During the "Kiangsi" period, in those areas of South China where local clan organisations or gentry leadership were

---

[2]Jan Myrdal, *Report From a Chinese Village* (London: Heinemann, 1965), p. 67. Emphasis added.

well developed and active, the early peasant associations found the job of political penetration rather difficult. Party organisers found their best opportunities in places where economic exploitation gave the Communists a good issue, and where peasant para-military forces had been able to intimidate or physically destroy the traditional organisations of control.[3] And in North China it was the Japanese invasion and "conditions of rural anarchy following the evacuation of local élites" that prepared the way for Communist political and military expansion.[4] The Japanese thus worked for the Party by breaking indigenous linkages of social control; and in the areas where this process had been most complete the Communists enjoyed their greatest successes.[5]

If undermining the Nationalist government's links to the people was one of their strategic aims, the Communists displayed an equal determination to re-establish and extend channels of political communication and control by building organisations of their own design.[6] From experiences dating back to the movement's early days in the Chingkang Mountains, Mao acquired a great sensitivity to the problem of maintaining popular support: "Wherever the Red Army goes, the masses are cold and aloof, and only after our propaganda do they slowly move into action. . . . We have an acute sense of our isolation which we keep hoping will end."[7] Much of the still-to-be-written history of communism in China concerns the development of the political institutions by which the Party was able effectively to link itself up with "the masses." We know from his famous "Hunan Report" that Mao was highly impressed with the capacity of organisation to focus popular political interests: "It was on the strength of their extensive organisation that the peasants went into action and within four months brought about a great revolution in the

---

[3]See Roy Mark Hofheinz, Jr., *The Peasant Movement and Rural Revolution: Chinese Communists in the Countryside (1923–1927)* (unpublished Ph.D. dissertation, Harvard University, 1966), pp. 218–220, and *passim*.

[4]Chalmers A. Johnson, *Peasant Nationalism and Communist Power: The Emergence of Revolutionary China, 1937–1945* (Stanford: Stanford University Press, 1962), p. 49.

[5]*Ibid.*, Chapters III and IV.

[6]A recent study of the Viet Cong has stressed the importance of building or re-building communication channels through organisational work as essential to the Communists' strategy of political insurgency: "In the hands of the Communists [revolutionary guerrilla warfare is] a form of aggression useful in nations characterised by people without communication, isolated by terrain, psychology, or politics, people inward turning. . . . The chief [communist] effort was communication; the chief medium was the especially created organisation; the chief daily activity of the cadres was agitation and propaganda work. Communication facilitated organisation, which facilitated mobilisation." Douglas Pike, *Viet Cong: The Organization and Techniques of The National Liberation Front of South Vietnam* (Cambridge, Mass.: The M.I.T. Press, 1966), p. 32.

[7]Mao, "The Struggle in The Chingkang Mountains," *Selected Works*, Vol. I, pp. 97–98.

countryside, a revolution without parallel in history."[8] And in the same report he also underlined the effectiveness of propaganda in mobilising popular support.

The Party has also shown a continuing concern with the development and maintenance of channels of vertical information to keep Party decision-makers well informed about popular attitudes and conditions. The stress the Communists have laid upon the dispatch of "survey" and "investigation" teams to the lower levels of operation not only reflects Mao's personal experience of having tapped a wealth of political support among the peasantry of Hunan, but also the Party's relative ignorance about the countryside.[9] Party training and policy documents continually exhort cadres to abandon "commandist" and "subjectivist" styles of leadership and to base their decisions on a thorough understanding of local problems. As Mao wrote in 1941, in the preface to "Rural Surveys":

> Many of our comrades still have a crude and careless style of work, do not seek to understand things thoroughly and may even be completely ignorant of conditions at the lower levels, and yet they are responsible for directing work. This is an extremely dangerous state of affairs. . . . The only way to know conditions is to make social investigations, to investigate the conditions of each social class in real life.[10]

The full integration and application of the Party's early techniques for political communication and control — propaganda work, the gathering of local intelligence, and the creation of organisation channels for the transmission and application of decisions from the Party centre—was attained during the war with Japan. The Communists not only developed channels of information which enabled them successfully to promote guerrilla warfare, to maintain a high level of intelligence about enemy military activities yet to deny such information to their opponents, but also created the political control structure which gave a sense of unity and co-ordination to the actions of a decentralised peasant political-military organisation. It was in no small measure through such organisation accomplishments that the Communists came to power in China.[11]

---

[8]Mao, "Report on An Investigation of The Peasant Movement in Hunan," *Selected Works*, Vol. 1, p. 25. The study by Hofheinz, *op. cit.*, has some very interesting material on the development of propaganda techniques during the early days of the peasant movement, especially pp. 94–116.

[9]See Hofheinz, *op. cit.*, p. 54.

[10]Mao, "Preface and Postscript to Rural Surveys," *Selected Works*, Vol. III, p. 11.

[11]Franz Schurmann has suggested that much of the Communist success during this period was related to their effective use of existing social organisation: "The linkage between war and production based on the natural village was one of the great organisational achievements of the Chinese Communists." *Ideology and Organization in Communist China*, p. 425.

## Gaps between Party and Masses

One of the more enduring slogans which runs through Chinese Communist Party educational documents and analyses of its style of leadership
is the phrase, "the Party must not cut itself off from the masses" (*t'uo-li
ch'ün-chung*). This frequently-invoked phrase is striking because it
echoes so strongly both the way that paternal authority "cut itself off"
from contact with its maturing sons, and the gap between peasantry and
government which the Communists exploited in their struggle for power.
Party leaders are concerned that pressures for radical social change will
once again create a gap of emotion and purpose between the political
élite and the people.[12] As documents from the rectification campaigns of
the early 1940s reveal, the Party has found it a most difficult job to
overcome the leadership style and communications habits characteristic
of the traditionally aloof and élitist political class. The answer which Mao
Tse-tung and other Party leaders have developed to prevent this kind
of breakdown in communication between leader and led is the notion of
the "mass line" (*ch'ün-chung lu-hsien*).[13]

> All correct leadership is necessarily "from the masses; to the masses."
> This means: take the ideas of the masses (scattered and unsystematic
> ideas) and concentrate them (through study turn them into concentrated
> and systematic ideas), then go to the masses and propagate and explain
> these ideas until the masses embrace them as their own, hold fast to
> them and translate them into action, and test the correctness of these
> ideas in such action. Then once again concentrate ideas from the
> masses and then once again go to the masses so that the ideas are
> persevered in and carried through. And so on, over and over again in
> an endless spiral. . . .[14]

The application of this conception, first articulated in 1943, to daily
political action has involved both organisational innovation and efforts to
change the attitudes of the leaders and the led. Perhaps most basic to
this conception of political action is the notion of being "positive" or
"active" (*chi-chi*). For those with political authority this has meant the
commitment to manipulate social institutions and individual attitudes and
habits so as to promote rapid change; for the led it has meant a forced

---

[12]See Liu Shao-ch'i, *Lun Ch'ün-chung Lu-hsien* (Hong Kong: Hsin-min Ch'u-pan
She, 1949), especially pp. 1–18.
[13]The two best English language studies of the "mass line" concept will be found
in: John Wilson Lewis, *Leadership in Communist China* (Ithaca: Cornell University Press, 1963), especially Chapter III; and James R. Townsend, *Political Participation in Communist China* (Berkeley and Los Angeles: University of California
Press, 1967), especially Chapter IV.
[14]Mao, "Some Questions Concerning Methods of Leadership," *Selected Works*,
Vol. III, p. 119.

mobilisation into the realm of political action. The Communists have sought to deny the individual the traditional option of non-participation in the "tiger world" of politics.

By bringing the individual into newly-enlarged processes of political communication the régime exposes him to new norms of social behaviour and political goals of its own definition. And by giving "the masses" a more active role in the process of political communication, largely by encouraging their criticism of the way Party cadres have *applied* Central Committee directives, the Party has sought to bind the people into a political process of its own creation and control. Literacy, which traditionally differentiated mass from élite, is now being spread throughout the country. Yet the extension of this skill appears to promote Party control more than the expression of popular opinion since the channels of communication remain firmly under Party direction. Participation in weekly "study" sessions or in the periodic mass movements exposes the individual to a continuing and often rapidly changing flow of official communication which he must actively assimilate and "feed back" to Party cadres or face a variety of sanctions.

That Party directives continue to speak of the problem of "the separation of theory from practice," and of the danger of the Party "cutting itself off from the masses" indicates that traditional attitudes towards the use of authority endure. And, as is suggested by such institutional efforts as the compulsory periods of physical labour for army officers and Party and government cadres, or the periodic *hsia-fang* movements to get Party operatives out into the countryside, and the formalised efforts to subject them to mass criticism, Party leaders remain ever-sensitive to a breakdown in communication between their cadres and "the masses." Mao's articles from the 1942 rectification campaign, "Oppose Stereotyped Party Writing" and "Talks at the Yenan Forum on Literature and Art", represent only the first of continuing efforts to promote a new style of political communication, oriented to mass consumption and unfettered by "sectarian" and élitist attitudes concerning the relationship of Party to people.

Party attention to building new "vertical" links between the leadership and the led, and with developing new habits of leader-led intercommunication, is perhaps second only to concern with developing lateral or "horizontal" communication and control structures. These are intended to knit the Communist Party together and to link Party to government and army, thus preventing the re-emergence of cliques and bases of autonomous political power—"independent kingdoms"—which might be used to challenge Party central authority. Efforts in this direction seem to have centred around the problem of breaking down the traditional purely hierarchical conception of authority and giving greater power to peer group structures. Shortly before "liberation" Mao complained that in many of the leadership organisations of the Party,

> it is the habitual practice for one individual to monopolise the conduct of affairs and decide important problems. Solutions to important problems are decided not by Party committee meetings but by one individual, and membership in the Party committee has become nominal. Differences of opinion among committee members cannot be resolved and are left unresolved for a long time. . . . [They] maintain only formal, not real, unity among themselves. This situation must be changed. From now on a sound system of Party committee meetings must be instituted in all leading bodies.[15]

Efforts to shift authority away from the individual and to the group, however, run up against the enduring habits of China's traditional political life—reliance on superiors for organisational initiative, and reluctance to criticise peers. Another essay of Mao's spells out in minute detail the proper norms for promoting openness in communication within Party committees:

> Place problems on the table . . . do not talk behind peoples' backs. Whenever problems arise call a meeting, place the problems on the table for discussion, take some decisions and the problems will be solved. "Exchange information." This means that members of a Party committee should keep each other informed and exchange views on matters that have come to their attention. This is of great importance in achieving a common language. . . .
> Ask your subordinates about matters you don't understand or don't know, and do not lightly express your approval or disapproval . . . and we should listen carefully to the views of the cadres at the lower levels.[16]

The organisational structures within which lateral communications have been promoted are primarily the study group (*hsiao-tzu*), Party committee meetings, and the more serious investigation meeting (*chien-t'ao hui*). Through the "criticism—self-criticism" technique, a resistant Party membership has been coerced into openly airing differences of opinion and criticising individual mistakes. Here again, the Party leadership has sought to deny its cadres the security of non-involvement and

---

[15]Mao, "On Strengthening The Party Committee System," *Selected Works*, Vol. IV, p. 267.
[16]Mao, "Methods of Work of Party Committees," *Selected Works*, Vol. IV, p. 377.

withdrawal by continually stimulating the open discussion of problems of work and group relations. One of our interviewees, a man who had been a field grade military officer under the Nationalist régime, and then a military instructor in the PLA gave us some insight into the effects of group criticism:

> [The cadres] have criticism meetings among themselves; they talk about their problems and develop a sense of unity. The Communists are always encouraging people to talk, to express their opinions. Originally there is no enmity among people, and if you talk about problems you can prevent misunderstandings and can maintain unity in work. During the National-ist era things were not this way; you would hold back your opinions and they would continuously get greater. The distance between you would get greater and you would eventually become enemies.

Fear that traditional attitudes will re-emerge has led to an almost com-pulsive attempt to organise every aspect of life on the mainland so that Party influence will penetrate all areas of daily activity. Propaganda workers stress the importance of eliminating "empty points" (*k'ung-tzu*) which would give "feudalism, capitalism, and freaks and monsters [a place] to sneak into"[17]: and communications cadres write proudly of having eliminated "empty areas" (*k'ung-pai ti-ch'ü*) where Party opinion and directives had not fully penetrated.[18]

## A "Cultural Revolution"?

Has the apparently far-reaching Party-led social transformation of the past eighteen years in China wrought a genuine change in peoples' atti-tudes and social behaviour; or do traditional political habits endure be-hind a façade of organisational manipulations? A full answer to such a question is clearly beyond the scope of this essay; yet the few detailed investigations that have been made strongly suggest that lasting change has been slow in coming. The domestic mainland press reveals that de-spite efforts by top Party leaders to promote a critical dialogue between the peasantry and its cadres, peasant anxieties about raising criticisms of those with immediate authority over them, and the unwillingness of the

---

[17]"Transform The Old Market Fairs: Propagate New Thinking," *Jen-min Jih-pao* (*People's Daily*), August 25, 1964, p. 2.
[18]See, "Management By The Entire Party Is The Basic Directive of Newspaper Work," *People's Daily*, June 12, 1960, p. 11. I am indebted to Dr. Alan Liu for having called to my attention Party concern with eliminating "empty points."

cadres to submit to such criticism, have attenuated the development of open communication.[19] "Formalism," *i.e.,* relying on organisational forms and personal authority, rather than implementing the spirit of the "mass line," has continued to frustrate the development of a sense of "voluntarism" and mass initiative.[20]

Until recently, the 1954 purge of Kao Kang and Jao Shu-shih, and Peng Teh-huai's removal in 1959 seemed relatively isolated events in what appeared from the outside to be a context of organisational unity.[21] The secret PLA "Work Bulletins" (*Kung-tso T'ung-hsun*) revealed however that at least as far back as 1960 Mao and the Party central apparently found themselves losing their grip over the army because of communication blockages and the wilful distortion of information by PLA political cadres. The Party's Military Affairs Commission, in attempting to correct this situation, stressed that, "Attention should always be paid to taking hold of the two ends: one end is to transmit and carry through the directives and decisions of the central authorities of the Party and the Military Affairs Commission; the other is to manage well the ideological activity of the army units. Messages from above must be carried below, and what happens below must be reported above. The levels in between should not block the flow of communication."[22] Resistance to Party control was apparently so great that the leadership had to demand that its political cadres "transmit at the right time directives and resolutions of the central authorities of the Party. . . . The directives of the central authorities of the Party and Chairman Mao must be seriously, responsibly, completely, and systematically passed down to the rank and file, level by level."[23] And the resolution went on to complain, "Some cadres . . . do not transmit the directives of the Party and of their superiors to their subordinates at the proper time, nor do they report to their superiors, or seek the latter's advice. . . . They have even reported to their superiors only things which are good and withheld from their superiors things which are bad. In a word, they have falsified the situation."

---

[19]The best overall review of Party efforts in this direction will be found in Townsend, *Political Participation in Communist China* (Berkeley, Calif.: University of California Press, 1967).

[20]*Ibid.,* pp. 116–117, 142–144.

[21]These challenges to Mao's leadership are discussed in Franz Schurmann, *Ideology and Organization in Communist China, op. cit.*

[22]"Resolution Made by the Enlarged Meeting of the Military Affairs Commission of the Central Authorities of the Chinese Communist Party on Strengthening Political and Ideological Work in the Army" (Peking, October 20, 1960), in *Bulletin of Activities*, No. 3, January 7, 1961. Translated in Chester Cheng, ed., *The Politics of The Chinese Red Army: A Translation of The Bulletin of Activities of The People's Liberation Army* (Stanford, California: The Hoover Institution, 1966), p. 68.

[23]*Ibid.,* pp. 70–71.

The full extent of resistance to Mao's policies, if not his personal leadership, has now been more fully revealed in the "Great Proletarian Cultural Revolution." This unprecedented upheaval, initiated by a leadership uncompromisingly committed to utopian goals, has exposed both Mao's impatience for change and the magnitude of resistance to a radical transformation of society. What is particularly interesting about the events of the past two years from the point of view of political communications is the degree to which control, distortion, and manipulation of information has been one of the chief weapons of Mao's opponents. The breakdown in relations among the top leadership was so great, and the "independent kingdom" which P'eng Chen had created within the Peking Party Committee was such a closed grouping that even Mao himself apparently could not publish his initial attacks against his opponents in November 1965 except by going to Shanghai. In essence "the emperor" had been cut off from access to the machinery of government by his "loyal ministers."

The fact that a large proportion of the men initially removed from positions of Party authority were engaged in propaganda activity, and the concomitant reorganisation of the editorial staffs of several major newspapers and numerous provincial ones, underlines the degree to which communication channels apparently had passed out of Maoist control. And the continuing heavy reliance on the wall poster in propagating official directives and information about daily events seems to indicate the continuing unreliability of the normal instruments of mass communication for the "revolutionary" cause. That Mao accuses many of his opponents of having "waved a 'red flag' to oppose *the* red flag" — that is, of having presented an appearance of supporting his policies, while in fact resisting them — gives further evidence of the degree to which Mao apparently found himself cut off from the reality of political control by a Party giving lip-service to the slogans of revolution. As had happened so often in China's political past, "name" (*ming*) and "reality" (*shih*) were out of joint and required rectification.

In Mao's response to this loss of political control, the "mass line" has acquired its most grotesque reality. The activities of the Red Guards seem to be the revolutionary's response to the threat of resurgent élitism within the Party. And by invoking the new literacy skills of "the masses" — the writing of wall posters critical of those "misusing" Party authority, and the incantation of "Quotations from Chairman Mao"—a political voice has been given to those who were traditionally dependent on the guidance of their elders.

Will the present turmoil produce an enduring institutionalisation of the "mass line"? Or will the Maoist conception of a mobilisation political culture attain its ultimate discredit in excess and social disruption? The weight of human experience inclines one toward the latter possibility. But the world can only wait and watch the playing out of this fantastic effort to create a truly participant political process that is not built on long-term investments in education and economic development, but rather on the unstable ground of manipulated emotions and "class" hatreds.[24]

[24]The role of stimulated hatreds in mass mobilisation in Communist China has been explored in my article "America's Revolutionary Alliance with Communist China," *Asian Survey*, December, 1967.

# POLITICAL INTEGRATION, POLITICAL STRUCTURE, AND THE ALLOCATION PROCESSES

Political integration generally refers to a relationship of community among groups of people within the boundaries of a political entity. By developing various ties with each other, members of a political system gradually acquire a sense of community, a feeling of identity, and an awareness of their common destination. It is with the development of this kind of community feeling among members of a political system that peaceful methods instead of violence will be used to resolve disputes, and the continuing existence of the system is assured.

In the case of Communist China, the political leaders attempted to achieve political integration by a variety of methods. The first method applied by the Chinese Communists was to eliminate elements in the Chinese society which might be disruptive to the social and political order of the newly established regime. They achieved this by executing, jailing, or sending to the labor camps those they considered to be "the enemies of the people," meaning former officials and officers of the Nationalist government, landlords, the urban bourgeoisie, and uncooperative intellectuals.

The second method used by the Chinese Communists to achieve integration, and probably the most important one, was to resort to political indoctrination. By making the learning of communist ideology the core of the curricula of the schools of all levels on mainland China, the Communists endeavored to produce a new generation of Chinese youth totally dedicated to the building of a communist society. In addition to the control of the educational system, monopoly of the mass media has been an important means of political control. Through the complete state control of the mass media, such as the newspapers, magazines, movies, and television, the Chinese Communists have been able not only to transmit to the people what the political authority wants them to see and hear, but have also prevented the people from getting any information from the outside world which might be detrimental to the indoctrination effort of the regime.

A third method to attain political integration was to rely on the political machines of the Chinese Communist party. By increasing the membership of the party, by placing party members in key positions in every social institution and political organization in mainland China, the Chinese Communists have obtained a degree of control seldom achieved by previous governments of China. Through the application of the principles of "democratic centralization," the Chinese Communists hoped to enlarge the level of participation of the Chinese people, communists or noncommunists, in the decision-making process. This did not mean, of course, that after a decision had already been made by the central authority, the people still had the right to ask for a change in that decision.

Finally, the leaders of Communist China tried to increase the support of the majority of the people on the mainland through the allocation or, to put it more precisely, the re-allocation of values in the Chinese society. They made fundamental changes in two areas, i.e., the distribution of welfare and allocation of justice. In regard to the distribution of welfare, the Chinese Communists attempted to change the distribution of wealth by adopting a combination of measures which included the nationalization of private industries, confiscation of lands of the landlords, and the establishment of the state-operated ration systems.

Available information on income distribution among various groups of people on the Chinese mainland has yielded evidence that the wealth is probably more evenly distributed in today's China than in the pre-1949 periods. But the same data also show that government and party officials, military officers and soldiers, university professors, scientists, and skilled, as well as unskilled workers still receive incomes substantially higher than that of the peasants who constitute the overwhelming majority of the population.

In regard to the allocation of justice, the practice of the Chinese Communists has been under strong influence of their ideology. According to Mao Tse-tung, there are two kinds of contradictions — the contradictions between the enemy and the "people," and the contradictions among the "people." The major function of the "people's court" system was to protect the "people" in their conflicts with the "enemy of the people," i.e., the "exploitive and reactionary" classes of China. Thus the laws in Communist China were not to be applied and interpreted strictly according to its language in the decision-making process of the legal system. Instead, both the laws and the court should be used as instruments of class struggle against the class enemies. Following this logic, it was only natural for the Chinese Communists to rely upon staged "mass trials" to get rid of the landlords, factory owners, anti-communist intellectuals and students.

In the mid-1950s some judges in Communist China made suggestions that the process of trials should be more "normalized," meaning a stricter adherence to the language and intention of the law in court decisions, instead of relying solely on political considerations. These suggestions, however, were condemned as being rightist tendencies and were dismissed by the party leaders. With the occurrence of the Great Cultural Revolution, the "normalization" efforts of the legal-minded judges were dealt a severe blow. The humiliation and prosecution of high-ranking officials in "mass meetings" during the Cultural Revolution was a clear indication that the Chinese Communists had little intention of giving up the emphasis of political and propagandist purposes in the process of the allocation of justice.

Until 1958, the Chinese Communist leaders had shown remarkable ability to hold the country together for the achieving of many ambitious programs of nation building. With the advent of the Great Leap Forward, differences and conflicts among various sections of the society as well as among various factions of the party had been developed. These differences and conflicts among various groups of people in Communist China reached a climax during the period of the Great Cultural Revolution.

So serious were the divisions and conflicts among various sections of the party and the society that at some points in the year of 1967, there were serious doubts among diplomats stationed in Peking whether the central government in Peking still had effective control over various parts of the Mainland. Although the turmoil caused by the Cultural Revolution has somewhat subsided, the movement has left deep scars on the internal cohesiveness of the system. The deeply rooted suspicions and hatred between various factions of the communist party during the Cultural Revolution, the generation gap between the old guardians of the Chinese Communist revolution and the younger generation brought up under communist rule after 1949, and the conflicts between the Han-Chinese and other racial and ethnic groups, are but some of the more obvious problems that the Chinese Communist leaders face in the arena of political integration. Whether leaders in Peking can successfully overcome these problems will be a determining factor in the political future of the communist system on the Chinese mainland.

# VIII
# Political Integration

## 20. Mao's Effort to Reintegrate the Chinese Polity

*Richard H. Solomon*

The factional conflict and sporadic violence which convulsed China from the summer of 1966 until early 1969 has called into question many of our assumptions about the degree of national unity and political centralization which the Communists apparently had achieved after nearly two decades of control on the mainland. The full meaning of the events of what was called "The Great Proletarian Cultural Revolution" is so profound and all encompassing in its implications regarding the changes that have, and have not, occurred in Chinese society in recent years that no one interpretation is likely to account for more than a facet of the whole. Furthermore, many of the data that would be necessary for a full understanding of Mao's efforts to "prevent a restoration of capitalism" in China, and to keep the Communist Party from "changing its color," have yet to be made public. Hence, with the full awareness that the following remarks can be considered only provisional and incomplete, we nonetheless want to suggest some hypotheses on the meaning of the Cultural Revolution for the question of China's political integration.

To at least one seasoned observer of the Chinese political scene, the public conflict which erupted on the mainland in the late summer of 1966 was yet another bursting out of that condition of chaos (*luan*) which has been so much a part of the rhythm of Chinese social life: "There is no real civil war. What is happening has happened many times before in the course of Chinese history. It is war welling up from below. It is disintegration."[1] Whatever general characterization is given to the Cultural Rev-

[1] *China News Analysis*, Hong Kong, No. 667 (July 6, 1967), p. 1.

Reprinted from Richard H. Solomon, "Mao's Effort to Reintegrate the Chinese Polity: Problems of Authority and Conflicts in Chinese Social Process," in A. Doak Barnett, ed., *Chinese Communist Politics in Action* (Seattle: University of Washington Press, 1969), pp. 340–51, by permission of the author and publisher. Revised and updated by the author.

olution years, it is clear that the basic issue of political integration was brought to the fore; and Mao's conception of how "People's China" should be restructured and driven forward to modernity was called into question.

Probing the meaning of the Cultural Revolution as it affects the matter of social integration requires analysis at two distinct levels. It is clear that preceding the public manifestation of conflict in China, beginning with the mass Red Guard rallies in August of 1966, there was a breakdown in the ability of the top Party leaders to cooperate among themselves.[2] Subsequently, as a result of this breakdown in relations among the country's leaders, public conflict was initiated and expanded in scope, in time coming to encompass the most basic levels of social organization, and giving an increasing quality of regional fragmentation and local chaos to mainland political life. The following analysis will proceed within the framework of these two levels of the Cultural Revolution.

In the light of recent events it appears that at least since 1957 — probably beginning with the failure of Mao's Hundred Flowers policy for dealing with the intellectuals — a series of fundamental policy miscalculations increasingly called into question the legitimacy of Mao's "revolutionary" style of leadership. The great costs of the dispute with the Soviet Union, the failure of the Great Leap Forward, and more recent foreign policy misadventures in the underdeveloped world undoubtedly created great strains among China's rulers, forcing a critical review of the country's most basic foreign and domestic policies. Yet for reasons that are only now becoming apparent, these tensions went well beyond dispute over specific policy issues; they shattered what so many observers of the mainland scene had come to see as a particular capacity of the Long March generation of leaders to resolve disputes with considerable give and take.

The critical factor contributing to this breakdown of Party leadership seems to have been the issue of succession, of who in time would attain Mao's position as leader of the Party and nation. More exactly, it seems that Mao, in his uncompromising determination to see his own style of leadership and authority maintained despite the resistance of long-time colleagues, first reacted to criticism of his policies as attacks on his leading role; and then he himself raised the conflict to the level of status relations by attempting to designate a new "close comrade in arms" to implement his policies and then carry them on after his death.

---

[2] A detailed analysis of the evolution of policy disputes among Party leaders since the mid-1950's which eventually led to the Cultural Revolution conflict is contained in Part IV of the study by Richard H. Solomon, *Mao's Revolution and the Chinese Political Culture* (Berkeley and Los Angeles: University of California Press, 1971).

That the Cultural Revolution has grown from a breakdown in elite relations, and embodies at its core the succession issue, is suggested by one of those ambiguous "esoteric" or Aesopian phrases found in an important political document which is as tantalizing in its implication as it is vague in its full meaning. In one of the major articles of the 1964 polemical exchanges with the Soviet Union occurs a detailed analysis of the conditions which Mao, or those writing in support of the Maoist position, saw as basic to maintaining proper revolutionary leadership in China.[3] Among the conditions specified for those who would be "revolutionary successors" (*chieh-pan jen*) to Party leadership were the following two:

> They [revolutionary successors] must be proletarian statesmen capable of uniting and working with the overwhelming majority. Not only must they unite with those who agree with them, *they must also be good at uniting with those who disagree and even with those who formerly opposed them and have since been proved wrong.* But they must especially watch out for careerists and conspirators like Khrushchev and prevent such bad elements from usurping the leadership of the Party and the government *at any level.*
>
> They must be models in applying the Party's democratic centralism, must master the method of leadership based on the principle of "from the masses, to the masses," and must cultivate a democratic style and be good at listening to the masses. *They must not be despotic like Khrushchev and violate the Party's centralism, make surprise attacks on comrades or act arbitrarily and dictatorially.*[4]

With the added clarity of hindsight, and on the basis of information subsequently revealed in the mainland press and in Red Guard newspapers, it seems that a likely interpretation of this ambiguous passage would run something as follows: Increasingly during the first five years of the decade of the sixties Mao found himself unable to translate his own will into implemented policy decisions. As a result of his establishment of what Red Guard newspapers have termed "first and second lines" of leadership within the Politburo's Standing Committee after 1958, Mao found himself increasingly cut off from the operational machinery of the Party, and saw his general policy directives distorted in application.[5] This loss of influence over the policy implementation process must have en-

---

[3]These measures were seen as necessary for preventing a "revisionist" usurpation of Party leadership such as had occurred, they said, in the case of Khrushchev's leadership of the Communist Party in the Soviet Union.

[4]The Editorial Departments of the *People's Daily* and *Red Flag*, "On Khrushchev's Phony Communism and Its Historical Lessons," July 14, 1964, trans. in *Current Background*, No. 737 (July 17, 1964).

[5]See these complaints in a speech attributed to Mao translated in *Current Scene* (Hong Kong), V, No. 9 (May 31, 1967), 6.

I would assume that Red Guard assertions that Mao was removed from the office of state chairman in December, 1958, are not accurate, but represent subsequent efforts by his supporters to undermine the position of his opponents. See a report of these charges in the *New York Times*, January 6, 1967, p. 1.

raged Mao,[6] and presented him not only with a threat to the implementation of his personal will, but also with a situation in which he saw the Party apparatus as increasingly bureaucratized and self-serving, full of "careerists and conspirators like Khrushchev." In a sense he must have seen the Party and governmental system turning into just the type of state apparatus that he had spent a lifetime working to destroy in the struggle for power with the Nationalists.

What is more, Mao evidently saw the cooperative-collectivist style of leadership, with openness of communication not only "vertically" between the different levels of the political system but more significantly in relations among his closest associates in the Party's leading bodies,[7] giving way to self-serving "revisionism" — cliquishness and the desire to protect personal bases of power in various governmental organizations.[8] This seems to be part of the burden of his remarks that "revolutionary successors" must be capable of "uniting with those who disagree and even with those who formerly opposed them and have since been proved wrong," and his warning that "careerists and conspirators like Khrushchev" must be prevented from "usurping the leadership of the Party and government at any level."

A more specific but conjectural interpretation of these last two intriguing phrases may be advanced in the light of evidence made public as a result of the Cultural Revolution struggle. Open attacks on Liu Shao-ch'i in the spring of 1967 assert that in 1962 he defended P'eng Teh-huai for his criticisms of the Great Leap Forward delivered at the 1959 Lushan Central Committee Plenum. Liu is also said to have "openly tried to reverse the verdict on P'eng Teh-huai at the enlarged Work Conference of the Party's Central Committee held in January 1962," and to have encouraged P'eng to write a defense of his own position which was circu-

---

[6] A Red Guard publication reported that Mao complained at a Central Committee meeting of October, 1966, that Liu Shao-ch'i and Teng Hsiao-p'ing had treated him "as if I were their dead parent at a funeral."

[7] Mao's frustration at the distortion of "vertical" communication flows within the political system, first revealed in the *Kung-tso T'ung-hsün*, has been discussed in my article, "Communication Patterns and the Chinese Revolution," pp. 108–9; and in Neuhauser, "Chinese Communist Party in the 1960's," p. 22 and *passim*, both in *The China Quarterly*, No. 32 (October–December, 1967).

More recent attacks on P'eng Teh-huai have asserted that he "either refused to transmit the directives of the Party Central Committee and Chairman Mao or distorted and emasculated them or obeyed them publicly while disobeying them in secret." He is also said to have "maintained illicit connections" with Soviet leaders: "In 1955, 1957, and 1959, taking advantage of his many trips abroad, P'eng Teh-huai made secret deals with Khrushchev." ("Principal Crimes of P'eng Teh-huai, Big Ambitionist and Schemer," Canton *Ching-kang-shan* and *Kuang-tung Wen-i Chan-pao* [Chingkang Mountains, and Kwang-tung Literary and Art Combat Bulletin], September 5, 1967, trans. in *SCMP*, No. 4047 [October 25, 1967], pp. 5, 8.)

[8] See Neuhauser, "Chinese Communist Party in the 1960's," pp. 17–18 and *passim* for a discussion of Party cadre efforts to prevent "rectification" or supervision by mass organizations during the early 1960's.

lated just before the Tenth Plenum in the fall of that year.[9] If these charges contain an element of fact, they suggest that Liu may have challenged Mao's authority during 1962 — or at least that Mao construed Liu's actions as indicating a lack of support for him and his policies. And while the Tenth Plenum of September, 1962, reaffirmed the leading role of the "thought of Mao Tse-tung" and attacked "modern revisionism," it appears that behind such expressions of support for the Party Chairman's policies were highly strained relations between Mao and Liu.

It apparently was not until 1964, however, that Mao felt he had sufficient support from his backers in the People's Liberation Army to challenge Liu and other opponents in the Party apparatus. This he may have done indirectly or "esoterically" in the context of the movement for "cultivating revolutionary successors" launched in the summer of that year — with Liu, at that time still designated as *the* successor to Mao's leadership position, being attacked by implication.[10]

Inasmuch as during the Cultural Revolution Liu was referred to in the public mainland press as "China's Khrushchev," it seems not unlikely that it was he who Mao had in mind in 1964 when he asserted that revolutionary successors "must especially watch out for careerists and conspirators *like Khrushchev* and prevent such bad elements from usurping the leadership of the Party and government *at any level*" (that is, even in the top leadership).[11]

---

[9]See the *Red Flag* editorial, "From the Defeat of P'eng Teh-huai to the Bankruptcy of China's Khrushchev," trans. in *Peking Review*, No. 34 (August 18, 1967), pp. 18–20, 35.

[10]The Baum and Teiwes study, *Ssu-Ch'ing*, pp. 26–46, strongly suggests that by mid-1964 Mao's counterchallenge was being mounted on a broad front: policy for the "Socialist Education Campaign" was adjusted in a more radical direction; the army was put forward as the model political organization to be emulated in the "Learn from the PLA" campaign (thus indirectly slighting the Party); and extensive efforts were made to promote the study of "Chairman Mao's Thought."

[11]By early 1965 Mao apparently was even more explicit in identifying the focus of his displeasure when it was noted, in the "Twenty-three Articles" of the socialist education campaign, that "there are some people . . . even in the work of . . . Central Committee departments, who oppose socialism." See *ibid.*, p. 37.

Since this analysis was first written in the spring of 1967, additional material has been published on the mainland which seems to confirm the interpretation we have given to these documents of 1964 and 1965. A *Red Flag* editorial of August, 1967, notes:

"The document *Some Current Problems Raised in the Socialist Education Movement in the Rural Areas*, referred to as the 23-article document, worked out under the personal guidance of Chairman Mao in January 1965, put it clearly for the first time: 'The main target of the present movement is those persons within the Party who are in authority and are taking the capitalist road.' China's Khrushchev [that is, Liu Shao-ch'i] is the one in the highest position among the persons mentioned here." ("Completely Smash the Bourgeois Headquarters," trans. in *Peking Review*, No. 33 [August 11, 1967], p. 7.)

If these tentative interpretations are correct,[12] it seems likely that by signaling, in 1964, that he was dissatisfied with Liu's status as his successor, Mao may have stimulated a premature succession struggle in which various leaders began to vie among themselves for Mao's blessing as *the* revolutionary successor.[13] Whether Mao did this deliberately as a way of breaking down his opposition, or as a strategy for entrapping his rivals by making them expose their ambitiousness prematurely, is something about which we can only speculate.

In addition, we can only infer to what degree it was Mao's own obduracy in continuing to insist on policies which had proven unworkable in practice, or his overweening belief that only his "thought" could guide China into the modern world, which provoked the opposition of longtime comrades.[14]

While it may be some time before we know with greater certainty the reality which lies behind these documentary materials, they do make it clear that cooperative relations among China's leaders were seriously compromised by late 1964. The main purpose of this interpretive exercise has been to detail the extent to which the Maoist *image* of a new style of leadership — of unity, cooperation, and openness in communication both within the Party and between mass and elite, of critical checks on lower level cadres wielding Party authority, in short, the set of leadership concepts which we explored in Part II — gradually fell by the wayside during the 1960's. What is more, serious factionalism, seen earlier in the purgings of Kao Kang and P'eng Teh-huai, once again threatened Party unity, as is now revealed in the attacks on P'eng Chen for having created an "independent kingdom" in the Peking Party committee.

As well, Mao evidently felt that his "revolutionary" goals were being threatened by a Party and governmental system increasingly resorting to what he interpreted as "traditional" misuses of authority. This would seem to be the burden of continuing attacks on Liu Shao-ch'i for having propagated a doctrine of "slavish obedience" to Party authority, and for

---

[12]This interpretation, developed in the early stage of the Cultural Revolution, has been strengthened by "Red Guard" documents which subsequently became available in the West. These materials, and a detailed analysis of themes only partially developed here, are contained in the study by Solomon, *Mao's Revolution and the Chinese Political Culture, op. cit.*

[13]In several public statements during late 1964, Mao disclosed that death and succession were very much on his mind. See Edgar Snow's interview with Mao, *New Republic* (February 27, 1965), pp. 17–23.

[14]The role that the propagation of "the thought of Mao Tse-tung" has played as an issue in the conflict between Mao and Liu is analyzed in an interesting article by Cheng Chu-yuan, "The Root of China's Cultural Revolution: The Feud Between Mao Tse-tung and Liu Shao-ch'i," *Orbis*, XI, No. 4 (Winter, 1968), 1160–78.

seeking to train cadres to be "docile tools" of the Party.[15] Such phrases certainly echo Mao's aversion to the dependency orientation toward authority which we explored above; and they may be additional indication of Mao's rage at those who sought to put the Party above his own authority.

Liu is also accused of wanting to play down the promotion of "class struggle," the criticism and confrontation of the enemies of change within China.[16] Mao apparently feared that his efforts to make mediated conflict and criticism an integral part of China's new political order were threatened by those men in power who, in his opinion, were still burdened with the "four olds" of the traditional culture. He saw their influence leading in time to a "restoration of capitalism," that is, a return to government by a narrow and privileged elite such as had characterized China at an earlier stage of her social development.

In any event, Mao and certain close supporters responded to what they saw as a challenge to their influence and style of leadership by turning for mass support to the first generation fully educated under China's new socialist order.[17] Mao's massive mobilization of the youth of the country into the Red Guard organizations during the summer and fall of 1966 has some of the quality of a reaching out for supporters wherever he could find them, as well as an effort to deny his opponents a source of organizational manpower; but it also seems to be a form of political combat in continuity with what we have detailed earlier as Mao's style of political action: the belief that change is most effectively promoted through active participation and "struggle," and the tendency to check those with operational political power by subjecting them to criticism from below.[18] And, as appears with such clarity in 1967, Mao as early as the summer of 1964 publicized his intention to rebuild the revolutionary vitality of the Chinese Communist Party through renewed storms of mass struggle which would

---

[15]See, for example, "Growing Mass Movement to Criticize and Repudiate the Book on 'Self-Cultivation' of Communists," *Peking Review*, No. 17 (April 21, 1967), pp. 14–15.

[16]See "Betrayal of Proletarian Dictatorship Is Essential Element in the Book on 'Self-Cultivation,'" by the editorial departments of *Red Flag* and *People's Daily*, trans. in *Peking Review*, No. 20 (May 12, 1967), pp. 7–11.

[17]These young people were mobilized by Mao's supporters in the one organization he evidently felt reliable, the People's Liberation Army. It should be noted, however, that the precise relationship between Mao and the army leadership, and Lin Piao in particular, remains one of the most obscure aspects of the Cultural Revolution.

[18]The similarity between Mao's use of the Red Guards to criticize Party cadres "from below," and earlier Maoist forms of political control such as the "Congresses of Poor and Lower-middle Peasants" mentioned above has also been noted and discussed by Philip Bridgham in "Mao's 'Cultural Revolution': Origin and Development," *China Quarterly*, No. 29 (January–March, 1967), pp. 10–11.

mobilize a new generation of "activist" cadres: "Successors to [lead the] revolutionary cause of the proletariat come forward in mass struggles and are tempered in the great storms of revolution. It is essential to test and know cadres and choose and train successors in the long course of mass struggle."[19]

From a psychological perspective the Cultural Revolution has the eerie quality of a psychological recapitulation of Mao's entire political career, for in mobilizing China's youth to attack the Party structure itself, and in telling them that the essence of Marxism is the notion that "to rebel is justified," Mao seems to be reliving vicariously, in the struggles of the younger generation, his own youthful rebellion against authority. What satisfaction (or sadness?) comes in seeing them attack the political structure of his own creation, an organization which apparently had come to represent for him all of the outrageous misuses of authority and power which he had spent a lifetime opposing in struggle?

There is, as well, a broader sense in which the Cultural Revolution recapitulates Mao's career: by re-exposing the fundamental political problems which have marked his rise to power. This is most obviously indicated by the republication of a whole series of his early articles dealing with the organizational and ideological "deviations" which had hampered the growth of the Communist Party.[20]

From the point of view of our focus on the problem of political integration, the Cultural Revolution has clearly revealed the shallowness of change, relative to Mao's revolutionary objectives, that in fact has occurred in China since 1949. Two problems stand out in particular: the inability of the younger generation to keep political conflict within the "principled" bounds of national policy objectives — to prevent the Cultural Revolution from degenerating into *luan*; and their continuing inability to prevent lateral social fragmentation by maintaining cooperative relationships among their peers.

One of the fundamental questions concerning interpretations of the Cultural Revolution is the degree to which it is a personalized struggle for power, or a conflict over policy and principle. While a mixture of both factors probably underlies the turmoil, it is evident from the docu-

---

[19]"On Khrushchev's Phony Communism . . ." in *Current Background*, No. 737 (July 17, 1964).

[20]Mao's 1929 article, "On Correcting Mistaken Ideas in the Party," was republished in February, 1967; his "Talks at the Yenan Forum on Literature and the Arts" (1942), was republished in May; a series of four other articles from the past three decades dealing with policy toward the arts was republished in late May; and the notable 1957 speech, "On the Correct Handling of Contradictions among the People," was republished in June, 1967. The "*san-lao*," "Serve the People" (1944), "In Memory of Norman Bethune" (1939), and "The Foolish Old Man Who Removed the Mountains" (1945) have been given particularly wide recirculation.

mentary material available that Mao has sought to define limits to the conflict within the context of an attempt to "prevent a restoration of capitalism," that is, to forestall the implementation of certain policies or the re-emergence of a style of political leadership which would lead to the re-establishment of a more "traditional" political order. The struggle of the Red Guards, in conception at least, is an ideological confrontation, or as the oft-repeated slogan goes, *"yao yung wen-tou, pu-yung wu-tou"* (we must use verbal struggle, not armed struggle).

The mass media have consistently revealed, however, that efforts to carry out the conflict within the bounds of political principle have from the start foundered on two rocks: the tendency of the Revolutionary Rebels to be indiscriminate (*luan*) in their attacks on authority;[21] and the (successful) efforts of Mao's opponents to defend themselves by forcing the conflict out of the realm of "principle" and into the arena of violence. Newspaper articles complain that those "taking the capitalist road" incite the masses to struggle among themselves, or provoke them into "directing the spearpoint of the struggle" against the PLA.

The Cultural Revolution has re-exposed the tendency of the society to fragment into self-serving cliques focused around individual authorities, and even the more anarchic tendency to reject the discipline of any authority whatsoever.[22] The response to this political fragmentation — to "bourgeois" manifestations of "individualism," "sectarianism," "particularism," "small group mentality," "departmentalism," "ultra-democracy," "liberalism," "reputationism" (*feng-t'ou-chu-yi*), "mountain strongholdism" (*shan-t'ou-chu-yi*) — has been an all too familiar cry: "Down with 'selfishness,' establish the collective (*p'o-szu, li-kung*), and establish a

---

[21]A *People's Daily* of early February, 1967, states with concern: "It is completely wrong to regard all persons in authority as untrustworthy and overthrow all of them indiscriminately. This idea of opposing, excluding and overthrowing all in discriminately and its implementation run completely counter to Marxism-Leninism, Mao Tse-tung's Thought." *People's Daily* editorial, "A Good Example in Struggle by Proletarian Revolutionaries to Seize Power," February 10, 1967, trans. in *Peking Review*, No. 8 (February 17, 1967), p. 19.
And Chiang Ch'ing appealed in April of 1967:
There is no contradiction in the struggle, criticism, and repudiation [carried out by the newly formed Peking City revolutionary committee], or in its work of criticizing the biggest authority in the Party taking the capitalist road [Liu Shao-ch'i]; this can be done with unity . . . But in doing this you must use your brains, think things through well. You must study well the works of Chairman Mao, and thoroughly carry out the work of investigation and research. You must keep cool (*yao yung leng-ching*), and be able to sit down and consult about things, and not continually be squabbling, or even worse get up and start fighting among yourselves. (*People's Daily*, April 21, 1967, p. 2).
[22]See, for example, the *People's Daily* editorial, "Down with Anarchism," April 26, 1967.

great proletarian unity through unending criticism — self-criticism."[23]
The plea is for a resolution of disputes among the fragmented "revolutionaries" through Mao's formula of "unity-criticism-unity"; otherwise
the future of the Cultural Revolution could only be the fighting of "civil
war" (*ta nei-chan*) and "armed struggle" (*wu-tou*).[24]

The outcome of the present political disintegration and conflict on the
mainland is obviously not something in the realm of predictable human
events; but in terms of our analytical focus on the problem of the reinte-
gration of the Chinese polity it seems clear that we are now witnessing a
return to more traditional forms of political control: the repersonalization
of a guiding authority ("defend Chairman Mao"); the increased use of
organizational measures to control individual behavior ("support the
army"); and the active promotion of "educational" procedures so as to
re-establish political discipline ("study the thought of Chairman Mao").
The alternatives to the use of such measures seem limited, for the "four
olds" of China's traditional customs and habits, culture and social
thought continue to exercise their influence. Indeed, Defense Minister Lin
Piao could even spell out one fearful prospect in symbols that must evoke
the image of the political fragmentation which characterized the warlordism of the 1920's:

> Our country is a great land of 700 million people; and the entire country
> must have unified thinking. If we unite on the basis of the thought of
> Mao Tse-tung, then we can have united action. But if a nation of 700
> million people does not have unified thinking then it will be just like a
> sheet of scattered sand.[25]

Only time will tell if the PLA, or some coalition of political forces,
has both the sense of internal unity and the capacity to coerce into being
and construct a new national political order. At various times during
the evolution of the Cultural Revolution, the Maoists sought to reassert
their authority through new structures of political control, most notably
the Paris Commune form of mass based government which was attempted in Shanghai in early 1967, and the subsequent "triple alliance"
*(san chieh-ho)* of loyal military and cadre leaders in combination with

---

[23]See, for example, the article by the Third Headquarters of the Capital Red
Guards, "Down with 'Selfishness,' Promote a Great Alliance of the Revolutionary
Rebel Groups," *People's Daily*, January 31, 1967, p. 3.

[24]See the *People's Daily* editorial, "Immediately Restrain Armed Struggle," May
22, 1967.

[25]*Red Flag* editorial, "Victoriously Advance on the Road of Mao Tse-tung's
Thought," No. 11 (1966), p. 21.

"revolutionary" mass organizations. Subsequently the "revolutionary committee" was put forward as the appropriate combination of military, "liberated" cadre, and mass power which would give life to Mao's dream of a truly participant and well-integrated polity.[26] And it was only in April of 1969, at the Chinese Communist Party's Ninth National Congress, that Mao indicated his intention of reviving the Party as an instrument of national political control.

The Ninth Party Congress affirmed Defense Minister Lin Piao as Mao's successor to Party leadership, and called for the gradual "liberation" of old Party cadres through a process of political revival termed "struggle-criticism-transformation." The slowness with which the Party organization is being rebuilt, however, suggests that it is no easy task to create institutions which will embody the "thought of Mao Tse-tung." Bureaucratic organizations inherently contain tendencies toward the "revisionism" which Mao sought to destroy with the Cultural Revolution; and one senses that the Chairman may seek to limit the growth of a new political bureaucracy through greater administrative decentralization. Should Mao die before the present period of institutional restructuring is completed, there seems to remain considerable likelihood of another disruptive succession struggle, if not repudiation of Mao's policies and his chosen successor.

Such imponderable dimensions of China's immediate political future only stress the uncertainties which continue to surround the evolution of the country's domestic governmental institutions, and the questionable degree of permanence of Mao Tse-tung's impact on China's continuing social revolution.

---

[26]See the *People's Daily*, *Red Flag*, and *Liberation Army Daily* editorial, "Revolutionary Committees are Fine," March 30, 1968, trans. in *Peking Review*, No. 14 (April 5, 1968), p. 6.

## 21. The Minority Groups and the Problems of Political Integration

*George Moseley*

### I

There have been enthusiastic reports in the Chinese Press about the collectivisation movement in agriculture and animal husbandry among the forty million people of the national minorities in China. But it now appears that the socialist revolution has not developed successfully in the non-Han frontier regions of the country. Premier Chou En-lai said, in his report to the National People's Congress in December 1964:

> to gain complete liberation, the people of all the minority nationalities in our country must rise in revolution under the leadership of the Communist Party. They must conduct and accomplish not only the democratic revolution, but also the socialist revolution, and carry them through to the end.[1]

This exhortation followed the Premier's revelation that the Panchen Lama, who had only recently been named to take over the functions of

---

[1]Chou En-lai, "Report on the Work of the Government to the 1st Session of the 3rd National People's Congress" (Summary), *New China News Agency* (NCNA), December 30, 1964.

Reprinted from George Moseley, "China's Fresh Approach to the National Minority Question," *The China Quarterly* 24 (October–December 1965): 15–27, by permission of the author and journal. The trend of developments since this article was completed in the middle of 1965 indicates an intensification of "struggle" in the national minority regions, and especially in Sinkiang and Tibet. It appears that the Party leadership has become more apprehensive about the security of its frontiers because of the increasingly serious international situation with which it is faced. The "socialist education" drive which has been carried forward throughout the country is another factor contributing to a harder approach to the national minorities.

309

the Dalai Lama as the head of the Preparatory Committee for the Tibet Autonomous Region, had had to be sacked because of his intrigues with "the reactionary clique of serf-owners."[2] Chou quoted Chairman Mao Tse-tung to the effect that the national minority problem was really a class problem; henceforth, he asserted, class struggle would be the main theme of the CCP's (Chinese Communist Party's) national minority policy.[3]

Premier Chou's statement helps to clarify a number of developments in the CCP's theoretical position on the national minority question during the past several years. With the progress of China's "socialist construction," the gap between the Han Chinese and the national minorities had, apparently, tended to widen rather than, as had been expected, to become narrower. Finally, a basic readjustment of the CCP's national minority policy had been required, for it had become obvious that the image of China's "great family of nationalities" advancing together on the socialist road was no longer tenable. But the implications of this policy readjustment went far beyond the immediate need to account for the lag in the development of the national minorities. The magnitude of the CCP's shift in policy is revealed in the changed notions of what constitutes a "contradiction" in nationality relations. As late as the end of 1961 a vice-chairman of the Nationality Affairs Commission could say that national differences constitute contradictions, whereas by 1963 it was being asserted that there are no contradictions between nationalities but only between classes.[4]

The CCP's new position on the national minority question may provide the basis for a stable relationship between the Han Chinese and China's non-Han peoples. It may also permit this vital area of domestic policy to develop in harmony with China's foreign policy, with the national minority regions assuming their traditional role as an intermediate zone between China proper (the China of the Han Chinese) and the states of Asia contiguous to China. In short, this new theoretical approach may well represent the key to a normalisation of China's position in Asia and the world. While there has been no formal announcement of a new policy, it seems clear that it entered a new phase in 1962 and that

---

[2]*Ibid.* Unlike the Dalai Lama, the Panchen Lama had been educated in China.

[3]The CCP credits Mao with having developed this thesis in 1963, at a reception for a group of African visitors. See *Jen-min Jih-pao* (*People's Daily*), August 9, 1963. But Mao had already raised the issue in September 1962 at the 10th Plenum of the Central Committee.

[4]Wang Feng, "To Better Understand the Party's Nationalities Policy," *Min-tsu T'uan-chieh* (*National Unity*), 1961, No. 10–11, p. 3. Mao initiated the new line in August 1963; it was fully developed by another Vice-Chairman of the Nationality Affairs Commission, Liu Ch'un, in an article in *Hung Ch'i* (*Red Flag*), 1964, No. 12, "Class Struggle and the National Question in Our Country at the Present Time," especially p. 25.

the magnitude of this shift was comparable to the great policy reappraisal of 1956-58. In 1956 the national minorities fell from the high estate which they had enjoyed since the "Liberation," and during the ensuing years of collectivisation and Great Leap Forward (1956-1960) they were treated very much like second-class citizens. In the perspective of the policy now in vogue, the 1949-1956 period was a "right" deviation (all unity and no struggle) and the 1956-1961 period a "left" deviation (all struggle and no unity).

In contrast to the Russian revolution, in which peoples other than the Great Russians played a significant role, the revolution in China was a purely Han Chinese affair. To employ a crude but useful distinction, it took place in "inner" China, for "outer" China (Mongolia, Sinkiang and Tibet) had already drifted beyond the reach of the Chinese government by the time the CCP came into being. The fringe areas of "inner" China, too, had become oriented outward, with, for instance, the T'ai regions of Yunnan and Kwangsi tending to fall under the influence of British Burma and French Indochina. Prior to the Long March, the CCP leadership had had no direct contact with the frontier regions where the non-Han people live, which occupy over half the total area of the country; during this period it was content to echo pronouncements on the national question by Stalin (the Georgian whom Lenin had picked to be Chairman of the People's Commissariat for Nationalities of the USSR) and to imitate, in its own programme for China, the federal structure of the Soviet Union. Nor was the CCP's 1936 appeal to the national minorities to unite with the Han Chinese in resisting Japan much more than a slogan, although a number of revolutionary workers from among the national minorities were trained at Yenan. And when the CCP came to power in 1949 it did so in China proper (including Manchuria), with the outlying national minority regions still to be occupied by the PLA (People's Liberation Army). That Inner Mongolia had fallen under the domination of the PLA early in the civil war was due less to the endeavors of the handful of Sinified Mongols who worked with the CCP than to the fact that Inner Mongolia was required as a military corridor between the northwest and Manchuria.

The national minority policy developed by the CCP during the formative years of the new régime was again an approximation of Soviet orthodoxy.[5] The Party's primary concern until 1956 was the reimposition of unchallengeable Han Chinese mastery of the frontier regions. The policy

---

[5]See G. F. Hudson, "The Nationalities of China," *St. Antony's Papers*, VII (London, 1960), pp. 51–61; and Roderick MacFarquhar, "The Minorities," in "Communist China's First Decade," *The New Leader*, Vol. 42, No. 23 (1959), pp. 17–21. For a superb discussion of the background of the problem, see John DeFrancis, "National and Minority Policies" in "Report on China," *Annals of the American Academy of Political and Social Science*, Vol. 277 (1951), pp. 146–155.

devised was essentially negative, seeking to undercut any resistance on the part of the minorities to the domination of their homelands by the PLA and the Central People's Government. Regional autonomy for the non-Han peoples was instituted precisely in order to permit the CCP to pursue a differentiated policy in the frontier regions as compared with China proper; it was not the objective of regional autonomy indefinitely to guarantee to the minorities a special status within the CPR (Chinese People's Republic). The establishment of autonomous areas was an essential device in the hands of the United Front Work Department of the CCP in its task of fostering a sense of identification with the new régime in Peking on the part of the national minorities, and especially their traditional leaders.

This policy of studied magnanimity was reversed in 1957, when the anti-rightist campaign launched in China proper took the form of an anti-local-nationalist campaign in the frontier regions.[6] With the frontier regions firmly under control, the government then attempted rapidly to carry out among the national minorities the socialist reforms that had been deferred since "liberation." Objections based on national distinctiveness were brushed aside. Han cadres took the place of nationality cadres who were purged in large numbers and a large-scale influx of Han settlers into the frontier regions commenced. Local nationalism, rather than Han chauvinism, was now held to be the principal obstacle to the success of the CCP's national minority policy. Indeed, the policy pursued during these years was really the negation of the national minority policy which had earlier been defined. This trend of Han assertiveness became even more acute with the "great leap forward" and the people's commune movements of 1958-1960. The Tibetan revolt was but the most spectacular expression of the disaffection which ensued. There was an exodus of T'ai peoples across the southern frontier in the course of the commune movement in Yunnan. The massive flight of Kazakhs to the Soviet Union in 1962 also had its roots in the CCP's repression of "local nationalism." Less overt manifestations of resistance to the hard line were evident throughout China's frontier regions.

But the campaign against local nationalism was not merely the negation of the earlier policy, for it did demonstrate the Party's determination that socialist reform would eventually be carried out in the national minority areas, just as, in the earlier period, it had been demonstrated that the frontier regions were irreversibly Chinese. On the other hand,

---

[6]In an unpublished master's dissertation (Georgetown University, Washington, D.C., 1959) entitled "Communist Policy in Inner Mongolia, 1947–1957" (p. 153), Thomas A. Metzger has traced the beginnings of this new policy to a nationalities work conference held in Tsingtao during July and August 1957.

the CCP's tacit admission, which followed upon the waning of the great leap forward, that reforms among the national minorities would be a long-term process, represented a victory for the national minorities. By 1961 a general relaxation in the CCP's approach to the national minority problem could be discerned, and in the following year a fresh policy was formulated.[7]

## II

This new policy rests on several concepts which reflect the experience of more than a decade in dealing with China's national minorities and which indicate that the CCP has arrived at a mature position with respect to the applicability of Soviet theory in this particular field of policy formulation. First in importance among these concepts is the idea that each of China's national minority peoples must develop into a "modern nationality" on its road to Socialism, Communism, and its ultimate disappearance as a distinct national group. Although this idea had been suggested by Liu Shao-ch'i in his report to the Eighth National Congress of the Party in 1956, it was only with the Tenth Plenum of the Eighth Central Committee, which met in Peking in September 1962, that it became prominent in policy discussions.[8] It is to be compared, on the one hand, with the view consistently advanced by the CCP during the decade 1950-1960: the national minorities must strive to "catch up with" the Han people, thereby wiping out the inequalities among China's nationalities inherited from history and making it possible for all of China's peoples, Han and non-Han, to advance together to socialist society. On the other hand, it is to be set against Stalin's familiar dictum of "national in form, socialist in content" which was intended to indicate the correct way of doing away with a nationality's identity while making it appear that this national identity was actually flourishing.

The difference between the older line of the CCP and the view expressed by Liu is that the latter recognises the fact that the "transforma-

---

[7]The shift in nationalities policy was part of a general policy review undertaken at the time, especially in the economic field. For a perceptive discussion of the period, see A. M. Halpern, "Between Plenums: A Second Look at the 1962 National People's Congress in China," *Asian Survey*, Vol. II, No. 9 (November 1962), pp. 1–10.

[8]Liu Shao-ch'i, "Political Report of the Central Committee to the Eighth National Congress of the CCP," *Eighth National Congress of the CCP* (Peking, 1956), p. 79. There is nothing of consequence in the Communiqué of the 10th Plenum (NCNA, September 28, 1962); the substance of the CCP's deliberations on nationalities policy at the meeting may be gleaned from an editorial in *Min-tsu T'uan-chieh*, No. 11, 1962: "In National Minority Areas Positively Implement the Spirit of the Party's 10th Plenum. . . ."

tion" of China's national minorities will be a long-term process and suggests, indeed, that they may never "catch up with" the Han people or only in the remote future. In other words, the "special characteristics" of the national minorities are organic to them; they are not residual or affective qualities which can be readily cast off. Quite aside from the question of their willingness to do so, they cannot become good Han-Chinese, not even good Han Chinese Communists. Therefore, attempts at Sinification will not hasten their journey along the road towards Socialism but will, on the contrary, retard it. They must be allowed, even encouraged, to take their own road to Socialism, for so deep is their psychological commitment to their specific customs and manners that they cannot function in a positive way if their social environment is hastily or forcibly altered. In essence, then, the CCP has admitted the existence of a contradiction between communisation and Sinification— which is precisely what the "local nationalists" had been urging several years previously.

The largest of China's national minorities, the Chuang, numbers 7.7 million, or only slightly over 1 per cent of the Han Chinese population, and there are only a few others, such as the Uighurs, Tibetans, Mongols, Hui and Koreans, which number more than one million. Taken together, China's national minorities comprise only about 6 per cent of the total population of the country. This situation is in marked contrast to that of Russia in 1917, where the Great Russians comprised less than half the population of the whole country. Furthermore, China's non-Han peoples are, by and large, extremely retarded as compared with Russia's nationalities. Then, too, the minorities in China are backward (in terms of Marxism-Leninism's own categories) as compared with the Han, for they are largely pastoralists. Only the Uighurs, with their oasis civilisation, the T'ai, with their Hinayana Buddhism, the Koreans of Manchuria, and a few heavily Sinified groups, such as the Min-chia of Yunnan, even approximate the cultural level of the Han people. It is clear, therefore, that the slogan "national in form, socialist in content" advanced by Stalin was designed for conditions altogether different from those in China. He could envisage the federated peoples of the Soviet Union advancing together towards Socialism, but such a thesis, as the CCP now recognises, is altogether inapplicable to China, where the development of the Han Chinese could not but be something qualitatively different from that of the national minorities.

Lenin, however, made one distinction between the Great Russians and the other peoples of the Soviet Union which the CCP has now seized upon: he referred to the first as a "nation" (*natsiya*) and to the others as "nationalities" (*narodnost*). Early in 1962 a controversy arose among

Party cadres engaged in nationalities work over the ambiguous use of the Chinese term "*min-tsu*" (nation, nationality, people) for rendering a variety of Russian and German terms:[9]

|              | Russian    | German       | Chinese   |
|--------------|------------|--------------|-----------|
| People       | *Narod*    | *Volk*       |           |
| Nation       | *Natsiya*  | *Nation*     | *Min-tsu* |
| Nationality  | *Narodnost* | *Nationalität* |         |

The conference at which this problem was discussed concluded that it was entirely proper to employ "*min-tsu*" for all of these terms. But in taking this position the Party's theoreticians looked for support to the German texts of Marx and Engels, where they found evidence for the view that the identification of a community as a nation does not depend first of all upon its stage of development but rather upon its inherent cohesion. Regardless of how retarded the development of a community might be, it was correct to refer to it as a nation so long as it was logical to suppose that it was destined to develop as a nation. Specifically, a community could constitute a nation while still being in a pre-capitalist stage of development.[10]

The controversy had arisen over the particular question (presumably advanced by national minority cadres) of whether or not it was correct to refer to the Han people as a nation (*min-tsu*), rather than as a nationality (*pu-tsu*, literally "tribe"), prior to its arrival at a capitalist level of development. Responding to this question in the affirmative, the conference went on to ascribe nation-status to all of China's "national" minorities. It was not denied, however, that the Han people conformed more completely to the idea of a nation than did the national minorities; it was simply more convenient, on the whole, consistently to use the term "*min-tsu*." A parallel was implicitly drawn between the national minorities in China and in Russia when it was noted by the conference that it had not been entirely wrong to translate as "*pu-tsu*" the term "*narodnost*" (nationality) which Stalin and Lenin had applied to peoples other than the

---

[9]Chang Lu, "The Situation with Regard to the Use and Translation of the Term '*Min-tsu*'," *Min-tsu T'uan-chieh*, No. 7, 1962, pp. 34–39.

[10]Some of the Soviet Union's "national minorities," notably in Siberia and Central Asia, were in a pre-capitalist stage of development at the time of the Revolution. As a result, Lenin had been obliged to distinguish between "nations" and "nationalities," as observed earlier. Apparently, however, the CCP was not satisfied with Lenin's theoretical formulation of the problem. On Stalin's muddled attempt to deal with this very murky problem, see Samad Shaheen, *The Communist (Bolshevik) Theory of National Self-Determination* (Bandung: Utrecht University Thesis, 1956) p. 51.

Great Russians. The conclusion apparently reached by the conferees, then, was that the "national minorities" are really nationalities, but that they should be called nations nevertheless.[11]

This position is, of course, heretical, for, in more traditional Marxist-Leninist theory, nationality is supposed to be a distinct attribute of the capitalist stage of development of a given people. But like the many other heresies committed by the CCP in applying Marxism-Leninism to China, it is vital. From this position, the CCP was able to advance to a comprehensive prognosis concerning the future evolution of China's multi-national state within the context of a general international movement towards Communism. Ultimately, all nations are destined to disappear, for national identity will be completely superseded when Communism has become world-wide. But some peoples, clearly, will attain Communism before others. As for China, the non-Han peoples will gradually merge with the Han people. At a still later stage, the people of China will lose their identity by entering the great sea of the world proletariat. Thus, the fusion of China's nationalities is a phenomenon to be consummated prior to the disappearance of all nationalities.[12]

The long-term nature of the effort to bring about the fusion of China's various peoples is a theme which recurs again and again in the policy discussions of 1962. Thus, we are told that so long as the national minorities retain distinctive languages and cultures, as they inevitably will for a long time to come, China's national question cannot be considered to have been completely resolved. Indeed, the stage of socialist transformation in the evolution of the national minorities defines the period during which their cultures are supposed to flourish, and this stage has only just arrived, signalled by the completion of democratic reform in Tibet, the most retarded area of China. It will not be consummated until the national minorities have been cleansed of the last vestiges of "capitalism." How long will this take? Individuals with an orientation towards capitalism can be expected to exist among the people of the national minorities as long as capitalism remains in the world, which may be "several decades or even longer."[13]

---

[11]In terms of Communist revolutionary practice, nations may form Communist Parties, but nationalities do not. Thus, the somewhat esoteric distinction here between nation and nationality is of considerable moment. The Russian and Chinese Communists shared the problem of how to preserve a multi-national state under the leadership of a single Communist Party; both denied the national minorities the right to form their own parties.

[12]This point is brought out in an article by Ku Feng in *Min-tsu T'uan-chieh*, No. 10, 1962, pp. 7–11, entitled "The Thorough Resolution of the National Question Is a Long Historical Process."

[13]*Ibid.* Ulanfu, the leading non-Han personality in the CCP, was perhaps more to the point when he observed in the October 1, 1959, issue of *Red Flag* that the influence of bourgeois ideology "will be stronger in its expression in the nationalities question than anywhere else, because the nationalities question provides it with a very good disguise."

Conforming to this theme, a nationalities work conference held in the spring of 1962 exhorted Party cadres to be patient and understanding in their nationalities work. The principal slogans of the conference were "ceaselessly strengthen nationalities' unity" and "develop the economies of the national minority areas." According to a dispatch in the *People's Daily*,

> The conference considered: that for the people of each nationality in our country to proceed in the direction of Socialism is unalterable. But nationalities work must genuinely be done well, adhering to the thought of Mao Tse-tung and truly taking cognisance of and correctly managing the national question in the stage of socialist revolution and the building of Socialism. In this stage, each nationality still has all its national characteristics: it is necessary, therefore, to pay attention to these characteristics, recognising the distinctiveness of nationalities and the long-term nature of these differences; to study and analyse correctly the peculiarities of the area and the economy of each national minority; clearly to recognise, with respect to the national minorities, the relationship between the religious question and the national question; and genuinely to respect the rights of equality and autonomy of the national minorities.[14]

In other words, the focus of change would henceforth have to be on the national minorities themselves, and development in their areas keyed more directly to their own interests and desires. This development would have a markedly national flavour, with the minorities, as they matured (in the socialist stage), possibly becoming even more differentiated from the Han. Only in the far-distant future, therefore, could it be anticipated that China's national minorities, having become "modern nationalities" (equivalent to "socialist" nationalities), would have prepared themselves for a loss of identity in the larger entity of the Chinese people. It is not surprising, then, that new prominence has been given to the role of the United Front Work Department in the gradual resolution of the national question in China. Representatives of this department from each province and autonomous region participated in the conference, and one of its principal speakers was the department's head, Li Wei-han.

The Party now looks to economic development in the national minority areas as the prime agent for bringing about the desired evolution in the relationship between the Han and non-Han peoples of China. This principle, too, was stated by Liu Shao-ch'i in his report to the Eighth National Congress of the Party and taken up by the Tenth Plenum:

> In order that the national minorities may grow into modern nationalities, the most fundamental thing, the key, besides carrying out social reforms, is to develop modern industries in the areas they inhabit.[15]

---

[14]*People's Daily*, June 3, 1962.
[15]Liu, *op. cit.*

That the establishment of modern industry in the comparatively backward national minority areas will in itself be a long-range task is acknowledged, for it must be built on the foundation of more efficient
agricultural, animal husbandry, forestry, and raw material production.
The national minorities must shoulder this task themselves, developing
their own resources with their own labour. Clearly, the Party has been
disabused of the notion that improvements in education and health will
lead magically to industrialisation.[16]

From these several concepts, (1) the development of each of China's
national minorities into a "modern nationality," (2) the identification of
China's non-Han peoples as nationalities rather than nations, and (3) the
long-range nature of the fusing together of all the national groups in
China, the theoretical framework for the new position on the national
minority problem can be discerned. Briefly stated, it envisages for each
of China's national minorities a unique and gradual process of moderni-
sation which will lead ultimately to its fusion with the Han people. There
is nothing in this general theory which contradicts the Party's basic thesis
on the national minority problem as developed in the early years of the
régime, but the emphasis of the new policy is radically different from that
of the old.

In recognising the fact that the development of the national minorities,
if they are to develop at all, will have to be related to the interests of the
people themselves as distinct national groups, the Party has admitted the
failure of its attempt to denationalise the national minorities by absorb-
ing their leaders in the United Front. The task of the United Front Work
Department with respect to the national minority problem had always
been viewed in terms of establishing an alliance with the upper strata of
the non-Han peoples, and it rested on the presumption of a natural
community of interest between the "labouring masses" of the national
minorities, on the one hand, and the alliance of Han Chinese workers
and peasants, on the other.[17] Implicit in the new position, on the contrary, is an acceptance of the fact that there is a natural community of
interest among the members of a given national minority without reference to class. Of course, the Party is determined that the socialist revolution, meaning class struggle, should be carried forward among the
national minorities, but this will now have the character of a true national
revolution, something distinct from the Han Chinese revolution. In the

---

[16]*Min-tsu T'uan-chieh* editorial, No. 11, 1962, *op. cit.*

[17]See, for instance, Chang Chih-i (Vice-Chairman of the United Front Work
Department), "Several Questions Concerning the People's Democratic United
Front," *Hsin Hua Pan-yueh K'an (New China Semi-monthly)* No. 11, 1957, pp.
67–71. As in all discussions of the problem, Chang speaks only of the upper strata
of the national minorities as an object of "unity-struggle-unity."

CCP's own terms, the changed character of the nationalities' united front
derives from the hypothesis that the revolutions of the nationalities have
developed from the "democratic" to the "socialist" stage: in the first the
united front is based on armed struggle (against imperialism and its
lackeys), while in the second it is based on Socialism, *i.e.*, on proletarian
unity. In these terms, then, the current problem in nationalities work is
that a working class outlook has been insufficiently developed among the
masses of the national minorities.

The distinctiveness now attributed to the socialist revolutions among
the national minorities is further emphasized by the Party's acknowledgment that it will require many years for them to reach the stage of
modern, socialist nationalities, at which point their fusion with the Han
Chinese will be practicable. Apparently the national minorities have not,
to the extent anticipated, benefited from or participated in the ecomonic
development of the country by the Han Chinese, including development
of the border regions inhabited by the national minorities. Although this
would be difficult if not impossible to verify, one suspects that the development of the border regions by the Chinese Communists has followed,
essentially, a colonial pattern, with the national minorities tending to
form relatively stagnant pockets, and that it is to remedy such a situation
that the Party is now urging the national minorities to push themselves
forward economically.

Finally, the identification of the national minorities as "nationalities"
rather than "nations" serves to place their revolutions in an intermediate
position between the Han Chinese and the independent states of Asia. It
must be a matter of deep satisfaction to the Chinese that their relationships with other peoples are once more, after a hundred years of confusion, falling into an ordered pattern. In fact, China's drive to restore
and reorder her position in Asia and the world must have been a major
motivating force in the CCP's shift in national minority policy. The new
policy fits logically into the general pattern of China's policy initiatives
during the several years since the rupture in the Sino-Soviet alliance, an
event which, for all the inconvenience it caused the CPR, for the first
time gave Peking a free hand in the international arena.

## III

In the course of his interview with Edgar Snow in January 1965 Chairman Mao Tse-tung referred to China's national minorities in comment-
ing upon Indonesia's withdrawal from the United Nations. Indonesia, he
said, felt that there was not much advantage in remaining in the UN.

As for China, was it not in itself a United Nations? Any one of several
of China's minority nationalities was larger in population and territory

than some states in the UN whose votes had helped deprive China of her seat there.[18]

The full significance of Mao's statement is only apparent when it is considered in relation to China's recent campaign for the establishment of a "revolutionary" united nations to serve the needs of the underdeveloped countries. A united front of peace-loving peoples comprising a united nations of Afro-Asian-Latin American states supported by China's own united nations (as its "base") is a kind of theoretical construction which has appealed to the Chinese Communist leadership in the past.[19]

Whatever the prospects for its eventual establishment, the projection of a "revolutionary" united nations under the tutelage of the CPR at once reflects a coherent theoretical assessment of the potential applicability of nationalities policy to foreign policy and suggests the influence which China's aims in the international field must have had on the CCP in arriving at its current position on the national minority question. Whereas China's national revolution had long been held up as an example to other peoples engaged in "wars of national liberation," the revolutionary united front of China's nationalities is now held to be a model for the collective struggle of the peoples of Asia, Africa and Latin America against the forces of world imperialism led by the United States and the forces of modern revisionism led by the Soviet Union.[20] As projected by the CCP, the two are structurally the same, with the ties between the underdeveloped country's feudal élite and the American imperialists corresponding to the ties between the national minority's feudal élite and the (pre-"liberation") reactionary ruling clique of the Han Chinese; just as the latter called forth a united front between the Han Chinese workers and peasants and the labouring masses of the national minorities, so the former demands a united front between the Afro-Asian-Latin American labouring masses and the Chinese People's Republic (the personification of 700 million proletarian friends).

In applying this model beyond China's frontiers, priority is given to Asia, where it has maximum relevance. A noteworthy feature of the

---

[18]Edgar Snow, "Interview with Mao," *The New Republic,* February 27, 1965. As Mr. Snow explains, Chairman Mao's answers as published are not direct quotations.

[19]The idea of a revolutionary united nations was advanced by Premier Chou En-lai in a statement made January 25 on the occasion of a visit to Peking of Dr. Subandrio, Foreign Minister of Indonesia. See *Le Monde,* January 26, 1965.

[20]This is the clear implication of Liu Ch'un's *Red Flag* article (see note 4, above) in which a summary of the requirements for an international united front introduces a detailed discussion of the success of China's united front of nationalities in overcoming feudalism, etc. For a thorough discussion of the Chinese revolution as a model for the "third world," see Philippe Richer, "Doctrine chinoise pour le Tiers Monde," *Politique étrangère,* 1965, No. 1, pp. 75–97.

CCP's approach to the national minority question, which may be traced back at least as far as the Yenan and Kiangsi periods, is the absence of a precise distinction between non-Han peoples of China and non-Han peoples of Asia. China is in the process of finding a new equilibrium between herself and her neighbours following the breakdown of the old order in Asia caused by the interregnum of European imperialism, during which the boundaries inherited by the CPR were imposed on a weak China. It is no accident that agreements on boundary questions between China and her neighbours—Burma, Nepal and Pakistan—have been accompanied by a new *modus vivendi* between the contracting parties marked by generally warmer relations and, particularly, by steps to establish overland trade.

Except in the north, China is "looking outward" once more, and her frontiers are again assuming a positive role, that of giving access to the outside world.[21] The Sino-Soviet frontier in Sinkiang, where "revisionist" *i.e.,* separatist tendencies among China's national minorities are most marked, has, by way of contrast, an almost wholly negative character. Without wishing to make too glib a comparison between old and new China, there does seem to be some reason to think that China's leaders today share with their imperial forerunners something of a Great Wall psychology, which manifests itself in a defensive posture in the north and a forward policy elsewhere. The states of Asia which at various times in the past have sent tribute missions to Peking are once more tending to draw closer to China, with the national minority regions again becoming an intermediate zone between the two. They also constitute an intermediate zone in Maoist theoretical terms, for the national minorities are now engaged in socialist transformation, whereas the Han people are already in the more advanced stage of socialist construction and the non-Communist states of Asia are still carrying out the national democratic revolution. And, according to the CCP, what distinguishes the Chinese world (China and the "third world") from the world of capitalism and revisionism, is that it is seriously engaged in class struggle. Chairman Mao's assertion that there are no contradictions between nations but only between classes was made in a statement supporting the struggle of American negroes to achieve equality. It was no mere coincidence that the Party, which could have found just as apt quotations from Lenin, seized upon this statement and made it the cornerstone of its current national minority policy.

To the extent that a new equilibrium has been established among domestic policy, national minority policy (*i.e.,* frontier [the *fan-pu* of the

[21]Owen Lattimore, *From China, Looking Outward* (inaugural lecture), (Leeds: Leeds Un. Press, 1964).

imperial system] policy), and foreign policy, it may be expected that policy towards the national minorities will be more sensitive to developments in the international arena than has been the case heretofore. For instance, if protracted U.S. involvement in South Vietnam leads to a lessening of Sino-Soviet differences and to a tougher Chinese foreign policy, the attitude of the CCP towards the national minorities will tend to harden. There is some evidence that such a chain reaction may already have been set off. On the other hand, the sensitivity of national minority policy to the vagaries of foreign policy is modified by Han colonisation of the frontier regions. Ultimately, the ethnic distinctiveness of China's frontiers will have diminished to the point where national minority policy will be of but marginal concern. However, the rate of Han emigration from China proper is not constant, being itself influenced by Party policy towards the national minorities.

# IX
# Political Structure

## 22. The Formal Political Structure

*Liu Shao-ch'i*

Now I should like to give some explanation of the basic content of the Draft Constitution under four headings:

### 1. The Character of Our State

Article 1 of the Draft Constitution lays down that "the People's Republic of China is a people's democratic state led by the working class and based on the alliance of workers and peasants." The Preamble and many other articles of the Draft Constitution clearly indicate that a broad people's democratic united front still exists under our country's system of people's democracy.

The truth that only by relying on the leadership of the working class is it possible for the Chinese people to win liberation from the oppression of imperialism, feudalism, and bureaucrat-capitalism has long since been proved by historical facts over a long period. After the people had won victory, a new problem cropped up, that is: Would the working class continue to be as capable and confident in leading national construction as it had been in the past? Some people may have adopted a wait-and-see attitude on this question in the beginning, but facts in the past five years have fully proved what unusual talent the working class possesses in leading the country. To secure the fruits of victory already won by the Chinese people, it is necessary to further consolidate and strengthen the working-class leadership of the state. Without such leadership, success

Reprinted from Liu Shao-ch'i, "Report on the Draft Constitution of the People's Republic of China" [September 15, 1954], *Documents of the First Session of the First National People's Congress of the People's Republic of China* (Peking: Foreign Languages Press, 1955).

in our cause of socialist construction and socialist transformation would be unthinkable. . . .


## 2. Steps to Be Taken in the Transition to a Socialist Society

Article 4 of the Draft Constitution states: "The People's Republic of China, by relying on the organs of state and the social forces, and by means of socialist industrialization and socialist transformation, insures the gradual abolition of systems of exploitation and the building of a socialist society."

To insure the thorough implementation of the policy laid down in Article 4, many provisions are made in other articles under the heading of General Principles. These provisions define both the general objective of building a socialist society and the concrete steps to be taken to build such a society.

In the transition period of our country there are still many different economic sectors. Ownership of the means of production in our country at present falls mainly into the following categories: state ownership, that is, ownership by the whole people; cooperative ownership, that is, collective ownership by the working masses; ownership by individual working people; and capitalist ownership. The task of the state is to strive to strengthen and extend the first two categories, that is, the socialist sector of our economy, and to bring about step by step the socialist transformation of the latter two categories, that is, the nonsocialist sector of our economy. Consequently, the state "insures priority for the development of the state sector of the economy" and pays special attention to the step-by-step building of heavy industry, the main economic foundation of socialism. The state "encourages, guides, and helps the development of the cooperative sector of the economy" and encourages and guides the transformation of capitalist industry and commerce "into various forms of state-capitalist economy, gradually replacing capitalist ownership with ownership by the whole people."

These provisions in the Draft Constitution are of course not based on imagination but on changes in social and economic relations that have actually taken place since the founding of the People's Republic of China, and on the experience of the masses. All of them are therefore practicable. With regard to these provisions, I should like to deal with the following questions.

The first is the question of forms of transition. As we are aware, the socialist transformation of agriculture, handicrafts, and capitalist industry and commerce is a very arduous task. We cannot hope to accomplish this transformation overnight. We must proceed step by step in the light of the experience and political consciousness of the masses and in accordance with what is possible in the actual situation. Our experience has proved that socialist transformation, either of agriculture and handicrafts or of capitalist industry and commerce, may have its transitional forms and that it is of primary necessity that the transitional forms we adopt be flexible and varied. . . .

### 3. Our Political System of People's Democracy and the People's Rights and Duties

Article 2 of the Draft Constitution lays it down that: "All power in the People's Republic of China belongs to the people. The organs through which the people exercise power are the National People's Congress and the local people's congresses." This provision and those contained in other articles specify that the political system of our country is that of people's congresses. In the light of long experience of political construction in our people's revolutionary bases and with the experience of the Soviet Union and other people's democracies as reference, our Common Program five years ago decided on this kind of political system for our country. Now, summing up the experience of the work of our organs of state and the experiences of all levels of the people's representative conferences of all circles in the past five years, the Draft Constitution makes more complete provision for the political system of our country. This political system which we have adopted is bound up with the fundamental nature of our state. It is this political system which we, the Chinese people, are adopting to insure our country's advance toward socialism.

The system of people's congresses is the proper political system for our country, because it helps the people to exercise their own power and participate constantly in running the state through this political system, thereby bringing into full play their initiative and creativeness. Clearly, if there is no suitable political system that enables the masses to use their abilities in running the state, it is impossible to mobilize and organize them effectively for the building of socialism. . . .

Paragraph 2 of Article 2 of the Draft Constitution declares: "The National People's Congress, the local people's congresses, and other organs of state practice democratic centralism." Our system of democratic centralism is explained by the fact that the exercise of state power is unified and concentrated in the system of people's congresses. A reactionary publication issued in Hong Kong asserted that our "system of people's congresses is a system of concentration of power by the central authority." These reactionaries seem to think they have found something to attack us with. However, we Marxist-Leninists have long since publicly declared that we stand for centralism. The question is, what kind of centralism — the despotic centralism of a handful of big feudal lords and capitalists, or the democratic centralism of the masses of the people led by the working class? These two systems of centralism are poles apart. In the Draft Constitution, we have combined a high degree of centralism with a high degree of democracy. Our political system has a high degree of centralism but it is based on a high degree of democracy.

While people are themselves still subjected to oppression, they cannot fully concentrate their will and strength. It is precisely for this reason that the Chinese people in the past were ridiculed as being like "loose sand." The revolution concentrated the people's will and strength and, having liberated themselves and set up their own state, the people naturally concentrated their whole will and strength on building up their state apparatus, making it a powerful weapon. The stronger the people's state apparatus, the more powerfully it can defend the people's interests, protect the people's democratic rights, and assure the building of socialism.

When Comrade Mao Tse-tung discussed the political system of our country in his work *On Coalition Government*, he stated clearly: "It is at once democratic and centralized, that is, centralized on the basis of democracy and democratic under centralized guidance" [Mao, *Selected Works*, IV, 272]. That is our principle.

Not a few people often mistakenly assume democracy and centralism to be two absolutely antagonistic things which cannot be combined. They think that where there is centralism there cannot be democracy. When they see the political unanimity of the people in our organs of state and find a highly unified leadership throughout the country, they try to show that "there is no democracy" here. The trouble with them is that they simply do not understand people's democracy, and consequently have no idea what centralism on the basis of people's democracy means.

The common interests of the people and their unity of will are the starting point of the work of the people's congresses and all other organs of state. Therefore, it is possible in all these organs of state to arrive at political unanimity of the people based on democracy. But political unanimity does not mean a lessening or elimination of criticism and self-criticism. On the contrary, criticism and self-criticism are most important expressions of our democratic life. In the work of all organs of state in our country there are bound to be defects and mistakes. Therefore, full scope must be given to criticism and self-criticism, at the sessions of the

National People's Congress, at the sessions of the local people's congresses, and at meetings of all organs of state, and in their daily activities. We must use the weapon of criticism and self-criticism to drive forward the work of the organs of state, constantly correcting defects and mistakes and fighting against bureaucratism, which spells departure from the masses, so that the organs of state can maintain regular and close contact with the masses and correctly reflect their will. If there is not full criticism and self-criticism, political unanimity of the people can neither be achieved nor maintained. Suppression of criticism in our organs of state is a legal offense. . . .

# 23. The Cultural Revolution in Structural Perspective

## Chalmers Johnson

During 1967, two major schools of interpretation emerged among "China Watchers" with reference to the Great Proletarian Cultural Revolution. The first and by far the most popular is the "End-of-a-Dynasty" view, according to which "China is slipping inexorably toward total collapse, with Chairman Mao fighting an ever-losing battle to impose his rebaptism of revolutionary purity."[1] The second view, which might be called the "Mao-as-scenarist" school, does not underestimate the chaos on the mainland but tends to see it as "controlled mayhem" and regards splits within the Maoist forces themselves as the only real signs that Mao may not always have been the organizational engineer in charge of turning the tempo up or down.[2]

The intepretation that seems most compatible with the known events of 1967, however, falls between these two poles. According to this view, Mao indeed began by exercising the controlling initiative in the Cultural Revolution, but unintended consequences of his initiatives have increasingly diverted the Maoist forces from their long-term goals into emer-

---

[1]Murrey Marder in *Japan Times*, September 29, 1967, p. 12. On the two schools of interpretation, see also *Asahi Shimbun* (Tokyo), October 4, 1967, p. 3. Two representative examples of the end-of-a-dynasty interpretation are: L. La Dany, "Mao's China: The Decline of a Dynasty," *Foreign Affairs*, XLV, No. 4 (July 1967), pp. 610–23; and Robert S. Elegant, "China's Next Phase," *ibid.*, XLVI, No. 1 (October 1967), pp. 137–50.

[2]For a valuable analysis, close to this position, see, e.g., Tadao Ishikawa, "Mō Taku-tō no kuni" (The Country of Mao Tse-tung), *Tokyo Shimbun*, April 28-May 11, 1967 (10 parts). Professor Ishikawa travelled on the mainland during the period April 12-24, 1967.

Reprinted from Chalmers Johnson, "China: The Cultural Revolution in Structural Perspective," *Asian Survey* 8 (January 1968): 1–15, by permission of the author and journal.

gency salvage operations. In order to present this view, let us recapitulate briefly how perceptions of the Cultural Revolution have changed from seeing it as an issue-based sacking of a few insubordinates to a structurally-oriented attack on the Communist Party itself.

During 1966, in the early phases of the Cultural Revolution, it seemed to many external observers that the struggle within the leadership concerned primarily differences over policies of the regime. Mao Tse-tung, having been kicked upstairs in 1959 as a result of the problems encountered in the Great Leap Forward, appeared to be attempting a comeback. It was thought that he planned to reverse the moderate policies, based on material incentives, that the Party had implemented since the Ninth Plenum (1961) and was continuing to implement despite its rhetorical support of the so-called Socialist Education Campaign (1962-66). In addition to this basic policy difference between the Leader and his Party, Mao was known to hold equally fundamentalist views on questions of international relations, the Sino-Soviet conflict, and the training of a successor generation—views which powerful members of the Political Bureau apparently did not support.

Mao has believed for a long time that Communism in the Soviet Union under Khrushchev genuinely degenerated into a form of neo-bourgeois capitalism and that this Soviet "modern revisionism" is the root cause of the Soviet Union's policy of peaceful coexistence with the United States, including policies such as the partial nuclear Test Ban Treaty of 1963 and the proposed nuclear non-proliferation treaty, which many Chinese Communists see as freezing the global status quo and working against China's national interests. Because of its revisionism the Soviet Union has, in Mao's eyes, forfeited all claims to lead or assist the international revolutionary movement.

It has been argued that Mao's judgment came under sharp attack in China during the winter of 1965-66, when it appeared that China itself might require the assistance of the USSR in case the Vietnam War developed into a Sino-American conflict. According to this view, Mao chose to continue his policy of sponsoring and endorsing "wars of national liberation," independent of the USSR's less warlike orientation, and he launched the Great Cultural Revolution to eliminate those Chinese leaders who wanted a reconciliation with Russia in order to enhance China's defenses. Mao is also said to have argued that the Cultural Revolution would steel China for guerrilla war in the event of an American attack.[3]

Mao's primary domestic ally in this purge and national mobilization was Defense Minister Lin Piao, whose reform of the People's Liberation

---

[3]For an analysis along these lines, see H. F. Schurmann, "The Upheaval in China: What It Means," *New York Review of Books*, October 20, 1966.

Army (PLA) during the period 1959-65 had recommended him as a truly devoted student of the Thought of Mao Tse-tung. The actual task forces of the purge were the Red Guards, students specially mobilized through the device of closing the schools, whose operations against Mao's enemies also served the secondary purpose of turning the youth of China away from an effete civilian life and imbuing them with the quasi-military qualities that Mao so much admires.

This was the way matters looked in 1966. No one imagined that Mao's purpose — or a possible consequence of his actions — was virtually to destroy the authority of the Communist Party within Communist China. By the end of 1967, however, this earlier estimate required radical revision. While it remains likely that disputes over policy contributed to the timing of the Cultural Revolution and that they served to catalyze the Leader and the Party into antagonistic positions, it became evident during 1967 that an irreducible component of the upheaval was a dispute over the very structure of the regime itself.

From the perspective of late 1967, it seemed that the Cultural Revolution was a desperate effort to solve certain fundamental structural problems of an aging Communist bureaucracy. Aging Communist parties are sometimes characterized as having become "bureaucratized," but this is a misnomer since all ruling Communist parties are bureaucracies from the start. What is meant by the term is that Communist bureaucracies sometimes become rigidified or ossified—that is, they suffer from the inescapable pressures on any bureaucracy, Communist or otherwise, to dilute the authority of the political leader over time in favor of the interests of entrenched office-holders. Anthony Downs has phrased one aspect of this problem in terms of general law: "All organizations tend to become more conservative as they get older, unless they experience periods of very rapid growth or internal turnover."[4]

The problem is not simply one of conservatism but also of what Downs calls "the rigidity cycle or the ossification syndrome," an anomaly of bureaucratic functioning which, he says:

> . . . is much more likely to appear in Communist countries than in most western nations for two reasons. First, most bureaus in nondemocratic countries receive weaker feedbacks [from the public]. Second, the bureaucracies in at least two Communist nations — China and Russia — are vastly larger in absolute size. Faced by enormous hierarchies with dozens of levels, top-ranking officials are compelled to establish giant monitoring bureaus that develop complex hierarchies of their own. . . . Bureaucracies in Communist nations are undoubtedly subject to at least

---

[4]*Inside Bureaucracy* (Boston: Little, Brown, and Co., 1967), p. 20.

some high-level control. But the leakage of authority in the whole structure is so great that the pressures felt by low-level officials are often
almost totally unrelated to the objectives of those at the top of the
pyramid.[5]

It is not necessary or appropriate in the present context to offer an
exhaustive list of the problems that are inherent in large, aging bureaucracies. Mao Tse-tung is quite willing to admit that these problems exist:

> With victory, certain moods may grow within the Party — arrogance, the
> airs of a self-styled hero, inertia and unwillingness to make progress,
> love of pleasure and distaste for continued hard living.[6]

These types of problems must be faced in all Communist bureaucracies;
however, the characteristic modes by which a Communist leader attempts
to prevent the ossification of his own Party bureaucracy may provide us
with criteria for distinguishing among Communist political systems. It is
true that all Communist elites, including the Chinese, resort to certain
common methods of escape from the normal rigidities of a large bureaucracy; the most obvious of these is the routine use of "campaigns" or
*yün-tung* in order to achieve key objectives. But the Chinese Communist
Party can be distinguished from the Communist Party of the Soviet
Union and most other ruling parties in terms of Mao's typical methods
for dealing with the problem of inner-Party bureaucratic rigidification.
Mao himself distinguishes his own party on this criterion: "Conscientious
practice of self-criticism is still another hallmark distinguishing our Party
from all other political parties."[7]

Whereas Stalin characteristically controlled his Party through the use
of an external monitoring agency with its own career path — the secret
police — Mao has sought ever since the Yenan rectification (*cheng-feng*)
to control his Party through such devices as self-criticism, mutual supervision through small group study sessions, thought reform, periodic status
reversal for cadres (*hsia-fang*), and internal criticism of upper ranks by
lower ones (e.g., PLA "democracy"). Unquestionably, Mao replied on
indoctrination rather than police monitoring during the Yenan period
partly because of the requirements of his mass-based, guerrilla warfare
strategy of revolution, a major point of differentiation between the Chi-

---

[5] *Ibid.*, p. 164.

[6] *Quotations from Chairman Mao Tse-tung* (Peking: Foreign Languages Press,
1966), p. 237. This is not a Mao quote selected out of context merely to support the
present argument; it is one that was highly salient in the press during 1967. See,
e.g., *Peking Review*, No. 43 (October 20, 1967), p. 25.

[7] *Quotations from Chairman Mao Tse-tung*, p. 259.

nese and Russian revolutions. But whatever the reasons for Mao's choice, he has normally shunned the use of extra-Party agencies to control his own Party.

The use of monitoring by police and a reliance upon indoctrination carry with them different unintended consequences.[8] Until approximately the time of the Hundred Flowers campaign of 1957, bureaucratic self-interest in the Chinese Party was not very important because the leadership had not split seriously over policies or policy failures and because the Yenan-type methods of control appeared to work quite well. The Hundred Flowers rectification campaign, however, marked a significant departure. For the first time Party leaders invited criticism of Party members from non-Party groups. This suggests that the Party bureaucracy had already begun to learn from experience how to protect itself from control through indoctrination. The "little red book" is instructive in this regard:

> Another point that should be mentioned in connection with inner-Party criticism is that some comrades ignore the major issues and confine their attention to minor points when they make their criticism. They do not understand that the main task of criticism is to point out political and organizational mistakes.[9]

The turning of the Hundred Flowers *cheng-feng* into the subsequent anti-rightist campaign tends to confirm this view. The non-Party intellectuals who were asked to criticize the Party revealed by their behavior the failure of their own "thought reform" a few years earlier, and the Party itself escaped meaningful rectification. From the Hundred Flowers period to the present, the leadership's policies and the results obtained from these policies have tended to exacerbate the growing structural problems of the Party organization. The Great Leap Forward enhanced the power of the Party over that of other hierarchies in China, and the failure of the Great Leap tended to divide the leadership, thereby putting an intolerable strain on the capacity of the regime to control the Party through indoctrination alone. Control through normative means is difficult enough when the indoctrinee is presented with a message on which there is widespread agreement. Under conditions of disunity, indoctrination rapidly degenerates into the formalistic recitation of slogans.

Efforts were made throughout the Socialist Education Campaign period to reinvigorate the indoctrination system. This was combined with a resort to *inner-Party* monitoring agencies such as the so-called "work

---

[8]For a theoretical analysis of the potentialities and problems of monitoring and of indoctrination, see Downs, *op. cit.*, pp. 148-53 and 233-36.

[9]*Quotations from Chairman Mao Tse-tung*, p. 263.

groups" employed in the "four cleanups" (*ssu-ch'ing*) movement. However, the top leadership remained divided—some leaders may even have contributed to subverting the Socialist Education Campaign (we do not possess detailed knowledge of the politics of this period)—and by 1965, a sizable gap had appeared between the rhetoric of the Party press and the practice of the Communist bureaucracy. The stage was thus set for the Great Proletarian Cultural Revolution. During 1967, the supreme leader launched an attack directly on the Communist Party utilizing non-Party forces—that is, he undertook a purge of the Party closer in form to Stalinist precedents than any previous organizational initiative of the Maoist era. The course of events during 1967 suggests, however, that the differences in terms of agents and methods between the Cultural Revolution and Stalinist-type purges — i.e., the use of the Army and the involvement of the masses in China — may have consequences for Communist China that are unprecedented in any Communist context.

## First Quarter: Revolutionary Rebels vs. Economism

The year 1967 opened with Mao's extra-Party forces going into action against the regional and local "power holders" of the Communist Party. Red Guard "little generals" from Peking joined with local low-level cadres and the rank-and-file of enterprises and offices—groups newly christened as "revolutionary rebels"—in order to purge the ruling Communist Party apparatus. They proclaimed:

> With Mao Tse-tung's thinking for our weapon, and with Chairman Mao's support for us revolutionary rebels, we dare to embrace the universe and seize the moon and the giant sea-turtle; we dare to touch the tiger's buttocks and put our hands in the hornets' nest; we dare to pull the local emperor off his horse.[10]

The rising of the local ranks to welcome and join the invading Red Guards revealed the crucial importance of control of the propaganda media as a source of political power in China. Mao began his purge in late 1965 and early 1966 by ousting the entire central propaganda establishment and turning it over to figures of his persuasion. The organ of Lin Piao's PLA, *Chieh-fang-chün Pao*, took the lead in exhorting the mass of the population to rebel and in reorganizing the other important newspapers in China. Supervising the entire operation were Mao's wife, Chiang Ch'ing, and his former secretary, Ch'en Po-ta. An event that in retrospect signalled the launching of the attack on the Party was the de-

---

[10]Radio Foochow, January 7, 1967.

nunciation, in December 1966, of T'ao Chu, Director of the CCP Central Propaganda Department during the previous six months, presumably because he had crossed Chiang Ch'ing on the question of the forthcoming "power seizures." With its monopoly over press and radio (but not over wall posters), the Maoist faction had access to the population at large; it instructed them incessantly to take power into their own hands, to kick out the local Party leaders, and to create new organs of local political and administrative power.

Not unexpectedly the local Party leaders, often incumbents in their offices for some seventeen or eighteen years, fought back. Among their several weapons was one that the Maoist press denounced as "economism" (*ching-chi chu-i*)—that is, "inciting work stoppages, strikes, and sabotage of production; handing out state money and train tickets; and persuading a number of Red Guard workers and persons misled by them to leave production posts without permission, under the pretext of going to Peking to complain about conditions."[11] Another anti-Maoist tactic was to invite educated youths and city-bred workers who had been sent to the countryside to return to the cities, thereby swamping transportation and distribution systems. In some cases local leaders used townsmen loyal to them to engage in physical combat with Red Guards coming in from the outside. Peking wall posters reported that in Nanking, for example, 54 persons were killed, 900 wounded, and 6,000 arrested in clashes that occurred on January 3, 5, and 6, between workers and Red Guards.

A more subtle but ultimately more damaging anti-Mao tactic was for local leaders to acquiesce in and then stage-manage a fake seizure of power. As the *Hupeh Jih Pao* reported:

> They pretend to welcome the taking-over, assuming an appearance of generosity and spontaneity. . . . You take over the factories, offices, shops! . . . Then they recede behind the scenes and with all their energy, carefully draw up schemes and play tricks, continuing to sabotage the Great Proletarian Cultural Revolution. . . . Some push all routine administrative matters onto the revolutionary rebel organizations, on the one hand trapping the revolutionary rebels in routine matters, making them busy all day long and dispersing their energies for carrying out political struggle; on the other hand, inciting a number of misled masses to go slow or even to stop production altogether. . . . The crimes of sabotaging and affecting work are imputed to the revolutionary rebels, damaging the reputation of the revolutionary rebel organizations and getting the revolutionary leftist into trouble.[12]

---

[11]*Ibid.*, January 12, 1967.
[12]Radio Wuhan, January 23, 1967.

On January 23, for example, a fake power seizure took place in the Canton Railroad Sub-bureau CCP Committee, which played havoc with transportation in that city until the Army finally placed the entire municipal administration under its direct control.[13]

From the Maoist point of view, the purge did not go smoothly during the first three weeks of the year. On January 21, Mao ordered Lin Piao to use the PLA to backstop the left-wing rebels in the Cultural Revolution. Two days later the CCP Central Committee, the State Council, the Military Affairs Committee and the Central Cultural Revolution Small Group jointly issued the following orders:

(a) The order that the Army should not become involved in Cultural Revolution manifestations is rescinded; (b) the Army must send troops to help any genuine revolutionary body which seeks help; (c) the Army must attack any counterrevolutionary elements which resort to arms; (d) the Army must not become "an air-raid shelter" for such counterrevolutionary elements; and (e) the Army should penetratingly carry out education [within its own ranks] for struggle between the proletarian revolutionary line represented by Chairman Mao and the bourgeois revisionist line represented by Liu Shao-ch'i and Teng Hsiao-p'ing.[14]

The concrete actions taken by the PLA in the period from January to March constitute one of the most complicated aspects of the Great Cultural Revolution. As a rule, the Army did not intervene directly but instead staged military parades as a warning that it would not tolerate overt defeat of the Red Guards and revolutionary rebels. For example, joint parades of revolutionary rebels and PLA troops in full combat gear were reported in Anhwei (January 26), Tsingtao (January 30), Kweichow (February 2), Ch'ang-ch'un (February 6), Fukien (February 10), and Kiangsi (February 15). These sorties were only a beginning, however. By the third quarter of the year the so-called "three-way coalition" between the PLA, revolutionary rebels, and pro-Mao Party members would become little more than a facade for direct military administration.

Maoists launched attacks on the Party in many scattered areas during the quarter. On March 6, Ch'en Tsai-tao, PLA commander in Wuhan and by July the most overt anti-Maoist in China, reported that:

---

[13]Radio Canton No. 2 (in Mandarin), March 27, 1967. There were over 30,000 Red Guard passengers per day at Canton railroad station during the tumultuous months of January and early February. Radio Canton City (Mandarin), April 2, 1967.

[14]These orders were printed in the Red Guard newspaper *Tung Fang Hung* (The East Is Red), No. 18, January 31, 1967.

The proletarian revolutionaries of Shanghai were the first to achieve great victory in the struggle to seize power. The storm of the January revolution has rapidly rolled through the whole country. The proletarian revolutionaries in Shansi, Kweichow, Heilungkiang, and Shantung have also scored great victories in the struggle to seize power.[15]

He did not say anything at all, however, about the 24 other provinces, municipalities, and autonomous regions, or about his own city of Wuhan.

The quarter ended with comparative restraint. Fearing damage to agricultural production if spring planting were neglected, on February 23 Chou En-lai and the Military Affairs Committee damped down the fires of Red Guard activism with a new slogan, allegedly the latest manifestation of the Thought of Mao Tse-tung—namely, "grasp revolution and boost production." The Army began to dispatch units all over the countryside to assist in agricultural work, and the press repeated the theme "it is absolutely impermissible to direct the spearhead of the struggle at [agricultural] production team cadres."[16] In Peking, the Red Guards were temporarily diverted from the difficulties of the purge by laying siege to the Soviet Embassy for two-and-a-half weeks. On February 15, *Pravda* published a 4,000-word editorial calling for the overthrow of Mao, and Sino-Soviet relations hit rock bottom. Internally, the provincial radios reported a few mutterings from dispossessed Party members who were promising to settle accounts after the autumn harvest, but the situation appeared to be in hand. A few China watchers even thought that the Cultural Revolution was coming to an end.

## Second Quarter: "China's Khrushchev"

On April 1, Mao opened his campaign against Liu Shao-ch'i in the mass media, thereby bringing the purge directly to bear on the highest-ranking bulwark of the Party organization and, incidentally, virtually insuring that the Chinese Communist regime will undergo a succession struggle upon Mao's death. Communist regimes suffer from difficulties in transferring leadership for the simple reason that they refuse to recognize that succession is a problem. According to Party statutes, the leader of the Party is nothing more than the chairman of the Central Committee, elected by that Committee, and in the event that the incumbent dies the Central Committee need only elect a replacement. But it has never worked that

---

[15]Radio Wuhan, March 6, 1967.
[16]Radio Nanchang, February 15, 1967.

way since the time of Lenin, and in this respect China is no different from the USSR.

During the 1950's, Mao showed commendable realism concerning the problem of succession by designating Liu as his successor. On April 1, however, he jettisoned Liu once and for all, thereby reopening the entire problem. Mao's present heir apparent is Lin Piao, but Lin has not so far displayed the kind of political acumen that would lead an observer of Chinese society to believe that he could fill Mao's shoes for long. Lin is also in poor health.

The public attack on Liu was one of the most bizarre campaigns in the history of Communist purges: it began with accusations that read more like lines from a gerontological comedy than the usual hyperbolic denunciations of the Stalinist tradition. It seems that back in 1950, Mao Tse-tung and his wife went to see a movie called *Ch'ing-kung mi-shih* (Inside Story of the Ch'ing Court), a film version of Yao Hsin-nung's well-known play about the Boxers and the intrigues of the Manchu court under Tz'u Hsi. The Maos didn't like it—they thought it was unpatriotic —but Lu Ting-i, Chou Yang, Hu Ch'iao-mu, and "the number one Party person in authority taking the capitalist road" (otherwise known to the press as "China's Khrushchev," but no longer by his real name, Liu Shao-ch'i) thought it was all right. Seventeen years later Mao and Chiang Ch'ing recalled the incident and argued, in effect, that anybody liking that movie must be a revisionist![17]

The greatest anomaly in the campaign against Liu is that he was not arrested or subjected to physical violence; in fact, according to Anna Louise Strong, he continues to draw his salary and lead a normal life.[18] This fact seems to indicate that the public attack on Liu, far from signalling his final downfall, was actually intended to supply new ammunition and renewed dedication to the Maoist forces working in the provinces, particularly because these groups were beginning to show an alarming tendency to fight among themselves and to allow the whole movement to degenerate into anarchism.[19]

The most serious consequences of Mao's purge methods became fully manifest in the second quarter of 1967. Individual Red Guard and revolutionary rebel units fought among themselves for political advantage; and there was no higher authority that could pass judgment on their ever-escalating charges and counter-charges, since each faction based its claim to preeminence on maxims from *Mao chu-hsi yü-lu* (Quotations

---

[17]Ch'i Pen-yü, "Patriotism or National Betrayal?" *Jen Min Jih Pao*, April 1, 1967.
[18]*Letter From China*, September 23, 1967.
[19]"Destroy Anarchism," editorial, *Jen Min Jih Pao*, April 26, 1967.

from Chairman Mao). *Hsin Kweichow Pao* described the situation as follows:

Some persons [in the revolutionary ranks] only talk about revolution, without putting it into effect in their actions. Their main characteristic is to put on ultra-leftist appearances and shout the most extreme-leftist slogans to deceive some of the masses who do not understand the true situation. . . . In their actions, they reverse the relationship between the enemy and ourselves and point the spearhead of struggle at the proletarian HQ, the PLA, and their own comrades-in-arms. . . . The thinking, words, and actions of the "verbal revolutionaries" cannot be separated from selfishness. They shout "everything for the Party and the revolution," but the moment the interests of themselves and their own little cliques crop up, they cannot sacrifice themselves and act for the Party and the revolution.[20]

These were the sorts of people whom the Army had supported in January and February; by summertime the military's patience had been exhausted.

One valuable side-effect of the attack on Liu was the revelation of many important details concerning the history of Political Bureau politics during the previous decade and the origins of the Cultural Revolution. *Hung-ch'i* published long excerpts from the Lushan Plenum of August 1959, revealed that Liu Shao-ch'i had defended P'eng Te-huai in 1962 when the latter had tried to exonerate himself, confirmed that the split in the leadership revolved primarily around the issues of the communes and the Sino-Soviet dispute, and indicated that the planning of the purge of anti-Maoist Party intellectuals began at least a year before 1965.[21] All of these and many other new details provided the most important materials on top-level Party decision-making yet obtained by analysts of Chinese Communism.

Not everybody in China spent the spring of 1967 arguing about who was or was not a good loyal follower of the "Great Helmsman." On June 17, scientific workers of the PLA detonated China's first hydrogen weapon, which testified to China's extremely rapid advances in the field of nuclear armaments and gave final confirmation, if any were needed, that elements in the regime intended to acquire a strategic nuclear capacity. In foreign affairs generally, it appeared as though the Red Guards had reverted to nineteenth-century Chinese xenophobia. Indian and Bulgarian diplomats were manhandled in Peking, Chinese Communists bombed and burned other Chinese in Hong Kong who did not agree with

[20]Radio Kweiyang, July 11, 1967.
[21]*Hung-ch'i*, No. 13 (1967); *Peking Review*, No. 34 (August 18, 1967); *Jen Min Jih Pao*, May 17 and 18, 1967; and *Peking Review*, No. 21 (May 19, 1967).

them, and Chinese relations with virtually all east Asian nations from Mongolia to Indonesia markedly worsened. Only Pakistan and North Vietnam continue to cultivate Peking, and the possibility of a Communist victory in Vietnam appears to be the only immediate development that could reestablish China's greatly diminished influence in Far Eastern international relations.

## Third Quarter: The Army Wavers and Mao Takes a Trip

During July and August the basic structural configuration of Mao Tse-tung's purge collapsed. As a result of opportunism, incompetence, and intrigues within the Red Guard and revolutionary rebel segments of the Maoist three-way alliances, the Army in several regions chose to support one faction over another on the basis of Army interests, personal ties, and a desire to restore order, rather than on the basis of Maoist ideology or Lin Piao's orders. This unexpected denouement of the Cultural Revolution began to emerge in early spring. During April, and particularly during May and June, the incidence of "struggle by force" between rival Red Guard battalions, murders, robberies, escapes of imprisoned "counterrevolutionaries," thefts of arms, and disorderly demonstrations increased all over the country. Heilungkiang, for example, reported that a mob had thrown Red Guards from the tops of buildings; four hundred rebels were said to have been burned alive in a multi-story building in Chengchow, Honan; and numerous incidents of "bloody violence" occurred in Peking itself.

Probably the most turbulent area was the rich, heavily populated southwestern province of Szechwan. Li Ching-ch'üan had ruled the area from 1950 as Political Commissar of the Chengtu Military Region and, since October 1961, as First Secretary of the Southwest Bureau of the CCP Central Committee. During April, Li reportedly arrested some 20,000 revolutionary rebels in Chengtu; and during early May his own "revolutionary" organization, the Production Army, opened fire with machine guns against revolutionary rebels in Chengtu, producing casualties running into the hundreds. On May 9, he was officially fired by the CCP Central Commitee and replaced by General Chang Kuo-hua from Tibet, but there is no evidence that his influence has been eliminated.[22]

From Szechwan the main focus of the mutiny moved to the vital industrial city of Wuhan, although serious incidents were taking place in virtually every area during this period. In Wuhan there were two major groups of allies claiming to represent the Thought of Mao Tse-tung. On

---

[22]Radio Kweiyang, June 4, 12, and 25, 1967; *Yunnan Jih Pao*, July 4, 1967; and *Joint Publications Research Service* (JPRS) 42,503, pp. 135–36.

the one hand, there was the San Kang (Three Steels), a 400,000-strong coalition of two workers' groups from the Wuhan Steelworks and one student group from three Wuhan colleges. On the other hand, there was a unit of 300,000 workers and public security employees calling themselves the Pai Wan Hsiung Shih (Million Heroes). The Million Heroes were allegedly organized and directed by former leaders from the trade union apparatus, and some reports indicate that this group had contact with the Production Army in Szechwan.[23]

On June 17, the Million Heroes reportedly occupied the Yangtze river bridge, and the Three Steels asked the military in Wuhan to dislodge them. Ch'en Tsai-tao, Commander since 1954 of the Wuhan Military Region, chose to support the Million Heroes and refused to assist the Three Steels. A month later, on July 16, Hsieh Fu-chih and Wang Li, representing the Central Cultural Revolution Small Group, arrived in Wuhan and delivered an order from Chou En-lai instructing the Army not to support the Million Heroes. Ch'en Tsai-tao's reaction was to seize Mao's two emissaries and have them "beaten and humiliated." On July 22, Hsieh and Wang were released, possibly because of the movement of five warships and paratroops to the city, possibly because of the "direct intervention" of Chou En-lai, or possibly both. The Maoists held massive rallies in Peking to welcome Hsieh and Wang back from the abyss, and the press denounced the "small handful in the Party and Army following the capitalist road in Wuhan." A few weeks later Tseng Ssu-yu replaced Ch'en Tsai-tao as Commander in Wuhan, and the Army began to support the Three Steels and try to woo back the "hoodwinked masses" of the Million Heroes.

Although the Maoist press passed off the July rebellion in Wuhan as a glorious victory, the precedent of Ch'en's mutiny seemed to cause the situation elsewhere to deteriorate alarmingly. During August, reports of riots, fires, gunfire, corpses hanging from trees, criminals breaking out of prison, and internal movements of refugees, flowed in from Hunan, Chekiang, Liaoning, Kirin, Shantung, Heilungkiang, Szechwan, Yunnan and, above all, Kwangtung. The situation in and around Canton became so bad that between August 9 and August 30 all radio stations in Canton ceased broadcasting local news.[24]

In September the brakes were applied. We do not know whether Mao and his associates chose to stop or whether they were forced to reverse their course due to regional Army pressure, but the new line they began to enunciate sounded more like the voice of conservative Army leaders than that of Mao and Lin. On September 8, *Jen Min Jih Pao* opened an

[23]*Mainichi Shimbun* (Tokyo), August 1, 1967, p. 4; *Jen Min Jih Pao*, July 26, 1967; *Hung-ch'i*, No. 12 (1967).
[24]See *Far Eastern Economic Review,* August 31, 1967, p. 408.

attack on the "extreme left" of the movement (i.e., the Red Guards and revolutionary rebels), accusing persons of this persuasion of being "T'ao Chu-type counterrevolutionaries." (According to Mao, during late 1966, T'ao Chu assumed a hyper-leftist stance as a tactic in his support of Liu Shao-ch'i; if T'ao could use these tactics, perhaps many extreme-leftist Red Guards were really counterrevolutionaries in disguise.) Extreme leftism, said the *People's Daily*, promoted attacks on the Army, led to struggle by violence and caused splits in the revolutionary ranks; it had to be suppressed. The paper also referred to a mysterious group called the "May 16 Detachment," apparently an extreme-leftist group made up of Peking Red Guards such as Miss Nieh Yüan-tzu of Peking University, who had launched the whole affair with her original *ta-tze-pao* (big character poster) attacking the administration of the University. According to the press, the May 16 Detachment, located in the capital, was under investigation and would be suppressed.

More important than these press announcements was a secret speech delivered by Chiang Ch'ing on September 5. Although her address has not been published, an order was printed instructing the entire nation to study it. Its gist, obtained from regional radio broadcasts, was that the Army would open fire on mobs that defied its authority or continued to cause disturbances in the face of orders to "form alliances."[25] At the same time that his wife was laying down the law, Mao Tse-tung took a flying trip to Honan, Hunan, Chekiang, Kiangsi, Hupeh and Shanghai — all places where serious disturbances had occurred. His visit was not announced in advance and went uncelebrated upon its completion; it seems likely that Mao was persuaded by his military colleagues to go and see for himself how far things had deteriorated. He may also have attempted to reconcile warring factions in the disturbed areas.

At the end of September the regime started to tidy up Peking for its eighteenth national day celebrations. On September 27, a mass rally in the capital condemned seven persons to death, perhaps in order to suggest that the new line was to be taken seriously; workmen began to scrub off the thousands of wall newspapers that had provided so much information on the regional struggles; and the ranks of the overly candid (from the Maoist point of view) Japanese journalists dwindled to four. Clearly a major battle, if not the war, had come to an end.

## Fourth Quarter: Help the Cadres Get Back on the Horse

On October 15, the Shanghai *Wen Hui Pao*, one of the two or three most important Maoist newspapers in China, entitled its editorial, "Be coura-

---

[25]*Jen Min Jih Pao*, September 17, 1967, p. 1.

geous in helping the revolutionary cadres mount the horse." With these new instructions to rebuild the cadre apparatus, Mao's purge appeared to enter its final phase. All over the country the Army suppressed revolutionary rebel organizations that refused to get into line and reopened the schools with PLA political commissars on hand to supervise both the instruction and the ex-Red Guard pupils. Many "leftists" (i.e., Red Guards and revolutionary rebels), frustrated by the realization that young members of the Party and not they themselves were to be the main beneficiaries of the purge, tried to keep the movement going with new accusations and demonstrations. The Army's decision, however, was perfectly clear. "Revolutionary cadres," said the *People's Daily* on October 21, "should be drawn into the revolutionary provisional organs of power because they have greater experience in the struggle, are more capable in organizational and other work, and have a relatively high level of understanding policy."

Particularly serious from the point of view of the Maoist activists was the order that "revolutionary alliances" (i.e., the subordination of all groups to the newly installed cadres and their Army backers) should be formed *"on the basis of systems."*[26] This meant that the technical and administrative hierarchies were to be reestablished and that revolutionary rebel organizations which cut across occupational and geographic lines should be broken up. On October 1, in his anniversary speech from the T'ien An Men, Lin Piao introduced a new, allegedly Maoist slogan that spelled the end of the revolutionary purges: *tou-ssu p'i-hsiu*, an acronym meaning "struggle against selfishness and criticize the revisionists," implying in its sequence the new order of priorities. The "selfishness" to be struggled against was Red Gaurd reluctance to subordinate themselves to the revolutionary cadres.

Is this the end that Mao had always envisioned for the Cultural Revolution —the elevation to power of a new group of cadres—or was this ending forced on him by the Army? It is too early to know. Some evidence for the former view can be found in the four categories of cadres that Mao identified in his original 16-point resolution on the Great Cultural Revolution (August 8, 1966). In Point 8 of that document, he described cadres as "(1) good; (2) comparatively good; (3) those who have made serious mistakes but have not become anti-Party, anti-Socialist Rightists; and (4) the small number of anti-Party, anti-Socialist Rightists." As early as February 14, according to the *Hsin Kweichow Pao* (that is, according to the Maoist newspaper in an area where a power seizure had just occurred), the cadre policy with regard to these

---

[26]See, e.g., *Jen Min Jih Pao*, November 14, 1967, p. 2 (italics added).

four types was to be one of "arrest, dismissal, promotion, retention, and transfer." Cadres in the fourth category who had committed criminal acts were to be arrested; cadres in the fourth category who were not accused of acting on their opposition to Mao were to be dismissed; cadres in the first category and a few in the second category were to be promoted; the rest of the cadres in the second and those in the third categories who were willing to reform were to be retained in their posts; and others in the third category were to be transferred, thereby "giving them a chance to make up for their mistakes."

If this was the original intention of the purge, then the Red Guards were merely instruments for carrying it out; and the whole Cultural Revolution was a device for promoting "good" (i.e., young[27]) cadres over older, less flexible bureaucrats. As if to confirm this view, on September 1, Chou En-lai put the entire upheaval in a cyclical perspective:

> For a year the whole country has been alight. . . . Now in the second year it is the year for grasping victory. . . . The third year is for winding up. Then after an interval of a few years we will start again.[28]

Even assuming that the primary purpose of the Cultural Revolution was to solve inner-Party problems of recruitment and retirement, we do not know whether the purge was a success or whether the Maoist faction called it off in September on its own initiative. The Maoists succeeded in setting up reformed governments in only about one quarter of China's provincial level administrative districts—i.e., in Heilungkiang (February 1), Shansi (February 12), Kweichow (February 14), Shantung (February 23), Shanghai (February 24), Peking (April 20), Tsinghai (August 12) and Inner Mongolia (November 2). The rest of the country appears to be ruled directly by the People's Liberation Army, and some areas may be in anti-Maoist hands. Even in areas where a Maoist seizure of power has occurred, the Army has become the most important political force supporting the new administration. Mao's pet schemes for the economy also do not appear to have been implemented. According to the press, the good harvest and the atomic bomb are "victories for the Thought of Mao Tse-tung," but many agricultural cadres, scientific workers, and their supervisors obviously know better. These vital sectors

---

[27]See Chou En-lai's speech, May 26, 1967, to a mass rally at the Chinese Academy of Sciences. *K'o-chi Chan Pao* (Scientific Fighters' News), June 2, 1967 (JPRS 42,977, pp. 21–27).

[28]Speech at enlarged conference of the Peking Municipal Revolutionary Committee. See *Jen Min Jih Pao*, September 4, 1967; and *Ta Kung Pao* (Hong Kong), September 12, 1967.

of the economy were relatively insulated from the disruptions of the Cultural Revolution from the outset.

The true gains in the Cultural Revolution appear to have been made by one of Mao's extra-Party monitoring agencies—namely, the PLA. If the Army remains unified, it is possible that it will replace the Party (or, in a sense, become the Party) and that a national, military-type of Communist regime, more analogous to many governments in the ex-colonial nations than to the USSR or the east European states, will emerge on the mainland. However, the cohesion of the PLA is by no means assured.[29] The most critical problem in China at the present time is a pervasive lack of authority or unity in the hands of any of the various hierarchies— Party, governmental, or Army.

Loyalty within China has become increasingly personal, focused on the figure of Mao Tse-tung himself, and the key to power is access to the Maoist press, where the Thought of Mao Tse-tung can be manipulated for concrete policy ends. On December 26, 1967, Mao was 74 years old. If he should die before the Party can be rehabilitated in some form, it may not be too far-fetched to foresee a recurrence of the fragmentation that followed the death in 1916 of another strongman toward whom loyalty among military men had become primarily personal—that is, the regionalism following the death of President Yüan Shih-k'ai.

---

[29]See Harald Munthe-Kaas, "Problems for the PLA," *Far Eastern Economic Review,* October 5, 1967, pp. 39–43.

# X

# Chinese Communist System in Action — the Allocation Processes

## 24. The Allocation of Income

*Yuan-li Wu*

### Principles in Income Distribution

There are few expressly formulated principles of income distribution in Communist China. However, it can perhaps be said that payment of labor according to work and the abolition of private property as a source of income constitute the major theoretical propositions. All other propositions are based on practical considerations of economic policy and the need to adjust practice to the stage of economic development and the prevailing political environment. Among such practical considerations are the maintenance of a high rate of investment and, by necessity, a low level of consumption, increase in labor productivity, observation of strict labor discipline, avoidance of gross popular discontent, and maintenance of some degree of equity in income distribution.

In the first place, the Communist regime's answer to the question "for whom to produce" is of course affected by the "national goals" the CPC has chosen for the economy. In particular we may single out the following:

First, since rapid and accelerated accumulation is desired, and since the total output of the economy is low, a high rate of saving can best be assured by pre-empting a large part of the national product for the purpose of investment before it can reach the individual consumer. Since the Communist society wishes to regulate the rate of collective consumption as well, and, even more, to channel it into very specific directions, it would be expedient to add to the share pre-empted for investment an amount set aside for collective consumption. The latter corresponds

Reprinted from Yuan-li Wu, *The Economy of Communist China: An Introduction* (New York: Praeger, 1965), pp. 72-86, by permission of the author, Praeger Publishers, Inc., and Pall Mall Press Ltd.

to expenditures for "defense," "government administration," and "social and cultural activities," all of which are standard expenditure categories in the state budget. The following description of the distribution process by an economist in Communist China is worth quoting:

> In the case of those peasants who have joined agricultural cooperatives, in the first phase of distribution of the national product created every year, a part of the product becomes the personal income of the peasants . . . another part constitutes the collective income of the cooperative farm. In the second stage of redistribution, a part of the collective income received by the collective farm during the first stage has to be forwarded to the treasury via the agricultural tax; the remainder will be used within the cooperative for investment in further production . . . and for expenditure on collective-welfare items for the benefit of the cooperative's members. . . . Furthermore, out of the national income annually produced by government industrial enterprises, during the first stage of distribution, a part consists of the workers' wages while the remainder constitutes the gross income of the enterprise. In the second stage of redistribution, with the exception of a part of the gross income retained as the "reward fund" of the enterprise, or profit reserved to it, which may be disposed of by the enterprise itself, the greater part is transmitted to the treasury either as tax or as profit. The wage income received by the employees in the first stage of the distribution may also be transferred to the government treasury or to the credit institution through purchase of bonds or savings deposits.[1]

The previous observation that a sizable portion of the national product has to be pre-empted for collective consumption or government investment means that the second stage of redistribution must produce large transfers of funds to the government.

In order to safeguard the share pre-empted for purposes of investment and collective consumption, it would be expedient if the amount of income distributed to the individuals could be closely regulated by the government. Within the framework of Marxian concepts, this proposition means that the amount of personal income distributed to the farmers or to the wage earners in the first stage of distribution preferably should be limited. Such a situation can be promoted by enlarging the relative share of wages in the national income, by correspondingly reducing both the share and the absolute amount of property income, and by careful government regulation of the form and structure of wage payments.

---

[1]Yang P'o, "Shih-lun Wo-kuo Kuo-min-shou-ju ti Fen-p'ei Wen-t'i" (On the Distribution of China's National Income), *Ching-chi Yen-chiu*, No. 6, 1957, pp. 1–11.

Since transition to socialism is a "national goal" of the CPC, national-ization of private property becomes an important means of reducing the relative and absolute amount of property income. Thus the pattern of income distribution to be established is invariably associated with the continual redistribution of wealth, which is in turn an integral part of the political and social revolution. In practice, since tactical considera-tions preclude the completion of the revolutionary process in one stroke, the redistribution of wealth and income must also proceed by stages. So long as property income is not completely eliminated, it will be necessary to regulate the size of the income, as well as its disposition, in order to safeguard the planned accumulation of resources and collec-tive consumption.

Finally, since equity is a major consideration in a socialist economy both for ideological and for practical political reasons, and since increase in labor productivity is a principal goal of a developing economy, the final pattern of income distribution has necessarily to be resolved in a tug of war between two forces—the provision of adequate incentive on the one hand and the desire for equity and limitation of individual con-sumption on the other. It is in this light that one has to evaluate the attempt of Chinese planners to predicate wage increments on increases in productivity, to institute appropriate wage differentials, and to create a workable and efficient system of nonmonetary rewards and punish-ments. How all these measures are implemented and what problems are encountered may be seen in the following sections. One may note in passing that most of the measures and problems are common to Soviet-type economies.

## Reduction of Property Income

The reduction of the share and absolute amount of property income goes hand in hand with the nationalization of private enterprise. The entire process may be conveniently explained with respect to the urban and rural areas separately.

The process of nationalization of nonagricultural enterprises in the urban areas proceeded by several stages during 1949-56. At the begin-ning of their rule, the Communist authorities took over the state enter-prises of the Nationalist regime and confiscated property owned by the so-called "counterrevolutionaries." The confiscation of banking and manufacturing interests of owners identified with the Nationalist govern-ment had the effect of giving the Communists a nucleus of important financial and manufacturing enterprises, in addition to the many former state-owned enterprises. Obviously, because of the political power wielded by the Communist Party, an enterprise would behave as if it were completely nationalized as soon as the Communist government had established a minority interest.

In the second stage, which happened during the first half of 1952, the nationalization process took place as a part of the "five-anti" campaign. The latter was an attempt to bring a larger number of private business enterprises under Communist control, ostensibly as a countermeasure to the efforts of the capitalists to undermine the new order as a class. The five economic "crimes" against which the campaign was directed were bribery of public officials, evasion of taxes, theft of government-owned assets, fraud in filling government contracts, and betrayal and misuse of the state's economic secrets. Prosecution of "offenders" served to cloak the government's real intention—i.e., an unprecedentedly large capital levy and the expansion of the sphere of joint and public enterprises. The large number of business firms investigated under this campaign probably included most of the larger firms. Infringement of government regulations was classified into several categories, and punishment ranging from fines to confiscation was meted out to the offenders by special tribunals.[2] The officially reported sharp decline of the proportion of capitalist enterprises in the gross value of industrial output (excluding handicrafts) from 28.7 per cent in 1951, to 17.1 per cent in 1952, and 14.0 per cent in 1953,[3] serves as an indication of the scale of socialization during the five-anti campaign and immediately afterward.

The third stage of socialization was reached in 1955-56, when businesses were brought under the aegis of whole or partial state ownership on a wholesale basis. At this time, joint enterprises were formed by entire trade groups. The same official statistics cited above show that the proportion of the capitalist enterprises in the gross value of output of industry had declined to .1 per cent by 1956.

With the virtual elimination of private enterprise in the nonagricultural sectors in 1956, the former owners of these enterprises were given a nominal "dividend" payment under a resolution passed by the State Council on February 8, 1956. A nominal "fixed interest" or "dividend" of 1-6 per cent a year, payable quarterly, regardless of the profit or loss of the enterprises in question, was promised to private stockholders for a period of six years. The amount was subsequently revised to a uniform 5 per cent per annum. Inasmuch as the payments were to be terminated at the end of six years, this arrangement was tantamount to confiscation with partial compensation at the rate of 30 per cent of the estimated value of the private owners' investment, payable over a six-year period. The value of the investment itself was, of course, subject to the arbitrary

---

[2] See Yuan-li Wu, *An Economic Survey of Communist China*, pp. 228–31.
[3] *Wei-ta ti Shih-nien* (*Great Ten Years*), Peking, 1959, p. 32.

influence and decision of the authorities. Prior to the 1956 regulation, it was customary to allot at least one quarter of the net profit of all joint enterprises to private stockholders. Thus, with the 1956 regulation, the source of property income in the urban sector was effectively eliminated.[4] Although the practice of paying 5 per cent a year to the original stockholders was extended in 1962 for another three years, compensation would still be limited to 45 per cent of the property value assigned to it by the authorities.

In the agricultural sector, socialization and the redistribution of wealth were also carried out in several stages. The first stage consisted of land reform, which began in 1950 under a new Land Reform Law. It was completed toward the end of 1952 and in 1953. Under the redistribution program, those farmers who leased land to others or had tenants, and some of the "rich peasants," were deprived of their land and other means of production. The latter were distributed to the poorer farmers and farm workers. The same reform also eliminated rental and interest payments as sources of income. However, nominally at any rate, the land received in distribution was to remain as the private property of the owner-cultivator. Thus property income was not entirely eliminated at this point.

The second stage of socialization, however, followed immediately after land reform. This phase was heralded by the establishment of "mutual-aid teams," which in turn led to the formation of agricultural cooperatives of the first degree. The mutual-aid teams were precisely what their name implied. They were formed by groups of farmers who h ; d one another with equipment or labor for specific purposes or at certain times of the year. In many ways they were a traditional form of mutual assistance among individual farmers. The important transition was from a temporary mutual-aid team to a permanent one, and then to the cooperative farm of the first degree. While the mutual-aid team served an average of 20 households each in 1952, the cooperative farm of the first degree comprised an average of 48 households in 1957, and the advanced cooperative farm, an average of 158 households.[5]

The mutual-aid teams were a form of organization of production only. Even the cooperative farms organized at that time still retained a category of property income, namely, a part of the output of the farm was

---

[4]*Fa-kuei Hui-pien*, January-June, 1956, pp. 282–83. Discussions on the theme of "fixed interest" may be found in various articles in *Ching-chi Yen-chiu*, No. 1, 1957. The further extension of the "dividend" payment measure for 1963–65 was reported at the end of the third session of the second National People's Congress, March 27–April 16, 1962. *People's Daily*, Peking, April 17, 1962.

[5]See *Ching-chi Chou-pao* (*Economic Weekly*), No. 38, 1952, p. 747, and Yuan-li Wu, "Some Economic Effects of Land 'Reform,' Agricultural Collectivization and the Commune System in Communist China," *Land Tenure, Industrialization and Social Stability: Experience and Prospects in Asia* (Milwaukee: The Marquette University Press, 1961), pp. 21–22.

distributed to the members on the basis of the land and other means of production they had contributed to the cooperative. However, such property income was not to exceed the amount distributed on the basis of labor performed.

The third stage of socialization was the formation of the advanced type collective farms. Distribution on the basis of property contribution was eliminated completely at this point. This stage of socialization in the agricultural sector corresponded roughly to the same time period as the completion of socialization in the nonagricultural sectors.

Then, in 1958, the communes were established,[6] and for a time income distribution was made up almost entirely of commodity supplies, so that some enthusiastic CPC members were able to claim that Communist China had already reached the ultimate phase of distribution according to need. The amount of money income was reduced to a minimum, and distribution was carried out largely without reference to the amount of work performed. Under the commune, which averaged 4,600 households in September, 1958,[7] the peasant members were organized into production brigades and teams. During the period when the commune was in full swing (April, 1958-April, 1959), the production brigade was solely a unit for production, corresponding roughly in size to the advanced cooperative farm, while the production team was a smaller unit under the brigade. After April, 1959, but only for a very short period, the production brigade was given the function of income distribution and made into an independent accounting unit.

Finally, beginning in the middle of 1961, and again in 1962, the method of distribution within the commune was once more readjusted to the same pattern that had existed prior to the formation of the more advanced cooperative. The category of property income was restored through the granting of private plots to the farmers, who were permitted to retain their own output either for personal consumption or for sale on the free market.

## Pre-emption of National Income for Accumulation

In the early years, when the Communist authorities were not yet in a position to control fully the allocation of resources and the flow of income, political means were employed to curtail consumption. Prior to the establishment of the First Five-Year Plan, police and parapolice methods were often employed to discourage persons from consuming

---

[6]The state farm may be regarded as the epitome of nationalization in agriculture, and differs from the communes of 1958 in ownership and management. It is an instance of state rather than collective ownership and is probably more centrally managed. It is also more mechanized. However, there were only 2,490 state farms at the end of 1960, accounting for 4.6 per cent of the total cultivated land.

[7]*T'ung-chi Kung-tso* (*Statistical Work*), Peking, No. 20, 1958, p. 23.

more than what was considered politically acceptable. People were afraid of being accused of the "crime" of conspicuous consmption; heavy taxation (including levies of "back-taxes"), compulsory bond purchases, and forced savings were also relied upon. Subsequently, as the scope of nationalization widened and greater control of the income flow was established, profit from the state enterprises and the depreciation fund became a major source of the investment fund. Reinforced by rationing and centralized distribution of various commodities, including food, clothing, and other basic consumer goods, the level of consumption was kept at an "acceptable" volume. At the same time, the level of investment was augmented by employing hitherto unemployed or semi-employed labor, including peasants, prisoner labor, and the Communist Chinese Army. These workers were employed in mass labor projects for water conservation, road and railway building, and other similar labor-intensive work; they numbered 23 million in 1953, according to one estimate.[8]

## The Principle of Low Wages

In the course of the program to establish control over resources for accumulation, a principle of low wages and low farm income was evolved. The system of low wages, according to Communist Chinese authors, is one under which all workers would have enough to eat while improvements in the standard of living would be gradual and would be granted only on the basis of further development in production. It is said to be the only principle which, under Communist China's present condition of low output, would permit the practice of rewarding labor according to the amount of work performed. To quote Hsü Kang, "Payment according to labor performed means that the compensation of the worker must be appropriate in the light of the productivity of all social labor. Furthermore, compensation to each individual worker must be in accordance with the amount and quality of the labor performed, subject to the condition that all workers must, as far as possible, be given enough food to eat."[9] The underlying idea that there should be sufficient wage differentials to reflect differences in productivity along with a total wage bill that would permit adequate accumulation is also brought out in the statement:

---

[8]Estimate by Li T'ien-min, quoted in Yuan-li Wu, *op. cit.*, 1956, pp. 322–23. A later *China Post* (Taipei, March 11, 1965) report puts the number of forced labor camps at over 350, and the cumulative total of inmates in fourteen years at 90 million. Seventeen labor reform farms are said to have a population of 2 million.

[9]Hsü Kang, "Lao-tung Kung-tzu Kung-tso Pi-hsü Tseng-hsü T'ung-ch'ou Chien-ku Ch'in-chien Chien-kuo ti Fang-tsun" (Pursuit of Labor and Wage Policy in the Light of the Over-all Policy of National Construction under Austerity), *Ching-chi Yen-chiu*, No. 2, 1958, pp. 21–30.

If we assume the lowest level of consumption that would accrue to a worker on the basis of the quantity and quality of his work or the lowest standard of living to be 3, even if the labor differentials should be $3:6:9:12$, the distribution of the consumption fund to the individuals need not maintain the differences of $3:6:9:12$ but may be at the ratios of $3:4:5:6$. This would reflect the principle of letting everybody have enough to eat and of distributing the rest on the basis of differences in the quality and quantity of labor. Such an arrangement would still satisfy the requirements of the law of distribution according to labor, but would at the same time allow for the low productivity of the economy. Therefore, a rational low wage system does not contravene the law of distribution according to labor . . . it is not equalitarianism.[10]

In the agricultural sector, even on a cooperative farm of the advanced type or in a commune, there exists some remnant of collective ownership instead of outright state ownership. An attempt must therefore be made to minimize the distribution of output as personal income and to provide appropriate differentials for the sake of safeguarding incentive. This dual purpose is realized in several ways, namely (1) by determining the real value of the wage unit after the total number of wage units is known and the amount available for distribution as personal income has been determined; (2) by requiring the collective farm or the commune and its subdivisions to pre-empt a certain amount of the gross output for collective consumption and investment purposes; (3) by requiring the same distribution units to set aside supplies allocated to the tax fund and for compulsory sales to the government, (4) in the case of the commune during 1958-60, by paying personal income mostly in kind, and (5) by specifying in advance the work unit for each person and for each job. As practiced by the cooperative farm and the commune prior to the latter's modification in 1961-62, this method of controlling personal consumption on the farm was probably no less effective in maintaining a high level of accumulation than the low wage policy practiced in the nonagricultural sectors.

## Labor Productivity and the Wage Rate

In practice, according to official statistics, the low-wage principle resulted in an annual increase of 14 per cent in the money-wage rate during 1952-56. The corresponding increase in the real-wage rate was 13

---

[10]T'ang Kuo-chün, "Wo-kuo Kuan-yü 'An-lao Fen-p'ei' ti T'ao-lun" (National Discussion on the Principle of Payment According to Work), *ibid.*, No. 7, 1958, pp. 72–76.

per cent. These rates may be compared with a 22 per cent annual increase of labor productivity in the material-production department. The official sources of these statistics also show that the annual increment was not at all even and that the ratio between the rates of increase in wages and in labor productivity at times varied violently. The most notorious example occurred in 1955 and 1956. During 1955, a 15 per cent increase in labor productivity over the corresponding level in 1954 was accompanied by a 1 per cent increase in real wages and a 3 per cent increase in money wages over the preceding year. On the other hand, in 1956, the rates of increase were 30 per cent in labor productivity (1955 = 100), 25 per cent in real wages, and 28 per cent in the money wage rate. In the case of individual industries, workers sometimes fared much worse than the average indicated.

However, while the increase in the wage rate may lag far behind that reported for labor productivity, the average lag being about 50 per cent or less, it is nevertheless possible for the wage-rate increase to exceed that of the supply of consumer goods on which wages are spent. This point is noted by Hsü Heng-mo,[11] according to whom retail prices rose precisely because of such a discrepancy. Employing what he alleges to be hypothetical figures, Hsü showed that if the increase in the total wage bill was 48 per cent in 1955-56 while the supply of consumer goods increased by only 32 per cent, an increase in retail prices might be expected. It is conceivable to have some price inflation even though the phenomenon can be largely suppressed by direct controls. The low wage policy does not always work out as well as it should in principle.

### The Wage System and Labor Incentive

Throughout the decade and a half of their rule, the problem of providing enough incentive for labor has incessantly plagued the Chinese Communists. The authorities oscillated between stressing material incentives and stressing nonmaterial incentives. The frequent back-and-forth swings between these two approaches mirror the state of the economy and its subjective interpretation by the Communist Party leaders. In the early years and through the First Five-Year Plan, primary emphasis was placed on the employment of material incentives, and considerable efforts were exerted in order gradually to evolve a wage system based primarily on piece rates and adequate wage differentials. Such a system, it was

---

[11]Hsü Heng-mo, "Ju-ho Fen-hsi Yen-chiu Chih-kung Kung-tzu Wen-t'i" (Method of Analysis of the Problem of Wages of Workers and Employees), *Tung-chi Kung-tso* (*Statistical Work*), No. 7, 1957, pp. 8–10.

thought, would be calculated to encourage workers to put forth their best effort. Toward the last two years of the First Five-Year Plan and during the Great Leap, the pendulum swung toward the nonmaterial incentives. Piece rates gave way to time rates, at least in principle, and to the time-worn "supply" or ration system, which provided for relatively equal distribution regardless of the amount of work completed or output produced. These measures were reintroduced in the commune, and, to a lesser extent, in the nonagricultural sectors. With the collapse of the Great Leap, the pendulum swung back to the material incentives, as may be noted in the restoration of piece rates and the permission granted the peasants to cultivate their private plots and to keep the produce for themselves. The most significant concessions were the reversion to output distribution by the production team on the basis of work units and setting a value on the work unit in advance.[12]

The regular material incentives in the nonagricultural sectors consist of the basic wage plus supplementary payments for overtime, night or holiday work, hazardous working conditions, regional allowances, and bonuses and other special emoluments. Subsidized housing and other welfare benefits provided under a labor insurance scheme are also part of the total compensation. According to official statistics, the number of workers under the labor-insurance system increased from 3.3 million in 1952 to 13.8 million in 1958;[13] the coverage includes maternity, injury, illness, and death benefits, although the level of benefits is necessarily very low. In addition, during the First Five-Year Plan, a system was evolved establishing awards for rationalization proposals, innovations, and inventions. These were generally based on the amount of cost savings to the enterprises.

The most notable advance in the development of the wage system, however, was made in June, 1956. The wage reform of that year consisted mainly of (1) the abolition of the former wage point system, which was introduced during a period of hyperinflation and under which the actual amount depended upon the monetary value of the wage point which varied with certain commodity prices, (2) the establishment of an eight-grade wage scale in money for most industries and enterprises, (3) the widening of wage differentials to correspond more closely to differences in skill and training, and (4) the establishment of common standards in differentiating the various grades in each industry. Wage rates of the highest grades in Manchurian industries[14] were about 2.5 to 3.2 times those of the lowest grades, while in general an average ratio of 1 to 3 prevailed. In particular, greater wage increases were granted to

---

[12]*People's Daily*, Peking, March 30, 1963.
[13]*Wei-ta ti Shih-nien* (*Great Ten Years*) (Peking, 1959), pp. 192–94.
[14]Charles Hoffmann, "Work Incentives in Communist China," Social Science Research Council, Berkeley, Calif., 1964.

workers employed in those industries that were deemed important in the priority scale of the economic plan — that is, workers in "heavy" rather than "light' industry; production workers rather than administrative workers; engineering, technical, and highly skilled managerial personnel rather than the ordinary administrative workers; professors, scientific researchers, and other intellectuals rather than the common run of workers.[15]

There were several reasons for the brief return to egalitarianism during the Great Leap. One of these was the ideological attitude that the communes represented a stage of development approaching real Communism and that compensation of labor according to work would be incongruent in these circumstances. Secondly, the industrial and agricultural output, partly due to faulty accounting and inaccurate records, was advancing at such a rate at the time that any attempt to maintain the same piece rates would have resulted in a very sharp increase in personal wage income and consumption. Hence, emphasis was shifted to ideological rewards and the psychic compensation that one should find in being a good Communist and an exemplary worker; the materialistic incentives, on the other hand, were denounced as unduly "bourgeois."

Where the nonmaterial incentives are employed, often they take the form of special honors given to "model workers," "labor heroes," and "advanced workers," who frequently are the winners of emulation campaigns and competitive drives conducted among different groups of workers either within the same industry or between industries. These emulation campaigns are comparable to the Stakhanovist drives of the Soviet Union. One disadvantage of such emulation campaigns and competitions, often not understood by planners and officials, is that such measures are disruptive of production based on predetermined plans. For, if such output drives are not to be stalled because of lack of raw material or spare parts, the participating enterprises and workers should have at their disposal a larger supply of raw materials and other inputs than what the plans call for. This would imply an increase in working-capital requirements. Since quality may also suffer in consequence of the output drive, the effort to increase labor productivity may actually end up in creating an increase in goods of dubious quality, aggravated by new bottlenecks.

Attention should also be called to the role of negative incentives. Strict labor discipline which cuts down absenteeism and forbids slowdowns and strikes is based both on the collective discipline exercised by the labor union and the ever-present threat that an unsatisfactory worker

---

[15]Ma Wen-jui, "Report to the Third Session of the First National People's Congress," *Current Background*, No. 405. See also the article by Charles Hoffmann, "Work Incentive Policy in Communist China," *The China Quarterly*, No. 17, January-March, 1964, pp. 92–110.

may be treated as a counterrevolutionary by the authorities. The penalties are both monetary and nonmonetary. The role of the trade union in Communist China, similar to that of other Communist countries, is no longer that of the guardian of the workers' interest, vis-à-vis the employer. In state-owned and -controlled industries, the workers, in their capacity as citizens, are said to be the real owners of the enterprises. Consequently, they would not want to strike against themselves. They must also be protected against such base feelings should they be so misguided as to regard themselves and management as opponents. The trade union, of course, performs certain welfare functions as agents of the state, dealing with such matters as labor insurance, safety, living conditions, mutual savings, female workers, health and hygiene, etc.[16]

Finally, although little is usually said of the forced-labor camps, such labor contingents under the direct control of the Ministry of Public Security exist in Communist China.[17] The possibility of direct allocation of forced labor to specific locations, enterprises, and industries, and the possibility of sending industrial workers to farms or to labor camps are very potent weapons of enforcement of labor discipline. These negative incentives are and can be used to supplement what an otherwise undesirable pattern and method of income distribution may fail to achieve, at least in the short run.

## Income Differentials Between Farmers and Industrial Workers

One of the principal "contradictions" that exist in the Communist Chinese society is the disparity between the incomes of industrial and farm workers. The phenomenon is well recognized by Mao Tse-tung and economists and officials. In 1952, the per-capita annual "consumption" of wage earners' families averaged 167.7 yuan, while the corresponding average consumption of farmers' families, including possibly some production costs, was only 72.8 yuan. In 1956, the corresponding values were 199.8 yuan per head for workers' families, while the per-capita value of farmers' families was 84.2 yuan. A ratio of 2.3:1 was maintained during the First Five-Year Plan. The preceding data are based on official figures that include collective consumption. The 1955 figures net

---

[16]The multifarious welfare and related functions of the union under the direction of the national and territorial federations of labor unions and the national industrial union are illustrated in Yuan-li Wu, *op. cit.*, pp. 426 ff.

[17]For a discussion on the "Regulations Governing Labor Service for Reform" proclaimed in 1954, see Yuan-li Wu, *op. cit.*, pp. 320–23.

of collective consumption, but inclusive of consumption of self-produced goods valued at retail prices, were 148 yuan per capita of personal income for workers' families and 138 yuan of per-capita expenditure, while the corresponding figures for farmers' families were 98 yuan of income (probably gross) and 93 yuan of expenditure. These figures exclude such items as rent, utilities, and transportation expenditures. If the latter were included, workers' families would have a per-capita income of 183 yuan and a per-capita expenditure of 173 yuan, while the corresponding figures for peasant families would be 102 yuan of income and 97 yuan of expenditure.[18] In any case, there was a large discrepancy of income and expenditure between farmers and nonfarmers. On the basis of the first set of figures, the discrepancy varied from 50 per cent of the farmers' income to 80 per cent of expenditure.[19] The discrepancy in income may also be seen in the larger relative expenditure of the farmers on staple foods and vegetables in comparison with a much larger expenditure on meat, cooking oil, and sugar by the urban workers.

During the first phase of the commune in 1958, when the peasants were paid mostly in kind, the per capita annual personal income of the commune members was estimated at 77 yuan in one study.[20] Of this amount, 51 yuan consisted of food rations; the remainder represented the sum total of monetary receipts, including both regular and bonus wages. The discrepancy between agricultural income and industrial wages was probably largest during this period.

Particularly annoying to the peasants was the higher income of the unskilled industrial workers. The inequity was recognized by the Communist authorities and partly corrected through a reduction of the basic wage of the lowest three grades of unskilled industrial workers. The wage and income differentials between farm and other workers have, however, persisted, and attempts are made by the authorities to explain them away. First, it is said that considerable differences in productivity exist between these two groups of workers. Secondly, it is pointed out

---

[18]At 1952 prices and in terms of the 1952 "product mix," 1 yuan would be equivalent to 33 cents in U.S. currency for industrial consumer goods, and 95 cents for agricultural products. See Yuan-li Wu, *et al.*, *op. cit.*, p. 353.

[19]See "Wo-kuo Kuo-min Shou-ju Sheng-ch'an ho Fen-p'ei ti Ts'u-pu Yen-chiu" (A Preliminary Study on the Distribution and Production of China's National Income), *T'ung-chi Yen-chiu*, No. 1, 1958, pp. 11–15, and "Kuan-yü Kung-nung Sheng-ho Shui-p'ing Wen-t'i" (On the Standards of Living of Workers and Peasants), *ibid.*, No. 13, 1957, pp. 4–5 and 24.

[20]Yuan-li Wu, "Some Economic Effects of Land 'Reform,' Agricultural Collectivization and the Commune System in Communist China," in *Land Tenure, Industrialization and Social Stability* (Milwaukee: The Marquette University Press, 1961), pp. 17–37.

that the income differences are to some extent offset by opposite price differences, so that the differences in real income are much less. Thirdly, farm workers allegedly do not have certain expenditures incurred by workers living in urban areas. The fact that the farmers may prefer to enjoy some of the urban amenities is not mentioned. The real issue, of course, is that there are too many farm workers, and any increase in their wages would lead to a sharp increase in potential consumption. Although it is conceivable to increase the farmers' pay and then try to tax away the excess income, this is a far less reliable method. The same consideration has probably caused the Communists to rely more on the turnover tax and the state's share of the profit margin rather than the direct income tax as a major source of government revenue, even though the price structure is unnecessarily distorted as a result and the indirect taxes are highly regressive. Since the lower income of the farmer is a reflection of China's excess farm population, the solution lies in the absorption of more farm labor by other sectors of employment. It was partly to resolve this problem . . . that the communes and the small-local-industry movement were initiated in 1958.

# 25. The Allocation of Justice

*Allan Spitz*

The system of people's courts in Communist China is an element of the total "political-legal" organ of the state which also includes the people's procuratorate and the state public security agencies. Collectively, this network performs a range of political and legal functions such as surveillance, intelligence, policing, and the administration of justice. The authority establishing the people's court system is found in article VI, sections 73-80, of the constitution of the People's Republic of China, and the structure and functions are set down in the Organic Law of the People's Courts.

People's courts exist at all levels of government in China, from the Supreme People's Court down to basic level people's courts. The president of each people's court is elected by the people's deputies at the appropriate level people's congress and may be dismissed by them. The judges of each court are appointed and dismissed by the administrative organ of the appropriate people's congress.[1]

Under article VI, section 80, of the constitution, "the Supreme People's Court is responsible and accountable to the National People's Congress, or when the NPC is not in session, to its Standing Committee. Local people's courts are responsible and accountable to local people's congresses at the corresponding levels."

This paper deals with the role and functions of the system of people's courts in Communist China. Its thesis is simple: that the courts represent the placing of "politics in command"—the application of the Maoist

---

[1]"A People's Court Must Report its Work to the People's Congress of the Corresponding Level," *Kuang Ming Jih Pao*, March 27, 1956 (*Survey of China Mainland Press* [*SCMP*] 1272, p. 5).

Reprinted from Allan Spitz, "Maoism and the People's Courts," *Asian Survey* 9 (April 1969): 255–63, by permission of the author and journal.

ideology to an organizational structure. The primary sources are articles from *Jen Min Jih Pao* and provincial people's dailies, as translated and reported in the *Survey of China Mainland Press*.

Any discussion of Chinese Communist politics depends upon an understanding of Maoist ideology. The appropriate point of departure is, therefore, the theory of contradictions and the concommitant concern with recognizing the two types of contradictions and the proper ways of handling them.

The people's courts are "tools of the proletarian dictatorship,"[2] and "weapons in the hands of the people."[3] As such, they must be concerned with resolving the two different types of contradictions which must arise, according to Mao, in any association of leaders and the led. Two functions of the system of people's courts, then, are to aid in the solution of contradictions arising either "between the enemy and the people" or "among the people."[4]

In 1926, writing in an essay entitled "An Analysis of the Social Classes in China," Mao laid the ideological foundations for the correct handling by the legal arm of the state of the two types of contradictions: "In dealing with the enemy we must speak in terms of power politics, and in dealing with the people we must speak in terms of justice."[5] In practice, a distinction has been made between common criminals, those guilty of minor "crimes against public peace and order," and "enemies of the people," including counterrevolutionaries, murderers, rapists, etc.[6] In 1958 there was some debate over the proper disposition of criminal cases by the courts. One view maintained that so long as a crime had been committed and a conviction returned, the case was a contradiction between the enemy and the people, to be dealt with by imposing a "dictatorship" (harsh punishment) over the offender. A second view held that a conviction did not necessarily mean that an antagonistic contradiction was involved—the crime might be of the nature of a contradiction among the people. A third position would have dealt with all crimes sternly, but

---

[2]"The Basic Experience on the Political and Legal Front," *Liaoning Jih Pao,* October 5, 1959 (*SCMP* 2142, p. 14).

[3]"The Giant Achievements on the Political and Legal Front of Anhwei in the Past Ten Years," *Anhwei Jih Pao,* October 1, 1959 (*SCMP* 2141, p. 48).

[4]"Defining the Two Types of Contradictions in Political Work and the Two Methods of Handling Them," Hao Chin-ch'ing and Wu Chien-fan, *Cheng-fa Yen-chiu,* No. 2, May 5, 1963, pp. 25–30 (*Joint Publications Research Service* [*JPRS*] Series 22989, No. 5303, March 1964, pp. 52–63).

[5]"Are All Criminal Cases to be Treated as Contradictions Between the Enemy and Ourselves?," *Cheng-fa Yen-chiu,* No. 3, June 20, 1958 (*Excerpts from China Mainland Magazines* [*ECMM*], No. 142, p. 10).

[6]"Give up Evil in Favor of Good, Be a New Man," *Shenshi Jih Pao,* September 29, 1959 (*SCMP* 2129, p. 24).

without concern for the nature of contradiction.[7] The second view would appear to have won out, judging from the reports of criminal proceedings contained in the Chinese mainland press and elsewhere, and judging also from the importance attached to the recognition of the differences between the two types of contradictions within the ideology.

There is no room within Chinese Communism for the peaceful accommodation of antagonistic contradictions. They must be dealt with through suppression, or, in the case of the courts, through the "exercise of dictatorship." Thus, incorrigible criminals, persistent counter-revolutionaries, and those guilty of other "serious" crimes such as murder, rape, etc., are subject to long prison terms or to the death penalty, while "rascals," thieves, and those adjudged guilty of other minor crimes are subjected to more lenient sentences.

Central to Chinese Communist practice, however, is the notion of "reform" — the view that one who holds ideas of a fundamentally antagonistic nature can, through the process of criticism, self-criticism, and indoctrination, be convinced of his error and gain re-entry into the ranks of the people. Provisions for such "rehabilitation" have been made within the court system under the policy of "combining leniency with punishment."[8] The criminal, after a specified period of detention under the policy of combining leniency with punishment and reform through labor with ideological education, is eligible for pardon under the authority of orders of amnesty granted from time to time by Chairman Mao and implemented through the courts.

An "Order of Amnesty by the Chairman of the People's Republic of China" was granted in 1959. According to the Chinese press, between September 17 and December 8 more than 2,400 counter-revolutionary criminals and more than 9,000 convicted or ordinary criminals were released from detention in the various provinces, municipalities and autonomous regions of China. A number of other prisoners were reported to have had their sentences commuted.[9] In November 1960, and again in December 1961, various kinds of criminals were pardoned under the authority of an amnesty order. It was noted in the press that the Supreme People's Court had pardoned twice as many war criminals in 1961 (68) as had been released in 1959 (33).[10] This fact was hailed

---

[7]*ECMM*, No. 142, p. 10.

[8]"Ten Proposals from the Representative Conference of Advanced Workers in Public Security, Procuratorial, and Judicial Organs of Hopei," *Hopei Jih Pao*, April 16, 1959 (*SCMP* 2037, p. 9).

[9]"First Batch of Counter-Revolutionaries and Criminals Pardoned in Various Provinces, Municipalities, and Autonomous Regions," December 8, 1959 (*SCMP* 2156, p. 1).

[10]"Chinese Supreme People's Court Pardons War Criminals," December 25, 1961 (*SCMP* 2650, p. 1).

as proof of the correctness of the policy of combining leniency with punishment in salvaging criminals. During the periods in which the courts are pardoning criminals, the press is rife with accounts of how "thankful to the Party under the leadership of Chairman Mao" the individual criminals and their families are because of the opportunity to "give up evil for good."

In line further with the theory of contradictions, there is evidence of an ideological difference between the use of punishment *per se* in the case of common criminals and in the case of "enemies of the people" guilty of serious crimes in opposition to the "socialist path." Stern punishment is justified for the latter type of criminal because those who persist in antagonistic behavior must be suppressed and the contradiction that they represent must be eliminated. In such cases legal punishment is seen as an appropriate aspect of the use of "power politics" which Chairman Mao has stated is the proper way in which to handle the enemy. For the common criminal, however, legal punishment is viewed as "only an auxiliary means to persuasion-education, the method to be used by the courts in solving the contradictions among the people."[11] The courts may fall back on coercive force in dealing with non-antagonistic contradictions "under relatively serious circumstances."[12]

The court system's function of suppressing the enemy, which is implicit in the application of the theory of contradictions, is viewed as an element of the class struggle. Indeed, President Shieh Chueh-tsai of the Supreme People's Court has referred to the suppression of the "destructive activities of counter-revolutionary and other serious criminal elements" as "the most acute form of class struggle."[13] Viewed as such, the "suppression" function takes on special significance within the context of the Communist doctrine of the "dictatorship of the proletariat" (recall that the courts are considered to be a weapon of the proletariat), as it imposes a "dictatorship" over the reactionary forces engaging in criminal activity. Here the "basic line of the People's Democratic Dictatorship" and the basic direction of the work of the people's courts— that is, the ideology of Communism and the function of a state organ —come very close together.[14]

In sum, the people's courts in China function to suppress the enemies of the state and to help solve the contradictions among the people. This

[11]*JPRS* Series 22989, No. 5303, March 1964, pp. 52–63.
[12]*Ibid.*
[13]"President Shieh Chueh-tsai's Report on the Work of the Supreme People's Court to the First Conference of the Third Session of the National People's Congress," December 26, 1964 (*JPRS* Series 33705, No. 4587-37, March 1965, pp. 1-15).
[14]*Ibid.*

dual function is a manifestation of the theory of contradictions contained within Maoist ideology.

The maintenance of at least the illusion of an intimate relationship between the party organization and the masses is vital if the party is to adhere to the "mass line" and retain its identity with the proletariat. Predictably, then, the system of people's courts plays a role as one of the elements in a complex communications network.

Shortly after the liberation, an *ad hoc* policy of people's assessors was instituted. The policy was formalized under the Organic Law of the People's Courts, adopted in September 1954. Locally elected assessors were to participate in the disposition of all except the most minor cases coming before the lower people's courts. The effectiveness of the assessors in the actual disposition of cases is highly questionable, since they were untrained in the law, compelled to leave their jobs, and probably had to bear the resentment of the judges. Nevertheless, as Townsend points out, the role of the assessors in giving a significant segment of the population some direct contact with basic level government was probably the most tenable one.[15] There is evidence in the press that the most important of the assessors' functions, as viewed from the higher levels of party leadership, was the propaganda role they played upon their return to the masses. Assessors were in a position to acquaint those around them with the legislation and directives filtering down from high party organs.[16] It has been claimed that such enhancement of the knowledge of the masses about the law and the courts serves to guard against violations of the law.[17]

A second, more obvious, propaganda-education function of the courts is carried out through the practice of public "judgment meetings." A 1956 article in *Liaoning Jih Pao*, reporting the activity of the people's courts within the province for the year, noted that a program of public disposition of cases had been implemented.[18] It was felt that through actual cases the people would become aware of the laws and the efficiency of the courts in distributing retribution, and thus the law-abiding discipline of the masses would be strengthened. The article further claimed that among 71 people's courts in the province, 774 speeches had been made between January and July in 1956 to an audience of more

---

[15]J. R. Townsend, *Political Participation in Communist China* (Berkeley: University of California Press, 1967), p. 142.

[16]"Bring Out the Full Functions of People's Assessors," *Kuang Ming Jih Pao,* January 28, 1956 (*SCMP* 1228, p. 4).

[17]*Ibid.*

[18]"Report on the Work of the Liaoning Higher People's Court for 1956," *Liaoning Jih Pao*, December 21, 1956 (*SCMP* 1484, p. 24).

than 200,000, urging the people to obey the law and to "raise their revolutionary vigilance."

Other examples of the use of "judgment meetings" were reported in December 1956 in an article noting the accomplishments of the Shensi Province People's Court[19] and in another article describing a meeting held before the Hai Hsi *chou* Intermediate People's Court in March 1958.[20] It was claimed that in Shensi Province in early 1955, 91 counter-revolutionaries were sentenced at a public meeting attended by 30,000 people. It was further alleged that 199 criminals were sentenced at another meeting that autumn with 20,000 in attendance. The role of the courts from a historical perspective will be examined later, but it should be noted that 1955 was seen as the high point of the socialist revolution as well as the peak of counter-revolutionary activity. During this period the press put heavy emphasis on the activities of the people's courts in sentencing "U.S.-Chiang agents" and other enemies of the people. In Hai Hsi, sentences were passed on "43 culprits" for sabotaging "the socialist cause and jeopardizing social order." One thousand people were reported to have watched the full process from indictment to execution, in some cases, of the sentences. In a speech before the meeting had begun, a ranking administrative officer of the *chou* addressed the people, calling on them to "raise their revolutionary vigilance, and deal determined blows to counter-revolutionaries and other criminal elements."

An even more direct approach to fostering a closer relationship between the government and the people, so the accounts run, was attempted with reported success in Shantung Province in 1958. Courts throughout the province adopted the method of holding popular debates over the disposition of some civil and criminal cases.[21] An example was cited of a case which had been dormant for six months before a public meeting was called. The case involved one T'ien Wan-ts'ai, whose house burned in September 1957. The fire also claimed 34 pieces of clothing in an adjacent laundry. The managers of the laundry brought suit to recover the damages, and the case was put aside. At the public debate, T'ien Wan-ts'ai was criticized for his "irresponsible attitude," but was not forced to pay damages because he lacked the resources. Moreover, the citizens in attendance directed the textile goods wholesale bureau to give the laundry managers cloth tickets to cover the extent of the damages.

[19]"Report on Work of People's Court in Shensi Province in Past Two Years," *Sian Jih Pao*, December 28, 1956 (*SCMP* 1465, p. 15).

[20]"43 Culprits Given Court Sentences in Hai Hsi," *Tsinghai Jih Pao*, March 14, 1958 (*SCMP* 1775, p. 19).

[21]"People's Courts in Shantung Mobilize Masses to Debate on Handling of Cases," *Jen Min Jih Pao* (*JMJP*), September 3, 1958 (*SCMP* 1858, p. 43).

This case demonstrated, according to the press, that the party policy of "calling upon the wisdom of the masses" to assist in the functions of basic level government was correct.

Some comments are in order regarding the role of the press in assisting the courts to carry out the propaganda-education function. Whenever the press reports on the activities of the people's courts, at whatever level, the article is drawn so as to convince the masses that they are living under a fair and impartial rule of law, and that the courts, under the leadership of Chairman Mao and the party, indeed exist to "protect the people." Particularly noteworthy in this connection are the accounts of amnestied prisoners and their families who heap plaudits upon the party and Chairman Mao for "making a new man" out of a husband, son, or brother.

During the One Hundred Flowers period, of course, there were numerous criticisms of the court system, including one from a disgruntled jurist who accused some of his colleagues of "failing to alight from their sedan chairs," thus attacking the aloofness of some of the cadres within the system. Such abusive language was more than balanced, however, by press concentration on the exposure and purge of "rightist elements" within the court system after the "100 Flowers" had turned to "noxious weeds."

The point is, of course, that what the people are told the courts do, perhaps more than what the courts *do* do, influences the reaction of the masses to party policy. When the people are told repeatedly that the judicial organ of the People's Democratic Dictatorship is guarding their interests, they learn to believe it.

In summary, the public education and propaganda functions of the courts are realized through (1) the direct involvement of the people's assessors, with the most significant educative function occurring after the assessor has performed his official duties; (2) the use of "judgment meetings," probably including both (a) speeches designed to inform and stimulate the audience to a greater level of political consciousness and (b) the actual disposition of cases designed to instill a "law-abiding discipline"; and (3) the rarer, but possibly more effective, public debate method of deciding cases. All are set within a system of public reporting that so colors the activities of the courts as to lead the people along the line of Communist Party policy and socialist construction.

In late 1959, officials of the high provincial people's courts in most provinces submitted reports to the provincial people's congresses, describing the political and legal accomplishments of the preceding ten years in commemoration of the 10th anniversary of the People's Republic of China. These reports provide evidence that another function of the court system in China, a function common to all state organs, operates at a more theoretical level. I refer to the role of aiding the progress of socialist construction in the wake of the people's democratic revolution.

The claim is made that the political and legal organs of the state comprise the superstructure of the socialist economic foundation.[22] As of 1959, the socialist economic foundation was seen as the direction of socialist construction. A pivotal consideration in the advancement of socialist construction is the consolidation of the power of the People's Democratic Dictatorship. Within this context, the functions of the political and legal organs of the state were to aid in the advancement in the direction of the economic foundation of the state—socialist construction.[23] It was noted in the reports of 1959 that the people's courts, by correctly identifying the two types of contradictions and knowing how to handle them, by acting to suppress the enemy and resolve the contradictions among the people, by "raising the revolutionary vigilance" of the masses, by instilling "law-abiding discipline" and respect for the policies and goals of the Chinese Communist Party, were thereby acting to consolidate the power of the People's Democratic Dictatorship and help clear the way for the progress of socialist construction.[24]

To understand fully the role of the people's courts in Communist China, it is vital that the specific functions and whatever ancillary functions might accompany them be seen within the scope of the broad functions, which are the advancement of whatever the policies and goals of the party leadership happen to be at a given time.

Implicit in this is the notion that the functions of the courts, as an element of the political-legal organ of the state, change when the policies of the state (party) change. In 1956, after Liu Shao-chi called for the creation of a totally new legal system in his address to the Eighth National People's Congress, the question "Why change the legal system?" arose. The question was answered by noting that the People's Republic of China had passed through its stormy revolutionary phase and was in transition to the period of socialist construction. The argument went that whereas during the revolution the primary concern had been with smashing the political and legal system of old China, attention in the future would be turned toward the "smooth progress of socialist construction."[25] It was noted that "the mass movement of revolution could

---

[22]*SCMP* 2141, p. 48.

[23]*Ibid.*

[24]"Review of Political and Legal Work in Heilungkiang Province in Recent Ten Years," *Heilungkiang Jih Pao*, September 27, 1959 (*SCMP* 2132, p. 20).

[25]"The Question of a Complete Legal System," *Chung Kuo Ching Nien Pao,* October 20, 1956 (*SCMP* 1413, p. 2).

not depend entirely on law." [26] To establish and maintain a period of consolidation and construction in the wake of a revolutionary period characterized by *ad hoc* laws, it was necessary to create a new, more formal, legal structure. It should be noted that "legal structure" in Communist China comprises more than merely the courts and the procuratorates. Rather, the legal system in the broadest sense includes nearly any political or governmental activity or organization.[27]

The result of all of this is that the courts, as an integral part of the political-legal front, operate in response to the policies and goals of the party in Communist China. In a period of high counter-revolutionary activity, such as occurred in 1955, stress was placed on the punishment of saboteurs, counter-revolutionaries, and other enemies of the people. In more peaceful times the courts turn to the additional tasks of resolving the contradictions among the people, raising revolutionary viligance, etc., in pursuit of socialist construction. Here rests the basis for the assertion, made in 1957, that legal cadres must not only know the law, but be aware of the current political situation as well, in order to understand the direction that the courts are expected to take in the advancement of the party's goals.[28]

In the aftermath of the "blooming and contending" period of Chinese Communist history, concern arose among party functionaries about the "rightist elements" present in the system of people's courts. These elements, the press reports indicate, asserted that the judiciary should operate independently of party leadership in accord with the provisions of the constitution and the Organic Law of the People's Courts, stating that "The people's courts administer justice independently and are subject only to the law." Judges in courts of all levels were charged in this period with treating counter-revolutionaries too leniently, e.g., by imposing prison sentences when death was the proper penalty, as determined by judicial committees of the people's congress on circuit. The rightists maintained that persons charged should be considered "innocent until found otherwise," and that "one should treat others with love." [29]

The party response to such arguments was unequivocal. The claim that the people's courts should operate independently from the party leadership was met by a definitive interpretation of the constitutional provision on which the argument was grounded. The Communists maintained

---

[26]*Ibid.*
[27]"The Legal System, Democracy, and Other Matters," *JMJP*, August 15, 1956 (*SCMP* 1358, p. 2).
[28]"Rightist Thought Hampers Progress of Political and Legal Work," *JMJP*, October 14, 1957 (*SCMP* 1638, p. 7).
[29]"Political and Law Departments Must be Thoroughly Reorganized," *JMJP*, December 20, 1957 (*SCMP* 1687, p. 2).

that the provision only distinguished the nature of the task of the people's court from the tasks of other organs of the state—in other words, that the people's courts "shall administer justice independently" did not mean independently from the party. Furthermore, they maintained that the provision provided that the people's courts, while administering justice, must do so without distorting the law or disregarding it, and that the lower people's courts are not bound by the orders or subject to the interference of superior people's courts. Finally, they argued that this provided only that the *people's courts*, not the judges, should administer justice independently. The party maintained that the structure of the courts, when coupled with the leadership from above, properly implemented the organizational concept of democratic centralism.[30] In response to the allegations that the proper function was to administer justice on the assumption of prior innocence, the party held that as an instrument of the people's democratic dictatorship, the function of the courts was to punish counter-revolutionaries and all others "who resist socialist transformation and sabotage socialist construction."[31]

In summary, during this period of exposure of rightist tendencies within the state organs, it was maintained that two tendencies must be overcome: (1) the tendency to neglect the dictatorship of reactionary elements — that is, a failure to recognize the antagonistic nature of certain contradictions and to deal with them properly; and (2) the tendency to neglect the leadership of the party and assert a claim to independence.[32]

The value of the dialogue that was conducted during 1957 lies in the insights gained into the actual relationship between the court system and party leadership. Lest there be any mistaken impression about the real power of the courts to dispense nonpolitical, independent justice, the dialogue helps to define the situation rather well.

---

[30]"No Perversion of the Character of the People's Court Allowed," *JMJP*, December 24, 1957 (*SCMP* 1686, p. 6).

[31]*Ibid.*

[32]"Overcome the Two Tendencies in Political and Legal Work," *JMJP*, October 14, 1957 (*SCMP* 1638, p. 1).

# EXTERNAL ENVIRONMENT AND THE PROBLEMS OF CAPABILITY AND STABILITY

In a world of constant interaction and interdependence between various societies and peoples, no political system can exist in complete isolation from other political systems. The output of a political system, such as policies and actions, constitutes, in one way or another, the input of other political systems as well as the international political system. Likewise, the output of other political systems and of the international system also become the input of a specific political system.

When the Chinese Communist political system came into being in 1949, it immediately generated serious repercussions in other political systems of the world, especially those in East and Southeast Asia. Through its participation in the Korean War, its split with the Soviet Union, its conflict with India, its development of nuclear weapons and satellites, and its support of insurgent activities in various developing nations, Communist China has made itself an important political and military power, which the leaders of nearly every nation of the world must reckon with in the formation as well as in the execution of their foreign policy.[1]

In an attempt at providing some theoretical basis for the interpretation of the international behavior of the Chinese Communists, students of Chinese affairs have developed several types of models. The first model, which may be called the "historical model," stresses the historical experience and cultural heritage of the Chinese polity in explaining the

---

[1]For the diplomatic relations between Communist China and other nations, see appendixes two and three.

reactions of the Chinese Communists toward the outside world. Students adopting this model look at the emergence of Communist China as the newest development of a long series of dynastic changes in China and try to relate the behavior of the Chinese Communists in international affairs to that of the previous dynasties and regimes. By examining the traditional patterns of Chinese response to other nations and peoples, they hope to draw some generalizations or to discover some parallels between the past and present.

The second model is built around the concept of national interest. Individuals endorsing the "national-interest model" assume that the orientation and behavior of the Chinese Communists are not different from those of the other nations of the world; that is, they are motivated by the pursuit and the safeguarding of their national interest. Thus the Chinese Communists' participation in the Korean War has been interpreted as a measure preventing a possible invasion of the Manchurian territories by the United States; the conflict with India as a means of securing control over Tibet; and the split with the Soviet Union as an unavoidable development from the age-old territorial disputes between China and Russia.

A third and probably the most frequently applied model is to interpret the international behavior of the Chinese Communists by their political ideology. Looking at the Chinese Communists as a group of revolutionaries devoted to the realization of a communist world, students of the "ideological model" find explanations of the policies and actions of Communist China in the writings of Marx, Engels, Lenin, and more recently, Mao Tse-tung. The aspect of Mao's version of communism which has received most attention among the ideological analyses of the international behavior of the Chinese Communists has been his theory of the "people's war of national liberation." The wars in Vietnam, Laos, and Cambodia and the guerrilla warfare in African and Latin American nations have provided ample opportunities for those applying the "ideological model" to test the validity of Mao's theory of protracted wars.

Whereas all the above models offer some plausible answers to the behavior of the Chinese Communists in international affairs, none of them has yielded a completely satisfactory interpretation. It seems that variables affecting the decision-making process of the leaders in Peking can probably be found in all these models. In other words, the international behavior of Communist China should probably be interpreted and predicted through a combination of concepts and perceptions of all three models—the ideological, the national-interest, and the historical.

One of the mistakes most frequently committed by some analysts of China's affairs is to interpret the international behavior of Communist China by its attitude toward the outside world as reflected by the official

Chinese Communist propaganda and the numerous demonstrations occurring in Communist China every year. One of the consequences of doing so is to equate the level of overt hostility of the Chinese with their readiness to take immediate action. The fact is that although the Chinese Communists have never given up their proclaimed goal of spreading their brand of communism to other parts of the world, their actions have so far fallen short of their expressed intentions. Other than their participation in the Korean War and the war with India, the Communist Chinese have pretty much kept their armed forces within their own territories. An examination of the external environment and the capacity of the Chinese Communist political system yields some obvious explanations for this exercise of military restraint by the leaders in Peking.

Let us first take a look at the immediate environment of Communist China. Except for the North Koreans in the northeast, the North Vietnamese in the south, and the Pakistanis on the southwest borders of mainland China, the Chinese Communists are surrounded by hostile neighbors. Foremost of the hostile neighbors are the Nationalists on Taiwan and the Russians in Siberia and Central Asia. Backed by a defense treaty with the United States and with one of the largest and best trained armed forces in Asia, the Nationalists pose a serious threat to the security of Communist China. Fearing a counterattack from the Nationalists, the Chinese Communists have deployed 53 of the 118 divisions of the People's Liberation Army along the coast provinces facing Taiwan as the first line of defense, and on the axis of the Canton-Wuhan railway as a second line of protection.[2]

As for the precautions against possible Russian invasion, four divisions are deployed in Sinkiang; another four are stationed in Inner Mongolia, and still another twenty-eight divisions are located in Manchuria and the Peking metropolitan regions. In addition to the huge number of troops committed to defense against Nationalist China and the Soviet Union, conflicts with India in the early 1960s have also necessitated that the Communist Chinese station four divisions in Tibet.[3] As a result of all these arrangements for self-defense, the amount of military force which the Communist Chinese can use to support their ambitious policy goals beyond their borders is rather limited.

In addition to Nationalist China, the Soviet Union, and India, the military presence of the United States in East and Southeast Asia is also a factor of grave concern for the Chinese Communist leaders. The fact that the U. S. Armed Forces have had nuclear warheads has served as one of the important deterrents against any large-scale aggression from Chinese Communists toward neighboring nations.

---

[2]According to data in *The Military Balance, 1969–1970* (London: The Institute for Strategic Studies, 1969), pp. 39–40.

[3]*Ibid.*

Other than the restrictions imposed upon the international behavior of Communist China by its hostile neighbors, the low level of economic development and military capability is another major factor preventing the Communist Chinese from taking more adventurous actions against other noncommunist nations. Despite its huge size and population, the gross national product of Communist China is only about seven percent of that of the United States and sixteen percent of that of the Soviet Union.[4] The GNP of Communist China is significantly smaller than those of France, Japan, and Italy.[5] The industrial outputs of Communist China are even more insignificant when compared with the above-mentioned Western nations. With this kind of GNP and economic structure, the capacity of Communist China to meet the demands of a large-scale war fought with modern military weapons is seriously restricted.

Certain Western observers have considered Communist China's huge population as an important asset to its military might. This observation, however, reveals only one side of the coin. Although the huge population on the Chinese mainland provides the Communist Chinese with a large reservoir of manpower, it also poses a tremendous demand for food, clothing, and other consumer goods. The huge population of mainland China and the low level of development make it impossible for the Communist Chinese to convert a larger portion of its GNP into war efforts.

One may point to the importance of the role of political indoctrination in Communist China in generating an intense feeling of loyalty and devotion to the goal of the communist system as a substitute and compensation for the lack of adequate technological support — a thesis which Mao Tse-tung has repeatedly belabored in his theory of a "People's War." It must be pointed out, however, that commitment to the system cannot always compensate for the lack of training and the inferiority of equipment. The disastrous defeat suffered by the air force of Communist China at the hands of the Nationalists in 1958 during the Taiwan Strait crisis was a clear example. Moreover, among experts in China studies, serious doubts have been raised about the invariability of devotion to the goal of the political system among the members of Communist China's armed forces. These doubts were raised by the contents of some secret military papers which were smuggled out of Communist China during the Great Leap Forward period.

In sum, the capability of Communist China to wage wars, especially wars outside its boundaries, seems to be rather limited.[6] So far as direct

---

[4]Computed from data in Alexander Eckstein, *Communist China's Economic Growth and Foreign Trade* (New York: McGraw-Hill, 1966), p. 249.
[5]*Ibid.*
[6]For the military capability of Communist China, see appendix five.

military action is concerned, the present threat of Communist China will be restricted to its immediate neighbors, such as Taiwan, Hong Kong, India, and Indo-China. Even in these areas, the Chinese Communists have thus far contented themselves with occasional threats, political maneuvers, and the support of insurgent activities rather than direct military intervention.

However, the picture may change quickly after a further cutback of U. S. military presence in Asia and more advanced development of middle-range and long-range nuclear missiles by Communist China.[7] If this is allowed to happen, the balance of power in Asia and even of the world would be affected, with the result that the security of all the noncommunist nations in the neighborhood of Communist China will be seriously threatened. This is the primary reason that leaders of some Asian nations, such as Singapore, Indonesia, and Japan, who were originally rather critical of the American military presence in Asia, have become increasingly concerned with the reduction of U. S. military might in this area.

More recently, Nixon's acceptance of an invitation to visit Peking by May 1972 has further complicated the power relationship in East and Southeast East Asia. Despite repeated U.S. assurance that her seeking of a new relationship with Peking would not be at the expense of old friends, nations surrounding Mainland China have been deeply disturbed.[8] Political leaders at Taipei, Tokyo, and Seoul are not at all convinced that a thaw between Washington and Peking will not turn out to be against their interests after they have allied with the former against the latter as a common enemy for so many years.

Meanwhile, developments within Mainland China continued to puzzle China watchers. Along with the cancellation of the October 1 rally and parade, the prolonged absence of Mao and Lin in public gatherings and a resurgence of refugees escaping from the Mainland to Hong Kong have generated much speculation as to the stability of the Chinese Communist regime. We should exercise some caution, therefore, in asserting that the seemingly conciliatory international gesture of the Chinese Communists is a reflection of the consolidation and maturity of the communist rule on Mainland China today.

---

[7]In a recent defense report to Congress, U.S. Defense Secretary Melvin R. Laird said that Communist China might already have deployed a limited number of medium range nuclear missiles aimed at a number of the great cities of Asia such as Tokyo, Manila, and Singapore. See UPI news release from Washington, D.C., March 9, 1971.

[8]See Hugh Sidney, "Asia Feels 'the Nixon Shock,'" *Life,* September 17, 1971, p. 4.

# XI
# Relations with Other Political Systems

## 26. Mao's Revolutionary Strategy and Peking's International Behavior

*Tang Tsou and Morton H. Halperin*

Despite its political implications, the recent explosion of an atomic device has not greatly altered China's present military position *vis-à-vis* the West. By all standards except population and size, Communist China is still not a first-rate power. But she has nevertheless proceeded to engage the two superpowers simultaneously in a contest from her position of military and economic weakness. What is equally undeniable is that the success of Peking's foreign policy in the struggle with both superpowers, though limited and perhaps only temporary, has considerably exceeded anticipations based on her military and economic strengths. It is the contention of this paper that an explanation of these two striking facts must be sought in the nature of Mao's revolutionary strategy in the Chinese internal political-military struggle and his belief in the applicability of this strategy to the international arena and to other countries, particularly those in the underdeveloped areas. Mao dared to challenge the militarily and economically strong United States because his revolutionary experience proved to his own satisfaction that his integrated and comprehensive strategy would enable him presently to score political gains from a position of military inferiority, and ultimately enable him to achieve highly ambitious objectives with initially meager means in a protracted struggle. This conviction also explains in part his willingness to challenge the Soviet policy of "peaceful coexistence" even at the cost of losing Soviet economic aid and at the risk of an open split in the international communist movement.

Reprinted from Tang Tsou and Morton H. Halperin, "Mao Tse-tung's Revolutionary Strategy and Peking's International Behavior," *American Political Science Review* 51 (March 1965): 80–83, by permission of the authors and The American Political Science Association.

The key to the understanding of Communist China's foreign policy lies, accordingly, in Mao's revolutionary strategy and its projection abroad. This paper begins with a brief examination of the various factors facilitating the Chinese Communists' projection of their revolutionary strategy abroad and with the enumeration of some items of evidence of this relationship between international behavior and revolutionary strategy. It then seeks to define the nature of Mao's revolutionary strategy by an end-means analysis and to show how the various elements of that strategy form a unified and intelligible structure. This reconstruction of Mao's revolutionary strategy on the basis of his writings and his actions is carried out with the hope that it might serve as an initial step in, and a provisional guide for, intensive rescarch on the Chinese Communist revolution. It might also help in future attempts to interpret Peking's foreign policy. This interpretation, if correct, will in turn raise certain theoretical questions about the foreign policy of revolutionary regimes and perhaps even about the international behavior of nations in general.

## 1. Revolutionary Strategy and International Behavior

All violent political revolutions start with a group of men who are initially weak in numbers and strength. But in the modern world, no other group of successful revolutionaries was confronted with greater odds, waged a more protracted armed struggle, and survived greater defeats than Mao Tse-tung and his comrades. In his tortuous road to ultimate victory, Mao followed a pattern of action and adopted a set of principles which, on many occasions, helped him to achieve political gain from a position of military weakness and which, over a period of time, enabled him to bridge the enormous gap between his highly ambitious goal and his early military political impotence.

This pattern of action and set of principles followed in time and in logical sequence Lenin's substitution of the conquest of political power for socialism as the end-in-view of the Communist movement and his use of military analogy for the analysis of the revolutionary situation and for the development of a theory of political strategy. This military analogy obliterated the analytic difference between political and military forms of the class struggle and called attention to the relevance of military analysis as a method of formulating programs to deal with political conflict.[1] But unlike Lenin, Mao was engaged in an intermittent civil war

---

[1]Andrew C. Janos, "The Communist Theory of the State and Revolution," in *Communism and Revolution*, ed. Cyril E. Black and Thomas P. Thornton (Princeton, N.J., Princeton University Press, 1964), pp. 32–6.

over a period of more than twenty years before the seizure of power. Thus, Mao went beyond Lenin in his emphasis on the importance of military power, laid down precepts for coordinating its use with political policies, developed the doctrine of protracted war, pursued a military strategy of surrounding the cities from the countryside, and exemplified in his strategies and tactics a combination of prudence with revolutionary enthusiasm. While Mao's doctrines and precepts are by no means profound, they were perfectly adapted to the objective conditions confronting him[2] and were in the best tradition of *Realpolitik* and the age-old military-political wisdom of China. They helped the Chinese Communists to win the most bitter and most protracted internal war in the twentieth century.

Furthermore, the Communists' theory of revolution, as Janos pointed out, is the theory of world revolution. To them the analytic categories relevant to domestic and international politics are identical.[3] From their viewpoint their revolution to overthrow the Kuomintang government was, among other things, a fight against the lackeys of Western imperialism, particularly American imperialism in the last few years of the struggle; and they have seen their attacks on the West, particularly on the United States, after their capture of power as merely a continuation of their previous struggle. The precarious balance of power in the Far East and Southeast Asia within a world-wide context of American military superiority must have seemed to them analogous to the siutation during the larger part of the civil war, when over-all Nationalist superiority was juxtaposed to local Communist strength in particular areas. Moreover, these long-standing principles which brought about ultimate success have a sacrosanct quality. They are immune from challenge by most of the now largely discredited traditional rules. They are not checked by any principles of the newly established social order, which they themselves helped to bring into existence. Their projection into the international arena is also helped by the relatively short but highly traumatic experience of China as a member of the family of nations. This experience militates against wholehearted acceptance of the system of national states and the rules governing nations in that system. The moral unanimity among the leaders who claim to know the absolute and universal truth reinforces the proverbial Chinese ethnocentrism and strengthens the tendency to view the foreign scene in the Chinese image and to judge alien things by Chinese standards. Thus, it is not surprising that many of Mao's principles and precepts of political-military actions have underlain Peking's policies, strategies, and tactics in the international arena and in each specific encounter with other nations.

---

[2]Thomas P. Thornton, "The Foundations of Communist Revolutionary Doctrine," *ibid.*, p. 66.

[3]Janos, *loc. cit.*, p. 40.

As early as August, 1946, Mao set down four theses on the international situation which, with some modifications, continued to guide his foreign policy. First, on all-out war between the United States and the Soviet Union in the immediate future was improbable. Second, the struggle in the immediate future between the socialist and imperialist camps would take place in "the vast zone" separating the United States and the Soviet Union which included "many capitalist, colonial and semi-colonial countries in Europe, Asia and Africa." This thesis was the origin of the controversial concept of the intermediate zone. Third, the atomic bomb is a "paper tiger" because "the outcome of war is decided by the people, not by one or two new types of weapons." Fourth, all reactionaries, including "the United States reactionaries" are paper tigers. "In appearance, the reactionaries are terrifying, but in reality they are not so powerful from the long-term point of view."[4] These four theses in what amounted to Mao's first independent assessment of the global situation confronting the international Communist movement[5] reflected his unified strategy in the Chinese revolution, particularly in the period between 1937 and 1945, which will be described later. This assessment of the global situation constituted Mao's justification of his acceptance in July, 1946 of all-out war with Chiang from the viewpoint of the international Communist movement as a whole and placed his revolutionary war within the context of the struggle between two camps.

Soon after the establishment of their regime, the Chinese Communists began to apply Mao's political-military strategy outside of China. In November, 1949, Liu Shao-ch'i, already the second ranking leader in the Chinese Communist Party, declared that the peoples of various colonial and semicolonial countries should follow the "path taken by the Chinese people in defeating imperialism and its lackeys." He specifically identified this path as consisting of Mao's three magic weapons: the united front, armed struggle, and party building.[6] In defeating General MacArthur's drive to the Yalu, the Chinese Communist forces successfully carried out Mao's strategy of retreating deep into one's base area,

---

[4]Mao Tse-tung, "Talk with the American Correspondent Anna Louise Strong," *Selected Works*, IV (Peking, Foreign Languages Press, 1963), pp. 97–101. Hereafter cited as Mao, *Selected Works*, IV (Peking), in order to distinguish it from the fourth volume of Mao's selected works published by Lawrence and Wishart which covers the period from 1941 to Aug. 9, 1945.

[5]Prior to that time, Mao's pronouncements on international questions generally followed the twists and turns of the Soviet line. See Tang Tsou, *America's Failure in China* (Chicago, University of Chicago Press, 1963), pp. 209–16.

[6]"Opening Speech by Liu Shao-ch'i at the Trade Union Congress of Asian and Australian Countries," *For a Lasting Peace, For a People's Democracy*, December 30, 1949, p. 14; H. Arthur Steiner, *The International Position of Communist China* (New York, Institute of Pacific Relations, 1958), pp. 8–15; A. M. Halpern, "The Foreign Policy Uses of the Chinese Revolutionary Model," *The China Quarterly* (July-Sept., 1961), pp. 1–16.

waiting for the enemy to commit mistakes and fighting a battle of quick decision as a prelude to a general counteroffensive.[7] In Indo-China, the Viet Minh applied to its own revolutionary war those Chinese methods and precepts suitable to Vietnamese conditions, perfected some new tactics of its own, and ultimately defeated the modern, fully trained, and excellently equipped French Expeditionary Corps.[8] In the Quemoy crisis of 1958, a timely retreat, an early offer to negotiate, and a unilateral declaration of ceasefire kept the military risks and political cost to a minimum and achieved some political gains.[9] In the military clash over the border with India in 1962, China inflicted a stinging defeat on Indian forces, and then declared a unilateral cease-fire, thereby exhibiting Mao's strategy of limited victory and restraint. The strategy and tactics of the Pathet Lao both in the coalition government and on the battlefield remind one of Mao's principles and precepts. Whether or not the Chinese Communists have given aid and advice to the rebels in the Congo, they certainly believe that their revolutionary experience holds important lessons for the Congolese.[10] Several documents issued in the dispute between the Communist Party of the Soviet Union and the Communist Party of China show that Mao is pursuing the global long-term strategy against the West of encircling the developed areas from the underdeveloped areas, which is a projection abroad of his strategy of surrounding the cities from the countryside in the Chinese civil war.[11]

The Chinese Communist leaders are highly self-conscious of their revolutionary mission. The late Marshal Lo Jung-huan told the cadres in the Political Academy in October, 1960: "At present, revisionism is

---

[7]For Mao's doctrine on this point, see Mao Tse-tung, "Problems of China's Revolutionary War," *Selected Works*, I (London, Lawrence and Wishart, 1955), pp. 210–53. On the actions of the Chinese Communist forces in Korea, see Roy E. Appleman, *South to the Naktong, North to the Yalu* (Washington, G.P.O., 1961), pp. 667–776; S. L. A. Marshall, *The River and the Gauntlet* (New York, 1953). For an interpretation, see Allen Whiting, *China Crosses the Yalu* (New York, 1960), pp. 130–50.

[8]George Modelski, "The Viet Minh Complex," in Black, ed., *op. cit.*, pp. 207–209; George K. Tanham, *Communist Revolutionary Warfare, the Viet Minh in Indo-China* (New York, 1961), pp. 23–8.

[9]Robert W. Barnett, "Quemoy: the Use and Consequences of Nuclear Deterrence" (mimeographed) (Cambridge, Center for International Affairs, Harvard University, 1960); Alice Langley Hsieh, *Communist China's Strategy in the Nuclear Era* (Englewood Cliffs, N. J., 1962), pp. 119–30; Donald Zagoria, *The Sino-Soviet Conflict, 1956–1961* (Princeton, Princeton University Press, 1962), pp. 213–215; John R. Thomas, "Soviet Behavior in the Quemoy Crisis of 1958," *Orbis* (Spring, 1962), pp. 38–9; Tang Tsou, *The Embroilment of Quemoy: Mao, Chiang, and Dulles* (Salt Lake City, University of Utah Press, 1959).

[10]Editorial, *Jen-min jih-pao*, June 24, 1964, p. 1.

[11]Tang Tsou, "Mao Tse-tung and Peaceful Coexistence," *Orbis* (Spring, 1964), pp. 36–51. For an interpretation of the struggle for power in China, see Tang Tsou, *America's Failure in China*, pp. 48–56, 127–141, 186–92, 300–311, 401–40.

spreading. The world revolution relies on the thought of Mao Tse-tung
. . . [The thought of Mao Tse-tung] belongs not only to China but also
has its international implications."[12] Another recent official analysis of
the international situation contains the following prognosis: "Peaceful
coexistence [with many countries other than the United States] or coexistence through stalemate [with the United States] is a transitional
form. So is pacifist neutralism. The life of imperialism will necessarily
come to an end; socialism will one day be realized throughout the
world."[13] Marshal Yeh Chien-ying declared:

> No other nation in the world has more experience [in fiighting a war]
> than we . . . . The nations which have not yet been liberated also want to
> overthrow imperialism and feudalism . . . and to wage armed struggle.
> They very much need our experience. Therefore, we should sum up our
> experience to hand it down to posterity and to present it to our friends.[14]

As this experience is most relevant to the struggle of the "national
liberation movement" in the underdeveloped areas, Peking accords a
high priority in her foreign policy to the support of these movements.
A military journal explained it this way:

> Toward national liberation movements in colonial and semi-colonial
> countries, there are two different attitudes. One makes the improvement
> of relations with the West a primary concern and does not support or
> gives small amount of support to the national liberation movements. The
> other makes support for national liberation movements a primary con-
> cern. It permits some proper dealings with the Western countries but
> considers this a secondary question. Our country adopts the latter atti-
> tude, firmly supporting the national liberation movements and opposing
> colonialism and imperialism. We may have dealings with Western coun-
> tries but do not bargain away our support for national liberation move-
> ments.[15]

So Peking's policy is actively to cultivate close relationships with countries in Asia, Africa, and Latin America, but not the Western countries,
particularly the United States. In 1961, Africa was regarded as the center of the anti-colonial struggle. "When the time is ripe, a revolutionary

---

[12]*Kung-tso t'ung-hsün* [*Work Correspondence*] no. 8 (Feb. 2, 1961), pp. 16, 17.
The *Work Correspondence* is a secret journal, designed for reading by the cadres
of the People's Liberation Army at the regimental level and above. Hereafter
cited as *Work Correspondence.*

[13]*Ibid.,* no. 17 (April 25, 1961), p. 20.

[14]*Ibid.,* no. 12 (March 10, 1961), p. 4.

[15]*Ibid.,* no. 17 (April 25, 1961), p. 22.

upsurge will engulf the African continent."[16] Even the Taiwan question is viewed in the broad context of the world-wide struggle against the United States in which "one incautious move will cause the loss of the game."[17] If Communist China, "a newly emerging socialist country," should yield to the United States and allow imperialist forces to hold her territory, Taiwan, "her international prestige will drop ten thousand feet."[18] By refusing to compromise on the issue of Taiwan and by keeping Sino-American relations in a stalemate, "we can keep the anti-imperialist banner, freely support the national liberation struggle in the colonial and semi-colonial countries, preserve our ability to attract political support, and stimulate our morale.[19] Marshal Chen Yi, the Foreign Minister, summed up Peking's approach to international affairs neatly when he affirmed in September, 1964, that Mao's strategical and tactical thinking, together with the policies and general lines of the Party center, were the principal guides for Communist China's analysis of international problems in the past fifteen years.[20] It is clear that Mao's revolutionary strategy in the struggle in China is a recurrent element in Peking's international behavior. . . .

---

[16]*Ibid.*, p. 23.
[17]*Ibid.*, p. 20.
[18]*Ibid.*, p. 25.
[19]*Ibid.*, p. 24.
[20]Chen Yi, "Commemorating the Thirtieth Anniversary of the Publication of the *Shih-chieh chih-shih*," *Shih-chieh chih-shih*, Sept. 10, 1964, p. 1.

## 27. The Objectives and Instrumentalities of Foreign Policy

*Harold C. Hinton*

Many of the puzzling peculiarities of Communist Chinese external behavior arise out of frustration at the considerable gap that exists between aims and desires, on the one hand, and available means and attainable results, on the other.

### Security

The first essential for any individual or collective entity is to survive, and therefore to achieve a tolerable degree of security from hostile external influences.

It might be argued that the CPR has no serious external security problem, and that this very fact permits the CPR to behave as it does in international affairs. Reasonable though this argument may appear, however, this does not seem to be the way in which the Communist Chinese leaders view their situation. Even apart from the tendency to fear aggression from the "imperialist camp," the United States in particular, on ideological grounds, it must be remembered that China is a divided country. The Communist regimes in all four of the divided countries — the others being Korea, Vietnam, and Germany — find the United States allied in one way or another with the non-Communist regimes and consider it as not only an obstacle to reunification but a threat to survival. In addition, East Germany, as well as the other East European countries and the Soviet Union itself, has a deep fear of West Germany's

Reprinted from Harold C. Hinton, *Communist China in World Politics* (Boston: Houghton Mifflin Company, 1966), pp. 107–21, by permission of the author and publisher.

military potential, even if unsupported by the United States. On a somewhat reduced scale, the Communist Chinese also fear Japan's military potential, particularly if it should be developed with American support. In all four Communist regimes in the divided countries, we find internal and external policies that are harsh and militant even by Communist standards. More than the others, the Chinese considers itself as overwhelmingly superior to its domestic opponent, and therefore as prevented from achieving territorial unification almost exclusively by the United States.

In terms of logical possibilities, the greatest threat to Chinese security would of course be a strategic attack with thermonuclear weapons. For the present and the indefinite future, such an attack could come only from the United States or the Soviet Union. Either possibility is remote, but it cannot safely be regarded by the CPC as zero, except probably for the case of a totally unprovoked attack by either of the two nuclear superpowers.

It is clear that Soviet bombers and missiles in the Far East are capable of hitting Chinese territory, and it has also become clear that a Sino-Soviet war cannot be dismissed as out of the question. The political deterrents to the use of nuclear weapons against a nonnuclear power being what they are, however, the most probable utility to the Soviet Union of its own nuclear weapons in the event of hostilities with the CPR would be to deter the latter from escalating the conflict beyond a fairly low level. Against the Soviet strategic military threat the CPR has no sure defense, since it obviously cannot rely on American protection, but it can clearly count under most circumstances on its own caution and on Soviet self-restraint.

An American attack presents a different problem. Although somewhat less unlikely, whether as an act of aggression or of retaliation, than a Soviet attack, an American decision to attack the CPR would have to reckon with the Sino-Soviet alliance. The alliance has been so eroded by tensions, however, that Soviet strategic protection of the CPR is at least open to doubt.[1] Indeed, it has apparently seemed doubtful to the CPC since about 1951, and since that time it has held its external be-

---

[1]Cf. "... the Peking leaders from time to time still utter highsounding hypocritical phrases that 'in the stern hour of trial' the CPR and the Soviet Union will always be together. But every sober-minded person will tell them: How do you intend to insure this when a filthy anti-Soviet propaganda campaign is going in China, when the most monstrous accusations are formulated against the Soviet Union from morning to night? Is not this dangerous political game, directed toward undermining the very foundations of Sino-Soviet friendship, too risky?" (Yu. Zhukov, "The Chinese Wall," *Pravda*, June 21, 1964).

havior down to a level at which complications were unlikely to arise that could not be managed if necessary by the CPR itself, unaided except by American belief in the validity of the Sino-Soviet alliance.[2] It seems likely, although it cannot be proven, that Soviet strategic protection or retaliation is available to the CPR only in three extremely improbable eventualities: an unprovoked American strategic attack on the CPR, a more localized air attack against targets near the Soviet border, or the landing of substantial American combat forces in Chinese territory anywhere near the Soviet border. In other cases, including an American strategic attack that was clearly provoked — and Chinese provocation of that order is another extremely improbable contingency — it is unlikely that the Soviet Union would do more than send military equipment and "volunteers" to help the CPR, as it hinted in 1962.[3] If the CPR were to disintegrate from internal weakness, accompanied perhaps by a Nationalist invasion, it is doubtful whether the Soviet Union would feel either able or obligated to restore the situation; it might confine itself to reestablishing spheres of influence in Manchuria and Sinkiang.

A more realistically possible threat to the security of the CPR than the ones so far mentioned is a Chinese Nationalist attack, timed probably to coincide with an internal crisis on the mainland, and supported by the United States, perhaps with tactical nuclear weapons. Against such a threat, which seems to have worried the CPC a great deal at certain times, Soviet protection is of doubtful availability, and the CPC must rely on maintaining domestic control, keeping its guard up, exercising due caution, and hoping for a continuation of real or assumed American irresolution.

In addition to strategic attack and local attack or border probes, the CPR is also nervous of the possibility that, as so often during the heyday of "imperialism," a strong foreign power might entrench itself on China's border and proceed to project a preponderant influence into the nearest region of China Proper. It should be borne in mind that China's frontier regions, apart from Manchuria, are in general sparsely populated by

---

[2]Cf. "In fighting imperialist aggression and defending its security, every socialist country has to rely in the first place on its own defense capability, and then — and only then — on assistance from fraternal countries and the people of the world" (Chinese government statement, August 15, 1963, New China News Agency dispatch, same date).

[3]Cf. M. Domogatskikh and V. Karymov, "An Instructive Lesson," *Pravda*, July 7, 1962. There were other articles to the same effect in the Soviet press at this time, which was the twenty-fifth anniversary of the Japanese attack on China. The articles recalled that the Soviet Union has sent arms and "volunteers" to China (Nationalist, not Communist, as the articles failed to mention) at that time.

restless minorities, backward, and poorly connected with the rest of the country. Manchuria, the traditional "cockpit of Asia" and the CPR's major heavy industrial region, is also considered vulnerable even though it is much more developed. By far the most important reason why the CPR intervened in the Korean War was the determination to prevent a powerful American army from entrenching itself on the Yalu River, with possibly serious effects on the CPR's hold on Manchuria. Similarly, the CPR was worried in 1962 by what seemed to it the overly close approach of the Indian Army to the border of restless Tibet, and the CPR would also take a very dim view of any intrusions by American ground forces into such regions bordering directly on the CPR as North Vietnam or Laos.

Another logically possible threat that worries the CPR is one from India to the security of China's Himalayan frontier and to Tibet, which is in a state of unrest. Such a threat from India would be serious, in all probability, only if it coincided by accident or design with a threat from some other quarter.

There is no doubt that the time of maximum danger to the CPR's security, to date, was the period from its intervention in the Korean War (October, 1950) to the termination of the war (July, 1953). A second period of considerable danger, or at least assumed danger, occurred in the spring of 1962. The domestic situation was bad. The Chinese Nationalists appeared to be girding for an attempt at invasion, perhaps with American support. The United States sent troops into Thailand. The Indian Army was moving into border areas claimed by the CPR. The Soviet Union was beginning to create trouble along the Sino-Soviet frontier and to collude with rebellious minorities in Sinkiang. How the CPR continued to maintain its external security during these periods, as well as others less critical, is discussed elsewhere.

There is no doubt that, in view of the unreliability and uncontrollability of Soviet protection, and in any case the undesirablility of being unduly dependent on it, the CPC believes that the best way to deter or combat threats to its security would be to acquire its own nuclear weapons and delivery systems, with a regional even if not an intercontinental range. Since this situation is some years in the future, the CPC generally behaves in a way that Mao has described as strategically bold but tactically cautious.

It should not necessarily be assumed that after the CPR acquires nuclear weapons its behavior, toward Taiwan or elsewhere, will become markedly bolder. Even the Soviet Union, after all, has succeeded since the Second World War in maintaining no more than an essentially minimum deterrent posture with respect to the United States.[4] This posture has proven to be an insufficient basis on which to make major strategic gains at the expense of the United States on those few occasions when an attempt has been made to do so, notably in Cuba in 1962. The addition of a nuclear Communist China to this situation need not make a decisive difference, since the United States clearly can more than match both the Communist powers combined in nuclear weapons for the indefinite future. Thus the gain to the CPR of a nuclear capability, and hence its main reason apart from prestige for seeking it, is likely to be more defensive than offensive.

It would clearly be a gain for the CPR's security, as well as for its influence in Asia, if American sea and air bases could be removed from the Far East and the Western Pacific. The CPC considers Japan to be the main such base; this is a reasonable view, especially when one realizes that when the CPC refers to Japan in this context it means to include Okinawa, with its huge complex of American bases.[5] Since the CPR is obviously in no position to remove these bases by force, it must content itself with essentially political maneuvers, such as efforts to inflame local public feeling against the bases.

The CPR denies that the United States has any right to maintain bases or forces in the Far East, but it cannot openly do the same for the Soviet Union. Nevertheless, the remote Soviet threat as well as the more immediate American threat to Chinese security would be substantially reduced if the Far East and the West Pacific became an atom-free zone, or better still a "peace zone" in which only indigenous states were allowed to have nuclear weapons. This consideration helps to explain the support, although a rather equivocal support, that the CPR has given to the concept of an atom-freeze zone since 1958.[6]

## Power

Although security is essential even if one lacks power, it is obvious that power is very helpful in the search for security.

An obvious element of future Chinese power, nuclear weapons, has already been mentioned. In addition, the CPR has maintained since 1949

---

[4]John R. Thomas, "The Role of Missile Defense in Soviet Strategy," *Military Review*, vol. xliv, no. 5 (May, 1964), pp. 46–58.

[5]Okinawa is the military keystone of American containment of the CPR.

[6]A Chinese government statement of July 31, 1963, demanded a "nuclear weapon-free zone of the Asian and Pacific region, including the United States, the Soviet Union, China, and Japan" (New China News Agency dispatch, same date).

the most powerful armed forces of any strictly Asian state, with the possible, partial, and recent exception of Indonesia.[7] From 1950 to 1960, the Communist Chinese armed forces were progressively modernized with Soviet aid, although the Soviet Union was careful to withhold from its Chinese ally, as it usually has from its other allies, any major, operational offensive weapons. After about 1955, the emphasis in the Soviet military aid program to the CPR shifted, as the Chinese desired, from weapons deliveries to aid in the construction of Chinese defense industries.[8] The entire program soon ran afoul of growing Sino-Soviet tensions, however, and was terminated during 1960. Since that time the absence of Soviet aid and spare parts deliveries and the continued weakness of the Chinese economy seem to have resulted in a fairly rapid obsolescence of Communist China's conventional military capabilities, except perhaps for the ground forces. The effort to acquire a nuclear capability undoubtedly continues.

Clearly the extent of the CPR's national power is affected by the degree to which it maintains internal political control and is believed abroad to maintain it. In this respect the CPR has had repeated, almost continuous, difficulties in the non-Chinese border areas, especially Tibet and Sinkiang, but much less trouble in China Proper. In the latter the most serious situation to date probably occurred in the spring of 1962, when the CPC was concerned not only about the external threats already mentioned but also apparently by the possibility, however slight, that party officials in relatively well-fed areas might withhold "surplus" grain from the famine areas.[9] This crisis, if such it was, passed without a dis-

---

[7]On Communist China's armed forces see, in addition to works already cited, Lt. Col. Robert B. Rigg, *Red China's Fighting Hordes*, Harrisburg, Pa.: The Military Service Publishing Company, 1951; Hanson W. Baldwin, "China as a Military Power," *Foreign Affairs*, vol. 30, no. 1 (October, 1951), pp. 51–62; P. G. Gittins, "The Red Dragon of China: A Brief Review of Communist China as a Military Power," *Australian Army Journal*, no. 132 (May, 1960), pp. 5–18; Allan S. Nanes, "Communist China's Armed Forces," *Current Scene* (Hong Kong), vol. i, no. 16 (October 25, 1961); Harold C. Hinton, "Communist China's Military Posture," *Current History*, vol. 43, no. 253 (September, 1962), pp. 149–155. On the political aspect see Harold C. Hinton in Harry L. Coles ed., *Total War and Cold War*, Ohio State University Press, 1962, pp. 266–292; Ralph L. Powell, *Politico-Military Relationships in Communist China*, Department of State: External Research Staff, 1963; J. Chester Cheng, "Problems of Chinese Communist Leadership as Seen in the Secret Military Papers," *Asian Survey*, vol. iv, no. 6 (June, 1964), pp. 861–872.

[8]Cf. Raymond L. Garthoff, "Sino-Soviet Military Relations," *The Annals of the American Academy of Political and Social Science*, vol. 349 (September, 1963), pp. 81–93. The CPR has stated, and the Soviet Union has not denied, that the Soviet Union agreed on October 15, 1957, to give the CPR at least token aid in the production of nuclear weapons but terminated the program on June 20, 1959, in the interest of Soviet-American relations (Chinese government statement of August 15, 1963, *loc. cit.*).

[9]Cf. *The Washington Post and Times Herald*, June 27, 1962.

aster, although not without lingering aftereffects. On the whole, especially in view of the size of the country and its population, the poor state of communications and technology in general, and the record of previous Chinese regimes, the CPC has been remarkably successful in acquiring and maintaining internal control. The main reason for this is the fact that it is a "homegrown" totalitarian regime, one that learned how to control and manipulate populations before coming to power over the country as a whole, rather than one that came to power suddenly as the result of some accident or of installation in power by the Soviet Union. The CPC's success in acquiring and maintaining internal control has unquestionably increased the CPR's national power to a significant degree.

Power in the modern world of course requires an economic base, communications and heavy industry in particular. Measured against the standards of the modern West (including the Soviet Union) or those of its own ambitions, the CPR is still seriously deficient in these respects. On the other hand, by comparison with pre-Communist China or with any other Asian country except Japan, its performance has been fairly impressive. The highway and to a lesser extent the rail systems are being steadily extended into the border regions and toward the frontiers, for economic reasons as well as for political and military ones, whether offensive or defensive.[10] Industrial growth, which was rapid although precarious down to 1960, was reversed by the crisis of that year, which was accentuated by the withdrawal of most Soviet aid, and it has not yet recovered from this disaster."[11]

---

[10]Cf. Denis Warner, "China's New Roads: Where Do They Lead?" *The Reporter*, September 26, 1963; *Christian Science Monitor*, February 8, 1964. There are road, rail, and air connections with all of the CPR's Communist neighbors (the Soviet Union, North Korea, Outer Mongolia, and North Vietnam). The connection with the Soviet Union (opened at the beginning of 1956) is broad gauge from the point where it begins in Inner Mongolia; this is the only case where the Soviet broad gauge has been projected outside the Soviet frontier, and was almost certainly due to the insistence of the Outer Mongols on this form of protection from Chinese infiltration. There are thus change of gauge points in Inner Mongolia, at the Soviet frontier in Manchuria, and at the North Vietnamese frontier (the North Vietnamese railways are narrow gauge). An additional Sino-Soviet rail link via Sinkiang is supposedly under construction, but it is far behind schedule. There are also external highway connections with India and Laos; connections are being constructed with Nepal, and perhaps with Afghanistan and Pakistan (cf. A. R. Field, "Strategic Development in Sinkiang," *Foreign Affairs*, vol. 39, no. 2 [January, 1961], pp. 312–318). A rail connection with Burma is projected (see *China: Provisional Atlas of Communist Administrative Units*, Washington: Central Intelligence Agency, 1959, Plate 3). There are air connections with Hong Kong, Burma, Cambodia, Pakistan, Ceylon, and Indonesia.

[11]Cf. "Plain Living and Hard Struggle: An Economic Assessment," *Current Scene* (Hong Kong), vol. ii, no. 28 (February 15, 1964).

The CPR's power, in the sense of the ability to enforce its will against objections or opposition, has almost certainly declined somewhat since 1960. Furthermore, it has never had the ability to project its power across salt water—to Japan, Taiwan (since 1950), or Indonesia, in particular. Nevertheless, and although the CPR still lives in the shadow of the vastly superior power of the United States and the Soviet Union, it remains the strongest strictly indigenous regime on the mainland of Asia, far ahead of its closest rivals, North and South Korea, North Vietnam, India, and Pakistan.

An important element of power is of course the extent to which the possessor is generally believed to be willing to use it. In this respect the CPC has been remarkably successful, even if one ignores its occasional remarks implying a bullish attitude toward a Third World War.[12] By means of repeated, carefully calculated resort to force — notably in Korea, over the offshore islands in 1954-55 and 1958, and along the Sino-Indian frontier in 1962 — the CPR has succeeded among other things in keeping alive a fairly general and somewhat exaggerated idea of its willingness to take its power out of reserve and commit it to action. This willingness, real and still more assumed, must be accounted a major component of the CPR's national power.

## Unification

There can be no doubt that territorial unification ranks high on the CPR's list of external objectives. There have been occasional intimations in official statements[13] and textbooks designed for internal circulation[14] that this objective might apply to the whole of the former Manchu empire, or even to the traditional tributary system at its maximum extent. Such statements appear, however, to be designed mainly for political effect, internal or external.

In reality the CPR's territorial claims are much more modest, nor is there any convincing evidence, apart from bombastic propaganda, that it is willing to take any serious risks in order to realize them. This objec-

---

[12]"Of course, whether or not the imperialists will unleash a war is not determined by us; we are, after all, not their chief-of-staff. . . . On the debris of imperialism, the victorious people would create very swiftly a civilization thousands of times higher than the capitalist system and a truly beautiful future for themselves" (*Long Live Leninism, op. cit.*, pp. 21–22).

[13]E.g., "A Comment on the Statement of the CPUSA," *People's Daily*, March 8, 1963.

[14]E.g., the one discussed in Jacques Jacquet-Francillon, "The Borders of China: Mao's Bold Challenge to Khrushchev," *The New Republic*, April 20, 1963, pp. 18–22.

tive, like the CPR's other objectives, is evidently expected to require a great deal of time for its fulfillment. Specifically, the CPR claims as of right, in addition to China Proper, Manchuria, Inner Mongolia, Sinkiang, Tibet, Taiwan (since the Cairo Declaration of 1943, as we have seen), and the Paracel and Spratly Islands in the South China Sea.[15] The first three of these regions were in Chinese Communist hands by the time of the end of the civil war on the mainland in 1949. Tibet was "liberated," by force, in 1950-51. Taiwan remains to be "liberated." The CPR does not appear as yet to have made any serious effort to establish control of the Paracel or Spratly Islands.

It is well known that the outer frontiers of these areas are not clear or generally agreed on in all cases. In fact, the CPR has or has had a border dispute of some sort with every country, Communist or non-Communist, on which it borders, with the apparent exception of North Vietnam.[16] In every case but two — India and the Soviet Union — these disputes have been settled through a compromise of one kind or another, sometimes to be sure after a crisis in which the CPR has employed considerable pressure. In none of these settlements does the CPR seem to have insisted on its maximum demands, and the latter must therefore be regarded mainly as bargaining devices. The Indian and Soviet disputes are still unresolved, but there is reason to think that the CPR would also settle these, under conditions it considered appropriate, on the basis of something less than its maximum demands.

Territorial unification is a major objective, then, but it is not a fetish, still less a be-all and end-all to be pursued at suicidal risk.

Something further needs to be said about Taiwan, in view of its peculiar position and importance as the seat of a rival government claiming jurisdiction over the whole of China.

Both the Communist and the Nationalist regimes regard Taiwan as Chinese territory, a view that is not necessarily shared by the indigenous Taiwanese. To the Communists, the "liberation" of Taiwan would constitute the biggest single step remaining to be taken toward the unification of China. It would confer on them unquestioned sole custody of the symbols of China's sovereignty and status, including general diplomatic recognition (except perhaps for that of the United States) and China's permanent seat on the United Nations Security Council, assuming that these had not already been acquired.

---

[15]On the CPR's claim to the Paracels and Spratlys, which obviously have potential naval importance, see Maps 33, 34, and 36 in *Atlas of the Northern Frontier of India*, New Delhi: Ministry of External Affairs, 1960.

[16]Cf. Guy Searls, "Communist China's Border Policy: Dragon Throne Imperialism?" *Current Scene* (Hong Kong), vol. ii, no. 12 (April 15, 1963).

On the other hand, the Chinese Communists clearly realize that a military "liberation" of Taiwan was rendered impossible by the extension of American protection to the island on June 27, 1950. For the present, this would cease to be true only if the Soviet Union were to lend active military support to a Communist attack on Taiwan.

It is equally clear that the Soviet Union has been most reluctant to become involved in the CPR's quest for the "liberation" of Taiwan and that the CPR has been determined to involve it. The CPR has consistently maintained since June, 1950, that the United States was committing aggression against the CPR by occupying, or in other words protecting, Taiwan, the clear implication being that the Soviet Union was obligated under the Sino-Soviet alliance to take whatever action might be necessary to eliminate the American presence from Taiwan and turn the island over to the control of the CPR.[17]

The situation might also change when and if the CPR acquires its own nuclear capability, but this is still some time in the future. The situation would certainly change if the United States withdrew its protection from Taiwan, but there is no sign of this despite the Communists' best efforts to erode the American military position in the Far East and the Western Pacific through political action.

Realistically speaking, there is no way at present for the Communists to "liberate" Taiwan except by means of a political arrangement with the Nationalists that would have as one of its main features a repudiation by the latter of American protection. The Communists have always been careful to keep open the possibility of such an accommodation. They have never demanded unconditional surrender — a meaningless term in the contemporary world, in any case — by the Nationalists. Rather, they have implicitly held up as a model, not the harsh terms proposed to Nationalist Acting President Li Tsung-jen in April, 1949, but the relatively moderate terms granted to General Fu Tso-i when he surrendered Peking in January, 1949. To date, the Nationalists on Taiwan are not known to have shown serious interest in Communist efforts to persuade

---

[17]Khrushchev once stated a willingness to give military support to the CPR in connection with the "liberation" of Taiwan in an interview with Governor Averell Harriman (see *Life*, July 13, 1959, p. 36), but this was almost certainly bluster for political effect. The main purpose was probably to deter the Chinese Nationalists and the United States from threatening the mainland when the Communists were involved in Tibet and on the Himalayan frontier. A secondary purpose was probably to support Marshal P'eng Te-huai, one of whose arguments in opposition to the policies being pursued by the CPC evidently was that Soviet protection could be relied on, provided the CPC did not antagonize the Soviet Union unduly, and that the CPR therefore did not have to strain its economy further in order to produce nuclear weapons.

them to accept a subordinate if allegedly secure place in the Communist system.[18]

The problem cannot be disposed of quite so simply, however. A curious dialogue takes place across the Taiwan Strait. Each side asserts and demonstrates, from time to time, its independence of its powerful ally and patron. The Communists' demonstration of independence has been wholly convincing since 1960, when they accepted the termination of Soviet economic and military aid rather than abandon their political pressures on the Russians. The Nationalists, as the weaker party, have not yet felt it feasible to give a comparable demonstration of independence. Their closest approach to one so far has been the Black Friday riots of May 24, 1957, in Taipei, which stemmed from anger at the refusal of the United States to pay to its Chinese ally the tribute it had paid to its Japanese former enemy, that of signing a status-of-forces agreement. It is a curious fact that most of the prominent individuals[19] who have gotten into serious political difficulties on either side of the Taiwan Strait have had closer-than-average connections with the foreign patron of each one's respective regime. Each party to the dialogue across the Taiwan Strait accuses the other of subservience to its patron — the Nationalists, to be sure, have modified their charges in the light of the Sino-Soviet dispute — not so much because it believes its own charges as to discredit the other and to evoke further demonstrations of independence from it.

Certainly many obstacles stand in the way of a political accommodation between Peking and Taipei, among them the convincing demonstration by the Communists in 1957, when they silenced and persecuted their "rightist" critics, that there is no secure place in the Communist system for the dissenter. On the other hand at least two obstacles, Mao Tse-tung and Chiang Kai-shek, will presumably not be operative much longer. Furthermore, the Nationalists must face the fact that the Communist regime shows no signs of internal collapse, that their own example and appeals have failed to capture the imagination of the mainland Chinese as an alternative to the Communist regime, and that they have little prospect of conquering the mainland by force.

---

[18]Cf. Lewis Gilbert, "Peking and Taipei," *The China Quarterly,* no. 15 (July-September, 1963), pp. 56–64. Chiang Kai-shek's memoirs, *Soviet Russia in China: A Summing-Up at Seventy,* New York: Farrar, Straus and Cudahy, 1957, represent among other things a rejection of Communist overtures, which were especially obvious in 1956, on the ground that the historical record shows that the good faith of neither the Chinese Communists nor the Soviet Union can be trusted.

[19]On the mainland: Kao Kang and P'eng Te-huai. On Taiwan: K. C. Wu, Sun Li-jen, and Lei Chen.

It appears, then, that neither side is in a position to impose its will on the other, and that the only workable alternative to the present state of suppressed war would be one that could be agreed to, tacitly at least, by both sides. One obvious possibility would be a "two Chinas situation," which would probably require among other things a Nationalist evacuation of the offshore islands, but neither side has so far given any persuasive evidence of willingness to accept such a solution. A more likely outcome, in the long run at any rate, and barring the collapse of either regime, would be reunification through some sort of accommodation.[20] If this materializes, it would be a striking vindication of General de Gaulle's belief that national identity is a more durable force than ideology.

### Influence

The CPR's objectives under the heading of influence may be discussed fairly briefly, since for the most part they have already been treated in the previous chapter.

The first is hegemony of some sort on at least the mainland of eastern Asia. As a first major step toward this goal, the CPR would probably like its land frontiers to be ringed, insofar as possible, with buffers, which need not be satellites. As usual, it has given no evidence of an intent to force this process at the cost of incurring serious risks. The process is going ahead, nonetheless, fairly slowly and as inconspicuously as possible. The CPC would also like the greatest influence attainable, again short of unacceptable risks or political costs, on the other Asian Communist Parties.

The CPC clearly aspires to a leading role, of some kind that it may not claim to be able to foresee, in the "socialist camp" and the international Communist movement. This has been conceded by most students of Sino-Soviet relations since 1963, when the CPC began seriously trying to set up an "international" of its own in rivalry with the parties that tend to support the Soviet Union. The CPC evidently expects, or at least claims to expect, that the Soviet-led coalition will disintegrate from its internal ideological errors and political weaknesses, so that the victory will fall to the CPC almost by default.

The CPC certainly aspires to provide a "model," or example, and if possible a degree of leadership, for the whole of the underdeveloped areas

---

[20]Speaking purely hypothetically, such an accommodation might involve political, economic, and military autonomy for Taiwan, perhaps under the guise of a federation with the mainland, at least nominal participation by its leaders in a unified coalition government, and a unified representation in foreign countries and the United Nations. There is an obvious likelihood that such an arrangement would prove to be no more than temporary.

(the "oppressed nations"). This implies the ultimate exclusion of Soviet as well as American influence from these regions.

The CPC apparently hopes to make China, by about the end of the twentieth century, a superpower comparable to the United States and the Soviet Union. This implies such things as the creation of a first-class industrial economy, although not necessarily of high living standards; a nuclear and space capability; United Nations representation and control of China's seat on the Security Council; and the right to an active role in the settlement of all major international issues.

The complete satisfaction of this desire for superpower status being unlikely, the CPR might decide that the best way to compensate for its limitations without entirely giving up its ambitions is to try to play the role of balancing power between the United States and the Soviet Union. Such a role, if it were actually attempted, would presumably require a lessening of Sino-American tension sufficient to allow the CPR to assume a posture of approximate equi-distance between the United States and the Soviet Union.

Finally, the CPC claims to anticipate and probably does anticipate the eventual worldwide triumph of "communism," however that term may be defined as a concept and organized as a system at the time of its hypothetical triumph.[21] The Chinese view of this subject, at least as expressed in 1958, differs significantly from older Marxist-Leninist formulations and from Khrushchev's recent interpretation of them by implying that a country need not be economically and culturally advanced in order to be said to have attained "communism," but may be "poor and blank," like China.[22]

## Policy Instrumentalities

The instrumentalities that the CPC has employed to date in pursuit of its external objectives occupy a rather wide spectrum with respect to the

---

[21]"However many twists and turns may await us on our forward journey, humanity will eventually reach its bright destiny — communism. There is no force that can stop it." ("More on the Historical Experience Concerning the Dictatorship of the Proletariat," *People's Daily*, December 29, 1956).

[22]The term "poor and blank" was first used by Mao Tse-tung ("Introducing a Cooperative," *Red Flag,* June 1, 1958) to describe the economic and cultural state of the Chinese people in 1958, when the CPC was claiming that "the attainment of communism in China is no longer a remote future event" (Decision of the Eighth Central Committee of the CPC, August 29, 1958 [New China News Agency dispatch, September 10, 1958]). Shortly afterward the time table was stretched out with the admission that "the socialist system will have to continue [in China] for a very long time" before the attainment of "communism" (resolution of the Sixth Plenary Session of the Eighth Central Committee of the CPC, December 10, 1958 [New China News Agency dispatch, December 18, 1958]), but the CPC has not admitted publicly that "communism" presupposes economic and cultural abundance.

degree of violence involved and can be categorized conveniently as violent, semiviolent and nonviolent.

Apart from intervention in Korea, which taught the CPC a painful lesson on the disadvantages of challenging American military power too forcefully, the Chinese employment of overt violence in external relations has consisted mainly of military actions in or near the Taiwan Strait (in 1954-55 and in 1958) and armed incursions into disputed border areas (India from 1950 on, Burma intermittently from about 1952 to 1961) or demilitarized zones (Nepal briefly in 1960). In each of these cases, the CPC was trying to eliminate or head off something that it regarded as a threat to its security, and in each case it employed subterfuges of one kind or another to confuse the opposition and minimize international ill will and the chances of unwanted escalation. Similar subterfuges can be expected in similar situations in the future. The CPC, for example, can deny that the incident occurred at all, assert that only Chinese "volunteers" and not regular troops were involved, claim that the incident took place on Chinese soil or in Chinese territorial waters, charge the other side with being the intruder or aggressor, or some combination of these.

In keeping with its typically communist desire to have the fruits of war without war, the CPC makes use of a number of ambiguous or borderline instrumentalities that may be called semiviolent. These include border disputes (mainly with India and the Soviet Union), subversion, threats of military action either by regular forces or "volunteers," military demonstrations (such as the heavy redeployment near the Taiwan Strait in the spring of 1962), and military aid and advice to communist allies (North Korea and North Vietnam) and foreign left-wing movements.

At the lower end of the spectrum of violence, the CPC of course makes use of a number of nonviolent instrumentalities, some of which are potentially applicable to any other country, others only to nearby Asian countries. Among the former category, the first is diplomacy; a good example of Chinese communist diplomacy is the effort in recent years to bolster China's political position in East Asia by establishing or strengthening friendly relations with countries that are either weak neutrals incapable of rivaling China for regional leadership (such as Burma and Cambodia), the enemies of China's enemies (such as Pakistan), or the objects of Soviet wooing (such as Indonesia). A second nonviolent instrumentality is Communist China's extensive program of "people's diplomacy" (cultural relations and propaganda) directed at groups, mainly but not exclusively leftist, whose opinions Peking wishes to influence or confirm.[23]

---

[23]For an excellent study of this see Herbert Passin, *China's Cultural Diplomacy*, New York: Praeger, 1963.

Thirdly, China attempts both to pressure and attract other countries, especially underdeveloped ones, through trade and aid, roughly one quarter of its activity in both fields being directed outside the Communist bloc down to about 1960. Since then, the emphasis has shifted to non-bloc countries. Since 1956, when it made its first aid commitment to a non-Communist country (Cambodia), the CPR has extended (down to mid-1964) credits of various kinds, often interest-free, totaling about half a billion dollars to Afro-Asian countries, as well as to Cuba. The recipients have generally drawn only a part of their credits, which of course can be used only for Chinese goods and services, and have often found these goods and services to be of inferior quality. The non-Communist Afro-Asian recipients of Chinese credits have been Burma, Laos, Cambodia, Indonesia, Ceylon, Nepal, Yemen, Algeria, Ghana, Guinea, Mali, Nigeria, Somalia, Zanzibar, Kenya, and Tanganyika. The Chinese aid program is far smaller than the American or Soviet program, with both of which it attempts to compete, and is conducted along different lines; it does not, for example, include aid in the field of heavy industry. While in Mali in January, 1964, Chou En-lai laid down "eight principles" governing the CPR's economic aid program: mutuality of benefit, "no strings," low interest or none, a goal of self-sufficiency rather than dependence, emphasis on light industry ("projects which require less investment while yielding quicker results"), valuations at international market prices (which are high when charged for generally inferior Chinese equipment), training of local personnel to operate the enterprises constructed with Chinese aid, and living standards for Chinese personnel no higher than those of corresponding personnel of the country in question.[24] To the extent that they are practiced, these principles are obviously not to be wholly condemned. On the other hand, the principles are designed to secure a maximum political return, including the fostering of the public sector in the economy of the aided country, from a modest economic outlay. In the case of industrial countries, including Japan, the CPR seeks trade (especially since 1960) not only for economic reasons but also to split the country in question from the United States, to increase the chances of diplomatic recognition, and to promote other such political objectives.

Fourthly, the CPC maintains liaison with most if not all foreign Communist Parties, by both covert and overt means. It tries to influence them in directions favorable to itself, or (since 1963) to split them and form pro-Chinese splinter parties. The CPC maintains covert party branches among overseas communities. Chou En-lai promised that they would be

---

[24]Chou's report on his trip to the Standing Committee of the National People's Congress (excerpts released by New China News Agency, April 25, 1964).

dissolved when he was in Southeast Asia at the end of 1956, but this does not appear to have been done.

In its dealings with nearby countries the CPC employs such special techniques as organized covert migration (to Burma), the harboring and exploitation of political exiles, the maintenance of "autonomous" minority areas near the border as a possible means of influencing kindred minorities across the frontier, and manipulation of various overseas Chinese communities within limits dictated by Chinese desire for good relations with indigenous governments and ethnic groups.

## The Relationship Between Objectives and Instrumentalities

In general, the CPC has tended to reserve overt violence for the defense of its security — as interpreted of course by itself — and has attempted to enhance its influence mainly through semiviolent and nonviolent means. On the other hand, whereas the CPC has shown itself to be willing to use violence in defense of its security, including violence of a preemptive or forestalling kind, it has always (except in the spring of 1951, in Korea) shown great caution in its employment of even defensive violence. The main, but not sole, restraint has been the fear of American retaliation. The same consideration has dictated even greater restraint on any unambiguously offensive use of force. Notwithstanding all the talk about Chinese bellicosity, one looks in vain for instances in recent years of Chinese military aggression, in the sense of attacks against neighboring countries or foreign forces that were not motivated, largely at least, by fear for Chinese security.[25] Offensive action is restrained not only by fear of American retaliation or other military consequences, but also by a realization that acts of aggression would adversely affect the prospects for achieving the CPR's long-term political objectives.

The CPC is apparently convinced, however, that the United States will not retaliate for anything less than an overt Chinese resort to violence. A combination of traditional Chinese arrogance and Communist doctrinarism, therefore, has produced a recurrent Chinese tendency to overestimate the extent to which the CPC's influence objectives, especially in the underdeveloped areas and Asia in particular, could be safely and advantageously promoted by a very energetic employment of ambiguous

---

[25]As will be shown later, these considerations apply essentially even to the CPC's policy toward Taiwan, the offshore islands, and the Sino-Indian frontier.

semiviolent techniques, as well as by nonviolent ones. When such an overestimate has occurred the result has generally been a setback.

On the whole, however, the record to date of Communist Chinese foreign policy in promoting the CPR's objectives, both national and revolutionary, has been fairly impressive.

# 28. The Sino-Soviet Conflict

*Harry Gelman*

In 1958 the Sino-Soviet struggle took on broader dimensions as new conflicts of national interest arose on several fronts. The three most important matters at issue were the military relationship between the two powers, the related question of Soviet conduct during the Taiwan Straits crisis, and Peking's radical new economic programs and the claims associated with them.

On the military issue, Peking's statement of last September, though not saying so explicitly, seeks to convey the impression that the Soviet Union, in the October 1957 defense assistance agreement, gave a firm commitment to help China attain an atomic weapons capability. This appears doubtful, however, particularly in view of the campaign launched by the (CCP)* in the summer of 1958 against Chinese military leaders charged with overemphasizing the importance of both atomic weapons and outside aid. The same Chinese statement further alleges that sometime (unspecified) in 1958 "the (CPSU)† put forward unreasonable demands designed to bring China under Soviet military control," and that these demands were "firmly rejected by the Chinese government." It is conceivable that the demands were linked by the Soviets to the question of atomic assistance to China, and that they were advanced by Khrushchev when he visited Peking in early August, at which time Soviet military assistance was reportedly discussed in the context of China's requirements for the impending Taiwan Straits venture.[1] In any event, the absence of any Soviet agreement to supply nuclear weapons to China

---

*Chinese Communist Party [Ed.]
†Communist Party of the Soviet Union [Ed.]
[1] See Raymond L. Garthoff, "Sino-Soviet Military Relations," *The Annals of the American Academy of Political and Social Science*, Vol. 349, Sept. 1963, p. 89.

Reprinted from Harry Gelman, "The Conflict: A Survey," *Problems of Communism* 13 (March-April 1964): 6–15, by permission of the journal.

was suggested shortly after Khrushchev's departure by an article in the CCP organ *Hung Ch'i* (August 16) prominently reasserting Mao's dictum that "the atomic bomb is a paper tiger."

If the Chinese were embittered by the evident Soviet reluctance to satisfy them in regard to the sharing of the USSR's nuclear might, that bitterness was further intensified by the hesitant backing China received from Moscow in the ensuing crisis in the Taiwan Straits. Confronted by American nuclear power, Peking apparently sought to obtain an early public commitment by the Soviet Union that would enable it to face down the United States and thus would make feasible Chinese military action to "liberate" the offshore islands. The Chinese government statement of September 1, 1963, charged that the Soviet Union had perfidiously withheld such a commitment until Moscow was sure that it could be given without risk — in other words, until it was too late to be of any assistance to the original Chinese goal.

The slow and deliberate course taken by Moscow in the Taiwan Straits crisis does, indeed, suggest that the Soviet leadership feared the possibility of being dragged into a nuclear conflict with the United States as a result of precipitate Chinese action taken in pursuit of interests not shared by the USSR. This interpretation would appear to derive support from the Chinese claim made last September (denied, unconvincingly, by Moscow) that Khrushchev, in his talks with Mao at Peking in October 1959, sought to remove Taiwan as "an incendiary factor in the international situation" by hinting that Peking ought to accept a "two-Chinas" solution.[2] At the same time, it seems likely that the Chinese Communist challenge to the United States in 1958 further reinforced Soviet reluctance to assist China in acquiring nuclear weapons.

A third new area of friction developed in connection with the radical turn in Chinese domestic policy during 1958, manifested in the launching of the communes program and the economic "Great Leap Forward." Chinese spokesmen exuberantly claimed that the communes, with their system of partial distribution according to need, contained "shoots" of communism, signifying that the final attainment of communism in China was no longer far off; that they represented an unprecedented achievement as well as a useful model for other countries. In these claims and the policies of the "Great Leap" as a whole, the CPSU saw a new and dangerous Chinese challenge to its leadership of the Communist world. As a Soviet comment stated in 1963, "things were depicted as though only they (the Chinese) were really engaged in communist construction,

---

[2]CPR government statement, Sept. 1, 1963. The same claim is made in *Jen-min Jih-pao* (People's Daily) and monthly *Hung Ch'i* (Red Flag), Sept. 6, 1963. (Hereafter cited as JMJP-HC joint editorial.)

leaving other countries behind," and the Chinese leaders tried to present their "totally unsound and harmful policy . . . as an objective law" and "as a prescription or recipe for other countries."[3]

According to one of the official Soviet statements issued last fall, Khrushchev personally protested these "innovations" in his talks with Mao in early August 1958.[4] For some time afterwards, however, the Soviet leaders continued to ignore the communes publicly, although their attitude was reflected in Soviet press comments criticizing the lack of material incentives characteristic of the commune system and emphasizing that the attainment of full communism required a level of production which was much closer to realization in the Soviet Union than in Communist China. Later, as the Sino-Soviet rift widened and as deteriorating economic conditions in China forced abandonment of the communes in all but name, Khrushchev repeatedly gibed at the Chinese with thinly-veiled references to Communist leaders who had become "estranged from the masses," disobedient "children" who had "burned their fingers," and to the fatuity of those who desired "pantless communism."

## Widening of the Breach

The year 1959 saw the deterioration of Sino-Soviet relations proceed at a markedly faster pace as dissensions over Soviet moves toward an easing of tensions with the United States and over Communist China's involvement in a border conflict with India still further widened the gap between the two Communist powers.

Moscow's intent to pursue more vigorously the "peaceful coexistence" strategy towards the West was signalled in January by Soviet Deputy Premier Anastas Mikoyan's exploratory visit to the United States, and was underlined later the same month by the ruling handed down by the 21st CPSU Congress that war between the capitalist and socialist states not only was not inevitable but might even be permanently avoided while capitalism still remained. Khrushchev's visit to the United States and his meeting with President Eisenhower followed in the fall, while Soviet propaganda during and after the visit took the softest line towards the West that it had displayed since World War II — or has taken since.

All this was naturally anathema to Peking, which considered the United States the principal obstacle to its ambitions in Asia and viewed the exertion of maximum Communist revolutionary pressure against the

---

[3]*Ekonomicheskaia gazeta* (Moscow), Sept. 28, 1963.
[4]Soviet government statement, Sept. 20, 1963.

US in all parts of world as essential to China's national interests.[5] Accordingly, Chinese Communist propaganda in the fall of 1959, while paying lip service to the principle of "peaceful coexistence," became more and more shrill in its warnings against perfidious American intentions to use negotiations and a relaxation of international tensions as a "smokescreen" to lull the peoples of the world into a false sense of security and thus facilitate US "aggression" against the national liberation movements in underdeveloped areas.

Other Soviet actions during the year aggravated old Chinese grievances or created new ones. Speaking publicly on July 18 at Poznan, Poland, Khrushchev — without referring to China by name — recalled the failure of the Soviet experiment with communes during the period of "war communism" and remarked that those who had wished to set them up "had a poor understanding of what communism is and how it is to be built."[6] Inasmuch as the CCP Central Committee was at that very moment meeting at Lushan to re-examine the communes program, Khrushchev's comment was regarded by the Chinese as a gratuitous attempt to intervene in Chinese internal affairs. There is also reason to suspect that the Soviets tried to intervene more directly by encouraging Chinese Communist Defense Minister Marshal P'eng Te-huai, during his visit to Eastern Europe in the spring of 1959, to oppose Maoist policies. It is believed that P'eng did challenge Mao's program at the Lushan meeting, and that this was responsible for his dismissal shortly thereafter, in September 1959.[7]

Meanwhile, Moscow continued to turn a deaf ear to Chinese appeals for assistance in the acquisition of nuclear weapons. According to the CCP, the Soviet Union in June 1959 finally rejected Peking's request that China be provided with "a sample of an atomic bomb" and thereby "unilaterally tore up" the 1957 Sino-Soviet agreement concerning "new technology for national defense."

On top of all this, the refusal of the Soviet leadership to stand beside Communist China in her border conflict with non-socialist, bourgeois India was viewed in Peking as an outright betrayal of the obligations of "proletarian internationalism." Following the outbreak of hostilities in

---

[5]In 1963, statements by Chilean and Costa Rican Communists alleged that CCP leaders had once told Latin American Communists visiting China that international tension was useful for the furtherance of revolutionary struggles. According to the Chileans, this statement was made early in 1959.

[6]Khrushchev's speech was simultaneously reported in *Pravda* (Moscow), *Trybuna Ludu* (Warsaw), and by the Soviet radio on July 21, after an unusual three-day delay.

[7]See David A. Charles, "The Dismissal of Marshal P'eng Te-huai," *The China Quarterly* (London), October-December 1961.

late August, the Soviet government on September 9 issued a public statement taking a neutral stand towards the conflict—this, the Chinese have since claimed, in spite of frantic last-minute efforts by themselves to dissuade Moscow from such action.[8] Not only did Moscow refuse to heed this appeal, but it later accused the Chinese of having deliberately timed their military action against India so as to embarrass Khrushchev on the eve of his trip to the United States.[9]

Khrushchev's visit to Peking at the end of September, on the heels of his US trip, apparently did more to accentuate than to assuage the grievances on both sides. Regarding the Sino-Indian conflict, Peking claims that the Chinese leaders "personally gave Comrade Khrushchev an explanation of the true situation" but that he "did not wish to know the true situation"; on the other hand, according to Moscow, the Soviet leader took the occasion to warn the Chinese that their course of action was "fraught with negative consequences not only for Sino-Indian relations, but also for the entire international situation." It was also at this time, as noted earlier, that Khrushchev allegedly suggested to Mao the desirability of accepting a two-Chinas solution of the Taiwan problem. Moreover, the Soviet leader further outraged his hosts by warning them, in a public address on September 30, against "testing by force the stability of the capitalist system."

## The War of Words

As the Chinese saw it, Khrushchev's actions during 1959 had set virtually a new record of error and betrayal: he had rebuffed them on the question of atomic military assistance, sought to interfere in Chinese internal affairs, hobnobbed with the leaders of "US imperialism," betrayed them in the Sino-Indian conflict, intimated that they should renounce their claim to Taiwan, and upbraided them publicly for their domestic and foreign policies. It is little wonder, therefore, that in April 1960 the CCP unleashed a massive propaganda assault aimed at the policies — and, implicitly, the authority—of the Soviet Communist Party.

Central to the many indirect but unmistakable indictments of Khrushchev's policies published in the leading organs of the CCP was the contention that the peaceful coexistence line as applied by the Soviet party was eroding the militancy of revolutionaries throughout the world. Now,

---

[8]Editorial article in *Jen-min Jih-pao*, Nov. 1, 1963.

[9]Article just cited claims that the Soviet charge was made in February 1960 in a private "verbal notification" to the CCP Central Committee. The Soviet government statement of Sept. 20, 1963, and other Soviet statements last year repeated the charge publicly.

for the first time, the Chinese systematically elaborated their objections to the arguments that the advent of nuclear weapons necessitated a change in Communist revolutionary strategy, that local wars involving the great powers would inevitably lead to world war, and that revolutionary armed struggles should not be so vigorously cultivated as to create a danger of nuclear conflict. While it was possible that world war could be averted, the Chinese contended, local anti-colonial or anti-imperialist wars of liberation could not, and the Communist policy should be to encourage and support such struggles without being inhibited by exaggerated fears of nuclear destruction or by a misguided desire to facilitate negotiations with the capitalist West.

Soon after the CCP campaign began, the position of the CPSU to defend its policies against the Chinese criticisms was measurably weakened as a result of the Soviet decision to publicly exploit the U-2 incident of May 1 whereas previous overflights had been ignored.[10] This decision set in motion a train of events which apparently led the Soviet leadership to conclude, after anguished debate,[11] that it would be politically harmful, in view of the Chinese offensive, to allow the scheduled summit conference with the Western leaders at Paris to take place. There is now substantive evidence that the CPSU leaders had the Chinese very much on their minds during the 16-day interval between the U-2 incident and Khrushchev's dynamiting of the summit parley. The Soviet party disclosed in April last year that on May 12, 1960 — four days before the Paris meeting was to open — Mao had been urgently invited to come to Moscow, but had refused.[12] Instead, on May 14, he made his first officially reported statement in two years, in which he professed to support a summit meeting but simultaneously gloated over the U-2 incident and implicitly taunted Khrushchev for having displayed "illusions" about imperialism.[13]

In early June the Chinese party carried its fight against the CPSU a step farther by utilizing the opportunity afforded by a meeting of the General Council of the World Federation of Trade Unions in Peking to conduct a campaign against the Soviet line among both Communist and

---

[10]See Allen Dulles, *The Craft of Intelligence*, Harper & Row, New York, 1963, p. 196, on Soviet reaction to previous overflights.

[11]*Ibid.* Mr. Dulles writes that "there is evidence of long debate in the Presidium during the first two weeks of May" over "whether to push the U-2 issue under the rug or use it to destroy the conference."

[12]CPSU Central Committee letter to the CCP, March 30, 1963, published in *Pravda,* April 3, 1963.

[13]Mao's statement was made in an interview with Latin American and Japanese visitors at Wuhan on May 14 and released the same day by NCNA. It was also quoted two days later in a *Jen-min Jih-pao* editorial.

non-Communist delegates. Shortly thereafter, according to the Chinese, the CPSU privately proposed to the CCP that steps be taken to organize a conference of all Communist parties for the purpose of ironing out differences, suggesting that a preparatory exchange of views take place in closed multi-party meetings during the impending Rumanian party congress.

When the CCP representatives went to Bucharest in the latter part of June, they were shocked to find themselves the target of a "surprise assault" allegedly concocted by the CPSU in order to browbeat them into submission. Khrushchev, according to the Chinese, first circulated a CPSU letter to the CCP, dated June 21, which attacked the Chinese party "all along the line." Then, in their speeches to the congress, Khrushchev and his supporters among the East European party leaders denounced the Chinese as Trotskyites and "madmen" seeking war, and further accused them of pursuing a selfishly "nationalistic" course in the Sino-Indian border conflict.[14] The Soviet leader is also alleged to have belittled Chinese military knowledge and the militia system, and to have criticized the purge of Marshal P'eng Te-huai. The CCP delegation, according to Peking, responded to the attacks with a "tit-for-tat struggle" and distributed a written statement of defiance at the close of the congress proceedings.

New Soviet acts of retaliation followed soon afterwards. According to the Chinese statements of last September, it was in July 1960 that Moscow "suddenly took a unilateral decision recalling all Soviet experts in China within one month." In addition, the Soviet government unilaterally cancelled the reciprocal publication of friendship magazines in both countries and demanded the recall of a member of the Chinese Embassy in Moscow.[15] It also appears from last year's statements by both sides that incidents began occurring on the Sino-Soviet border about this time, each side charging the other with having provoked them.

Meanwhile, the war of words continued with mounting intensity. In early August, Soviet party journals began claiming for the first time that peaceful coexistence represented the general foreign policy line of the *entire* Communist bloc, thus implicitly asserting the authority of the CPSU to define bloc foreign policy and the obligation of bloc members to accept such definition as a matter of Communist discipline. This was to be a recurrent Soviet motif in the Sino-Soviet polemic of subsequent

---

[14]JMJP-HC joint editorial, Sept. 6, 1963.
[15]*Ibid.* (This statement does not indicate what reason was given for the Soviet recall demand, but it seems quite possible that the expelled diplomatic official may have been guilty of disseminating Chinese anti-Soviet propaganda material in Moscow. This was the charge later made in connection with the expulsion of CPR officials from the USSR in 1963.)

years, receding in periods of Soviet retreat but reappearing when Moscow returned to the attack.

On September 10, the CCP replied to the CPSU letter of June 21 with a letter of rebuttal which called upon Moscow to restore bloc unity by abandoning not only its "erroneous" policy line but all efforts to exert its authority over Peking. That same month a Chinese delegation went to Moscow for fruitless private talks with CPSU leaders, and in Hanoi Soviet and Chinese party representatives again vied for support among the delegates to the Vietnamese party congress.

## The 1960 Communist Conference

In October 1960 there was another skirmish between the two antagonists in the 26-party committee which met in Moscow to prepare a draft declaration for submission to the scheduled November conference of Communist parties. Agreement was eventually reached on the bulk of a draft text, but not on certain key issues. In connection with this meeting, the Chinese claimed last September that Khrushchev, upon returning from the United Nations session in New York, "even scrapped agreements that had already been reached on some questions"—suggesting that some of the CPSU leaders were more willing than Khrushchev to make concessions to the Chinese for the sake of unity.[16]

When the conference proper convened, according to Peking, the Soviets again started things off, as at Bucharest, by distributing among the delegates a new 60,000-word CPSU "letter" attacking the CCP (and the Albanian party) "more savagely than ever." In the conference debate also, the Chinese claim, the CPSU mustered its adherents and "engineered converging assaults on the CCP" in an attempt to force it to yield. In the end, an ambiguous document was produced and signed, embodying the mutually contradictory positions of the two parties on many issues. While the CPSU perhaps succeeded in getting more of its points included than did the Chinese, it nevertheless suffered a major defeat on the central issue of authority in that it failed to obtain either a condemnation of (Chinese-Albanian) "factional activities" or an endorsement of the Soviet thesis that peaceful coexistence was the "general line" of bloc foreign policy. The Chinese have since boasted that this

---

[16]*Ibid.* Further evidence of disagreement within the CPSU over tactics towards the Chinese was provided by the handling of the much-discussed Titarenko article of August 1960, which for the first time named and threatened China with isolation from the Communist bloc. This article appeared in identical form throughout the Soviet provincial press with the single exception of the Leningrad party organization organ, *Leningradskaia pravda*, which omitted the passage identifying China.

was "an event of great historical significance" because it "changed the previous highly abnormal situation in which not even the slightest criticism of the errors of the CPSU leadership was tolerated and its word was final."[17]

The signature of the conference declaration was accompanied by the customary public pledges of undying solidarity and mutual affection, but privately neither Moscow nor Peking regarded the compromise as anything but a temporary makeshift, nor did either intend to abandon the struggle.[18] Right after the conference, in fact, Khrushchev renewed his attack on the Chinese position at what he evidently regarded as its weakest point — Albania. The Albanians, who had been the most vociferous supporters of the Chinese at Bucharest and the November Moscow conference, were now subjected to an extension of the Soviet economic pressures that had been initiated in the summer of 1960. These reprisals culminated in the withdrawal of all Soviet technicians and the complete termination of Soviet economic aid to Albania in April 1961, followed by the withdrawal of Soviet naval units from Vlore in May. An acrimonious exchange of messages between Moscow and Tirana was climaxed by a violent letter addressed to the Albanian party by the CPSU Central Committee on August 24, 1961. The Chinese, fully conscious of the fact that the Soviet pressures against Albania were aimed as much against themselves, countered by providing their East European ally with economic aid and technicians to replace those withdrawn by Moscow. Peking has since revealed that the CCP urged the Soviet party early in 1961 to take steps to improve Soviet-Albanian relations, and that it repeated this advice on the eve of the 22nd CPSU Congress in October,[19] apparently in an effort to head off the all-out Soviet attack on Albania that seemed foreshadowed by the August 24 CPSU letter to Tirana.

## The 22nd Congress and After

As events soon proved, however, the Soviet leadership was determined to force the Albanian issue into the open, evidently hoping thereby to recoup the damage done to its authority by the Chinese at the November 1960 conference of Communist parties. Thus, the 22nd Congress wit-

---

[17]*Ibid.*

[18]The Albanian party organ *Zeri i Popullit* (Dec. 6, 1961) claimed that Khrushchev had called the declaration "a compromise document of short duration." Similarly, according to a TASS report of October 12, 1963, Australian Communist sources quoted Mao as having said on the eve of the Moscow conference that "a temporary agreement" might possibly be reached, "but not durable unity."

[19]*Jen-min Jih-pao*, Feb. 27, 1963.

nessed an unprecedented torrent of abuse hurled publicly at the Albanians by CPSU spokesmen, most of all by Khrushchev, who in his speech of October 27 went so far as to call explicitly for the overthrow of Albanian party leaders Hoxha and Shehu.

Besides the assault on the Albanians, there were other moves at the congress which appeared aimed, at least implicitly, at various aspects of the Chinese position. The first was the renewed attack on Stalin, which flouted the position taken by the CCP ever since the 20th Congress. The second was the new, intensified offensive unleashed against the "anti-party group," and particularly against Molotov, who—it was repeatedly intimated by congress speakers — had been encouraged by the Chinese to attack Khrushchev's policies on two occasions, once in April 1960 (when Molotov was still ambassador to Outer Mongolia) and again just before the 22nd Congress.[20] The third was the effort to present the new CPSU Program, which the congress was to ratify, as a "new Communist Manifesto" justifying the claim of the Soviet party to world Communist leadership. On top of all this, the Chinese claim that Khrushchev, in his private meetings with Premier Chou En-lai during the congress, "expressed undisguised support for anti-party [*i.e.*, revisionist] elements in the CCP."[21]

As leader of the Chinese delegation, Chou responded to the Soviet moves by reproving Khrushchev before the congress for his open attack on the Albanian party, by demonstratively laying a wreath on Stalin's tomb, and by suddenly leaving for Peking before the conclusion of the congress. According to Chinese statements, he also "frankly criticized the errors of the CPSU leadership" in private conversations with Khrushchev and other Soviet leaders.

Following the congress, the CPSU stepped up its campaign to mobilize the bulk of the world's Communist parties in a solid front against the Albanians — and hence, implicitly, against the Chinese. Although all the East European parties and some of the non-bloc parties had backed the Soviet attack on Albania at the congress, many of the latter— as well as the North Korean and North Vietnamese parties—had failed to do so. During the next three months, however, in response to evident Soviet pressures, the great majority of the non-Asian Communist parties went on record with some form of rebuke to the Albanians. The Soviet

---

[20]Among the speakers who attacked Molotov were Ilichev, who cited Molotov's submission of a "dogmatic" article to *Kommunist* in April 1960; Satyukov and Pospelov, who told of a letter sent by Molotov to the Central Committee on the eve of the 22nd Congress attacking the draft CPSU program in terms similar to those later made explicit by the Chinese; and by Kuusinen, who accused Molotov of fishing in "foreign waters."

[21]JMJP-HC joint editorial, Sept. 6, 1963.

press avidly republished these statements, as it did the statements (after mid-November) of some of the foreign parties mildly but explicitly criticizing the Chinese for opposing criticism of the Albanians. In December, diplomatic relations between Moscow and Tirana were, in effect, ruptured.

Meanwhile, the Chinese Communist press maintained a spurious Olympian attitude, reprinting both the attacks on Albania and the ferocious Albanian replies — but of course giving greater prominence to the latter. Ample publicity was also given to statements by various Asian parties which declined to follow the Soviet lead. The North Vietnamese party, alarmed at the drift of events, took the initiative in January 1962 in privately urging the combatants to agree to the holding of a new world Communist conference "to settle the discord" and in proposing that "pending such a meeting the parties cease attacking one another in the press and over the radio."[22] Similar proposals were put forward, apparently also privately, by the Indonesian party, and publicly by the New Zealand CP.

## Jockeying for Position

By February 1962 it was evident to the CPSU that its campaign not only had failed to isolate the Albanians and Chinese but even had resulted in setbacks to its position, primarily among the Asian parties but also to some extent elsewhere. On February 21, the Soviet party climaxed its drive with an imposing two-page spread in *Pravda* summarizing the support it had received, citing Lenin on the necessity of subordination "to the international discipline of the revolutionary proletariat," and insisting that "only open, uncompromising criticism of the anti-socialist, nationalist actions of the Hoxha-Shehu group can secure the unity of our movement."

The very next day, February 22, the CPSU dispatched a secret letter to Peking which — as discreetly summarized by the Russians last July[23] —"drew the attention of the CCP" to the dangerous consequences of disunity and urged "more effective measures" for coordinating the positions of the two parties in the various world front organizations and elsewhere. According to the more outspoken Chinese summary, the CPSU letter accused the Chinese of taking "a special stand of their own"

[22]Statement of the Political Bureau of the Vietnamese Worker's Party, Feb. 10, 1963, reported by Hanoi Radio, same date.
[23]CPSU Open Letter of July 13, 1963: in *Pravda* same date.

in opposition to the world movement, "even made a crime" of the CCP's support for the Albanians, and demanded that Peking abandon its position and embrace Moscow's "erroneous line" as "preconditions" for an improvement of Sino-Soviet relations.[24]

In April the CCP replied with a letter favoring a new general conference of Communist parties, concurring with the North Vietnamese proposal for a truce in polemics, and calling for bilateral or multilateral talks to prepare for a world meeting. These Chinese also blandly advised the Soviet party to "take the initiative" in seeking a settlement of its differences with the Albanians.[25] Late in May, the CPSU again returned the ball to Peking with a note which, according to Moscow, reiterated the main points of the February 22 letter. The Soviet party also claimed last year that it had agreed in May 1962 to the convocation of a new Communist conference;[26] but the Chinese assert that the CPSU made an Albanian surrender the "precondition" for such a conference.[27]

Meanwhile, Moscow and Peking seemed to have agreed, at least for the time being, to heed the North Vietnamese appeal and apply the brake to public polemics against each other. Mutual recriminations were, in fact, greatly toned down during the spring of 1962 — although never quite eliminated. Public pronouncements on both sides sought to convey to the West an impression of restored harmony and unity — an effort which, as an American scholar of Communist affairs has noted, was assisted by Communist news correspondents in Moscow,[28] and which was rather naively taken at face value by some sections of the Western press.

Again, the reality was very different. According to the Chinese statement of last September 6, it was precisely during this period of seeming calm (April-May 1962) that "the leaders of the CPSU used their organs and personnel in Sinkiang, China, to carry out large-scale subversive activities in the Ili region, and enticed and coerced several tens of thousands of Chinese citizens into going into the Soviet Union," subsequently refusing to return them to Chinese territory despite Peking's protests.[29] These events were presumably related to the subsequently reported action of the CPR government closing Soviet consulates in China. Soviet press reports last September confirmed that a mass flight

[24]JMJP-HC joint editorial, Sept. 6, 1963.
[25]CCP letter to the CPSU of March 9, 1963: in *Peking Review,* March 22, 1963.
[26]CPSU letter to the CCP of Feb. 21, 1963: in *Pravda,* March 13, 1963.
[27]JMJP-HC joint editorial, Sept. 6, 1963.
[28]William E. Griffith, *Albania and the Sino-Soviet Rift,* Cambridge, Massachusetts Institute of Technology Press, 1963, pp. 143–44.
[29]JMJP-HC joint editorial, Sept. 6, 1963.

of Chinese across the Sino-Soviet border had in fact taken place, adding further lurid details which contradicted the Peking version.[30]

## Renewal of Hostilities

At the end of the summer of 1962, the Chinese fired the opening salvos in a renewed anti-Soviet campaign which has gone on continuously ever since. On three separate occasions, at the Rumanian (August 23), Vietnamese (September 1), and Bulgarian (September 8) national anniversary receptions held in Peking, Foreign Minister Chen Yi alluded to socialist countries which attempted to forcibly impose . . . [their] views on others" and "replaced comradelike discussions . . . with interference in [others'] internal affairs." Soon afterwards, in mid-September, the Chinese and Albanian press launched an obviously coordinated and violent assault on "modern revisionism," timed to coincide with the visit of Leonid Brezhnev, Chairman of the Presidium of the USSR Supreme Soviet, to Yugoslavia.

Curiously, Soviet propaganda displayed remarkable restraint as the Chinese attacks continued, and there was even an attempt to appease Peking. In meetings with the departing Chinese Ambassador Liu Hsiao on October 13 and 14, Khrushchev, according to Soviet statements last year, asked that Mao forget the past and "start our relations with a clear page."[31] Moreover, according to the Chinese, the Soviet leader expressed complete sympathy for Peking's stand on the border conflict with India, implicitly endorsed the Chinese intention to use force in that conflict, and promised to stand by Peking if hostilities again arose.[32] These private statements by Khrushchev were followed on October 25 by an equally remarkable editorial in *Pravda* which, for the first and last time in the three years of the Sino-Indian border controversy, sided with Peking. One can only speculate that the adoption by Moscow of a conciliatory posture was motivated by the approach of the Cuban crisis, which erupted into the open on October 22 — that is, by Soviet desire to assure bloc solidarity at a time of military crisis and also, perhaps, to

---

[30]*E.g.*, see *Kazakhstanskaia Pravda*, Sept. 29, 1963. The Soviet government statement of Sept. 20, 1963, claimed that there had been 5,000 Chinese violations of the Soviet border in 1962.

[31]CPSU Open Letter of July 13, 1963, *Pravda*, July 14, 1963. It is interesting to note that this document obscures the date of the conversations, referring to them merely as having occurred "in the autumn" of 1962. The JMJP-HC joint editorial identifies them as having taken place in October 1962, thus pinning them down to the Khrushchev-Liu interviews of October 13 and 14.

[32]*Jen-min Jih-pao* editorial, Nov. 1, 1963.

buy Chinese forbearance if it should become necessary to back down over the issue of Cuba.

As it turned out, the Soviets did have to back down, but the Chinese did not forbear and instead proceeded to belabor Khrushchev unmercifully for his "betrayal" of Castro. Placed on the defensive, Moscow edged back toward its previous neutral position vis-à-vis the Sino-Indian border conflict and then organized a thoroughgoing counterattack against the Chinese party.

The counterattack was pressed with mounting intensity throughout November and the first week of December at the successive congresses of the Bulgarian, Hungarian, Czechoslovakian and Italian Communist parties, each of these meetings witnessing the dragooning of a still larger number of the CPSU's foreign adherents into joining a chorus of denunciation first against the Albanians and later against the Chinese as well. The climax was reached in early December with the extremely violent anti-Albanian-and-Chinese speeches delivered by the Czechoslovak and Italian party secretaries, Koucky and Pajetta. There followed the elaborate state visit of Tito to the Soviet Union, where on December 12 the Yugoslav leader heard Khrushchev deliver an angry speech before the Supreme Soviet impugning Chinese motives and policies.

Mao's response was to open the sluice gates. In a succession of articles published between mid-December 1962 and March 1963, the CCP completed the process it had begun in 1956, gradually making explicit its past grievances and present ambitions. The Chinese party called on the Communists of the world to revolt against the "baton" of the CPSU; it derided the Soviet "temporary majority"; and it challenged Moscow to convene a meeting of the world movement, thus repeating publicly the demand made privately early in 1962. At last, Peking attacked, by name, the CPSU and its leading adherents in the West as betrayers of the revolution, simultaneously elaborating its 1960 thesis that the real focus of revolutionary struggle against "imperialism" was now in the underdeveloped areas of the world and that the real leader of this struggle was the Chinese Communist Party.

In response, Moscow began in February 1963 to intimate that its adversary was seeking to divide the revolutionary movement along geographical and racial lines—a complaint which was eventually expanded into thunderous denunciations of Chinese "racism," coupled with charges that Peking was attempting to isolate the European "socialist" states from the "national liberation movement" and to distort reality by claiming that imperialism's main conflict was now with the underdeveloped world (led by Peking's rhetoric) rather than with the bloc (led by Soviet military might).

In the meantime, however, it became clear early in 1963 that the Chinese public demand for a world Communist meeting had embarrassed the CPSU. In his January address to the East German party congress, Khrushchev not only proposed — as if it were his own idea — a suspension of polemics between the two factions, but also acknowledged the existence of pressure on him from "some comrades" to convene a world conference. He insisted, however, that the time was not ripe for such a meeting. The Soviet leader then went on to declare that he had no desire to excommunicate the Albanians from the bloc and challenged the Chinese to treat the Yugoslavs similarly. But even while extending this olive branch to Mao, Khrushchev could not forbear striking him with it: the East German congress was made the occasion for new attacks on the Albanians and the Chinese, and the CCP delegate was interrupted and subjected to apparently well-organized booing and hissing, an unprecedented insult to the Chinese party. Nevertheless, in February, the CPSU retreated a step further and sent Peking a fairly mild letter agreeing in principle to a world meeting and proposing bilateral talks to prepare for it.

The Chinese, however, were in no conciliatory mood and — as the Soviets later said — took Moscow's offer as a sign of weakness. They were by then in the midst of a vast new offensive against the CPSU and were vigorously proselytising in every part of the world. To this end, the various CCP statements and editorials were being assembled in brochures and distributed in many languages. In February, the Chinese openly attacked Soviet influence at a Tanganyika meeting of the Afro-Asian Solidarity Organization (using racial arguments, the Soviets said), and at the same time they began setting up counterparts to the existing world front organizations, excluding the Soviets from participation in the new bodies.

After receiving the CPSU letter of late February, the Chinese party responded with new public attacks of still greater violence. It was at this time that the CCP initiated the practice of publishing its current communications to the CPSU (forcing the Soviet party to do likewise), so that even the exchanges between the two Central Committees, hitherto kept in the form of confidential letters, now became a part of the open polemic. Thus, in spite of a promise given on March 9 that it would desist from further public attacks, Peking clearly had no intention of doing so.

## Moving Toward Schism

This was dramatically demonstrated on the eve of a CPSU Central Committee plenum and three weeks before the scheduled opening of bilateral Sino-Soviet talks in Moscow, when the Chinese distributed in the Soviet capital — and subsequently throughout the rest of the world — the CCP letter of June 14, 1963, explicitly indicting Soviet domestic policies for the first time and announcing Peking's intention to split every Communist party whose leadership continued to support Moscow. In this proclamation of Peking's "general line" for the Communists of the world, the Chinese also promised to anoint as honorary Marxists-Leninists all revolutionaries now *outside* the Communist movement who would carry their banner.

The Soviet leadership now reacted forcefully. The Chinese officials who had distributed the CCP letter in the Soviet Union were formally expelled, and after the Central Committee had pondered its course at the mid-June plenum, the Soviet case against the CCP was placed before the world in the form of a CPSU "Open Letter" released on July 13. A highly emotional speech delivered by Khrushchev six days later, on July 19, made it clear that he regarded the Chinese action as nothing less than an attempt to subvert his position at home and abroad.

Meanwhile, CPSU and CCP representatives opened their scheduled bilateral talks in Moscow, but even as the talks ground on toward eventual fruitless suspension, the Soviet government concluded a partial nuclear test-ban agreement with the United States on terms which it had previously rejected. Throughout the summer and autumn Soviet propaganda heavily exploited this agreement in an effort to isolate the Chinese, who were placed in the vulnerable position of having to defend before world opinion their determination to acquire nuclear weapons and their refusal to adhere to the test-ban treaty.

Sino-Soviet relations had now reached a point where both sides were caricaturing and attacking each other's leaders by name, and where both proceeded to publish statements revealing hitherto secret aspects of their dealings with each other since the beginning of the dispute. The Soviets spoke of Mao as a senile "Trotskyite" tyrant and racist who sought world war, who had made monumental blunders in domestic policy, and whose government maintained "concentration camps" and massacred minority peoples, forcing them to seek haven in the USSR. The Chinese, in turn, characterized Khrushchev as a cowardly traitor allied with "imperialism" who was striving to restore capitalism in the Soviet Union and to undermine Marxism-Leninism throughout the world.

In September-October 1963 there were reports in the Western press, supported circumstantially by hints in Soviet propaganda, which suggested that the CPSU was almost reconciled to the consequences of a schism and was now considering the convocation of a world Communist meeting at which the Chinese and their supporters would be called upon to recant their factional activity or depart. In late October, however, the CPSU — apparently again under pressure from members of its own camp — temporarily abandoned this intention and instead began calling once again for an end to public polemics.

The CCP, however, would not relent, and by late January 1964 Peking had begun to announce formal recognition of pro-Chinese factions which had rebelled and seceded from the established Communist parties of such countries as Ceylon, Peru, Belgium, and Switzerland as *the* official Communist parties in those countries. These ominous organizational measures were followed in early February by a new Chinese pronouncement — the most outspoken to date — which proclaimed Peking's intention to recognize and support such "revolutionary" Communist parties everywhere.[33]

The formalization of the worldwide Communist schism had now begun.

---

[33]Editorial article jointly published in *Jen-min Jih-pao* and *Hung-Ch'i*, Feb. 4, 1964.

# XII
# The Chinese Communist Political System: Problems of Capability and Stability

## 29. Communist China's Economic Development and International Capabilities

*Alexander Eckstein*

In the conduct of its foreign relations, Communist China can and does use military force, the threat of force, trade and aid, moral suasion, and propaganda appeals. Its ability to employ all these means, however, is in one way or another affected by the size of its national product, the structure of its economy, the state of its economic development, and the rate at which its economy is growing and being transformed from a backward and preponderantly agricultural economy into a modern, industrialized one. The relationships are most direct, of course, in the field of trade and aid. Yet they are also of major importance with respect to the country's military posture. On the other hand, they carry less decisive weight as far as propaganda capabilities are concerned.

In appraising the potency of economic instruments in the conduct of Chinese Communist foreign policy, it is important to start with a brief analysis of the present state of the mainland economy, its strengths and weaknesses, its accomplishments and its unresolved problems as brought out at greater length in the different chapters of this study.

Undoubtedly the most fundamental and intractable problem facing economic policy makers in China is that of population and food. On the basis of highly fragmentary and rather unreliable data, mainland China's population in 1964 was estimated to be about 730 million. This vast population is supposed to be growing at an average annual rate of 2 per cent or more. Thus, about 15 million people are added each year. Maintaining such a rapidly growing population just at the prevailing standards of living entails heroic efforts. It requires an average annual rate of

Reprinted from Alexander Eckstein, *Communist China's Economic Growth and Foreign Trade* (New York: McGraw-Hill, 1966), pp. 245–59, by permission of the author and publisher. Copyright© 1966 by Council of Foreign Relations, Inc.

growth in food supply of 2-3 per cent; it places a heavy demand on investment resources for housing, school construction, hospitals, and other educational, health, and welfare facilities.

This population has high birth rates and fairly high death rates — *i.e.*, it is a preponderantly young population with a high ratio of consumers to producers. These characteristics are conducive to high consumption and low saving. Furthermore, a sizable share of savings needs to be channeled into investment in social overhead rather than production facilities.

These relationships pose a series of dilemmas, which are common to all economies subject to acute population pressure. At the end of the First Five Year Plan period (1957), it seemed that China might be on the way to breaking out of this vicious circle of backwardness. Seen from the perspective of 1965, one can be much less certain of this.

There is no doubt that the Chinese Communist leadership is fully conscious of the problem and is trying to attack it from two directions simultaneously. As was shown in Chapters 2 and 3, it has in recent years accorded high priority to agricultural development. At the same time, it has embarked on a program of family planning, thus far largely confined to the urban areas.

Present indications are that this two-pronged attack has produced some recovery and progress. However, unless there is a miraculous boon in the form of unusually good harvests or foreign aid on a large scale, further economic growth and advance in China may be expected to be significantly slower than in the 1950s. Correspondingly, the Chinese Communist vision of becoming a top-ranking industrial nation may have to be postponed for a long time to come.

This prospect could be altered if Communist China were to gain access to foreign credits or grants. In this respect, China is in a unique situation, for it is perhaps the only underdeveloped country today that has no long-term credits or foreign aid to draw upon. On the contrary, since 1955 it has been a net exporter of capital. These capital exports have been used to amortize the Soviet loans and to finance Chinese foreign aid programs. It would seem that in contributing to rising Sino-Soviet tensions, the Chinese Communist leadership must have chosen to buy increasing self-reliance and freedom of action in foreign affairs at the price of economic development at home.

China's development prospects could also be altered markedly by changes in domestic policy. In recent years, the Chinese Communists have pursued a prudent and more or less conservative economic policy — easing the tax and collection pressure on the peasantry, trying to foster a generally more favorable incentive system for agriculture, keeping the savings burden down, and channeling a large share of investment to agriculture and agriculture-supporting industries. However, this policy yields a pattern of resource allocation which runs strongly counter to the ideological and programmatic commitments of the leadership. It tends to produce a lower rate of investment and a lower rate of industrial growth. Therefore, the current economic policies are in many ways distasteful to the regime — so much so that they become a continuing source of tension between what the leadership desires and hopes for and what it considers possible and necessary. This tension may in turn tempt the leadership to resort once more to bold measures to break out of the vise of backwardness. Such attempts could easily lead to another economic breakdown and crisis. Consequently, one of the most serious problems for the leadership is to curb its own sense of impatience.

According to some assessments, the very intractability of the population-food dilemma might drive the Chinese Communists into adventurism, particularly in Southeast Asia. The adherents of this view maintain that Communist China's current interest in Vietnam is at least partly motivated by a desire to gain access to the rice surpluses and the rich mineral resources of Southeast Asia. However, it is difficult to see what the economic gains of conquest would be. What could China obtain through conquest of this region that she cannot now get through the normal processes of international trade?

Implicit in this view is an assumption that the Chinese Communists could move in and confiscate the rice and other commodities. This region, however, depends on rice and mineral exports for essential imports. If Communist China conquered the region, she would have to assume responsibility for maintaining economic and political stability. This task would mean assuring a modicum of incentives to farmers to induce them at least to maintain, if not expand, production. Forced confiscation might yield some produce for a year or two but would unquestionably be counterproductive in the long run. The Chinese Communists have a great deal of difficulty with their own peasantry. It is hard to believe that they would expect to overcome these difficulties with a conquered peasantry.

For these reasons one probably has to look to historical, cultural, ideological, and strategic considerations rather than to economic motivations for the primary explanation for Communist China's interest in Southeast Asia.

## The Economic Base for Military Power

In terms of total size, mainland China's economy definitely is among the 10 largest in the world. According to the data in Table 1, China in 1962

TABLE 1.
The Gross National Product of Communist China
and Selected Countries
(in billions of U.S. dollars)

| Country | 1962 GNP (at 1961 prices) |
|---|---|
| United States | 551.8 |
| U.S.S.R. | 256.3 |
| Germany (Federal Republic) | 96.2 |
| United Kingdom | 91.5 |
| France | 83.6 |
| Japan | 77.0 |
| Italy | 52.8 |
| China[a] | |
| 1957 | 40.0 |
| 1960 | 50.0 |
| 1962 | 42.0 |

[a]The estimates are for gross domestic products at 1952 prices; however, the figures would not be significantly altered even if they were stated in 1961 prices.

Sources: The 1957 estimate for China is based on the estimate of T. C. Liu and K. C. Yeh, *The Economy of the Chinese Mainland: National Income and Economic Development, 1933–1959* (Princeton University Press, 1965) as adjusted in Table D-1* and converted into dollars at the official rate of exchange. This method of conversion introduces a sizable margin of error; however, it is far from clear whether this leads to an overvaluation or undervaluation of China's product in comparison with that of other countries. The official exchange rate of 2.62 yuan to the dollar probably undervalues China's agricultural product and overvalues the output of the investment goods industries. The direction of the bias is less clear for the other sectors. Thus, it is not possible to determine — short of a detailed national income estimate weighted both in Chinese and U.S. prices — the extent of the bias for national product as a whole. The 1960 estimate is based on the 1959 Liu-Yeh figure as adjusted in Table D-1 and then rounded upward to allow for some assumed expansion between these two years. The 1962 figure is a guess based on qualitative indicators of economic trends between 1960 and 1962.

The data for other countries are much more reliable than those for China. They were taken from U.S. Congress, Joint Economic Committee, *Annual Economic Indicators for the U.S.S.R.*, 88th Congress, 2d sess. (Washington, D.C.: GPO, 1964), p. 96.

*Editor's Note: See Alexander Eckstein, *Communist China's Economic Growth and Foreign Trade* (New York: McGraw-Hill, 1966), p. 302.

was outranked in total production by the United States by a ratio of nearly 14:1, by the Soviet Union by about 6:1, by Germany, Britain, France, and Japan by about 1.8-2.3:1, and by Italy barely at all.

Taken by themselves, however, these figures are misleading, for they overstate China's economic capabilities as compared to those of the more highly developed and more industrialized countries. Roughly 40 per cent of mainland China's national product never enters marketing channels, while in the United States the figure is only about 5 per cent. The other countries listed in Table 1 lie between these two extremes. Therefore, a sizable share of the goods and services produced in China are "frozen" within the household and cannot readily be mobilized or reallocated to alternative uses. *Pari passu* resources are "tied" to specific patterns of use which cannot be shifted into the military sector.

Bearing this fact in mind, we may perhaps better approach an analysis of relative capabilities by comparing the size of the industrial product

**TABLE 2.**
**Comparative Industrial Production of Communist China**
**and Selected Countries, 1962**
**(in billions of U.S. dollars)**

| Country | Industrial Product[a] |
|---------|----------------------|
| United States | 180.2 |
| U.S.S.R. | 86.7 |
| United Kingdom | 39.3 |
| Germany (Federal Republic) | 32.8 |
| France | 21.3 |
| Japan | 18.4 |
| Italy | 15.0 |
| China | |
| 1957 | 8 |
| 1960 | 13 |
| 1962 | 10 |

[a]Value added in manufacturing, mining, and public utilities.
*Sources:* See Table 1.

of China with that of the other countries. This measure encompasses only "modern" economic sectors which are fully commercialized and monetized. Within industry, therefore, factors can be more rapidly reallocated between branches in response to changing needs. Moreover, military capability is more directly related to industrial production than to any other branch of the economy. Analyzing the data in Table 2, then, we find that the conclusions emerging from Table 1 are indeed modified. That is, the gap between China and the other countries is significantly greater in terms of industrial product alone than it is if gauged by national product as a whole.

While in terms of the foregoing indicators, China is outranked by all the large industrial countries, her economy seems vast indeed in relation to other underdeveloped areas — that is, all of Asia (except Japan), Africa, and Latin America. The implications of size are further underlined by the apparent fact that pre-World War II Japan was capable of engaging in a major world conflict and sustaining it more or less successfully for four-five years with a total industrial product which probably was smaller than Communist China's is today. Admittedly, Japan was even then much more advanced technologically and much more highly industrialized than China is now. Furthermore, prewar Japan had a much smaller population to care for than China does, so it could allocate a much larger share of its total industrial product to expanding the military and closely related sectors. Therefore, one certainly could not conclude from this comparison that what Japan was capable of doing then, China could do now. Nevertheless, the comparison does suggest that if China continues on her industrialization path, it may not be too long before her war-making power may match that of Japan in the 1930s.

One of the most critical questions is whether population size should be treated as a source of weakness or strength. If one compares Communist China with her immediate continental neighbors, who are roughly at the same stage of development as she is, there is no doubt that population size represents an element of strength and power. If one compares Communist China with the United States and Russia, population size might represent an element of strength in the context of conventional warfare waged on the Asian continent. Within certain limits, sheer manpower might serve as a substitute for firepower. In a nuclear confrontation, however, it might have no effect at all, except in the macabre sense that a vast population has a somewhat better chance of leaving behind survivors.

Viewed in the above light, the economy — as underdeveloped as it is — is capable of providing Communist China with a military potential which can, and indeed has, signficantly altered the power balance on the Asian continent despite the fact that it may not permit the Chinese to challenge the Soviet Union and the United States in other parts of the world.

## Trade and Aid as Instruments of Foreign Policy

While China's size alone — its land area, population, and economy — gives it a significant weight in international affairs, this very size combined with the country's relative backwardness has tended to reduce its participation in world trade and thereby to reduce the importance of international trade as an instrument of Chinese Communist foreign policy. A vast country necessarily will tend to be more self-sufficient and to rely principally on internal markets and sources of supply. For this reason, its exports and imports will tend to be small relative to the total flow of goods and services produced in the economy. At the same time, the absolute level of foreign trade, regardless of its share in the national product, will tend to be a function of the country's stage of development. Thus, of two countries with roughly the same size of population, the one with the higher per capita income will tend to have the larger trade volume. It is not surprising, therefore, that even in its peak trade year of 1959, Communist China ranked only 12th in world imports and 13th in world exports.[1] A number of smaller but highly developed countries outranked her. West Germany and the United Kingdom, with gross national products about twice as large as that of mainland China, carried on a volume of trade that was four to five times as large. Even a country as small as The Netherlands carried on a volume of foreign trade twice as large.

These discrepancies were greatly magnified in the 1960s by the sharp slump in China's foreign trade under the impact of the economic crisis. As a result, by 1962 China slipped to 18th place in world rank with respect to exports and 30th place with respect to imports. This slump further curtailed the effectiveness of trade as a tool of foreign policy.

Foreign trade can provide a country with maximum power leverage if that country serves as the market for a vast share of another country's exports without itself being too dependent on these or, alternatively, if that country becomes a major source of its trading partner's supplies of imports without being too dependent on this market. Short of these circumstances, however, economic power can still be translated into political power via foreign trade when a country serves as a major market for another's principal exports or as a leading source of vital raw materials for the other's industries. For example, various agreements for a guaranteed market or for preclusive purchase can be of significant aid to particular industries or economic interests. Such a situation can be used to gain influence and to exercise pressure — if need be by threatening a sudden trade rupture with its attendant dislocations.

In the Chinese case, only for one country — namely, the Soviet Union — did mainland China constitute both a truly major market for exports and an important source of supply. Yet even in this instance, China's trade dependence on the Soviet Union during the 1950s was two to three times greater than vice versa. Moreover, the disparity in trade dependence increased in the 1960s, for China's share in Soviet foreign trade dropped to around 5 per cent while the Soviet Union's share in mainland commerce was still around 20 per cent. Before 1960, about 30-60 per cent of Russia's exports to China consisted of plant and transport equipment and machinery. The drastic curtailment in the purchase of these items in the 1960s might have led to some disruption in the Soviet machine-building industry. One cannot, for example, rule out the possi-

---

[1]These and subsequent rankings are based upon a comparison of my figures for Communist China's foreign trade with those of the foreign trade of other countries as reported in United Nations, *Yearbook of International Trade Statistics, 1963* (New York: Author, 1965). Table A, pp. 12–17.

bility that this curtailment of purchases may in the short run have placed a considerable burden of adjustment on individual factories producing for the China market. Nevertheless, the effect on the industry as a whole could not have been too serious, for by 1962-63 less than 1 per cent of its output was exported to China.

The only other area with a major trade orientation toward China has been Hong Kong. The latter obtains about 20 per cent of its imports from China, while the mainland now buys only a negligible share of its supplies from the colony. In and of itself, this situation gives the Chinese Communist regime limited leverage over Hong Kong, for the colony can find alternative sources of supply for its food and raw materials, although some inconvenience and possibly higher costs might be involved. Moreover, Hong Kong's dependence on Chinese supplies is counterbalanced by China's dependence on the colony as its principal source of foreign exchange. What this situation suggests is not that Communist China has no power or influence in Hong Kong but rather that its influence rests primarily on military and political — not economic — factors.

In addition, for several countries trade with mainland China has been of considerable importance to particular sectors rather than to the economy as a whole. Such, for instance, is the case with respect to grain exports from Canada and Australia. Both these countries had accumulated large grain surpluses, so Chinese purchases on a large scale offered definite relief to the farmers and traders of the two countries. The significance of these purchases can best be illustrated by the fact that since 1961 China has absorbed large shares of Australian and Canadian wheat exports. Although the Chinese are quite dependent on this grain, they have neutralized some of the effects of this dependence by fostering among the suppliers a spirit of competition for the China market. For example, they opened negotiations to buy a million tons of wheat from the French, who in 1964 were reported to have about two million tons of surplus wheat for export.[2]

The situation of the chemical fertilizer industry in Japan is analogous. It had been operating well below capacity, but its fortunes have undoubtedly been improved by a three-year fertilizer agreement concluded with China in 1964. According to this agreement, China will purchase a substantial share of Japan's total production of fertilizer and of its fertilizer exports.

Czechoslovakia's engineering industry was in a somewhat similar position. This industry is quite dependent on exports, and its products

---

[2]*The New York Times,* November 20, 1964.

account for a large portion of the country's total export earnings. Up to 1960, about 15 per cent of Czech engineering exports were sold to China. Moreover, the 1961-65 Czech plan envisaged a sizable expansion of these exports to China. Therefore, the collapse of the China market, as the result of deteriorating Sino-Soviet relations and the curtailment of the demand for investment goods within the country, was a serious blow to this industry.[3] The sudden reduction in China's agricultural exports to Czechoslovakia, moreover, aggravated the already precarious food supply situation in the latter country.

If one grants that particular economic branches in some countries can become more or less dependent on trade with the mainland, how can China use such dependence as an instrument of foreign policy? The potentialities and the limitations of trade as such an instrument perhaps can best be illustrated in the Southeast Asian context — that is, a region of vital concern to China. The mainland relies upon this region for its supply of rubber, which is produced in China only on a limited scale. For many years, she has been bartering rice for rubber from Ceylon. In this way, China has been providing a guaranteed market for about 25-30 per cent of Ceylonese rubber exports. Rubber, in turn, contributed about 15-20 per cent of Ceylon's total export earnings.[4] China, therefore, constitutes a significant factor in Ceylon's rubber market. In the absence of other purchases, however, China's importance from the standpoint of Ceylon's total earnings of foreign exchange is quite limited. On the other side of the ledger, China supplied about 50 per cent of Ceylon's imports of rice as of 1963,[5] but Ceylon could obtain this rice elsewhere. Therefore, these exports to Ceylon do not provide China with strong bargaining power. They may more properly be viewed as a form of payment Ceylon was willing to accept in order to find an outlet for her rubber.

By far the most important of Ceylon's exports is tea, which China herself exports. Besides rice, other significant items among Ceylon's imports are wheat and wheat flour, petroleum and petroleum products, chemicals, textiles, and machinery. In the case of petroleum and products, China too is an importer. She exports most of the other items, but all these are available from other sources as well. Whether and in what

---

[3] I am indebted to Professor J. M. Montias of Yale for calling this point to my attention.

[4] See various issues of the *Rubber Statistical Bulletin* (London), published by the International Rubber Study Group, and the *Yearbook of International Trade Statistics, 1963*, cited. All subsequent references to the total exports of any country except Communist China are based upon data in the latter source.

[5] See United Nations, *Commodity Trade Statistics*. Most subsequent references to the commodity composition of the trade of any country except Communist China are based upon data in this source.

quantities they will be purchased from the mainland will thus depend on relative cost considerations.

Other suppliers of rubber in the region are Indonesia, Malaysia, and to a lesser extent Cambodia. China could easily purchase all of Cambodia's rubber exports, but only at the cost of reducing her purchases from Ceylon. She could use the threat of such a shift as an instrument of foreign policy vis-à-vis both countries, but the threat could be effective in relation to both countries simultaneously only as long as it was not carried out. In the case of Indonesia, rubber contributes about 35-45 per cent of total exports. Were China to purchase all her imported rubber from Indonesia, she could not absorb more than 5 per cent of the country's total rubber crop.

Similarly, if China bought all her imports of petroleum and oil products solely from Indonesia, the purchases would constitute no more than one-fifth to one-fourth of the latter's total sales. The same general picture applies to Indonesia's other exports and imports. That is, China can buy only limited quantities of exports which are vital to Indonesia, while imports which China can supply are usually obtainable elsewhere — frequently on better, or at least no worse, terms.

The situation is rather different with respect to Cambodia, a small country with a small total volume of exports and imports. If Communist China wished, she could supply Cambodia, and in recent years has increasingly done so, with its modest imports of foodstuffs, textiles, and iron and steel. Similarly, she could buy all of Cambodia's rubber, rice, and corn surpluses. The additional costs thus incurred would undoubtedly be modest and could be borne if the political returns seemed promising enough.

What are the implications of this analysis for China's ability to use trade as an instrument in the conduct of its foreign relations? It is evident from these cases that the moderate size of total mainland exports and imports makes it difficult for China to impose a pattern of economic dependence and thereby to gain dominance over a country through trade. From China's point of view, the primary function of trade is to facilitate the maintenance of economic stability and to foster economic development at home. If at the same time trade can open new channels of communication for the spread of propaganda and political influence, so much the better. In other words, imports must be purchased from countries which can provide them on the most favorable terms, and exports must be sold in such a way as to maximize earnings of foreign exchange.

Therefore, China cannot afford to use import orders or export supplies just to impose patterns of economic dependence. I do not mean that trade cannot be used as a weapon in special cases where the additional costs incurred might be modest — either because economic and foreign policy considerations happen to coincide or because the country concerned is small (*e.g.*, Cambodia). Occasionally, for example, China may engage in preclusive buying at prices higher than world market prices or sell in specific markets at prices lower than world market prices. To the extent that China uses the trade weapon in one place, however, her capability of using it in other places is correspondingly reduced.

For all these reasons combined, trade is best suited to perform a supporting rather than independent role in the Chinese Communists' pursuit of their foreign policy objectives. It is really of importance in two rather different contexts. In countries where China has already made heavy inroads through the use of a whole arsenal of weapons, trade may serve to reinforce and accelerate an ongoing trend. In highly industrialized countries, it can serve as a prime avenue for gaining a certain measure of influence by creating the illusion of enormous trading potentials even in the face of currently modest trading levels. The ever-present lure of a "market with hundreds of millions of customers" seems to be just as strong today as it was in the 19th century. China's sheer size and population magnetically attract traders who do not want to miss possible opportunities and do not want possible competitors to get there ahead of them. In making certain policy moves, therefore, trading countries may consider it opportune to take into account the possible reactions of the Chinese Communists. This statement would certainly apply to Japan and perhaps to a lesser extent to Canada, Australia, Britain, France, and some additional European countries. But in none of these cases is trade of such importance as to provide Communist China with enough political bargaining power to impose a sharp turn in the direction of foreign policy.

The same general conclusions hold true with respect to China's economic aid capabilities. China's aid program is quite modest as compared with those of the United States and the Soviet Union. To some extent, the Chinese Communists seem to have succeeded in "packaging" their relatively small program in such a way as to maximize the political returns from their investment. In some African countries, for example, the aid and the Chinese Communist technicians who came with it apparently went some way in buying good-will and in counterbalancing Soviet influence. They may even have swayed a few votes on the question of the admission of Communist China to the United Nations. The Chinese aid program also has had a definite political impact in Southeast Asia, particularly in Cambodia and Burma. In both these cases, however, aid seems to have followed rather than led the way. That is, Chinese economic aid became important only after the governments concerned had made a political decision to pursue a more neutral-ist or pro-Chinese policy. Such decisions were then also reflected in the forced withdrawal of U.S. aid from these countries.

Chinese economic aid enjoys a near-monopoly position in only two countries, Albania and North Vietnam. In neither case was political dependence on China bought by economic dependence. Political de-pendence in the first case is based on a complex maze of political rela-tionships involving Yugoslavia and the Soviet Union, and in the second case on the military conflict with South Vietnam and the United States and on geographic proximity to mainland China.

## Communist China as a Development Model

To the extent that China does not rely upon force or the threat thereof — whether military or economic in nature — ideological appeal plays a significant role in its foreign policy arsenal. An important ingredient of this ideological appeal is what may be termed the "development-model effect." Depending upon the actual course of economic development on the mainland, the way this reality is handled in Chinese Communist propaganda, and the way it is perceived by the countries toward which the propaganda is directed, the effect may be either positive or negative. Here we are concerned only with the first aspect of this problem — namely, what this model effect might be in the absence of any propa-ganda effort based on it.

During the first decade of its existence, the Chinese Communist re-gime succeeded in creating an image of a vigorous, dynamic, and rapidly growing economy with some singular accomplishments to its credit. First of all, the regime rapidly restored the war-devastated economy and brought the prolonged inflation and hyperinflation to a halt. Monetary and fiscal stability was thus achieved despite the resource drain imposed by the Korean War. Moreover, a land redistribution program with sig-nificant appeal not only internally but externally was carried out during the same period.

This image was greatly reinforced by what at the time appeared to be a gradual and successful program of agrarian transformation based on an increasing degree of producer cooperation. As a result, strong senti-ment in favor of learning from the Chinese experience and emulating at least some aspects of it began to develop in India in the mid-fifties. Two official Indian delegations visited China. One was concerned primarily with problems of agricultural production, and the other with problems of agricultural organization.

Rapid industrial growth coupled with the aforementioned agrarian transformation caused many to believe that the Chinese Communists had succeeded in adapting the Soviet growth model to the conditions of an underdeveloped, densely populated economy. Since 1958, however, this image seems to have been tarnished. The extreme regimentation of the communes and the mass labor mobilization projects of the Great Leap seem to have had a negative external impact. More importantly, the profound economic crisis of 1960-62 dramatized the fact that the Chinese Communist regime had paid relatively little attention to agricultural development. At the same time, it again drove home the lesson that agricultural development is a necessary condition for economic development in densely populated, low-income countries.

The appeal of the Chinese Communist development model has no doubt been undermined by the economic setbacks on the mainland. Yet the force of the initial successes lingers on — partly because of an information lag, partly because of a statistical blackout since early 1960 which has helped to conceal the extent of the economic difficulties, and partly because of agricultural stagnation and difficulties of food supply in other underdeveloped countries (particularly India).

# 30. China's Conventional Military Capability

*Frank E. Armbruster*

The capability of modern China to wage conventional (classical, standard-formation, non-nuclear) war continues to be a topic of vital interest but one which perhaps still receives inadequate detailed attention. Traditionally, Chinese troops had been thought to suffer by comparison to Western troops and Western-type units. And perhaps the defeat of Chinese armies at the hands of the Japanese in the 1930's tended to confirm this opinion about modern China. The subsequent victories of these same Japanese armies over British and American-Philippine troops in Malaya and the Islands, however, pointed up the exceptional capability of this enemy; and British Field Marshal Viscount Slim said Chinese soldiers under him fought well in Burma.[1] When the Chinese soldier is a member of a good, well-organized, and well-led unit, his record is not one of inevitable failure; seldom in modern times has he had the type of disciplined, centrally controlled organization behind him that he has now. He is basically a hard-working, long-suffering, far from cowardly individual, and today he is said to be "in general . . . loyal to the regime and delighted to be in the army."[2]

The current conventional military capability of the Chinese Communist regime is held in very high esteem — in fact it may now be held in

---

[1]For Slim's evaluation of Chinese troops see Field Marshal the Viscount Slim, *Defeat into Victory* (New York: David McKay Company, Inc., 1961), pp. 12, 46–47.

[2]Chalmers Johnson, "How Sharp Are the Dragon's Claws?" *New York Times Magazine*, February 28, 1965, p. 22.

Reprinted from Frank E. Armbruster, "China's Conventional Military Capability," in Tang Tsou, ed., *China in Crisis* (Chicago: University of Chicago Press, 1968), 2: 161–66, 194–96, by permission of the author and publisher. The author wishes to acknowledge the research and editorial assistance of Doris Yokelson Batra.

such high esteem that there may be a danger of some error in this direction. There may even be a tendency to overlook some of the distinctions that are essential to assessments of military competence; that is, for example, distinctions between offensive and defensive capability, between different geographic areas in which the power is to be used, between different types of military organizations that might be the opponents, etc. This discussion of Communist China's conventional military capability is an attempt to view the subject in the light of the record of her forces as Peking may see it and in the context of the environment in which these forces may be called into action in the future. It emphasizes factors of geography, logistics, politics, and the required coordinated efforts of the Red Chinese Army, Navy, and Air Force.

Discussions of Red Chinese military power are of course influenced by the number of troops and the troop potential of the vast Chinese population. But emphasis on numbers can be unfortunate.[3] Numbers of troops are best considered only in relation to the factors mentioned above. Rather than "change format" in a discussion of Red China's conventional military power, however, let us cover the question of numbers and proceed to other issues that may be more significant, at least from the point of view of China's neighbors and the United States.

## People's Liberation Army

The primary conventional military capability of Red China lies in the People's Liberation Army (PLA). This army is occasionally visualized as consisting of (or potentially consisting of) hordes of fighting men — and to the small nations on her border it may appear so. Such estimates may not appear unfounded when one considers the fact that there are 125 million men of military age in Red China. Furthermore, the Chinese People's Republic has a vast militia which has been said to have had 220 or even 250 million men and women in its ranks (one of every three people) at one time or another. In 1964 the "basic" militia and "general" militia were said to include 200 million people. But these numbers alone are a somewhat shaky basis for estimating Chinese classical, overall, ground-force capability.

---

[3]It may be, however, as one work states, that the size of Red China's large land army, plus its record of successes, makes it appear to its neighbors to be invincible in any of its border areas against any foe (Morton H. Halperin and Dwight H. Perkins, *Communist China and Arms Control* [Cambridge, Mass.: East Asian Research Center, Center for International Affairs, Harvard University, 1965], p. 77).

The militia is no military body per se. It appears to be useful primarily as a means of controlling and directing the population in efforts to support the national and local economic plans, etc. About fifteen per cent of the men (and women) in the militia do receive military training, but the level of training is seldom high. This is not to say that there is no mission for the militia in time of war. First of all, it forms a somewhat "trained" reserve to provide replacements for the regular army (PLA), and indeed the basic militia is made up of army reservists, cadres and party members.[4] Second, in case of an actual invasion of the homeland, the militia may have the mission of defending the communes until overrun,[5] then acting as guerrilla support for the regular army. Under this plan, the militia would be expected to cooperate in the "protracted conflict" role and "bleed" the enemy, through guerrilla action, while the army retreats inland until the invading army is weakened and overextended — at which point the PLA is supposed to turn on the enemy and destroy him.[6] Or, to use Mao's phrase, the militia's job is to "drown" the enemy in "a sea of humanity."[7] This theory of a militia mission does provide a use (defensive only) for large numbers of untrained, quasimilitary people. But even it does not provide a use for unarmed people, the category into which the majority of militia men fall.[8]

The 125 million men of military age, therefore, are just that — 125 million men of military age. They are not armed, and except for militia and PLA services, they are not trained. They are neither organized nor equipped; in short, they are not an army. Nor does China have the capability to arm a vast army quickly. Even to adequately arm a large ground force at a slower pace would be a terrible drain on her very weak economy. Developing a modern army with high conventional combat capability requires the support of a highly developed economic and industrial base. To date China still has not achieved this goal. Crucial military support industries were hurt by the disorganization of the "Great Leap." With the Russian withdrawal of assistance (including fuel oil),[9] the

---

[4]John Gittings, "China's Militia," *The China Quarterly*, no. 18 (April-June, 1964), pp. 104, 110, 114; Edgar O'Ballance, *The Red Army of China* (London: Faber and Faber, 1962), pp. 204, 205; Johnson, *New York Times Magazine*, February 28, 1965, p. 22.

[5]O'Ballance, *The Red Army of China*, pp. 204, 205.

[6]"China: Dangers of Misunderstanding," *Newsweek*, March 7, 1966, p. 40.

[7]Gittings, *China Quarterly*, no. 18 (April-June, 1964), p. 106; and Johnson, *New York Times Magazine*, February 28, 1965, p. 85.

[8]One of the problems about issuing guns to this vast horde of people may be doubts about the loyalty of some of them. See O'Ballance, *The Red Army of China*, p. 205.

[9]Alice Langley Hsieh, "China's Secret Military Papers: Military Doctrine and Strategy," *China Quarterly*, no. 18 (April-June, 1964), p. 95.

Chinese experienced a deterioration of their forces in being. They are said to have made considerable efforts to overcome this handicap since 1961, but at least until 1965 without giving the military priority over economic development.[10] Nevertheless, China showed an inability in the early sixties to produce even such basic instruments of war as heavy artillery, although she has produced medium artillery and "some tanks."[11]

China's industrial base is currently expanding somewhat, but it is shaky, and in 1966 output was still placed below that of 1960.[12] China's population is also growing, bringing greater and greater demands on this same industrial base. The result seems to be that China's army has serious deficiencies, e.g., she lacks heavy and self-propelled artillery; her armored forces are far too few in number and they depend on World War II and some fine but not the most modern later Russian tank models.[13]

Radical and large-scale changes in this situation will require considerable time and effort. Furthermore, the "delivery system" of a conventional army is initially the indigenous transport system of the homeland. In China this system is totally inadequate to China's economic and military tasks. The railroad system is not fully developed, and the shortage of motor transport probably still restricts "strategic mobility."[14] Travelers report that the age-old curse of China, lack of transport, is still with her. Demands on the transport system increase daily, and the bottleneck in this area should remain for some time.

The Chinese Army, therefore, is very much smaller than the huge pool of men of military age might lead one to expect. It has 2½ million men grouped primarily into 30 field armies of three divisions each. There are said to be a total of 120 divisions of about 12,000 men each in the table of organization.[15] But, as in all military tables of organization, even this

[10]Halperin and Perkins, *Communist China and Arms Control*, p. 38.

[11]O'Ballance, *The Red Army of China*, p. 207; *The Military Balance, 1965-1966* (London: Institute of Strategic Studies, 1965), p. 9.

[12]"Since the disasters of the Great Leap, the Peking leaders have not known how to . . . promote sustained economic development. A process of modest growth is under way once again but . . . total agricultural output today is at approximately the level it reached almost a decade ago; in per-capita terms it is even lower. And despite renewed industrial growth in a few key fields, overall industrial production is still below its 1960 peak. There is good reason to believe that . . . Communist China has not really had any effective, long-term national economic plan in operation for over eight years . . ." (A. Doak Barnett, "China After Mao," *Look*, November 15, 1966, p. 33).

[13]O'Ballance, *The Red Army of China*, p. 207; *The Military Balance, 1967-1968* (London: The Institute for Strategic Studies, 1967), p. 10. She has shipped eighty T59 tanks, her version of the Soviet T54/T55 models, to Pakistan.

[14]*The Military Balance, 1965-1966*, p. 9.

[15]*The Military Balance, 1967-1968*, p. 10.

may not give the real strength of the army. In this army, the divisional "slice" of manpower would amount to about 20,000 men. That could mean a very thin army without sufficient supporting services; it could mean that some of the 120 divisions are not combat-ready and must be filled out in times of crises; or it could even mean that "line of communication troops" are not counted in the numbers one sees.[16] The second explanation may be the best. In any event, the army is known to be primarily made up of light infantry divisions (including two airborne divisions) with little mechanized equipment. There are thought to be only four "full-scale" armored divisions in the whole army, and her airlift capability for her airborne outfits is "probably limited to a few battalions."[17]

## The Navy

The navy of Red China consists of a very small, modern surface fleet (4 destroyers, 4-5 destroyer escorts, and 11 frigate escorts); a moderate underseas fleet (31-34 Soviet- and Chinese-built submarines); and a large fleet of small craft (18-19 minesweepers, 60 landing ships, 150 torpedo boats, a conglomeration of new-to-ancient gunboats, etc.). The submarines (21 to 23 of which are post-World War II Soviet "W" class boats assembled in Chinese yards)[18] present the main threat to a modern naval power. The training and competency of the submarine crews are somewhat unknown factors,[19] as is the actual capability of these Chinese-assembled vessels. They are fitted for mine laying and might play a significant role against an invasion fleet as well as cause casualties among the merchant fleet of the attacker, but they present no tool of conquest for the Chinese armed forces. The Red Chinese Navy does not have the

---

[16]See O'Ballance, *The Red Army of China*, p. 200; see also Johnson, *New York Times Magazine*, February 28, 1965, p. 87.

[17]*The Military Balance, 1967-1968*, pp. 10, 11; Halperin and Perkins, p. 36; Raymond L. Garthoff, "Sino-Soviet Military Relations," *Annals of the American Academy of Political and Social Science*, vol. 349 (September, 1963), p. 81.

[18]*Jane's Fighting Ships, 1967-1968* (New York: McGraw-Hill, 1967-1968), pp. 54–58. There have been reports that China has launched one and is building a second "G" class (Soviet-style) submarine that can carry three 400-mile surface-to-surface ballistic missiles. One submarine is now reported to be operational but presumably still lacks her missiles (*The Military Balance, 1967–1968*, p. 11).

[19]In the words of one "naval expert": "The Chinese have absolutely no deep-water submarine experience and their subs are confined mostly to coastal waters. They are not much of a threat and they won't be until they develop some seamanship and some technology in the field" ("China: Dangers of Misunderstanding," *Newsweek*, March 7, 1966, p. 38).

capability to carry out and protect a sizable amphibious operation. It cannot support China's primary military force, the PLA, in an offensive across any sizable water barrier in the face of an adequately equipped, determined opponent.

## The Air Force

The current Chinese Air Force consists of about 2,500 operable aircraft of which up to 150 are the obsolescent, light, jet bomber, the Il28 ("Beagle"), such as the one the Soviets put into Cuba. The fighters are MiG 15's, 17's, and a lesser number of 19's and supersonic MiG 21's. (The Chinese Navy has a land-based air arm of 150 Il28 torpedo planes and "substantial numbers" of MiG 15's and MiG 17's.)[20] The Shenyang Aircraft plant builds high-performance aircraft of Russian design, the MiG 17, MiG 15UTI, and "what is thought to be a simplified version of the MiG 21."[21] China is deficient in aviation fuel and in the past was heavily dependent upon the Soviet Union for its supplies. Since the Sino-Soviet split, training programs (at least until the mid-1960's) are said to have suffered from the shortage of fuel and spare parts.[22] . . .

## Conclusions

Chinese conventional warfare capability does not lend itself to large offensive operations outside its borders against a resolute large power. The effort required to radically change this posture is massive, and at least in the near future — except possibly with aid from abroad or at significant cost to her economic well-being — perhaps beyond China's power.

China will, however, experience some increase in her conventional capability, not only because of improvements in her conventional forces, but also as a result of her efforts in the economic area. Her economic plans require an increase in transport capacity which has military significance. Motor transport has the flexibility required for expeditionary forces, and rail transport produces traffic volume to support large-scale

---

[20]*The Military Balance, 1967-1968*, pp. 11, 12.

[21]*Jane's All the World's Aircraft, 1967-1968* (New York: McGraw-Hill, 1967-1968), p. 26. China has shipped some MiG 19's to Pakistan (*The Military Balance, 1966-1967*, p. 10).

[22]Johnson, *New York Times Magazine*, February 28, 1965, pp. 85, 86.

logistics at the border. But the roads on and just outside her borders, which are generally not affected by her economic development, in most cases will not support more than a moderate amount of military traffic. Changing that condition is a large-scale program and may even require cooperation from some potential victim states. Increasing rail capacity in many areas, critical from the point of view of possible offensive military operations, also would frequently fail to coincide with China's economic requirements and would sometimes represent expensive, very difficult construction (e.g., in South China).

In addition to the extensive transport equipment and engineering programs required, a major improvement of the air force and perhaps the entire Chinese aircraft industry is necessary to enable China to use her army beyond her borders. This requirement may make the other programs seem simple by comparison. It draws on all the resources that are so scarce in China: highly technical industrial capacity in machine tools, electronics and metallurgy, as well as items in short supply, such as aviation fuels, skilled technicians, qualified training pilots, etc. Yet without this arm of the service, her large land army is severely limited in projecting its power beyond her borders, particularly on the open plains and highlands from Tibet to Manchuria and across open water from her coast.

The same holds true for her navy; although, of course, if her air arm were overwhelming she could do with a less efficient surface fleet (at least for close-in operations). As things now stand, any amphibious force that China might choose to launch would be at the mercy of the air and sea forces awaiting it out on the blue waters off her coast. Increasing her surface navy without increasing her air force would be the height of folly. Without air cover, surface ships can become nothing more than targets. Nor does anti-aircraft missile technology of the level displayed in Vietnam provide an adequate substitute; and China probably has at present inadequate capability to produce even these ground-to-air missile systems in quantity, to say nothing of seaborne systems. She has therefore not made the great sacrifices in her industry which would have been required to increase significantly her surface navy. Her efforts on her submarine force have also been modest, although this primarily defensive force predominates in her navy.

The Red Chinese may well lack more than the equipment required for modern conventional warfare. The good quality of the individual soldiers and at least the junior officers of the light infantry units of the PLA notwithstanding, the Chinese may lack qualified personnel and know-how. Chinese pilots have in the past seemed inadequate to the task of conventional air action, and it appears they could not be counted on to cope with the pilots of a nation with a modern air arm, including Nationalist China. Nor is there any reason to feel that the Chinese naval units would fare any better against modern navies.[23] Furthermore, though the PLA is credited with great endurance, "marked stubbornness and persistence" in infantry battles, great bravery and clever tactics and propaganda, the Red Chinese are said to have "little knowledge of combined operations, including navy and air forces,"[24] which are the backbone of modern conventional operations.

The conclusion that one might draw from a study of Chinese conventional military capability is that — because of factors of geography and inadequacy of transportation, mechanized, air and naval forces, and joint operational capability — its role, when confronting larger powers, is primarily defensive. Indeed, as indicated earlier, there is evidence that the Chinese leaders do not view large-scale offensive conventional warfare as a practical mission of the armed forces.[25] This is not to say that had she the choice, China would prefer this weak offensive position; but it does provide a logical explanation for Chinese caution in the crises since Korea.

In conventional warfare, therefore, limited wars for limited objectives are the most practical kind of offensive operations for China. Even if some of the physical constraints on her mentioned earlier did not exist, extensive offensive operations might still be considered undesirable because of their great cost and because of China's precarious economic position.

In a defensive mode of conventional warfare, China's land army would have significant capability despite enemy control of the air. The difficulties of terrain which work to her disadvantage in offensive operations would to some degree prove advantageous to China defensively. The invader would now have the logistic problems, while the PLA fell back on its supply dumps. Also, China's militia would have a meaningful role; and, if her government could maintain control of the population, an invader would have to be prepared for a great, hard war if it wished to subjugate China.

---

[23]The navy did not seem to impede the supplying of Quemoy in 1958, and the Nationalists claim that several Communist surface craft were sunk during the crisis (*China Yearbook*, 1958-59, p. 3). This may, however, have been an unfair test of Communist capability against the Nationalists, because the presence of the United States Seventh Fleet in the Taiwan Strait may have deterred large-scale Communist naval operations.

[24]Johnson, *New York Times Magazine*, February 28, 1965. See insert on p. 85 of this issue for a Japanese estimate of the Red Chinese military capability.

[25]See p. 172 of this chapter for Hsieh's conclusions drawn from "China's Secret Military Papers: Military Doctrine and Strategy," *The China Quarterly*, no. 18. Meklin cites critics of our training of South Vietnamese troops for conventional war as stating that "floods of intelligence" indicated that the "Communists had concluded after Korea that it was an error to challenge Western industrial power in conventional warfare" (John Meklin, *Mission in Torment* [Garden City, New York: Doubleday & Co., Inc., 1965], p. 11).

# 31. Chinese Attitudes Toward Nuclear Weapons

*Morton H. Halperin*

The 1960's have been marked by three major events which affected the Chinese attitude toward nuclear weapons: the changes in American policy instituted by the Kennedy-Johnson administration, the growing Sino-Soviet rift, and the Chinese nuclear detonations.

The Peking leadership looked with some trepidation upon the changes in military strategy planned by the Kennedy administration. Kennedy and his advisers had campaigned on a platform which suggested that the Eisenhower administration had been unable to use its military power effectively to halt Communist aggression. From Peking's perspectives Kennedy appeared to be committed to finding a way to make credible the threat of the use of American nuclear power. According to analysis published by the Chinese Communists, American doctrine went through three distinct phases in the 1960's. The first phase the Chinese refer to as that of "flexible response." Under this strategy the United States sought to build up its military power across the board in order to prevent successful Communist revolution, particularly in Vietnam, the focus of Peking's analysis of American strategy. The United States aimed at suppressing revolutionary war by conventional means. When it recognized the failure of this strategy, the American government turned to its second strategic innovation, that of "counter-insurgency." With the inevitable failure of this effort from Peking's perspective, American strat-

---

Reprinted from Morton H. Halperin, "Chinese Attitudes Toward the Use and Control of Nuclear Weapons," in Tang Tsou, ed., *China in Crisis* (Chicago: University of Chicago Press, 1968), 2: 151–57, by permission of the author and publisher.

egy evolved into the third stage which persists until the present time —
the strategy of "escalation." In one of its rare references to American
strategic analysts Peking attributed this strategy to the writings of Her-
man Kahn.

Peking describes this strategy as an effort to defeat a revolutionary
war by engaging in larger and larger escalations ultimately ending up
with the threat of nuclear strikes against the Chinese mainland. The
question of whether or not the United States would actually carry the
war to China and engage in nuclear attacks on Chinese military and
civilian centers has been extensively debated in Peking. In the period
1965-66 most Chinese leaders appeared to have concluded that the
United States was on the verge of launching a nuclear attack against
China. Peking had no reason to believe that the Soviet Union would assist
in its defense and in fact its public statements implied a belief that the
Soviet Union might launch a simultaneous attack in the Sino-Soviet
border area. Nor at this time had Peking developed its own nuclear
capability to the point where China could count on this as a deterrent
against an American attack.

This situation brought on another round in the debate over the most
effective means to deal with a nuclear attack. The leadership was caught
in a dilemma. On the one hand, it desired to underplay the likely effect
of a nuclear attack on China in order to contribute to the deterrence of
American action. On the other hand, it wanted to arouse the people to
take the necessary steps in preparation for an attack. In this situation
Peking for the first time appears to have decided to present the Chinese
public with a fairly precise estimate of its own internal calculations. The
press and radio informed the Chinese people that an American nuclear
attack was probable if not inevitable and said that such an attack would
do great damage to China. Nevertheless, it asserted that the revolution
would go on, that the Chinese leaders would, if necessary, take to the
hills and direct the revolution from there, that American nuclear power,
even if aided by Soviet nuclear power and followed up by a ground
attack by the two countries, could not succeed in destroying the Chinese
revolution. While there was agreement on this analysis of the situation,
the Chinese leadership was divided on the best way to prepare for American attack. The professional military argument was that if an attack indeed was imminent China should seek to make use of its conventional
military forces which had been built up over the years. This force could,
of course, not be used in any way to defeat an American missile attack,
but it should be the main force to resist the land invasion which the
Chinese believe would follow a nuclear attack. Mao, with perhaps a
greater sense of the futility of the attempt to engage in conventional war-

fare against a nuclear power, argued that the People's Liberation Army (PLA) did not have a major role to play in defending China against an American nuclear attack. Rather the only hope lay in a withdrawal from the main centers of population both by the political leadership and by the PLA. The party and the army would return to the hills to preserve themselves intact and to prepare the campaign to ultimately drive the Americans out of China. At the same time the peasants organized in the form of the militia would bear the brunt of attempting to fight off the American invaders and harassing their advance. After some dispute, this line again won out and emphasis was put on preparing the people psychologically for an American attack and training elements of the militia to resist the attack. Mao's attitudes on nuclear war were put to one of their greatest tests during this period, but he and his associates appear to remain firmly convinced that in the end the revolution in China could not be suppressed by an American nuclear attack although such an attack could do great damage to all that had been created in China in the period since 1949.

By the middle of 1966, the Chinese leadership had come to recognize that the United States was not planning to escalate the war indefinitely and launch a nuclear attack against China. At the same time the frenzy of its internal activity was to give the leadership less time to deal with this issue.

The changes in American policy discussed above were paralleled by the rapid deterioration of Sino-Soviet relations to the point where Peking could no longer believe that Soviet nuclear power provided a significant deterrent against an American attack on China. Thus the need for a Chinese nuclear capability increased in Peking's view, at the very time when Soviet aid was cut off and China was forced to go it alone.

The Sino-Soviet rift also caused Peking to discuss in much greater detail than it ever had previously its views on nuclear weapons and to seek to clarify what its differences with the Soviet Union were. Peking faced the problem that all governments face in such a situation, namely the problem of multiple audiences. Peking had to direct its words simultaneously to its potential supporters in the Soviet Union, to other ruling and non-ruling Communist parties, to its own people, and to its potential enemies whose use of nuclear weapons it sought to deter. This problem was complicated by the line that the Soviet Union was taking. Having developed what it considered to be an adequate deterrent, the Soviet leadership was beginning to argue that nuclear weapons had changed the laws of history and that nuclear war had to be avoided at all costs. In order to justify this position, particularly within the international Communist movement, Khrushchev sought to stress the great destruction which would result from a nuclear war and to accuse the Chinese of not understanding the destructive power of nuclear weapons. This charge had the added appeal of painting the Chinese as irrational, thereby demonstrating Khrushchev's real desire for peaceful coexistence with the West and undercutting the Chinese position with other Communist parties and non-Communist nations.

In seeking to answer these charges, Mao faced a dilemma. If he chose to emphasize, as did the Soviet leadership, that nuclear war would be very destructive, he would simply be inviting the West to take advantage of China's weakness to put pressure on Peking. Yet Mao was not prepared to deny the power of nuclear weapons while devoting great resources to their production. Moreover, Peking recognized that to deny the destructive power of nuclear weapons was to be branded as irrational and hence to court the danger that China's nuclear capability would be destroyed in a preemptive strike.

In the face of this dilemma, the Peking leadership held to a statement of its own beliefs about nuclear weapons but with a change in nuance as the decade developed. In the late 1950's and into the early 1960's Peking emphasized its belief that socialism, but not capitalism, would survive a nuclear war. Peking discussed the results of a nuclear war in terms which led some critics to believe that China actually desired such a war and underestimated the destruction which would result. This posture had the value of rallying around Peking those who were opposed to Khrushchev's attempts to change Marxist-Leninist doctrine and it also was in line with the Chinese belief that man would ultimately triumph over weapons. However, it served to alienate large parts of the world Communist movement and to produce apprehensions in the West which Peking feared might lead to an attack on China's developing nuclear capability. By 1962 Peking had switched to a new tack in which it emphasized China's understanding of nuclear war and the great destructive power of nuclear weapons. This posture was to reach a crescendo at the time of the Chinese nuclear detonations.

The progress which China has made in developing nuclear weapons makes it unmistakably clear that the Peking leadership has devoted very substantial resources to a Chinese nuclear program, at least since the mid-1950's. In the 1960's China was forced to proceed without Soviet assistance, and this undoubtedly required an even greater domestic effort channeling a large percentage of China's scientific and technical manpower into a nuclear program. Viewed from Peking, this program of developing nuclear weapons was not without its risks. As the time of its first nuclear detonation came near, Peking began to fear that either the United States or the Soviet Union might decide to destroy the embryonic Chinese nuclear capability. This apprehension led Peking to move very cautiously in the period immediately preceding its detonation and to surround the detonation with a series of statements stressing China's reasonableness: that China would never be the first to use nuclear weapons, and that China understood the destructive power of these weapons. Fear of a preemptive nuclear attack not only forced Peking into cautious posture for several years but also gave added emphasis to a desire to get an operational nuclear capability as soon as possible. Only when China had such capability could she hope to deter an American attack, first by threatening to destroy American bases and the Seventh Fleet and ultimately by threatening to destroy American cities.

If Peking was forced to say a great deal more about nuclear weapons in the 1960's, so also was China forced to articulate in much more detail its own position on matters of arms control and disarmament. For one thing, China was no longer prepared simply to give lip service to the Soviet positions. For another, the United States and the Soviet Union were beginning to make progress on disarmament, and Peking was confronted with real measures to which she had to react. Finally, the Chinese sought to use their new disarmament policy as part of their effort to deter the use of nuclear weapons against them.

The Peking leadership viewed with grave misgivings the movement of the Soviet Union, beginning in 1955-56, away from a purely propaganda interest in arms control and disarmament measures toward some interest in actually signing limited nuclear arms control measures with the United States. The signing of the three environment test ban treaty in 1963 was a major turning point in Sino-Soviet relations and produced a series of bitter exchanges between the two governments. Peking viewed Moscow's adherence to the treaty as a logical extension of Khrushchev's belief that a fundamental change had taken place in the world situation, a belief which Peking of course rejected. If there were no fundamental change, then it was impossible to come to serious agreements with capitalist nations on a matter as vital as the most powerful weapons available to each side. Thus Soviet adherence to the treaty was taken as a sell-out, not only of Soviet interests, but those of the world Communist movement.

In responding to the Soviet adherence to the test ban treaty, Peking spelled out in some detail its own position on disarmament. In short, it argued that the only valuable nuclear agreement was one which brought about the total and complete destruction of nuclear weapons. Peking argued that such an agreement would only be possible when "imperialism" had been totally defeated. In other words Peking argued that arms control and disarmament was a sham unless it was an accompaniment of world revolution. To accept arms control agreements in the interim, which affected the capability of Communist nations, was to sell out the revolution because of a misconception of the role of nuclear weapons in world history.

Peking did propose one specific arms control agreement which she was to push vigorously over the next several years. This was an agreement to ban the first use of nuclear weapons. Peking could hardly expect such an agreement to have a real and lasting meaning, nor could she expect that it would be observed at the height of a large-scale military conflict. What Peking did seek by putting forward such an agreement was a propaganda answer to the charge that she was not prepared to sign the test ban treaty. Peking was probably quite prepared to sign a no-first-use agreement. Such an agreement in her eyes would not at all reduce Peking's flexibility, but would perhaps make it somewhat more difficult for the United States to make even the implicit threats of the use of nuclear weapons that Peking had come to fear over the years. Moreover, it would make it less likely that either Russia or the United States would launch a preemptive nuclear attack designed to destroy China's nuclear installations. In short, Peking's support of a no-first-use agreement harked back to the same motivations which guided the Soviets in the late forties and early fifties, namely a desire to reduce the likelihood that the West would use nuclear weapons, while gaining the support of adherents of "peace" and answering the West's disarmament proposals without accepting them.

Peking's disarmament campaign reached a climax at the time of the Chinese first and second nuclear detonations and was clearly designed to reduce the likelihood that the United States or the Soviet Union would attack China's nuclear capability. In 1966 Peking lost interest in its disarmament campaign, as China's interest in the world at large faded.

## The Future

Given the uncertain nature of conditions in Peking, it would be hazardous to make any firm predictions about the likely evolution of Chinese attitudes toward the use and control of nuclear weapons. However, it is perhaps worth emphasizing that all of those now competing for power in Peking have been debating the role of nuclear weapons for some time. All of them have understood the great destructive power of nuclear weapons. If there has been any dispute, it has been over how fundamental the change is. There is no doubt that all the leaders in Peking understand that a nuclear war would mean the destruction of all the modern sectors of society which Peking has built up since 1949. There is perhaps the danger that the Maoist faction, if it comes to believe that it has no alternative between war and capitulation, will decide that the continuation of the ideology in its pure form is worth even the total destruction of the modern sector of China. However, if both the United States and Soviet Union can refrain from confronting Peking with what appears to be an unacceptable ultimatum, we can expect, even from the Mao-Lin leadership, a continuing caution and a desire to avoid a nuclear confrontation.

# 32. Communist Rule in China: A Review

*Parris Chang*

Twenty years ago, when the establishment of the Chinese People's Republic (CPR) was proclaimed in Peking on October 1, 1949, China was a country that had been ravaged by decades of civil war, foreign invasion and social upheavals, a country whose economy had been disrupted and many of its industrial centers damaged or destroyed. Within ten years after they took power, however, the Chinese Communists had succeeded in recreating a centralized and efficient, albeit totalitarian, apparatus that unified and exercised effective control over the Chinese mainland. They had also brought order out of economic chaos and launched a succession of ambitious development programs which not only restructured the nation's economy but laid the foundations for building a substantial, modern industrial base. Furthermore, the Peking regime had impressively demonstrated its military might to the Western world in the Korean War of the early 1950's.

Thus, by October 1959, when Peking celebrated with great fanfare the conclusion of "a great decade" of the Chinese Communist revolution, China had risen to the status of a major world power. Leaders in many of the newly-independent and developing societies were looking towards Communist China as a source of inspiration and as a model to be emulated, and most outside observers were genuinely impressed by the remarkable achievements wrought by the Chinese Communist leadership,[1] even though those achievements fell short of the proclaimed goals of the regime.

---

[1]See, *e.g.*, Howard L. Boorman, "China and the Global Revolution"; C. F. Fitzgerald, "Order, Power and Modernization"; and Benjamin Schwartz, "Totalitarian Consolidation and the Chinese Model" — all in *The China Quarterly* (London), January-March 1960.

Reprinted from Parris H. Chang, "The Second Decade of Maoist Rule," *Problems of Communism,* November-December 1969, pp. 1-11, by permission of the author and journal.

As the Peking regime celebrates its 20th anniversary on October 1 this year, its situation stands in striking contrast to that of ten years ago. As a consequence of the Great Proletarian Cultural Revolution (GPCR) and the political turmoil it generated over the past three years, the once coherent and self-confident leadership of the Chinese Communist Party (CCP) has been shattered, and the tightly centralized party apparatus of the first decade has been fragmented and replaced by a new regionally-based and military-dominated power structure. China's economy, after barely recovering from the serious dislocations of the Great Leap Forward of 1958, has also been adversely affected by the disruptions of the past three years, forcing the apparent abandonment of the third Five-Year Plan, which was scheduled to enter into operation in 1966. In external affairs, too, the last decade has seen Communist China fall into a state of increasing diplomatic isolation, with her international prestige and influence undergoing a marked decline.

This article proposes, first, to survey the major developments both on the domestic scene and in the foreign relations of Communist China during the period 1959-1969, and second, to analyze current political trends in the People's Republic following the Ninth Party Congress of last April.

## The Economy in Review

While the first decade of Communist rule produced, on balance, a substantial record of achievement in the development of the mainland economy, the second decade has been beset with enormous economic difficulties from the very start. In 1958, Mao Tse-tung, dissatisfied with the progress of the economy during the first Five-Year Plan (1953-1957), had launched the "Great Leap Forward" program, intended to "transform China from an agricultural into an industrial country" virtually overnight. The already ambitious output targets previously set were scrapped in favor of higher goals which then were successively raised even higher, projecting rates of development that were unprecedented in China or anywhere else. To speed industrialization, the regime initiated a reckless drive to mobilize millions of rural villagers throughout China, using local resources, to build small backyard factories for the production of pig iron, steel, and other commodities. Most startling of all, within the brief span of a few months, in the fall of 1958, China's almost 750,000 collective farms were amalgamated into some 26,000 much larger communes in a move propagandized as a giant advance towards full communism but primarily designed to enhance the regime's ability to mobilize rural manpower and resources for state-directed projects.

Catastrophe soon followed. Agricultural failures and serious economic dislocations caused by the excesses and irrationalities of the Great Leap and commune movements, further aggravated by the sudden withdrawal of Soviet technical aid in 1960 and by natural calamities in 1959 and 1960, produced an economic crisis of major proportions in China during 1960-62. Food rations sank to subsistence levels for the nation as a whole, and there was outright starvation in some areas.

In order to salvage the situation, the regime found itself compelled, in the latter half of 1960, virtually to dismantle the grandiose Great Leap and communes programs. To camouflage this retreat, the leadership put forward a new slogan: "Agriculture is the foundation and industry the leading factor in the economy" — which meant in practice that priority was to be shifted to agriculture and more attention paid to light and consumer goods industries (especially those serving agriculture), with a corresponding slowdown in capital construction for heavy industry. By 1962, overall industrial production had declined to the 1957 level.[2]

The commune system was simultaneously abandoned in fact, if not in name. By 1962, the "production teams," generally consisting of 20-30 households and constituting the lowest level of the three-layer commune structure, had again been made the owners of the means of production and the basic accounting units in the commune, thus reverting in effect to the pre-1958 system of elementary agricultural cooperatives. To solve the desperate food situation, the regime was also obliged to make important concessions to the peasantry, principally the so-called "three freedoms and one guarantee."[3] In various provinces, public land was allocated or divided among individual peasant households, and the latter were allowed to "go it alone" (engage in private farming) — a cardinal sin in the collective economy. Teng Hsiao-p'ing, then Secretary-General of the party, is said to have justified this retreat from the principle of collectivization with the remark: "So long as it raises output, going it alone is permissible. White or black, so long as the cats catch mice, they are good cats."[4]

From 1963 on, thanks largely to the more pragmatic measures successfully advocated by the moderate elements in the leadership, grain

---

[2]For an excellent analysis of the Chinese economy in this period, see Choh-ming Li, "China's Industrial Development, 1958-63," in Roderick MacFarquhar (ed.), *China Under Mao: Politics Takes Command*, Cambridge, Mass., MIT Press, 1960, pp. 147–62.

[3]The "three freedoms" were the freedom to cultivate private plots, the freedom to trade in rural markets, and the freedom to engage in subsidiary enterprises. The "one guarantee" referred to the production quotas underwritten by individual peasant households, with rewards for overfulfillment of quotas.

[4]See "Struggle in China's Countryside Between the Two Roads," *Jen-min Jih-pao* (Peking), Nov. 23, 1967.

production increased, and the food shortage eased. Capital construction in the crucial chemical-fertilizer and petroleum industries went up. By the end of 1965, China's economy had at last recovered lost ground and, in some sectors, even scored notable gains over pre-Leap levels.[5] Peking announced the beginning of the third Five-Year Plan in January 1966 but failed to make public any specific production targets. This reticence probably reflected sharp disagreement within the leadership over the goals and methods of the plan, with Mao and the militants apparently demanding a return to the Great Leap approach and the moderates urging a continuation of the pragmatic policies that had put the economy back on an even keel.

Since 1966, the disorder and violence accompanying the GPCR have once again given rise to serious economic difficulties. Industrial production in 1967 — hard hit by transport tie-ups, coal shortages, and labor strikes and unrest — dropped some 15 percent below 1966, and it is estimated that industrial output in 1968 only approximated or slightly exceeded the level of 1967.[6] In agriculture, a bumper harvest in 1967 thanks to excellent weather served to brighten an otherwise gloomy economic picture;[7] but in 1968 agricultural output again dropped off as a result of less favorable weather conditions, fertilizer shortages, and the deteriorating morale of the cadres in rural areas.[8]

Meanwhile, Communist China's foreign trade is estimated to have declined from US $4.3 billion in 1966 (the peak year) to US $3.8 billion in 1967, and US $3.6 billion in 1968.[9] It is interesting to note in this connection that whereas the Soviet Union was Communist China's biggest

---

[5]Overall industrial output in 1965 was perhaps 50 percent above the 1957 level, with greater increases in specific sectors. *E.g.*, estimated steel output reached 10 million tons (or as much as 15 million tons, according to the US Bureau of Mines), doubling (or trebling) the 1957 output of 5.35 million tons; and estimated electric power output reached 35 million kilowatt-hours, an increase of 74 percent over the 1957 figure of 19 million kilowatt-hours. In agriculture, however, total 1965 grain output, estimated at 200 million tons, exceeded the 1957 figure of 185 million tons by a relatively narrow margin. For these and other production statistics, see Edwin F. Jones, "The Emerging Pattern of China's Economic Revolution," and Ta-chung Liu, "The Tempo of Economic Development of the Chinese Mainland, 1949-1965," both in US Congress Joint Economic Committee Report, *An Economic Profile of Mainland China*, Washington, DC, US Government Printing Office, 1967, Vol. I, pp. 71, 85, and 93–95.

[6]"China's Economy in 1968," *Current Scene* (Hong Kong), Vol. VII, No. 9, May 3, 1969.

[7]See John R. Wenmohs, "Agriculture in Mainland China — 1967: Cultural Revolution Versus Favorable Weather," *ibid.*, Vol. V, No. 21, December 15, 1967.

[8]Grain production for 1968 is estimated at 182 million tons, as compared with 190 million tons in 1967. Output of "economic" crops — cotton, oilseeds, sugar, tobacco, etc. — is also believed to have fallen below 1967 levels. See "China's Economy in 1968," *loc. cit.*

[9]"China's Foreign Trade in 1968," *ibid.*, Vol. VII, No. 13, July 1, 1969.

trading partner during the period 1950-59 (the USSR, in 1959, supplied 47.4 percent of China's total imports and took 49.5 percent of her total exports), the direction of Chinese trade changed markedly after 1960 because of the Sino-Soviet conflict, with Japan, Hong Kong, West Germany, Singapore, Canada, the United Kingdom, France, Australia and Italy becoming China's most important trading partners in recent years.

## Political Developments

With the harmful consequences of the Great Leap and communes adventures becoming increasingly evident, the first real challenge to Mao's leadership was already taking shape as the 1949-59 decade neared its close. A preliminary inkling of this came in December 1958 when Mao suddenly relinquished the chairmanship of the republic in favor of Liu Shao-ch'i (though remaining as head of the party). Although this was variously interpreted at the time, Red Guard posters displayed in Peking during the GPCR quoted Mao as stating that he had been forced out as chief of state in 1958 by Liu and other opposition leaders, who treated him like a "dead parent at a funeral" and subsequently failed to consult him on policy matters.[10] Whether or not Mao's reported claim is true cannot be determined with certainty; nevertheless, it is clear that his political authority and control over government policy began declining in 1959.

The rising opposition to Mao was confirmed at the August 1959 Plenum of the CCP Central Committee at Lushan, when a wide range of Maoist policies came under vigorous attack by P'eng Teh-huai, then Minister of Defense; Huang Ko-cheng, Army Chief of Staff; and a number of other military and party leaders.[11] Although P'eng and his "antiparty clique" went down to final defeat and disgrace after a tumultuous session, Mao's prestige and self-esteem were badly scarred in the confrontation. Moreover, the increasingly severe aftereffects of the Great Leap and communes programs proved P'eng's indictment at the Lushan Plenum to have been largely correct, with the probable result that not a few of those who sided with Mao and condemned P'eng in 1959 subsequently came to feel that they had done an injustice to P'eng.

---

[10]See Tokyo dispatches in *The New York Times*, Jan. 6, 1967.

[11]A considerable amount of generally credible new information concerning the Lushan showdown has come to light in the course of the GPCR. P'eng Teh-huai's "Letter of Opinion," in which he set forth his criticisms of Maoist policies, and other relevant materials are translated in *Current Background* (Hong Kong: hereafter cited as *CB*), No. 851, April 28, 1968. Chinese Communist official sources have also published the formal party resolution that repudiated P'eng in 1959, and other informative materials (see *Peking Review*, No. 34, Aug. 18, 1967).

According to later charges by the Maoists, a desire to vindicate P'eng and discredit Mao inspired the writing of a historical play, "The Dismissal of Hai Jui," which was performed throughout China during 1961-62. Written by Wu Han, a Deputy Mayor of Peking and a well-known playwright and historian, the play related the story of a righteous Ming Dynasty minister who returned land to the peasants and brought oppressive and corrupted officials to justice, only to be cashiered for his efforts through court intrigue.[12] There now seems to be little doubt that this play was in fact a veiled indictment of P'eng's 1959 dismissal and hence an attack on Mao's leadership. At any rate, it was a critique of Wu Han's play, reportedly written at Mao's instigation and published in a Shanghai newspaper in November 1965,[13] that proved to be the opening shot in the GPCR.

The cleverly-concealed attacks on Maoist leadership written by Wu Han and other dissident intellectuals,[14] coupled with the fact that they could be published without hindrance by the official censors, clearly attested to the decline of Mao's prestige and of his grip on the party and state apparatus. Whether it was because of opposition pressure within the leadership, of preoccupation with the widening Sino-Soviet rift, or of his unwillingness to preside over the liquidation of his utopian programs — or, more probably, because of a combination of all these factors — Mao abstained to a considerable degree, after 1959, from active participation in the day-to-day formulation and implementation of domestic policy. Although his formal approval of major policy decisions was apparently sought by his colleagues, it seems clear that he had temporarily lost a large measure of control over the decision-making process.

As soon as the national economy showed signs of recovery, however, Mao attempted to make the party once again responsive to his will. During a party conference in Peitaiho in August 1962 and again at the 10th Plenum of the Central Committee the following month, he demanded the rescission or restriction of the "revisionist" measures that had been taken to salvage the disasters of the three preceding years and the launching of a new campaign to revive ideological enthusiasm and restore discipline among party cadres at all levels. This time, however, Mao's intervention was only partially successful. For while the Plenum went along with his demand for an intensified campaign of "socialist

---

[12]Wu Han, *Hai Jui Pa Kuan* (The Dismissal of Hai Jui), Peking, Peking Ch'u-pan-she, 1961.

[13]Yao Wen-yuan, "A Criticism of the New Historical Play, 'The Dismissal of Hai Jui,' " *Wen Hui Pao* (Shanghai), Nov. 10, 1965; reprinted in *Jen-min Jih-pao* (Peking), Nov. 30, 1965.

[14]On the anti-Maoist writings of Wu Han and others, see Harry Gelman, "Mao and the Permanent Purge," *Problems of Communism,* No. 6 (November-December), 1966, p. 4.

education," most of the remedial measures that had contributed significantly to China's economic recovery were left intact. Thus, it would appear that some of Mao's former loyal supporters in the central leadership, such as Liu Shao-ch'i, Teng Hsiao-p'ing and P'eng Chen (a Politburo member and First Secretary of the Peking Party Committee), as well as many provincial party chiefs who had supported his radical policies in the 1950's, were now no longer inclined to follow his lead uncritically.

The implementation of the intensified socialist education campaign, which began in May 1963 and dragged on into 1965, itself provided fresh evidence of the growing fissures behind the central leadership's outer facade of unity. There were abrupt and bewildering shifts in the emphasis, targets, and objectives of the campaign as first Mao and his supporters, then Liu and Teng (the party's "organization men"), and finally the Maoists again, apparently gained the upper hand in issuing successive, conflicting instructions or directives in the name of the Central Committee. Although it was Mao who had the final word in this protracted, seesaw battle, the last of the Central Committee directives on the socialist education campaign — issued in January 1965 and believed to have been chiefly Mao's handiwork — seemed to reflect his conviction that the existing party organization could no longer be relied upon to act as a faithful executor of his will. The directive sounded a new and startling note in referring to "persons in authority within the party taking the capitalist road" — a phrase that was to become a *leitmotif* of the much larger struggle that began unfolding in 1966 — the Great Proletarian Cultural Revolution.[15]

The GPCR, without question, has been the most important development of the last decade in the politics of Communist China. The causes, evolution, and impact of this unprecedented upheaval have been explored in detail by many specialists on Chinese Communist affairs in this journal and elsewhere,[16] and they therefore need not be reviewed here. Suffice it to note that the serious conflicts which developed within the

---

[15]For a succinct account of the conflicting central directives on the socialist education campaign between May 1963 and January 1965, see Charles Neuhauser, "The Chinese Communist Party in the 1960's: Prelude to the Cultural Revolution," *The China Quarterly,* No. 32, October-December 1967, pp. 11–13. A detailed study of the campaign may be found in Richard Baum and Frederick C. Teiwes, *Ssuch'ing: The Socialist Education Campaign of 1962-1966,* Berkeley, University of California Center for Chinese Studies, 1968.

[16]In addition to the articles by Mr. Gelman and Mr. Neuhauser cited in footnotes 14 and 15, a partial listing of articles on the Cultural Revolution is as follows: Philip Bridgham, "Mao's Cultural Revolution: Origin and Development," *The China Quarterly,* No. 29, January-March 1967; Richard D. Baum, "Ideology Redivivus," and Franz Michael, "The Struggle for Power," *Problems of Communism,* No. 3 (May-June) 1967; and Parris H. Chang, "Mao's Great Purge: A Political Balance Sheet," *ibid.,* No. 2 (March-April) 1969.

CCP leadership in 1965 over a broad range of domestic issues (particularly, the socialist education campaign, rectification in the field of art and literature, and the strategy of economic development) as well as over foreign policy (especially the war in Vietnam and Sino-Soviet relations), and which immediately precipitated the GPCR, were essentially a continuation of earlier dissensions among the leaders, whose area of consensus had steadily narrowed over the years. In a fundamental sense, then, the GPCR represented a final, extreme effort by Mao to ferret out the opposition to his program and recapture control of the future direction of the Chinese revolution.

## Foreign Relations

The Sino-Soviet conflict has clearly been the most crucial foreign policy issue facing the Chinese leaders in the last decade—as well as one of the most portentous developments in the international politics of the 1960's. When Communist China emerged on the world scene in 1949, the CCP leaders adopted a policy of "leaning to one side" in world affairs and formed an alliance with the Soviet Union—a relationship which they believed would enable China not only to obtain Soviet material and technical assistance for her domestic economic and military construction but also to extend her international influence. Even before the first decade drew to a close, however, Peking found its hopes in the former area dashed by Moscow's unwillingness to extend further aid to China's economic development and to assist her in developing nuclear weapons, and in the international sphere by Soviet failure to back China more positively in the 1958 Quemoy crisis and the 1959 border conflict with India, as well as by Khrushchev's efforts to develop a "peaceful coexistence" dialogue with the United States.

In 1960, Peking's increasingly vociferous demands for Communist militancy against the West finally erupted into open polemics with Moscow. From then on, Chinese policy moved rapidly toward an open political and ideological break with the Soviet Union, finally consummated by Chinese charges of the "capitalist degeneration" of the Soviet system and denunciations of Khrushchev as a traitor to the cause of Communist world revolution. The Sino-Soviet conflict was certainly a key factor in reinforcing Peking's highly militant international posture during the first half of the 1960's, which saw the Chinese Communists attempt to assume the leading role in pressing the cause of anti-imperialism and wars of "national liberation" both in colonial areas and among the emergent countries of Asia, Africa, and Latin America.

China's effort to forge a new anti-imperialist alliance among the underdeveloped countries of Africa and Asia did, indeed, produce results for a time. By 1965, Peking had established cordial relations with a number of sympathetic—though non-Communist—Afro-Asian states, such as Sukarno's Indonesia, Nkrumah's Ghana, Sekou Touré's Guinea, Ben Bella's Algeria, Nasser's Egypt, Ayub Khan's Pakistan, Sihanouk's Cambodia, and Ne Win's Burma. Meanwhile, the CCP had also secured the backing and allegiance of most, if not all, the Asian Communist Parties —including the North Korean, North Vietnamese, Indonesian, and Japanese—in its competition with Moscow for leadership of the international Communist movement. The image of Communist China's power was also enhanced considerably in the Third World with the successful detonation, in October 1964, of China's first atomic device, making her the first non-Western nuclear power. China's international influence was thus at its peak in early 1965.

However, the Chinese Communist leaders dogmatic concept of the anti-imperialist solidarity of the underdeveloped nations often blinded them to the national interests of the countries and governments they sought to influence. Thus, for example, Premier Chou En-lai found on his African tour in 1964 that Peking's denunciations of the United Nations and of the partial nuclear test-ban treaty fell on unreceptive ears; and in 1965, when the Chinese attempted to turn the projected Second Bandung Conference into an anti-American and anti-Soviet demonstration, many non-Communist Afro-Asian delegations refused to go along. Peking's professions of friendship for the national regimes of Third World countries were belied, moreover, by a strategy of fomenting local Communist subversion against some of the very governments it was seeking to line up in the united front against imperialism. The bankruptcy of China's Third World policies was sharply underscored by the political demise of some of Peking's best friends—leaders like Ben Bella in Algeria, Sukarno in Indonesia,[17] and Nkrumah in Ghana. From 1965 onward, China's relations with a number of Afro-Asian countries, as well as with Cuba, deteriorated sharply.[18]

China's militant anti-imperialist policies in the Third World and her challenge to Soviet hegemony in the international Communist movement were not decided without debate in her leadership councils. Premier Chou's accusation in December 1964 that some misguided comrades

---

[17]The importance of the Communist debacle of September 1965 in Indonesia cannot be overstated. The abortive Communist attempt to stage a *coup d'état* resulted in the virtual destruction of the Indonesian Communist Party and the overthrow of Sukarno, under whose protection the Communists had seemed on the verge of a complete takeover. Sukarno's replacement by an anti-Communist military regime effectively terminated the so-called "Peking-Djakarta axis."

[18]For a general assessment of Peking's foreign policy goals and performance, see Richard Lowenthal, "Communist China's Foreign Policy," in Tang Tsou (ed.), *China's Policies in Asia and America's Alternatives,* Chicago, University of Chicago Press, 1968, pp. 1–18.

had advocated a capitulationist line of "three reconciliations and one reduction" (*i.e.*, reconciliation with reactionaries at home and with revisionists and imperialists abroad; and reduction of assistance to foreign
revolutionaries) strongly suggested that the militant foreign policy line
was not supported by every segment of the leadership.[19]

The escalation of the war in Vietnam after February 1965 appears to
have markedly intensified the debate in Peking. A careful analyst of
Chinese foreign policy has cited evidence for the conclusion that some
military leaders, led by the then Chief of Staff Lo Jui-ch'ing (since
purged), pressed for a reconciliation with Moscow in order to bolster
China's national defense, coupled with more aggressive policy to forestall an American victory in Vietnam; and that a civilian faction within
the leadership, consisting of Liu Shao-ch'i, Teng Hsiao-p'ing, P'eng Chen
and others, likewise urged a rapprochement with Moscow, primarily with
a view to regaining Soviet assistance in China's domestic economic development.[20] According to the same analyst, however, the faction led by
Mao, Lin Piao, and Chou En-lai won out in the debate, rejecting both
the demand for a hard line in Vietnam because it would greatly increase
the risk of war with the US, and the demand for reconciliation with Moscow because Mao regarded the Soviets and Soviet revisionism as an even
greater enemy than the Americans. Subsequently, in the spring of 1966,
Peking turned down a proposal advanced by the Japanese Communist
Party, with the approval of North Korea and North Vietnam, urging
Chinese participation with the USSR in a united Communist front on
Vietnam. The CCP's intransigent posture embittered Hanoi and strained
Peking's relations with North Korea and the JCP.

During the GPCR, Peking's international position suffered further. By
the end of 1967, almost all of China's ambassadors and key diplomatic
officials abroad (except her ambassador in Cairo) had been recalled to
undergo ideological "rectification," and Chinese Communist embassies
everywhere were being operated by low-level officials. Not only that, but
with a new group of militants temporarily running the Foreign Ministry
in Peking, the Chinese government showed itself unwilling or unable to
abide by the accepted norms of international diplomacy (including those
assuring protection for diplomats), which were denounced as a relic of
bourgeois institutions.[21] In July and August of 1967, when the GPCR

---

[19]Chou En-lai's "Report on Government Work" (delivered to the 1st session of
the 3rd National People's Congress on Dec. 21–22, 1964), *People's Handbook
1965*, Peking, Ta Kung Pao She, 1965, p. 12.

[20]Donald Zagoria, "The Strategic Debate in Peking," in Tang Tsou, *op cit.*,
pp. 237–68.

[21]See Robert A Scalapino, "The Cultural Revolution and Chinese Foreign Policy," in *The Cultural Revolution: 1967 in Review*, Ann Arbor, Mich., 1968, pp.
72–96.

reached its peak of violence and disorder, Red Guard mobs sacked and burned the British Embassy in Peking and harassed the embassies and diplomats of many other countires, while Chinese diplomatic personnel rioted in a number of foreign capitals.

Since mid-1968, Peking has moved to restore some semblance of order in its foreign relations. Particularly after the close of the Ninth Party Congress in April 1969, Communist China sent 17 ambassadors back to their posts abroad and resumed more normal diplomatic relations with a few selected European countries (France, Rumania and Sweden, in addition to Albania) and more than a dozen Afro-Asian countries. Despite these efforts, Peking's diplomacy remains far from restabilized, with little or no indication that the revamped leadership installed by the Ninth Party Congress has agreed upon any new, long-range foreign policy.[22]

## Rise of the Military

The political turmoil and breakdown of public order brought on by the GPCR had as their end result the rise of the People's Liberation Army (PLA) to an unprecedented position of political ascendancy in Communist China. Today, not only is the PLA the real locus of power in an overwhelming majority of the 29 revolutionary committees which are now the ruling political-administrative organs in all the provinces of the People's Republic; but it also has primary responsibility for implementing the regime's policies in factory, school and commune. The rise of the military to their present political preeminence did not, however, begin only with the GPCR. The assumption of political functions by the PLA and the process of gradual militarization of the system were already well under way.

The process can, in fact, be traced back to the replacement of P'eng Teh-huai by Lin Piao as Minister of Defense in September 1959. In his first public statement as head of the military establishment, Lin pledged the "unconditional loyalty of the People's Liberation Army to the party and to Comrade Mao,"[23] and from 1960 onward he carried out an intensive campaign of political indoctrinaton in the PLA, centering on the study and application of the thought of Mao.[24] Mao evidently adjudged

[22]Ch'en Yi was not reelected to the CCP Politburo by the Ninth Congress and appears to have relinquished his role as Foreign Minister. Finance Minister Li Hsien-nien has recently been performing Ch'en's former diplomatic duties.

[23]Lin Piao, "March Ahead under the Red Flag of the Party's General Line and Mao Tse-tung's Military Thought," *Jen-min Jih-pao*, Sept. 31, 1959.

[24]See "The Resolution of the Enlarged Session of the Military Affairs Committee Concerning the Strengthening of Indoctrination Work in Troop Units" (Oct. 20, 1960), in J. Chester Cheng, (ed.), *PLA Kung-tso Tung-hsun: The Politics of the Chinese Red Army*, Stanford, Hoover Institution, 1966, p. 64.

the army's campaign much more effective than those which had been carried out in the non-military sectors of society in the first half of the 1960's, such as the socialist education campaign and the ideological rectification campaign in arts and literature. Accordingly, the PLA was held up before the nation as the paradigm of the correct "Communist work style," and individual soldiers said to have distinguished themselves by their selflessness and ideological dedication, such as Lei Feng and Wang Chieh, were made models for emulation campaigns.

Further evidence that Lin Piao and the PLA were now the repositories of Mao's highest confidence was provided by the latter's call in December 1963 for the whole country to "learn from the PLA," with all political, economic and social organizations directed to study and emulate the army's methods of organization, operation, and ideological training. That this call was an indirect rebuke to the party for having not done its job properly is unmistakable in retrospect. Even more important, from 1964 on, steps were taken to establish a network of "political work departments," clearly modelled after the PLA's political commissar system, in party and government organizations. These departments were staffed primarily by political cadres transferred from the PLA, and PLA veterans also took over many other positions in government, party and industry normally held by civilians,[25] while civilian cadres in the economy were sent to PLA schools for training.

It is tempting to view the present political prominence of the PLA simply as the end result of the developments just discussed; yet to do so would be to ignore the special and largely unforeseen circumstances that came into being with the unfolding of the GPCR. Although Lin Piao and the PLA played a substantial role in helping Mao launch the GPCR in the summer of 1966,[26] extensive PLA intervention in the GPCR was evidently not planned from the outset. In fact, it appears that many of the PLA's commanding officers were opposed to army involvement in what they considered to be an intraparty dispute and initially adopted a hands-off policy. Thus, when the Red Guards, following the 11th Plenum, launched their assaults on "capitalist-leaning powerholders" in

---

[25] It was disclosed in 1965 that some 200,000 ex-PLA officers and men were working in the "political departments" and other branches of government trade and finance institutions. See *Jen-min Jih-pao*, May 18, 1965.

[26] It was *Chieh-fang Chün Pao*, the organ of the PLA, that set the pace in the attacks on Mao's leading intellectual critics and their supporters within the party hierarchy (such as P'eng Chen and Lu Ting-yi) in the spring of 1966; and without the backing of Lin Piao and the PLA, Mao certainly could not have defeated and demoted such powerful party figures as Liu Shao-ch'i and Teng Hsiao-p'ing at the 11th CC Plenum in August 1966. The PLA was also instrumental in organizing and providing transport and logistical support for the hordes of Red Guards who journeyed to Peking in 1966.

the regional, provincial and local party structures, the PLA units on the spot stayed on the sidelines.

However, the intrigues, incompetence, factional infighting, and almost unlimited license of the Red Guard and "rebel" organizations soon disrupted economic production and public order, while little headway was made in the struggle to wrest control from the provincial power structures. It was only after the failure of Mao's grand strategy of placing major reliance on the spontaneous forces of the "revolutionary masses" that he turned to the PLA in January 1967 and directed it to intervene on the side of the "leftist" revolutionaries, thus opening the way for the army to become the dominant force not only in the GPCR but in post-GPCR Chinese politics.[27] There is little reason to believe that this outcome—so contrary to Mao's own dictum that the party must direct the gun—was anticipated by Mao or is desired by him today.

## China's New Leadership

The Ninth Congress of the CCP, which met from April 1 to 24 this year and elected a new leadership, was supposed to symbolize the "victorious close" of the GPCR and mark the beginnning of a "new" political era. However, the distribution of power that underlies the post-Congress political order remains essentially the same as that which came into being during the past two years: that is to say, it is one in which the military-regional forces, generally articulating conservative viewpoints and opposed to measures that threaten local stability, occupy a predominant position.

In the 25-man Politburo (21 full members and 4 alternates) elected last April, representatives of military-regional forces overshadow those of other political groups.[28] More specifically, 13 of the 25 — Lin Piao, Yeh Chun, Yeh Chien-ying, Liu Po-cheng, Hsu Shih-yu, Ch'en Hsi-lien, Li Tso-p'eng, Wu Fa-shien, Chiu Hui-tso, Hung Yung-sheng, Hsieh Fu-chih, Li Teh-sheng, and Wang Tung-hsing — actually wear PLA uni-

---

[27]"Decision of the CCP Central Committee, the State Council, the Military Affairs Committee of the Central Committee, and the Cultural Revolution Group under the Central Committee on Resolute Support for the Revolutionary Masses of the Left" (Jan. 23, 1967), translated in *CB*, No. 852, p. 49. This directive nullified the PLA's previous "non-intervention" policy and ordered army units to support the leftists by force, if necessary.

[28]This feature is even more conspicuous in the make-up of the full Central Committee. Out of the 279 (170 full and 109 alternate) members, 46 percent or 127 (76 full and 51 alternate) members are from PLA ranks. Another 127 are representatives of the provincial Revolutionary Committees, but of these, 71 are PLA men concurrently holding army and committee posts. [See appendix one. Ed.]

form.[29] Four of these — Hsu, Ch'en, Huang and Li Teh-sheng — are army district commanders and concurrently chairmen of provincial Revolutionary Committees.

Mao, Chiang Ch'ing, Chang Ch'un-ch'iao, Yao Wen-yuan, and K'ang Sheng constitute the hard core of the leftist elements in the new Politburo, while the usually more moderate civilian officials of the State Council are represented only by Chou En-lai and Li Hsien-nien. Two patriarchal figures of the regime, Chu Teh, 83, and Tung Pi-wu, 82, are also included in the membership but are not likely to participate actively in the decision-making process because of their advanced age.

In terms of political orientation, the new Politburo represents a balance of power between radical and conservative forces, with the scale slightly tipped in favor of the conservatives (most of the military members must be regarded as falling in the conservative camp). While it is true that on the Politburo's five-man Standing Committee, which presumably is the supreme policy-making body, the radicals outnumber the conservatives by three to two, it seems unlikely that this body will formulate policies contrary to the will of the majority of the Politburo. It is probably equally true that the Politburo would find it impossible to carry out policies inimical to the interests of a large number of Central Committee members, particularly those military-regional members who occupy key positions in the administrative apparatus counted upon to implement central directives. It is important to note, in this connection, that the dissension within the top leadership during the last few years not only has brought about a marked expansion of the arena of political conflict, but has also resulted in easier and wider access from below to political influence.[30] Consequently, those situated in the secondary and lower levels of the leadership hierarchy are now in a position to par-

---

[29]The appearance of Hsieh and Wang in PLA uniforms is somewhat surprising since they had not previously been identified publicly as holding army positions. One source suggests that they may hold top positions in the PLA's security apparatus (see Ting Wang, "Issues Revealed in the Documentary Film of the Ninth CCP Congress," *Ming Pao* (Hong Kong), June 22-23, 1969).

[30]The latter is evidenced by the unusually large representation of mass organizations (other than the Red Guards) in the newly-elected Central Committee: 32 full members and 23 alternates, and possibly most of the 24 members whose background is not known. It would be a mistake to view all these people as mere window-dressing without any political weight. In the course of the GPCR, the political role of social groups, particularly the workers, increased substantially. In fact, in late 1966 and early 1967, the provincial party authorities and the Maoists actively sought and competed for the support of various mass organizations, and since 1968 some regional military authorities and newly-established Revolutionary Committees have reportedly organized so-called "Workers' Provost Corps" to help maintain order and subdue the radical Maoist rebels. The bargaining power of the mass organization has thus been enhanced, and it may be assumed that many, if not most, of the mass-organization representatives in the Central Committee play important roles in local politics, even though they are not well-known national political figures.

ticipate to a greater degree in the decision-making process and the resolution of conflicts.

## Recent Political Trends

When Mao addressed the Ninth Party Congress at its opening session
on April 1, he reportedly urged the Congress to become "a congress of
unity and a congress of victory."[31] However, the unity and victory that
the Congress was called upon to forge seem to have proven elusive, for
two months later Mao issued another appeal in the form of a major editorial pronouncement.[32] This "latest directive" of the party Chairman
was apparently made necessary by a resurgence of violent disorders in
various parts of the country, where ultra-leftist "rebel" factions launched
new attacks on the provincial Revolutionary Committees, provoking the
constituted authorities to respond to the attacks with severe counter-
measures.[33]

One of the main reasons for the resurgence of disorders has been the
widespread dissatisfaction among the young "rebels" over the campaign
to rehabilitate many of the party cadres who were ousted from office
during the GPCR. This process had already been going on in the provinces for some time, but it was elevated to the status of an official policy
by Lin Piao's Political Report to the Ninth Party Congress.[34] The central leadership has thus recognized that the administrative ability and
experience of the former cadres are vitally needed in order to reestablish
viable governing institutions throughout the nation. The reinstatement of
large numbers of cadres, however, will inevitably entail a further weakening of the position of the "rebel" organizations in the Revolutionary
Committees.

Judging from the harsh tone of another major editorial published on
Army Day (August 1),[35] and from many recent provincial radio broadcasts attacking "anarchy," "factionalism," and "splittism" and appealing

---

[31]"Press Communique of the Secretariat of the Presidium of the Ninth National
Congress of the CCP" (April 14, 1969), *Peking Review*, No. 18, April 30, 1969,
p. 42.

[32]Joint editorial, "Hold Aloft the Banner of Unity of the Ninth Party Congress
to Strive for Still Greater Victory," published in *Jen-min Jih-pao, Hung Ch'i*, and
*Chieh-fang Chün Pao*, June 9, 1969.

[33]In Chekiang province, oubreaks of violent factional fighting in April and May
led the *Chekiang Jih-pao* (May 8) to call for stringent measures to curb "class
enemies" (actually, extreme pro-Maoist "rebel" groups) who were "sabotaging"
party policies. For other examples of attacks on the resurgent activities of "ultra-
leftists," see Hunan Provincial Radio broadcast of May 27 and *Nan-fang Jih-Pao*
(Canton) editorial of June 2, 1969 (broadcast by Radio Canton the same day).

[34]See text of Lin's report in *Peking Review*, No. 18, April 30, 1969, pp. 16–35.

[35]Joint editorial, "The People's Army is Invincible," published in *Jen-min Jih-pao,
Hung Ch'i*, and *Chieh-fang Chün Pao*, Aug. 1, 1969.

to the public to observe "revolutionary discipline," Mao's pleas for national unity and for a measure of compromise between radicals and conservatives in the interest of such unity have not as yet quieted political unrest in the country.

Moreover, dissension does not seem to be confined to the lower levels of the political structure. The slow progress that is being made in reconstructing the shattered party apparatus strongly suggests that there are divergences of view within the top leadership as well. While Mao and his radical supporters in the Politburo are anxious to see the party organization rebuilt with their own followers in key positions, the military have displayed no enthusiasm for party reconstruction.[36]

The almost total absence of concrete policy proposals in Lin Piao's Congress report further strengthens the impression of a lack of consensus within the top leadership on China's future course. This uncertainty is as evident in the economic as it is in the political sphere. Denunciations of "revisionist" measures such as the earlier-mentioned system of "three freedoms and one guarantee" in agriculture and bonus incentives for workers in industry have been rare in recent months, and earlier moves toward launching a new leap forward in the economy along the lines of 1958-59 have apparently been abandoned, most likely because of opposition from the conservative elements in the leadership. The lack of consensus on economic policy is bound to impede the formulation and execution of a long-range policy of economic development. Those immediately in charge of operating economic units have been functioning during the past two or three years largely on the basis of stop-gap measures. It may perhaps be true, as Allen Whiting suggests, that in China's highly atomized, agricultural economy, local management can keep minimum needs in balance and maintain a reasonable level of productive activity for an indefinite period, barring natural calamities.[37] Still, without overall national planning and direction, China's economic growth is likely to be much slower, and the regime will find it ever harder to meet the needs of the mushrooming population.

## Looking Ahead

For the next few years the attention of the Chinese Communist leadership seems likely to be focussed more on internal problems and the

[36]This impression stems from the fact that the recent major pronouncements of the regime have paid surprisingly little attention to matters involving the party. For example, Lin Piao's 24,000-word Political Report to the Ninth Congress devoted only a few thousand words to party affairs, and the joint Army Day editorial mentioned party reconstruction only in passing, including it in a list of tasks to be fulfilled by the PLA.

[37]Allen S. Whiting, "China's Ninth Party Congress—'A Unity of Opposites,'" Part 3, *The Mainichi Daily News* (Tokyo), June 3, 1969.

building of "socialism in China." Reconstruction of the party machinery, reinvigoration of the economy and the restoration of production to pre-GPCR levels, the re-instilling of discipline in the youth who have enjoyed too much freedom in the past few years, and the reimposition of tight social controls—these are likely to be the national priorities of the leadership for some time to come. It is quite probable that this will mean a curtailment of aid to foreign revolutionaries and possibly some reduction of defense spending in order to channel more resources into economic development at home, no matter how stridently the national propaganda media may trumpet Mao's and/or Lin's militant international line. Despite the current tensions on the Sino-Soviet borders, China's military leaders are too well aware of the vulnerability of China's ground and air power—not to mention her own nuclear weapons centers—to sanction a policy that would risk war with the Soviet Union or the United States.

While a Sino-Soviet reconciliation is almost certainly out of the question as long as Mao remains on the scene, the future relationships between the two major Communist powers and between China and the United States will become much more fluid after Mao is gone. Much, of course, will depend on Soviet and American policies and on future developments in the general international situation. Some purged Chinese military leaders such as P'eng Teh-huai and Lo Jui-ch'ing once argued for the maintenance of close ties with Moscow in order to obtain Soviet aid in advanced weapons development and bolster China's defense position vis-à-vis the United States, while other members of the leadership advocated a reduction of tensions with both Moscow and Washington in order to give China a much-needed breathing spell for solving her economic problems at home. Policy alternatives such as these are virtually certain to be put forward again, even though their advocates may now be in disgrace or discreetly silent.

That the new post-GPCR leadership has already been engaged in debate on the future course of Chinese communism was suggested by a lengthy theoretical discussion of Mao's doctrine of "uninterrupted revolution" which appeared in *Jen-min Jih-pao* on July 5, 1969. Purportedly written by a member of a PLA Rear Service unit, the article referred back significantly to the Sixth Central Committee Plenum of December 1958 (which toned down the Great Leap and communes programs and approved Mao's "retirement" as chief of state) and went on to warn against leftist errors, emphasizing that revolution must proceed in orderly stages. The article also invoked the hallowed authority of Lenin in support of the doctrine that "socialist revolution could first win victory in one country," thus implicitly taking issue with a statement on "uninterrupted revolution" which Lin Piao attributed to Mao in his Ninth Congress report.

All this suggests that Chinese policy today is in a state of flux, and that changes are certainly within the realm of possibility—at least after Mao's death, if not before.

# COMPOSITION OF THE CCP POLITBURO

(As elected by the Ninth Party Congress)

| Members | Basic Position(s) |
|---|---|
| Mao Tse-tung*† | Chairman of the CCP |
| Lin Piao*† | Vice-Chairman of the CCP; Vice-Premier; Minister of Defense |
| Yeh Chun (wife of Lin Piao) | Director, Staff Office of the Military Affairs Committee (MAC) |
| Yeh Chien-ying† | Vice-Chairman of the MAC |
| Liu Po-cheng† | Vice-Chairman of the MAC |
| Chiang Ch'ing (wife of Mao) | 1st Deputy Director, Cultural Revolution Group (CRG) |
| Chu Teh† | Chairman, National People's Congress |
| Hsu Shih-yu | Commander, Nanking Military Region; Chairman of the Kiangsu Revolutionary Committee (RC) |
| Ch'en Po-ta*† | Director, CRG |
| Ch'en Hsi-lien | Commander, Shenyang Military Region; Chairman, Lioaning RC |
| Li Hsien-nien† | Vice-Premier; Minister of Finance |
| Li Tso-peng | 1st Political Commissar of the Navy |
| Wu Fa-hsien | Commander of the Air Force |
| Chang Ch'un-ch'iao | Deputy-Director, CRG; Chairman of the Shanghai RC |

Reprinted from *Problems of Communism* 13 (March-April 1964): 9.

Chiu Hui-tso — Deputy-Chief of Staff and Director, General Rear Service Department, PLA

Chou En-lai*† — Premier

Yao Wen-yuan — Member of the CRG; Vice-Chairman of the Shanghai RC

K'ang Sheng*† — Adviser to the CRG

Huang Yung-sheng — Chief of Staff, PLA; Chairman of the Kwangtung RC

Tung Pi-wu† — Vice-Chairman of the Republic

Hsieh Fu-chih† — Vice-Premier; Minister of Public Security; Commander of Public Security Forces; Member, MAC Standing Committee

## Alternate Members

Chi Teng-kuei — Vice-Chairman of the Honan RC

Li Hsueh-feng† — Chairman of the Hopei RC

Li Teh-sheng — Commander, Anhwei Military District; Chairman, Anhwei RC

Wang Tung-hsing — Director, Staff Office of the CC; Vice-Minister of Public Security; Member, MAC Standing Committee (?)

*Members of the Standing Committee of the Politburo
†Members of the preceding Politburo
NOTE: Except for Mao and Lin Piao, all names are listed in the Chinese equivalent of alphabetical order (*i.e.*, in order of the number of brush strokes in the Chinese ideograph for the surname).

# DILPOMATIC RELATIONS OF THE REPUBLIC OF CHINA AND THE PEOPLE'S REPUBLIC OF CHINA

(As of October 2, 1971)

### Countries having diplomatic relations with the Republic of China (Nationalist China)

*U.N. Members*

| | | | |
|---|---|---|---|
| Argentina | Ecuador | Malawi | Swaziland |
| Australia | El Salvador | Maldive Islands | Thailand |
| Barbados | Gabon | Malta | Togo |
| Belgium | The Gambia | Mexico | Turkey |
| Bolivia | Greece | New Zealand | United States |
| Botswana | Guatemala | Nicaragua | Upper Volta |
| Brazil | Haiti | Niger | Uruguay |
| Central African | Honduras | Panama | Venezuela |
|   Republic | Ivory Coast | Paraguay | |
| Chad | Jamaica | Peru | *Non-U.N. Members* |
| Colombia | Japan | Philippines | South Korea |
| Congo (Kinshasa) | Jordan | Portugal | South Viet-Nam |
| Costa Rica | Lebanon | Rwanda | Vatican City |
| Cyprus | Lesotho | Saudi Arabia | |
| Dahomey | Liberia | Sierra Leone | |
| Dominican | Luxembourg | South Africa | |
|   Republic | Malagasy Republic | Spain | |

Based upon data in *Issues in United States Foreign Policy: No. 4. Communist China* (Washington, D. C.: Dept. of State, 1969), p. 32, and *Voting Records on the So-Called "Problem of China's Representation in the U.N." (21–24 Session in the General Assembly)* (Taipei: Dept. of International Organizations, Ministry of Foreign Affairs, 1970). Updated by the editor.

## Countries having diplomatic relations with the People's Republic of China (Communist China)

*U.N. Members*

| Afghanistan | Equatorial Guinea | Mauritania | Turkey |
|---|---|---|---|
| Albania | Ethiopia | Mongolia | Uganda |
| Algeria | Finland | Morocco | United Arab Rep. |
| Bulgaria | France | Nepal | United Kingdom |
| Burma | Guinea | Netherlands | U.S.S.R. |
| Cambodia | Hungary | Norway | Yemen |
| Cameroon | India | Pakistan | Yugoslavia |
| Canada | Iran | Poland | Zambia |
| Ceylon | Iraq | Romania | |
| Chile | Italy | Somalia | |
| Congo | Kenya | Southern Yemen | *Non-U.N. Membe* |
| (Brazzaville) | Kuwait | Sudan | East Germany |
| Cuba | Laos | Sweden | North Korea |
| Czechoslovakia | Libya | Syria | North Viet-Nam |
| Denmark | Mali | Tanzania | Switzerland |

## Countries recognizing neither

*U.N. Members*                                      *Non-U.N. Members*

| Austria | Malaysia | Andorra | Monaco |
|---|---|---|---|
| Guyana | Singapore | Bhutan | San Marino |
| Iceland | Trinidad and Tobago | Liechtenstein | West Germany |
| Ireland | | | |

## Countries recognizing the People's Republic of China but having no diplomatic relations

| Burundi | Indonesia | Mauritius | Tunisia |
|---|---|---|---|
| Ghana | Israel | Senegal | |

## Country recognizing the Republic of China but having no diplomatic relations

Senegal

# VOTE ON CHINA'S REPRESENTATION IN THE U.N.

| Year | Membership | For Communist China | Against Communist China | Abstentions | Absent |
|------|-----------|--------------------|-------------------------|-------------|--------|
| 1950 | 59 | 16 | 33 | 10 | 0 |
| 1951 | 60 | 11 | 37 | 4 | no roll call |
| 1952 | 60 | 7 | 42 | 11 | 0 |
| 1953 | 60 | 10 | 44 | 2 | 4 |
| 1954 | 60 | 11 | 43 | 6 | 0 |
| 1955 | 60 | 12 | 42 | 6 | 0 |
| 1956 | 79 | 24 | 47 | 8 | 0 |
| 1957 | 82 | 27 | 48 | 6 | 1 |
| 1958 | 81 | 28 | 44 | 9 | 0 |
| 1959 | 82 | 29 | 44 | 9 | 0 |
| 1960 | 98 | 34 | 42 | 22 | 0 |
| 1961 | 104 | 36 | 48 | 20 | 0 |
| 1962 | 110 | 42 | 56 | 12 | 0 |
| 1963 | 111 | 41 | 57 | 12 | 1 |
| 1964 | no vote taken | | | | |
| 1965 | 117 | 47 | 47 | 20 | 3 |
| 1966 | 121 | 46 | 57 | 17 | 1 |
| 1967 | 122 | 45 | 58 | 17 | 2 |
| 1968 | 126 | 44 | 58 | 23 | 1 |
| 1969 | 126 | 48 | 56 | 21 | 1 |
| 1970 | 127 | 51 | 49 | 25 | 2 |
| 1971 | 131 | 76 | 35 | 17 | 3 |

## The Vote in 1971

Editor's Note: By passing the Albanian resolution which calls for the "restoration" of lawful right of the People's Republic of China in the United Nations on October 25, 1971, the members of the U.N. in effect invited the representatives of the People's Republic of China to represent China and expelled the delegation from the Republic of China. The delegation from the Republic of China, however, technically defeated the expulsion attempt by withdrawing from U.N. membership minutes before the vote on the Albanian resolution. A U.S.-initiated resolution which would have made the expulsion of the Republic of China an "important question" requiring a two-thirds vote to pass had been defeated by a vote of 55 to 59 with 15 abstentions. The roll call vote on the Albanian resolution is as follows:

### For (76)

Afghanistan, Albania, Algeria, Austria, Belgium, Bhutan, Botswana, Bulgaria, Burma, Burundi, Byelorussia, Cameroon, Canada, Ceylon, Chile, Cuba, Czechoslovakia, Denmark, Ecuador, Egypt, Equatorial Guinea, Guyana, Hungary, Iceland, India, Iran, Iraq, Ireland, Israel, Italy, Kenya, Kuwait, Laos, Libya, Malaysia, Mali, Mauritania, Mexico, Mongolia, Morocco, Nepal, The Netherlands, Nigeria, Norway, Pakistan, People's Democratic Republic of Yemen, People's Republic of Congo, Peru, Poland, Portugal, Romania, Rwanda, Senegal, Sierra Leone, Singapore, Somalia, Sudan, Sweden, Syria, Tanzania, Togo, Trinidad and Tobago, Tunisia, Turkey, Uganda, Ukraine, Soviet Union, United Kingdom, Yemen, Yugoslavia and Zambia.

### Against (35)

Bolivia, Brazil, Central African Republic, Chad, Democratic Republic of Congo, Costa Rica, Dahomey, Dominican Republic, El Salvador, Gabon, Gambia, Guatemala, Haiti, Honduras, Ivory Coast, Japan, Khmer (Cambodia), Lesotho, Liberia, Madagascar, Malawi, Malta, New Zealand, Nicaragua, Niger, Paraguay, Philippines, Saudi Arabia, South Africa, Swaziland, United States, Upper Volta, Uruguay and Venezuela.

### Abstentions (17)

Argentina, Bahrain, Barbados, Colombia, Cyprus, Fiji, Greece, Indonesia, Jamaica, Jordan, Lebanon, Luxembourg, Mauritius, Panama, Qator, Spain and Thailand.

### Absent (3)

(Nationalist) China, Maldvies, Oman.

# MAINLAND CHINA VERSUS

# REPUBLIC OF CHINA: A

# COMPARISON OF VITAL

# STATISTICS

|  | Mainland China | Republic of China |
|---|---|---|
| Size of Territories under control (sq. miles) | 3,700,000 | 13,945 |
| Cultivated Land (sq. miles) | 444,000 | 3,360 |
| Population | 750,000,000 | 14,554,050 |
| Density (per sq. mile) | 216 | 819 |
| Density (per cultivated sq. mile) | 1,800 | 4,331 |
| Growth rates, annual | 2.25% | 2.8% |
| Adult Literacy | About 40% | 83% |
| Labor Force | 350,000,000 | 4,300,000 |
| Agriculture | 85% | 43% |
| Industrial and Other | 15% | 57% |
| Gross National Product | $80 billion | $4.2 billion |
| GNP per capita | $100 | $300 |
| Crude Steel per capita | 33 lbs. | 64.4 lbs. |
| Telephones per capita | 1:3,380 | 1:60 |
| Radios per capita | 1:145 | 1:10 |
| Food: per capita daily calories intake | 2,000 | 2,350 |

Data sources: *Issues in United States Foreign Policy: No. 4. Communist China* (Washington, D. C.: Dept. of State, 1969), p. 14; *1968 Taiwan Demographic Fact Book* (Taichung, Taiwan: Dept. of Civil Affairs, Taiwan Provincial Government, 1969); and *Facts About Free China* (Taipei, Taiwan: China Publishing Company, 1969).

# COMMUNIST CHINA VERSUS NATIONALIST CHINA: THE MILITARY BALANCE

| Types of Armed Forces | Communist China | Nationalist China |
|---|---|---|
| Army | | |
| Total Strength | 2,500,000 | 400,000 |
| Infantry Divisions | 108 | 15 |
| Armored Divisions | 5 | 2 |
| Armored Cavalry Divisions | —— | 2 |
| Cavalry Divisions | 3 | —— |
| Airborne Divisions | 2 | —— |
| Parachute Brigades | —— | 1 |
| Light Divisions | —— | 6 |
| Special Forces Groups | —— | 4 |
| Navy | | |
| Total Strength (men) | 141,000 | 70,000 |
| Vessels | 969 | 251 |
| Airforce | | |
| Total Strength | 180,000 | 85,000 |
| Combat Aircraft | 2,800 | 375 |

| *Types of Armed Forces* | *Communist China* | *Nationalist China* |
|---|---|---|
| Total Regular Forces | 2,281,000[1] | 555,000 |
| Percentage of Population in the Armed Forces[2] | 0.37% | 4% |

[1]Although the numerical strength of the military power of mainland China is far larger than that of the Republic of China on Taiwan, it is generally agreed among western military experts that the Chinese Nationalist armed forces, especially its air force, are better trained and equipped.

[2]Computed by dividing the total regular forces of Communist China and Nationalist China by the total populations on the Chinese Mainland (750 millions) and Taiwan (14 millions).

Based upon data in *The Military Balance, 1969–1970* (London: Institute for Strategic Studies, 1969), pp. 38–43.